BaseBall america®
2010 DIRECTORY

YOUR DEFINITIVE GUIDE TO THE GAME

Detailed Information On Baseball In All Leagues At All Levels

Majors

Minors

Independent

International

College

Amateur

BASEBALL AMERICA INC. · DURHAM, N.C.

Connect to Cooperstown...

...Just a click away

ROBERTO CLEMENTE WALKER
PITTSBURGH N. L. 1955-1972
MEMBER OF EXCLUSIVE 3,000-HIT CLUB. LED
NATIONAL LEAGUE IN BATTING FOUR TIMES. HAD
FOUR SEASONS WITH 200 OR MORE HITS WHILE
POSTING LIFETIME .317 AVERAGE AND 240 HOME
RUNS. WON MOST VALUABLE PLAYER AWARD 1966.
RIFLE-ARMED DEFENSIVE STAR SET N. L. MARK BY
PACING OUTFIELDERS IN ASSISTS FIVE YEARS.
BATTED .362 IN TWO WORLD SERIES, HITTING IN
ALL 14 GAMES.

baseballhall.org

**Preserving History. Honoring Excellence.
Connecting Generations.**

BaseBall america®
2010 DIRECTORY

Editor
JOSH LEVENTHAL

Assistant Editors
BEN BADLER, J.J. COOPER, AARON FITT,
CONOR GLASSEY, WILL LINGO, NATHAN RODE, JIM SHONERD, HOFFMAN WOLFF

Database and Application Development
GREG LEVINE, BRENT LEWIS

Photo Editor
NATHAN RODE

Design & Production
SARA HIATT MCDANIEL, TIFFANY SCHWARZ, LINWOOD WEBB

Programming & Technical Development
GREG LEVINE, BRENT LEWIS

Cover Photo
LARRY GOREN

BaseBall america

PRESIDENT/PUBLISHER: LEE FOLGER
EDITORS IN CHIEF: WILL LINGO, JOHN MANUEL
EXECUTIVE EDITOR: JIM CALLIS
DESIGN & PRODUCTION DIRECTOR: SARA HIATT MCDANIEL
TECHNOLOGY MANAGER: GREG LEVINE

DISTRIBUTED BY SIMON & SCHUSTER
ISBN-13: 978-1-932391-30-5

BaseballAmerica.com

TABLE OF CONTENTS

Nationals Park

ED WOLFSTEIN

Target Field

MAJOR LEAGUES

BALLPARK: Minnesota Twins—Target Field.

DOUBLE-A

BALLPARK: Tulsa Drillers (Texas)—ONEOK Field.

FRANCHISE MOVE: Connecticut Defenders (Eastern) to Richmond Flying Squirrels (Richmond, Va.).

HIGH CLASS A

AFFILIATION CHANGES: Lynchburg Hillcats (Carolina) from Pirates to Reds, Sarasota Reds (Florida State) from Reds to Pirates.

FRANCHISE MOVE: Sarasota Reds (Florida State) to Bradenton Marauders (Bradenton, Fla.).

BALLPARK: Winston-Salem Dash—Winston-Salem Downtown Ballpark.

LOW CLASS A

LEAGUE REALIGNMENT: Bowling Green Hot Rods and Lake County Captains from South Atlantic to Midwest.

SHORT-SEASON

BALLPARK: Eugene Emeralds—PK Park.

ROOKIE

REALIGNMENT: Cincinnati Reds from Gulf Coast League to Arizona League.

Map illustrations by Paul Trap

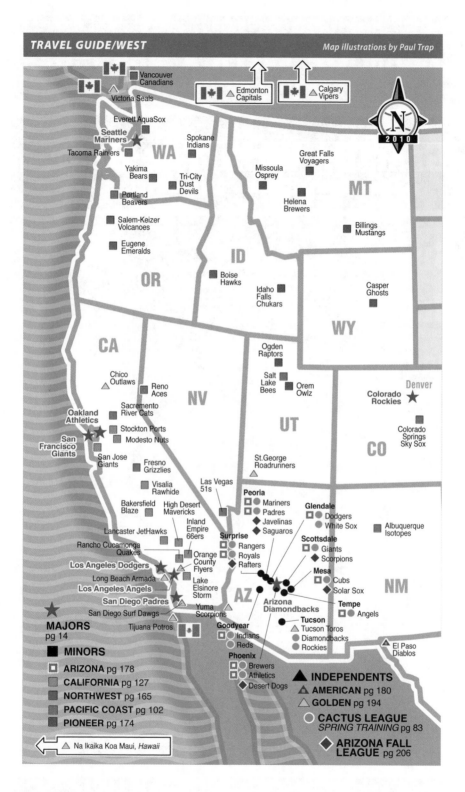

Vancouver Canadians
Victoria Seals
Everett AquaSox
Seattle Mariners
Tacoma Rainiers
WA
Spokane Indians
Yakima Bears
Tri-City Dust Devils
Portland Beavers
Salem-Keizer Volcanoes
Eugene Emeralds
OR

Edmonton Capitals
Calgary Vipers

N 2010

Great Falls Voyagers
Missoula Osprey
MT
Helena Brewers
Billings Mustangs

Boise Hawks
ID
Idaho Falls Chukars
Casper Ghosts
WY

CA
Chico Outlaws
Reno Aces
NV
Sacramento River Cats
Oakland Athletics
Stockton Ports
Modesto Nuts
San Francisco Giants
San Jose Giants
Fresno Grizzlies
Visalia Rawhide
Bakersfield Blaze
High Desert Mavericks
Lancaster JetHawks
Inland Empire 66ers
Rancho Cucamonga Quakes
Los Angeles Dodgers
Long Beach Armada
Los Angeles Angels
San Diego Padres
San Diego Surf Dawgs
Tijuana Potros
Orange County Flyers
Lake Elsinore Storm
Yuma Scorpions

Ogden Raptors
Salt Lake Bees
Orem Owlz
UT
St.George Roadrunners
Las Vegas 51s

Denver
Colorado Rockies
Colorado Springs Sky Sox
CO

Albuquerque Isotopes
NM
El Paso Diablos

Peoria
Mariners
Padres
Javelinas
Saguaros
Surprise
Rangers
Royals
Rafters
Glendale
Dodgers
White Sox
Scottsdale
Giants
Scorpions
Mesa
Cubs
Solar Sox
Tempe
Angels
AZ
Arizona Diamondbacks
Tucson
Tucson Toros
Diamondbacks
Rockies
Goodyear
Indians
Reds
Phoenix
Brewers
Athletics
Desert Dogs

MAJORS pg 14

MINORS
ARIZONA pg 178
CALIFORNIA pg 127
NORTHWEST pg 165
PACIFIC COAST pg 102
PIONEER pg 174

Na Ikaika Koa Maui, *Hawaii*

INDEPENDENTS
AMERICAN pg 180
GOLDEN pg 194

CACTUS LEAGUE
SPRING TRAINING pg 83

ARIZONA FALL LEAGUE pg 206

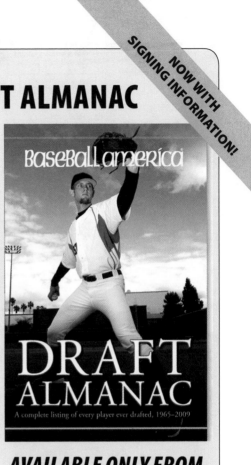

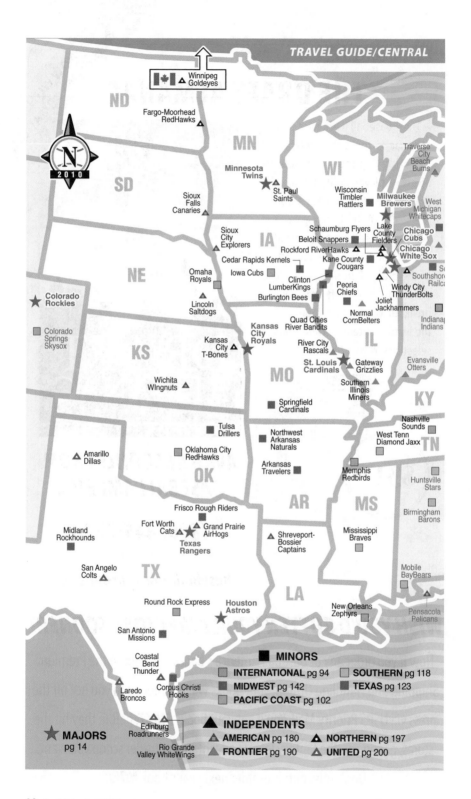

Winnipeg Goldeyes

ND

Fargo-Moorhead RedHawks

MN

Minnesota Twins

WI

Traverse City Beach Bums

SD

St. Paul Saints

Sioux Falls Canaries

Wisconsin Timber Rattlers

Milwaukee Brewers

West Michigan Whitecaps

Sioux City Explorers

IA

Schaumburg Flyers

Beloit Snappers

Lake County Fielders

Chicago Cubs

Rockford RiverHawks

Cedar Rapids Kernels

Kane County Cougars

Chicago White Sox

NE

Omaha Royals

Iowa Cubs

Clinton LumberKings

Peoria Chiefs

Southshore Railca

Colorado Rockies

Lincoln Saltdogs

Burlington Bees

Quad Cities River Bandits

Normal CornBelters

Windy City ThunderBolts

Joliet Jackhammers

IL

Indiana Indians

Colorado Springs Skysox

KS

Kansas City Royals

Kansas City T-Bones

River City Rascals

MO

St. Louis Cardinals

Gateway Grizzlies

Evansville Otters

Wichita WIngnuts

Springfield Cardinals

Southern Illinois Miners

KY

Nashville Sounds

Tulsa Drillers

Northwest Arkansas Naturals

West Tenn Diamond Jaxx

TN

Amarillo Dillas

Oklahoma City RedHawks

Arkansas Travelers

Memphis Redbirds

Huntsville Stars

OK

AR

MS

Birmingham Barons

Frisco Rough Riders

Fort Worth Cats

Grand Prairie AirHogs

Shreveport-Bossier Captains

Mississippi Braves

Midland Rockhounds

Texas Rangers

San Angelo Colts

TX

Mobile BayBears

LA

Round Rock Express

Houston Astros

New Orleans Zephyrs

Pensacola Pelicans

San Antonio Missions

Coastal Bend Thunder

Laredo Broncos

Corpus Christi Hooks

Edinburg Roadrunners

Rio Grande Valley WhiteWings

MAJORS
pg 14

■ MINORS

■ INTERNATIONAL pg 94	□ SOUTHERN pg 118
■ MIDWEST pg 142	■ TEXAS pg 123
■ PACIFIC COAST pg 102	

▲ INDEPENDENTS

| ▲ AMERICAN pg 180 | ▲ NORTHERN pg 197 |
| ▲ FRONTIER pg 190 | △ UNITED pg 200 |

N 2010

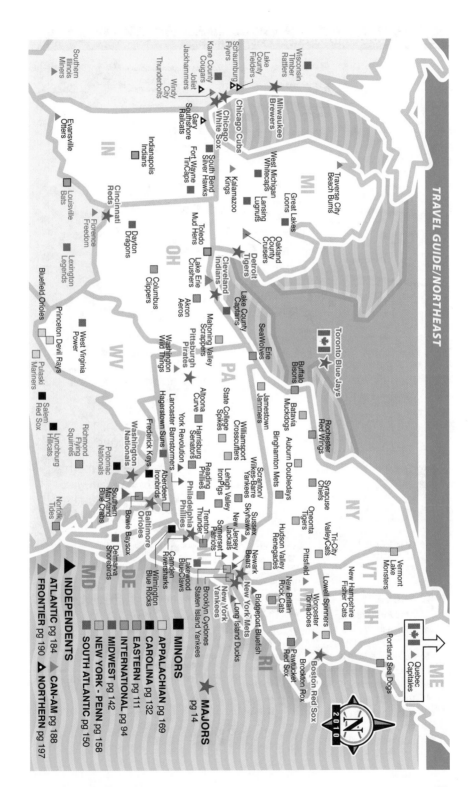

Southern Illinois Miners

Kane County Cougars
Schaumburg Flyers
Joliet Jackhammers
Windy City Thunderbolts
Gary Southshore Railcats
Evansville Otters

Wisconsin Timber Rattlers
Lake County Fielders
Milwaukee Brewers
Chicago White Sox
Chicago Cubs
West Michigan Whitecaps

IN
Indianapolis Indians
South Bend Silver Hawks
Fort Wayne TinCaps
Louisville Bats

Traverse City Beach Bums
MI
Great Lakes Loons
Oakland County Cruisers
Kalamazoo Kings
Lansing Lugnuts
Cincinnati Reds
Florence Freedom
Dayton Dragons
OH
Toledo Mud Hens
Lake Erie Crushers
Cleveland Indians
Detroit Tigers
Lake County Captains
Akron Aeros
Columbus Clippers
Lexington Legends
Bluefield Orioles
Princeton Devil Rays
West Virginia Power
WV
Mahoning Valley Scrappers
Pittsburgh Pirates
Washington Wild Things
Hagerstown Suns
Lancaster Barnstormers
PA
Altoona Curve
Harrisburg Senators
York Revolution
Reading Phillies
Pulaski Mariners
Salem Red Sox
Richmond Flying Squirrels
Lynchburg Hillcats
Frederick Keys
Aberdeen Ironbirds
Washington Nationals
Potomac Nationals
Norfolk Tides

Erie SeaWolves
Jamestown Jammers
Williamsport Crosscutters
State College Spikes
Lehigh Valley IronPigs
Trenton Thunder
Philadelphia Phillies
Scranton/Wilkes-Barre Yankees
Binghamton Mets
Auburn Doubledays
Buffalo Bisons
Batavia Muckdogs
Rochester Red Wings
Syracuse Chiefs
Oneonta Tigers
NY
New Jersey Jackals
Sussex Skyhawks
Somerset Patriots
Newark Bears
Hudson Valley Renegades
Pittsfield
Tri-City ValleyCats

Toronto Blue Jays

Bowie Baysox
Baltimore Orioles
Southern Maryland Blue Crabs
Delmarva Shorebirds
MD
Wilmington Blue Rocks
DE
Camden Riversharks
Lakewood BlueClaws
New York Mets
New York Yankees
Staten Island Yankees
Brooklyn Cyclones
Long Island Ducks
Bridgeport Bluefish
New Britain Rock Cats
Pawtucket Red Sox
Boston Red Sox
Brockton Rox
RI
New Hampshire Fisher Cats
Lowell Spinners
Worcester Tornadoes
VT
Vermont Lake Monsters
NH
MA
ME
Portland Sea Dogs

Quebec Capitales

2010

N

MAJORS
pg 14

MINORS
APPALACHIAN pg 169
CAROLINA pg 132
EASTERN pg 111
INTERNATIONAL pg 94
MIDWEST pg 142
NEW YORK - PENN pg 158
SOUTH ATLANTIC pg 150

INDEPENDENTS
ATLANTIC pg 184
FRONTIER pg 190
CAN-AM pg 188
NORTHERN pg 197

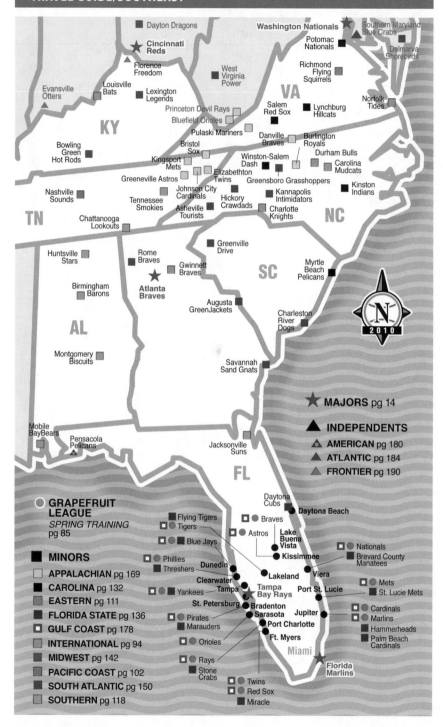

Dayton Dragons
Cincinnati Reds
Washington Nationals
Southern Maryland Blue Crabs
Potomac Nationals
Delmarva Shorebirds
Florence Freedom
West Virginia Power
Richmond Flying Squirrels
Evansville Otters
Louisville Bats
Lexington Legends
VA
Salem Red Sox
Lynchburg Hillcats
Norfolk Tides
Princeton Devil Rays
Bluefield Orioles
KY
Pulaski Mariners
Danville Braves
Burlington Royals
Bowling Green Hot Rods
Bristol Sox
Winston-Salem Dash
Durham Bulls
Kingsport Mets
Carolina Mudcats
Greeneville Astros
Elizabethton Twins
Greensboro Grasshoppers
Nashville Sounds
Johnson City Cardinals
Kannapolis Intimidators
Kinston Indians
Tennessee Smokies
Hickory Crawdads
Asheville Tourists
Charlotte Knights
NC
TN
Chattanooga Lookouts
Greenville Drive
Huntsville Stars
Rome Braves
Gwinnett Braves
SC
Myrtle Beach Pelicans
Birmingham Barons
Atlanta Braves
AL
Augusta GreenJackets
Charleston River Dogs
N 2010
Montgomery Biscuits
Savannah Sand Gnats
★ **MAJORS** pg 14

▲ **INDEPENDENTS**
Mobile BayBears
Pensacola Pelicans
Jacksonville Suns
△ **AMERICAN** pg 180
△ **ATLANTIC** pg 184
△ **FRONTIER** pg 190
FL

○ **GRAPEFRUIT LEAGUE**
SPRING TRAINING pg 85

Daytona Cubs
Daytona Beach
Flying Tigers
Tigers
Braves
Astros
Lake Buena Vista
Nationals
Brevard County Manatees

■ **MINORS**

☐ **APPALACHIAN** pg 169
Blue Jays
Kissimmee
Viera
☐ **CAROLINA** pg 132
Phillies
Threshers
Dunedin
Mets
St. Lucie Mets
Port St. Lucie
■ **EASTERN** pg 111
Clearwater
Lakeland
■ **FLORIDA STATE** pg 136
Yankees
Tampa
Tampa Bay Rays
☐ **GULF COAST** pg 178
St. Petersburg
Bradenton
Cardinals
☐ **INTERNATIONAL** pg 94
Pirates
Marauders
Sarasota
Jupiter
Marlins
■ **MIDWEST** pg 142
Port Charlotte
Hammerheads
Palm Beach Cardinals
■ **PACIFIC COAST** pg 102
Orioles
Ft. Myers
Miami
■ **SOUTH ATLANTIC** pg 150
Rays
Stone Crabs
Florida Marlins
☐ **SOUTHERN** pg 118
Twins
Red Sox
Miracle

MAJOR LEAGUES

MAJOR LEAGUE BASEBALL

Mailing Address: 245 Park Ave. New York, NY 10167.
Telephone: (212) 931-7800.
Website: www.mlb.com.
Commissioner: Allan H. "Bud" Selig.
President/Chief Operating Officer: Bob DuPuy. **Executive Vice President, Business:** Tim Brosnan. **Executive VP, Labor Relations/Human Resources:** Robert Manfred. **Executive VP, Finance:** Jonathan Mariner. **Executive VP, Administration/Chief Information Officer:** John McHale. **Executive VP, Baseball Operations:** Jimmie Lee Solomon.

Bud Selig

BASEBALL OPERATIONS

Senior Vice President, Baseball Operations: Joe Garagiola Jr.
VP, Baseball Operations/Administration: Ed Burns. **VP, International Baseball Operations:** Lou Melendez. **VP, Umpiring:** Mike Port. **VP, On-Field Operations:** Bob Watson.
Senior Director, Major League Operations: Roy Krasik. **Senior Director, Urban Youth Academy:** Darrell Miller. **Director, Operations Initiatives:** Sylvia Lind. **Senior Manager, Baseball Operations:** Jeff Pfeifer.
Manager, Dominican Operations: Ronaldo Peralta. **Manager, Minor League Operations:** Fred Seymour. **Senior Specialist, On-Field Operations:** Darryl Hamilton. **Specialist, Minor League Operations/ Initiatives:** Pat Scott.
Specialist, Amateur Player Administration: Chuck Fox. **Specialist, On-Field Operations:** Matt McKendry. **Specialist, Umpire Administration:** Cathy Davis. **Specialist, International Operations:** Joel Araujo. **Coordinator, Major League Operations:** Gina Liento. **Supervisor, Umpiring:** Larry Young. **Director, Umpire Administration:** Tom Lepperd. **Director, Umpire Medical Services:** Mark Letendre. **Umpiring Supervisors:** Rich Garcia, Cris Jones, Jim McKean, Steve Palermo, Rich Rieker, Marty Springstead. **Director, Arizona Fall League:** Steve Cobb. **Director, Major League Scouting Bureau:** Frank Marcos. **Assistant Director, Scouting Bureau:** Rick Oliver.

Security
Vice President, Security/Facility Management: Earnell Lucas.
Director, Facility Operations: Linda Pantell. **Senior Manager, Facility Operations:** Bob Campbell. **Supervisor, Executive Offices Security Operations:** William Diaz. **Managing Director, Security:** John Skinner. **Supervisor, Executive Protection:** Charles Hargrove. **Coordinator, Security/Facility Management:** Yenifer Nunez. **Assistant to VP, Security/ Facility Management:** Danielle Beckom.

Investigations
Senior Vice President, Investigations: Dan Mullin.
Vice President, Investigations: George Hanna. **Manager, Investigations:** Nancy Zamudio.

Bob DuPuy

Public Relations
Telephone: (212) 931-7878. **Fax:** (212) 949-5654.
Senior Vice President, Public Relations: Richard Levin.
VP, Public Relations Operations: Patrick Courtney. **VP, Business Public Relations:** Matt Bourne. **Director, Media Relations:** John Blundell. **Senior Project Manager, Baseball Information:** Rob Doelger. **Manager, Media Relations:** Michael Teevan. **Managers, Business Public Relations:** Jeff Heckelman, Daniel Queen. **Specialists, Business Public Relations:** Steven Arocho, Lauren Verrusio. **Coordinator, Media Relations:** Donald Muller. **Coordinator, Business Public Relations:** Sarah Leer. **Senior Administrative Assistant:** Heather Flock. **Administrative Assistant:** Raquel Ramos. **Official Baseball Historian:** Jerome Holtzman.

Club Relations
Senior Vice President, Scheduling/Club Relations: Katy Feeney. **Senior Administrative Assistant, Scheduling/ Club Relations:** Raxel Concepcion. **Coordinator, Club Relations:** Bennett Shields. **Senior Vice President, Club Relations:** Phyllis Merhige. **Senior Administrative Assistant, Club Relations:** Angelica Cintron. **Club Relations Assistant:** Greg Domino.

Licensing
Senior Vice President, Licensing: Howard Smith.
VP, Domestic Licensing: Steve Armus. **Senior Director, Consumer Products, Retail Marketing:** Adam Blinderman. **Director, Licensing/Minor Leagues:** Eliot Runyon. **Director, Gifts/Novelties:** Maureen Mason. **Director, Hard Goods:** Mike Napolitano. **Director, Non-Authentics:** Greg Sim. **Director, Authentic Collection:** Ryan Samuelson. **Senior Manager, Presence Marketing:** Robin Jaffe.

Publishing and Photographs
Vice President, Publishing/Photographs: Don Hintze.
Editorial Director: Mike McCormick. **Art Director, Publications:** Faith Rittenberg. **Director, MLB Photographs:** Rich Pilling.

Special Events
Senior Vice President, Special Events: Marla Miller.
Senior Director, Special Events: Brian O'Gara. **Directors, Special Events:** Eileen Buser, Jacqueline Secaira-Cotto.

MAJOR LEAGUES

Senior Manager, Special Events: Rob Capilli. **Managers, Special Events:** Joe Fitzgerald, Jennifer Jacobson.

Broadcasting
Senior Vice President, Broadcasting: Chris Tully.
VP, Broadcast Administration/Operations: Bernadette McDonald. **Director, Broadcast Administration/Operations:** Chuck Torres.

Corporate Sales/Marketing
Senior Vice President, Corporate Sales/Marketing: John Brody.
Vice President, Corporate Sales/Marketing: Jeremy Cohen. **Vice President, Corporate Sales/Marketing:** Ari Roitman.

Advertising
Senior Vice President, Advertising/Marketing: Jacqueline Parkes.
Vice President, Research/Strategic Planning: Dan Derian. **Research Manager, Advertising:** Marc Beck. **Vice President, Design Services:** Anne Occi.

Community Affairs/Educational Programming
Vice President, Community Affairs: Tom Brasuell. **Director, Community Relations:** Celia Bobrowsky.

General Administration
Senior Vice President, Accounting/Treasurer: Bob Clark. **Senior Vice President/General Counsel, Labor Relations:** Dan Halem. **Senior VP/General Counsel, Business:** Ethan Orlinsky. **Senior Vice President/General Counsel, BOC:** Tom Ostertag. **Senior VP, Finance:** Kathleen Torres. **Vice President, Application Development:** Mike Morris. **VP, Deputy General Counsel:** Domna Candido. **Senior VP, Diversity/Strategic Alliances:** Wendy Lewis. **VP, Human Resources:** Ray Scott. **Vice President/Deputy General Counsel:** Jennifer Simms. **VP, Operations/Tech Support:** Peter Surhoff. **Director, Baseball Assistance Team:** Joe Grippo. **Senior Director, Office Operations:** Donna Hoder. **Senior Director, Quality Control:** Peggy O'Neill-Janosik.
Vice President, Recruitment: John Quinones. **Director, Risk Management/Financial Reporting:** Anthony Avitabile. **Senior Manager, Records:** Mildred Delgado. **Director, Payroll/Pension:** Rich Hunt. **Director, Benefits/HRIS:** Diane Cuddy.

International
Mailing Address: 245 Park Ave., 31st Floor, New York, NY 10167. **Telephone:** (212) 931-7500. **Fax:** (212) 949-5795.
Senior Vice President, International Business Operations: Paul Archey.
Vice President, International Licensing: Denis Nolan. **VP/Executive Producer:** Russell Gabay. **Tournament Director, World Baseball Classic:** James Pearce. **Director, International Licensing:** Josephine Fuzesi. **Director, International Marketing/Advertising:** Jacquelyn Walsh. **Vice President, International Broadcast Sales:** Frank Uddo. **Senior Director, International Sponsorship/Communications:** Dominick Balsamo. **VP/Managing Director, MLB Japan:** Jim Small. **Director, China Operations:** Michael Marone. **Director, Australian Operations:** Thomas Nicholson. **Director, European Operations:** Clive Russell.

MLB Western Operations
Office Address: 2415 East Camelback Rd., Suite 850, Phoenix, AZ 85016.
Telephone: (602) 281-7300. **Fax:** (602) 281-7313.
Vice President, Western Operations/Special Projects: Laurel Prieb.
Office Coordinator: Valerie Dietrich.

Major League Baseball Productions
Office Address: One MLB Network Plaza, Secaucus, NJ 07094-2403. **Telephone:** (201) 751-8500. **Fax:** (201) 751-8568.
Vice President/Executive In Charge of Production: David Gavant. **VP, Programming/Business Affairs:** Elizabeth Scott. **Executive Producer:** David Check. **Senior Director, Operations:** Shannon Valine. **Coordinating Producer:** Adam Schlackman. **Coordinating Producer, Field Production:** Robert Haddad.

Umpires
Lance Barksdale, Ted Barrett, Wally Bell, C.B. Bucknor, Mark Carlson, Gary Cederstrom, Eric Cooper, Derryl Cousins, Jerry Crawford, Fieldin Culbreth, Phil Cuzzi, Kerwin Danley, Gary Darling, Bob Davidson, Gerry Davis, Dana DeMuth, Laz Diaz, Mike DiMuro, Bruce Dreckman, Doug Eddings, Paul Emmel, Mike Everitt, Andy Fletcher, Marty Foster, Greg Gibson, Brian Gorman, Chris Guccione, Tom Hallion, Angel Hernandez, Ed Hickox, John Hirschbeck, Bill Hohn, Sam Holbrook, Marvin Hudson, Dan Iassogna, Jim Joyce, Jeff Kellogg, Ron Kulpa, Jerry Layne, Alfonso Marquez, Randy Marsh, Tim McClelland, Jerry Meals, Chuck Meriwether, Bill Miller, Ed Montague, Paul Nauert, Jeff Nelson, Brian O'Nora, Tony Randazzo, Ed Rapuano, Rick Reed, Mike Reilly, Charlie Reliford, Jim Reynolds, Brian Runge, Paul Schrieber, Dale Scott, Tim Timmons, Tim Tschida, Larry Vanover, Mark Wegner, Bill Welke, Tim Welke, Hunter Wendelstedt, Joe West, Mike Winters, Jim Wolf.

Events
2010 All-Star Game: July 13 at Angel Stadium, Anaheim, CA.
2010 World Series: TBD.

AMERICAN LEAGUE

Years League Active: 1901-.
2010 Opening Date: April 4. **Closing Date:** Oct 3.
Regular Season: 162 games.
Division Structure: East—Baltimore, Boston, New York, Tampa Bay, Toronto. Central—Chicago, Cleveland, Detroit, Kansas City, Minnesota. West—Los Angeles, Oakland, Seattle, Texas.
Playoff Format: Three division champions and second-place team with best record meet in two best-of-five Division Series. Winners meet in best-of-seven League Championship Series.
All-Star Game: July 13, Angel Stadium, Anaheim (National League vs American League).
Roster Limit: 25, through Aug. 31 when rosters expand to 40.
Brand of Baseball: Rawlings.
Statistician: MLB Advanced Media, 75 Ninth Ave., 5th Floor, New York, NY 10011.

STADIUM INFORMATION

Team	Stadium	Dimensions			Capacity	2009 Att.
		LF	CF	RF		
Baltimore	Camden Yards	333	410	318	48,190	1,907,163
Boston	Fenway Park	315	390	302	36,525	3,062,699
Chicago	U.S. Cellular Field	330	400	335	40,615	2,284,164
Cleveland	Progressive Field	325	405	325	43,545	1,766,242
Detroit	Comerica Park	345	420	330	41,000	2,567,185
Kansas City	Kauffman Stadium	330	410	330	38,177	1,797,887
Los Angeles	Angel Stadium	333	404	333	45,050	3,240,386
Minnesota	Target Field	339	404	328	40,000	*2,416,237
New York	Yankee Stadium	318	408	314	52,325	3,719,358
Oakland	McAfee Coliseum	330	400	367	34,077	1,408,783
Seattle	Safeco Field	331	405	326	47,447	2,195,284
Tampa Bay	Tropicana Field	315	404	322	41,315	1,874,962
Texas	Rangers Ballpark in Arlington	332	400	325	48,911	2,156,016
Toronto	Rogers Centre	328	400	328	49,539	1,876,129

*Denotes attendance at Hubert H. Humphrey Metrodome

NATIONAL LEAGUE

Years League Active: 1876-.
2010 Opening Date: April 5. **Closing Date:** Oct 3.
Regular Season: 162 games.
Division Structure: East—Atlanta, Florida, New York, Philadelphia, Washington. Central—Chicago, Cincinnati, Houston, Milwaukee, Pittsburgh, St. Louis. West—Arizona, Colorado, Los Angeles, San Diego, San Francisco.
Playoff Format: Three division champions and second-place team with best record meet in two best-of-five Division Series. Winners meet in best-of-seven League Championship Series.
All-Star Game: July 13, Angel Stadium, Anaheim (National League vs. American League).
Roster Limit: 25, through Aug. 31 when rosters expand to 40.
Brand of Baseball: Rawlings.
Statistician: MLB Advanced Media, 75 Ninth Ave., 5th Floor, New York, NY 10011.

STADIUM INFORMATION

Team	Stadium	Dimensions			Capacity	2009 Att.
		LF	CF	RF		
Arizona	Chase Field	330	407	334	49,033	2,128,765
Atlanta	Turner Field	335	400	330	49,743	2,373,631
Chicago	Wrigley Field	355	400	353	41,160	3,168,859
Cincinnati	Great American Ball Park	328	404	325	42,319	1,747,919
Colorado	Coors Field	347	415	350	50,499	2,665,080
Florida	Sun Life Stadium	330	434	345	38,560	1,464,109
Houston	Minute Maid Park	315	435	326	40,976	2,521,076
Los Angeles	Dodger Stadium	330	395	330	56,000	3,761,655
Milwaukee	Miller Park	344	400	345	41,900	3,037,451
New York	Citi Field	335	408	330	42,000	3,168,571
Philadelphia	Citizens Bank Park	329	401	330	43,647	3,600,693
Pittsburgh	PNC Park	325	399	320	38,362	1,577,853
St. Louis	Busch Stadium	336	400	335	43,975	3,343,252
San Diego	PETCO Park	336	396	322	42,685	1,919,603
San Francisco	AT&T Park	339	399	309	41,503	2,862,110
Washington	Nationals Park	336	404	335	42,000	1,817,226

Arizona Diamondbacks

Office Address: Chase Field, 401 E. Jefferson St, Phoenix, AZ 85004.
Mailing Address: P.O. Box 2095, Phoenix, AZ 58001.
Telephone: (602) 462-6500. **Fax:** (602) 462-6599. **Website:** www.dbacks.com

Ownership
Managing General Partner: Ken Kendrick. **General Partners:** Mike Chipman, Dale Jensen, Jeff Royer.

BUSINESS OPERATIONS
President/CEO: Derrick Hall. **Executive Assistant to President/CEO:** Brooke Mitchell.
Special Assistants to President/CEO: Luis Gonzalez, Roland Hemond.

Broadcasting
Vice President, Broadcasting: Scott Geyer.

Corporate Partnerships/Marketing
Executive Vice President, Business Operations: Cullen Maxey.
Senior Director, Marketing: Karina Bohn. **Brand Director:** Doug Alkire. **Directors, Corporate Partnerships:** Tim Emory, Steve Mullins. **Director, Hispanic Sales/Marketing:** Julie Romero.

Finance/Legal
Executive Vice President/CFO: Tom Harris. **Executive Assistant to Managing General Partner/CFO:** Sandy Cox. **VP, Finance:** Craig Bradley. **VP/General Counsel:** Nona Lee. **Associate General Counsel:** Caleb Jay. **Legal Secretary:** Candace Kerege.

Ken Kendrick

Community Affairs
Director, Community Affairs: Kristine Hedlund. **Senior Coordinator, Community Affairs:** Tara Trzinski.

Communications/Media Relations
Telephone: (602) 462-6519. **Fax:** (602) 462-6527.
Vice President, Communications: Shaun Rachau. **Director, Player/Media Relations:** Mike McNally. **Manager, Corporate Communications:** Tina Manzo. **Manager, Player/Media Relations:** Casey Wilcox. **Coordinator, Player/Media Relations:** Morgan Ballard. **Director, Publications:** Greg Salvatore.

Stadium Operations
Vice President, Facility/Event Services: Russ Amaral. **Director, Security:** Sean Maguire. **Manager, Security:** Greg Green. **Senior Director, Suite/Premium Services:** Diney Ransford. **Director, Building Services:** Jim Hawkins. **Director, Engineering:** Jim White. **Director, Event Services:** Bryan White. **Event Coordinator:** Stephanie Scheidler. **Head Groundskeeper:** Grant Trenbeath. **Official Scorer:** Rodney Johnson.
Manager, Spring Training Operations: Bonnie Faircloth.

2010 SCHEDULE
Standard Game Times: 6:40 p.m.; Sun. 1:10.

APRIL		
5-7 . . . . San Diego	21-23 . . . . Toronto	5-7 . . . . . . Chicago (NL)	30-31 . . . . . . San Diego
9-11 . . . . Pittsburgh	25-27 . . . . . . at Colorado	8-11 . . . . Florida	
13-15 . at Los Angeles (NL)	28-30 . . . at San Francisco	16-18 . . . . . at San Diego	**SEPTEMBER**
16-18 . . . . . at San Diego	31 . . . at Los Angeles (NL)	19-21 . . . .New York (NL)	1 . . . . San Diego
19-21 . . . . St. Louis		22-25 . . . . . San Francisco	3-5 . . . . Houston
23-25 . . . .Philadelphia	**JUNE**	27-29 . . . . at Philadelphia	6-8 . . . . . . San Francisco
26-28 . . . . . at Colorado	1-2 . . at Los Angeles (NL)	30-31 . . . at New York (NL)	10-12 . . . . . at Colorado
29-30 . . . .at Chicago (NL)	4-6 . . . . Colorado		13-16 . . . . . .at Cincinnati
	7-10 . . . . Atlanta	**AUGUST**	17-19 . . . . . at Pittsburgh
MAY	11-13 . . . . . . St. Louis	1 . . . . . . at New York (NL)	21-23 . . . . .Colorado
1-2 . . . . . at Chicago (NL)	15-17 . . . . .at Boston	2-5 . . . . Washington	24-26 . . . Los Angeles (NL)
3-6 . . . . .at Houston	18-20 . . . . .at Detroit	6-8 . . . . San Diego	28-30 . . . at San Francisco
7-9 . . . . .Milwaukee	21-23 . . . . .New York (AL)	9-12 . . . . . at Milwaukee	
10-12 . . Los Angeles (NL)	25-27 . . . . . at Tampa Bay	13-15 . . . at Washington	**OCTOBER**
14-16 . . . . . . at Atlanta	28-30 . . . . .at St. Louis	17-19 . . . . . . Cincinnati	1-3 . . . at Los Angeles (NL)
17-18 . . . . .at Florida		20-22 . . . . .Colorado	
19-20 . . . . . San Francisco	**JULY**	24-26 . . . . . at San Diego	
	2-4 . . . . . Los Angeles (NL)	27-29 . . . at San Francisco	

GENERAL INFORMATION
Stadium (year opened): Chase Field (1998).
Team Colors: Red, sand and black.

Player Representative: Unavailable.
Home Dugout: Third Base.
Playing Surface: Grass.

Ticketing
Telephone: (602) 514-8400. **Fax:** (602) 462-4141.
Vice President, Ticket Sales/Service: John Fisher. **Senior Director, Suite/Premium Services:** Diney Ransford. **Director, Group/Suite Sales:** Scott Worden. **Director, Season Ticket/Inside Sales:** Jason Howard. **Assistant Director, Ticket Operations:** Luis Calderon. **Director, Ticket Development/Operations:** Kenny Farrell.

Travel, Clubhouse
Senior Director, Team Travel: Roger Riley. **Manager, Equipment/Visiting Clubhouse:** Bob Doty.

BASEBALL OPERATIONS
Telephone: (602) 462-6500. **Fax:** (602) 462-6425.
Executive Vice President/General Manager: Josh Byrnes.
VP/Assistant GM: Peter Woodfork. **VP, Special Assistant to GM:** Bob Gebhard. **Director, Baseball Operations:** Shiraz Rehman. **Baseball Operations Video Coordinator:** Jim Currigan. **Advance Scout/Consultant to Major League Staff:** David Parrish. **Baseball Operations Assistant:** Brendan Domaracki.

Josh Byrnes

Major League Staff
Manager: A.J. Hinch.
Coaches: Bench—Kirk Gibson; Pitching—Mel Stottlemyre, Jr.; Batting—Jack Howell; First Base—Matt Williams; Third Base—Bo Porter; Bullpen—Glenn Sherlock.

Medical, Training
Club Physicians: Dr. Michael Lee, Dr. Roger McCoy. **Head Trainer:** Ken Crenshaw.
Assistant Trainer: Dave Edwards. **Strength/Conditioning Coach:** Nate Shaw.

Minor Leagues
Telephone: (602) 462-4400. **Fax:** (602) 462-6425.
Director, Player Development: Mike Berger.
Assistant Director, Player Development: Charles Alberts.
Manager, Minor League Administration: Susan Webner.
Coordinators: Mike Bell (field), Jeff Pico (pitching), Dave Hansen (hitting), Tony Perezchica (infield), Joel Youngblood (outfield/baserunning), Bill Plummer (catching), Hatuey Mendoza (Latin liaison). **Advance Scout/Consultant to Major League Staff:** David Parrish. **Tucson Complex Coordinator:** Bob Bensinger. **Medical Coordinator:** PJ Mainville. **Assistant Medical Coordinator:** Jimmy Southard. **Strength/Conditioning Coordinator:** Brett McCabe.

Farm System

Class	Club (League)	Manager	Coach	Pitching Coach
Triple-A	Reno (PCL)	Brett Butler	Rick Burleson	Mike Parrott
Double-A	Mobile (SL)	Rico Brogna	Turner Ward	Dan Carlson
High A	Visalia (CAL)	Audo Vicente	Alan Zinter	Erik Sabel
Low A	South Bend (MWL)	Mark Haley	Francisco Morales	Wellington Cepeda
Short-season	Yakima (NWL)	Bob Didier	Andy Abad	Doug Drabek
Rookie	Missoula (PIO)	Hector de la Cruz	Jason Hardtke	Gil Heredia

Scouting
Telephone: (602) 462-6518. **Fax:** (602) 462-6527.
Vice President, Player Personnel: Jerry Dipoto.
Special Assistant to GM, Latin American Operations: Junior Noboa (Dominican Republic).
Director, Scouting: Tom Allison.
Director, International Scouting: Chad MacDonald.
Scouting Administrator: Jennifer Blatt. **Scouting Coordinator:** Helen Zelman.
Director, Pacific Rim Operations: Mack Hayashi. **Special Assistant, Pacific Rim Operations:** Jim Marshall.
Scouting Supervisors: Joe Bohringer (De Kalb, IL); Greg Lonigro (Connellsville, PA), Steve McAllister (Chillicothe, IL), Howard McCullough (Greenville, NC); Bob Minor (Garden Grove, CA), Mike Piatnik (Winter Haven, FL), Tim Schmidt (San Bernardino, CA).
Scouts: Shawn Barton (Reading, PA), Ray Blanco (Miami, FL), Darold Brown (Elk Grove, CA), Jeff Cirillo (Medina, WA), Trip Couch (Sugar Land, TX), Mike Daughtry (St. Charles, IL), Rodney Davis (Glendale, AZ), Jim Dedrick (Granite Falls, WA), Denney Kyle (Carl Junction, MO), Todd Donovan (East Lyme, CT), Micah Franklin (Gilbert, AZ), Carlos Gomez (Atlanta, GA), Muzzy Jackson (Key Biscayne, FL), Kevin Jarvis (Franklin, TN), Hal Kurtzman (Lake Balboa, CA), T.R. Lewis (Marietta, GA), Matt Merullo (Madison, CT), Jeff Mousser (Huntington Beach, CA), Pat Murtaugh (West Lafayette, IN), Joe Robinson (St. Louis, MO), Mike Sgobba (Scottsdale, AZ), Rick Short (Peoria, IL), George Swain (Wilmington, NC), Frankie Thon, Jr. (Louisville, KY), Luke Wrenn (Lakeland, FL).
Part-Time Scouts: Homer Newlin (Tallahassee, FL), Juan Gonzalez (Puerto Rico).
International Scouts: Supervisor—Luis Baez (Santo Domingo, DR). Dominican Republic—Gabriel Berroa, José Ortiz, Rafael Mateo. Panama—José Díaz Perez. Nicaragua—Julio Sanchez. Colombia—Luis Gonzalez. Venezuela—Ubaldo Heredia, Marlon Urdaneta.

Atlanta Braves

Office Address: 755 Hank Aaron Dr, Atlanta, GA 30315.
Mailing Address: PO Box 4064, Atlanta, GA 30302.
Telephone: (404) 522-7630. **Fax:** (404) 614-1391.
Website: www.braves.com.

Ownership
Operated/Owned By: Liberty Media.
Chairman Emeritus: Bill Bartholomay. **Chairman/CEO:** Terry McGuirk.
President: John Schuerholz. **Senior Vice President:** Henry Aaron.

BUSINESS OPERATIONS
Executive Vice President, Business Operations: Mike Plant.
VP/General Counsel: Greg Heller.

Finance
Senior Vice President, Chief Financial Officer: Chip Moore.

Marketing, Sales
Executive Vice President, Sales/Marketing: Derek Schiller. **Executive Director, Marketing:** Gus Eurton. **Senior Director, Ticket Sales:** Paul Adams. **Senior Director, Corporate Sales:** Jim Allen.

Terry McGuirk

Media Relations/Public Relations
Telephone: (404) 614-1556. **Fax:** (404) 614-1391.
Director, Media Relations: Brad Hainje. **Director, Public Relations:** Beth Marshall.
Publications Manager: Andy Pressley. **Public Relations Manager:** Meagan Swingle. **Media Relations Coordinators:** Adrienne Midgley, Jim Misudek.

Stadium Operations
Director, Stadium Operations/Security: Larry Bowman.
Field Director: Ed Mangan. **Director, Game Entertainment:** Scott Cunningham. **PA Announcer:** Casey Motter.
Official Scorers: Mike Stamus, Jack Wilkinson.

Ticketing
Telephone: (800) 745-3000. **Fax:** (404) 614-2480.
Director, Ticket Operations: Anthony Esposito.

Travel, Clubhouse
Director, Team Travel/Equipment Manager: Bill Acree.
Visiting Clubhouse Manager: John Holland.

2010 SCHEDULE
Standard Game Times: 7:10 p.m.; Fri. 7:35; Sun. 1:35.

APRIL
5 . . . . Chicago (NL)
7-8 . . . . . . Chicago (NL)
9-11 . . . . at San Francisco
12 . . . . at San Diego
14-15 . . . . . at San Diego
16-18 . . . . Colorado
20-22 . . . . . Philadelphia
23-25 . . at New York (NL)
26-29 . . . . . at St. Louis
30 . . . . Houston

MAY
1-2 . . . . Houston
4-6 . . . . . at Washington
7-9 . . . . at Philadelphia
10-12 . . . . . at Milwaukee

14-16 . . . . Arizona
17-18 . . . New York (NL)
19-20 . . . . . . Cincinnati
21-23 . . . . . at Pittsburgh
25-27 . . . . . . at Florida
28-30 . . . . . . Pittsburgh
31 . . . . Philadelphia

JUNE
1-2 . . . . . . Philadelphia
3-6 . . at Los Angeles (NL)
7-10 . . . . at Arizona
11-13 . . . . at Minnesota
15-17 . . . . . Tampa Bay
18-20 . . . . . Kansas City
22-24 . . at Chicago (AL)
25-27 . . . . Detroit
28-30 . . . . . Washington

JULY
2-4 . . . . Florida
5-7 . . . . at Philadelphia
9-11 . . . at New York (NL)
15-18 . . . . . Milwaukee
20-22 . . . . . San Diego
23-25 . . . . . at Florida
27-29 . . . at Washington
30-31 . . . . at Cincinnati

AUGUST
1 . . . . at Cincinnati
2-4 . . . . New York (NL)
5-8 . . . . San Francisco
9-11 . . . . . . at Houston
13-16 . . Los Angeles (NL)
17-19 . . . . . Washington

20-22 . . . at Chicago (NL)
23-25 . . . . . at Colorado
27-29 . . . . Florida
30-31 . . . New York (NL)

SEPTEMBER
1-2 . . . . . New York (NL)
3-5 . . . . at Florida
6-8 . . . . . at Pittsburgh
9-12 . . . . St. Louis
13-15 . . . . . Washington
17-19 . . at New York (NL)
20-22 . . at Philadelphia
24-26 . . at Washington
27-29 . . . . Florida

OCTOBER
1-3 . . . . . . Philadelphia

GENERAL INFORMATION
Stadium (year opened): Turner Field (1997).
Team Colors: Red, white and blue.

Player Representative: Unavailable.
Home Dugout: First Base.
Playing Surface: Grass.

BASEBALL OPERATIONS

Telephone: (404) 522-7630. **Fax:** (404) 614-3308.
Executive Vice President/General Manager: Frank Wren.
Assistant GM: Bruce Manno.
Director, Baseball Administration: John Coppolella.
Executive Assistants: Annie Lee, Chris Rice.

Frank Wren

Major League Staff

Manager: Bobby Cox.
Coaches: Bench—Chino Cadahia; Pitching—Roger McDowell; Batting—Terry Pendleton; First Base—Glenn Hubbard; Third Base—Brian Snitker; Bullpen—Eddie Perez.

Medical, Training

Head Team Physician: Dr. Xavier Duralde.
Trainer: Jeff Porter. **Assistant Trainer:** Jim Lovell.
Strength/Conditioning Coach: Phil Falco.

Player Development

Telephone: (404) 522-7630. **Fax:** (404) 614-1350.
Director, Player Development: Kurt Kemp.
Assistant Director, Player Development: Ronnie Richardson. **Special Assistant to the GM, Player Development:** Jose Martinez. **Administrative Assistant:** Vickie Griffin.
Minor League Field Coordinator: Tommy Shields. **Pitching Coordinator:** Dave Wallace. **Hitting Coordinator:** Leon Roberts. **Roving Instructors:** Mike Alvarez (pitching), Joe Breeden (catching), Lynn Jones (outfield/base running), Jonathan Schuerholz (infield), Luckie Dacosta (strength/conditioning).

Farm System

Class	Club (League)	Manager	Coach	Pitching Coach
Triple-A	Gwinnett (IL)	Dave Brundage	Jamie Dismuke	Derek Botelho
Double-A	Mississippi (SL)	Phillip Wellman	Garey Ingram	Marty Reed
High A	Myrtle Beach (CL)	Rocket Wheeler	Rick Albert	Kent Willis
Low A	Rome (SAL)	Randy Ingle	Bobby Moore	Jim Czajkowski
Rookie	Danville (APP)	Paul Runge	Carlos Mendez	Derrick Lewis
Rookie	Braves (GCL)	Luis Ortiz	Sixto Lezcano	Gabe Luckert
Rookie	Braves (DSL)	Jose Tartabull	Unavailable	William Martinez

Scouting

Telephone: (404) 614-1359. **Fax:** (404) 614-1350.
Director, Scouting: Tony DeMacio. **Office Coordinator, Scouting:** Dixie Keller.
Advance Scout: Bobby Wine (Norristown, PA). **Special Assistants to GM/Major League Scouts:** Dick Balderson (Englewood, CO), Dom Chiti (Auburndale, FL), Tim Conroy (Monroeville, PA), Jim Fregosi (Tarpon Springs, FL), Guy Hansen (Manakin Sabot, VA), Chuck McMichael (Keller, TX), Jeff Wren (Senoia, GA).
Professional Scouts: Rod Gilbreath (Lilburn, GA), Lloyd Merritt (Myrtle Beach, SC), John Stewart (Granville, NY). **National Crosscheckers:** John Flannery (Austin, TX), Deron Rombach (Mansfield, TX). **Regional Crosscheckers:** West—Tom Davis (Ripon, CA), Southwest–James "Bump" Merriweather (Glendale, AZ), East—Steve Fleming (Louisa, VA), Midwest—Terry R. Tripp (Harrisburg, IL).
Area Scouts: John Barron (Cameron, TX), Kevin Barry (Cream Ridge, NJ), Billy Best (Holly Spings, NC), Bill Bliss (Cincinnati, OH), Brian Bridges (Rome, GA), Stu Cann (Bradley, IL), Brett Evert (Salem, OR), Ralph Garr (Richmond, TX), Buddy Hernandez (Orlando, FL), Brian Hunter (Lakewood, CA), Gene Kerns (Hagerstown, MD), Chris Knabenshue (Fort Collins, CO), Steve Leavitt (Huntington Beach, CA), Tim Moore (Sacramento, CA), Don Thomas (Geismar, LA), Terry C. Tripp (Raleigh, IL), Gerald Turner (Bedford, TX). **Part-Time Scouts:** Hugh Buchanan (Snellville, GA), Dewayne Kitts (Moncks Corner, SC), Abraham Martinez (Santa Isabel, PR), Brendan Sagara (Wahiawa, HI), Lou Sanchez (Miami, FL).
Director, International Scouting: Johnny Almaraz. **Assistant Director, International Scouting/Operations:** Jose Martinez.
International Coordinators: Latin America—Roberto Aquino (Santo Domingo, Dominican Republic), Eastern Rim—Phil Dale (Victoria, Australia).
International Area Supervisors: Hiroyuki Oya (Japan), Luis Ortiz (Panama), Rolando Petit (Venezuela), Manuel Samaniego (Mexico). **Part-Time Scouts:** Eduardo Becerra (Venezuela), Neil Burke (Australia), Nehomar Caldera (Venezuela), Junior Carrion (Dominican Republic), Jeremy Chou (Taiwan), Carlos Garcia Roque (Colombia), Raul Gonzalez (Panama), Jose Guzman (Dominican Republic), Matias Laureano (Dominican Republic), Duk Lee (South Korea), Alfredo Molina (Ecuador), Rafael Motooka (Brazil), Nestor Perez (Spain), Jefferson Romero D'Lima (Venezuela), Eduardo Rosario (Venezuela), Miguel Theran (Colombia), Marvin Throneberry (Nicaragua), Carlos Torres (Venezuela).

Baltimore Orioles

Office Address: 333 W. Camden St, Baltimore, MD 21201.
Telephone: (888) 848-BIRD. **Fax:** (410) 547-6272.
E-mail Address: birdmail@orioles.com. **Website:** www.orioles.com.

Ownership

Operated By: The Baltimore Orioles Limited Partnership Inc.
Chairman/CEO: Peter Angelos.

BUSINESS OPERATIONS

Executive Vice President: John Angelos. **VP/Special Liaison to Chairman:** Lou Kousouris.
General Legal Counsel: Russell Smouse. **Director, Human Resources:** Lisa Tolson. **Director, Information Systems:** James Kline.

Finance

Vice President/CFO: Robert Ames.

Public Relations/Communications

Telephone: (410) 547-6150. **Fax:** (410) 547-6272.
Director, Communications: Greg Bader. **Director, Public Relations:** Monica Barlow.
Manager, Media Relations: Jeff Lantz. **Coordinator, Baseball Information:** Jay Moskowitz.
Director, Promotion/Community Initiatives: Kristen Schultz.

Peter Angelos

Ballpark Operations

Director, Ballpark Operations: Ray Trifari.
Assistant Director, Ballpark Operations: Kevin Cummings. **Head Groundskeeper:** Nicole Sherry.
PA Announcer: David McGowan. **Official Scorers:** Jim Henneman, Marc Jacobsen.

Ticketing

Telephone: (888) 848-BIRD. **Fax:** (410) 547-6270.
Director, Sales/Fan Services: Neil Aloise. **Assistant Director, Sales:** Mark Hromalik. **Ticket Manager:** Audrey Brown.

Travel/Clubhouse

Coordinator, Team Travel: Kevin Buck.
Equipment Manager (Home): Jim Tyler. **Equipment Manager (Road):** Fred Tyler. **Umpires, Field Attendant:** Ernie Tyler.

2010 SCHEDULE

Standard Game Times: 7:05 p.m; Sun. 1:35

APRIL
6-8 . . . . . . at Tampa Bay
9-11 . . . . Toronto
12-14 . . . . . Tampa Bay
15-18 . . . . . at Oakland
19-21 . . . . . . at Seattle
23-25 . . . . . . at Boston
27-29 . . . . New York (AL)
30 . . . . Boston

MAY
1-2 . . . . Boston
3-5 . . . . at New York (AL)
6-9 . . . . . at Minnesota
11-13 . . . . Seattle
14-16 . . . . . . Cleveland
17-18 . . . . . Kansas City

19-20 . . . . at Texas
21-23 . . . at Washington
25-27 . . . . . . Oakland
28-30 . . . . at Toronto

JUNE
1-3 . . at New York (AL)
4-6 . . . . Boston
8-10 . . . New York (AL)
11-13 . . . New York (NL)
14-16 . . at San Francisco
18-20 . . . . at San Diego
22-24 . . . . . . Florida
25-27 . . . . . Washington
29-30 . . . . . . Oakland

JULY
1 . . . . Oakland

2-4 . . . . at Boston
5-7 . . . . at Detroit
8-11 . . . . at Texas
16-18 . . . . . . Toronto
19-21 . . . . . Tampa Bay
22-25 . . . . . Minnesota
26-28 . . . . at Toronto
29-31 . . . at Kansas City

AUGUST
1 . . . . . . at Kansas City
3-5 . . . Los Angeles (AL)
6-9 . . . . . Chicago (AL)
10-12 . . . at Cleveland
13-15 . . . at Tampa Bay
16-18 . . . . . . Seattle
19-22 . . . . Texas

24-26 . . . at Chicago (AL)
27-29 . at Los Angeles (AL)
31 . . . . Boston

SEPTEMBER
1-2 . . . . Boston
3-5 . . . . . . Tampa Bay
6-8 . . . at New York (AL)
10-12 . . . . . at Detroit
13-15 . . . . . . Toronto
17-19 . . . New York (AL)
20-22 . . . . . at Boston
24-26 . . . . at Toronto
27-29 . . . . at Tampa Bay
30 . . . . Detroit

OCTOBER
1-3 . . . . Detroit

GENERAL INFORMATION

Stadium (year opened): Oriole Park at Camden Yards (1992).
Team Colors: Orange, black and white.

Player Representative: Unavailable.
Home Dugout: First Base.
Playing Surface: Grass.

BASEBALL OPERATIONS

Telephone: (410) 547-6121. **Fax:** (410) 547-6271.
President, Baseball Operations: Andy MacPhail.
Director, Baseball Operations: Matt Klentak.

Major League Staff

Manager: Dave Trembley.
Coaches: Bench—Jeff Datz; Pitching—Rick Kranitz; Batting—Terry Crowley; First Base—John Shelby; Third Base—Juan Samuel; Bullpen—Alan Dunn.

Medical, Training

Club Physician: Dr. William Goldiner. **Club Physician, Orthopedics:** Dr. John Wilckens.
Head Athletic Trainer: Richie Bancells. **Assistant Athletic Trainer:** Brian Ebel.
Strength/Conditioning Coach: Joe Hogarty.

Andy MacPhail

Minor Leagues

Telephone: (410) 547-6120. **Fax:** (410) 547-6298.
Director, Player Development: David Stockstill. **Assistant Director, Player Development:** Tripp Norton. **Coordinator, Minor League Instruction:** Brian Graham. **Pitching Coordinator:** Dave Schmidt. **Medical Coordinator:** Dave Walker. **Latin American Medical Coordinator:** Manny Lopez.
Roving Instructors: Butch Davis (outfield/baserunning), Larry Jaster (pitching coordinator, Florida operations), Denny Walling (hitting), Don Werner (catching), Mike Bordick (Offensive Instructor), Bobby Dickerson (Infield Coordinator).

Farm System

Class	Club (League)	Manager	Coach	Pitching Coach
Triple-A	Norfolk (IL)	Gary Allenson	Richie Hebner	Mike Griffin
Double-A	Bowie (EL)	Brad Komminsk	Moe Hill	Kennie Steenstra
High A	Frederick (CL)	Orlando Gomez	Denny Hocking	Blaine Beatty
Low A	Delmarva (SAL)	Ryan Minor	Mike Devereaux	Troy Mattes
Short-season	Aberdeen (NYP)	Gary Kendall	C. Devarez/J. Alfaro	Scott McGregor
Rookie	Bluefield (APP)	Einar Diaz	Leo Gomez	Larry McCall
Rookie	Orioles (GCL)	Ramon Sambo	Milt May	Calvin Maduro
Rookie	Orioles (DSL)	Miguel Jabalera	B. Adames/R. Lubo	R. Perez/D. Pascual

Professional Scouting

Telephone: (410) 547-6121. **Fax:** (410) 547-6298.
Director, International Scouting: John Stockstill.
Director, Professional Scouting: Lee MacPhail IV.
Major League Advance Scout: Jim Thrift. **Major League Scouts:** Dave Engle (San Diego, CA), Bruce Kison (Bradenton, FL). **Professional Scouts:** Todd Frohwirth (Waukesha, WI), Jim Howard (Clifton Park, NY), Deacon Jones (Sugar Land, TX), Ted Lakas (Worcester, MA), Bobby Myrick (Colonial Heights, VA), Gary Roenicke (Nevada City, CA), Fred Uhlman Sr. (Baltimore, MD).

Amateur Scouting

Telephone: (410) 547-6187. **Fax:** (410) 547-6298.
Director, Amateur Scouting: Joe Jordan. **Scouting Administrator:** Marcy Zerhusen.
National Crosschecker: Matt Reubel (Oklahoma City, OK). **Regional Crosscheckers:** East—Nick Presto (Palm Beach Garden, FL), Dean Albany (Baltimore, MD), Central—Jim Richardson (Marlow, OK), West—David Blume (Elk Grove, CA).
Full-Time Scouts: Keith Connolly (Fair Haven, NJ), Adrian Dorsey (Florence, KY), Christopher Gayle (Baltimore, MD), John Gillette (Gilbert, AZ), Ernest Jacobs (Wichita, KS), David Jennings (Spanish Fort, AL), James Keller (Sacremento, CA), Gilbert Kubski (Huntington Beach, CA), John Martin (Tampa, FL), Rich Morales (Kemah, TX), Mark Ralston (San Diego, CA), Bob Szymkowski (Chicago, IL), Mike Tullier (River Ridge, NC), Dominic Viola (Cary, NC).
Dominican Summer League, Camp Coordinator: Felipe Alou Jr.
International Scouts: Salvador Ramirez (Dominican), Carlos Bernhardt (Dominican).

Boston Red Sox

Office Address: Fenway Park, 4 Yawkey Way, Boston, MA 02215.
Telephone: (617) 226-6000. **Fax:** (617) 226-6416.
Website: www.redsox.com

Ownership
Principal Owner: John Henry. **Chairman:** Thomas Werner. **Vice Chairman:** David Ginsberg, Phillip Morse. **President/CEO:** Larry Lucchino.

BUSINESS OPERATIONS
Executive VP/Chief Operating Officer: Sam Kennedy. **EVP, Business Affairs:** Jonathan Gilula. **SVP, Fenway Affairs:** Larry Cancro. **Manager, Fenway Affairs:** Beth Krudys. **SVP, Corporate Relations/Executive Director, Red Sox Foundation:** Meg Vaillancourt. **Executive Consultant:** Lou Gorman. **Director, Business Development:** Tim Zue. **Senior Advisor/Baseball Projects:** Jeremy Kapstein. **Senior Advisor/Strategic Planning:** Michael Porter. **General Counsel, NESV:** Ed Weiss. **SVP/Assistant General Counsel:** Jennifer Flynn. **SVP, Special Counsel:** David Friedman. **VP, Club Counsel:** Elaine Steward.

Larry Lucchino

Finance/Human Resources/Information Technology
CFO: Steve Fitch. **Senior Advisor, Finance/Accounting:** Bob Furbush. **Controller:** Mark Solitro. **Director, Finance:** Ryan Oremus. **Payroll Administrator:** Mauricio Rosas. **Senior Manager, Accounting:** Cathy Fahy. **Senior Tax Accountant:** Erin Walsh. **Senior Accountant:** Tom Williams. **VP, Human Resources/Office Administration:** Mary Sprong. **Human Resources Manager:** Patty Moseley. **Director, IT:** Steve Conley. **Senior Systems Analyst:** Randy George.

Sales/Corporate Marketing/Fenway Enterprises
VP, Corporate Partnerships: Joe Januszewski. **VP, Client Services:** Troup Parkinson. **Director, Client Services:** Marcell Bhangoo. **Senior Manager, Club Services:** Carole Alkins. **Manager, Suite Services:** Kim Cameron. **Manager, Dugout Services:** Erin Burgoyne.

Public Affairs/Media/Broadcasting/Marketing/Community Relations
SVP, Public Affairs/Marketing: Susan Goodenow. **Director, Media Relations:** Pam Ganley. **Manager, Media Relations:** Leah Tobin. **Managers, Public Affairs:** Marty Ray, Mike Olano. **Manager, Photography:** Mike Ivins. **VP, Publications/Archives:** Dick Bresciani. **Director, Publications:** Debbie Matson. **Director, Marketing/Broadcast Services:** Colin Burch. **Manager, Marketing:** Monne Williams. **Senior Manager, Community Relations:** Sarah Stevenson.

Business/Ballpark Operations/Development
Director, Planning/Development: Paul Hanlon. **Director, Fenway Operations:** Pete Nesbit. **Director, Concessions/Merchandise Operations:** Jeff Goldenberg. **Director, Grounds:** Dave Mellor. **Director Emeritus, Grounds:** Joe Mooney. **Assistant Director, Grounds:** Jason Griffeth. **Manager, Grounds:** Weston Appelfeller. **Facilities Superintendent:** Donnie Gardner. **Manager, Facilities:** Glen McGlinchey. **Manager, Security Services:** Mark Cacciatore. **Director, Florida**

2010 SCHEDULE
Standard Game Times: 7:10 p.m.; Sun. 1:35

APRIL
5	New York (AL)
7-8	New York (AL)
9-11	at Kansas City
12	at Minnesota
14-15	at Minnesota
16-19	Tampa Bay
20-22	Texas
23-25	Baltimore
26-28	at Toronto
30	at Baltimore

MAY
1-2	at Baltimore
3-6	Los Angeles (AL)
7-9	New York (AL)
10-12	Toronto
14-16	at Detroit
17-18	at New York (AL)
19-20	Minnesota
21-23	at Philadelphia
24-26	at Tampa Bay
27-30	Kansas City

JUNE
1-3	Oakland
4-6	at Baltimore
7-10	at Cleveland
11-13	Philadelphia
15-17	Arizona
18-20	Los Angeles (NL)
22-24	at Colorado
25-27	at San Francisco
29-30	Tampa Bay

JULY
2-4	Baltimore
5-7	at Tampa Bay
9-11	at Toronto
15-18	Texas
19-21	at Oakland
22-25	at Seattle
26-28	at Los Angeles (AL)
30-31	Detroit

AUGUST
1	Detroit
2-5	Cleveland
6-9	at New York (AL)
10-12	at Toronto
13-15	at Texas
17-19	Los Angeles (AL)

20-22	Toronto
23-25	Seattle
27-29	at Tampa Bay
31	at Baltimore

SEPTEMBER
1-2	at Baltimore
3-5	Chicago (AL)
6-8	Tampa Bay
10-12	at Oakland
13-15	at Seattle
17-19	Toronto
20-22	Baltimore
24-26	at New York (AL)
27-30	at Chicago (AL)

OCTOBER
1-3	New York (AL)

GENERAL INFORMATION
Stadium (year opened): Fenway Park (1912).   **Home Dugout:** First Base.
Team Colors: Navy blue, red and white.   **Playing Surface:** Grass.
Player Representative: Unavailable.

Operations: Katie Haas. **VP, Fan Services/Entertainment:** Sarah McKenna. **Manager, Entertainment/Special Event Operations:** Dan Lyons. **Manager, Fan Services/Entertainment:** Stephanie Maneikis. **Senior Manager, Television Production:** John Carter. **Senior Manager, Video Operations/Scoreboard:** Sarah Logan. **PA Announcer:** Carl Beane.

Ticketing Services/Operations
Telephone: 877-REDSOX9. **FAX:** (617) 226-6640.
VP, Ticketing: Ron Bumgarner. **Director, Ticketing:** Richard Beaton. **Assistant Director, Ticketing:** Naomi Calder. **Assistant Director, Season Ticket Services:** Joe Matthews. **Manager, Ticket Operations:** Gary Goldberg. **Manager, Ticket Services:** Jenean Rombola. **Manager, Ticket Accounting:** Sean Carragher. **Manager, Ticket Fulfillment/Systems:** Peter Fahey. **Senior Manager, Premium Sales:** Corey Bowdre. **Manager, Premium Sales:** William Droste.

BASEBALL OPERATIONS

Telephone: (617) 226-6000. **FAX:** (617) 226-6695.
Executive VP/General Manager: Theo Epstein.
Senior VP/Assistant GM: Ben Cherington. **Senior VP, International Scouting:** Craig Shipley. **Assistant to GM:** Allard Baird. **Special Assistant to GM:** Dave Finley. **Director, Baseball Operations:** Brian O'Halloran. **Director, Baseball Information Services:** Tom Tippett. **Assistant Director, Baseball Operations:** Zack Scott. **Traveling Secretary:** Jack McCormick. **Executive Assistant:** Erin Cox. **Senior Advisor:** Bill James. **Special Assistant:** Alex Ochoa.

Major League Staff
Manager: Terry Francona.
Coaches: Bench—DeMarlo Hale; Pitching—John Farrell; Batting—Dave Magadan; First Base—Ron Johnson; Third Base—Tim Bogar; Bullpen—Gary Tuck. **Staff Assistant:** Rob Leary.

Theo Epstein

Medical/Training
Medical Director: Dr. Thomas Gill. **Internist:** Dr. Larry Ronan. **Head Trainer/Assistant Director, Medical Services:** Mike Reinold. **Medical Operations Coordinator:** Jim Rowe. **Assistant Athletic Trainers:** Greg Barajas, Masai Takahashi. **Strength/Conditioning Coach:** Dave Page.

Player Development
Telephone: (617) 226-6000. **FAX:** (617) 226-6695.
Director, Player Development: Mike Hazen. **Director, Minor League Operations:** Raquel Ferreira. **Assistant Director, Player Development:** Ben Crockett. **Assistant Director, Florida Baseball Operations:** Ethan Faggett. **Assistant Director, Latin American Operations:** Eddie Romero. **Field Coordinator:** David Howard. **Director, Dominican Operations:** Jesus Alou. **Latin American Field Coordinator:** Jose Zapata. **Latin American Pitching Coordinator:** Goose Gregson. **Strength/Conditioning Coordinator:** Pat Sandora. **Rehab Coordinator:** Chip Simpson. **Minor League Training Coordinator:** Brad Pearson. **Mental Skills Coordinator:** Bob Tewksbury. **Coordinator, Player Development Programs:** Duncan Webb. **Roving Instructors:** Gary DiSarcina (infield), Chad Epperson (catching), Tom Goodwin (outfield/baserunning), Victor Rodriguez (hitting), Ralph Treuel (pitching).

Farm System

Class	Club (League)	Manager	Coach(es)	Pitching Coach
Triple-A	Pawtucket (IL)	Torey Lovullo	Gerald Perry	Rich Sauveur
Double-A	Portland (EL)	Arnie Beyeler	Dave Joppie	Bob Kipper
High A	Salem (CL)	Kevin Boles	Carlos Febles	Dick Such
Low A	Greenville (SAL)	Billy McMillon	Luis Lopez	Kevin Walker
Short-season	Lowell (NYP)	Bruce Crabbe	George Lombard	Unavailable
Rookie	Red Sox (GCL)	Dave Tomlin	U.L. Washington	Walter Miranda
Rookie	Red Sox (DSL)	Jose Zapata	Nelson Paulino	J. Gonzalez/A. Telemaco

Scouting
Director, Amateur Scouting: Amiel Sawdaye. **Assistant Director, Professional Scouting:** Jared Porter. **Advance Scouting Coordinator:** Steve Langone. **Assistant, Amateur Scouting:** Jared Banner. **Assistant, International Scouting:** Fernando Tamayo. **Advance Scouts:** Dana LeVangie (East Bridgewater, MA), Mike Cather (Roswell, GA). **Special Assignment Scout:** Mark Wasinger (El Paso, TX). **Special Assignment Pitching Evaluator:** Al Nipper (Chesterfield, MO). **Major League Scouts:** Galen Carr (Burlington, VT), Kyle Evans (Boston, MA), Gus Quattlebaum (Long Beach, CA). **Pro Scouts:** Jaymie Bane (Parrish, FL), Dean Decillis (Weston, FL), Dave Klipstein (Roanoke, TX), Bill Latham (Trussville, AL), Joe McDonald (Lakeland, FL), Steve Peck (Scottsdale, AZ). **Consultants:** Curtis Leskanic (Orlando, FL), Jerry Stephenson (Fullerton, CA). **National Crosschecker:** Mike Rikard (Durham, NC). **Regional Crosscheckers:** East—Danny Haas (Ft. Myers, FL), Midwest—Fred Petersen (Horshoe Bay, TX), West—Dan Madsen (Murrieta, CA). Area Scouts: Tom Battista (Thousand Oaks, CA), Quincy Boyd (Harrisburg, NC), Chris Calciano (Ocean View, DE), Matt Dorey (Houston, TX), Raymond Fagnant (East Granby, CT), Laz Gutierrez (Miramar, FL), Blair Henry (Naperville, IL), Tim Hyers (Loganville, GA), Matt Mahoney (Scottsdale, AZ), Chris Mears (Oklahoma City, OK), Edgar Perez (Vega Baja, PR), Pat Portugal (Seattle, WA), Sam Ray (Cincinnati, OH), Demond Smith (Sacramento, CA), Jim Robinson (Arlington, TX), Anthony Turco (Tampa, FL), Danny Watkins (Tuscaloosa, AL), Jim Woodward (Claremont, CA).
Coordinator, Latin American Scouting/International Crosschecker: Todd Claus. **Coordinator, Pacific Rim Scouting:** Jon Deeble. **Coordinator, European Scouting:** Mike Lord. **Venezuela Scouting Supervisor:** Ernesto Gomez. **Dominican Scouting Supervisor:** Manny Nanita. **International Scouts:** Jose Cabrera (Mexico), Luciano Del Rosario (Dominican), Angel Escobar (Venezuela), Brian Farley (Europe), Julio Guevara (Venezuela), John Kim (Korea), Niko Lin (Taiwan), Santiago Prada (Columbia), Luis Prieto (Venezuela), Juan Carlos Pringle (Panama), Antonio Simon (Curacao), Victor Torres (Dominican), Fernando Veracierto (Venezuela).

Chicago Cubs

Office Address: Wrigley Field, 1060 W. Addison St, Chicago, IL 60613.
Telephone: (773) 404-2827. **Fax:** (773) 404-4129.
E-mail Address: cubs@cubs.com. **Website:** www.cubs.com.

Ownership
Chairman: Tom Ricketts. **Board Members:** Laura Ricketts, Peter Ricketts, Todd Ricketts. **President:** Crane Kenney.

BUSINESS OPERATIONS

Tom Ricketts

Phone: (773) 404-2827. **Fax:** (773) 404-4111.
Executive Vice President, Business Operations: Mark McGuire.
Executive Vice President, Chief Sales/Marketing Officer: Wally Hayward. **Executive Coordinator, Business Operations:** Sarah Poontong.

Accounting/Human Resources
Director, Finance: Jodi Reischl. **Accounting Manager:** Mike Van Poucke. **Finance Manager:** Jaime Norton. **Payroll Administrator:** Theresa Bacholzky. **Senior Accountants:** Marian Greene, Aimee Sison. **Senior Director, Human Resources:** Jenifer Surma. **Employment Manager:** Marisol Widmayer. **Coordinator, Human Resources/Stadium Operations:** Danielle Alexa.

Event Operations/Security
Manager, Event Operations/Security: Mike Hill. **Coordinator, Event Operations/Security:** Julius Farrell. **Stadium Operations Management Assistant:** Russell Johnson. **Coordinator, Exterior Operations:** Mary Kusmirek. **Switchboard Operator/Receptionist:** Brenda Morgan.

Facility Management/Information Technology
Senior Director, Facility Management/Information Technology: Carl Rice. **Information Systems Analyst:** Sean True. **Information Systems Support Specialist:** Lucas Luecke. **Coordinator, Office Services:** Randy Skocz. **Head Groundskeeper:** Roger Baird. **Facility Supervisor:** Bill Scott.

Legal/Community Affairs
Senior Vice President, Community Affairs/General Counsel: Michael Lufrano. **Managers, Community Affairs:** Mary Dosek, Jill Lawlor. **Senior Coordinator, Community Affairs/Neighborhood Relations:** Jennifer Dedes Nowak.

Marketing/Broadcasting
Director, Sales/Promotions: Matthew Wszolek. **Assistant Director, Sponsorship Sales:** Samantha Coghill. **Manager, Mezzanine Suites:** Louis Artiaga. **Manager, Special Events/Player Relations/Entertainment:** Joe Rios. **Senior Account Executive:** Andrea Burke.

Media Relations/Publications
Telephone: (773) 404-4191. **Fax:** (773) 404-4129.

2010 SCHEDULE
Standard Game Times: 1:20 p.m., 7:05.

APRIL		
5 . . . . at Atlanta
7-8 . . . . at Atlanta
9-11 . . . . . . at Cincinnati
12 . . . . Milwaukee
14-15 . . . . . . Milwaukee
16-18 . . . . . . Houston
19-22 . . at New York (NL)
23-25 . . . at Milwaukee
26-28 . . . . . Washington
29-30 . . . . Arizona

MAY
1-2 . . . . Arizona
4-6 . . . . . at Pittsburgh
7-9 . . . . . at Cincinnati
10-12 . . . . . . Florida
14-16 . . . . . . Pittsburgh

JUNE
17-18 . . . . . . Colorado
19-20 . . . at Philadelphia
21-23 . . . . at Texas
25-27 . . Los Angeles (NL)
28-30 . . . . St. Louis
31 . . . . at Pittsburgh
1-2 . . . . . . at Pittsburgh
4-6 . . . . at Houston
8-10 . . . . . at Milwaukee
11-13 . . . . Chicago (AL)
15-17 . . . . Oakland
18-20 . . Los Angeles (AL)
22-24 . . . . . . at Seattle
25-27 . . at Chicago (AL)
28-30 . . . . . . Pittsburgh

JULY		
1-4 . . . . Cincinnati
5-7 . . . . at Arizona
8-11 . . at Los Angeles (NL)
15-18 . . . . Philadelphia
19-21 . . . . Houston
23-25 . . . . . . St. Louis
26-28 . . . . . at Houston
30-31 . . . . . at Colorado

AUGUST
1 . . . . at Colorado
2-4 . . . . . . Milwaukee
6-8 . . . . Cincinnati
9-12 . . . at San Francisco
13-15 . . . . . at St. Louis
16-19 . . . . . San Diego
20-22 . . . . Atlanta

23-25 . . . . at Washington
27-29 . . . . . at Cincinnati
30-31 . . . . Pittsburgh

SEPTEMBER
1 . . . . Pittsburgh
3-5 . . . . . New York (NL)
6-8 . . . . Houston
10-12 . . . at Milwaukee
13-15 . . . . . at St. Louis
17-19 . . . . . . at Florida
21-23 . . . San Francisco
24-26 . . . . St. Louis
27-30 . . . . at San Diego

OCTOBER
1-3 . . . . at Houston

GENERAL INFORMATION

Stadium (year opened): Wrigley Field (1914).
Team Colors: Royal blue, red and white.

Player Representative: Unavailable.
Home Dugout: Third Base.
Playing Surface: Grass.

Director, Media Relations: Peter Chase. **Assistant Director, Media Relations:** Jason Carr. **Coordinator, Media Relations:** Dani Holmes. **Assistant, Media Relations:** Dusty Harrington. **Director, Publications/Creative Services:** Lena McDonagh. **Manager, Editorial Projects:** Michael Huang. **Editorial Project Specialist:** Sean Ahmed. **Manager, Design/Production:** Juan Alberto Castillo. **Design/Creative Services Specialist:** Joaquin Castillo.

Ticket Operations
Telephone: (773) 404-2827. **Fax:** (773) 404-4014.
Director, Ticket Operations: Frank Maloney. **Assistant Director, Ticket Sales:** Brian Garza. **Assistant Director, Ticket Services:** Joe Kirchen. **Vault Room Supervisor:** Cherie Blake. **Coordinator, Ticket Orders:** Jan Jotzat. **Coordinator, Ticket Sales:** Karry Kerness. **Senior Ticket Sales Representative:** Kevin Enerson.

Game Day Operations
PA Announcers: Paul Friedman. **Clubhouse Manager:** Tom Hellmann. **Visiting Clubhouse Manager:** Michael Burkhart. **Home Clubhouse Assistant:** Gary Stark.

BASEBALL OPERATIONS
Telephone: (773) 404-2827. **Fax:** (773) 404-4111.
Vice President/General Manager: Jim Hendry. **Assistant GM:** Randy Bush. **Director, Baseball Administration:** Scott Nelson. **Senior Advisor:** Billy Williams. **Special Assistants:** Gary Hughes, Ken Kravec, Dave Littlefield, Louie Elijua. **Major League Scouts:** Bill Harford, Brad Kelley. **Manager, Baseball Information:** Chuck Wasserstrom. **Traveling Secretary:** Jimmy Bank. **Major League Advance Scout:** Keith Stohr. **Major League Video Coordinator:** Naoto Masamoto. **Japanese Interpreter/Media Assistant:** Hiro Aoyama. **Executive Assistant to VP/GM:** Hayley DeWitte.

Jim Hendry

Major League Staff
Manager: Lou Piniella
Coaches: Pitching—Larry Rothschild; Hitting—Rudy Jaramillo; Bench—Alan Trammell; Third Base—Mike Quade; First Base—Ivan De Jesus; Bullpen—Lester Strode; Special Assistant—Matt Sinatro.

Medical/Training
Team Physician: Dr. Stephen Adams. **Team Orthopedist:** Dr. Stephen Gryzlo.
Orthopedic Consultant: Dr. Michael Schafer. **Director, Athletic Training:** Mark O'Neal. **Assistant Athletic Trainers:** Ed Halbur, Yoshi Nakazawa. **Major League Strength/Conditioning Coordinator:** Tim Buss.

Player Development
Telephone: (773) 404-4035. **Fax:** (773) 404-4147
Vice President, Player Personnel: Oneri Fleita.
Coordinators: Dave Bialas (field), Mark Riggins (pitching), Bobby Dernier (outfield/baserunning), Franklin Font (infield), Dave Keller (hitting) Jody Davis (catching). **Latin American Field Coordinator:** Carmelo Martinez. **Minor League Training Coordinator:** Justin Sharpe. **Assistant Training Coordinator:** Chuck Baughman. **Strength/Conditioning Coordinator:** Doug Jarrow. **Strength/Conditioning Coach:** Scott Weberg. **Manager, Player Development Administration:** Patti James. **Equipment Manager:** Dana Noeltner. **Baseball Operations Asstant:** Alex Suarez.

Farm System

Class	Club (League)	Manager	Hitting Coach	Pitching Coach
Triple-A	Iowa (PCL)	Ryne Sandberg	Von Joshua	Mike Mason
Double-A	Tennessee (SL)	Bill Dancy	Tom Beyers	Dennis Lewallyn
High Class A	Daytona (FSL)	Buddy Bailey	Richie Zisk	Tom Pratt
Low Class A	Peoria (MWL)	Casey Kopitzke	Barbaro Garbey	David Rosario
Short-season	Bosie (NWL)	Jody Davis	Ricardo Medina	Jeff Fassero
Rookie	Cubs (AZL)	Juan Cabreja	Desi Wilson	Rick Tronerud
Rookie	Cubs I (DSL)	Manuel Callado	Alberto Garcia	Leo Hernandez
Rookie	Cubs II (DSL)	Yudith Ozorio	Leo Perez	Anderson Tavares

Scouting
Telephone: (773) 404-2827. **Fax:** (773) 404-4147.
Director, Amateur/Professional Scouting: Tim Wilken (Dunedin, FL).
Director, International Scouting: Paul Weaver. **Special Assistant:** Steve Hinton (Mather, CA). **Senior Advisor:** Jim Crawford (Madison, MS). **Player Development/Scouting Assistant:** Jake Ciarrachi. **Administrative Assistant:** Patricia Honzik.
Pro Scouts: Tom Bourque (Cambridge, MA), Joe Housey (Hollywood, FL), Demie Mainieri (Ft. Lauderdale, FL), Mark Servais (LaCrosse, WI). **Special Assignment Scouts:** Bob Lofrano (Woodland Hills, CA), Glen Van Proyan (Lisle, IL). **National Crosschecker:** Sam Hughes (Atlanta, GA). **Crosscheckers:** East—Charles Aliano (Land O'Lakes, FL), Midwest— Steve Riha (Houston, TX), West—Mark Adair (Phoenix, AZ), Canadian/U.S./International: Ron Tostenson (El Dorado Hills, CA). **Area Scouts:** Tim Adkins (Huntington, WV), John Bartsch (Rocklin, CA), Billy Blitzer (Brooklyn, NY), Tom Clark (Lake City, FL), Trey Forkerway (Houston, TX), Steve Fuller (Seal Beach, CA), Al Geddes (Canby, OR), Antonio Grissom (College Park, GA), Denny Henderson (Orange, CA), Steve McFarland (Scottsdale, AZ), Lukas McKnight (Safety Harbour, FL), Ty Nichols (Broken Arrow, OK), Keith Ryman (Jefferson City, TN), Billy Swoope (Norfolk, VA), Stan Zielinski (Winfield, IL). **International Scouts:** Hector Ortega (Venezuela), Jose Serra (Dominican Republic), Steve Wilson (Pacific Rim).

Chicago White Sox

Office Address: 333 W. 35th St., Chicago, IL 60616.
Telephone: (312) 674-1000. **Fax:** (312) 674-5116.
Website: www.whitesox.com.

Ownership
Chairman: Jerry Reinsdorf. **Vice Chairman:** Eddie Einhorn.
Board of Directors: Robert Judelson, Judd Malkin, Robert Mazer, Allan Muchin, Jay Pinsky, Larry Pogofsky, Lee Stern, Sanford Takiff, Burton Ury, Charles Walsh.
Special Assistant to Chairman: Dennis Gilbert. **Assistant to Chairman:** Anita Fasano.

BUSINESS OPERATIONS
Executive Vice President: Howard Pizer.
Senior Director, Information Services: Don Brown. **Senior Director, Human Resources:** Moira Foy. **Administrators, Human Resources:** Leslie Gaggiano, J.J. Krane.

Finance
Senior Vice President, Administration/Finance: Tim Buzard. **Senior Director, Finance:** Bill Waters. **Accounting Manager:** Chris Taylor.

Marketing/Sales
Chief Marketing Officer/Vice President, Marketing: Brooks Boyer. **Senior Director, Business Development/Broadcasting:** Bob Grim. **Manager, Scoreboard Operations/Production:** Jeff Szynal. **Director, Game Operations:** Nichole Manning. **Manager, Game Operations:** Amy Sheridan. **Coordinator, Game Operations:** Dan Mielke.

Jerry Reinsdorf

Senior Director, Corporate Partnerships: Jim Muno. **Managers, Corporate Partnerships:** George McDoniel, Gail Tucker, Brad Dreher. **Manager, Client Services:** Stephanie Johnson. **Coordinator, Corporate Partnership Services:** Jorie Sax.
Director, Ticket Sales: Tom Sheridan. **Manager, Premium Seating Service:** Deb Theobald. **Senior Director, Community Relations:** Christine O'Reilly.
Director, Mass Communications: Maggie Luellen. **Manager, Design Services:** Gareth Breunlin. **Senior Coordinator, Design Services:** Matt Peterson. **Manager, Community Relations:** Danielle Disch. **Senior Coordinator, Community Relations:** Laina Myers. **Coordinators, Community Relations:** Stacy Tsihlopoulos, Dan Puente.

Public Relations
Telephone: (312) 674-5300. **Fax:** (312) 674-5116.
Vice President, Communications: Scott Reifert.
Director, Media Relations: Bob Beghtol. **Director, Public Relations:** Lou Hernandez. **Assistant Director, Media Relations:** Pat O'Connell. **Coordinator, Public Relations:** Marty Maloney. **Coordinator, Media Services:** Ray Garcia.

2010 SCHEDULE
Standard Game Times: 7:10 p.m.; Sun. 1:05.

APRIL
5 . . . . at Atlanta
7-8 . . . . at Atlanta
9-11 . . . . . . at Cincinnati
12 . . . . Milwaukee
14-15 . . . . . . Milwaukee
16-18 . . . . . . Houston
19-22 . . at New York (NL)
23-25 . . . . at Milwaukee
26-28 . . . . . Washington
29-30 . . . . Arizona

MAY
1-2 . . . . Arizona
4-6 . . . . at Pittsburgh
7-9 . . . . . at Cincinnati
10-12 . . . . Florida

14-16 . . . . . . Pittsburgh
17-18 . . . . . . Colorado
19-20 . . . at Philadelphia
21-23 . . . . at Texas
25-27 . . Los Angeles (NL)
28-30 . . . . . . St. Louis
31 . . . . . . at Pittsburgh

JUNE
1-2 . . . . . . at Pittsburgh
4-6 . . . . . . at Houston
8-10 . . . . at Milwaukee
11-13 . . . . Chicago (AL)
15-17 . . . . . . Oakland
18-20 . . Los Angeles (AL)
22-24 . . . . . . at Seattle
25-27 . . at Chicago (AL)
28-30 . . . . . . Pittsburgh

JULY
1-4 . . . . Cincinnati
5-7 . . . . at Arizona
8-11 . . at Los Angeles (NL)
15-18 . . . . Philadelphia
19-21 . . . . . . Houston
23-25 . . . . . . St. Louis
26-28 . . . . at Houston
30-31 . . . . at Colorado

AUGUST
1 . . . . at Colorado
2-4 . . . . . . Milwaukee
6-8 . . . . . . Cincinnati
9-12 . . . at San Francisco
13-15 . . . . at St. Louis
16-19 . . . . . San Diego

20-22 . . . . Atlanta
23-25 . . . at Washington
27-29 . . . at Cincinnati
30-31 . . . . . Pittsburgh

SEPTEMBER
1 . . . . Pittsburgh
3-5 . . . . New York (NL)
6-8 . . . . Houston
10-12 . . at Milwaukee
13-15 . . . . at St. Louis
17-19 . . . . . at Florida
21-23 . . San Francisco
24-26 . . . . . St. Louis
27-30 . . . at San Diego

OCTOBER
1-3 . . . . . . at Houston

GENERAL INFORMATION
Stadium (year opened): U.S. Cellular Field (1991).
Team Colors: Black, white and silver.

Player Representative: Unavailable.
Home Dugout: Third Base.
Playing Surface: Grass.

Stadium Operations
Senior Vice President, Stadium Operations: Terry Savarise. **Senior Director, Event Operations:** Troy Brown. **Senior Director, Guest Services/Diamond Suite Operations:** Julie Taylor. **Head Groundskeeper:** Roger Bossard. **PA Announcer:** Gene Honda. **Official Scorer:** Bob Rosenberg, Don Friske.

Ticketing
Telephone: (312) 674-1000. **Fax:** (312) 674-5102.
Director, Ticket Operations: Mike Mazza. **Manager, Ticket Accounting Administration:** Ken Wisz.

Travel/Clubhouse
Director, Team Travel: Ed Cassin.
Manager, White Sox Clubhouse: Vince Fresso. **Manager, Visiting Clubhouse:** Gabe Morell. **Manager, Umpires Clubhouse:** Joe McNamara Jr.

BASEBALL OPERATIONS
Senior Vice President/General Manager: Ken Williams.
VP/Assistant GM: Rick Hahn. **Special Assistants:** Bill Scherrer, Dave Yoakum. **Executive Assistant to GM:** Nancy Nesnidal. **Director, Baseball Operations:** Dan Fabian. **Assistant Director, Baseball Operations:** Daniel Zien. **Special Assignment Scout:** Alan Regier.

Ken Williams

Major League Staff
Manager: Ozzie Guillen.
Coaches: Bench—Joey Cora; Pitching—Don Cooper; Batting—Greg Walker; First Base—Harold Baines; Third Base—Jeff Cox; Bullpen—Juan Nieves.

Medical, Training
Senior Team Physician: Dr. Charles Bush-Joseph.
Head Athletic Trainer: Herm Schneider. **Assistant Athletic Trainer:** Brian Ball.
Director, Conditioning: Allen Thomas.

Player Development
Telephone: (312) 674-1000. **Fax:** (312) 674-5105.
Director, Player Development: Buddy Bell.
Senior Director, Minor League Operations: Grace Guerrero Zwit. **Assistant Director, Player Development/Scouting:** Del Matthews. **Senior Coordinator, Minor League Administration:** Kathy Potoski. **Manager, Clubhouse/Equipment:** Dan Flood.
Minor League Field Coordinator: Nick Capra. **Roving Instructors:** Daryl Boston (outfield), Kirk Champion (pitching), Jeff Manto (hitting), Ron Oester (infield), John Orton (catching), Manny Trillo (baserunning/bunting), Dale Torborg (conditioning coordinator). **Latin Roving Instructor:** Jose Bautista. **Dominican Player Development/Scouting Supervisor:** Rafael Santana. **Coordinator, Minor League Trainers/Rehabilitation:** Scott Takao. **Coaching Assistant:** Tommy Thompson. **Dominican Coordinator:** Julio Valdez.

Farm System

Class	Club (League)	Manager	Coach	Pitching Coach
Triple-A	Charlotte (IL)	Chris Chambliss	Gary Ward	Richard Dotson
Double-A	Birmingham (SL)	Everardo Magallanes	Andy Tomberlin	J.R. Perdew
High A	Winston-Salem (CL)	Joe McEwing	Robert Sasser	Bobby Thigpen
Low A	Kannapolis (SAL)	Ernie Young	Greg Briley	Larry Owens
Rookie	Bristol Sox (APP)	Ryan Newman	Jerry Hairston	Curt Hasler
Rookie	Great Falls (PIO)	Chris Cron	Eric Hollis	Brian Drahman
Rookie	White Sox (DSL)	Fermin Urbi	Domingo Michel	Melido Perez

Scouting
Telephone: (312) 674-1000. **Fax:** (312) 674-5105.
Pro Scouts: Joe Butler (Long Beach, CA), Gary Pellant (Chandler, AZ), Paul Provas (Arlington, TX), Daraka Shaheed (Vallejo, CA), Bill Young (Scottsdale, AZ), John Tumminia (Newburgh, NY), Dedrick Williams (Chicago, IL).
Director, Amateur Scouting: Doug Laumann (Florence, KY).
Assistant Director, Scouting/Player Development: J.J. Lally. **National Crosscheckers:** Nathan Durst (Sycamore, IL), Ed Pebley (Brigham City, UT). **Regional Crosscheckers:** East—Nick Hostetler (Union, KY), West—Derek Valenzuela (Temecula, CA). **Advisor to Baseball Department:** Larry Monroe (Schaumburg, IL).
Area Scouts: Mike Baker (Santa Ana, CA), Kevin Burrell (Sharpsburg, GA), Alex Cosmidis (Raleigh, NC), Ryan Dorsey (Frederick, MD), Dan Durst (Rockford, IL), Phil Gulley (Morehead, KY), Warren Hughes (Mobile, AL), George Kachigian (Coronado, CA), John Kazanas (Phoenix, AZ), Jose Ortega (Fort Lauderdale, FL), Clay Overcash (Oologan, OK), Andrew Pinter (Raleigh, NC), Mike Shirley (Anderson, IN), Joe Siers (Wesley Chapel, FL), Keith Staab (College Station, TX), Adam Virchis (Modesto, CA), Gary Woods (Solvang, CA).
Part-Time Scouts: Tommy Butler (East Rancho Dominguez, CA), Karl Carswell (Kansas City, MO), Javier Centeno (Guaynabo, PR), John Doldoorian (Whitinsville, MA), Trent Eckstaine (Lemars, IA), Cade Griffis (Addison, TX), Jack Jolly (Murfreeboro, TN), Jason Morvant (Abbeville, LA), Glenn Murdock (Livonia, MI), Howard Nakagama (Salt Lake City, UT), Al Otto (Schaumburg, IL), Mike Paris (Boone, IA).
International Scouts: Marino DeLeon (Dominican Republic), Miguel Peguero (Dominican Republic), Adriano Rodriguez (Dominican Republic), Amador Arias (Venezuela), Ehire Adrianza (Venezuela).

Cincinnati Reds

Office Address: 100 Joe Nuxhall Way, Cincinnati, OH 45202.
Telephone: (513) 765-7000. **Fax:** (513) 765-7342.
Website: www.reds.com.

Ownership
Operated by: The Cincinnati Reds LLC.
President/CEO: Robert Castellini. **Chairman:** Joseph Williams Jr. **Vice Chairman/Treasurer:** Thomas Williams. **COO:** Phillip Castellini. **Executive Assistant to COO:** Sally Greytak. **Secretary:** Christopher Fister.

BUSINESS OPERATIONS
Senior Vice President, Business Operations: Karen Forgus. **Senior Director, Business Development:** Lauren Werner. **Business Operations Assistant/Speakers Bureau:** Emily Chalfant. **Business/Broadcasting Administrator:** Ginny Kamp.

Finance/Administration
Vice President, Finance/CFO: Doug Healy. **VP/General Counsel:** James Marx. **Controller:** Bentley Viator. **Accounting Manager:** Jill Niemeyer. **Director, Human Resources:** Teddi Mangas-Coon. **Human Resources Manager:** John Hale. **Benefits Coordinator:** Allison Spurlock. **Director, Information Technology:** Brian Keys.

Bob Castellini

Sales
Senior Director, Ticket Sales: John Davis. **Business Development Manager:** Jodi Czanik. **Director, Group Sales:** David Ziegler. **Group Sales Manager:** Ryan Niemeyer. **Suite/Premium Services Manager:** Emily Tincher. **Premium Sales Managers:** Christopher Bausano, Ryan Rizzo. **Season Sales Manager:** Chris Herrell. **Season Ticket Manager:** Bev Bonavita. **Group Ticket Manager:** Brad Callahan. **Group Ticket Coordinator:** John Rieder. **Season Ticket Coordinator:** Shelley Volpenhein. **Director, Special Events:** Jennifer Green. **Event Services Coordinator:** Anne Kirby. **Director, Ticket Client Services:** Craig Warman. **Supervisor, Ticket Client Services:** Nancy Bloss.

Ticket Operations
Director, Ticket Operations: John O'Brien. **Assistant Director, Ticket Operations:** Ken Ayer. **Ticket Operations Administration Manager:** Hallie Kinney.

Media Relations
Director, Media Relations: Rob Butcher. **Assistant Directors, Media Relations:** Larry Herms, Jamie Ramsey.

Communications/Marketing
Director, Creative Services: Ralph Mitchell. **Managing Editor:** Jarrod Rollins. **Senior Director, Entertainment/Events/Production:** Jennifer Berger. **Promotional Events Manager:** Zach Bonkowski. **Media Production Manager:** David Storm. **Coordinator, Events/Community:** Kathryn Braun. **Manager, Public Relations:** Michael Anderson.

2010 SCHEDULE
Standard Game Times: 7:10 p.m.; Sun. 1:10

APRIL			JULY		SEPTEMBER

APRIL
5 . . . . St. Louis
7-8 . . . . St. Louis
9-11 . . . . Chicago (NL)
12-15 . . . . at Florida
16-18 . . . . at Pittsburgh
20-22 . . Los Angeles (NL)
23-25 . . . . . . San Diego
27-29 . . . . . at Houston
30 . . . . at St. Louis

MAY
1-2 . . . . at St. Louis
3-5 . . . . . New York (NL)
7-9 . . . . . Chicago (NL)
10-12 . . . . at Pittsburgh
14-16 . . . . St. Louis

17-18 . . . . . . Milwaukee
19-20 . . . . . . at Atlanta
21-23 . . . . at Cleveland
24-27 . . . . . . Pittsburgh
28-30 . . . . Houston
31 . . . . at St. Louis

JUNE
1-2 . . . . . . at St. Louis
4-6 . . . . . at Washington
7-10 . . . . . San Francisco
11-13 . . . . . Kansas City
15-17 . . Los Angeles (NL)
18-20 . . . . . . at Seattle
21-23 . . . . at Oakland
25-27 . . . . . . Cleveland
28-30 . . . . . Philadelphia

JULY
1-4 . . . . at Chicago (NL)
5-7 . . . . at New York (NL)
8-11 . . . . at Philadelphia
16-18 . . . . . . Colorado
19-22 . . . . . Washington
23-25 . . . . . . at Houston
26-28 . . . . . at Milwaukee
30-31 . . . . Atlanta

AUGUST
1 . . . . Atlanta
2-4 . . . . . at Pittsburgh
6-8 . . . . at Chicago (NL)
9-11 . . . . St. Louis
13-15 . . . . Florida
17-19 . . . . . . at Arizona

20-22 . at Los Angeles (NL)
23-25 . . . at San Francisco
27-29 . . . . . Chicago (NL)
30-31 . . . . . Milwaukee

SEPTEMBER
1 . . . . Milwaukee
3-5 . . . . at St. Louis
6-9 . . . . . . at Colorado
10-12 . . . . . . Pittsburgh
13-16 . . . . Arizona
17-19 . . . . . at Houston
20-22 . . . . at Milwaukee
24-26 . . . . at San Diego
28-30 . . . . Houston

OCTOBER
1-3 . . . . Milwaukee

GENERAL INFORMATION
Stadium (year opened): Great American Ball Park (2003).
Team Colors: Red, white and black.

Player Representative: Unavailable.
Home Dugout: First Base.
Playing Surface: Grass.

Marketing Manager: Lisa Braun.

Community Relations
Director, Community Relations: Lorrie Platt. **Community Fund Executive Director:** Charley Frank. **Executive Director, Reds Hall of Fame:** Rick Walls. **Operations Manager/Chief Curator, Reds Hall of Fame:** Chris Eckes.

Corporate Sales
Vice President, Corporate Sales: Bill Reinberger. **Assistant, Corporate Sales:** Denise Lockwood. **Corporate Sales Managers:** Dave Collins, Dan Lewis, Mark Scherer. **Broadcast/Affiliates Manager:** Joe Zerhusen.

Ballpark Operations
Vice President, Ballpark Operations: Declan Mullin.
Director, Ballpark Operations: Sean Brown. **Ballpark Operations Manager:** Colleen Rodenberg. **Ballpark Operations Superintendent:** Bob Harrison. **Manager, Technology Business Center:** Chris Campbell. **Chief Engineer:** Roger Smith. **Head Groundskeeper:** Doug Gallant. **Assistant Groundskeeper:** Jon Phelps.

BASEBALL OPERATIONS
President, Baseball Operations/GM: Walt Jocketty.
Director, Major League Administration: Debbie Bent. **Vice President/Assistant GM:** Bob Miller. **VP, Scouting/Player Development/International Operations:** Bill Bavasi. **VP/Special Assistant:** Jerry Walker. **Special Assistants:** Eric Davis, Mario Soto. **VP, Baseball Operations:** Dick Williams. **Assistant Director, Baseball Operations:** Nick Krall. **Manager, Video Scouting:** Rob Coughlin. **Manager, Baseball Research/Analysis:** Sam Grossman. **Baseball Operations Assistant:** Stephanie Ben.

Walt Jocketty

Major League Staff
Manager: Dusty Baker.
Coaches: Bench—Chris Speier; Pitching—Bryan Price; Batting—Brook Jacoby; First Base—Billy Hatcher; Third Base—Mark Berry; Bullpen—Juan Lopez.

Player Development
Telephone: (513) 765-7700. **Fax:** (513) 765-7799.
Senior Director, Player Development/Global Scouting: Terry Reynolds.
Director, Minor League Administration: Lori Hudson. **Player Development Administrator:** Jeff Graupe. **Arizona Operations Manager:** Mike Saverino. **Coordinator, Arizona Marketing/Operations:** Lisa Lantz.
Field Coordinator: Freddie Benavides. **Assistant Field Coordinator, Instruction:** Bill Doran. **Coordinators:** Ronnie Ortegon (hitting), Mack Jenkins (pitching), Darren Bragg (outfield/baserunning), Pat Kelly (catching). **Director, Dominican Republic Academy:** Juan Peralta. **Assistant Field Coordinator, Dominican Republic:** Joel Noboa. **Director, Venezuela Academy:** Jose Fuentes. **Venezuela Field Coordinators:** Jose Miguel Nieves. **Medical Coordinator:** Richard Stark. **Medical Administrator:** Patrick Serbus. **Strength/Conditioning Coordinator:** Sean Marohn. **Rehab/Physical Therapist:** Andrew McNally. **Rehab/Physical Therapist:** Brad Epstein. Strength/Conditioning Coach: Zach Gjestvang.

Farm System

Class	Club (League)	Manager	Coach	Pitching Coach
Triple-A	Louisville (IL)	Rick Sweet	Adrian Garrett	Ted Power
Double-A	Carolina (SL)	David Bell	Ryan Jackson	Tom Browning
High A	Lynchburg (CAR)	Pat Kelly	Tony Jaramillo	Rigo Beltran
Low A	Dayton (MWL)	Todd Benzinger	Ken Griffey Sr.	Tony Fossas
Rookie	Billings (PIO)	Delino DeShields	Alex Pelaez	Bob Forsch
Rookie	Reds (AZL)	Julio Garcia	Jorge Orta	Tom Browning
Rookie	Reds (DSL)	Jose Noboa	Nilson Antiqua	Francisco Trejo

Scouting
Telephone: (513) 765-7000. **Fax:** (513) 765-7799.
Senior Director, Amateur Scouting: Chris Buckley. **Assistant Director, Amateur Scouting:** Paul Pierson.
Senior Special Assistant, Pro Scouting: Gene Bennett. **Senior Special Assistant, Player Personnel:** Cam Bonifay. **Special Assistants:** J Harrison, Mike Squires. **Major League Advance Scout:** Shawn Pender. **Pro Scouts:** Jeff Morris, John Morris, Tom Shafer, Jeff Taylor. **National Crosscheckers:** Wayne Britton (Waynesboro, VA), Mark McKnight (Tega Cay, SC), Mark Snipp (Humble, TX). **Crosschecker:** Jeff Barton (Gilbert, AZ). **Scouting Supervisors:** Tony Arias (Miami, FL), Jason Baker (Salem, OR), Rich Bordi (Rohnert Park, CA), Jeff Brookens (Chambersburg, PA), Bill Byckowski (Ontario, Canada), Clark Crist (Tucson, AZ), Rex De La Nuez (Burbank, CA), Jerry Flowers (Cypress, TX), Tyler Jennings (Daphne, AL), Joe Katuska (Cincinnati, OH), Mike Keenan (Manhattan, KS), Brad Meador (Cincinnati, OH), Mike Misuraca (Murrieta, CA), John Poloni (Tarpon Springs, FL), Lee Seras (Flanders, NJ), Perry Smith (Charlotte, NC), Andy Stack (Hartford, WI), Greg Zunino (Cape Coral, FL). **Part-Time Scouts:** Edwin Daub (Binghamton, NY), Jim Grief (Paducha, KY), Bill Killian (Stanwood, MI), Ed Mathes (Westbury, NY), Denny Nagel (Cincinnati, OH), Marlon Styles (Cincinnati, OH), Mike Wallace (Escondido, CA), John Walsh (Windsor, CT), Roger Weberg (Bemidji, MN).
Director, Latin American Scouting: Tony Arias. **Director, Global Scouting:** Jim Stoeckel. **Assistant Director, Latin America Scouting:** Miguel Machado. **Coordinator, Dominican Republic Scouting:** Richard Jimenez.
International Scouts: Carlos Batista (Dominican), Geronimo Blanco (Colombia), Bill Byckowski (Canada), Cesar Castro (Dominican), Andy Chen (Taiwan), Nick Dempsey (South Africa), Jose Fuentes (Venezuela), Jason Hewitt (Australia), Evert Jan't Hoen (Netherlands), Bob Lindsey (Germany), Robert Morillo (Venezuela), Victor Oramas (Venezuela), Camilo Pina (Dominican), Luke Prokopec (Australia), Anibal Reluz (Panama), Sal Varriale (Italy), Anibal Vega (Nicaragua), Everth Velasquez (Venezuela), Miguel Victor Pol (Dominican), Randy Yamashiro (Hawaii/Japan).

Cleveland Indians

Office Address: Progressive Field, 2401 Ontario St, Cleveland, OH 44115.
Telephone: (216) 420-4200. **Fax:** (216) 420-4396.
Website: www.indians.com.

Ownership
Owner, CEO: Lawrence Dolan. **President:** Paul Dolan.

BUSINESS OPERATIONS

Executive Vice President, Business: Dennis Lehman. **Executive Administrative Assistant, Business:** Dru Kosik.

Corporate Marketing/Finance
Director, Corporate Sales: Ted Baugh. **Manager, New Business Development:** Sheff Webb. **Senior VP, Finance/CFO:** Ken Stefanov. **VP/General Counsel:** Joe Znidarsic. **Controller:** Sarah Taylor. **Director, Planning/Analysis/Reporting:** Rich Dorffer. **Manager, Accounting:** Karen Menzing. **Manager, Payroll Accounting:** Mary Forkapa.

Human Resources
Senior Director, Human Resources/Benefits: Sara Lehrke. **Director, Training/Recruitment:** Susie Downey. **Technology Trainer:** Jennifer Gibson. **Coordinator, Benefits:** Crystal Basile. **Coordinator, Human Resources:** Melissa Painter.

Larry Dolan

Marketing/Merchandising
Senior VP, Sales/Marketing: Vic Gregovits. **Director, Marketing:** Sanaa Julien. **Manager, Promotions:** Jason Kidik. **Manager, Productions:** Justin White. **Manager, In-Game Entertainment:** Annie Merovich. **Broadcast Engineer:** Jim Rosenhaus. **Coordinator, Marketing/Copywriting:** Anne Madzelan. **Senior Director, Merchandising:** Kurt Schloss. **Merchandise Manager:** Karen Fox.

Public Relations, Communications
Telephone: (216) 420-4380. **Fax:** (216) 420-4396.
Vice President, Public Relations: Bob DiBiasio. **Director, Media Relations:** Bart Swain. **Manager, Media Relations/Administration:** Susie Giuliano. **Manager, Media Relations:** Jeff Sibel. **Director, Communications/Creative Services:** Curtis Danburg. **Coordinator, Communications:** Danielle Cherry. **Team Photographer:** Dan Mendlik.

Ballpark Operations
Vice President, Ballpark Operations: Jim Folk.
Director, Facility Maintenance: Chris Donahoe. **Head Groundskeeper:** Brandon Koehnke. **Director, Ballpark Operations:** Jerry Crabb. **Assistant Director, Ballpark Operations:** Brad Mohr. **Assistant Director, Facility Maintenance:** Seth Cooper. **Coordinator, Game Day Staff:** Trevina Johnson.

2010 SCHEDULE

Standard Game Times: 7:05 p.m.; Sun. 1:05.

APRIL
5 . . . . . . at Chicago (AL)
7-8 . . . . at Chicago (AL)
9-11 . . . . at Detroit
12 . . . . Texas
14-15 . . . . Texas
16-18 . . . . . Chicago (AL)
20-22 . . . . . at Minnesota
23-25 . . . . . . at Oakland
26-28 at Los Angeles (AL)
30 . . . . Minnesota

MAY
1-2 . . . . Minnesota
3-5 . . . . Toronto
7-9 . . . . Detroit
11-13 . . . . at Kansas City
14-16 . . . . . at Baltimore

17-18 . . . . . at Tampa Bay
19-20 . . . . . Kansas City
21-23 . . . . Cincinnati
24-26 . . . . . Chicago (AL)
28-31 . . at New York (AL)

JUNE
1-3 . . . . at Detroit
4-6 . . . . at Chicago (AL)
7-10 . . . . Boston
11-13 . . . . . Washington
15-17 . . . . New York (NL)
18-20 . . . . . at Pittsburgh
22-24 . . . . at Philadelphia
25-27 . . . . . at Cincinnati
28-30 . . . . Toronto

JULY
1 . . . . Toronto
2-4 . . . . Oakland
5-7 . . . . at Texas
8-11 . . . . . at Tampa Bay
16-18 . . . . Detroit
19-21 . . . . at Minnesota
23-25 . . . . . Tampa Bay
26-29 . . . . New York (AL)
30-31 . . . . . at Toronto

AUGUST
1 . . . . at Toronto
2-5 . . . . at Boston
6-8 . . . . Minnesota
10-12 . . . . . . Baltimore
13-15 . . . . Seattle
17-19 . . . . at Kansas City

20-22 . . . . at Detroit
24-26 . . . . Oakland
27-29 . . . . . Kansas City
30-31 . . . . . Chicago (AL)

SEPTEMBER
1 . . . . Chicago (AL)
2-5 . . . . at Seattle
6-8 . . at Los Angeles (AL)
10-12 . . . . . Minnesota
14-16 . . . Los Angeles (AL)
17-19 . . . . at Kansas City
20-22 . . . . at Minnesota
23-26 . . . . . Kansas City
27-29 . . . . Detroit

OCTOBER
1-3 . . . . at Chicago (AL)

GENERAL INFORMATION
Stadium (year opened): Progressive Field (1994).
Team Colors: Navy blue, red and silver.

Player Representative: Jake Westbrook.
Home Dugout: Third Base.
Playing Surface: Grass.

Information Systems

Senior Director, Information Systems: Dave Powell. **Manager, Systems Development:** Matt Tagliaferri. **Manager, End-User Support:** Dan Mendlik. **Network Manager:** Whitney Kuszmaul. **Programmer Analyst:** Plamen Kouzov.

Ticketing

Telephone: (216) 420-4487. **Fax:** (216) 420-4481.

Director, Ticket Services: Gene Connelly. **Manager, Ticket Services:** David Pike. **Manager, Ticket Office:** Ryan Beech. **Manager, Ticket Operations:** Andrea Zagger. **Senior Director, Tickets/Premium Sales:** Mike Mulhall. **Director, Fan Services:** Dave Murray.

Spring Training/Arizona Operations:

Manager, Arizona Operations: Ryan Lantz. **Manager, Home Clubhouse:** Fletcher Wilkes. **Manager, Equipment Acquisitions:** Jeff Sipos.

Travel, Clubhouse

Director, Team Travel: Mike Seghi. **Home Clubhouse/Equipment Manager:** Tony Amato. **Manager, Video Operations:** Bob Chester. **Visiting Clubhouse Manager:** Willie Jenks.

BASEBALL OPERATIONS

Telephone: (216) 420-4200. **Fax:** (216) 420-4321.

Executive Vice President/General Manager: Mark Shapiro.

VP, Baseball Operations/Assistant GM: Chris Antonetti.

Director, Player Personnel: Steve Lubratich. **Director, Baseball Operations:** Mike Chernoff. **Director, Baseball Administration:** Wendy Hoppel. **Manager, Baseball Research/Analytics:** Keith Woolner. **Assistant Director, Baseball Operations:** Andrew Miller. **Assistant, Baseball Research/Analysis:** Jason Pare. **Executive Administrative Assistant:** Marlene Lehky. **Administrative Assistant:** Barbara Lessman. **Sports Psychologist:** Dr. Charles Maher.

Major League Staff

Manager: Manny Acta.

Coaches: Bench—Tim Tolman, Pitching—Tim Belcher, Hitting—Jon Nunnally, First Base— Sandy Alomar Jr., Third Base/Infield—Steve Smith, Bullpen—Scott Radinsky.

Mark Shapiro

Assistants, Major League Staff: Ruben Niebla, Dave Wallace.

Medical, Training

Head Team Physician: Dr. Mark Schickendantz. **Director, Medical Services/Head Trainer:** Lonnie Soloff. **Assistant Athletic Trainers:** Rick Jameyson, Jeff Desjardins. **Strength/Conditioning Coach:** Joe Kessler.

Player Development

Telephone: (216) 420-4308. **Fax:** (216) 420-4321.

Director, Player Development: Ross Atkins.

Assistant, Player Development: Meka Asonye. **Administrative Assistant:** Nilda Taffanelli. **Advisor, Player Development:** Johnny Goryl. **Director, Latin American Operations:** Ramon Pena. **Field Coordinator:** Dave Hudgens. **Coordinators:** Dave Miller (pitching), Bruce Fields (hitting), Gary Thurman (outfield/baserunning), Chris Tremie (catching), Jake Beiting (strength/conditioning), Julio Rangel (mental skills). **Field Coordinator, Latin America:** Minnie Mendoza.

Farm System

Class	Club	Manager	Coach	Pitching Coach
Triple-A	Columbus (IL)	Mike Sarbaugh	Lee May Jr.	Charles Nagy
Double-A	Akron (EL)	Joel Skinner	Jim Rickon	Greg Hibbard
High A	Kinston (CL)	Aaron Holbert	Rouglas Odor	Tony Arnold
Low A	Lake County (MWL)	Ted Kubiak	Phil Clark	Mickey Callaway
Short-season	Mahoning Valley (NYP)	Travis Fryman	Dennis Malave	Ken Rowe
Rookie	Indians (AZL)	Chris Tremie	Anthony Medrano	Jeff Harris
Rookie	Indians (DSL)	Wilfredo Tejada	G. Jabalera/C. Fermin	Mario Brito

Scouting

Telephone: (216) 420-4309. **Fax:** (216) 420-4321.

Assistant General Manager/Scouting Operations: John Mirabelli.

Director, Amateur Scouting: Brad Grant. **Assistant Director, Scouting:** Paul Gillispie. **Assistant, Scouting Operations:** Derek Falvey. **Assistant, Professional Scouting:** Carter Hawkins. **Major League Scouts:** Dave Malpass (Huntington Beach, CA), Don Poplin (Norwood, NC), Chris Smith (Montgomery, TX). **Pro Scouts:** Doug Carpenter (North Palm Beach, FL), Jim Cuthbert (Chapel Hill, NC), Steve Lyons (Lake Mary, FL).

National Crosschecker: Chuck Ricci (Greencastle, PA). **Regional Crosscheckers:** Scott Barnsby (Huntsville, AL), Paul Cogan (Rocklin, CA), Scott Meaney (Apex, NC), Derrick Ross (Lake Orion, MI). **Area Scouts:** Steve Abney (Lawrence, KS), Corteze Armstrong (Willowbrook, IL), Chuck Bartlett (Starkville, MS), Kevin Cullen (Dallas, TX), Byron Ewing (Goodyear, AZ), Don Lyle (Sacramento, CA), Bob Mayer (Somerset, PA), Junie Melendez (Lorain, OH), Les Pajari (Conroe, TX), Vince Sagisi (Encino, CA), Jason Smith (Long Beach, CA), Mike Soper (Tampa, FL), Brad Tyler (Bishop, GA), Jack Uhey (Ridgefiled, WA), Brent Urcheck (Philadelphia, PA). **Latin America Crosschecker:** Cesar Geronimo (Aventura, FL).

Colorado Rockies

Office Address: 2001 Blake St., Denver, CO 80205.
Telephone: (303) 292-0200. **Fax:** (303) 312-2116.
Website: www.coloradorockies.com.

Ownership
Operated by: Colorado Rockies Baseball Club Ltd.
Vice Chairman/CEO: Charles Monfort. **Vice Chairman:** Richard Monfort.
Executive Assistant to Vice Chairmen: Patricia Penfold.

BUSINESS OPERATIONS

Charles Monfort

President: Keli McGregor. **Executive Assistant to President:** Terry Douglass. **Executive Vice President, Business Operations:** Greg Feasel. **Assistant to Executive VP, Business Operations:** Kim Olson. **VP, Human Resources:** Elizabeth Stecklein.

Finance
Senior Vice President/CFO: Hal Roth. **VP, Finance:** Michael Kent. **Senior Director, Purchasing:** Gary Lawrence. **Purchasing Assistant:** Gloria Giraldi. **Director, Accounting:** Phil Emerson. **Accountants:** Joel Binfet, Laine Campbell. **Payroll Administrator:** Juli Daedelow.

Marketing/Sales
VP, Corporate Sales: Marcy English-Glasser. **Director, New Partner Development:** Brendan Falvey. **Director, Promotions/Special Events:** Jason Fleming. **Coordinator, Promotions/Special Events:** Liz Coates. **Assistant Director, In-Game Entertainment/Broadcasting:** Kent Krosbakken. **VP, Community/Retail Operations:** Jim Kellogg. **Managers, Community Affairs:** Dallas Davis, Antigone Vigil. **Manager, Community Fields Program/Historian:** Paul Parker. **Director, Retail Operations:** Aaron Heinrich. **Director, Information Systems:** Bill Stephani. **Senior Director, Advertising/Marketing:** Jill Campbell. **Coordinator, Advertising/Marketing:** Sarah Topf. **Assistant, Advertising/Marketing:** Marisol Villagomez. **Assistant Editor, Publications:** Paul Swydan.

Public Relations/Communications
Telephone: (303) 312-2325. **Fax:** (303) 312-2319.
VP, Communications/Public Relations: Jay Alves. **Assistant to the VP, Communications/Public Relations:** Irma Castañeda. **Manager, Communications/Public Relations:** Charlie Hepp. **Coordinator, Communications/Public Relations:** Nick Piburn.

Stadium Operations
Senior Director, Food Service Operations/Development: Albert Valdes. **VP, Ballpark Operations:** Kevin Kahn. **Manager, Ballpark Services:** Mary Beth Benner. **Senior Director, Guest Services:** Steven Burke. **Director, Security:** Don Lyon. **Senior Director, Engineering/Facilities:** James Wiener. **Director, Engineering:** Randy Carlill. **Director, Facilities:**

2010 SCHEDULE

Standard Game Times: 6:40 p.m.; Fri. 7:10; Sat. 6:10; Sun. 1:10.

APRIL
5-7	at Milwaukee
9-11	San Diego
13-15	New York (NL)
16-18	at Atlanta
19-22	at Washington
23-25	Florida
26-28	Arizona
30	at San Francisco

MAY
1-2	at San Francisco
3-5	at San Diego
7-9	at Los Angeles (NL)
10-12	Philadelphia
13-16	Washington
17-18	at Chicago (NL)

19-20	at Houston
21-23	at Kansas City
25-27	Arizona
28-30	Los Angeles (NL)
31	at San Francisco

JUNE
1-2	at San Francisco
4-6	at Arizona
7-10	Houston
11-13	Toronto
15-17	at Minnesota
18-20	Milwaukee
22-24	Boston
25-27	at Los Angeles (AL)
28-30	at San Diego

JULY
1-4	San Francisco
6-8	St. Louis
9-11	San Diego
16-18	at Cincinnati
19-22	at Florida
23-26	at Philadelphia
27-29	Pittsburgh
30-31	Chicago (NL)

AUGUST
1	Chicago (NL)
3-4	San Francisco
5-8	at Pittsburgh
10-12	at New York (NL)
13-15	Milwaukee
17-19	at Los Angeles (NL)
20-22	at Arizona

23-25	Atlanta
27-29	Los Angeles (NL)
30-31	at San Francisco

SEPTEMBER
1	at San Francisco
3-5	at San Diego
6-9	Cincinnati
10-12	Arizona
13-15	San Diego
17-19	at Los Angeles (NL)
21-23	at Arizona
24-26	San Francisco
27-29	Los Angeles (NL)
30	at St. Louis

OCTOBER
1-3	at St. Louis

GENERAL INFORMATION
Stadium (year opened): Coors Field (1995).
Team Colors: Purple, black and silver.
Player Representative: Troy Tulowitzki.
Home Dugout: First Base.
Playing Surface: Grass.

Oly Olsen. **Head Groundskeeper:** Mark Razum. **PA Announcer:** Reed Saunders. **Official Scorers:** Dave Einspahr, Dave Plati.

Ticketing
   Telephone: (303) 762-5437, (800) 388-7625. **Fax:** (303) 312-2115.
   VP, Ticket Operations, Sales/Services: Sue Ann McClaren. **Senior Director, Ticket Operations/Sales/Services:** Kevin Fenton. **Director, Ticket Operations/Finances:** Kent Hakes. **Assistant Director, Ticket Operations:** Scott Donaldson. **Manager, Ticket Operations:** Kevin Flood. **Supervisor, Ticket Operations:** Mandy Stecklein. **Representative, Ticket Operations/Spring Training Promotions/Group Sales:** Andy Finley. **Director, Season Tickets/Group Sales:** Jeff Benner. **Manager, Season Tickets:** Farrah Magee. **Supervisor, Outbound Sales/Suites:** Matt Haddad. **Account Representatives, Ticket Sales:** Grayson Beatty, Ryan Dillon, Jason Regan. **Client Services Representative, Season Tickets:** Bobby Dicroce.

Travel/Clubhouse
   Director, Major League Operations: Paul Egins.
   Director, Clubhouse Operations: Keith Schulz. **Assistant to Director, Clubhouse Operations:** Joe Diaz.
   Visiting Clubhouse Manager: Alan Bossart.

BASEBALL OPERATIONS
   Telephone: (303) 292-0200. **Fax:** (303) 312-2320.
   Executive VP/General Manager: Dan O'Dowd. **Assistant to Executive VP/GM:** Adele Armagost. **VP/Assistant GM:** Bill Geivett. **Director, Baseball Operations:** Jeff Bridich. **Assistant, Baseball Operations/General Counsel:** Zack Rosenthal. **Special Assistants to GM:** Pat Daugherty (Aurora, CO), Dave Holliday (Tulsa, OK), Marcel Lachemann (Penryn, CA).

Dan O'Dowd

Major League Staff
   Manager: Jim Tracy.
   Coaches: Bench—Tom Runnells; Pitching—Bob Apodaca; Hitting—Don Baylor; First Base—Glenallen Hill; Third Base—Rich Dauer; Bullpen—Jim Wright; Bullpen Catcher—Mark Strittmatter; Strength/Conditioning—Brian Jordan; Video—Brian Jones.

Medical/Training
   Director, Medical Operations: Tom Probst. **Medical Director:** Dr. Thomas Noonan. **Club Physicians:** Dr. Allen Schreiber, Dr. Douglas Wyland. **Head Trainer:** Keith Dugger.

Player Development
   Telephone: (303) 292-0200. **Fax:** (303) 312-2320.
   Senior Director, Player Development: Marc Gustafson.
   Assistant, Player Development: Walter Sylvester. **Field Coordinator:** Ron Gideon. **Roving Instructors:** Scott Fletcher (infield), Marv Foley (catching), Trenidad Hubbard (outfield/baserunning), Jim Johnson (hitting), Bo McLaughlin (pitching). **Special Assistant, Baseball Operations:** Rick Mathews. **Senior Advisor, Player Development:** Bobby Knoop. **Video Coordinator:** Jimmy Hartley. **Strength/Conditioning Coordinator:** Gabe Bauer. **Mental Skills Coach:** Ronn Svetich. **Rehab Coordinator:** Scott Murayama. **Cultural Development Coordinator:** Daniel Pace. **Equipment Manager:** Jerry Bass.

Farm System

Class	Club (League)	Manager	Coach	Pitching Coach
Triple-A	Colorado Springs (PCL)	Stu Cole	Rene Lachemann	Doug Linton
Double-A	Tulsa (TL)	Ron Gideon	Dave Hajek	Bryan Harvey
High A	Modesto (CAL)	Jerry Weinstein	Duane Espy	Darryl Scott
Low A	Asheville (SAL)	Joe Mikulik	Houston Jimenez	Dave Schuler
Short-season	Tri-City (NWL)	Fred Ocasio	Anthony Sanders	Joey Eischen
Rookie	Casper (PIO)	Tony Diaz	Kevin Riggs	Craig Bjornson
Rookie	Rockies (DSL)	Mauricio Gonzalez	F. Nunez/E. Jose	Edison Lora

Scouting
   Telephone: (303) 292-0200. **Fax:** (303) 312-2320.
   Vice President, Scouting: Bill Schmidt. **Assistant Director, Scouting:** Danny Montgomery. **Manager, Scouting:** Zach Wilson. **Director, Pro Scouting:** Jon Weil. **Advance Scout:** Chris Warren. **Major League Scouts:** Will George (Woolwich Township, NJ). **Pro Scouts:** Ty Coslow (Louisville, KY), Jack Gillis (Sarasota, FL), Mike Hamilton (Dallas, TX), Mike Paul (Tucson, AZ). **Special Assignment Scout:** Terry Wetzel (Overland Park, KS).
   National Crosschecker: Mike Ericson (Phoenix, AZ). **Scouting Adviser:** Dave Snow (Seal Beach, CA).
   Area Scouts: John Cedarburg (Fort Myers, FL), Scott Corman (Lexington, KY), Dar Cox (Frisco, TX), Jeff Edwards (Humble, TX), Chris Forbes (AZ), Mike Garlatti (Edison, NJ), Mark Germann (Atkins, IA), Matt Hattabaugh (Westminster, CA), Damon Iannelli (Brandon, MS), Jon Lukens (San Diego, CA), Alan Matthews (Atlanta, GA), Jay Matthews (Concord, NC), Jorge de Posada (Rio Piedras, PR), Ed Santa (Powell, OH), Gary Wilson (Sacramento, CA). **Part-Time Scouts:** Norm DeBriyn (Fayetteville, AR), Jeff Hipps (Millbrae, CA), Marc Johnson (Centennial, CO), Dave McQueen (Bossier City, LA), Greg Pullia (Plymouth, MA).
   Director, International Operations: Rolando Fernandez. **Director, Venezuelan Operations:** Francisco Cartaya. **Manager, Dominican Operations:** Jhonathan Leyba. **Manager, Pacific Rim Operations:** Ming Harbor. **International Scouts:** Phil Allen (Australia), Martin Cabrera (Dominican Republic), Claudino Hernandez (Panama), Carlos Gomez (Venezuela), Orlando Medina (Venezuela), Frank Roa (Dominican Republic), Chi-Sheng Tsai (Taiwan).

Detroit Tigers

Office Address: 2100 Woodward Ave, Detroit, MI 48201.
Telephone: (313) 471-2000. **Fax:** (313) 471-2138. **Website:** www.tigers.com

Ownership
Operated By: Detroit Tigers Inc. **Owner:** Michael Ilitch.
President/CEO/General Manager: David Dombrowski. **Special Assistants to President:** Al Kaline, Willie Horton.
Executive Assistant to President/CEO/GM: Marty Lyon. **Senior Vice President:** Jim Devellano.

BUSINESS OPERATIONS
Senior Vice President, Business Operations: Duane McLean.
Executive Assistant to Senior VP, Business Operations: Peggy Bacarella.

Finance
VP/CFO: Stephen Quinn. **Senior Director, Finance:** Kelli Kollman. **Director, Purchasing/Supplier Diversity:** DeAndre Berry. **Accounting Manager:** Sheila Robine. **Financial Analyst:** Kristin Jorgensen. **Accounts Payable Coordinator:** Debbie Sword. **Accounts Receivable Coordinator:** Sharon Szkarlat. **Administrative Assistant:** Tracy Rice. **Director, Human Resources:** Karen Gruca. **Senior Manager, Payroll Administration:** Maureen Kraatz. **Director, Information Technology:** Scott Wruble.

Public, Community Affairs
VP, Community/Public Affairs: Elaine Lewis. **Manager, Player Relations, Sports/Youth Programs:** Sam Abrams. **Director, Tigers Foundation:** Jordan Field. **Manager, Community Affairs:** Alexandrea Thrubis. **Community Affairs Coordinator:** Kristen Joe. **Administrative Assistant:** Audrey Zielinski.

Sales, Marketing
VP, Corporate Partnerships/Ticket Sales: Steve Harms. **Senior Director, Corporate Sales:** Kurt Buhler. **Corporate Sales Managers:** Zach Wagner, John Wolski. **Sponsorship Services Manager:** Amy Peterson. **Sponsorship Services Coordinator:** Mallory Seide. **VP, Marketing:** Ellen Hill Zeringue. **Director, Marketing:** Ron Wade. **Director, Promotions/In-Game Entertainment:** Eli Bayless. **Promotions Coordinator:** Jared Karner. **VP, Suite Sales/Services:** Scot Pett.

Media Relations, Communications
Telephone: (313) 471-2114. **Fax:** (313) 471-2138.
VP, Communications: Ron Colangelo. **Director, Baseball Media Relations:** Brian Britten. **Manager, Baseball Media Relations:** Rick Thompson. **Coordinator, Baseball Media Relations:** Russell Carlton. **Director, Broadcasting:** Molly Light.

Ballpark Operations
VP, Park Operations: Michael Healy. **Head Groundskeeper:** Heather Nabozny. **Assistant Groundskeeper:** Gail DeGennaro. **Senior Manager, Park Operations:** Ed Goward. **Manager, Event/Guest Services:** Jill Baran. **Park**

Mike Ilitch

2010 SCHEDULE
Standard Game Times: 7:05 p.m.; Sun. 1:05.

APRIL
5	at Kansas City
7-8	at Kansas City
9-11	Cleveland
12-14	Kansas City
16-18	at Seattle
19-22	at Los Angeles (AL)
23-26	at Texas
27-29	Minnesota
30	Los Angeles (AL)

MAY
1-2	Los Angeles (AL)
3-5	at Minnesota
7-9	at Cleveland
10-13	New York (AL)
14-16	Boston
17-18	Chicago (AL)
19-20	at Oakland
21-23	at Los Angeles (NL)
25-26	at Seattle
28-31	Oakland

JUNE
1-3	Cleveland
4-6	at Kansas City
8-10	at Chicago (AL)
11-13	Pittsburgh
15-17	Washington
18-20	Arizona
22-24	at New York (NL)
25-27	at Atlanta
28-30	at Minnesota

JULY
2-4	Seattle
5-7	Baltimore
9-11	Minnesota
16-18	at Cleveland
19-21	Texas
22-25	Toronto
26-29	at Tampa Bay
30-31	at Boston

AUGUST
1	at Boston
3-5	Chicago (AL)
6-8	Los Angeles (AL)
9-11	Tampa Bay
13-15	at Chicago (AL)
16-19	at New York (AL)
20-22	Cleveland
23-25	Kansas City
26-29	at Toronto
31	at Minnesota

SEPTEMBER
1-2	at Minnesota
3-5	at Kansas City
6-9	Chicago (AL)
10-12	Baltimore
14-15	at Texas
17-19	at Chicago (AL)
20-22	Kansas City
24-26	Minnesota
27-29	at Cleveland
30	at Baltimore

OCTOBER
1-3	at Baltimore

GENERAL INFORMATION
Stadium (year opened): Comerica Park (2000).
Team Colors: Navy blue, orange and white.

Player Representative: Unavailable.
Home Dugout: Third Base.
Playing Surface: Grass.

Operations Manager: Allan Carrise. **Scoreboard Operations Manager:** Robb Wilson. **Event Services Coordinator:** Rofeal Daniels.

Ticketing
Telephone: (313) 471-2255.
Director, Ticket Sales: Steve Fox. **Director, Group Sales:** Dwain Lewis. **Senior Director, Ticket Services:** Victor Gonzalez.

Travel, Clubhouse
Traveling Secretary: Bill Brown. **Manager, Home Clubhouse:** Jim Schmakel. **Assistant Manager, Visiting Clubhouse:** John Nelson. **Clubhouse Assistant:** Tyson Steele. **Baseball Video Operations:** Jeremy Kelch. **Assistant, Baseball Video Operations:** Andy Bjornstad, Tim Janicki.

BASEBALL OPERATIONS

Dave Dombrowski

Telephone: (313) 471-2000. **Fax:** (313) 471-2099.
General Manager: David Dombrowski.
VP/Assistant GM: Al Avila. **VP/Legal Counsel:** John Westhoff. **VP, Player Personnel:** Scott Reid. **Special Assistant:** Dick Egan. **Director, Baseball Operations:** Mike Smith. **Executive Assistant to President/GM:** Marty Lyon. **Executive Assistant:** Eileen Surma.

Major League Staff
Manager: Jim Leyland.
Coaches: Pitching—Rick Knapp; Batting—Lloyd McClendon; Infield—Rafael Belliard; First Base—Tom Brookens; Third Base—Gene Lamont; Bullpen—Jeff Jones.

Medical, Training
Director, Medical Services/Head Athletic Trainer: Kevin Rand. **Assistant Athletic Trainers:** Steve Carter, Doug Teter. **Strength/Conditioning Coach:** Javair Gillett. **Team Physicians:** Dr. Michael Workings, Dr. Stephen Lemos, Dr. Louis Saco (Florida). **Coordinator, Medical Services:** Gwen Keating.

Player Development
Telephone: (863) 686-8075. **Fax:** (863) 688-9589.
Director, Minor League Operations: Dan Lunetta. **Director, Player Development:** Glenn Ezell. **Director, Minor League/Scouting Administration:** Cheryl Evans. **Director, Dominican Republic Operations:** Ramon Perez. **Director, International Operations:** Tom Moore. **Pacific Rim Coordinator:** Kevin Hooker. **Director, Latin American Player Development:** Manny Crespo.
Minor League Operations Coordinator: Avi Becher. **Minor League Operations Administrative Assistant:** Marilyn Acevedo. **Minor League Field Coordinator:** Mike Rojas. **Minor League Medical Coordinator:** Dustin Campbell. **Minor League Strength/Conditioning Coordinator:** Chris Walter. **Assistant Minor League Strength/Conditioning Coordinator:** Steve Chase.
Roving Instructors: Toby Harrah (hitting), Jon Matlack (pitching), Kevin Bradshaw (infield), Andrew Graham (catching), Gene Roof (outfield/baserunning), Brian Peterson (performance enhancement).

Farm System

Class	Club	Manager	Coach	Pitching Coach
Triple-A	Toledo (IL)	Larry Parrish	Leon Durham	A.J. Sager
Double-A	Erie (EL)	Phil Nevin	Glenn Adams	Ray Burris
High A	Lakeland (FSL)	Andy Barkett	Larry Herndon	Joe Coleman
Low A	West Michigan (MWL)	Joe DePastino	Luis Quinones	Mark Johnson
Short-season	Oneonta (NYP)	Howard Bushong	Scott Dwyer	Jorge Cordova
Rookie	Tigers (GCL)	Basilio Cabrera	Andrew Graham	Greg Sabat
Rookie	Tigers (DSL)	Frey Peniche	Rafael Martinez	Jose Parra
Rookie	Tigers (VSL)	Josman Robles	Carlos Quintero	Carlos Bohorquez

Scouting
Telephone: (863) 413-4112. **Fax:** (863) 413-1954.
VP, Amateur Scouting: David Chadd. **Assistant Director, Amateur Scouting:** James Orr.
Major League Scouts: Scott Bream (Phoenix, AZ), Jim Olander (Vail, AZ), Mike Russell (Gulf Breeze, FL), Bruce Tanner (New Castle, PA), Jeff Wetherby (Wesley Chapel, FL).
National Crosscheckers: Ray Crone (Cedar Hill, TX), Scott Pleis (Lake St. Louis, MO). **Regional Crosscheckers:** East—Murray Cook (Orlando, FL); Central—Tom Osowski (Franklin, WI); Midwest—Mike Hankins (Lee's Summit, MO); West—Tim McWilliam (San Diego, CA). **Area Scouts:** Bryson Barber (Pensacola, FL), Grant Brittain (Hickory, NC), Bill Buck (Manassas, VA), Rolando Casanova (Miami, FL), Scott Cerny (Rocklin, CA), Tim Grieve (New Braunfels, TX), Garrett Guest (Lockport, IL), Phil Huttmann (Pasadena, CA), Ryan Johnson (Oregon City, OR), Marty Miller (Chicago, IL), Steve Pack (San Marcos, CA), Brian Reid (Laveen, AZ), Jim Rough (Sharpsburg, GA), Chris Wimmer (Yukon, OK), Harold Zonder (Louisville, KY).
Director, International Operations: Tom Moore. **Director, Latin American Development:** Manny Crespo. **Director, Latin American Scouting:** Miguel Garcia. **Coordinator, Pacific Rim Scouting:** Kevin Hooker. **Director, Dominican Operations:** Ramon Perez. **Coordinator, Dominican Academy:** Oliver Arias. **Venezuelan Scouting Supervisor:** Pedro Chavez. **Coordinator, Venezuelan Academy:** Oscar Garcia.

Florida Marlins

Office Address: Sun Life Stadium, 2267 Dan Marino Blvd. Miami, FL 33056.
Telephone: (305) 626-7400. **Fax:** (305) 626-7302.
Website: www.marlins.com.

Ownership

Owner/CEO: Jeffrey Loria. **Vice Chairman:** Joel Mael.
President: David Samson. **Special Assistants to President:** Jeff Conine, Andre Dawson, Tony Perez. **Special Advisor to Owner:** Jack McKeon. **Executive Assistant to Owner/Vice Chairman/President:** Beth McConville.

BUSINESS OPERATIONS

Executive Vice President/CFO: Michel Bussiere. **Executive Assistant to the Executive VP/ CFO:** Lisa Milk. **Executive Vice President, Ballpark Development:** Claude Delorme. **Executive Assistant:** Ingrid Rodriguez. **Manager, Game Services:** Antonio Torres-Roman. **Coordinator, Ballpark Development:** Victoria Mathias.
 Senior Director, Human Resources: Ana Hernandez. **Coordinator, Human Resources:** Brian Estes. **Administrator, Benefits:** Ruby Mattei. **Supervisor, Office Services:** Karl Heard. **Assistant, Office Services:** Donna Kirton. **Senior Receptionist:** Kathy Lanza. **Receptionist:** Dianette Oliva.

Finance

 Senior VP, Finance: Susan Jaison. **Controller:** Alina Trigo. **Administrator, Payroll:** Carolina Calderon. **Accountant:** Alina Quiros. **Coordinator, Accounts Payable:** Marva Alexander. **Coordinator, Finance:** Diana Jorge. **Assistant, Accounting:** Thomas Lundstedt. **Director, IT:** David Enriquez. **Manager, Technical Support:** David Kuan. **Network Engineer:** Ozzie Macias. **Manager, Telecommunications:** Sam Mora. **IT Technician:** Alexis Farres.

Jeffrey Loria

Marketing

 VP, Marketing: Sean Flynn. **Manager, Retail Operations:** Robyn Feinstein. **Director, Multicultural Marketing:** Juan Martinez. **Director, Marketing/Promotions:** Matt Britten. **Coordinator, Marketing:** Boris Menier. **Coordinator, Promotions:** Rafael Capdevila. **Coordinator, Mermaids:** Jose Guerrero. **Coordinator, Marlins en Miami:** Danny Vargas.

Sales

 VP, Business Development: Dale Hendricks. **VP, Sales:** Brendan Cunningham. **Manager, Corporate Sales:** Tony Tome. **Corporate Sales Account Executives:** Brian Schutz, Bob Eisenberg, David Goldberg. **Coordinators, Corporate Sales:** Sheri Talerico, Christina Brito. **Executive Assistant, Corporate Sales:** Judy Cavanagh. **Director, Customer Service:** Spencer Linden. **Senior Account Executive, Group Sales/Special Events:** Mario Signorello. **Manager, Group Sales/Special Events:** Charles Sano. **Senior Account Executives, Group Sales/Special Events:** Bray LaDow, Kathleen Massolio, Anthony Jabara. **Senior Account Executives:** Sean Flood, Orestes Hernandez.

2010 SCHEDULE

Standard Game Times: 7:10 p.m.; Sun. 1:10

APRIL		
5 . . . . . . at New York (NL)	19-20 . . . . . . at St. Louis	JULY
7-8 . . . . at New York (NL)	21-23 . . . at Chicago (AL)	2-4 . . . . at Atlanta
9-11 . . . Los Angeles (NL)	25-27 . . . . Atlanta	5-7 . . at Los Angeles (NL)
12-15 . . . . Cincinnati	28-30 . . . . . Philadelphia	8-11 . . . . at Arizona
16-18 . . . . at Philadelphia	31 . . . . Milwaukee	16-18 . . . . . Washington
20-22 . . . . . . at Houston		19-22 . . . . . . Colorado
23-25 . . . . . at Colorado	JUNE	23-25 . . . . Atlanta
26-28 . . . . . . San Diego	1-3 . . . . . . Milwaukee	26-29 . . . at San Francisco
30 . . . . Washington	4-6 . . . at New York (NL)	30-31 . . . . . at San Diego
	8-10 . . . . at Philadelphia	
MAY	11-13 . . . . at Tampa Bay	AUGUST
1-2 . . . . Washington	15-17 . . . . Texas	1 . . . . at San Diego
4-6 . . . . . San Francisco	18-20 . . . . . Tampa Bay	3-5 . . . . . Philadelphia
7-9 . . . . at Washington	22-24 . . . . . at Baltimore	6-8 . . . . St. Louis
10-12 . . . at Chicago (NL)	25-27 . . . . . . San Diego	10-12 . . . at Washington
13-16 . . . New York (NL)	28-30 . . . . New York (NL)	13-15 . . . . at Cincinnati
17-18 . . . . Arizona		16-19 . . . . at Pittsburgh
		20-22 . . . . Houston

24-26 . . . at New York (NL)	
27-29 . . . . at Atlanta	
30-31 . . . . . . Washington	
SEPTEMBER	
1 . . . . Washington	
3-5 . . . . Atlanta	
6-8 . . . . at Philadelphia	
10-12 . . . at Washington	
13-15 . . . . . Philadelphia	
17-19 . . . . Chicago (NL)	
21-22 . . . New York (NL)	
23-26 . . . . at Milwaukee	
27-29 . . . . at Atlanta	
30 . . . . Pittsburgh	
OCTOBER	
1-3 . . . . Pittsburgh	

GENERAL INFORMATION

Stadium (year opened): Sun Life Stadium (1993).

Team Colors: Teal, black, white and silver.
Player Representative: Unavailable.

Media Relations, Communications

Telephone: (305) 626-7492. **Fax:** (305) 626-7302.

Senior VP, Communications/Broadcasting: P.J. Loyello. **Director, Media Relations:** Matthew Roebuck. **Manager, Media Relations:** Marty Sewell. **Administrative Assistant, Media Relations:** Maria Armella. **Director, Broadcasting:** Emmanuel Munoz. **Manager, Broadcasting:** Karen Deery. **Director, Business Communications:** Carolina Perrina. **Director, Community Outreach:** Angela Smith. **Coordinator, Player Relations:** Alex Morin. **Assistant, Community Outreach/Youth Baseball:** Juan Garciga. **Executive Director, Marlins Community Foundation:** Nancy Olson. **Director, Foundation Development:** Jennifer Dilliz. .

In-Game Entertainment

Director, Game Presentation/Events: Larry Blocker. **Manager, Game Presentation/Events:** Eric Ramirez. **Director, Creative Services:** Alfred Hernandez. **Mascot:** John DeCicco. **PA Announcer:** Dick Sanford.

Travel, Clubhouse

Senior Director, Team Travel: Bill Beck. **Equipment Manager:** John Silverman. **Visiting Clubhouse Manager:** Michael Rock Hughes.

BASEBALL OPERATIONS

Larry Beinfest

Telephone: 305-626-7400; Fax: 305-626-7433
President, Baseball Operations: Larry Beinfest.
Vice President/General Manager: Michael Hill. **Executive Assistant to the President, Baseball Operations/VP/GM:** Rita Filbert. **VP, Player Development/Scouting/Assistant GM:** Jim Fleming. **VP, Player Personnel/Assistant GM:** Dan Jennings. **Special Assistants to GM/Pro Scout:** Orrin Freeman, Mark Wiley. **Video Coordinator:** Cullen McRae. **VP/General Counsel:** Derek Jackson. **Executive Assistant to the VP/General Counsel:** A'kyra Thomas.

Major League Staff

Manager: Fredi Gonzalez.
Coaches: Bench—Carlos Tosca; Pitching—Randy St. Claire; Hitting—Jim Presley; First Base/Infield—Dave Collins; Third Base—Joe Espada; Bullpen—Reid Cornelius; Bullpen Coordinator—Pierre Arsenault.

Medical, Training

Head Trainer: Sean Cunningham. **Assistant Trainer:** Mike Kozak. **Director, Strength/Conditioning:** Paul Fournier.

Player Development

VP, Player Development/Scouting/Assistant GM: Jim Fleming. **Director, Player Development:** Brian Chattin. **Manager, Player Development/International Operations:** Manny Colon. **Assistant, Baseball Operations:** Marc Lippman. **Assistant, Player Development/Scouting:** Michael Youngberg.
Field Coordinator: John Pierson. **Coordinators:** Gene Basham (training/rehabilitation), Tarrik Brock (Roving outfield/baserunning), Tim Cossins (roving catching), John Mallee (hitting), Wayne Rosenthal (pitching), Josh Seligman (Strength/conditioning), Brandon Hyde (infield).
Minor League Equipment Manager: Mark Brown. **Minor League Clubhouse Manager:** Lou Assalone.

Farm System

Class	Club (League)	Manager	Coach	Pitching Coach
Triple-A	New Orleans (PCL)	Edwin Rodriguez	Unavailable	Scott Mitchell
Double-A	Jacksonville (SL)	Tim Leiper	Corey Hart	John Duffy
High A	Jupiter (FSL)	Ron Hassey	Robert Bell	Steve Doc Watson
Low A	Greensboro (SAL)	Andy Haines	Kevin Randel	Charlie Corbell Jr.
Short-season	Jamestown (NYP)	Dave Berg	Frank Moore	Unavailable
Rookie	Jupiter (GCL)	Jorge Hernandez	Angel Espada	Jeff Schwarz
Rookie	Marlins (DSL)	Ray Nunez	Luis Brito	Edison Santana

Scouting

Telephone: (561) 630-1816/Pro (561) 630-1809.
Director, Scouting: Stan Meek.
Assistant Director, Scouting: Gregg Leonard. **Pro Scouting Assistant:** Dan Noffsinger. **Advance Scout:** Joel Moeller (San Clemente, CA). **Pro Scouts:** Roger Jongewaard (Fallbrook, CA), Dave Roberts (Fort Worth, TX), Phil Rossi (Jessup, PA), Tommy Thompson (Greenville, NC), Michael White (Lakewood Ranch, FL).
National Crosschecker: David Crowson (College Station, TX). **Regional Supervisors:** East—Matt Haas (Cincinnati, OH); Central—Ray Hayward (Norman, OK); West—Scott Goldby (Yuba City, CA); Canada—Steve Payne (Barrington, RI).
Area Scouts: Matt Anderson (Williamsport, PA), Carlos Berroa (Caguas, PR), Carmen Carcone (Canton, GA), Robby Corsaro (Victorville, CA), John Hughes (Walnut Creek, CA), Kevin Ibach (Arlington Heights, IL), Brian Kraft (Auburndale, FL), Joel Matthews (Concord, NC), Tim McDonnell (Westminster, CA), Gabe Sandy (Damascus, OR), Scott Stanley (Peoria, AZ), Steve Taylor (Shawnee, OK), Ryan Wardinsky (Edmond, OK), Mark Willoughby (Hammond, LA), Nick Zumsande (Fairfax, IA).
Director, International Operations: Albert Gonzalez. **International Supervisors:** Sandy Nin (Santo Domingo, Dominican Republic), Wilmer Castillo (Maracay, VZ). **International Scouts:** Luis Cordoba (Panama), Willie Marrugo (Cartagena, Colombia), Alix Martinez (San Pedro de Macoris, DR), Hugo Martinez (Santiago, DR), Victor Montoya (Caracas, VZ), Domingo Ortega (Santo Domingo, DR), Robin Torres (Zulia, VZ).

Houston Astros

Office Address: Minute Maid Park, Union Station, 501 Crawford, Suite 400, Houston, TX 77002.
Mailing Address: P.O. Box 288, Houston, TX 77001.
Telephone: (713) 259-8000. **Fax:** (713) 259-8981.
E-mail Address: fanfeedback@astros.mlb.com. **Website:** www.astros.com.

Ownership

Operated By: McLane Group LP.
Chairman/CEO: Drayton McLane.
Board of Directors: Bob McClaren, G.W. Sanford, Webb Stickney.

BUSINESS OPERATIONS

President, Business Operations: Pam Gardner. **Executive Assistant:** Eileen Colgin.
Senior Vice President, Finance/Administration: Jackie Traywick. **Senior Director, Risk Management:** Monica Rusch. **Controller:** Jonathan Germer. **Director, Treasury/Office Services:** Damian Babin. **Senior Accountant:** Monique Sam. **Accounts Payable Coordinator:** Nestor Lopez. **VP, Human Resources:** Larry Stokes. **Human Resources Manager:** Chanda Lawdermilk. **Director, Payroll/Employee Benefits:** Ruth Kelly.

Drayton McLane

Marketing/Sales

Senior VP, Sponsorship/Ticket Sales: Tom Garrity. **Senior VP, Premium Sponsorships:** Jamie Hildreth. **VP, Sponsorships/Business Development:** John Sorrentino. **VP, Market Development:** Rosi Hernandez. **VP, Marketing:** Jennifer Germer. **Director, Marketing/ Promotions:** Clint Pasche. **Director, Sponsorship Sales:** Shane Hildreth.

Public Relations/Communications

Telephone: (713) 259-8900. **Fax:** (713) 259-8981.
Senior VP, Communications: Jay Lucas. **Director, Media Relations:** Gene Dias. **Assistant Director, Media Relations:** Sally Gunter. **Media Relations Coordinators:** Stephen Grande, MJ Trahan. **VP, Foundation Development:** Marian Harper. **Assistant Director, Foundation Development:** Marisa Lopez. **Director, Community Affairs:** Shawn Bertani. **Coordinator, Community Affairs:** Dairanetta Spain. **Director, Procurement:** Seth Courtney. **Director, Information Technology:** Steve Reese. **Senior Network Administrator:** Michael Hovan. **IT Coordinator:** Ken Bellinger.

Stadium Operations

VP, Building Operations: Bobby Forrest. **VP, Special Events:** Kala Sorenson. **VP, Guest Services:** Marty Price. **Director, Engineering/Maintenance:** David McKenzie. **Audio-Visual Coordinator:** James Sorensen. **Assistant Director, Building Operations:** Austin Malone. **Senior Director, Creative Services:** Kirby Kander. **Director, Ballpark Entertainment:** Brock Jessel. **Production Coordinator:** Joey Graham. **Director, Affiliate Relations:** Mike Cannon. **Radio Broadcast Engineer:** Lowell Matheny. **Director, Telecommunications/Executive Assistant:** Tracy Faucette. **Director, Guest Services:** Michael Kenny. **Authentications Manager:** Mike Acosta. **Assistant Director, Special Events:** Jonathan Sterchy. **Assistant Sales**

2010 SCHEDULE

Standard Game Times: 7:05 p.m.; Sat. 6:05; Sun. 1:05.

APRIL
5-7	San Francisco
9-11	Philadelphia
12	at St. Louis
14-15	at St. Louis
16-18	at Chicago (NL)
20-22	Florida
23-25	Pittsburgh
27-29	Cincinnati
30	at Atlanta

MAY
1-2	at Atlanta
3-6	Arizona
7-9	San Diego
11-13	at St. Louis
14-16	at San Francisco

17-18	at Los Angeles (NL)
19-20	Colorado
21-23	Tampa Bay
25-27	at Milwaukee
28-30	at Cincinnati
31	Washington

JUNE
1-3	Washington
4-6	Chicago (NL)
7-10	at Colorado
11-13	at New York (AL)
15-17	at Kansas City
18-20	Texas
22-24	San Francisco
25-27	at Texas
28-30	at Milwaukee

JULY
1-4	at San Diego
6-8	Pittsburgh
9-11	St. Louis
16-18	at Pittsburgh
19-21	at Chicago (NL)
23-25	Cincinnati
26-28	Chicago (NL)
30-31	Milwaukee

AUGUST
1	Milwaukee
2-4	at St. Louis
6-8	at Milwaukee
9-11	Atlanta
13-15	Pittsburgh
16-19	New York (NL)

20-22	at Florida
23-26	at Philadelphia
27-29	at New York (NL)
30-31	St. Louis

SEPTEMBER
1	St. Louis
3-5	at Arizona
6-8	at Chicago (NL)
9-12	Los Angeles (NL)
13-15	Milwaukee
17-19	Cincinnati
20-23	at Washington
24-26	at Pittsburgh
28-30	at Cincinnati

OCTOBER
1-3	Chicago (NL)

GENERAL INFORMATION

Stadium (year opened): Minute Maid Park (2000).
Team Colors: Brick red, sand and black.

Player Representative: Unavailable.
Home Dugout: First Base.
Playing Surface: Grass.

Director, Special Events: Katy Preisler. **Director, Major League Field Operations:** Dan Bergstrom. **Groundskeeper:** Willie Berry. **PA Announcer:** Bob Ford. **Official Scorers:** Rick Blount, Ivy McLemore, Greg Porzucek, Trey Wilkinson.

Ticketing
Telephone: (713) 259-8500. **Fax:** (713) 259-8326.
Senior Director, Ticket Sales: Bill Goren. **Senior Director, Ticket Services:** Brooke Ellenberger. **Director, Ticket Operations:** Marcia Coronado. **Director, Box Office Operations:** Bill Cannon. **Manager, Premium Sales:** Clay Kowalski. **Manager, Ticket Services:** Adam Eiseman. **Manager, Ticket Systems/Customer Retention:** Jolene Sherman.

Travel/Clubhouse
Director, Team Travel: Barry Waters.
Equipment Manager: Dennis Liborio. **Assistant Equipment Manager:** Carl Schneider. **Visiting Clubhouse Manager:** Steve Perry. **Umpire/Clubhouse Assistant:** Chuck New.

BASEBALL OPERATIONS
Telephone: (713) 259-8000. **Fax:** (713) 259-8600.
President, Baseball Operations: Tal Smith.
General Manager: Ed Wade.
Assistant GM/Player Relations: David Gottfried. **Director, Baseball Research/Pro Scouting Coordinator:** Charlie Norton. **Executive Assistant:** Traci Dearing. **Video Coordinator:** Jim Summers.

Ed Wade

Major League Staff
Manager: Brad Mills.
Coaches: Bench—Al Pedrique; Pitching—Brad Arnsberg; Hitting—Sean Berry; First Base—Bobby Meacham, Sr.; Third Base—Dave Clark; Bullpen—Jamie Quirk.

Medical, Training
Medical Director: Dr. David Lintner. **Team Physicians:** Dr. Tom Mehlhoff, Dr. Jim Muntz.
Head Trainer: Nathan Lucero. **Assistant Trainer:** Rex Jones. **Strength/Conditioning Coach:** Dr. Gene Coleman.

Player Development
Telephone: (713) 259-8920. **Fax:** (713) 259-8600.
Assistant GM/Director, Player Development: Ricky Bennett. **Director, Florida Operations:** Jay Edmiston. **Coordinator, Player Development:** Allen Rowin. **Field Coordinator:** Dick Scott. **Minor League Coordinators:** Mike Barnett (hitting), Britt Burns (pitching), Jaime Garcia (assistant pitching), Eric Young (outfield/baserunning), Danny Sheaffer (catching), Jim Pankovits (Infield), Pete Fagan (training/rehabilitation), Mike Smith (strength/conditioning).

Farm System

Class	Club	Manager	Hitting Coach	Pitching Coach
Triple-A	Round Rock (PCL)	Marc Bombard	Keith Bodie	Burt Hooton
Double-A	Corpus Christi (TL)	Wes Clements	Mark Bailey	Travis Driskill
High A	Lancaster (CAL)	Tom Lawless	Darryl Robinson	Don Alexander
Low A	Lexington (SAL)	Rodney Linares	Stubby Clapp	Rick Aponte
Short-season	Tri-City (NYP)	Jim Pankovits	Joel Chimelis	Gary Ruby
Rookie	Greeneville (APP)	Ed Romero	Pete Rancont	Dave Borkowski
Rookie	Astros (GCL)	Omar Lopez	D.J. Boston	unavailable
Rookie	Astros (DSL)	Luis Martinez	Luis Mateo	Fermin Ward

Scouting
Telephone: (713) 259-8925. **Fax:** (713) 259-8600.
Assistant GM, Amateur Scouting: Bobby Heck. **Special Assistant to the GM–Latin America:** Felix Francisco. **Director, Pacific Rim Scouting:** Glen Barker. **Director, Major League Scouting:** Fred Nelson. **Coordinator, Amateur Scouting:** Mike Burns. **Major League Scouts:** Gene DeBoer (Brandon, WI), Jack Lind (Mesa, AZ), Walt Matthews (Texarkana, TX), Paul Ricciarini (Pittsfield, MA), Bob Skinner (San Diego, CA), Fred Nelson (Missouri City, TX), Ken Califano (Stafford, VA), Matt Galante (Staten Island, NY). **Professional Scouts:** Ruben Amaro Sr. (Weston, FL), Bob Rossi (Baton Rouge, LA), Scipio Spinks (Missouri City, TX), Tad Slowik (Arlington Heights, IL), Hank Allen (Malboro, MD), Tom Weidenbauer (Ormond Beach, FL).
National Crosschecker: David Post (Canton, GA). **Regional Supervisors:** Midwest—Ralph Bratton (Dripping Springs, TX); West—Mark Ross (Tucson, AZ); East—Clarence Johns (Atlanta, GA). **Area Scouts:** J.D. Alleva (Charlotte, NC), Keith Bogan (Ridgeland, MS), Greg Brown (Davie, FL), Mike Brown (Chandler, AZ), Brad Budzinski (Huntington Beach, CA), Tim Costic (Stevenson Ranch, CA), Paul Gale (Keizer, OR), Joe Graham (Sacramento, CA), Matt Heath (Tampa, FL), Troy Hoerner (Middleton, WI), John Kosciak (Milford, MA), Lincoln Martin (Douglasville, GA), Rusty Pendergrass (Missouri City, TX), Jim Stevenson (Tulsa, OK), Everett Stull (Richmond, VA), Nick Venuto (Newton Falls, OH).
Senior Advising Scouts: Bob King (La Mesa, CA), Bob Poole (Redwood City, CA).
Part-time Scouts: Ed Fastaia (Lake Ronkonkoma, NY), Tom McCormack (University City, MO), Joey Sola (Caguas, PR). **International Scouts:** Venezuela: Daniel Acuna, Oscar Alvarado, Miguel Chacoa, Joan Fernandez, Johan Maya, Luimac Quero. **Dominican Republic:** Rafael Belen, Julio De La Cruz, Jose Lima, Francis Mojica, Jose Ortiz. **Colombia:** Carlos Martinez. **Europe:** Mauro Mazzotti. **Panama:** Jose Luis Santos. **Nicaragua:** Leocadio Guevara. **Curacao:** Wellington Herrera.

Kansas City Royals

Office Address: One Royal Way, Kansas City, MO 64129.
Mailing Address: P.O. Box 419969, Kansas City, MO 64141.
Telephone: (816) 921-8000. **Fax:** (816) 924-0347. **Website:** www.royals.com

Ownership

Operated By: Kansas City Royals Baseball Club Inc.
Chairman/CEO: David Glass. **President:** Dan Glass. **Board of Directors:** Ruth Glass, Don Glass, Dayna Martz, Julia Kauffman, Herk Robinson, Dale Rohr. **Executive Administrative Assistant (Executive Staff):** Ginger Salem.

BUSINESS OPERATIONS

Senior Vice President, Business Operations: Kevin Uhlich. **Executive Administrative Assistant:** Cindy Hamilton.

Finance/Administration

Vice President, Finance/Administration: David Laverentz. **Director, Finance:** Adam Tyhurst. **Director, Renovation Accounting/Risk Management:** Patrick Fleischmann. **Senior Director, Payroll/Benefits/Human Resources:** Tom Pfannenstiel. **Senior Director, Information Systems:** Brian Himstedt.
Senior Director, Ticket Operations: Larry Chu. **Director, Ticket Operations:** Chris Darr.

Communications/Broadcasting

Vice President, Communications/Broadcasting: Mike Swanson. **Director, Broadcast Services/Royals Alumni:** Fred White. **Manager, Radio Network Operations:** Don Free.

David Glass

Media Relations

Director, Media Relations: David Holtzman. **Coordinator, Media Services:** Dina Wathan. **Coordinator, Communications/Broadcasting:** Colby Curry.

Publicity/Community Relations

Vice President, Community Affairs/Publicity: Toby Cook. **Senior Director, Community Relations:** Ben Aken. **Senior Director, Publicity:** Lora Grosshans. **Senior Director, Royals Charities:** Joy Sedlacek. **Director, Community Outreach:** Betty Kaegel.

Ballpark Operations

Vice President, Ballpark Operations/Development: Bob Rice. **Director, Event Operations:** Renee VanLaningham. **Director, Fan Experience/Hospitality:** Carrie Bligh. **Director, Groundskeeping/Landscaping:** Trevor Vance. **Manager, Groundskeeping:** Justin Scott. **Director, Ballpark Services:** Johnny Williams. **Manager, Ballpark Services:** Isaac Riffel. **Director, Stadium Engineering/Maintenance:** Todd Burrow.

2010 SCHEDULE

Standard Game Times: 7:10 p.m.; Sat. 6:10; Sun. 1:10.

APRIL
5 . . . . Detroit
7-8 . . . . Detroit
9-11 . . . . Boston
12-14 . . . . at Detroit
16-18 . . . . at Minnesota
19-21 . . . . . at Toronto
23-25 . . . . . Minnesota
26-28 . . . . . . Seattle
29-30 . . . at Tampa Bay

MAY
1-2 . . . . . at Tampa Bay
3-5 . . . . at Chicago (AL)
6-9 . . . . at Texas
11-13 . . . . . . Cleveland
14-16 . . . . Chicago (AL)
17-18 . . . . . at Baltimore

19-20 . . . . . at Cleveland
21-23 . . . . . . Colorado
25-26 . . . . Texas
27-30 . . . . . . at Boston
31 . . . . . Los Angeles (AL)

JUNE
1-3 . . . Los Angeles (AL)
4-6 . . . . Detroit
8-10 . . . . . at Minnesota
11-13 . . . . at Cincinnati
15-17 . . . . Houston
18-20 . . . . . . at Atlanta
21-23 . . . at Washington
25-27 . . . . . . St. Louis
28-30 . . . . . Chicago (AL)

JULY
2-4 . . at Los Angeles (AL)
5-7 . . . . at Seattle
9-11 . . . at Chicago (AL)
16-18 . . . . Oakland
19-21 . . . . Toronto
22-25 . . at New York (AL)
26-28 . . . . . Minnesota
29-31 . . . . . . Baltimore

AUGUST
1 . . . . Baltimore
2-4 . . . . . . at Oakland
6-8 . . . . . . at Seattle
9-11 . . at Los Angeles (AL)
12-15 . . . New York (AL)
17-19 . . . . . Cleveland
20-22 . . . . Chicago (AL)

23-25 . . . . at Detroit
27-29 . . . . at Cleveland
30-31 . . . . Texas

SEPTEMBER
1 . . . . Texas
3-5 . . . . Detroit
6-8 . . . . . at Minnesota
10-12 . . at Chicago (AL)
13-15 . . . . Oakland
17-19 . . . . . Cleveland
20-22 . . . . . at Detroit
23-26 . . . . at Cleveland
27-29 . . . . . Minnesota
30 . . . . . . Tampa Bay

OCTOBER
1-3 . . . . Tampa Bay

GENERAL INFORMATION

Stadium (year opened): Ewing M. Kauffman Stadium (1973).
Team Colors: Royal blue and white.

Player Representative: Unavailable.
Home Dugout: First Base.
Playing Surface: Grass.

Sales

Senior Director, Ticket Sales/Services: Dawson Hughes. **Director, Sales:** Theodore Hodges. **Senior Director, Ticket Operations:** Larry Chu. **Director, Ticket Operations:** Chris Darr. **Director, Ticket Services:** Scott Wadsworth.

Marketing/Business Development

Vice President, Marketing/Business Development: Michael Bucek. **Senior Director, Event Presentation/ Production:** Don Costante. **Director, Event Presentation/Production:** Chris DeRuyscher. **Senior Director, Corporate Sales Partnerships:** Mitch Wheeler. **Senior Director, Corporate Sponsorship Relations:** Michele Kammerer.

BASEBALL OPERATIONS

Dayton Moore

Telephone: (816) 921-8000. **Fax:** (816) 924-0347.
Senior Vice President, Baseball Operations/General Manager: Dayton Moore.
VP, Baseball Operations/Assistant GM: Dean Taylor. **Assistant GM, Scouting/Player Development:** J.J. Picollo. **Senior Advisor to GM/Scouting Player Development:** Mike Arbuckle. **Director, Baseball Administration:** Jin Wong. **Director, Baseball Operations:** Lonnie Goldberg. **Baseball Operations Assistant:** Kyle Vena. **Administrative Assistants, Baseball Operations:** Emily Penning, Mike Groopman.
Manager, Arizona Operations: Nick Leto. **Coordinator, Pro Scouting:** Gene Watson. **Senior Advisors:** Art Stewart, Donnie Williams. **Assistant to GM:** Brian Murphy. **Special Assistant to GM, International Operations:** Rene Francisco. **Special Assistant/Player Personnel:** Louie Medina. **VP, Baseball Operations:** George Brett. **Special Assistants to GM:** Pat Jones, Rusty Kuntz, Mike Toomey. **Special Advisor to GM:** Ned Yost. **Team Travel:** Jeff Davenport. **Video Coordinator:** Mark Topping.

Major League Staff

Manager: Trey Hillman.
Coaches: Bench—John Gibbons; Pitching—Bob McClure; Batting—Kevin Seitzer; First Base—Eddie Rodriguez; Third Base—Dave Owen; Bullpen—Steve Foster.

Medical/Training

Team Physician: Dr. Steven Joyce. **Athletic Trainer:** Nick Kenney. Assistant Athletic Trainer: Kyle Turner.

Player Development

Telephone: (816) 921-8000. **Fax:** (816) 924-0347.
Director, Minor League Operations: Scott Sharp. **Special Assistants:** Jack Maloof (hitting), Bill Fischer (pitching). **Special Assistant to Player Development/Scouting:** John Wathan. **Coordinators:** Doug Sisson (field), Tony Tijerina (assistant field/catching), Mark Harris (infield), Luis Silverio (outfield), Quilvio Veras (baserunning/bunting). **Rehab Pitching Coach:** Carlos Reyes.

Farm System

Class	Club (League)	Manager	Coach	Pitching Coach
Triple-A	Omaha (PCL)	Mike Jirschele	Tommy Gregg	Doug Henry
Double-A	Northwest Arkansas (TL)	Brian Poldberg	Terry Bradshaw	Larry Carter
High A	Wilmington (CL)	Brian Rupp	Justin Gemoll	Steve Luebber
Low A	Burlington (MWL)	Jim Gabella	Omar Ramirez	Jerry Nyman
Rookie	Idaho Falls (PIO)	Brian Buchanan	Julio Bruno	Carlos Martinez
Rookie	Burlington (APP)	Nelson Liriano	Unavailable	Bobby St. Pierre
Rookie	Royals (AZL)	Darryl Kennedy	A. David/J. Williams	C. Reyes/M. Davis
Rookie	Royals (DSL)	Jose Mejia	Larry Sutton	Rafael Roque

Scouting

Telephone: (816) 921-8000. **Fax:** (816) 924-0347.
Manager, Scouting Operations: Linda Smith.
Major League Scouts: Charles Bolton (Indianapolis, IN), Matt Price (Atlanta, GA), Mike Pazik (Bethesda, MD). **Advance Scout:** Kelly Heath (Palm Harbor, FL).
National Supervisors: Marty Maier (Chesterfield, MO), Junior Vizcaino (Raleigh, NC), Dennis Woody (Danville, AR). **Regional Supervisors:** Gregg Kilby (Tampa, Florida), Dan Ontiveros (Laguna Niguel, CA), Sean Rooney (Pompton Lake, NJ), Mitch Webster (Kansas City, MO).
Area Scouts: Rich Amaral (Huntington Beach, CA), Jason Bryans (Windsor, Canada), Dennis Cardoza (Boyd, TX), Casey Fahy (Apex, NC), Jim Farr (Williamsburg, VA), Sean Gibbs (Canton, GA), Colin Gonzales (Orlando, FL), Steve Gossett (Fremont, NE), Scott Groot (Mission Viejo, CA), Ben Jones (Ft. Wayne, IN), Scott Melvin (Quincy, IL), Alex Mesa (Miami, FL), Ken Munoz (Scottsdale, AZ), Johnny Ramos (Carolina, PR), Scott Ramsay (Valley, WA), Brian Rhees (Live Oak, TX), Rick Schroeder (Pleasanton, CA), Dennis Sheehan (Glasco, NY), Lloyd Simmons (Oklahoma City, OK).
Latin America Supervisor: Orlando Estevez. **International Scouts:** Richard Castro (Venezuela), Salvador Donadelli (Venezuela), Juan Indriago (Venezuela), Joelvis Gonzalez (Venezuela), Charlie Kim (Korea), Juan Lopez (Nicaragua), Nathan Miller (Taiwan), Rafael Miranda (Colombia), Fausto Morel (Dominican), Ricardo Ortiz (Panama), Edis Perez (Dominican), Hector Pineda (Dominican), Mike Randall (South Africa), Rafael Vasquez (Dominican), Franco Wawoe (Curacao).

Los Angeles Angels

Office Address: 2000 Gene Autry Way, Anaheim, CA 92806.
Mailing Address: P.O. Box 2000, Anaheim, CA 92803.
Telephone: (714) 940-2000. **Fax:** (714) 940-2205.
Website: www.angelsbaseball.com.

Ownership
Owner: Arte Moreno. **Chairman:** Dennis Kuhl. **President:** John Carpino.

BUSINESS OPERATIONS

Chief Financial Officer: Bill Beverage. **Vice President, Finance/Administration:** Molly Taylor Jolly. **Controller:** Cris Fisher. **Accountants:** Lorelei Largey, Kylie McManus, Jennifer Whynott. **Assistant, Accounting:** Linda Chubak. **Director, Human Resources:** Jenny Price. **Benefits Coordinator:** Cecilia Schneider. **Human Resources Representative:** Arianna Fernandez. **Manager, Recruitment/Training:** Brittany Johnson. **Manager, Information Services:** Al Castro. **Senior Network Engineer:** Neil Farris. **Senior Customer Support Analyst:** David Yun. **Assistant Network Administrator:** Paramjit Singh. **Travel Account Manager:** Chantelle Ball.

Marketing/Corporate Sales
VP, Corporate Sales: Richard McClemmy. **Corporate Sales Account Executives:** Jennifer Soliman, Rick Turner, Carla Enriquez, Rob Aylesworth. **Sponsorship Services Manager:** Cesar Sanchez. **Senior Sponsorship Services Coordinator:** Maria Dinh. **Sponsorship Services Coordinators:** Derek Ohta, Jackie Perkins.

Arte Moreno

VP, Marketing/Ticket Sales: Robert Alvarado. **Senior Marketing Manager:** Matt Artin. **Marketing Manager:** Ernie Prukner. **Promotions Representative:** John Rozak. **Marketing Coordinator/Graphic Designer:** Jeff Lee. **Ticket Sales Manager:** Tom DeTemple.

Director, Client Services: Brian Sanders. **Event Manager:** Manny Almaraz. **Client Services Representatives:** Arthur Felix, Ashley Green, Justin Hallenbeck, Alisa Moreno, Shawn Meyer, Adrieanna Ryan, Matt Swanson, Kellie Wardecki. **Group Sales Account Executive:** Angel Rodriguez. **Premium Sales/Service Manager:** Brian Lawrence. **Ticket Sales Account Executives:** Clint Blevins, Jeff Leuenberger, Jasmin Matthews, Scott Tarlo. **Administrative Assistant, Marketing:** Monica Campanis. **Administrative Assistant, Ticket Sales:** Pat Lissy.

Public/Media Relations/Communications
Telephone: (714) 940-2014. **Fax:** (714) 940-2205.
Vice President, Communications: Tim Mead. **Communications Manager:** Eric Kay. **Administrative Assistant, Communications:** Jennifer Hoyer. **Community Relations Coordinator:** Lindsay McHolm. **Publications Manager:** Doug Ward. **Media Relations Representative:** Ryan Cavinder. **Traveling Secretary:** Tom Taylor. **Club Photographers:** Debora Robinson, John Cordes, Bob Binder.

2010 SCHEDULE
Standard Game Times: 7:05 p.m.; Sun. 12:35.

APRIL			
5-8 . . . . Minnesota	21-23 . . . . . . .at St. Louis	2-4. . . . . . . Kansas City	27-29 . . . . . . Baltimore
9-11 . . . . Oakland	24-26 . . . . .Toronto	5-8. . . . .at Chicago (AL)	30-31 . . . . . . .at Seattle
13-15 . . . at New York (AL)	28-30 . . . . Seattle	9-11 . . . . . . .at Oakland	
16-18 . . . . . . at Toronto	31 . . . . . .at Kansas City	15-18 . . . . Seattle	**SEPTEMBER**
19-22 . . . . Detroit		20-21 . . . at New York (AL)	1 . . . . .at Seattle
23-25 . . . .New York (AL)	**JUNE**	22-25 . . . . .at Texas	3-5. . . . . . . .at Oakland
26-28 . . . . . . Cleveland	1-3. . . . . .at Kansas City	26-28 . . . . Boston	6-8. . . . . Cleveland
30 . . . . .at Detroit	4-6. . . . . .at Seattle	30-31 . . . . Texas	10-12 . . . . Seattle
	7-10 . . . . . .at Oakland		14-16 . . . . . .at Cleveland
MAY	11-13 . at Los Angeles (NL)	**AUGUST**	17-19 . . . . at Tampa Bay
1-2. . . . . . . .at Detroit	14-16 . . . . . .Milwaukee	1 . . . . Texas	20-22 . . . . Texas
3-6. . . . . . . .at Boston	18-20 . . .at Chicago (NL)	3-5. . . . . . at Baltimore	24-26 . . . . Chicago (AL)
7-9. . . . . . . .at Seattle	22-24 . . Los Angeles (NL)	6-8. . . . . . . .at Detroit	27-29 . . . . . . Oakland
10-12 . . . . . .Tampa Bay	25-27 . . . . . .Colorado	9-11 . . . . . Kansas City	30 . . . . .at Texas
14-16 . . . . . . Oakland	29-30 . . . . Texas	13-15 . . . . .Toronto	
17-18 . . . . . . .at Texas		17-19 . . . . . . .at Boston	**OCTOBER**
19-20 . . . .at Chicago (AL)	**JULY**	20-22 . . . . at Minnesota	1-3. . . . . .at Texas
	1 . . . . Texas	23-25 . . . . . .Tampa Bay	

GENERAL INFORMATION

Stadium (year opened): Angel Stadium (2004).
Team Colors: Red, dark red, blue and silver.

Player Representative: Unavailable.
Home Dugout: Third Base.
Playing Surface: Grass.

Ballpark Operations/Facilities

Director, Ballpark Operations: Sam Maida. **Director, Facility Services:** Mike McKay. **Event Manager:** Calvin Ching. **Manager, Security:** Keith Cleary.

Maintenance Manager, Field/Ground: Barney Lopas. **Assistant Manager, Facility Services:** Linda Fitzgerald. **Maintenance Supervisor:** David Tamblyn. **Purchasing Manager:** Ron Sparks. **Purchasing Assistant:** Suzanne Peters. **Receptionists:** Sandy Sanford, Margie Walsh.

Manager, Entertainment/Production: Peter Bull. **Producer, Video Operations:** David Tsuruda. **Associate Producer:** Danny Pitts. **Entertainment Supervisor:** Heather Capizzi. **PA Announcer:** David Courtney.

Ticketing

Manager, Ticket Operations: Sheila Brazelton. **Assistant Ticket Manager:** Susan Weiss. **Ticketing Supervisor:** Ryan Vance. **Ticketing Representatives:** Cyndi Nguyen, Clancy Holligan, Kim Weaver.

Travel/Clubhouse

Clubhouse Manager: Keith Tarter.

Assistant Clubhouse Manager: Shane Demmitt. **Visiting Clubhouse Manager:** Brian Harkins. **Senior Video Coordinator:** Diego Lopez. **Video Coordinator:** Ruben Montano.

BASEBALL OPERATIONS

General Manager: Tony Reagins.

Assistant GM: Ken Forsch. **Special Advisor:** Bill Stoneman. **Special Assistant to GM:** Gary Sutherland. **Manager, Baseball Operations:** Tory Hernandez.

Tony Reagins

Major League Staff

Manager: Mike Scioscia. **Coaches:** Bench—Ron Roenicke; Pitching—Mike Butcher; Batting—Mickey Hatcher; First Base—Alfredo Griffin; Third Base—Dino Ebel; Bullpen—Orlando Mercado; Bullpen Catcher—Steve Soliz.

Medical/Training

Medical Director: Dr. Lewis Yocum. **Team Physician:** Dr. Craig Milhouse.

Head Athletic Trainer: Ned Bergert. **Athletic Trainer:** Rick Smith. **Assistant Athletic Trainer:** Adam Nevala. **Minor League Physical Therapist:** David Hogarth. **Strength/Conditioning Coach:** T.J. Harrington. **Director, Legal Affairs/Risk Management:** David Cohen. **Administrative Assistant, Trainers:** Chris Titchenal.

Player Development

Director, Player Development: Abe Flores.

Assistant, Player Development/Scouting: Justin Hollander. **Administrative Assistant:** Kathy Mair.

Administration Manager, Arizona: Eric Blum.

Field Coordinator/Hitting Instructor: Todd Takayoshi. **Roving Instructors:** Tom Gregorio (catching), Geoff Hostetter (training coordinator), Bill Lachemann (catching/special assignment), Eric Owens (outfield/baserunning/bunting), Rob Picciolo (infield), Kernan Ronan (pitching).

Farm System

Class	Club	Manager	Coach	Pitching Coach
Triple-A	Salt Lake (PCL)	Bobby Mitchell	Jim Eppard	Erik Bennett
Double-A	Arkansas (TL)	Bobby Magallanes	Francisco Matos	Ken Patterson
High A	R. Cucamonga (CAL)	Keith Johnson	Damon Mashore	Daniel Ricabal
Low A	Cedar Rapids (MWL)	Bill Mosiello	Brent Del Chiaro	Brandon Emanuel
Rookie	Orem (PIO)	Tom Kotchman	Mike Eylward	Zeke Zimmerman
Rookie	Angels (AZL)	Ty Boykin	Dick Schofield	Trevor Wilson
Rookie	Angels (DSL)	Charlie Romero	Edgal Rodriguez	Santos Alcala

Scouting

Telephone: 714-940-2130, 714-940-2061. **Fax:** (714) 940-2203.

Director, Amateur Scouting: Eddie Bane. **Assistant, Scouting:** Kathy Mair.

Major League Scouts: Rich Schlenker (Walnut Creek, CA), Jeff Schugel (Denver, CO), Brad Sloan (Brimfield, IL), Dale Sutherland (La Crescenta, CA).

National Crosscheckers: Jeff Malinoff (Lopez, WA), Ric Wilson (Chandler, AZ). **Regional Supervisors:** East—Mike Silvestri (Davie, FL); Midwest—Ron Marigny (New Orleans, LA); West—Bo Hughes (Sherman Oaks, CA).

Area Scouts: Arnold Brathwaite (Grand Prairie, TX), Bart Braun Jr. (Davie, FL), Jim Bryant (Mobile, AL), John Burden (Fairfield, OH), Tim Corcoran (Le Verne, CA), Bobby DeJardin (San Clemente, CA), John Gracio (Mesa, AZ), Kevin Ham (El Paso, TX), Casey Harvie (Lake Stevens, WA), Tom Kotchman (Seminole, FL), Chris McAlpin (Norman Park, GA), Greg Morhardt (So. Windsor, CT), Joel Murrie (Evergreen, CO), Dan Radcliff (Palmyra, VA), Scott Richardson (Elk Grove, CA), Jeff Scholzen (Santa Clara, UT), Rob Wilfong (San Dimas, CA).

Director, International Scouting: Marc Russo. **International Scouts:** Mario Mendoza (Mexico), Grant Weir (Australia).

Los Angeles Dodgers

Office Address: 1000 Elysian Park Ave, Los Angeles, CA 90090.
Telephone: (323) 224-1500. **Fax:** (323) 224-1269.
Website: www.dodgers.com

Ownership

Owner and Chairman: Frank McCourt. **Special Advisors to Chairman:** Tommy Lasorda, Dr. Frank Jobe, Don Newcombe.

BUSINESS OPERATIONS

President: Dennis Mannion. **COO:** Geoff Wharton. **Senior Vice President/General Counsel:** Sam Fernandez. **VP, Organizational Development/Fan Services:** Joe Walsh. **Chief Revenue Officer:** Michael Young.

Finance

CFO: Peter Wilhelm. **VP Finance:** Marlo Vandemore.

Sales/Advertising/Client Services

Vice President, Partnership Management: Steve Spartin. **Senior Director, Consumer Development:** Harlan Hendrickson. **Director, Ticket Sales:** David Siegel.

Communications

VP, Communications: Josh Rawitch. **Assistant Director, Public Relations:** Joe Jareck. **Assistant Director, Business/Multicultural PR:** Yvonne Carrasco. **Supervisor, Public Relations:** Amy Summers. **Director, Publications:** Jorge Martin.

Frank McCourt

Stadium Operations

VP, Security: Ray Maytorena. **Director, Security/Guest Services:** Shahram Ariane. **Director, Stadium Operations:** Francine Hughes. **Assistant Director, Turf/Grounds:** Eric Hansen. **PA Announcer:** Eric Smith. **Official Scorers:** Don Hartack, Ed Munson. **Organist:** Nancy Bea Hefley.

Ticketing

Telephone: (323) 224-1471. **Fax:** (323) 224-2609.
VP, Ticket Operations: Billy Hunter. **Assistant Director, Ticket Operations:** Seth Bluman.

Travel, Clubhouse

Manager, Team Travel: Scott Akasaki.
Home Clubhouse Manager: Mitch Poole. **Visiting Clubhouse Manager:** Jerry Turner. **Advisor, Team Travel:** Billy DeLury.

2010 SCHEDULE

Standard Game Times: 7:10 p.m.; Sun. 1:10

APRIL
5 . . . . at Pittsburgh
7-8 . . . . . . at Pittsburgh
9-11 . . . . .at Florida
13-15 . . . . Arizona
16-18 . . . . . San Francisco
20-22 . . . . . .at Cincinnati
23-25 . . . at Washington
26-28 . . . at New York (NL)
29-30 . . . . Pittsburgh

MAY
1-2 . . . . Pittsburgh
4-6 . . . . .Milwaukee
7-9 . . . . .Colorado
10-12 . . . . at Arizona
14-16 . . . at San Diego
17-18 . . . . Houston

19-20 . . . . . . San Diego
21-23 . . . . Detroit
25-27 . . . .at Chicago (NL)
28-30 . . . . . at Colorado
31 . . . . Arizona

JUNE
1-2 . . . . .Arizona
3-6 . . . . Atlanta
7-9 . . . . St. Louis
11-13 . . . Los Angeles (AL)
15-17 . . . . . .at Cincinnati
18-20 . . . . .at Boston
22-24 . at Los Angeles (AL)
25-27 . . . . .New York (AL)
28-30 . . . at San Francisco

JULY
2-4. . . . . at Arizona
5-7. . . . . Florida
8-11 . . . . . Chicago (NL)
15-18 . . . . . .at St. Louis
19-21 . . . . San Francisco
22-25 . . . .New York (NL)
27-29 . . . . at San Diego
30-31 . . . at San Francisco

AUGUST
1 . . . . . . at San Francisco
2-5. . . . . San Diego
6-8. . . . . Washington
10-12 . . . . at Philadelphia
13-16 . . . . at Atlanta
17-19 . . . . . . .Colorado
20-22 . . . . Cincinnati

24-26 . . . . . at Milwaukee
27-29 . . . . . at Colorado
30-31 . . . . . .Philadelphia

SEPTEMBER
1 . . . . .Philadelphia
3-5. . . . . . . San Francisco
6-8. . . . . . at San Diego
9-12 . . . . . . .at Houston
14-16 . . at San Francisco
17-19 . . . . . . .Colorado
21-23 . . . . . . San Diego
24-26 . . . . . . at Arizona
27-29 . . . . at Colorado

OCTOBER
1-3. . . . . .Arizona

GENERAL INFORMATION

Stadium (year opened): Dodger Stadium (1962).
Team Colors: Dodger blue and white.

Player Representative: Russell Martin.
Home Dugout: Third Base.
Playing Surface: Grass.

BASEBALL OPERATIONS

Telephone: (323) 224-1500. **Fax:** (323) 224-1463.
General Manager: Ned Colletti.
Vice President/Assistant GM: Kim Ng. **Special Assistants to GM:** Ken Bracey, Bill Mueller, Rick Ragazzo. **Special Assistant to GM/Director, Pro Scouting:** Vance Lovelace. **Special Assistant to GM/Advance Scout:** Mark Weidemaier. **Director, Baseball Operations:** Ellen Harrigan. **Director, Asian Operations:** Acey Kohrogi. **Director, International Operations:** Joseph Reaves. **Manager, Team Travel:** Scott Akasaki. **Special Assistant, Baseball Operations:** Mark Sweeney. **Baseball Operations Assistants:** Roman Barinas, Chris Madden, Matt Marks, Will Sharp.

Ned Colletti

Major League Staff

Manager: Joe Torre.
Coaches: Bench—Bob Schaefer; Pitching—Rick Honeycutt; Hitting—Don Mattingly; First Base—Mariano Duncan; Third Base—Larry Bowa; Bullpen—Ken Howell. **Major League Hitting Instructor:** Jeff Pentland. **Major League Instructor:** Manny Mota.

Medical/Training

Team Physicians: Dr. Neal ElAttrache, Dr. Ken Landis.
Director, Medical Services/Head Trainer: Stan Conte. **Assistant Athletic Trainer:** Todd Tomczyk. **Strength/Conditioning Coach:** Brendon Huttmann. **Physical Therapist:** Sue Falsone. **Massage Therapist:** Ichiro Tani. **Minor League Strength Coordinator:** Mike Winkler. **Minor League Physical Therapist:** Jeremiah Randall. **Minor League Medical Coordinator:** Jim Young.

Player Development

Telephone: (323) 224-1431. **Fax:** (323) 224-1359.
Assistant GM, Player Development: De Jon Watson.
Assistant Director, Player Development: Chris Haydock. **Special Assistant, Baseball Operations:** Jose Vizcaino. **Coordinator, Minor League Administration:** Adriana Urzua. **Field Coordinator:** Bruce Hines. **Hitting Coordinator:** Gene Clines. **Pitching Coordinator:** Rafael Chaves. **Outfield/Baserunning Coordinator:** Rodney McCray. **Infield Coordinator:** Matt Martin. **Catching Coordinator:** Travis Barbary. **Campo Las Palmas Coordinator:** Henry Cruz. **Field Coordinator, Campo Las Palmas:** Antonio Bautista.

Farm System

Class	Club (League)	Manager	Coach	Pitching Coach
Triple-A	Albuquerque (PCL)	Tim Wallach	John Moses	Jim Slaton
Double-A	Chattanooga (SL)	Carlos Subero	John Valentin	Danny Darwin
High A	Inland Empire (CAL)	Jeff Carter	Franklin Stubbs	Charlie Hough
Low A	Great Lakes (MWL)	Juan Bustabad	Michael Boughton	Chuck Crim
Rookie	Ogden (PIO)	Damon Berryhill	Johnny Washington	Kremlin Martinez
Rookie	Dodgers (AZL)	Lorenzo Bundy	Leo Garcia	Glen Dishman
Rookie	Dodgers (DSL)	Pedro Mega	Tony Mota	Unavailable

Scouting

Assistant GM, Scouting: Logan White.
Director, Amateur Scouting: Tim Hallgren.
Special Advisor/National Crosschecker: Gib Bodet (San Clemente, CA). **National Crosscheckers:** Paul Fryer (Calabasas, CA), Larry Barton (Leona Valley, CA).
Manager, Scouting: Jane Capobianco. **Scouting Coordinator:** Trey Magnuson.
East Coast Supervisor: John Green (Tucson, AZ). **Midwest Supervisor:** Gary Nickels (Naperville, IL). **West Coast Supervisor:** Brian Stephenson (Chandler, AZ).
Major League Scouts: Jon Debus, Carl Loewenstine, Al La Macchia, Billy Merkel, Ron Rizzi, John Sanders.
Area Scouts: Clint Bowers (Hewitt, TX), Bobby Darwin (Cerritos, CA), Rich Delucia (Reading, PA), Manny Estrada (Longwood, FL), Scott Hennessey (Ponte Vedra, FL), Orsino Hill (Des Moines, IA), Calvin Jones (Highland Village, TX), Henry Jones (Vancouver, WA), Lon Joyce (Spartanburg, SC), Scott Little (Jackson, MO), Marty Lamb (Nicholasville, KY), Dennis Moeller (Santa Clarita, CA), Matthew Paul (Slidell, LA), Clair Rierson (Frederick, MD), Chet Sergo (Stoughton, WI), Tom Thomas (Phoenix, AZ).
International Scouts: Ralph Avila (Dominican Republic), Elvio Jimenez (Dominican Republic), Gustavo Zapata (Central America), Rolando Chirino (Curacao), Ezequiel Sepulveda (Dominican Republic), Rafael Rijo (Dominican Republic), Bienvenido Tavarez (Dominican Republic), Wilton Guerrero (Dominican Republic), Keiichi Kojima (Japan), Byung-Hwan An (Korea), Mike Brito (Mexico), Camilo Pascual (Venezuela), Bernardo Torres (Venezuela), Oswaldo Villalobos (Venezuela), Maximo Gross (Dominican Republic).
Part-Time Scouts: George Genovese, Artie Harris, Luis Faccio, Greg Goodwin.

Milwaukee Brewers

Office Address: Miller Park, One Brewers Way, Milwaukee, WI 53214.
Telephone: (414) 902-4400. **Fax:** (414) 902-4053.
Website: www.brewers.com.

Ownership
Operated By: Milwaukee Brewers Baseball Club.
Chairman/Principal Owner: Mark Attanasio.

BUSINESS OPERATIONS

Executive Vice President, Business Operations: Rick Schlesinger. **Executive VP, Finance/ Administration:** Bob Quinn. **VP, General Counsel:** Marti Wronski. **Director, Business Operations:** Teddy Werner. **Executive Assistant, Business Operations:** Adela Reeve. **Executive Assistant, Ownership Group:** Samantha Ernest.

Mark Attanasio

Finance/Accounting
Vice President/Controller: Joe Zidanic. **Director, Reporting/Special Projects:** Steve O'Connell. **Accounting Manager:** Vicki Wise. **Staff Accountant:** Meredith Zaffrann.
Vice President, Human Resources/Office Management: Sally Andrist. **Human Resources Assistant:** Zendy Hernandez.
Vice President, Technology/Information Systems: John Winborn. **Network Administrator:** Corey Kmichik. **Application Developer:** Tod Johnson. **Systems Support Specialist:** Adam Bauer.

Marketing/Corporate Sponsorships
Vice President, Corporate Marketing: Tom Hecht. **Senior Director, Corporate Marketing:** Greg Hilt. **Directors, Corporate Marketing:** Sarah Holbrook, Andrew Pauls, Dave Tamburrino. **Vice President, Consumer Marketing:** Todd Taylor. **Senior Director, Marketing:** Kathy Schwab. **Director, Merchandise Branding:** Jill Aronoff. **Director, Corporate Suite Services:** Shaunna Richardson.
Senior Director, Broadcasting/Entertainment: Aleta Mercer. **Director, Audio/Video Productions:** Deron Anderson. **Manager, Entertainment/Broadcasting:** Andrew Olson. **Coordinator, Audio/Video Production:** Cory Wilson.

Media Relations/Communications
Telephone: (414) 902-4500. **Fax:** (414) 902-4053.
Vice President, Communications: Tyler Barnes. **Director, Media Relations:** Mike Vassallo. **Manager, Media Relations:** John Steinmiller. **Coordinator, Media Relations:** Ken Spindler.
Director, Community Relations: Katina Shaw. **Community Relations Assistant:** Erica Bowring. **Manager, Youth Outreach:** Larry Hisle. **Executive Director, Brewers Community Foundation:** Cecelia Gore.

Stadium Operations
Director, Stadium Operations: Bob Hallas. **Director, Event Services:** Matt Kenny. **Director, Grounds:** Gary

2010 SCHEDULE
Standard Game Times: 7:10 p.m.; Sun. 1:10.

APRIL		JULY	
5-7 . . . . Colorado	17-18 . . . . . at Cincinnati	1-4 . . . . .at St. Louis	20-22 . . . . San Diego
9-11 . . . . St. Louis	19-20 . . . . . at Pittsburgh	5-8 . . . . . . San Francisco	24-26 . . . Los Angeles (NL)
12 . . . . .at Chicago (NL)	21-23 . . . . . at Minnesota	9-11 . . . . Pittsburgh	27-29 . . . . Pittsburgh
14-15 . . . .at Chicago (NL)	25-27 . . . . Houston	9-11 . . . . Pittsburgh	30-31 . . . . .at Cincinnati
16-18 . . . at Washington	28-30 . . . . .New York (NL)	15-18 . . . . . . at Atlanta	
20-22 . . . . at Pittsburgh	31 . . . . .at Florida	19-22 . . . . at Pittsburgh	SEPTEMBER
23-25 . . . . Chicago (NL)		23-25 . . . . . Washington	1 . . . . .at Cincinnati
26-28 . . . . . Pittsburgh	JUNE	26-28 . . . . . . Cincinnati	3-5 . . . . . at Philadelphia
29-30 . . . . at San Diego	1-3 . . . . .at Florida	30-31 . . . . . .at Houston	6-8 . . . . St. Louis
	4-6 . . . . .at St. Louis		10-12 . . . . Chicago (NL)
MAY	8-10 . . . . . Chicago (NL)	AUGUST	13-15 . . . . . . .at Houston
1-2 . . . . . . at San Diego	11-13 . . . . Texas	1 . . . . .at Houston	17-19 . . . at San Francisco
4-6 . . . at Los Angeles (NL)	14-16 . at Los Angeles (AL)	2-4 . . . . .at Chicago (NL)	20-22 . . . . . . Cincinnati
7-9 . . . . at Arizona	18-20 . . . . . . at Colorado	6-8 . . . . Houston	23-26 . . . . Florida
10-12 . . . . Atlanta	22-24 . . . . . . Minnesota	9-12 . . . . .Arizona	27-30 . . . at New York (NL)
14-16 . . . . .Philadelphia	25-27 . . . . Seattle	13-15 . . . . at Colorado	
	28-30 . . . . Houston	17-18 . . . . . .at St. Louis	OCTOBER
			1-3 . . . . . . .at Cincinnati

GENERAL INFORMATION
Stadium (year opened): Miller Park (2001).
Team Colors: Navy blue, gold and white.
Player Representative: Unavailable.
Home Dugout: First Base.
Playing Surface: Grass.

Vanden Berg. **Landscape Manager:** Miranda Bintley. **Supervisor, Warehouse:** Patrick Rogo. **Vice President, Brewers Enterprises:** Jason Hartlund. **Manager, Event Services:** Jennacy Cruz. **Receptionists:** Willa Oden, Jody McBee.

Ticketing
Telephone: (414) 902-4000. **Fax:** (414) 902-4100.
Senior Director, Ticket Sales: Jim Bathey. **Director, Group Sales:** Chris Barlow. **Director, Season Ticket Sales:** Billy Freiss. **Director, Ticket Operations:** Regis Bane. **Administrative Assistant:** Irene Bolton. **Assistant Director, Ticket Services:** Nancy Jorgensen. **Manager, Ticket Operations:** Chad Olson.

BASEBALL OPERATIONS

Telephone: (414) 902-4400. **Fax:** (414) 902-4059.
Executive Vice President/General Manager: Doug Melvin.
VP/Assistant GM: Gord Ash. **Special Assistant to GM/Baseball Operations:** Dan O'Brien.
Director, Baseball Operations: Tom Flanagan. **Manager, Advance Scouting/Baseball Research:** Karl Mueller. **Coordinator, Advance Scouting/Baseball Research:** Scott Campbell. **Manager, Coaching Assistant/Digital Media Coordinator:** Joe Crawford. **Senior Administrator, Baseball Operations:** Barb Stark.

Major League Staff
Manager: Ken Macha.
Coaches: Bench—Willie Randolph; Pitching—Rick Peterson; Hitting—Dale Sveum; First Base—Ed Sedar; Third Base—Brad Fischer; Bullpen—Stan Kyles.

Doug Melvin

Medical, Training
Head Team Physician: Dr. William Raasch. **Head Athletic Trainer:** Roger Caplinger. **Assistant Athletic Trainer/ Strength/Conditioning Coordinator:** Dan Wright.

Player Development
Special Assistant to GM/Director, Player Development: Reid Nichols (Phoenix, AZ).
Business Manager: Scott Martens. **Assistant Director, Player Development:** Tony Diggs. **Coordinator, Administration/Player Development:** Mark Mueller. **Field/Catching Coordinator:** Charlie Greene. **Coordinators:** Frank Neville (athletic training), Lee Tunnell (pitching), Darnell Coles (hitting). **Roving Instructors:** Garth Iorg (roving infield), Reggie Williams (roving outfield/baserunning).

Farm System

Class	Club (League)	Manager	Coach	Pitching Coach
Triple-A	Nashville (PCL)	Don Money	Sandy Guerrero	Rich Gale
Double-A	Huntsville (SL)	Mike Guerrero	Al Leboeuf	John Curtis
High A	Brevard County (FSL)	Bob Miscik	Dwayne Hosey	Fred Dabney
Low A	Wisconsin (MWL)	Jeff Isom	Matt Erickson	Chris Hook
Rookie	Helena (PIO)	Joe Ayrault	Ned Yost IV	Elvin Nina
Rookie	Brewers (AZL)	Tony Diggs	Kenny Dominguez	Steve Cline
Rookie	Brewers (DSL)	Nestor Corredor	Luis De Los Santos	Jose Nunez

Scouting
Telephone: (414) 902-4400. **Fax:** (414) 902-4059.
Special Assistant to GM/Director, Professional Scouting: Dick Groch (Marysville, MI).
Director, Amateur Scouting: Bruce Seid. **Assistant Director, Amateur Scouting:** Ray Montgomery. **Manager, Minor League Scouting Personnel/Coordinator, Pro Scouting:** Zack Minasian. **Coordinator, Administration/Amateur Scouting:** Amanda Kropp.
Roving Crosschecker: Jim Rooney (Scottsdale, AZ). **Regional Supervisors:** West—Corey Rodriguez (Redondo Beach, CA); Midwest—Ray Montgomery (Simsbury, CT); East—Doug Reynolds (Tallahassee, FL).
Pro Scouts: Lary Aaron (Atlanta, GA), Brad Belbarba (Ft. Mitchell, KY), Bryan Gale (Chicago, IL), Cory Melvin (Tampa, FL), Dick Groch (St. Claire, MI), Ben Mclure (Hummelstown, PA), Zack Minasian (Milwaukee, WI), Tom Mooney (Pittsfield, MA), Ross Sapp (Cherry Valley, CA), Marv Thompson (West Jordan, UT), Derek Watson (Charlotte, NC), Tom Wheeler (Martinez, CA), Leon Wurth (Paducah, KY).
Area Scouts: Josh Belovsky (Orange, CA), Jeremy Booth (Houston, TX), Kevin Clouser (Phoenix, AZ), Tim Collinsworth (Rowlett, TX), Mike Farrell (Indianapolis, IN), Manolo Hernandez (Puerto Rico), Dan Huston (Thousand Oaks, CA), Harvey Kuenn, Jr. (New Berlin, WI), Jay Lapp (London, Ontario, Canada), Marty Lehn (White Rock, British Columbia, Canada), Joe Mason (Millbrook, AL), Justin McCray (Davis, CA), Tim McIlvaine (Tampa, FL), Dan Nellum (Crofton, MD), Brandon Newell (Bellingham, WA), Ryan Robinson (Tallahassee, FL), Brian Sankey (Yarmouth Port, MA), Charles Sullivan (Weston, FL).
Part-time Scouts: John Bushart (West Hills, CA), Richard Colpaert (Shelby Township, MI), Don Fontana (Pittsburgh, PA), John Haar (Burnaby, British Columbia, Canada), Joe Hodges (Rockwood, TN), Roger Janeway (Englewood, OH), Johnny Logan (Milwaukee, WI), J.P. Roy (Saint Nicolas, Quebec, Canada), J.R. Salinas (Houston, TX), Lee Seid (Las Vegas, NV), Brad Stoll (Lawrence, KS), Nathan Trosky (Carmel, CA).
Latin American Supervisor: Fernando Arango (Davie, FL). **International Scouts:** Manny Batista (Dominican Republic/ Venezuela/Puerto Rico), Freddy Torres (Venezuela), Rafael Espinal (Dominican Republic), Jose Guarache (Venezuela).

Minnesota Twins

Office Address: Target Field, 1 Twins Way, Minneapolis, MN 55403.
Telephone: (612) 659-3400. **Fax:** 612-659-4025. **Website:** www.twinsbaseball.com.

Ownership
Operated By: The Minnesota Twins.
Chief Executive Officer: Jim Pohlad.
Chairman, Executive Committee: Howard Fox. **Executive Board:** James Pohlad, Robert Pohlad, William Pohlad, Dave St. Peter.

BUSINESS OPERATIONS

Jim Pohlad

President, Minnesota Twins: Dave St. Peter. **President, Twins Sports Inc.:** Jerry Bell. **Senior Vice President, Business Development:** Laura Day. **Senior Vice President, Business Administration/CFO:** Kip Elliott.

Target Field Development
Construction Consultant: Dick Strassburg. **Project Manager:** Paul Johnson. **Director, New Ballpark Development:** Scott O'Connell. **Development, Finance/Accounting:** Dan Starkey.

Human Resources/Finance/Technology
VP, Human Resources/Diversity: Raenell Dorn. **Payroll Manager:** Lori Beasley. **Benefits Manager:** Leticia Silva. **Human Resources Generalist:** Holly Corbin.
Senior Director, Finance: Andy Weinstein. **Manager, Ticket Accounting:** Jerry McLaughlin. **Accountant:** Lyndsey Taylor. **Manager, Finance Planning/Analysis:** Amy Fong-Christianson. **Manager, Accounting:** Lori Windschitl. **Director, Purchasing:** Bud Hanley. **Administrative Assistant:** Ka Her. **Vice President, Technology:** John Avenson. **Director, Technology:** Wade Navratil. **Manager, Technology Infrastructure:** Tony Persio.

Marketing/Broadcasting
VP, Marketing: Patrick Klinger. **Senior Director, Advertising:** Nancy O'Brien. **Director, Event Marketing:** Heidi Sammon. **Promotions Manager:** Julie Rohloff. **Manager, Emerging Markets:** Miguel Ramos. **Director, Broadcasting/Game Presentation:** Andy Price. **Radio Network Producer:** Mark Genosky.

Corporate Partnerships
VP, Corporate Partnerships: Eric Curry. **Senior Manager, Client Services:** Bodie Forsling. **Manager, Corporate Client Services:** Katie Beaulieu. **Coordinator, Corporate Client Services:** Paulette Cheatham. **Coordinator, Traffic/Service:** Amy Johnson.

Communications
Telephone: (612) 659-3475. **Fax:** (612) 659-3472.
Director, Baseball Communications: Mike Herman. **Senior Manager, Baseball Communications:** Dustin Morse.

2010 SCHEDULE
Standard Game Times: 7:10 p.m.; Sun 1:10.

APRIL		
5-8. . . at Los Angeles (AL)	19-20 . . . . . . .at Boston	**JULY**
9-11 . . . . .at Chicago (AL)	21-23 . . . . . .Milwaukee	1-4. . . . . .Tampa Bay
12 . . . . Boston	25-27 . . . .New York (AL)	6-8. . . . . at Toronto
14-15 . . . . Boston	28-30 . . . . Texas	9-11 . . . . .at Detroit
16-18 . . . . . Kansas City	31 . . . . .at Seattle	15-18 . . . . Chicago (AL)
20-22 . . . . . . Cleveland		19-21 . . . . . . Cleveland
23-25 . . .at Kansas City	**JUNE**	22-25 . . . . .at Baltimore
27-29 . . . . . . .at Detroit	1-3. . . . . .at Seattle	26-28 . . . .at Kansas City
30 . . . . . . .at Cleveland	4-6. . . . . . . .at Oakland	30-31 . . . . Seattle
	8-10 . . . . . . Kansas City	
MAY	11-13 . . . . Atlanta	**AUGUST**
1-2. . . . . . .at Cleveland	15-17 . . . . .Colorado	1 . . . . Seattle
3-5. . . . . Detroit	18-20 . . . .at Philadelphia	2-5. . . . . . at Tampa Bay
6-9. . . . . Baltimore	22-24 . . . . . at Milwaukee	6-8. . . . . . .at Cleveland
11-12 . . . . . . Chicago (AL)	25-27 . . .at New York (NL)	10-12 . . . .at Chicago (AL)
14-16 . . . at New York (AL)	28-30 . . . . Detroit	13-15 . . . . Oakland
17-18 . . . . at Toronto		17-19 . . . . . Chicago (AL)
		20-22 . . . Los Angeles (AL)

23-26 . . . . .at Texas		
27-29 . . . . . . .at Seattle		
31 . . . . Detroit		
SEPTEMBER		
1-2. . . . . Detroit		
3-5. . . . . Texas		
6-8. . . . . . . Kansas City		
10-12 . . . . .at Cleveland		
14-16 . . . .at Chicago (AL)		
17-19 . . . . Oakland		
20-22 . . . . . . Cleveland		
24-26 . . . . . . .at Detroit		
27-29 . . . .at Kansas City		
30 . . . . .Toronto		
OCTOBER		
1-3. . . . . .Toronto		

GENERAL INFORMATION
Stadium (year opened): Target Field (2010). **Home Dugout:** First Base.
Team Colors: Red, navy blue and white. **Playing Surface:** Natural Grass.
Player Representative: Michael Cuddyer.

Manager, Publications/Media Services: Molly Gallatin. **Coordinator, Baseball Communications:** Mitch Hestad.

Public Affairs
    Executive Director, Public Affairs/Twins Community Fund: Kevin Smith. **Director, Community Affairs:** Bryan Donaldson. **Manager, Corporate Communications:** Chris Iles.

Ticketing
    Telephone: 1-800-33-TWINS. **Fax:** (612) 659-4030.
    VP, Ticket Sales/Service: Steve Smith. **Manager, Ticket Sales/Service:** Eric Hudson. **Manager, Group Ticket Sales:** Rob Malec. **Manager, Communications/Support:** Beth Vail. **Database Marketing Coordinator:** Brandon Johnson. **Senior Director, Ticket Operations:** Paul Froehle. **Senior Manager, Box Office:** Mike Stiles.

Stadium Operations
    VP, Operations: Matt Hoy. **Director, Stadium Operations:** Dave Horsman. **Manager, Stadium Operations:** Dan Smoliak. **Manager, Security:** Dick Dugan. **PA Announcer:** Adam Abrams. **Equipment Manager:** Rod McCormick. **Visitors Clubhouse:** Troy Matchan. **Manager, Major League Video:** Sean Harlin. **Head Groundskeeper:** Larry DiVito.

BASEBALL OPERATIONS

    Telephone: (612) 659-3485. **Fax:** (612) 659-4026.
    Senior Vice President/General Manager: Bill Smith.
    VP, Player Personnel: Mike Radcliff. **Assistant GM:** Rob Antony. **Senior Advisor:** Terry Ryan. **Special Assistants:** Joe McIlvaine, Tom Kelly. **Director, Baseball Operations:** Brad Steil. **Manager, Major League Administration:** Jack Goin. **Director, Team Travel:** Remzi Kiratli.

Major League Staff
    Manager: Ron Gardenhire.
    Coaches: Bench—Steve Liddle; Pitching—Rick Anderson; Batting—Joe Varva; First Base—Jerry White; Third Base—Scott Ullger; Bullpen—Rick Stelmaszek.

Medical, Training
    Club Physicians: Dr. Dan Buss, Dr. Vijay Eyunni, Dr. Tom Jetzer, Dr. John Steubs, Dr. Jon Hallberg, Dr. Gustavo Navarrete. **Head Trainer:** Rick McWane. **Assistant Trainer:** Dave Pruemer. **Strength/Conditioning Coach:** Perry Castellano.

Bill Smith

Player Development
    Telephone: (612) 659-3480. **Fax:** (612) 659-4026.
    Director, Minor Leagues: Jim Rantz. **Manager, Minor League Administration:** Kate Townley. **Minor League Coordinators:** Joel Lepel (field), Eric Rasmussen (pitching), Bill Springman (hitting), Paul Molitor (infield/baserunning).

Farm System

Class	Club	Manager	Coach	Pitching Coach
Triple-A	Rochester (IL)	Tom Nieto	F. Rayford/R. Ingram	Bobby Cuellar
Double-A	New Britain (EL)	Jeff Smith	Rudy Hernandez	Stu Cliburn
High A	Fort Myers (FSL)	Jake Mauer	Jim Dwyer	Steve Mintz
Low A	Beloit (MWL)	Nelson Prada	Tommy Watkins	Gary Lucas
Rookie	Elizabethton (APP)	Ray Smith	Jeff Reed	Jim Shellenback
Rookie	Twins (GCL)	Chris Heintz	M. Cuyler/R. Borrego	Ivan Arteaga
Rookie	Twins (DSL)	Unavailable	J. Alvarez/O. Rogers	Unavailable
Rookie	Twins (VSL)	Asdrubal Estrada	Unavailable	Luis Ramirez

Scouting
    Telephone: (612) 659-3490. **Fax:** (612) 659-4025.
    Director, Scouting: Deron Johnson (Sacramento, CA).
    Special Assignment Scouts: Tom Kelly (Maplewood, MN), Joe McIlvaine (Newton Square, PA).
    Major League Scouts: Ken Compton (Cypress, CA), Earl Frishman (Tampa, FL), Bob Hegman (Lee's Summit, MO).
    Coordinator, Professional Scouting: Vern Followell (Buena Park, CA).
    Pro Scout: Bill Milos (Crown Point, IN). **Advance Scout:** Shaun McGinn (Kansas City, MO).
    Scouting Supervisors: East—Mark Quimuyog (Lynn Haven, FL), West—Sean Johnson (Chandler, AZ), Mideast—Tim O'Neil (Lexington, KY), Midwest—Mike Ruth (Lee's Summit, MO).
    Area Scouts: Trevor Brown (Eugene, OR), Billy Corrigan (Tampa, FL), JR DiMercurio (Kansas City, MO), Mike Eaglin (Los Angeles, CA), Marty Esposito (Robinson, TX), John Leavitt (Garden Grove, CA), Hector Otero (Miami, FL), Jeff Pohl (Evansville, IN), Jack Powell (Sweetwater, TN), Greg Runser (The Woodlands, TX), Elliott Strankman (Walnut Creek, CA), Ricky Taylor (Hickory, NC), Jay Weitzel (Ridgway, PA), Ted Williams (Peoria, AZ), John Wilson (Hampton, NJ), Mark Wilson (Lindstrom, MN) Earl Winn (Bowling Green, KY).
    Coordinator, International Scouting: Howard Norsetter (Australia).
    Coordinator, Latin American Scouting: Jose Marzan (Ft. Myers, FL).
    International Scouts—Full-Time: Cary Broder (Taiwan), Glenn Godwin (Europe, Africa), Fred Guerrero (Dominican Republic), David Kim (South Korea), Jose Leon (Venezuela, Panama), Francisco Tejeda (Dominican Republic).
    International Scouts—Part-Time: Vicente Arias (Dominican Republic), John Cortese (Italy), Eric Espinosa (Panama), Eurey Luis Haslen (Dominican Republic), Andy Johnson (Europe), Nelson Meneses (Venezuela), Juan Padilla (Venezuela), Franklin Parra (Venezuela), Yan-Yu "Kenny" Su (Taiwan), Koji Takahashi (Japan), Pablo Torres (Venezuela), Lester Victoria (Curacao), Akihiro Yamaguchi (Japan).

New York Mets

Office Address: Citi Field, 126th Street, Flushing, NY 11368.
Telephone: (718) 507-6387. **Fax:** (718) 507-6395.
Website: www.mets.com, www.losmets.com.

Ownership
Operated By: Sterling Mets LP.
Chairman/Chief Executive Officer: Fred Wilpon. **President:** Saul Katz. **Chief Operating Officer:** Jeff Wilpon. **Board of Directors:** Fred Wilpon, Saul Katz, Jeff Wilpon, Richard Wilpon, Michael Katz, David Katz, Tom Osterman, Arthur Friedman, Steve Greenberg, Stuart Sucherman.

BUSINESS OPERATIONS

Fred Wilpon

Executive Vice President, Business Operations: David Howard. **Executive Vice President/General Counsel:** David Cohen.

Finance
CFO: Mark Peskin. **VP/Controller:** Len Labita. **Assistant Controller/Director:** Rebecca Landau-Mahadeva. **Director, Baseball Accounting:** Robert Gerbe.

Marketing, Sales
Senior VP, Marketing/Communications: David Newman. **Senior Director, Marketing:** Tina Mannix. **Senior Director, Marketing Productions:** Tim Gunkel. **Director, Broadcasting/Special Events:** Lorraine Hamilton. **Director, Marketing Communications:** Jill Grabill. **Director, Community Outreach:** Jill Knee. **Senior VP, Corporate Sales/Services:** Paul Asencio. **VP, Venue Services:** Mike Landeen. **Directors, Corporate Sales/Partnerships:** Pete Helfer, Matthew Soloff. **Director, Suite Sales/Services:** Patrick Jones.

Media Relations
Telephone: (718) 565-4330. **Fax:** (718) 639-3619.
VP, Media Relations: Jay Horwitz. **Director, Media Relations:** Shannon Forde. **Manager, Media Relations:** Ethan Wilson. **Media Relations Coordinators:** Billy Harner, Nicole Chayet. **Media Relations Assistant:** Jon Kerber.

Ballpark Operations
VP, Facilities: Karl Smolarz. **VP, Operations:** Pat McGovern. **Director, Ballpark Operations:** Sue Lucchi. **Assistant Ballpark Manager:** Mike Dohnert. **Manager, Field Operations:** Bill Deacon. **Senior Director, Information Technology:** Joe Milone. **Director, Information Technology:** Robert Gradante. **PA Announcer:** Alex Anthony. **Official Scores:** Bill Shannon, Howie Karpin, Jordan Sprechman, David Freeman, Billy Altman.

Ticketing
Telephone: (718) 507-8499. **Fax:** (718) 507-6369.
Vice President, Ticket Sales/Services: Bill Ianniciello. **Senior Director, Ticket Operations:** Joan Sullivan. **Senior**

2010 SCHEDULE
Standard Game Times: 7:10 p.m.; Sun. 1:10.

APRIL
5 . . . . Florida
7-8 . . . . Florida
9-11 . . . . Washington
13-15 . . . . . . at Colorado
16-18 . . . . . .at St. Louis
19-22 . . . . . Chicago (NL)
23-25 . . . . Atlanta
26-28 . . . Los Angeles (NL)
30 . . . . . . at Philadelphia

MAY
1-2 . . . . . at Philadelphia
3-5 . . . . . . .at Cincinnati
7-9 . . . . . . San Francisco
10-12 . . . . . Washington
13-16 . . . . . . .at Florida

17-18 . . . . at Atlanta
19-20 . . . . at Washington
21-23 . . . . .New York (AL)
25-27 . . . . .Philadelphia
28-30 . . . . . at Milwaukee
31 . . . . at San Diego

JUNE
1-2 . . . . . . at San Diego
4-6 . . . . Florida
8-10 . . . . San Diego
11-13 . . . . . .at Baltimore
15-17 . . . . .at Cleveland
18-20 . . at New York (AL)
22-24 . . . . Detroit
25-27 . . . . . .Minnesota
28-30 . . . . . . .at Florida

JULY
1-4 . . . . . at Washington
5-7 . . . . Cincinnati
9-11 . . . . Atlanta
15-18 . . . at San Francisco
19-21 . . . . . . at Arizona
22-25 . at Los Angeles (NL)
27-29 . . . . St. Louis
30-31 . . . . Arizona

AUGUST
1 . . . . Arizona
2-4 . . . . at Atlanta
6-8 . . . . . at Philadelphia
10-12 . . . . Colorado
13-15 . . . . . .Philadelphia
16-19 . . . . . .at Houston

20-22 . . . . . at Pittsburgh
24-26 . . . . Florida
27-29 . . . . Houston
30-31 . . . . at Atlanta

SEPTEMBER
1-2 . . . . at Atlanta
3-5 . . . . . .at Chicago (NL)
6-8 . . . . . . at Washington
10-12 . . . . .Philadelphia
13-16 . . . . . . .Pittsburgh
17-19 . . . . Atlanta
21-22 . . . . . . .at Florida
24-26 . . . . at Philadelphia
27-30 . . . . . . .Milwaukee

OCTOBER
1-3 . . . . Washington

GENERAL INFORMATION
Stadium (year opened): Citi Field (2009).
Team Colors: Blue and orange.
Player Representative: David Wright.
Home Dugout: First Base.
Playing Surface: Grass.

Director, Group Sales/Ticket Sales Services: Tom Fersch. **Director, Ticket Sales Development:** Jamie Ozure. **Director, Ticket Operations:** John Giglio.

Venue Services
Vice President, Venue Services: Mike Landeen. **Vice President, Guest Experience:** Craig Marino. **Director, Venue Services:** Paul Schwartz. **Director, Hospitality/Catering Events:** Heather Collamore.

Travel, Clubhouse
Clubhouse Manager/Associate Travel Director: Charlie Samuels. **Assistant Equipment Manager:** Dave Berni. **Visiting Clubhouse Manager:** Tony Carullo. **Video Editor:** Joe Scarola.

BASEBALL OPERATIONS
Telephone: (718) 565-4315. **Fax:** (718) 507-6391.
Executive Vice President/General Manager: Omar Minaya.
VP/Assistant GM: John Ricco. **Special Assistants to GM:** Sandy, Johson, Wayne Krivsky, Bryan Lambe. **Manager, Baseball Administration:** Leonor Barua. **Executive Assistant to GM:** Diana Parra-Gonzalez. **Manager, Baseball Operations:** Adam Fisher. **Statistical Analyst:** Ben Baumer.

Major League Staff
Manger: Jerry Manuel.
Coaches: Bench—Dave Jauss; Pitching—Dan Warthen; Batting—Howard Johnson; First Base—Razor Shines; Third Base—Chip Hale; Bullpen—Randy Niemann.

Omar Minaya

Medical, Training
Medical Director: Dr. David Altchek. **Physician:** Dr. Struan Coleman. **Trainer:** Ray Ramirez.

Player Development
Telephone: (718) 565-4302. **Fax:** (718) 205-7920.
Director, Minor League Operations: Adam Wogan. **Director, International Operations:** Rafael Perez. **Coordinator, Minor League Operations:** Jon Miller. **Assistant, Player Development:** Michele Holmes. **FL/GCL Administrator:** Ronny Reyes. **Video Coordinator:** TJ Barra. **Field Coordinator:** Terry Collins. **Coordinator, Instruction/Infield:** Kevin Morgan. **Hitting Coordinator:** Lamar Johnson. **Pitching Coordinator:** Rick Waits. **Catching Coordinator:** Bob Natal. **Outfield/Baserunning Coordinator:** Mookie Wilson. **Medical Coordinator:** Mark Rogow. **Rehab/Physical Therapist:** Dave Pearson. **Strength/Conditioning:** Jason Craig. **Rehab Pitching Coordinator:** Frank Fultz. **Senior Advisor:** Guy Conti. **Pitching Consultant:** Al Jackson. **Special Instructor:** Bobby Floyd. **Hitting Instructor:** Tom McCraw. **International Field Coordinator:** Rafael Landestoy. **International Hitting Coordinator:** Pablo Cruz. **International Catching Instructor:** Ozzie Virgil. **Equipment/Clubhouse Manager:** Kevin Kierst.

Farm System

Class	Club	Manager	Coach(es)	Pitching Coach
Triple-A	Buffalo (IL)	Ken Oberkfell	Jack Voigt	Ricky Bones
Double-A	Binghamton (EL)	Tim Teufel	Luis Natera	Mark Brewer
High A	St. Lucie (FSL)	Edgar Alfonzo	G. Greer/J. Carreno	Phil Regan
Low A	Savannah (SAL)	Pedro Lopez	R. Ellis/L. Rojas	Marc Valdez
Short-season	Brooklyn (NYP)	Wally Backman	B. Distefano/J. Fuentes	Rick Tomlin
Rookie	Kingsport (APP)	Mike DiFelice	B. Malek/J. Lopez	Jonathan Hurst
Rookie	Mets (GCL)	Sandy Alomar Sr.	D. Mitchell	Hector Berrios
Rookie	Mets (DSL)	Francisco Cabrera	C. Capellan	Benjamin Marte
Rookie	Mets (DSL2)	Yunior Garcia	L. Hernandez/D. Davalillo	Rafael Lazo

Scouting
Telephone: (718) 565-4311. **Fax:** (718) 205-7920.
Director, Amateur Scouting: Rudy Terrasas. **Assistant, Amateur Scouting:** Elizabeth Gadsden. **Coordinator, Amateur Scouting:** Ian Levin. **Assistant, Professional/International Scouting:** Diana Parra-Gonzalez. **Advance Scout:** Bob Johnson (University Park, FL). **Pro Scouts:** Mack Babitt (Richmond, CA), Russ Bove (Longwood, FL), Roland Johnson (Newington, CT), David Keller (Phoenix, AZ), Duane Larson (Knoxville, TN), Bob Melvin (Long Beach, CA), Harry Minor (Long Beach, CA), Isao O'Jimi (Japan). **National Crosschecker:** David Lakey (Kingwood, TX). **Regional Supervisors:** Southeast—Steve Barningham (Land O'Lakes, FL), West—Tim Fortugno (Elk Grove, CA), Northeast—Scott Hunter (Mount Laurel, NJ), Midwest—Mac Seibert (Cantonment, FL).
Area Supervisors: Erwin Bryant (Lexington, KY), Larry Chase (Pearcy, AR), Ray Corbett (College Station, TX), Spencer Graham (San Dimas, CA), Jon Heuerman (Chandler, AZ), Larry Izzo, Jr. (Deer Park, NY), Tommy Jackson (Hoover, AL), Fred Mazuca (Tustin, CA), Marlin McPhail (Irmo, SC), Steve Nichols (Mount Dora, FL), Les Parker (Hudson, FL), Claude Pelletier (St. Lazare, Quebec), Art Pontarelli (Lincoln, RI), Jim Reeves (Camas, WA), Junior Roman (San Sebastian, Puerto Rico), Max Semler (Allen, TX), Jim Thompson (Wallingford, PA), Doug Thurman (San Jose, CA), Scott Trcka (Hobart, IN).
Director, Latin American Scouting: Ismael Cruz. **Area Supervisor, Venezuela:** Robert Alfonzo. **International Scouts:** Modesto Abreu (Dominican Republic), Imberwer Alvarez (Venezuela), Marciano Alvarez (Dominican Republic), Gerardo Cabrera (Dominican Republic), Carlos Capellan (Dominican Republic), Lionel Chatelle (Germany), Ender Chavez (Venezuela), Harold Herrera (Colombia), Rafael Jimenez (Venezuela), Gabriel Low (Mexico), Jimmy Oliver (South Korea), Camilo Pina (Dominican Republic), Hector Rincones (Venezuela), Jose Sandy Rosario (Dominican Republic), Luis Schecker (Dominican Republic), Edgar Suarez (Venezuela), Jossef Suarez (Venezuela), Caryl Van Zanten (Curacao), Alex Zapata (Panama).

New York Yankees

Office Address: Yankee Stadium, One East 161st Street, Bronx, NY 10451.
Telephone: (718) 293-4300. **Fax:** (718) 293-8431. **Website:** www.yankees.com; www.yankeesbeisbol.com.

OWNERSHIP

Principal Owner/Chairperson: George M. Steinbrenner III.
Managing General Partner/Co-Chairperson: Harold Z. Steinbrenner.
General Partner/Co-Chairperson: Henry G. Steinbrenner. **General Partner/Vice Chairperson:** Jennifer Steinbrenner Swindal. **General Partner/Vice Chairperson:** Jessica Steinbrenner. **Vice Chairperson:** Joan Steinbrenner. **Senior Vice President:** Felix Lopez.

BUSINESS OPERATIONS

President: Randy Levine, Esq.
COO: Lonn A. Trost, Esq.
Senior Vice President, Strategic Ventures: Marty Greenspun. **Senior VP, Chief Security Officer:** Sonny Hight. **Senior VP/Chief Financial Officer, Yankee Global Enterprises:** Anthony Bruno. **Senior VP, Business Development:** Jim Ross. **Senior VP, Corporate/Community Relations:** Brian Smith. **Senior VP, Corporate Sales/Sponsorship:** Michael Tusiani. **Senior VP, Marketing:** Deborah Tymon. **VP/Assistant GM:** Jean Afterman. **Vice President/CFO, Accounting:** Robert Brown. **CFO/VP, Financial Operations:** Scott Krug. **Deputy General Counsel/VP, Legal Affairs:** Alan Chang. **Controller:** Derrick Baio.

George Steinbrenner

Business Development

Executive Director, Premium Sales: Christopher Gallagher. **Senior Director, Client Relations:** Jennifer Reilly. **Director, Premium Services:** Harvey Winston.

Corporate Sales/Sponsorships

Directors, Corporate Sales/Sponsorships: Brian Calka, John Penhollow. **Director, Sponsorship Services:** Nicole Arceneaux.

Media Relations/Publicity

Telephone: (718) 579-4460. **Fax:** (718) 293-8414.
Director, Media Relations/Publicity: Jason Zillo. **Managers, Media Relations/Publicity:** Jason Latimer, Michael Margolis. **Coordinators, Media Relations/Publicity:** Loran Moran, Connie Schwab. **Assistant, Media Relations/Publicity:** Kenny Leandry. **Administrative Assistant, Media Relations/Publicity:** Dolores Hernandez. **Director, Publications:** Afred Santasiere III.

Office Operations

Director, Human Resources: Betsy Peluso. **Senior Director, Technology:** Mike Lane. **General Counsel:** Rachel M. Cohen, Esq. **Director, Creative Services:** Kara Mooney. **Director, Client Relations:** Jennifer Reilly.

2010 SCHEDULE

Standard Game Times: 7:05 p.m.; Sat.-Sun. 1:05.

APRIL				
4 . . . . .at Boston	17-18 . . . . Boston	**JULY**		20-22 . . . . Seattle
6-7 . . . . .at Boston	19-20 . . . . . .Tampa Bay	1 . . . . Seattle		23-25 . . . . . at Toronto
9-11 . . . . . at Tampa Bay	21-23 . . . at New York (NL)	2-4 . . . . .Toronto		27-29 . . . .at Chicago (AL)
13-15 . . . Los Angeles (AL)	25-27 . . . . . at Minnesota	5-7 . . . . .at Oakland		30-31 . . . . Oakland
16-18 . . . . Texas	28-31 . . . . Cleveland	8-11 . . . . .at Seattle		
20-22 . . . . . .at Oakland		16-18 . . . . . .Tampa Bay		**SEPTEMBER**
23-25 . at Los Angeles (AL)	**JUNE**	20-21 . . . Los Angeles (AL)		1-2 . . . . Oakland
27-29 . . . . . at Baltimore	1-3 . . . . Baltimore	22-25 . . . . . . Kansas City		3-5 . . . . .Toronto
30 . . . . Chicago (AL)	4-6 . . . . at Toronto	26-29 . . . .at Cleveland		6-8 . . . . Baltimore
	8-10 . . . . . . .at Baltimore	30-31 . . . . . at Tampa Bay		10-12 . . . . .at Texas
MAY	11-13 . . . . Houston			13-15 . . . . . at Tampa Bay
1-2 . . . . Chicago (AL)	15-17 . . . . .Philadelphia	**AUGUST**		17-19 . . . . .at Baltimore
3-5 . . . . Baltimore	18-20 . . . . .New York (NL)	1 . . . . at Tampa Bay		20-23 . . . . . .Tampa Bay
7-9 . . . . .at Boston	21-23 . . . . . at Arizona	2-4 . . . . .Toronto		24-26 . . . . Boston
10-13 . . . . . . .at Detroit	25-27 . at Los Angeles (NL)	6-9 . . . . Boston		27-29 . . . . . . at Toronto
14-16 . . . . . . Minnesota	29-30 . . . . Seattle	10-11 . . . . .at Texas		
		12-15 . . . .at Kansas City		**OCTOBER**
		16-19 . . . . Detroit		1-3 . . . . .at Boston

GENERAL INFORMATION

Stadium (year opened): Yankee Stadium (2009).
Team Colors: Navy blue and white.

Player Representative: Unavailable.
Home Dugout: First Base.
Playing Surface: Grass.

Scoreboard/Broadcasting
Senior Director, Scoreboard/Broadcasting: Michael Bonner.

Security/Stadium Operations
Executive Director, Stadium/Event Security: Todd Lechter. Stadium Superintendent: Pete Pullara. Senior Director, Stadium Operations: Doug Behar.

Ticket Operations
Telephone: (718) 293-6000. Fax: (718) 293-4841.
Senior Director, Ticket Operations: Irfan Kirimca. Executive Director, Ticket Operations: Kevin Dart.

BASEBALL OPERATIONS

Telephone: (718) 293-4300. Fax: (718) 293-0015.
Senior Vice President/General Manager: Brian Cashman.
VP/Assistant GM: Jean Afterman, Esq.
Senior VP/Special Advisor: Gene Michael. Special Advisors: Reggie Jackson, Yogi Berra.
Special Assistants: Gordon Blakeley, Tino Martinez, Stump Merrill.
Director, Quantitative Analysis: Michael Fishman. Director, Mental Conditioning: Chad Bohling. Coordinator, Mental Conditioning: Chris Passarella. Assistant, Baseball Operations: Steve Martone. Systems Architect: Brian Nicosia. Research Assistant: Jim Logue. Administrative Assistant: Mary Pellino.

Brian Cashman

Major League Staff
Manager: Joe Girardi.
Coaches: Bench—Tony Pena; Pitching—Dave Eiland; Batting—Kevin Long; First Base—Mick Kelleher; Third Base—Rob Thomson; Bullpen—Mike Harkey.

Medical/Training
Team Physician, New York: Dr. Christopher Ahmad. Senior Advisor, Orthopedics: Stuart Hershon. Team Physician, Tampa: Dr. Andrew Boyer.
Head Athletic Trainer: Gene Monahan. Assistant Athletic Trainer: Steve Donohue. Strength/Conditioning Coordinator: Dana Cavalea.

Player Development
Telephone: (813) 875-7569. Fax: (813) 873-2302.
Senior Vice President, Baseball Operations: Mark Newman. Vice President, Player Personnel: Billy Connors. Director, Player Development: Pat Roessler. Assistant Director, Baseball Operations: Eric Schmitt. Administrative Assistant: Jackie Williams. Minor League Coordinators: Nardi Contreras (pitching), James Rowson (hitting), Jody Reed (defensive), Julio Mosquera (Catching), Jack Hubbard (outfield).

Farm System

Class	Club	Manager	Hitting Coach	Pitching Coach
Triple-A	Scranton/WB (IL)	Dave Miley	Butch Wynegar	Scott Aldred
Double-A	Trenton (EL)	Tony Franklin	Frank Menechino	Tom Phelps
High A	Tampa (FSL)	Torre Tyson	Julius Matos	Greg Pavlick
Low A	Charleston (SAL)	Greg Colbrunn	Justin Turner	Jeff Ware
Short-season	Staten Island (NYP)	Josh Paul	Ty Hawkins	Pat Daneker
Rookie	Tampa (GCL)	Tom Slater	Unavailable	Carlos Chantres
Rookie	Yankees I (DSL)	Carlos Mota	Freddie Tiburcio	Wilfredo Cordova
Rookie	Yankees II (DSL)	Raul Dominguez	Roy Gomez	Jose Duran

Scouting
Telephone: (813) 875-7569. Fax: (813) 873-2302.
VP, Amateur Scouting: Damon Oppenheimer. Assistant Director, Amateur Scouting: John Kremer.
Senior Director, Pro Personnel: Billy Eppler. Assistant, Professional Scouting: Will Kuntz.
Professional Scouts: Ron Brand (Plano, TX), Joe Caro (Tampa, FL), Jay Darnell (San Diego, CA), Gary Denbo (Tampa, FL), Bill Emslie (Tampa, FL), Dan Freed (Lexington, IL), Jalal Leach (Sacramento, CA), Bill Livesey (St. Petersburg, FL), Bill Mele (Boston, MA), Tim Naehring (Cincinnati, OH), Greg Orr (Sacramento, CA), Kevin Reese (Sterling, VA), Rick Williams (Tampa, FL), Tom Wilson (Lake Havasu, AZ), Bob Miske (part-time, Amherst, NY). Amateur Scouting, National Crosscheckers: Brian Barber, Kendall Carter, Tim Kelly. Area Scouts: Mark Batchko (Arlington, TX), Steve Boros (Kingwood, TX), Andy Cannizaro (Mandeville, LA), Jeff Deardorff (Clermont, FL), Mike Gibbons (Liberty Township, OH), Matt Hyde (Canton, MA.), David Keith (Anaheim, CA), Steve Kmetko (Phoenix, AZ), Steve Lemke (Geneva, IL), Scott Lovekamp (Lynchburg, VA), Carlos Marti (Miramar, FL), Tim McIntosh (–Stockton, CA), Darryl Monroe (Decatur, GA), Jeff Patterson (Yorba Linda, CA), Cesar Presbott (Bronx, NY), Dennis Twombley (Redondo Beach, CA), D.J. Svihlik (Birmingham, AL), Mike Thurman (West Linn, OR).
Director, International Scouting: Danny Rowland. Assistant Director, International Operations: Alex Cotto. Coordinator, International Player Development: Pat McMahon. International Scouting Supervisors: Victor Mata (Dominican Republic), Ricardo Final (Venezuela).
Scouting Development Coaches: Argenis Paulino, Jonnathan Saturria.
Dominican Scouts: Angel Ovalles, Juan Rosario, Jose Sabino, Raymond Sanchez. Venezuelan Scouts: Alan Atacho, Darwin Bracho, Jose Gavidea, Cesar Suarez. International Scouts: Chairon Isenia (Curacao), Jason Lee (Korea), Carlos Levy (Panama), Edgar Rodriguez (Nicaragua), Luis Sierra (Colombia), Lee Sigmen (Mexico), Ken Su (Pacific Rim), John Wadsworth (Australia).

Oakland Athletics

Office Address: 7000 Coliseum Way, Oakland, CA 94621.
Telephone: (510) 638-4900. **Fax:** (510) 562-1633. **Website:** www.oaklandathletics.com

Ownership
Co-Owner, Managing Partner: Lewis Wolff.

BUSINESS OPERATIONS

President: Michael Crowley. **Executive Assistant to President:** Carolyn Jones.
Legal General Counsel: Steve Johnston. **Assistant General Counsel:** Neil Kraetsch.

Finance/Administration
Vice President, Finance: Paul Wong.
Director, Finance: Kasey Jarcik. **Payroll Manager:** Kathy Leviege. **Senior Accountant, Accounts Payable:** Isabelle Mahaffey. **Accounting Analyst:** Ling Ding. **Ticket Office Accountant:** Scott Zumsteg. **Accounts Receivable Specialist:** John Anki. **Staff Accountant:** Lance Louie. **Manager, Human Resources:** Kim Kubo. **Assistant, Human Resources:** Michaele Smith. **Manager, Information Systems Manager:** Nathan Hayes. **Travel Specialist:** Colleen Osterberg.

Lew Wolff

Sales/Marketing
VP, Sales/Marketing: Jim Leahey. **Assistant, Sales/Marketing:** Breanne Pund. **Director, Corporate Sales:** Franklin Lowe. **Corporate Account Managers:** Matthew Gallagher, Jill Golden, Meredith Hartery. **Manager, Marketing/Advertising:** Zachary Glare. **Manager, Creative Services:** Mike Ono. **Coordinator, Advertising:** Amy MacEwen. **Manager, Promotions/Special Events:** Heather Rajeski.

Public Relations/Communications
Telephone: (510) 563-2207. **Fax:** (510) 562-1633.
VP, Broadcasting/Communications: Ken Pries. **Manager, Broadcast Services:** Warren Chu. **Director, Public Relations:** Bob Rose. **Manager, Baseball Information:** Mike Selleck. **Manager, Media/Player Relations:** Kristy Fick. **Manager, Media Services:** Debbie Gallas. **Team Photographer:** Michael Zagaris. **Director, Community Relations:** Detra Paige. **Coordinator, Community Relations:** Erik Farrell.
Senior Director, In-Stadium Entertainment: Troy Smith. **Senior Director, Multimedia Services:** David Don. **PA Announcers:** Roy Steele, Dick Callahan. **Official Scorers:** Chuck Dybdal, David Feldman, Michael Duca.

Stadium Operations
VP, Stadium Operations: David Rinetti. **Senior Manager, Stadium Operations:** Paul LeVeau. **Manager, Stadium Services:** Randy Duran. **Manager, Events:** Kristy Ledbetter. **Coordinator, Guest Services:** Whitney Tool. **Coordinator, Stadium Operations:** Meghan Mahrholz. **Head Groundskeeper:** Clay Wood. **Arizona Groundskeeper:** Chad Huss.

2010 SCHEDULE
Standard Game Times: 7:05 p.m.; Sat./Sun. 1:05.

APRIL		
5-8 . . . . Seattle	19-20 . . . . Detroit	2-4 . . . . .at Cleveland	24-26 . . . . . .at Cleveland

APRIL
5-8 . . . . Seattle
9-11 . . at Los Angeles (AL)
12-14 . . . . .at Seattle
15-18 . . . . . . Baltimore
20-22 . . . . .New York (AL)
23-25 . . . . . . Cleveland
27-28 . . . . at Tampa Bay
29-30 . . . . . . at Toronto

MAY
1-2 . . . . at Toronto
3-5 . . . . Texas
7-9 . . . . .Tampa Bay
11-13 . . . . .at Texas
14-16 . at Los Angeles (AL)
17-18 . . . . Seattle

19-20 . . . . Detroit
21-23 . . . . . San Francisco
25-27 . . . . . .at Baltimore
28-31 . . . . .at Detroit

JUNE
1-3 . . . . .at Boston
4-6 . . . . .Minnesota
7-10 . . . Los Angeles (AL)
11-13 . . at San Francisco
15-17 . . . .at Chicago (NL)
18-20 . . . . . .at St. Louis
21-23 . . . . . . Cincinnati
25-27 . . . . . . Pittsburgh
29-30 . . . . . .at Baltimore

JULY
1 . . . . .at Baltimore

2-4 . . . . .at Cleveland
5-7 . . . . . .New York (AL)
9-11 . . . . Los Angeles (AL)
16-18 . . . .at Kansas City
19-21 . . . . Boston
23-25 . . . . Chicago (AL)
27-29 . . . . .at Texas
30-31 . . . .at Chicago (AL)

AUGUST
1 . . . . . . .at Chicago (AL)
2-4 . . . . Kansas City
6-8 . . . . Texas
9-11 . . . . .at Seattle
13-15 . . . at Minnesota
16-18 . . . . .Toronto
19-22 . . . . . .Tampa Bay

24-26 . . . . .at Cleveland
27-29 . . . . .at Texas
30-31 . . . at New York (AL)

SEPTEMBER
1-2 . . . . . at New York (AL)
3-5 . . . . . Los Angeles (AL)
6-8 . . . . Seattle
10-12 . . . . Boston
13-15 . . . .at Kansas City
17-19 . . . . . at Minnesota
20-22 . . . . Chicago (AL)
23-26 . . . . Texas
27-29 . at Los Angeles (AL)
30 . . . . .at Seattle

OCTOBER
1-3 . . . . .at Seattle

GENERAL INFORMATION
Stadium (year opened): McAfee Coliseum (1968). **Team Colors:** Kelly green and gold.

Player Representative: Unavailable.
Home Dugout: Third Base.
Playing Surface: Grass.

Ticketing
  Manager, Season Ticket Sales: Brian DiTucci. **Manager, Premium Seat Sales:** Chris Van Dyne. **Manager, Group Sales:** Kati Ayres. **Manager, Luxury Suite Sales:** Parker Newton. **Manager, Inside Sales:** Aaron Dragomir. **Senior Account Manager, Season Ticket Sales:** Phil Chapman.

Ticket Operations
  Senior Director, Ticket Operations: Steve Fanelli. **Senior Manager, Ticket Services:** Josh Ziegenbusch. **Manager, Ticket Operations:** David Adame. **Manager, Box Office:** Anthony Silva. **Coordinator, Ticket Operations:** Anthony Blue. **Manager, Spring Operations/Ticket Services:** Travis LaDolce. **Coordinator, Database:** Faizan Subhani. **Supervisor, Ticket Services:** Catherine Glazer. **Senior Manager, Premium Seating Services:** Susie Weiss.

Travel/Clubhouse
  Director, Team Travel: Mickey Morabito. **Equipment Manager:** Steve Vucinich. **Visitors Clubhouse:** Mike Thalblum. **Assistant Equipment Manager:** Brian Davis. **Umpires Assistant:** Matt Weiss. **Clubhouse Assistant:** William Angel.

BASEBALL OPERATIONS
  VP/General Manager: Billy Beane.
  Assistant GM: David Forst. **Director, Player Personnel:** Billy Owens. **Special Assistant to GM:** Randy Johnson. **Executive Assistant:** Betty Shinoda. **Director, Baseball Administration:** Pamela Pitts. **Director, Baseball Operations:** Farhan Zaidi. **Video Coordinator:** Adam Rhoden.

Billy Beane

Major League Staff
  Manager: Bob Geren.
  Coaches: Bench—Tye Waller; Pitching—Curt Young; Batting—Jim Skaalen; First Base—Todd Steverson; Third Base—Mike Gallego; Bullpen—Ron Romanick.

Medical, Training
  Head Athletic Trainer: Steve Sayles. **Assistant Athletic Trainer:** Walt Horn. **Director, Strength/Conditioning:** Bob Alejo. **Major League Massage Therapist:** Ozzie Lyles. **Coordinator, Medical Services:** Larry Davis. **Team Physicians:** Dr. Allan Pont, Dr. Robert Napoles, Dr. Elliott Schwartz. **Team Orthopedist:** Dr. John Frazier. **Consulting Orthopedists:** Dr. Thomas Peatman, Dr. Lewis Yocum, Dr. Stephen Viess, Dr. Joseph Donnelly. **Arizona Team Physicians:** Dr. Fred Dicke, Dr. Doug Freedberg.

Player Development
  Telephone: (510) 638-4900. **Fax:** (510) 563-2376.
  Director, Player Development: Keith Lieppman. **Director, Minor League Operations:** Ted Polakowski. **Administrative Assistant, Player Development:** Valerie Vander Heyden. **Minor League Roving Instructors:** Juan Navarrete (infield), Ron Plaza (infield), Gil Patterson (pitching), Greg Sparks (hitting). **Minor League Instructor:** Ruben Escalera. **Minor League Video Coordinator:** Mark Smith. **Minor League Medical Coordinator:** Jeff Collins. **Coordinator, Medical Services:** Larry Davis. **Minor League Coordinator, Strength/Conditioning:** Judd Hawkins. **Coordinator, Minor League Pitching Rehab:** Garvin Alston. **Supervisor, Arizona Clubhouse:** Jesse Sotomayor. **Manager, Arizona Clubhouse:** James Gibson. **Staff, Arizona Clubhouse:** Chad Yaconetti.

Farm System

Class	Club (League)	Manager	Coach	Pitching Coach
Triple-A	Sacramento (PCL)	Tony DeFrancesco	Brian McArn	Rick Rodriguez
Double-A	Midland (TL)	Darren Bush	Webster Garrison	Scott Emerson
High A	Stockton (CL)	Steve Scarsone	Tim Garland	Don Schulze
Low A	Kane County (MWL)	Aaron Nieckula	Haas Pratt	Jimmy Escalante
Short-season	Vancouver (NWL)	Rick Magnante	Casey Myers	Craig Lefferts
Rookie	Athletics (AZL)	Marcus Jensen	Juan Dilone	Ariel Prieto
Rookie	Athletics (DSL)	Ruben Escalera	Rahdames Perez	David Brito

Scouting
  Telephone: (510) 638-4900. **Fax:** (510) 563-2376.
  Director, Scouting: Eric Kubota (Rocklin, CA).
  Assistant Director, Scouting: Michael Holmes. **Director, Pro Scouting:** Chris Pittaro (Hamilton, NJ). **Coordinator, Scouting:** Sam Geaney. **Major League Advance Scout:** Joe Sparks (Phoenix, AZ). **National Crosschecker:** Ron Vaughn (Corona, CA). **Western Crosschecker:** Scott Kidd (Folsom, CA). **Midwest Crosschecker:** Steve Bowden (Oklahoma City, OK). **Pro Scouts:** Bryn Alderson (San Francisco, CA), Jeff Bittiger (Saylorsburg, PA), Will Schock (Oakland, CA), Craig Weissmann (San Diego, CA), Mike Ziegler (Orlando, FL).
  Area Scouts: Neil Avent (Greensboro, NC), Yancy Ayres (Topeka, KS), Armann Brown (Texas City, TX), Marcus Cayenne (Nashville, TN), Jermaine Clark (Livermore, CA), Jim Coffman (Portland, OR), Matt Higginson (Oakville, ON), Rick Magnante (Sherman Oaks, CA), Eric Martins (Diamond Bar, CA), Kevin Mello (Champaign, IL), Kelcey Mucker (Baton Rouge, LA), Matt Ranson (Kennesaw, GA), Marc Sauer (Cliffwood Beach, NJ), Trevor Schaffer (Belleair, FL), Jeremy Schied (Queen Creek, AZ), Rich Sparks (Sterling Heights, MI), J.T. Stotts (Moorpark, CA).
  Director, Latin American Operations: Raymond Abreu (Santo Domingo, DR). **Coordinator, International Operations/Baseball Operations Analyst:** Dan Kantrovitz (San Francisco, CA). **Coordinator, Latin American Scouting:** Julio Franco (Caracas, VZ).
  International Scouts: Ruben Barradas (VZ), Juan Carlos De La Cruz (DR), Angel Eusebio (DR), Andri Garcia (VZ), Tom Gillespie (Europe), Adam Hislop (Taiwan), Lewis Kim (South Korea), Pablo Marmol (DR), Amaury Reyes (DR), Russell Spear (Australia), Oswaldo Troconis (VZ), Juan Villanueva (VZ).

Philadelphia Phillies

Office Address: Citizens Bank Park, One Citizens Bank Way, Philadelphia, PA 19148.
Telephone: (215) 463-6000. **Website:** www.phillies.com.

Ownership
Operated By: The Phillies.
President/CEO: David Montgomery. **Chairman:** Bill Giles.

BUSINESS OPERATIONS
Vice President/General Counsel: Rick Strouse. **Vice President, Phillies Enterprises:** Richard Deats. **Vice President, Employee/Customer Services:** Kathy Killian. **Director, Ballpark Enterprises/Business Development:** Joe Giles. **Director, Information Systems:** Brian Lamoreaux. **Director, Employee Benefits/Services:** JoAnn Marano.

Ballpark Operations
Senior Vice President, Administration/Operations: Michael Stiles. **Director, Ballpark Operations:** Mike DiMuzio. **Director, Event Operations:** Eric Tobin. **Manager, Ballpark Operations/Security:** Sal DeAngelis. **Manager, Concessions Development:** Bruce Leith. **Head Groundskeeper:** Mike Boekholder. **PA Announcer:** Dan Baker. **Official Scorers:** Jay Dunn, Mike Maconi, Joseph Bellina.

David Montgomery

Communications
Telephone: (215) 463-6000. **Fax:** (215) 389-3050.
Vice President, Communications: Bonnie Clark. **Director, Baseball Communications:** Greg Casterioto. **Coordinator, Baseball Communications:** Kevin Gregg. **Baseball Communications Assistant:** Craig Hughner. **Communications Assistant:** Deanna Sabec.

Finance
Senior Vice President, Business/Finance: Jerry Clothier. **Vice President/CFO:** John Nickolas.
Director, Payroll Services: Karen Wright.

Marketing/Promotions
Senior Vice President, Marketing/Sales: David Buck. **Manager, Client Services/Alumni Relations:** Debbie Nocito. **Director, Corporate Partnership:** Rob MacPherson. **Director, Advertising Sales:** Brian Mahoney. **Managers, Advertising Sales:** Scott Nickle, Tom Sullivan. **Director, Marketing Programs/Events:** Kurt Funk. **Director, Entertainment:** Chris Long. **Manager, Broadcasting:** Rob Brooks. **Manager, Advertising/Internet Services:** Jo-Anne Levy-Lamoreaux.

Sales/Tickets
Telephone: (215) 463-1000. **Fax:** (215) 463-9878.
Vice President, Sales/Ticket Operations: John Weber. **Director, Ticket Department:** Dan Goroff. **Director, Ticket Technology/Development:** Chris Pohl. **Director, Season Ticket Sales:** Derek Schuster. **Manager, Suite Sales/Services:**

2010 SCHEDULE
Standard Game Times: 7:05 p.m.; Sun. 1:35

APRIL		
5 . . . . at Washington	17-18 . . . . . . Pittsburgh	JULY
7-8 . . . . . at Washington	19-20 . . . . . Chicago (NL)	1-4 . . . . at Pittsburgh
9-11 . . . . . . .at Houston	21-23 . . . . Boston	5-7 . . . . Atlanta
12 . . . . Washington	25-27 . . . at New York (NL)	8-11 . . . . Cincinnati
14-15 . . . . . Washington	28-30 . . . . .at Florida	15-18 . . . .at Chicago (NL)
16-18 . . . . Florida	31 . . . . at Atlanta	19-22 . . . . . . .at St. Louis
20-22 . . . . at Atlanta		23-26 . . . . .Colorado
23-25 . . . . at Arizona	JUNE	27-29 . . . . Arizona
26-28 . . . at San Francisco	1-2 . . . . at Atlanta	30-31 . . . . at Washington
30 . . . . . . .New York (NL)	4-7 . . . . San Diego	
	8-10 . . . . Florida	AUGUST
	11-13 . . . . .at Boston	1 . . . . at Washington
MAY	15-17 . . . at New York (AL)	3-5 . . . . .at Florida
1-2 . . . . . .New York (NL)	18-20 . . . . . . Minnesota	6-8 . . . . . .New York (NL)
3-6 . . . . St. Louis	22-24 . . . . Cleveland	10-12 . . . Los Angeles (NL)
7-9 . . . . Atlanta	25-27 . . . . . . at Toronto	13-15 . . . at New York (NL)
10-12 . . . . . at Colorado	28-30 . . . . . .at Cincinnati	17-19 . . . . . San Francisco
14-16 . . . . . at Milwaukee		20-22 . . . . . . Washington

23-26 . . . . Houston	
27-29 . . . . . at San Diego	
30-31 . at Los Angeles (NL)	
SEPTEMBER	
1 . . . at Los Angeles (NL)	
3-5 . . . . .Milwaukee	
6-8 . . . . Florida	
10-12 . . . at New York (NL)	
13-15 . . . . .at Florida	
17-19 . . . . . Washington	
20-22 . . . . Atlanta	
24-26 . . . .New York (NL)	
27-29 . . . . at Washington	
OCTOBER	
1-3 . . . . at Atlanta	

GENERAL INFORMATION
Stadium (year opened): Citizens Bank Park (2004).
Team Colors: Red, white and blue.

Player Representative: Unavailable.
Home Dugout: First Base.
Playing Surface: Natural Grass

Tom Mashek. **Manager, Phone Center:** Phil Feather. **Manager, Season Ticket Services:** Mike Holdren.

Travel/Clubhouse
Director, Team Travel/Clubhouse Services: Frank Coppenbarger.
Manager, Visiting Clubhouse: Kevin Steinhour. **Manager, Home Clubhouse:** Phil Sheridan. **Manager, Equipment/ Umpire Services:** Dan O'Rourke.

BASEBALL OPERATIONS
Senior VP/General Manager: Ruben Amaro Jr. **Assistant GM:** Scott Proefrock. **Assistant GM, Player Personnel:** Benny Looper. **Assistant GM, Player Development/Scouting:** Chuck LaMar. **Director, Baseball Administration:** Susan Ingersoll Papaneri. **Baseball Information Analyst:** Jay McLaughlin. **Senior Advisor to GM:** Dallas Green. **Senior Advisor to the President/GM:** Pat Gillick. **Special Assistant to GM:** Charley Kerfeld.

Ruben Amaro, Jr.

Major League Staff
Manager: Charlie Manuel.
Coaches: Bench—Pete Mackanin; Pitching—Rich Dubee; Batting—Milt Thompson; First Base—Davey Lopes; Third Base—Sam Perlozzo; Bullpen Coach—Mick Billmeyer; Bullpen Catcher—Jesus Tiamo.

Medical/Training
Director, Medical Services: Dr. Michael Ciccotti. **Head Athletic Trainer:** Scott Sheridan. **Assistant Athletic Trainer:** Mark Andersen. **Strength/Conditioning Coordinator:** Doug Lien. **Employee Assistance Professional:** Dickie Noles.

Player Development
Telephone: (215) 463-6000. **Fax:** (215) 755-9324.
Assistant GM, Player Personnel: Benny Looper. **Assistant GM, Player Development/Scouting:** Chuck LaMar. **Assistant Directors, Minor League Operations:** Steve Noworyta, Lee McDaniel. **Administrative Assistant, Minor League Operations:** Jose Duverge. **Pro Scouting Coordinator:** Mike Ondo. **Director, Florida Operations:** John Timberlake.
Field Coordinator: Mike Compton. **Coordinators:** Brian Cammarota (trainer), Ernie Whitt (catching), Gorman Heimueller (pitching), Shawn Fcasni (conditioning), Sal Rende (hitting), Steve Henderson (outfield/baserunning), Doug Mansolino (infield).

Farm System

Class	Club (League)	Manager	Coach	Pitching Coach
Triple-A	Lehigh Valley (IL)	Dave Huppert	Gregg Gross	Rod Nichols
Double-A	Reading (EL)	Steve Roadcap	Frank Cacciatore	Bob Milacki
High A	Clearwater (FSL)	Dusty Wathan	Kevin Jordan	Dave Lundquist
Low A	Lakewood (SAL)	Mark Parent	Greg Legg	Steve Schrenk
Short-season	Williamsport (NYP)	Chris Truby	Jorge Velandia	Lance Carter
Rookie	Clearwater(GCL)	Roly DeArmas	Donnie Sadler	Chuck Hernandez
Rookie	Phillies (DSL)	Manny Amador	Luis Arzeno	Cesar Mejia
Rookie	Phillies (VSL)	Rafael DeLima	Silverio Navas	Les Straker

Scouting
Director, Scouting: Marti Wolever (Papillion, NE). **Assistant Director, Scouting:** Rob Holiday.
Coordinators, Scouting: Mike Ledna (Arlington Heights, ILL), Bill Moore (Alta Loma, CA).
Regional Supervisors: Gene Schall (East/Harleysville, PA), Brian Kohlscheen (Central/Norman, OK), Darrell Conner (West/Riverside, CA).
Area Scouts: Steve Cohen (Spring, TX), Joey Davis (Ranco Murrieta, CA), Nate Dion (West Chester, OH), Ellis Dungan (Charlotte, NC), Mike Garcia (Moreno Valley CA), Brad Holland (Gilbert AZ), Tim Kissner (Kirkland WA), Chip Lawrence (Palmetto, FL), Paul Murphy (Wilmington, DE), Demerius Pittman (Corona CA), Paul Scott (Rockwall, TX), David Seifert (Paw Paw, IL), Mike Stauffer (Ridgeland, MS), Eric Valent (Wernersville PA).
International Supervisor: Sal Agostinelli (Kings Park (NY).
International Scouts: Alex Agostino (Canada), Norman Anciani (Panama), Nathan Davison (Australia), Arnold Elles (Columbia), Tomas Herrera (Mexico), Paul Hsu (Taiwan), Eric Jacques (Europe), Allan Lewis (Panama, Central America), Jesus Mendez (Venezuela), Manabu Noto (Japan), Koby Perez (Dominican Republic), Darryn Smith (South Africa).
Director, Major League Scouting: Gordon Lakey (Barker, TX). **Advance Scout:** Craig Colbert. **Major League Scouts:** Jim Fregosi Jr. (Murrieta, CA), Howie Frieling. **Professional Scouts:** Sonny Bowers (Hewitt, TX), Dave Hollins (Orchard Park, NY), Dean Jongewaard (Fountain Valley, CA), Jon Mercurio (Coraopolis, PA), Roy Tanner (North Charleston, SC), Del Unser (Scottsdale, AZ), Dan Wright (Cave Springs, AR).

Pittsburgh Pirates

Office Address: PNC Park at North Shore, 115 Federal St, Pittsburgh, PA 15212.
Mailing Address: P.O. Box 7000, Pittsburgh, PA 15212.
Telephone: (412) 323-5000. **Fax:** (412) 325-4412. **Website:** www.pirates.com

Ownership
Chairman of the Board: Robert Nutting.
Board of Directors: Donald Beaver, G. Ogden Nutting, Robert Nutting, William Nutting, Duane Wittman.

Executive
President: Frank Coonelly.
Executive Vice President/CFO: Jim Plake. **Executive VP/General Manager, PNC Park:** Dennis DaPra. **Executive VP/Chief Marketing Officer:** Lou DePaoli. **Senior VP/General Counsel:** Larry Silverman.

BUSINESS OPERATIONS

Finance/Administration/Information Technology
Senior Director, Human Resources: Pam Nelson Minteer. **Senior Director, Information Technology:** Terry Zeigler. **Director, Employee Services:** Patti Mistick. **Director, Baseball Systems Development:** Dan Fox.

Communications
Fax: (412) 325-4413.
Senior Director, Communications: Brian Warecki. **Director, Media Relations:** Jim Trdinich. **Director, Broadcasting:** Marc Garda. **Manager, Media Services:** Dan Hart. **Manager, Business Communications:** Matt Nordby.

Frank Coonelly

Community Relations
VP, Community/Public Affairs: Patty Paytas. **Director, Development of Pirates Charities:** Denise Balkovec. **Manager, Community Relations:** Michelle Mejia. **Manager, Diversity Initiatives:** Chaz Kellem.

Marketing/Sales
Senior Director, Marketing/Special Events: Brian Chiera. **Senior Director, Corporate Partnerships:** Mike Egan. **Director, Alumni Affairs, Promotions/Licensing:** Joe Billetdeaux. **Director, Advertising/Creative Services:** Kiley Cauvel. **Manager, Special Events:** Christine Serkoch. **Manager, Promotions:** Dan Millar. **Manager, In-Game Entertainment:** Eric Wolff. **Media Producer:** Ken Brown. **Manager, Promotions/Licensing:** Megan Vizzini. **Manager, PNC Park Events:** Ann Elder. **Managers, Client Services:** Mike DeMars, Dana Geary.

Stadium Operations
Senior Director, Ballpark Operations: Chris Hunter. **Senior Director, Security/Contract Services:** Jeff Podobnik.

2010 SCHEDULE
Standard Game Times: 7:05 p.m.; Sun. 1:35.

APRIL		
5 . . . . . . Los Angeles (NL)		
7-8. . . . . Los Angeles (NL)		
9-11 . . . . . . at Arizona		
12-14 . . . at San Francisco		
16-18 . . . . Cincinnati		
20-22 . . . . . . Milwaukee		
23-25 . . . . . . at Houston		
26-28 . . . . at Milwaukee		
29-30 . at Los Angeles (NL)		

MAY		
1-2. . . at Los Angeles (NL)		
4-6. . . . . . . Chicago (NL)		
7-9. . . . . St. Louis		
10-12 . . . . Cincinnati		
14-16 . . . .at Chicago (NL)		
17-18 . . . . at Philadelphia		

JUNE		
19-20 . . . . . . .Milwaukee		
21-23 . . . . Atlanta		
24-27 . . . . . .at Cincinnati		
28-30 . . . . . at Atlanta		
31 . . . . Chicago (NL)		

JUNE		
1-2. . . . . . . Chicago (NL)		
4-6. . . . . . San Francisco		
8-10 . . . . . at Washington		
11-13 . . . . . . .at Detroit		
15-17 . . . . Chicago (AL)		
18-20 . . . . Cleveland		
22-24 . . . . .at Texas		
25-27 . . . . .at Oakland		
28-30 . . . .at Chicago (NL)		

JULY		
1-4. . . . . . .Philadelphia		
6-8. . . . . . . .at Houston		
9-11 . . . . . at Milwaukee		
16-18 . . . . Houston		
19-22 . . . . Milwaukee		
23-25 . . . . . . San Diego		
27-29 . . . . . at Colorado		
30-31 . . . . .at St. Louis		

AUGUST		
1 . . . . .at St. Louis		
2-4. . . . . Cincinnati		
5-8. . . . . .Colorado		
10-12 . . . at San Diego		
13-15 . . . . . .at Houston		
16-19 . . . . Florida		
20-22 . . . . .New York (NL)		

23-25 . . . . St. Louis		
27-29 . . . . at Milwaukee		
30-31 . . . .at Chicago (NL)		

SEPTEMBER		
1 . . . . . . .at Chicago (NL)		
3-5. . . . . . . .Washington		
6-8. . . . . Atlanta		
10-12 . . . . .at Cincinnati		
13-16 . . . at New York (NL)		
17-19 . . . . Arizona		
21-23 . . . . St. Louis		
24-26 . . . . Houston		
27-29 . . . . . .at St. Louis		
30 . . . . .at Florida		

OCTOBER		
1-3. . . . . .at Florida		

GENERAL INFORMATION
Stadium (year opened): PNC Park (2001). **Home Dugout:** Third Base.
Team Colors: Black and gold. **Playing Surface:** Grass.
Player Representative: Paul Maholm.

Manager, Security/Service Operations: Mark Weaver. **Director, Field Operations:** Manny Lopez. **Operations Manager:** Ben Fortun. **Guest Relations Manager:** Melissa Cushey.

Ticketing
 Telephone: (800) 289-2827. **Fax:** (412) 325-4404.
 Senior Director, Ticket Sales/Services: Christopher Zaber. **Senior Director, Market Analytics/Business Development:** Jim Alexander. **Manager, Ticket Services:** Dave Wysocki. **Director, Suite Sales/Service:** Terri Smith. **Director, Ticket Development:** Jim Popovich. **Manager, Inside Sales:** Justin Gurney. **Manager, Ticket Services/Retention:** Raven Jemison. **Inside Sales Manager:** Travis Apple.

Travel/Clubhouse
 Traveling Secretary: Greg Johnson.
 Equipment Manager/Home Clubhouse Operations: Scott Bonnett. **Visitors Clubhouse Manager:** Kevin Conrad.

BASEBALL OPERATIONS
 Senior VP/General Manager: Neal Huntington. **Director, Player Personnel:** Doug Strange. **Director, Baseball Operations:** Tyrone Brooks. **Director, Baseball Systems Development:** Dan Fox. **Assistant Director, Baseball Operations:** Kevan Graves. **Special Assistants to GM:** Jim Benedict, Larry Corrigan, Marc DelPiano, Jax Robertson, Pete Vuckovich. **Major League Scouts:** Mike Basso, Keith Champion, Joe Ferrone, Steve Williams. **Senior Advisors:** Bill Lajoie, Chuck Tanner. **Assistant, Baseball Operations:** Alex Langsam. **Baseball Operations Data Analyst:** Joe Sheehan. **Video Coordinator:** Kevin Roach. **Video Advance Scout:** Simon Ferrer.

Neal Huntington

Major League Staff
 Manager: John Russell.
 Coaches: Bench—Gary Varsho; Pitching—Joe Kerrigan; Hitting—Don Long; First Base—Carlos Garcia; Third Base—Tony Beasley; Bullpen—Luis Dorante; Coach— Ray Searage.

Medical/Training
 Medical Director: Dr. Patrick DeMeo. **Team Physician:** Dr. Edward Snell. **Head Athletic Trainer:** Brad Henderson. **Assistant Athletic Trainer:** Mike Sandoval. **Strength/Conditioning Coordinator:** Frank Velasquez. **Latin American Strength/Conditioning Coordinator:** Kiyoshi Momose. **Physical Therapist/Rehab Coordinator:** Erwin Valencia.

Minor Leagues
 Director, Player Development: Kyle Stark.
 Minor League Field Coordinator: Jeff Bannister. **Outfield/Baserunning Coordinator:** Kimera Bartee. **Pitching Coordinator:** Jim Benedict. **Infield Coordinator:** Steve Lombardozzi. **Hitting Coordinator:** Gregg Ritchie. **Latin American Field Coordinator:** Euclides Rojas. **Personal Development Coordinator:** Anthony Telford. **Athletic Training Coordinator:** Carl Randolph. **Strength/Conditioning Coordinator:** Chris Sobonya. **Rehab Coordinator:** Marc Oceguera. **Mental Conditioning Coordinator:** Bernie Holliday. **Minor League Administrator:** Diane DePasquale.

Farm System

Class	Club (League)	Manager	Coach(es)	Pitching Coach
Triple-A	Indianapolis (IL)	Frank Kremblas	Jeff Branson	Dean Treanor
Double-A	Altoona (EL)	Matt Walbeck	Ryan Long	Tom Filer
High A	Bradenton (FSL)	P.J. Forbes	Dave Howard	Wally Whitehurst
Low A	West Virginia (SAL)	Gary Green	Edgar Varela	Jeff Johnson
Short-season	State College (NYP)	Gary Robinson	Brandon Moore	Mike Steele
Rookie	Bradenton (GCL)	Tom Prince	R. Pena/W. Huyke/M. Lum	Miguel Bonilla
Rookie	Pirates (DSL)	Ramon Zapata	C. Beltre/R. Carrion	Henry Corniel
Rookie	Pirates (VSL)	Osmin Melendez	I. Colmenares/J. Prieto	Dan Urbina

Scouting
 Fax: (412) 325-4414.
 Director, Scouting: Greg Smith. **Assistant Director, Scouting:** Joe Delli Carri. **Scouting Administrator:** Jim Asher.
 National Supervisors: Jack Bowen (Bethel Park, PA), Jimmy Lester (Columbus, GA).
 Director, Latin American Scouting: Rene Gayo. **Regional Supervisors:** Jesse Flores (Sacramento, CA), Rob Guzik (Latrobe, PA), Rodney Henderson (Lexington, KY), Everett Russell (Thibodaux, LA).
 Area Supervisors: Rick Allen (Agoura Hills, CA), Matt Bimeal (Baldwin City, KS), Larry Broadway (Glendale, AZ), Sean Campbell (Corona Del Mar, CA), Jerome Cochran (Slidell, LA), Trevor Haley (Conroe, TX), Greg Hopkins (Beaverton, OR), Chris Kline (Northampton, MA), Mike Leuzinger (Canton, TX), Darren Mazeroski (Panama City Beach, FL), Hal Morris (Palo Alto, CA), Rolando Pino (Pembroke Pines, FL), Greg Schilz (Atlanta, GA), Brian Tracy (Mason, OH), Matt Wondolowski (Herndon, VA), Anthony Wycklendt (Grafton, WI).
 Part-Time Scouts: Elmer Gray (Pittsburgh, PA), Jose Rosario (Bayamon, PR), George Vranau (S. California).
 Full-Time Scouts: Orlando Covo (Colombia), Nelson Llenas (Dominican Republic), Ellis Pena (Dominican Republic), Rodolfo Petit (Venezuela), Cristino Valdez (Dominican Republic), Jesus Chino Valdez (Mexico).
 Part-Time Scouts: Marcos Briseno (Dominican Republic), Luis Campusano (Dominican Republic), Pablo Csorgi (Venezuela), Denny Diaz (Dominican Republic), Daniel Garcia (Colombia), Fernando Hernandez (Mexico), Jhoan Hidalgo (Venezuela), Jose Lavagnino (Mexico), Javier Magdaleno (Venezuela), Alcides Melendez (Venezuela), Jose Pineda (Panama), Placido Pinto (Mexico), Marino Tejada (Dominican Republic), David Urias (Mexico), Francisco Valdez (Dominican Republic), Marc Van Zanten (Netherlands Antilles), Darryl Yrausquin (Aruba).
 International Scouts: Fu-Chun Chiang (Taiwan), Tony Harris (Australia), Tom Randolph (International).

St. Louis Cardinals

Office Address: 700 Clark Street, St. Louis MO 63102.
Telephone: (314) 345-9600. **Fax:** (314) 345-9523. **Website:** www.stlcardinals.com.

Ownership
Operated By: St. Louis Cardinals, LLC.
Chairman: Bill DeWitt, Jr.
Vice Chairman: Fred Hanser. **Secretary/Treasurer:** Andrew Baur. **President:** Bill DeWitt III. **Senior Administrative Assistant to Chairman:** Grace Pak. **Senior Administrative Assistant to President:** Julie Laningham.

BUSINESS OPERATIONS
Vice President, Event Services: Vicki Bryant. **Manager, Event Services:** Missy Tobey. **Director, Human Resources:** Christine Nelson. **Manager, Office Administration/Human Resources Specialist:** Karen Brown.

Finance
Fax: (314) 345-9520.
Senior VP/Chief Financial Officer: Brad Wood. **Director, Finance:** Rex Carter.

Marketing/Sales
Fax: (314) 345-9529.
Senior VP, Sales/Marketing: Dan Farrell. **Administrative Assistant, Corporate Sales:** Gail Ruhling. **VP, Corporate Sales/Marketing/Stadium Entertainment:** Thane van Breusegen. **Senior Account Executive, Corporate Sales:** Jeff Floerke.

Bill DeWitt III

Media Relations/Community Relations
Fax: (314) 345-9530.
Director, Media Relations: Brian Bartow. **Manager, Media Relations/New Media:** Melody Yount. **Director, Public Relations/Government Affairs:** Ron Watermon. **Director, Publications:** Steve Zesch. **Publication Assistants:** Lauren Anderson, Larry State. **Vice President, Cardinals Care/Community Relations:** Michael Hall. **Administrative Assistant:** Jama Fabry. **Director, Target Marketing:** Ted Savage. **Youth Baseball Commissioner, Cardinals Care:** Keith Brooks. **Coordinator, Cardinals Care:** Lucretia Payne. **Supervisor, Community Relations:** Jessica Illert. **Community Relations Specialist:** Mark Taylor.

Stadium Operations
Fax: (314) 345-9535.
Vice President, Stadium Operations: Joe Abernathy. **Administrative Assistant:** Hope Baker. **Director, Stadium Operations:** Mike Bertani. **Director, Security/Special Services:** Joe Walsh. **Director, Quality Assurance/Guest Services:** Mike Ball. **Manager, Stadium Operations:** Cindy Richards. **Head Groundskeeper:** Bill Findley. **Assistant Head Groundskeeper:** Chad Casella. **PA Announcer:** John Ulett. **Official Scorers:** Gary Muller, Jeff Durbin, Mike Smith.

2010 SCHEDULE
Standard Game Times: 7:15 p.m.; Sun. 1:15.

APRIL		
7-8 . . . . .at Cincinnati		
9-11 . . . . . . at Milwaukee		
12 . . . . Houston		
14-15 . . . . Houston		
16-18 . . . . .New York (NL)		
19-21 . . . . . . at Arizona		
23-25 . . . at San Francisco		
26-29 . . . . Atlanta		
30 . . . . Cincinnati		

MAY		
1-2 . . . . Cincinnati		
3-6 . . . . . at Philadelphia		
7-9 . . . . . . at Pittsburgh		
11-13 . . . . Houston		
14-16 . . . . .at Cincinnati		
17-18 . . . . . . Washington		

19-20 . . . . Florida
21-23 . . . Los Angeles (AL)
25-27 . . . . . at San Diego
28-30 . . . .at Chicago (NL)
31 . . . . Cincinnati

JUNE
1-2 . . . . Cincinnati
4-6 . . . . .Milwaukee
7-9 . . . at Los Angeles (NL)
11-13 . . . . . . at Arizona
15-17 . . . . Seattle
18-20 . . . . Oakland
22-24 . . . . . . at Toronto
25-27 . . . .at Kansas City
28-30 . . . . Arizona

JULY
1-4 . . . . .Milwaukee
6-8 . . . . at Colorado
9-11 . . . . .at Houston
15-18 . . . Los Angeles (NL)
19-22 . . . . . .Philadelphia
23-25 . . . .at Chicago (NL)
27-29 . . . at New York (NL)
30-31 . . . . Pittsburgh

AUGUST
1 . . . . Pittsburgh
2-4 . . . . Houston
6-8 . . . . .at Florida
9-11 . . . . . .at Cincinnati
13-15 . . . . Chicago (NL)
17-18 . . . . . .Milwaukee
20-22 . . . . . San Francisco

23-25 . . . . . at Pittsburgh
26-29 . . . . at Washington
30-31 . . . . . . .at Houston

SEPTEMBER
1 . . . . .at Houston
3-5 . . . . Cincinnati
6-8 . . . . . . at Milwaukee
9-12 . . . . at Atlanta
13-15 . . . . Chicago (NL)
16-19 . . . . San Diego
21-23 . . . . at Pittsburgh
24-26 . . .at Chicago (NL)
27-29 . . . . . . Pittsburgh
30 . . . . .Colorado

OCTOBER
1-3 . . . . Colorado

GENERAL INFORMATION
Stadium (year opened): Busch Stadium (2006).
Team Colors: Red and white.

Player Representative: Unavailable.
Home Dugout: First Base.
Playing Surface: Grass.

Ticketing
Fax: (314) 345-9522.
VP, Ticket Sales/Service: Joe Strohm. **Director, Ticket Services:** Derek Thornburg. **Manager, Ticket Services:** Brady Bruhn. **Manager, Premium Ticket Sales:** Delores Scanlon. **Manager, Season Ticket Sales/Services:** Jamie Brickler. **Manager, Ticket Technology:** Jennifer Needham. **Manager, Small Groups:** Mary Clare Bena. **Director, Fan Development/Alumni Relations:** Martin Coco. **Supervisor, Receptionist:** Marilyn Mathews.

Travel, Clubhouse
Fax: (314) 345-9523.
Traveling Secretary: C.J. Cherre. **Equipment Manager:** Rip Rowan. **Assistant Equipment Manager:** Ernie Moore. **Visiting Clubhouse Manger:** Jerry Risch. **Video Coordinator:** Chad Blair.

BASEBALL OPERATIONS
Fax: (314) 345-9525.
VP, General Manager: John Mozeliak.
Assistant GM: John Abbamondi. **Executive Assistan:** Linda Brauer. **Special Assistants to GM:** Gary LaRocque, Mike Jorgensen, Matt Slater. **Director, Baseball Development:** Mike Girsch. **Director, Major League Administration:** Judy Carpenter-Barada. **Manager, Professional Scouting:** Matt Carroll. **Coordinator, Baseball Operations:** Ellen Gingles. **Director, International Operations:** Moises Rodriguez. **Manager, Baseball Information:** Jeremy Cohen. **Senior Quantitative Analyst:** Sig Mejdal. **Quantitative Analyst:** Chris Correa.

John Mozeliak

Player Development
Fax: (314) 345-9519.
Vice President, Amateur Scouting/Player Development: Jeff Luhnow. **Director, Minor League Operations:** John Vuch. **Coordinators:** Dyar Miller (Pitching), Brent Strom (Pitching Instruction), Dann Bilardello (Roving Catching), Keith Joynt (Minor League Medical Coordinator), Rene Pena (Strength/Conditioning Coordinator), Blaise Ilsley (Complex Pitching Coordinator).
Minor League Equipment Manager: Buddy Bates.

Major League Staff
Telephone: (314) 345-9600.
Manager: Tony La Russa.
Coaches: Bench—Joe Pettini; Pitching—Dave Duncan; Batting—Mark McGwire; First Base—Dave McKay; Third Base—Jose Oquendo; Bullpen—Marty Mason. **Hitting Instructor:** Mike Aldrete.

Medical/Training
Medical Advisor: Dr. George Paletta. **Head Trainer:** Barry Weinberg. **Assistant Trainer:** Greg Hauck. **Assistant Trainer/Rehabilitation Coordinator:** Adam Olsen.

Class	Club (League)	Manager	Coach	Pitching Coach
Triple-A	Memphis (PCL)	Chris Maloney	Mark Budaska	Derek Lilliquist
Double-A	Springfield (TL)	Ron Warner	Derrick May	Dennis Martinez
High A	Palm Beach (FSL)	Luis Aquayo	Jeff Albert	Bryan Eversgerd
Low A	Quad Cities (MWL)	Johnny Rodriquez	Unavailable	Tim Leveque
Short-season	Batavia (NYP)	Dann Bilardello	Joe Kruzel	Arthur Adams
Rookie	Johnson City (APP)	Mike Shildt	Ramon Ortiz	Doug White
Rookie	Cardinals (GCL)	Steve Turco	Unavailable	Henderson Lugo
Rookie	Cardinals (DSL)	Claudio Almonte	Rene Rojas	Bill Villanueva
Rookie	Cardinals (VSL)	Unavailable	Jesus Laya	Dernier Orozco

Scouting
Telephone: (314) 345-9358. **Fax:** (314) 345-9525.
Coordinator, Pro Scouting: Matt Carroll (St. Louis, MO).
Professional Scouts: Bruce Benedict (Atlanta, GA), Alan Benes (Town & Country, MO), Matt Carroll (St. Louis, MO), Chuck Fick (Newbury Park, CA), Mike Jorgensen (Fenton, MO), Marty Keough (Scottsdale, AZ), Gary LaRocque (Browns Summit, NC), Deric McKamey (Buffton, OH), Joe Rigoli (Parsippany, NJ), Matt Slater (Stevenson Ranch, CA).
Crosscheckers: Joe Almaraz (San Antonio, TX), Mike Roberts (Hot Springs, AR), Roger Smith (Eastman, GA).
Area Supervisors: Matt Blood (New Orleans, LA), Jay Catalano (Joelton, TN), Mike Elias (Oakton, VA), Rob Fidler (Atlanta, GA), Ralph Garr, Jr. (Houston, TX), Charlie Gonzalez (Weston, FL), Kris Gross (Chicago, IL), Brian Hopkins (Brunswick, OH), Jeff Ishii (Chino, CA), Mike Juhl (Indian Trail, NC), Aaron Krawiec (Gilbert, AZ), Aaron Looper (Shawnee, OK), Sean Moran (Levittown, PA), Jamal Strong (Victorville, CA), Matt Swanson (Ripon, CA).
Part-Time Scouts: Alec Adame (Los Angeles, CA), Vince Bailey (Renton, WA), Manny Guerra (Las Vegas, NV), Jimmy Matthews (Athens, GA), Keith Prager (La Verne, CA), Juan Ramos Carolina, Puerto Rico), John Ramirez (Springfield, MA).
Director, International Operations: Moises Rodriguez. **Latin American Supervisor:** Juan Mercado. **Administrator, VZ Operations:** Indira Robleto. **Administrator, Dominican Republic Operations:** Aaron Rodriguez.
International Scouts: Domingo Garcia (Dominican Republic), Jose Gregorio Gonzalez (Venezuela), Carlos Heron (Panama), Neder Horta (Colombia), Carlos Lugo (Dominican Republic), Rene Rojas (Dominican Republic), Crysthiam Blanco (Nicaragua), Fermin Coronel (Curacao).

San Diego Padres

Office Address: PETCO Park, 100 Park Blvd, San Diego, CA 92101.
Mailing Address: P.O. Box 122000, San Diego, CA 92112.
Telephone: (619) 795-5000.
E-mail address: comments@padres.com. **Website:** www.padres.com.

Ownership
Operated By: Padres LP.
Chairman: John Moores. **Vice Chairman/COO:** Jeff Moorad.
President/COO: Tom Garfinkel.

BUSINESS OPERATIONS
Executive VP/General Counsel: Katie Pothier. **Executive VP/Senior Advisor:** Dave Winfield.

Finance
Executive VP/CFO: Fred Gerson. **Director, Corporate/Suite Sales:** Marty Gorsich. **Director, Financial Analysis/Reporting:** Beth Brandsford. **Director, Information Systems:** Joe Lewis.

Media Relations/Community Relations
Telephone: (619) 795-5265. **Fax:** (619) 795-5266.
Director, Media Relations: Warren Miller. **Manager, Media Relations:** Bret Picciolo. **Assistant, Media Relations:** Josh Ishoo. **Club Photographer:** Chris Hardy. **Director, Padres Foundation:** Sue Botos. **Manager, Community Relations:** Nhu Tran.

Jeff Moorad

Stadium Operations
Executive VP, Ballpark Management/General Manager, PETCO Park: Richard Andersen. **VP, Ballpark Operations:** Mark Guglielmo.
Director, Security/Transportation: Ken Kawachi. **Director, Landscape/Field Maintenance:** Luke Yoder. **Director, Guest Services:** Kameron Durham. **PA Announcer:** Frank Anthony. **Official Scorers:** Bill Zavestoski, Jack Murray, Tim Powers.

Ticketing
Telephone: (619) 795-5500. **Fax:** (619) 795-5034.
VP, Ticket Sales/Service: Jarrod Dillon.
Executive Director, Ticket Operations: Jim Kiersnowski. **Director, Season Ticket Sales:** Jonathan Tillman. **Director, Group Ticket Sales:** Amy Saxon.
Manager, Group Sales: Ryan Ross. **Manager, Inside Sales:** Robert Davis. **Director, Ticket Customer Services:** Laura Evans.

2010 SCHEDULE
Standard Game Times: 7:05 p.m.; Sun. 1:05

APRIL
5-7 . . . . at Arizona
9-11 . . . . . . at Colorado
12 . . . . Atlanta
14-15 . . . . Atlanta
16-18 . . . . .Arizona
19-21 . . . . San Francisco
23-25 . . . . .at Cincinnati
26-28 . . . . . . .at Florida
29-30 . . . . . .Milwaukee

MAY
1-2. . . . . . . .Milwaukee
3-5. . . . . .Colorado
7-9. . . . . . . .at Houston
11-13 . . . at San Francisco
14-16 . . . Los Angeles (NL)
17-18 . . . . . San Francisco

19-20 . at Los Angeles (NL)
21-23 . . . . . . .at Seattle
25-27 . . . . St. Louis
28-30 . . . . . Washington
31 . . . . . . .New York (NL)

JUNE
1-2 . . . . . .New York (NL)
4-7 . . . . . at Philadelphia
8-10 . . . . at New York (NL)
11-13 . . . . Seattle
14-16 . . . . .Toronto
18-20 . . . . . . Baltimore
22-24 . . . . . at Tampa Bay
25-27 . . . . . . .at Florida
28-30 . . . . .Colorado

JULY
1-4. . . . . Houston
6-8. . . . . at Washington
9-11 . . . . . at Colorado
16-18 . . . . .Arizona
20-22 . . . . . . at Atlanta
23-25 . . . . at Pittsburgh
27-29 . . . Los Angeles (NL)
30-31 . . . . Florida

AUGUST
1 . . . . Florida
2-5. . . at Los Angeles (NL)
6-8. . . . . at Arizona
9-12 . . . . Pittsburgh
13-15 . . . at San Francisco
16-19 . . . .at Chicago (NL)
20-22 . . . . . at Milwaukee

24-26 . . . . Arizona
27-29 . . . . .Philadelphia
30-31 . . . . at Arizona

SEPTEMBER
1 . . . . at Arizona
3-5. . . . . .Colorado
6-8. . . . . Los Angeles (NL)
9-12 . . . . . San Francisco
13-15 . . . . . at Colorado
16-19 . . . . . .at St. Louis
21-23 . at Los Angeles (NL)
24-26 . . . . . . .Cincinnati
27-30 . . . . Chicago (NL)

OCTOBER
1-3. . . . . at San Francisco

GENERAL INFORMATION

Stadium (year opened): Petco Park (2004).
Team Colors: Padres sand, navy blue and sky blue.

Player Representative: Unavailable.
Home Dugout: First Base.
Playing Surface: Grass.

Travel, Clubhouse
Director, Team Travel/Equipment Manager: Brian Prilaman.
Assistant Clubhouse Manager: Tony Petricca. **Assistant to the Equipment Manager:** Spencer Dallin. **Visiting Clubhouse Manager:** David Bacharach.

BASEBALL OPERATIONS
Telephone: (619) 795-5076. **Fax:** (619) 795-5361.
Executive Vice President/General Manager: Jed Hoyer.
Executive VP: Paul DePodesta. **VP/Assistant GMs:** Fred Uhlman Jr, Jason McLeod. **Special Assistant to GM/Major League Scout:** Bill Bryk. **Director, Baseball Operations:** Josh Stein. **Director, Player Personnel:** Chris Gwynn. **Special Assistant, Baseball Operations:** Dave Roberts. **Assistant:** Ryan Isaac.

Jed Hoyer

Major League Staff
Manager: Bud Black.
Coaches: Bench—Ted Simmons; Pitching—Darren Balsley; Hitting—Jim Lefebvre; First Base—Rick Renteria; Third Base—Glenn Hoffman; Bullpen—Darrel Akerfelds.

Medical/Training
Club Physician: Scripps Clinic Medical staff.
Head Athletic Trainer: Todd Hutcheson. **Assistant Athletic Trainer:** Paul Navarro. **Strength/Conditioning Coach:** Jim Malone.

Player Development
Telephone: (619) 795-5343. **Fax:** (619) 795-5036.
Vice President, Scouting/Player Development: Jason McLeod. **Director, Player Development:** Randy Smith.
Director, Minor League Operations: Mike Wickham. **Coordinator, Latin American Operations:** Juan Lara. **Administrator, Dominican Republic Operations:** Cesar Rizik. **Coordinator, Scouting/Player Development:** Ilana Miller.
Roving Instructors: Mike Couchee (pitching), Tony Muser (hitting), Tom Gamboa (field coordinator), Duffy Dyer (catching), Gary Jones (infield), Matt Wilson (trainer coordinator), Dan Morrison (strength/conditioning), Matt Neiberg (rehab).

Farm System

Class	Farm Club (League)	Manager	Coach	Pitching Coach
Triple-A	Portland (PCL)	Terry Kennedy	Orv Franchuck	Steve Webber
Double-A	San Antonio (TL)	Doug Dascenzo	Max Venable	Glenn Abbott
High A	Lake Elsinore (CAL)	Carlos Lezcano	Bob Skube	Dave Rajsich
Low A	Fort Wayne (MWL)	Jose Flores	Tom Tornncasa	Bronswell Patrick
Short-season	Eugene (NW)	Greg Riddoch	Shawn Wooten	Tom Bradley
Rookie	Padres (AZL)	Ivan Cruz	Kory Dehaan	Jimmy Jones
Rookie	Padres (DSL)	Evaristo Lantigua	J. Rosario/J. Amancio	C. Reyes/J. Mateo

Scouting
Telephone: (619) 795-5343. **Fax:** (619) 795-5036.
Director, Scouting: Jaron Madison.
Director, International Scouting/Major League Scout: Randy Smith.
Assistant Director, Scouting: Pete DeYoung.
Major League Scouts: Ray Crone (Waxahachie, TX), Bill Bryk (Schereville, IL).
Professional Scouts: John Vander Wal (Grand Rapids, MI), Van Smith (Belleville, IL), Joe Bochy (Plant City, FL).
Special Assignment Scout: Bill "Chief" Gayton (San Diego, CA).
National Supervisor: Bob Filotei (Mobile, AL).
Regional Supervisors: Pete DeYoung (La Jolla, CA), Tim Holt (Allen, TX), Ash Lawson (Athens, TN).
Amateur Scouts: Justin Baughman (Portland, OR), Adam Bourassa (Raleigh, NC), Jim Bretz (South Windsor, CT), Mark Conner (Aiken, SC), Jeff Curtis (Hurst, TX), Lane Decker (Piedmont, OK), Kevin Ellis (Katy, TX), Josh Emmerick (Oceanside, CA), David Francia (Dickinson, AL), Brendan Hause (Carlsbad, CA), Noah Jackson (Mill Valley, CA), Dave Lottsfeldt (Castle Rock, CO), Shane Monahan (Woodstock, GA), Andrew Salvo (Manassas, VA), Rob Sidwell (Windermere, FL), Jeff Stewart (Normal, IL). **Part-Time Scouts:** Robert Gutierrez (Carol City, FL), Hank Krause (Akron, IA), Willie Ronda (Las Lomas Rio Piedras, Puerto Rico), Cam Walker (Centerville, IA), Murray Zuk (Souris, Manitoba).
Coordinator, Latin American Scouting: Felix Feliz, Trevor Schumm (Pacific Rim), Yfrain Linares (Venezuela), Robert Rowley (Mexico, Central/South America).
International Scouts: Antonio Alejos (Venezuela), Milton Croes (Aruba), Marcial Del Valle (Colombia), Emenejildo Diaz (Dominican Republic), Elvin Jarquin (Nicaragua), Martin Jose (Dominican Republic), Victor Magdaleno (Venezuela), Ricardo Montenegro (Panama), Luis Prieto (Venezuela), Ysreal Rojas (Dominican Republic), Jose Salado (Dominican Republic).

San Francisco Giants

Office Address: AT&T Park, 24 Willie Mays Plaza, San Francisco, CA 94107.
Telephone: (415) 972-2000. **Fax:** (415) 947-2800. **Website:** sfgiants.com, sfgigantes.com.

Ownership
Operated by: San Francisco Baseball Associates L.P.
Chief Executive Officer: William H. Neukom. **Special Assistant:** Willie Mays. **Senior Advisor:** Willie McCovey.

BUSINESS OPERATIONS

Bill Neukom

President/Chief Operating Officer: Laurence M. Baer. **Senior VP/General Counsel:** Jack F. Bair. **Chief People Officer:** Leilani Gayles.

Finance
SVP/Chief Financial Officer: John F. Yee. **Senior VP/Chief Information Officer:** Bill Schlough. **Senior Director, Information Technology:** Ken Logan. **Senior VP, Facilities:** Alfonso G. Felder. **VP, Finance:** Lisa Pantages.

Marketing/Sales
Senior VP, Corporate Marketing: Mario Alioto. **VP, Corporate Sponsorship:** Jason Pearl. **Director, Special Events:** Valerie McGuire. **Senior VP, Consumer Marketing:** Tom McDonald. **Senior Director, Marketing/Entertainment:** Chris Gargano. **VP, Client Relations:** Annemarie Hastings. **VP, Sales:** Jeff Tucker. **Manager, Season Ticket Sales:** Craig Solomon. **General Manager, Retail:** Dave Martinez. **Director, Retail Operations:** Bonnie MacInnes.

Media Relations/Community Relations
Telephone: (415) 972-2445. **Fax:** (415) 947-2800.
Senior VP, Communications: Staci Slaughter. **Senior Director, Broadcast Services:** Maria Jacinto. **Senior Director, Media Relations:** Jim Moorehead. **Senior Media Relations Coordinator:** Matt Chisholm. **Hispanic Media Relations Coordinator/Spanish Language Broadcaster:** Erwin Higueros. **Media Relations Assistant:** Eric Smith. **Vice President, Print Publications/Creative Services:** Nancy Donati. **Director, Public Affairs/Community Relations:** Shana Daum. **Director, Photography/Archives:** Missy Mikulecky.

Ballpark Operations
Senior VP, Ballpark Operations: Jorge Costa. **VP, Guest Services:** Rick Mears. **Senior Director, Ballpark Operations:** Gene Telucci. **Senior Director, Security:** Tinie Roberson. **Head Groundskeeper:** Greg Elliott. **PA Announcer:** Renel Brooks-Moon. **Official Scorers:** Chuck Dybdal, Art Santo Domingo, Michael Duca, Dave Feldman.

Ticketing
Telephone: (415) 972-2000. **Fax:** (415) 972-2500.
Managing VP, Ticket Services/Client Relations: Russ Stanley. **Director, Ticket Services:** Devin Lutes. **Senior Ticket Accounting Manager:** Kem Easley. **Senior Ticket Operations Manager:** Anita Sprinkles. **Senior Box Office Manager:** Todd Pierce.

2010 SCHEDULE
Standard Game Times: 7:15 p.m.; Sun. 1:05

APRIL
5-7 . . . . .at Houston
9-11 . . . . Atlanta
12-14 . . . . . . .Pittsburgh
16-18 . at Los Angeles (NL)
19-21 . . . . . at San Diego
23-25 . . . . St. Louis
26-28 . . . . .Philadelphia
30 . . . . Colorado

MAY
1-2 . . . . .Colorado
4-6 . . . . .at Florida
7-9 . . . . at New York (NL)
11-13 . . . . . . San Diego
14-16 . . . . Houston
17-18 . . . . at San Diego

19-20 . . . . at Arizona
21-23 . . . . . .at Oakland
25-27 . . . . . Washington
28-30 . . . . .Arizona
31 . . . . .Colorado

JUNE
1-2 . . . . .Colorado
4-6 . . . . . . at Pittsburgh
7-10 . . . . . .at Cincinnati
11-13 . . . . Oakland
14-16 . . . . . . Baltimore
18-20 . . . . . . at Toronto
22-24 . . . . . .at Houston
25-27 . . . . Boston
28-30 . . . Los Angeles (NL)

JULY
1-4 . . . . at Colorado
5-8 . . . . . . at Milwaukee
9-11 . . . . at Washington
15-18 . . . . .New York (NL)
19-21 . at Los Angeles (NL)
22-25 . . . . at Arizona
26-29 . . . . Florida
30-31 . . . Los Angeles (NL)

AUGUST
1 . . . . . .Los Angeles (NL)
3-4 . . . . at Colorado
5-8 . . . . at Atlanta
9-12 . . . . . . Chicago (NL)
13-15 . . . . San Diego
17-19 . . . . at Philadelphia

20-22 . . . . . . .at St. Louis
23-25 . . . . Cincinnati
27-29 . . . . .Arizona
30-31 . . . . .Colorado

SEPTEMBER
1 . . . . .Colorado
3-5 . . . at Los Angeles (NL)
6-8 . . . . at Arizona
9-12 . . . . . . at San Diego
14-16 . . . Los Angeles (NL)
17-19 . . . . . .Milwaukee
21-23 . . . .at Chicago (NL)
24-26 . . . . at Colorado
28-30 . . . . .Arizona

OCTOBER
1-3 . . . . San Diego

GENERAL INFORMATION
Stadium (year opened): AT&T Park (2000).
Team Colors: Black, orange and cream.
Player Representative: Unavailable.
Home Dugout: Third Base.
Playing Surface: Grass.

Travel/Clubhouse

Coordinator, Team Travel: Michael King. **Coordinator, Organizational Travel:** Mike Scardino. **Giants Equipment Manager:** Miguel Murphy. **Visitors Clubhouse Manager:** Harvey Hodgerney. **Assistant Equipment Manager:** Ron Garcia.

BASEBALL OPERATIONS

Telephone: (415) 972-1922. **Fax:** (415) 947-2929.
Senior VP/General Manager: Brian R. Sabean.
VP, Player Personnel: Dick Tidrow. **VP, Baseball Operations:** Bobby Evans. **Special Assistant to the GM:** Felipe Alou. **Senior Advisor, Baseball Operations:** Tony Siegle. **Senior Director, Baseball Operations/Pro Scouting:** Jeremy Shelley. **Director, Minor League Operations/Quantitative Analysis:** Yeshayah Goldfarb. **Executive Assistant to the GM:** Karen Sweeney. **Coordinator, Video Operations:** Danny Martin.

Major League Staff

Manager: Bruce Bochy
Coaches: Bench—Ron Wotus; Pitching—Dave Righetti; Hitting—Hensley Meulens; First Base—Roberto Kelly; Third Base—Tim Flannery; Bullpen—Mark Gardner, Bill Hayes.

Brian Sabean

Medical Training

Team Physicians: Dr. Robert Murray, Dr. Ken Akizuki, Dr. Anthony Saglimbeni. **Head Trainer:** Dave Groeschner. **Assistant Trainers:** Mark Gruesbeck, Ben Potenziano. **Coordinator, Medical Administration:** Chrissy Yuen.

Player Development

Director, Player Development: Fred Stanley.
Senior Consultant, Player Personnel: Jack Hiatt. **Special Assistants:** Joe Amalfitano, Jim Davenport. **Director, Arizona Operations:** Alan Lee. **Minor League Operations Assistant:** Eric Flemming. **Coordinator, Player Personnel Administration:** Clara Ho. **Arizona Operations Assistant:** Gabriel Alvarez. **Coordinator, Instruction:** Shane Turner. **Coordinator, Minor League Pitching:** Bert Bradley. **Coordinator, Minor League Hitting:** Bob Mariano.
Minor League Roving Instructors: Henry Cotto (Baserunning/Outfield), Jose Alguacil (Infield), Lee Smith (Pitching), Kirt Manwaring (Catching).

Farm System

Class	Farm Club (League)	Manager	Coach	Pitching Coach
Triple-A	Fresno (PCL)	Steve Decker	Ken Joyce	Pat Rice
Double-A	Richmond (EL)	Andy Skeels	Russ Morman	Ross Grimsley
High A	San Jose (CAL)	Brian Harper	Gary Davenport	Jerry Cram
Low A	Augusta (SAL)	Dave Machemer	Lipso Nava	Steve Kline
Short-season	Salem-Keizer (NWL)	Tom Trebelhorn	R. Ward/D. McMain	Brian Cooper
Rookie	Giants (AZL)	Mike Goff	Victor Torres	M. Caldwell/M. Garcia
Rookie	Giants (DSL)	Jesus Tavarez	C. Valderrama/H. Borg	Marcos Aguasvivas

Scouting

Telephone: (415) 972-2360. **Fax:** (415) 947-2929.
Special Assistant to GM, Scouting: John Barr (Haddonfield, NJ).
Senior Advisors, Scouting: Ed Creech (Moultrie, GA), Joe Lefebvre (Hookset, NH), Matt Nerland (Clayton, CA), Paul Turco Sr. (Sarasota, FL).
Coordinator, Amateur Scouting: Doug Mapson (Chandler, AZ). **Special Assignment Scout:** Tom Korenek (Houston, TX), Darren Wittcke (Gresham, OR). **Major League Scouts:** Steve Balboni (Murray Hill, NJ), Lee Elder (Evans, GA), Brian Johnson (Detroit, MI), Stan Saleski (Dayton, OH), Rudy Santin (Miami, FL), Tom Zimmer (Seminole, FL). **Senior Consultants, Scouting:** Dick Cole (Costa Mesa, CA), Bo Osborne (Woodstock, CA). **Scouting Assistant:** Adam Nieting.
Supervisors: Northeast—John Castleberry (High Point, NC); Midwest—Joe Strain (Englewood, CO); Southeast—Paul Turco Jr. (Tampa, FL). **Territorial Scouts:** Northeast Region—Kevin Christman (Noblesville, IN), John DiCarlo (Glenwood, NJ), Jeremy Cleveland (Oakton, VA), Glenn Tufts (Bridgewater, MA).
Southeast Region—Andrew Jefferson (Mobile, AL), Ronnie Merrill (Tampa, FL), Mike Metcalf (Lakeland, FL), Sean O'Connor (Cartersville, GA); Midwest Region—Lou Colletti (Elk Grove Village, IL), Chuck Hensley (Erie, CO), Todd Thomas (Dallas, TX), Hugh Walker (Jonesboro, AR); West Region—Brad Cameron (Los Alamitos, CA), Michael Kendall (Rancho Palos Verde, CA), John Shafer (Portland, OR), Keith Snider (Stockton, CA), Matt Woodward (Vancouver, WA). **Part Time Scouts:** Bob Barth (Williamstown, NJ), Jim Chapman (Langley, BC), Ray Callari (Cote St. Luc, Quebec), Felix Negron (Bayamon, PR), Tim Rock (Orlando, FL).
Director, Dominican Operations: Pablo Peguero. **Venezuela Supervisor:** Ciro Villalobos.
Coordinator, Pacific Rim Scouting: John Cox. **Latin America Crosschecker:** Joe Salermo (Hallandale Beach, FL). **Coordinator, Japan Operations:** Shun Kakazu.
International Scouts: Mateo Alou (Dominican Republic), Jonathan Arraiz (Venezuela), Jonathan Bautista (Dominican Republic),Phillip Elhage (Curacao/Bonaire/Aruba), Edgar Fernandez (Venezuela), Ricardo Heron (Panama), Juan Marquez (Venezuela), Sebastian Martinez (Venezuela), Daniel Mavarez (Colombia), Sandy Moreno (Nicaragua), Jim Patterson (Australia), Felix Peguero (Dominican Republic), Luis Pena (Mexico), Jesus Stephens (Dominican Republic).

Seattle Mariners

Office Address: 1250 First Avenue South, Seattle, WA 98134.
Mailing Address: P.O. Box 4100, Seattle, WA 98194.
Telephone: (206) 346-4000. **Fax:** (206) 346-4400.
Website: www.mariners.com.

Ownership
Board of Directors: Minoru Arakawa, John Ellis, Chris Larson, Howard Lincoln, Wayne Perry, Frank Shrontz, Craig Watjen.
Chair/CEO: Howard Lincoln
President/Chief Operating Officer: Chuck Armstrong.

BUSINESS OPERATIONS

Chuck Armstrong

Finance
Executive Vice President, Finance/Ballpark Operations: Kevin Mather. **VP, Finance:** Tim Kornegay. **Controller:** Greg Massey. **VP, Human Resources:** Marianne Short.

Marketing, Sales
Executive Vice President, Business/Operations: Bob Aylward. **VP, Corporate Business/Community Relations:** Joe Chard. **Director, Corporate Business:** Ingrid Russell-Narcisse. **VP, Marketing:** Kevin Martinez. **Director, Marketing:** Gregg Greene. **Senior Director, Merchandise:** Jim La Shell.
Vice President, Sales: Frances Traisman. **Director, Group/Season Ticket Sales:** Bob Hellinger. **Director, Private Suite Sales:** Steve Camp. **Suite Sales:** Moose Clausen, Jill Dahlen.

Baseball Information, Communications
Telephone: (206) 346-4000. **Fax:** (206) 346-4400.
Vice President, Communications: Randy Adamack.
Director, Baseball Information: Tim Hevly. **Manager, Baseball Information:** Jeff Evans. **Coordinator, Baseball Information:** Kelly Munro. **Assistant, Baseball Information:** Fernando Alcala.
Director, Public Information: Rebecca Hale. **Director, Graphic Design:** Carl Morton. **Director, Community Relations:** Gina Hasson. **Manager, Community Programs:** Sean Grindley.

Ticketing
Telephone: (206) 346-4001. **Fax:** (206) 346-4100.
Director, Ticketing/Parking Operations: Malcolm Rogel. **Director, Ticket Services:** Jennifer Sweigert. **Manager, Group/Suite Ticket Services:** Steve Belling. **Manager, Box Office:** Malcolm Rogel.

Stadium Operations
Vice President, Ballpark Operations: Scott Jenkins. **Senior Director, Safeco Field Operations:** Tony Pereira.

2010 SCHEDULE
Standard Game Times: 7:10 p.m.; Sun. 1:10.

APRIL
5-8 . . . . .at Oakland
9-11 . . . . .at Texas
12-14 . . . . Oakland
16-18 . . . . Detroit
19-21 . . . . Baltimore
23-25 . . . . at Chicago (AL)
26-28 . . . .at Kansas City
30 . . . . Texas

MAY
1-2 . . . . Texas
4-6 . . . . .Tampa Bay
7-9 . . . . . Los Angeles (AL)
11-13 . . . . . .at Baltimore
14-16 . . . . . at Tampa Bay
17-18 . . . . . .at Oakland
19-20 . . . . .Toronto

21-23 . . . . . . San Diego
25-26 . . . . Detroit
28-30 . at Los Angeles (AL)
31 . . . . Minnesota

JUNE
1-3 . . . . .Minnesota
4-6 . . . . . Los Angeles (AL)
7-10 . . . . .at Texas
11-13 . . . at San Diego
15-17 . . . . . .at St. Louis
18-20 . . . . Cincinnati
22-24 . . . . Chicago (NL)
25-27 . . . . at Milwaukee
29-30 . . at New York (AL)

JULY
1 . . . . . . at New York (AL)

2-4 . . . . .at Detroit
5-7 . . . . . . Kansas City
8-11 . . . . .New York (AL)
15-18 . at Los Angeles (AL)
19-21 . . . . . Chicago (AL)
22-25 . . . . Boston
26-29 . . . .at Chicago (AL)
30-31 . . . . at Minnesota

AUGUST
1 . . . . at Minnesota
3-5 . . . . Texas
6-8 . . . . Kansas City
9-11 . . . . Oakland
13-15 . . . .at Cleveland
16-18 . . . . .at Baltimore
20-22 . . . at New York (AL)

23-25 . . . . . . .at Boston
27-29 . . . . . .Minnesota
30-31 . . . Los Angeles (AL)

SEPTEMBER
1 . . . . . . Los Angeles (AL)
2-5 . . . . Cleveland
6-8 . . . . .at Oakland
10-12 . at Los Angeles (AL)
13-15 . . . . Boston
17-19 . . . . Texas
21-23 . . . . . . at Toronto
24-26 . . . . . at Tampa Bay
27-29 . . . . . .at Texas
30 . . . . Oakland

OCTOBER
1-3 . . . . Oakland

GENERAL INFORMATION
Stadium (year opened): Safeco Field (1999).
Team Colors: Northwest green, silver and navy blue.

Player Representative: Unavailable.
Home Dugout: First Base.
Playing Surface: Grass.

Director, Security: Sly Servance. **Director, Events:** Jill Hashimoto.
Vice President, Information Services: Dave Curry. **Director, PBX/Retail Systems:** Oliver Roy. **Director, Procurement:** Sandy Fielder.
Head Groundskeeper: Bob Christofferson. **Assistant Head Groundskeepers:** Tim Wilson, Leo Liebert. **PA Announcer:** Tom Hutyler. **Official Scorer:** Eric Radovich.

Travel, Clubhouse

Director, Team Travel: Ron Spellecy.
Clubhouse Manager: Ted Walsh. **Visiting Clubhouse Manager:** Henry Genzale. **Video Coordinator:** Carl Hamilton.

BASEBALL OPERATIONS

Executive Vice President/General Manager: Jack Zduriencik.
Assistant GM: Jeff Kingston. **Special Assistants:** Tony Blengino, John Boles, Ken Madeja.
Administrator, Baseball Operations: Debbie Larsen.

Major League Staff

Manager: Don Wakamatsu.
Coaches: Bench—Ty Van Burkleo; Pitching— Rick Adair; Batting—Alan Cockrell; First Base—Lee Tinsley; Third Base—Mike Brumley; Bullpen—John Wetteland.

Medical, Training

Medical Director: Dr. Edward Khalfayan. **Club Physician:** Dr. Mitchel Storey. **Head Trainer:** Rick Griffin. **Assistant Trainers:** Rob Nodine, Takayoshi Morimoto. **Stength/Conditioning:** Allen Wirtala.

Jack Zduriencik

Player Development

Telephone: (206) 346-4316. **Fax:** (206) 346-4300.
Director, Minor League Operations: Pedro Grifol. **Director, Minor League/International Administration:** Hide Sueyoshi. **Administrator, Minor League Operations:** Jan Plein. **Assistant, Minor League Operations:** Casey Brett. **Coordinator, Minor League Instruction:** Andy Stankiewicz. **Trainer Coordinator:** Mickey Clarizio. **Physical Therapist:** Sean McQueeney. **Roving Instructors:** James Clifford (strength/conditioning), Darrin Garner (infield/baserunning), Roger Hansen (catching), Jose Castro/Phil Plantier (hitting), Carl Willis (pitching), Mike Tosar (Latin America field coordinator), Nasusel Cabrera (Latin America pitching coordinator).

Farm System

Class	Club (League)	Manager	Coach	Pitching Coach
Triple-A	Tacoma (PCL)	Daren Brown	Alonzo Powell	Jaime Navarro
Double-A	West Tenn (EL)	Tim Laker	Andy Fox	Lance Painter
High A	High Desert (CAL)	Jim Horner	Tommy Cruz	Tom Dettore
Low A	Clinton (MWL)	John Tamargo	Terry Pollreisz	Dwight Bernard
Short-season	Everett (NWL)	Jose Moreno	Scott Steinmann	Rich Dorman
Rookie	Pulaski (APP)	Eddie Menchaca	Rafael Santo Domingo	Andrew Lorraine
Rookie	Peoria (AZL)	Jesus Azuaje	Andy Bottin	Gary Wheelock
Rookie	Mariners (DSL)	Francisco Gerez	J.Guerrero/M.Pimentel	Danielin Acevedo
Rookie	Mariners (VSL)	Russell Vasquez	W.Oropeza/J.Umbria	Carlos Hernandez

Scouting

Telephone: (206) 346-4000. **Fax:** (206) 346-4300.
Director, Amateur Scouting: Tom McNamara. **Director, Pro Scouting:** Carmen Fusco. **Scouting Administrator:** Hallie Larson.
Major League Scouts: John Boles (West Melbourne, FL), Todd Greene (Alpharetta, GA), Bob Harrison (Long Beach, CA), Jordan Horne (Cincinnati, OH), Greg Hunter (Seattle, WA), Steve Jongewaard (Napa, CA), Bill Kearns (Milton, MA), John McMichen (Treasure Island, FL), Ken Madeja (Novi, MI), Bill Masse (Manchester, CT), Frank Mattox (Peoria, AZ), Joe Nigro (Staten Island, NY), Steve Pope (Asheville, NC), Duane Shaffer (Anaheim, CA), John Stearns (Port St. Lucie, FL), Woody Woodward (Palm Coast, FL).
National Crosschecker: Mike Cadahia (Miami Springs, FL).
Territorial Supervisors: West—Butch Baccala (Weimar, CA), East—Paul Gibson (Center Moriches, NY), Midwest— Mark Lummus (Cleburne, TX).
Area Supervisors: Dave Alexander (Lafayette, IN), Garrett Ball (Sandy Springs, GA), Jesse Kapellusch (Hays, KS), Devitt Moore (Gulfport, MS), Mike Moriarty (Edison, NJ), Rob Mummau (Stephens City, VA), Brian Nichols (Taunton, MA), Chris Pelekoudas (Goodyear, AZ), Stacey Pettis (Antioch, CA), John Ramey (Wildomar, CA), Alvin Rittman (Memphis, TN), Joe Ross (Kirkland, WA), Tony Russo (Fayetteville, NC), Bob Steinkamp (Beatrice, NE), Mike Tosar (Miami, FL), Kyle Van Hook (Brenham, TX), Greg Whitworth (Los Angeles, CA), Brian Williams (Cincinnati, OH).
Vice President, International Operations: Bob Engle (Tampa, FL).
Coordinator, Special Projects International: Ted Heid (Glendale, AZ). **Coordinator, Pacific Rim:** Pat Kelly (Leabrook, S. Australia). **Coordinator, Canada/Europe:** Wayne Norton (Port Moody, British Columbia).
Supervisors, International Scouting: Emilio Carrasquel (Venezuela), Patrick Guerrero (Dominican Republic), Jamey Storvick (Taiwan), Curtis Wallace (Colombia), Yasushi Yamamoto (Japan).

Tampa Bay Rays

Office Address: Tropicana Field, One Tropicana Drive, St. Petersburg, FL 33705.
Telephone: (727) 825-3137. **Fax:** (727) 825-3111. **Website:** www.raysbaseball.com

Ownership

Principal Owner: Stuart Sternberg. **President:** Matt Silverman.

BUSINESS OPERATIONS

Senior Vice President, Administration/General Counsel: John Higgins. **Senior VP, Business Operations:** Brian Auld. **Senior VP/Chief Sales Officer:** Mark Fernandez. **Senior VP, Development/Business Affairs:** Michael Kalt. **VP, Development:** Melanie Lenz. **Director, Development:** William Walsh. **Senior Director, Procurement/Business Services:** Bill Wiener, Jr. **Director, Partner/VIP Relations:** Cass Halpin. **Senior Director, Information Technology:** Juan Ramirez.

Finance

VP, Finance: Rob Gagliardi. **Controller:** Patrick Smith.

Marketing/Community Relations

VP, Marketing/Community Relations: Tom Hoof. **Senior Director, Marketing:** Brian Killingsworth. **Senior Director, Community Relations:** Suzanne Murchland.

Stuart Sternberg

Communications/Broadcasting

Phone: (727) 825-3242.
VP, Communications: Rick Vaughn. **Director, Communications:** Chris Costello. **Senior Director, Broadcasting:** Larry McCabe. **Director, Radio Operations:** Rich Herrera.

Corporate Partnerships

Senior Directors, Corporate Partnerships: Aaron Cohn, Wes Engram. **Director, Corporate Partnership Services:** Jason Wilmoth.

Ticket Sales

Phone: (888) FAN-RAYS.
VP, Sales/Service: Brian Richeson. **Senior Director, Group/Suite Sales:** Clark Beacom. **Director, Season Ticket Sales/Service:** Jeff Tanzer. **Director, Ticket Operations:** Robert Bennett. **Assistant Director, Ticket Operations:** Ken Mallory.

Stadium Operations

VP, Operations/Facilities: Rick Nafe. **Senior Director, Building Operations:** Scott Kelyman. **Director, Event Operations:** Tom Karac. **Director, Building Operations:** Chris Raineri. **Director, Audio/Visual Services:** Ron Golick. **Head Groundskeeper:** Dan Moeller. **VP, Branding/Fan Experience:** Darcy Raymond. **Director, In-Game Entertainment:**

2010 SCHEDULE

Standard Game Times: 7:10 p.m.; Sun. 1:40.

APRIL
6-8 . . . . Baltimore
9-11 . . . . . New York (AL)
12-14 . . . . . at Baltimore
16-19 . . . . . . .at Boston
20-22 . . . .at Chicago (AL)
23-25 . . . . .Toronto
27-28 . . . . Oakland
29-30 . . . . . Kansas City

MAY
1-2 . . . . Kansas City
4-6 . . . . .at Seattle
7-9 . . . . .at Oakland
10-12 . at Los Angeles (AL)
14-16 . . . . Seattle
17-18 . . . . Cleveland

19-20 . . . at New York (AL)
21-23 . . . . . .at Houston
24-26 . . . . Boston
27-30 . . . . . Chicago (AL)
31 . . . . at Toronto

JUNE
1-2 . . . . at Toronto
4-6 . . . . .at Texas
8-10 . . . . .Toronto
11-13 . . . . Florida
15-17 . . . . . . at Atlanta
18-20 . . . . . .at Florida
22-24 . . . . . . San Diego
25-27 . . . . .Arizona
29-30 . . . . . . .at Boston

JULY
1-4 . . . . . . at Minnesota
5-7 . . . . Boston
8-11 . . . . Cleveland
16-18 . . . at New York (AL)
19-21 . . . . . .at Baltimore
23-25 . . . . .at Cleveland
26-29 . . . . Detroit
30-31 . . . .New York (AL)

AUGUST
1 . . . . . . .New York (AL)
2-5 . . . . .Minnesota
6-8 . . . . at Toronto
9-11 . . . . .at Detroit
13-15 . . . . Baltimore
16-18 . . . . Texas
19-22 . . . . . .at Oakland

23-25 . at Los Angeles (AL)
27-29 . . . . Boston
30-31 . . . . .Toronto

SEPTEMBER
1 . . . . .Toronto
3-5 . . . . .at Baltimore
6-8 . . . . .at Boston
10-12 . . . . . . at Toronto
13-15 . . . . .New York (AL)
17-19 . . . Los Angeles (AL)
20-23 . . . at New York (AL)
24-26 . . . . Seattle
27-29 . . . . . . Baltimore
30 . . . . . . .at Kansas City

OCTOBER
1-3 . . . . . . .at Kansas City

GENERAL INFORMATION

Stadium (year opened): Tropicana Field (1998).
Team Colors: Dark blue, light blue, yellow.

Player Representative: Evan Longoria.
Home Dugout: First Base.
Playing Surface: FieldTurf Duofilament.

Lou Costanza. **Director, Customer Service:** Eric Weisberg.

Travel, Clubhouse
Director, Team Travel: Jeff Ziegler. **Equipment Manager, Home Clubhouse:** Chris Westmoreland. **Video Coordinator:** Chris Fernandez.

BASEBALL OPERATIONS

Executive VP, Baseball Operations: Andrew Friedman. **Senior VP, Baseball Operations:** Gerry Hunsicker.
Director, Baseball Operations: Dan Feinstein. **Director, Major League Administration:** Sandy Dengler. **Senior Baseball Advisor:** Don Zimmer. **Senior Programmer:** Brian Plexico. **Managers, Baseball Research/ Development:** James Click, Erik Neander. **Assistant, Baseball Operations:** Matt Hahn.

Major League Staff
Manager: Joe Maddon.
Coaches: Bench—Dave Martinez; Pitching—Jim Hickey; Hitting—Derek Shelton; First Base—George Hendrick; Third Base—Tom Foley; Bullpen—Bobby Ramos; Assistant Pitching— Stan Boroski.

Andrew Friedman

Medical/Training
Medical Director: Dr. James Andrews. **Medical Team Physician:** Dr. Michael Reilly. **Orthopedic Team Physician:** Dr. Koco Eaton. **Head Athletic Trainer:** Ron Porterfield. **Assistant Athletic Trainers:** Paul Harker, Nick Paparesta. **Strength/ Conditioning Coach:** Kevin Barr.

Minor Leagues
Telephone: (727) 825-3267. **Fax:** (727) 825-3493.
Director, Minor League Operations: Mitch Lukevics. **Assistant Director, Minor League Operations:** Chaim Bloom. **Administrator, Player Development:** Giovanna Rodriguez.
Field Coordinators: Jim Hoff, Bill Evers. **Minor League Coordinators:** Skeeter Barnes (outfield/baserunning), Dick Bosman (pitching), Steve Livesey (hitting), Jamie Nelson (catching), Matt Quatraro (hitting), Dewey Robinson (pitching), Mark Vinson (medical training), Joel Smith (rehabilitation/athletic training), Trung Cao (strength/conditioning).
Equipment Manager: Tim McKechney. **Assistant Equipment Manager:** Shane Rossetti.

Farm System

Class	Club(League)	Manager	Coach	Pitching Coach
Triple-A	Durham (IL)	Charlie Montoyo	Dave Myers	Xavier Hernandez
Double-A	Montgomery (SL)	Billy Gardner Jr.	Ozzie Timmons	Bill Moloney
High A	Charlotte (FSL)	Jim Morrison	Joe Szekely	Neil Allen
Low A	Bowling Green (MWL)	Brady Williams	Manny Castillo	R.C. Lichtenstein
Short-season	Hudson Valley (NYP)	Jared Sandberg	Reinaldo Ruiz	Jack Giese
Rookie	Princeton (APP)	Michael Johns	Wuarner Rincones	Marty DeMerritt
Rookie	Rays (GCL)	Joe Alvarez	D. DeMent/H. Torres	Darwin Peguero
Rookie	Rays (DSL)	Julio Zorrilla	E. Del Rosario/J. Martinez	Manuel Esquivia
Rookie	Rays (VSL)	Esteban Gonzalez	M. Holder/G. Omaña	Pablo Pacheco

Scouting
Telephone: (727) 825-3241. **Fax:** (727) 825-3493.
Director, Scouting: R.J. Harrison (Phoenix, AZ).
Administrator, Scouting: Nancy Berry. **Assistant, Scouting/Minor League Operations:** Rob Metzler.
Director, Pro Scouting: Matt Arnold. **Coordinator, Advance Scouting:** Mike Calitri. **Special Assignment Scouts:** Bart Braun (Vallejo, CA), Mike Cubbage (Keswick, VA), Larry Doughty (Leawood, KS). **Major League Scout:** Gene Glynn (Weseca, MN). **Professional Scouts:** Gail Henley (La Verne, CA), Jason Karegeannes (Dallas, TX), Brian Keegan (Matthews, NC), Jeff McAvoy (Palmer, MA), Jim Pransky (Davenport, IA), Elanis Westbrooks (Houston, TX).
National Crosscheckers: Jeff Cornell (Lee's Summitt, MO), Tim Huff (Cave Creek, AZ). **East Coast Crosschecker:** Kevin Elfering (Wesley Chapel, FL). **Midwest Crosschecker:** Ken Stauffer (Katy, TX). **West Coast Crosschecker:** Fred Repke (Carson City, NV). **Area Scouts:** James Bonnici (Davison, MI), Evan Brannon (St. Petersburg, FL), John Ceprini (Massapequa, NY), Tom Couston (Chicago, IL), Rickey Drexler (New Iberia, LA), Jayson Durocher (Cave Creek, AZ), Brian Hickman (Sapulpa, OK), Milt Hill (Cumming, GA), Paul Kirsch (Sherwood, OR), Brad Matthews (Concord, NC), Robbie Moen (Playa del Rey, CA), Brian Morrison (Fairfield, CA), Pat Murphy (Marble Falls, TX), Lou Wieben (Little Ferry, NJ), Jake Wilson (Carlsbad, CA). **International Scout:** Tateki Uchibori (Japan).
Part-Time Area Scouts: Terry Brewer (Monroe, NC), Jose Hernandez (Miami, FL), Jim Lief (Wellington, FL), Gil Martinez (San Juan, PR), Graig Merritt (Pitts Meadow, Canada), Casey Onaga (Aiea, HI), Donald Turley (Spring, TX).
Director, International Operations: Carlos Alfonso (Naples, FL). **Director, Dominican Republic Operations:** Eddy Toledo. **Director, Venezuelan Operations:** Ronnie Blanco. **Pacific Rim Coordinator:** Tim Ireland. **Special Assistant, Baseball Operations:** Andres Reiner. **Assistant, International Operations:** Nelson Montes de Oca. **Consultant, International Operations:** John Gilmore.

Texas Rangers

Office Address: 1000 Ballpark Way, Arlington, TX 76011.
Mailing Address: P.O. Box 90111, Arlington, TX 76011.
Telephone: (817) 273-5222. **Fax:** (817) 273-5110. **Website:** www.texasrangers.com.

Ownership
Owner: Hicks Holdings.
Chairman of the Board: Tom Hicks. **President:** Nolan Ryan.

BUSINESS OPERATIONS
Senior Executive VP: Jim Sundberg. **Executive VP, Hicks Holdings LLC:** Casey Coffman. **Executive VP, Sales:** Andy Silverman. **Executive VP, Ballpark Operations:** Rob Matwick. **Executive VP, Marketing/Community Development:** Dale Petroskey. **Executive VP, Communications:** John Blake. **Executive VP, Finance & CFO:** Kellie Fischer. **VP, Hicks Holdings LLC:** Thomas Hicks Jr. **Assistant VP, Rangers:** Alex Hicks.

Tom Hicks

Finance/Accounting
Assistant VP, Controller: Starr Pritchard. **Payroll Manager:** Donna Ebersole.

Human Resources/Legal/Information Technology
VP, Human Resources: Terry Turner. **Associate Counsel:** Kate Jett. **Immigration Counsel:** Steve Ladik. **Supervisor, Staffing/Development:** Shannon Abbott. **Assistant VP, Information Technology:** Mike Bullock. **Manager, Application Systems:** Bill Edevane.

Business/Event Operations
VP, Event Operations/Security: John Hardin. **Senior Director, Customer Service:** Donnie Pordash. **Director, Event Operations:** Danielle Cornwell.

Communications/Community Relations
Phone: (817) 273-5203. **Fax:** (817) 273-5110.
Senior Director, Media Relations: Rich Rice. **Assistant VP, Player/Community Relations:** Taunee Taylor. **Assistant Director, Player/Community Relations:** Jenny Martin. **Director, Broadcasting:** Angie Swint. **Manager, Media Relations:** Court Berry-Tripp. **Creative Director, Media:** Rush Olson. **Assistant, Community Relations:** Ashleigh Greathouse. **Coordinator, Media Relations:** Brian SanFilippo.

Facilities
Assistant VP, Facilities Operations: Gib Searight. **Director, Grounds:** Dennis Klein. **Director, Maintenance:** Mike Call.

Marketing/Community Development
Assistant VP, Marketing: Kelly Calvert. **Senior Creative Director, Graphic Design:** Rainer Uhlir. **Manager, Marketing:** Kaylan Eastepp. **Executive Director, Foundation/Hispanic Marketing:** Karin Morris.

2010 SCHEDULE
Standard Game Times: 7:05 p.m.; Sun. 1:05.

APRIL			
5 . . . . Toronto	14-16 . . . . at Toronto	**JULY**	19-22 . . . . . . at Baltimore
7-8 . . . . Toronto	17-18 . . . Los Angeles (AL)	1 . . . . at Los Angeles (AL)	23-26 . . . . Minnesota
9-11 . . . . Seattle	19-20 . . . . . . Baltimore	2-4 . . . . Chicago (AL)	27-29 . . . . Oakland
12 . . . . .at Cleveland	21-23 . . . . . Chicago (NL)	5-7 . . . . Cleveland	30-31 . . . . .at Kansas City
14-15 . . . . . . .at Cleveland	25-26 . . . . .at Kansas City	8-11 . . . . Baltimore	
16-18 . . . at New York (AL)	28-30 . . . . at Minnesota	15-18 . . . . .at Boston	**SEPTEMBER**
20-22 . . . . .at Boston		19-21 . . . . .at Detroit	1 . . . . .at Kansas City
23-26 . . . . Detroit	**JUNE**	22-25 . . . Los Angeles (AL)	3-5 . . . . . . at Minnesota
27-29 . . . . . Chicago (AL)	1-3 . . . . .at Chicago (AL)	27-29 . . . . Oakland	6-9 . . . . at Toronto
30 . . . . .at Seattle	4-6 . . . . Tampa Bay	30-31 . at Los Angeles (AL)	10-12 . . . .New York (AL)
	7-10 . . . . Seattle		14-15 . . . . Detroit
MAY	11-13 . . . . . at Milwaukee	**AUGUST**	17-19 . . . . .at Seattle
1-2 . . . . .at Seattle	15-17 . . . . .at Florida	1 . . . . at Los Angeles (AL)	20-22 . at Los Angeles (AL)
3-5 . . . . .at Oakland	18-20 . . . . . .at Houston	3-5 . . . . .at Seattle	23-26 . . . . . . .at Oakland
6-9 . . . . Kansas City	22-24 . . . . . . Pittsburgh	6-8 . . . . .at Oakland	27-29 . . . . Seattle
11-13 . . . . Oakland	25-27 . . . . Houston	10-11 . . . . .New York (AL)	30 . . . . . Los Angeles (AL)
	29-30 . at Los Angeles (AL)	13-15 . . . . Boston	
		16-18 . . . . . at Tampa Bay	**OCTOBER**
			1-3 . . . . . Los Angeles (AL)

GENERAL INFORMATION
Stadium (year opened): Rangers Ballpark in Arlington (1994).
Team Colors: Royal blue and red.

Player Representative: Unavailable.
Home Dugout: First Base.
Playing Surface: Grass.

Merchandising
Assistant VP, Merchandising: Diane Atkinson. Director, Merchandising: Stephen Moore. Manager, Warehouse Merchandise: Randy Wolveck. Retail Manager: Eric Garcia.

Ticket Sales
VP, Suite Sales/Premium Services: Paige Farragut. Senior Director, Baseball Programs/Youth Ballpark/Corporate Clinics: Breon Dennis. Director, Inside Sales: Chip Kisabeth. Director, Dallas/Fort Worth Outside Sales: Coty Kaptain.

Ticket Operations
Director, Ticket Operations: Mike Lentz. Manager, Ticket Operations: Ben Rogers. Coordinator, Season Tickets: Jace Sanders. Coordinator, Group Tickets: Cale Vennum. Coordinator, Ticket Accounting Administration: Ranae Lewis.

BASEBALL OPERATIONS

Telephone: (817) 273-5222. Fax: (817) 273-5285.
General Manager: Jon Daniels.
Assistant GM: Thad Levine. Senior Advisor to the GM: John Hart. Senior Director, Baseball Operations: Don Welke. Senior Advisor to GM: Tom Giordano. Special Assistant to the GM: Ron Hopkins. Special Assistant, Baseball Operations: Scott Littlefield. Director, Baseball Operations: Matt Vinnola. Assistant, Baseball Operations: Matt Klotsche. Executive Assistant to GM: Barbara Pappenfus.

Major League Staff
Manager: Ron Washington.
Coaches: Bench—Jackie Moore; Pitching—Mike Maddux; Hitting—Clint Hurdle; First Base—Gary Pettis; Third Base—Dave Anderson; Bullpen—Andy Hawkins; Special Assignment Coach—Johnny Narron.

Jon Daniels

Medical, Training
Team Physician: Dr. Keith Meister. Team Internist: Dr. David Hunter. Spine Consultant: Dr. Andrew Dossett. Head Trainer/Medical Director: Jamie Reed. Assistant Trainer: Kevin Harmon. Director, Strength/Conditioning: Jose Vazquez.

Player Development
Telephone: (817) 273-5224. Fax: (817) 273-5285.
Director, Player Development: Scott Servais.
Assistant Director, Player Development: Jake Krug. Special Assistant, Player Development: Mark Connor, Harry Spilman. Manager, Cultural Enhancement: Bill McLaughlin. Roving Instructors: Mike Micucci (Field Coordinator), Danny Clark (Pitching Coordinator), Spike Owen (Infield Coordinator), Mike Boulanger (Hitting Coordinator), Luis Ortiz (Hitting Instructor), Keith Comstock (Rehab Pitching Coordinator), Wayne Kirby (Baserunning/Outfield Coordinator), Napoleon Pichardo (Strength/Conditioning), Matthew Lucero (Medical Coordinator), Brian Bobier (Rehab Coordinator).
Manager, Minor League Complex Operations: Chris Guth. Assistant Equipment Manager: Russ Oliver.

Farm System

Class	Club (League)	Manager	Coach	Pitching Coach
Triple-A	Oklahoma City (PCL)	Bobby Jones	Scott Coolbaugh	Terry Clark
Double-A	Frisco (TL)	Steve Buechele	Brant Brown	Jeff Andrews
High A	Bakersfield (CAL)	Bill Haselman	Jason Wood	Dave Chavarria
Low A	Hickory (SAL)	Bill Richardson	Jason Hart	Brad Holman
Short-season	Spokane (NWL)	Tim Hulett	J. Perez/B. Dayette	Justin Thompson
Rookie	Rangers (AZL)	Jayce Tingler	H. Ortiz/O. Bernard	R. O'Malley/J. Jaimes
Rookie	Rangers (DSL)	Kenny Holmberg	A. Infante/R. Westman	Pablo Blanco

Scouting
Telephone: (817) 273-5277. Fax: (817) 273-5285.
Senior Director, Player Personnel: A.J. Preller.
Director, Amateur Scouting: Kip Fagg. Director, Pro Scouting: Josh Boyd.
Manager, Amateur Scouting: Bobby Crook.
Professional Scouts: Mike Anderson (Austin, TX), Russ Ardolina (Rockville, MD), Keith Boeck (Chandler, AZ), John Booher (Buda, TX), Scot Engler (Montgomery, IL), Greg Smith (Davenport, WA), Todd Walther (Dallas, TX).
Western Crosschecker: Kevin Bootay (Elk Grove, CA). Central Crosschecker: Mike Grouse (Olathe, KS). Eastern Crosschecker: Phil Geisler (Mount Horeb, WI).
Area Scouts: Juan Alvarez (Miami, FL), Ryan Coe (Ackworth, GA), Roger Coryell (Ypsilanti, MI), Jay Eddings (Sperry, OK), Steve Flores (Temecula, CA), Todd Guggiana (Long Beach, CA), Jay Heafner (Morris Plain, NJ), Chris Kemp (Spartanburg, SC), Derek Lee (Frankfurt, IL), Rick Matsko (Johnstown, PA), Mike McAbee (Euless, TX), Gary McGraw (Gaston, OR), Butch Metzger (Sacramento, CA), Andy Pratt (Scottsdale, AZ), Dustin Smith (Emporia, KS), Randy Taylor (Katy, TX), Frankie Thon (Guaynabo, Puerto Rico), Jeff Wood (Birmingham, AL).
Director, International Scouting: Mike Daly. Director, Pacific Rim Operations: Jim Colborn. Coordinator, Pacific Rim Operations: Joe Furukawa (Japan). Dominican Program Coordinator: Danilo Troncoso. International Scouts: Pedro Avila (Venezuela), Daniel Floyd (West Australia), Chu Halabi (Curacao), Barry Holland (Australia), Gil Kim (Mexico), Jesus Ovalle (Dominican Republic), Rodolfo Rosario (Dominican Republic), Joel Ronda (Puerto Rico), Rafic Saab (Venezuela), Hamilton Sarabia (Colombia), Eduardo Thomas (Panama), Hajime Watabe (Japan).

Toronto Blue Jays

Office/Mailing Address: 1 Blue Jays Way, Suite 3200, Toronto, Ontario M5V 1J1.
Telephone: (416) 341-1000. **Fax:** (416) 341-1250. **Website:** www.bluejays.com.

Ownership
Operated by: Toronto Blue Jays Baseball Club. **Principal Owner:** Rogers Communications Inc.

BUSINESS OPERATIONS

President/CEO, Rogers Media: Tony Viner. **President/CEO, Toronto Blue Jays:** Paul Beeston.
Senior Vice President, Stadium Operations: Richard Wong. **VP, Special Projects:** Howard Starkman. **Executive Assistant to the President/CEO:** Sue Cannell.

Finance
VP, Finance/Administration: Stephen Brooks. **Executive Administrative Assistant:** Donna Kuzoff. **Controller:** Lynda Kolody. **Director, Payroll/Benefits:** Brenda Dimmer. **Director, Risk Management:** Suzanne Joncas. **Financial Business Managers:** Leslie Galant-Gardiner, Tanya Proctor. **Manager, Ticket Receipts/Vault Services:** Joseph Roach. **Manager, Financial Planning:** Ciaran Keegan. **Manager, Stadium Payroll:** Sharon Dykstra. **Financial Analysts:** Melissa Paterson, Cecil Vellinga, Craig Whitmore. **Payroll Finance Analyst:** Tony Phung. **Payroll Analyst:** Joyce Chan. **Director, Human Resources:** Claudia Livadas. **Senior Manager, Human Resources:** Fiona Nugent. **Advisor, Human Resources:** Gurpreet Singh. **Director, Information Technology:** Jacques Farand. **IT Project Manager:** Anthony Miranda. **Senior Technical Analyst:** Vidal Abad.

Paul Beeston

Marketing/Community Relations
VP, Marketing/Merchandising: Anthony Partipilo. **Executive Assistant, Marketing:** Maria Cresswell. **Director, Community Initiatives/Amateur Baeball:** Michael Volpatti. **Director, Stadium Entertainment:** Marnie Starkman.
Executive Director, Jays Care Foundation: Danielle Silverstein.
Vice President, Sales, Rogers Sports/Entertainment: Gary Murphy. **Director, Business Development:** John Griffin. **Director, Marketing Solutions:** Kelly Gianopoulos. **Director, Strategic Marketing Partnerships:** Krista Semotiuk. **Senior Manager, Business Development:** Honsing Leung. **Manager, Sales Support:** Nicole MacKellar..

Communications
Telephone: (416) 341-1301/1302/1303. **Fax:** (416) 341-1250.
Vice President, Communications: Jay Stenhouse.
Manager, Baseball Information: Mal Romanin. **Coordinator, Baseball Information:** Erik Grosman. **Coordinators, Communications:** Kendra Hunter, Sue Mallabon.

2010 SCHEDULE
Standard Game Times: 7:07 p.m.; Sat/Sun: 1:07

APRIL		
5 . . . . .at Texas		
7-8 . . . . .at Texas		
9-11 . . . . . .at Baltimore		
12-15 . . . . . Chicago (AL)		
16-18 . . . Los Angeles (AL)		
19-21 . . . . . Kansas City		
23-25 . . . . . at Tampa Bay		
26-28 . . . . Boston		
29-30 . . . . Oakland		

MAY		
1-2 . . . . Oakland		
3-5 . . . . .at Cleveland		
6-9 . . . . . .at Chicago (AL)		
10-12 . . . . .at Boston		
14-16 . . . . Texas		
17-18 . . . . . . Minnesota		

APRIL (cont.)
19-20 . . . . . . .at Seattle
21-23 . . . . . . at Arizona
24-26 . at Los Angeles (AL)
28-30 . . . . . . Baltimore
31 . . . . .Tampa Bay

JUNE
1-2 . . . . .Tampa Bay
4-6 . . . . . .New York (AL)
8-10 . . . . at Tampa Bay
11-13 . . . . at Colorado
14-16 . . . . at San Diego
18-20 . . . . San Francisco
22-24 . . . . . . St. Louis
25-27 . . . . .Philadelphia
28-30 . . . . .at Cleveland

JULY
1 . . . . .at Cleveland

JULY (cont.)
2-4. . . . at New York (AL)
6-8 . . . . Minnesota
9-11 . . . . Boston
16-18 . . . . . .at Baltimore
19-21 . . . . .at Kansas City
22-25 . . . . . . .at Detroit
26-28 . . . . . . Baltimore
30-31 . . . . Cleveland

AUGUST
1 . . . . Cleveland
2-4. . . . at New York (AL)
6-8 . . . . .Tampa Bay
10-12 . . . . Boston
13-15 . at Los Angeles (AL)
16-18 . . . . . . .at Oakland
20-22 . . . . . . .at Boston
23-25 . . . . .New York (AL)

AUGUST (cont.)
26-29 . . . . Detroit
30-31 . . . . at Tampa Bay

SEPTEMBER
1 . . . . at Tampa Bay
3-5 . . . . . at New York (AL)
6-9 . . . . Texas
10-12 . . . . . .Tampa Bay
13-15 . . . . . .at Baltimore
17-19 . . . . .at Boston
21-23 . . . . Seattle
24-26 . . . . . . Baltimore
27-29 . . . . .New York (AL)
30 . . . . at Minnesota

OCTOBER
1-3 . . . . at Minnesota

GENERAL INFORMATION
Stadium (year opened): Rogers Centre (1989).
Team Colors: Blue, silver, white
and black.
Home Dugout: Third Base.
Playing Surface: Artificial.

Stadium Operations
Vice President, Stadium Operations/Security: Mario Coutinho. **Executive Assistant, Stadium Operations/Security:** June Sym. **Manager, Game Operations:** Karyn Gottschalk. **Head Groundskeeper:** Tom Farrell.

Ticketing
Telephone: (416) 341-1234. **Fax:** (416) 341-1177.
VP, Ticket Sales/Service: Jason Diplock. **Director, Ticket/Guest Services:** Sheila Stella. **Director, Premium Sales:** Mike Hook. **Director, Ticket Operations:** Doug Barr. **Director, Ticket Sales/Service:** Franc Rota. **Executive Administrative Assistants:** Leigh-Ann Milbourne, Stacey Jackson. **Manager, Box Office:** Scott Hext.

Travel/Clubhouse
Manager, Team Travel: Mike Shaw.
Equipment Manager: Jeff Ross. **Clubhouse Manager:** Kevin Malloy. **Visiting Clubhouse Manager:** Len Frejlich. **Video Operations:** Robert Baumander. **Video Operations Assistant:** Brian Abraham.

BASEBALL OPERATIONS
Senior VP, Baseball Operations/General Manager: Alex Anthopoulos. **VP, Baseball Operations/Assistant GM:** Tony LaCava. **Special Assistant to GM:** Dana Brown. **Assistant to GM/Pro Scout:** Jon Lalonde. **Executive Assistant, Major League Operations:** Heather Connolly.

Major League Staff
Manager: Cito Gaston.
Coaches: Bench—Nick Leyva; Pitching—Bruce Walton; Hitting—Dwayne Murphy; First Base—Omar Malave; Third Base—Brian Butterfield; Bullpen—Rick Langford.

Medical, Training
Medical Advisor: Dr. Bernie Gosevitz. **Team Physician:** Dr. Ron Taylor.
Head Trainer: George Poulis. **Assistant Trainer:** Mike Frostad. **Strength/Conditioning Coordinator:** Bryan King. **Director, Team Safety:** Ron Sandelli.

Alex Anthopoulos

Player Development
Telephone: (727) 734-8007. **Fax:** (727) 734-8162.
Director, Minor League Operations: Charlie Wilson.
Director, Employee Assistance Program: Ray Karesky. **Minor League Field Coordinator:** Doug Davis.
Assistant, Latin American Operations: Jeff Roemer. **Coordinator, Minor League Administration:** Joanna Nelson. **Administrative Assistant:** Kim Marsh. **Senior Advisors, Player Development:** Mel Didier, Mel Queen.
Roving Instructors: Anthony Iapoce (hitting), Mike Mordecai (infield), Rich Miller (outfield/baserunning), Dane Johnson (pitching), Pete Walker (rehab pitching). **Minor League Coordinators:** Hap Hudson (athletic training/rehab), Donovan Santas (strength/conditioning), Billy Wardlow (equipment).

Farm System

Class	Club (League)	Manager	Coach	Pitching Coach
Triple-A	Las Vegas (PCL)	Dan Rohn	Chad Mottola	Dave LaRoche
Double-A	New Hampshire (EL)	Luis Rivera	Ralph Dickenson	Tom Signore
High A	Dunedin (FSL)	Clayton McCullough	Justin Mashore	Darold Knowles
Low A	Lansing (MWL)	Sal Fasano	John Tamargo Jr.	Antonio Caceres
Short-season	Auburn (NYP)	Dennis Holmberg	Kenny Graham	Vince Horsman
Rookie	Blue Jays (GCL)	John Schneider	D. Pano/D. Solano	John Wesley
Rookie	Blue Jays (DSL)	Guillermo Peralta	Luis Rodriguez	Oswald Peraza

Scouting
Telephone: (416) 341-1229. **Fax:** (416) 341-1245.
Director, Amateur Scouting: Andrew Tinnish. **Director, Pro Scouting:** Perry Minasian.
Coordinator, Amateur Scouting: Ryan Mittleman. **Coordinator, Professional Scouting:** Harry Einbinder. **Video Coordinators:** Thom Dreier (Houston, TX), Matt O'Brien (Clermont, FL), Matt Sherman (Los Angeles, CA).
Major League Scouts: Sal Butera, Ed Lynch, Roy Smith. **Professional Crosscheckers:** Mike Mangan, Gary Rajsich.
Professional Scouts: Kevin Briand, John Brickley, Tom Clark, Steve Connelly, Kimball Crossley, Jim D'Aloia, Rick Down, Bob Hamelin, John Lombardo, David May Jr., Wayne Morgan, Brian Parker, Marteese Robinson, Steve Springer, Doug Witt.
National Crosscheckers: Billy Gasparino, Tommy Tanous, Marc Tramuta. **Regional Crosscheckers:** Matt Briggs, Tom Burns, Dan Cholowsky, Bob Fontaine, Brandon Mozley. **Area Scouts:** Chris Becerra (San Francisco, CA), Jon Bunnell (Overland Park, KS), Dan Cox (Santa Ana, CA), Blake Crosby (Santa Maria, CA), Mark Flatten (Phoenix, AZ), Ryan Fox (Yakima, WA), Bobby Gandolfo (Lansdale, PA), Joel Grampietro (Tampa, FL), John Hendricks (Mocksville, NC), Aaron Jersild (Houston, TX), Randy Kramer (Aptos, CA), Nick Manno (North Royalton, OH), Eric McQueen (Acworth, GA), Mike Medici (Chicago, IL), Steve Miller (Plano, TX), Nate Murrie (Nashville, TN), Cliff Pastornicky (Birmingham, AL), Wes Penick (Clive, IA), Michael Pesce (Long Island, NY), Jorge Rivera (Puerto Nuevo, PR), Carlos Rodriguez (Miami, FL), Tim Rooney (Los Angeles, CA), Rob St. Julien (Lafayette, LA), Darin Vaughan (Tulsa, OK).
Canada Scouts: Don Cowan (Delta, BC), Jamie Lehman (Brampton, Ontario). **Ambassador, Canadian Amateur Baseball:** Jim Fanning.
Director, Latin American Operations: Marco Paddy. **International Scouts:** Miguel Bernard (Dominican Republic), Robinson Garces (Venezuela), Pablo Leal (Venezuela), Erick Medina (Colombia), Rafael Moncada (Venezuela), Lorenzo Perez (Dominican Republic), Hilario Soriano (Dominican Republic), Greg Wade (Australia).

Washington Nationals

Office Address: 1500 South Capitol St. SE, Washington, DC 20003.
Telephone: (202) 640-7000. **Fax:** (202) 547-0025.
Website: www.nationals.com

Ownership
Managing Principal Owner: Theodore Lerner.
Principal Owners: Annette Lerner, Mark Lerner, Marla Lerner Tanenbaum, Debra Lerner Cohen, Robert Tanenbaum, Edward Cohen, Judy Lenkin Lerner.

BUSINESS OPERATIONS
President: Stan Kasten. **Executive Vice President:** Bob Wolfe. **Vice President, Administration:** Elise Holman. **Vice Preisdent, Government/Municipal Affairs:** Gregory McCarthy. **Executive Assistant to President/Executive Vice President:** Cheryl Rampy.

Legal/Business Affairs
Senior Director, Business Development/Ballpark Enterprises: Catherine Silver. **Director, Ballpark Enterprises:** Heather Westrom. **Manager Ballpark Enterprises:** Maggie Gessner. **Vice President/General Counsel:** Damon Jones. **Assistant Counsel:** Amy Inlander.

Finance/Human Resources
Chief Financial Officer: Lori Creasy. **Controller:** Ted Towne. **Director, Accounting:** Kelly Pitchford. **Senior Accountants:** Ross Hollander, Rachel Proctor. **Payroll Administrator:** Katelyn Carenza. **Baseball Analyst:** Michael Page. **Vice President, Human Resources:** Bettina Deynes. **Benefits Administrator:** Stephanie Giroux. **Coordinator, Human Resources:** Alan Gromest. **Assistant, Human Resources:** Jimel Virges.

Stan Kasten

Media Relations/Communications
Senior Director, Baseball Media Relations: John Dever. **Director, Baseball Media Relations:** Mike Gazda. **Coordinator, Baseball Media Relations:** Bill Gluvna. **Vice President, Communications/Community Relations:** Chartese Burnett. **Manager, Communications:** Lisa Pagano. **Assistant Communications:** Christina Miller.

Community Relations
Director, Community Relations: Israel Negron. **Manager, Community Relations:** Nadia Wajid. **Coordinator, Community Relations:** Jennifer Jopling.

Marketing/Broadcasting
Vice President, Marketing/Broadcasting: John Guagliano. **Senior Director, Production/Entertainment:** Jacqueline Coleman. **Manager, Creative Services/Broadcasting:** Daniel Kasper. **Manager, Consumer Marketing:** Scot Lewis. **Scoreboard Producer:** Dave Lundin. **Associate Producer:** Benjamin Smith. **Production Coordinator:** Kellee Mickens, Graphic Designer: Eric Soderberg. **Coordinator, Entertainment:** Thomas Davis.
Director, Partner Service: Allison Grinham.

2010 SCHEDULE
Standard Game Times: 7:05 p.m.; Sun. 1:35

APRIL
5 . . . . .Philadelphia
7-8 . . . . .Philadelphia
9-11 . . . . at New York (NL)
12 . . . . . . at Philadelphia
14-15 . . . . at Philadelphia
16-18 . . . . . . .Milwaukee
19-22 . . . . .Colorado
23-25 . . . Los Angeles (NL)
26-28 . . . .at Chicago (NL)
30 . . . . .at Florida

MAY
1-2 . . . . .at Florida
4-6 . . . . .Atlanta
7-9 . . . . Florida
10-12 . . . at New York (NL)
13-16 . . . . . . at Colorado

17-18 . . . . . . .at St. Louis
19-20 . . . .New York (NL)
21-23 . . . . . . Baltimore
25-27 . . . at San Francisco
28-30 . . . . . at San Diego
31 . . . . .at Houston

JUNE
1-3 . . . . .at Houston
4-6 . . . . Cincinnati
8-10 . . . . Pittsburgh
11-13 . . . .at Cleveland
15-17 . . . . . . .at Detroit
18-20 . . . . . Chicago (AL)
21-23 . . . . Kansas City
25-27 . . . . .at Baltimore
28-30 . . . . at Atlanta

JULY
1-4 . . . . . . .New York (NL)
6-8 . . . . San Diego
9-11 . . . . . . San Francisco
16-18 . . . . .at Florida
19-22 . . . .at Cincinnati
23-25 . . . . . at Milwaukee
27-29 . . . . Atlanta
30-31 . . . . .Philadelphia

AUGUST
1 . . . . .Philadelphia
2-5 . . . . at Arizona
6-8 . . . at Los Angeles (NL)
10-12 . . . . Florida
13-15 . . . . .Arizona
17-19 . . . . . . at Atlanta
20-22 . . . . at Philadelphia

23-25 . . . . . Chicago (NL)
26-29 . . . . St. Louis
30-31 . . . . . . .at Florida

SEPTEMBER
1 . . . . .at Florida
3-5 . . . . . . at Pittsburgh
6-8 . . . . . .New York (NL)
10-12 . . . . Florida
13-15 . . . . at Atlanta
17-19 . . . at Philadelphia
20-23 . . . . Houston
24-26 . . . . Atlanta
27-29 . . . . .Philadelphia

OCTOBER
1-3 . . . . . . .New York (NL)

GENERAL INFORMATION
Stadium (year opened): Nationals Park (2008).
Team Colors: Red, white and blue.
Player Representative: Unavailable.
Home Dugout: First Base.
Playing Surface: Grass.

Ticketing
Vice President/Managing Director, Sales/Marketing: Chris Gargani. **Director, Ticket Operations:** Derek Younger. **Executive Director, Client Services:** Stacey Marthaler. **Manager, Premium Ticket Services:** Dave Wredberg. **Manager, Box Office:** Tyler Hubbard.

Ballpark Operations
Director, Ballpark Operations: Matthew Blush. **Director, Guest Services:** Kynneth Sutton. **Manager, Event Operations:** Adam Lasky. **Director, Florida Operations:** Thomas Bell. **Manager, Florida Operations:** Jared Lyon.

Travel/Clubhouse
Director, Team Travel: Rob McDonald. **Clubhouse Manager:** Mike Wallace. **Visiting Clubhouse Manager:** Matt Rosenthal.

BASEBALL OPERATIONS
Senior VP/General Manager: Mike Rizzo.
Assistant GM: Bryan Minniti. **Executive Assistant to GM:** Harolyn Cardozo. **Senior Advisor to GM:** Davey Johnson. **Director, Baseball Operations:** Jay Sartori. **Director, Team Travel:** Rob McDonald. **Assistant Director, Baseball Operations:** Adam Cromie. **Coordinator, Advance Scouting:** Erick Dalton. **Assistant, Advance Scouting:** Mike Mazur.

Mike Rizzo

Major League Staff
Manager: Jim Riggleman.
Coaches: Bench—John McLaren; Pitching—Steve McCatty; Hitting—Rick Eckstein; First Base—Dan Radison; Third Base—Pat Listach; Bullpen—Jim Lett.

Medical, Training
Team Medical Director: Dr. Wiemi Duoghui. **Head Trainer:** Lee Kuntz. **Assistant Trainer:** Mike McGowen. **Strength/Conditioning Coach:** John Philbin.

Player Development
Assistant GM/VP, Player Development: Bob Boone. **Senior Assistant to GM, Player Development:** Tim Foli. **Senior Assistant, Player Development:** Pat Corrales. **Director, Player Development:** Doug Harris. **Director, Minor League Operations:** Mark Scialabba. **Director, Florida Operations:** Thomas Bell. **Dominican Republic Academy Administrator:** Fausto Severeno. **Coordinator, Player Development/Scouting:** Jason Choi. **Coordinator, Minor League Operations:** Ryan Thomas. **Coordinators:** Bobby Henley (Field), Spin Williams (Pitching), Rick Schu (Hitting), Devon White (Outfield/Baserunning), Mark Grater (Rehab Pitching), Steve Gober (Medical/Rehab), Landon Brandes (Strength/Conditioning), Minor League Equipment/Clubhouse Manager: John Mullin.

Farm System

Class	Club	Manager	Coach(es)	Pitching Coach
Triple-A	Syracuse (IL)	Trent Jewett	Jerry Browne	Greg Booker
Double-A	Harrisburg (EL)	Randy Knorr	Troy Gingrich	Randy Tomlin
High A	Potomac (CL)	Gary Gathcart	Matt Nokes	Paul Menhart
Low A	Hagerstown (SAL)	Matt LeCroy	Tony Tarasco	Chris Michalak
Short-season	Vermont (NYP)	Jeff Garber	Paul Sanagorski	Franklyn Bravo
Rookie	Nationals (GCL)	Bobby Williams	Sergio Mendez	J. Poppert/J. Sanchez

Scouting
Assistant GM/VP, Player Personnel: Roy Clark. **Director, Scouting:** Kris Kline. **Scouting Coordinator:** Reed Dunn. **Director, Pro Scouting:** Bill Singer. **Director, Player Procurement:** Kasey McKeon. **Director, Latin American Operations:** Johnny DiPuglia. **Special Advisor to GM:** Ron Schueler. **Special Assistants to GM:** Jay Robertson, Phil Rizzo. **Special Assignment Pro Scout:** Deric Ladnier, Wade Taylor. **Crosscheckers:** Jeff Zona (National/East), Jimmy Gonzales (Midwest), Mark Baca (West). **Special Assignment/Area Scout:** Paul Trinnell (Bradenton, FL). Mike Alberts (Worcester, MA), Tony Arango (Davie, FL), Steve Arnieri (Barrington, IL), Fred Costello (Livermore, CA), Paul Faulk (Little River, SC), Kerrick Jackson (Kirkwood, MO), Craig Kornfield (Rancho Santa Margarita, CA), Bob Laurie (Plano, TX), Timothy Reynolds (Irvine, CA), Eric Robinson (Hiram, GA), Alex Smith (Abingdon, MD), Mitch Sokol (Phoenix, AZ), Tyler Wilt (Montgomery, TX).
Dominican Republic Scouting Supervisor: Moises De La Mota. **Venezuela Scouting Supervisor:** German Robles. **International Scouts:** Modesto Ullo (Dominican Republic), Bernardina Valera (Dominican Republic). **Part-Time Scouts:** Rafael Hernandez (Colombia), Juan Munoz (Venezuela).

NATIONAL MEDIA INFORMATION

BASEBALL STATISTICS

ELIAS SPORTS BUREAU INC.
Official Major League Statistician
Mailing Address: 500 Fifth Ave., Suite 2140, New York, NY 10110. **Telephone:** (212) 869-1530. **Fax:** (212) 354-0980.
Website: www.esb.com.
President: Seymour Siwoff.
Executive Vice President: Steve Hirdt. **Vice President:** Peter Hirdt. **Data Processing Manager:** Chris Thorn.

MAJOR LEAGUE BASEBALL ADVANCED MEDIA
Official Minor League Statistician
Mailing Address: 75 Ninth Ave., New York, NY 10011. **Telephone:** (212) 485-3444. **Fax:** (212) 485-3456.
Deputy Project Manager: Nathan Blackmon. **Senior Project Manager:** Sammy Arena. **Senior Editorial Producer:** Jason Ratliff. **Senior Manager, Statistics Operations:** Chris Lentine. **Senior Reporter:** Jonathan Mayo. **Reporters:** Kevin Czerwinski, Lisa Winston.

STATS Inc.
Mailing Address: 2775 Shermer Road, Northbrook, IL 60062. **Telephone:** (847) 583-2100. **Fax:** (847) 470-9140.
Website: biz.stats.com.
CEO: Gary Walrath. **Executive Vice Presidents:** Steve Byrd, Robert Schur. **Directors, Sales:** Jim Capuano, Vin Bagnaturo, Eric Kutzin, Greg Kirkorsky. **Director, Marketing:** Walter Lis. **Director, Sports Operations:** Allan Spear. **Manager, Baseball Operations:** Jeff Chernow.

TELEVISION NETWORKS

ESPN/ESPN2
Mailing Address, ESPN Connecticut: ESPN Plaza, Bristol, CT 06010. **Telephone:** (860) 766-2000. **Fax:** (860) 766-2213.
Mailing Address, ESPN New York Executive Offices: 77 W. 66th St., New York, NY, 10023. **Telephone:** (212) 456-7777. **Fax:** (212) 456-2930.
President, ESPN/ABC Sports: George Bodenheimer.
Executive Vice President, Administration: Ed Durso. **Executive VP, Content:** John Skipper. **Executive VP, Production:** Norby Williamson. **Senior VP, Programming/Acquisitions:** Len DeLuca. **VP, Programming:** Mike Ryan. **Senior VP/Executive Producer, Remote Production:** Jed Drake. **Senior Coordinating Producer, Remote Production:** Tim Scanlan. **Coordinating Producer, Event Production:** Matt Sandulli. **Senior VP/Managing Editor, Studio Production:** Mark Gross. **Senior Coordinating Producer, Baseball Tonight:** Jay Levy.
Senior VP, Operations: Jodi Markley.

ESPN CLASSIC, ESPNEWS
Vice President, Programming/Acquisitions: John Papa. **Senior Coordinating Producer, ESPNEWS:** David Roberts.

ESPN INTERNATIONAL, ESPN DEPORTES
Executive VP/Managing Director, ESPN International: Russell Wolff.
Senior VP, ESPN Radio/ESPN Deportes: Traug Keller. **General Manager, ESPN Deportes:** Lino Garcia. **VP, International Production/Operations:** Chris Calcinari.

FOX SPORTS
Mailing Address, Los Angeles: Fox Network Center, Building 101, Fifth floor, 10201 West Pico Blvd., Los Angeles, CA 90035. **Telephone:** (310) 369-6000. **Fax:** (310) 969-6700.
Mailing Address, New York: 1211 Avenue of the Americas, 20th Floor, New York, NY 10036. **Telephone:** (212) 556-2500. **Fax:** (212) 354-6902. **Website:** www.foxsports.com.
Chairman/CEO, Fox Sports Television Group: David Hill. **President/Executive Producer:** Ed Goren. **COO:** Larry Jones. **Executive VP, Production/Coordinating Studio Producer:** Scott Ackerson. **Executive VP, Production/Field Operations:** Bill Brown. **Executive VP, Programming/Production:** George Greenberg. **Executive VP, Creative Director:** Gary Hartley. **Senior VP, Production:** Jack Simmons. **Senior VP, Field/Technical Opearations, MLB on Fox:** Jerry Steinberg. **Senior VP, Research/Programming:** Bill Wagner. **Coordinating Producer, MLB on Fox:** Pete Macheska. **Director, Game Production, MLB on Fox:** Jacob Ullman.
Senior VP, Communcations: Lou D'Ermilio. **VP, Communications:** Dan Bell. **Director, Communications:** Ileana Pena. **Publicists:** Eddie Motl, Bob Broderick.

MLB NETWORK
Mailing Address: 40 Hartz Way, Suite 10, Secaucus, NJ 07094. **Telephone:** (201) 520-6400.
President/CEO: Tony Petitti. **Executive VP, Advertising/Sales:** Bill Morningstar. **Senior VP, Marketing/Promotion:** Mary Beck. **Senior VP, Production:** John Entz. **Senior VP, Distribution, Affiliate Sales/Marketing:** Art Marquez. **Senior VP, Programming/Business Affairs:** Rob McGlarry. **Senior VP, Finance/Administration:** Tony Santomauro. **VP, Programming:** Andy Butters. **VP, Engineering/I.T.:** Mark Haden. **VP, Remote Production:** Susan Stone. **Director, Remote Operations:** Tom Guidice. **Director, Studio:** Karen Whritner. **VP, Business Public Relations, Major League Baseball:** Matt Bourne. **Specialist, Business Public Relations, Major League Baseball:** Lauren Verrusio.

TURNER SPORTS
    Mailing Address: 1015 Techwood Drive, Atlanta, GA 30318. **Telephone:** (404) 827-1700. **Fax:** (404) 827-1339. **Website:** www.tbs.com.
    President: David Levy. **Senior VP, Executive Producer:** Jeff Behnke. **Senior VP, Sports Marketing/Programming:** Jennifer Storms. **Senior VP, Sports Production/New Media:** Lenny Daniels. **VP, Sports Program Planning:** John Vandegrift. **Executive VP, Turner Sports Ad Sales/Marketing:** Jon Diament. **VP, Production:** Howard Zalkowitz. **Senior VP, Public Relations:** Sal Petruzzi. **Senior Director, Public Relations:** Jeff Pomeroy.

FOX SPORTS NET
    Mailing Address: 10201 W. Pico Blvd., Building 103, Los Angeles, CA 90035. **Telephone:** (310) 369-1000. **Fax:** (310) 969-6049.
    President/CEO, Fox Sports Television Group: David Hill. **President, Fox National Cable Networks:** Bob Thompson. **President, Fox Regional Cable Sports Networks:** Randy Freer. **Executive VP, Production:** Doug Sellars. **Senior VP, Communicatioins:** Lou D'Ermilio. **Senior VP, LA News Resource Center:** Rick Jaffe.

OTHER TELEVISION NETWORKS

CBS SPORTS
    Mailing Address: 51 W. 52nd St., New York, NY 10019. **Telephone:** (212) 975-5230. **Fax:** (212) 975-4063.
    President, CBS Sports: Sean McManus. **Senior Vice Presidents, Programming:** Mike Aresco, Rob Correa. **Vice President, Communications:** Leslie Anne Wade.

CNN SPORTS
    Mailing Address: One CNN Center, Atlanta, GA 30303. **Telephone:** (404) 878-1600. **Fax:** (404) 878-0011.
    Vice President, Production: Jeffrey Green.

HBO SPORTS
    Mailing Address: 1100 Avenue of the Americas, New York, NY 10036. **Telephone:** (212) 512-1000. **Fax:** (212) 512-1751.
    President, HBO Sports: Ross Greenburg.

NBC SPORTS
    Mailing Address: 30 Rockefeller Plaza, Suite 1558, New York, NY 10112. **Telephone:** (212) 664-2014. **Fax:** (212) 664-6365.
    Chairman, NBC Sports: Dick Ebersol. **President, NBC Sports:** Ken Schanzer.
    VP, Sports Communications: Mike McCarley.

ROGERS SPORTSNET (Canada)
    Mailing Address: 9 Channel Nine Court, Toronto, ON M1S 4B5. **Telephone:** (416) 332-5600. **Fax:** (416) 332-5629. **Website:** www.sportsnet.ca.
    President, Rogers Media: Tony Viner. **President, Rogers Sportsnet:** Doug Beeforth. **Director, Communications/Promotions:** Dave Rashford.

THE SPORTS NETWORK (Canada)
    Mailing Address: 9 Channel Nine Court, Toronto, ON M1S 4B5. **Telephone:** (416) 384-5000. **Fax:** (416) 332-4337. **Website:** www.tsn.ca
    Executive Producer: Jim Marshall.

RADIO NETWORKS

ESPN RADIO
    Address: ESPN Plaza, 935 Middle St., Bristol, CT 06010. **Telephone:** (860) 766-2000, (800) 999-9985. **Fax:** (860) 589-5523. **Website:** espnradio.espn.go.com/espnradio/index.
    GM, ESPN Radio Network: Mo Davenport. **Senior Director, Operations:** Scott Masteller. **Senior Director, Operations/Events:** Keith Goralski. **Senior Director, Radio Content/Operations:** Peter Gianesini. **Senior Director, Marketing/Integration:** Freddy Rolon. **Executive Producer, Event Production:** John Martin. **Senior Director, Engineering:** Kevin Plumb. **Executive Director, Affiliate Relations:** Jim Roberts.

MLB ADVANCED MEDIA MULTIMEDIA
    Mailing Address: 75 Ninth Ave., New York, NY 10011. **Telephone:** (212) 485-3444. **Fax:** (212) 485-3456. **E-Mail Address:** radio@mlb.com. **Website:** www.mlb.com.
    Senior Vice President, Multimedia/Distribution: Joe Inzerillo. **VP/Executive Producer, Content:** Jim Jenks. **Senior Director, Production:** Daria Debuono. **Director, Remote Programming:** Mike Siano. **Director, Studio Programming:** Richard Bush. **Video Acquisition:** Stephanie Gentile. **Audio Acquisition:** Scott Majeska.
    Talent: John Marzano, Billy Sample, Hal Bodley, Seth Everett, Vinny Micucci, Casey Stern, Ed Randall, Jim Salisbury, Peter McCarthy, Noah Coslov.

XM SATELLITE RADIO
    Mailing Address: 1500 Eckington Place NE, Washington, DC 20002. **Telephone:** (202) 380-4000. **Fax:** 202-380-4500. **E-Mail Address:** mlb@xmradio.com. **Website:** www.xmradio.com.
    President/Chief Conent Officer: Scott Greenstein. **Senior VP, Sports:** Steve Cohen. **Senior Director, MLB Programming:** Chuck Dickemann. **Senior Director, Communications/Sports Programming:** Andrew Fitzpatrick. **Executive Producer, MLB Home Plate:** Chris Eno.

GENERAL INFORMATION

MAJOR LEAGUE BASEBALL PLAYERS ASSOCIATION
Mailing Address: 12 E. 49th St., 24th Floor, New York, NY 10017. **Telephone:** (212) 826-0808. **Fax:** (212) 752-4378.
E-Mail Address: feedback@mlbpa.org. **Website:** www.mlbplayers.com.
Year Founded: 1966.
Executive Director/General Counsel: Michael Weiner.
Chief Operating Officer: Gene Orza. **Chief Labor Counsel:** David Prouty.
Assistant General Counsels: Doyle Pryor, Robert Lenaghan, Jeff Fannell, Emily Cabrera, Timothy Slavin. **Senior Executive:** Rick Shapiro. **Chief Administrative Officer:** Martha Child. **Chief Financial Officer:** Marietta DiCamillo.
Special Assistants to Executive Director: Bobby Bonilla, Phil Bradley, Rick Helling, Stan Javier, Mike Myers Steve Rogers. **Player Relations:** Allyne Price, Virginia Carballo. **Contract Administrator:** Cindy Abercrombie. **Director, Communications:** Greg Bouris. **Manager, Player Trust:** Melissa Persaud. **Accounting Assistants:** Terri Hinkley, Yolanda Largo. **Program Coordinator:** Hillary Falk. **Administrative Assistants:** Aisha Hope, Melba Markowitz, Sharon O'Donnell, Lisa Pepin, Deirdre Sweeney. **Receptionist:** Rebecca Rivera.
General Manager, Licensing: Richard White. **Category Director, Interactive Media:** Michael Amin. **New Media Content Director:** Chris Dahl. **Category Director, Trading Cards/Collectibles/New Business Development:** Evan Kaplan. **Retail Development Director/Category Director, Apparel:** Nancy Willis. **Category Manager, Novelties/Hard Goods:** Josh Orenstein. **Business Services Manager:** Heather Gould. **Licensing Assistants:** Paul McNeill, Eric Rivera. **Licensing Assistant, Sponsorship:** Ed Cerulo. **Manager, Office Services:** Victor Lugo. **Executive Secretary/Licensing:** Sheila Peters.
Executive Board: Player representatives of the 30 major league clubs.
MLBPA Representatives: Curtis Granderson, Mark Loretta. **MLBPA Alternate Representatives:** Mark Teixeira, Craig Counsell.

SCOUTING

MAJOR LEAGUE BASEBALL SCOUTING BUREAU
Mailing Address: 3500 Porsche Way, Suite 100, Ontario, CA 91764. **Telephone:** (909) 980-1881. **Fax:** (909) 980-7794.
Year Founded: 1974.
Director: Frank Marcos. **Assistant Director:** Rick Oliver. **Office Coordinator:** Debbie Keedy: Administrative Assistant: **Adam Cali.**
Board of Directors: Ed Burns (Major League Baseball), Dave Dombrowski (Tigers), Bob Gebhard (Diamondbacks), Roland Hemond (White Sox), Frank Marcos (MLBSB), Alex Anthopoulos (Blue Jays), Randy Smith (Padres), Art Stewart (Royals), Kevin Towers (Padres).
Scouts: Rick Arnold (Spring Mills, PA), Matt Barnicle (Huntington Beach, CA), Andy Campbell (Chandler, AZ), Mike Childers (Lexington, KY), Craig Conklin (Cayucos, CA), Dan Dixon (Temecula, CA), Jim Elliott (Winston-Salem, NC), Brad Fidler (Douglassville, PA), Art Gardner (Walnut Grove, MS), Rusty Gerhardt (New London, TX), Dennis Haren (San Diego, CA), Chris Heidt (Cherry Valley, IL), Don Jacoby (Winter Haven, FL), Don Kohler (Asbury, NJ), Mike Larson (Waseca, MN), Johnny Martinez (Overland Park, KS), Wayne Mathis (Cuero, TX), Steve Merriman (Grandville, MI), Paul Mirocke (Lutz, FL), Carl Moesche (Gresham, OR), Tim Osborne (Woodstock, GA), Gary Randall (Rock Hill, SC), Willie Romay (Miami Springs, FL), Kevin Saucier (Pensacola, FL), Harry Shelton (Ocoee, FL), Pat Shortt (South Hempstead, NY), Craig Smajstrla (Pearland, TX), Christie Stancil (Raleigh, NC), Ed Sukla (Irvine, CA), Charles Peterson (Pembina, ND), Jim Walton (Shattuck, OK).
Supervisor, Canada: Walt Burrows (Brentwood Bay, B.C.). **Canadian Scouts:** Curtis Bailey (Red Deer, Alberta), Jason Chee-Aloy (Toronto, Ontario), Bill Green (Vancouver, B.C.), Andrew Halpenny (Winnipeg, Manitoba), Ian Jordan (Kirkland, Quebec), Ken Lenihan (Bedford, Nova Scotia), Chris Kemlo (Ontario), Todd Plaxton (Saskatoon, Sask.), Jasmin Roy (Longueuil, Quebec), Bob Smyth (Ladysmith, B.C.), Tony Wylie (Anchorage, AK).
Supervisor, Puerto Rico: Pepito Centeno (Cidra, PR).

PROFESSIONAL BASEBALL SCOUTS FOUNDATION
Mailing Address: 5190 Parkway Calabasas, Calabasas, CA 91302. **Telephone:** (818) 224-3906. **Fax:** (818) 267-5516.
E-Mail: cindy.pbsf@yahoo.com and/or Dennis.Gilbert.PBSF@gmail.com. **Website:** www.pbsfonline.com.
Chairman: Dennis Gilbert. **Director:** Cindy Picerni.
Board of Directors: Bill Gayton, Pat Gillick, Derrick Hall, Roland Hemond, Gary Hughes, Lisa Jackson, J.J. Lally, Tommy Lasorda, Roberta Mazur, Harry Minor, Bob Nightengale, Dana Pump, Tracy Ringolsby, John Scotti, Dale Sutherland, Kevin Towers, Dave Yoakum, John Young.

SCOUT OF THE YEAR FOUNDATION
Mailing Address: P.O. Box 211585, West Palm Beach, FL 33421. **Telephone:** (561) 798-5897, (561) 818-4329. **Fax:** (561) 798-4644. E-Mail Address: bertmazur@aol.com.
President: Roberta Mazur. **Vice President:** Tracy Ringolsby. **Treasurer:** Ron Mazur II.
Board of Advisers: Pat Gillick, Roland Hemond, Gary Hughes, Tommy Lasorda.
Scout of the Year Program Advisory Board: Joe Klein, Roland Hemond, Gary Hughes, Dan Jennings, Linda Pereira.

UMPIRES

PROFESSIONAL BASEBALL UMPIRE CORPORATION
Office Address: 9550 16th Street North, St. Petersburg, FL 33716. **Mailing Address:** P.O. Box A, St. Petersburg, FL 33731. **Telephone:** (727) 822-6937. **Fax:** (727) 821-5819.

President: Pat O'Conner. **Treasurer/Vice President Administration:** Tim Purpura. **Secretary/Vice President, Legal Affairs/General Counsel:** D. **Scott Poley. Executive Director, PBUC:** Justin Klemm (Branchburg, NJ). **Chief, Instruction/ Field Evaluator:** Mike Felt (Lansing, MI).

Field Evaluators/Instructors: Jorge Bauza (San Juan, PR), Larry Reveal (Chesapeake, VA). **Evaluator:** Dusty Dellinger (China Grove, NC). **Special Assistant, PBUC:** Lillian Patterson.

JIM EVANS ACADEMY OF PROFESSIONAL UMPIRING

Mailing Address: 200 South Wilcox St., #508, Castle Rock, CO 80104. **Telephone:** (303) 290-7411. **E-Mail Address:** jeapu@umpireacademy.com. **Website:** www.umpireacademy.com.

Operator: Jim Evans.

TRAINERS

PROFESSIONAL BASEBALL ATHLETIC TRAINERS SOCIETY

Mailing Address: 400 Colony Square, Suite 1750, 1201 Peachtree St., Atlanta, GA 30361. **Telephone:** (404) 875-4000, ext. 1. **Fax:** (404) 892-8560. **E-Mail Address:** rmallernee@mallernee-branch.com. **Website:** www.pbats.com.

Year Founded: 1983.

President: Richie Bancells (Baltimore Orioles). **Secretary:** Mark O'Neal (Chicago Cubs). **Treasurer:** Jeff Porter (Atlanta Braves). **American League Head Athletic Trainer Representative:** Ron Porterfield (Tampa Bay Rays). **American League Assistant Athletic Trainer Representative:** Rob Nodine (Seattle Mariners). **National League Head Athletic Trainer Representative:** Roger Caplinger (Milwaukee Brewers). **National League Assistant Athletic Trainer Representative:** Mike Kozak (Florida Marlins). **Immediate Past President:** Jamie Reed (Texas Rangers).

General Counsel: Rollin Mallernee.

RESEARCH

SOCIETY FOR AMERICAN BASEBALL RESEARCH

Mailing Address: 812 Huron Rd. E., Suite 719, Cleveland, OH 44115. **Telephone:** (216) 575-0500. **Fax:** (216) 575-0502. **Website:** www.sabr.org.

Year Founded: 1971.

President: Andy McCue. **Vice President:** Bill Nowlin. **Secretary:** Vince Gennaro. **Treasurer:** F.X. Flinn. **Directors:** Gary Gillette, Tom Hufford, Paul Hirsch, Anthony Salazar.

Executive Director: John Zajc. **Director, Publications:** Nick Frankovich. **Director, Knowledge Management:** Peter Garver. **Publicity/Member Services Manager:** Susan Petrone. **Membership Services Associate:** Eileen Canepari.

ALUMNI ASSOCIATIONS

MAJOR LEAGUE BASEBALL PLAYERS ALUMNI ASSOCIATION

Mailing Address: 1631 Mesa Ave., Suite B, Colorado Springs, CO 80906. **Telephone:** (719) 477-1870. **Fax:** (719) 477-1875. **E-Mail Address:** postoffice@mlbpaa.com. **Website:** www.baseballalumni.com.

President: Brooks Robinson. **Chief Executive Officer:** Dan Foster. **Board of Directors:** Sandy Alderson, John Doherty, Denny Doyle, Brian Fisher, Jim "Mudcat" Grant, Rich Hand, Jim Hannan (chairman), Steve Rogers, Will Royster, Jim Sadowski, Jose Valdivielso, Fred Valentine (vice chairman).

Legal Counsel: Sam Moore. **Vice President, Legends Entertainment Group:** Chris Torgusen. **Chief Operating Officer:** Geoffrey Hixson. **Director, Special Events:** Mike Groll. **Vice President, Development:** Lance James. **Administration:** Mary Russel Baucom. **Director, Memorabilia:** Matt Hazzard. **Coordinator, Memorabilia:** Billy Horn.

ASSOCIATION OF PROFESSIONAL BALL PLAYERS OF AMERICA

Mailing Address: 101 S. Kraemer Blvd. Suite 223. **Telephone:** (714) 528-2012. **Fax:** (714) 528-2037.

E-Mail Address: ballplayersassn@aol.com. **Website:** www.apbpa.org.

Year Founded: 1924.

President: Roland Hemond. **First Vice President:** Tal Smith. **Second VP:** Stephen Cobb. **Third VP:** Tony Siegle. **Secretary/Treasurer:** Dick Beverage. **Membership Services Administrator:** Jennifer Joost.

Directors: Sparky Anderson, Tony Gwynn, Whitey Herzog, Tony La Russa, Tom Lasorda, Brooks Robinson, Nolan Ryan, Tom Seaver, James Leyland, Mike Scioscia.

BASEBALL ASSISTANCE TEAM (BAT)

Mailing Address: 245 Park Ave., 34th Floor, New York, NY 10167. **Telephone:** (212) 931-7822, Fax: (212) 949-5433. **Website:** www.baseballassistanceteam.com. **Year Founded:** 1986. **To Make a Donation:** (866) 605-4594.

President: Ted Sizemore. **Chief Executive Officer:** James Martin. **Vice Presidents:** Bob Gibson (HOF), Frank Torre, Greg Wilcox. **Board of Directors:** Ruben Amaro, Sr., Steve Garvey, Luis Gonzalez, Joe Morgan (HOF), Jim Pongracz, Robin Roberts (HOF), Octavio "Cookie" Rojas, Gary Thorne, Randy Winn.

Executive Director: Joseph Grippo. **Secretary:** Thomas Ostertag. **Treasurer:** Scott Stamp. **Consultant:** Sam McDowell. **Operations:** Dominique Correa, Erik Nilsen.

MINOR LEAGUE BASEBALL ALUMNI ASSOCIATION

Mailing Address: P.O. Box A, St. Petersburg, FL 33731. **Telephone:** (727) 822-6937. **Fax:** (727) 821-5819. **E-Mail Address:** alumni@minorleaguebaseball.com. **Website:** www.milb.com.

Manager, Exhibiton Services/Alumni Association: Noreen Brantner.

MINISTRY

BASEBALL CHAPEL
Mailing Address: P.O. Box 302, Springfield, PA 19064. **Telephone:** (610) 690-2477. **E-Mail Address:** office@baseball-chapel.org. **Website:** www.baseballchapel.org.
Year Founded: 1973.
President: Vince Nauss.
Director, Hispanic Ministry: Rich Sparling. **Director, Ministry Operations:** Rob Crose. **Director, Player Relations:** Steve Sisco.
Board of Directors: Don Christensen, Greg Groh, Dave Howard, Vince Nauss, Bill Sampen, Walt Wiley.

TRADE/EMPLOYMENT

BASEBALL WINTER MEETINGS
Mailing Address: P.O. Box A, St. Petersburg, FL 33731. **Telephone:** (727) 822-6937. **Fax:** (727) 821-5819. **Website:** www.baseballwintermeetings.com
2010 Convention: Dec. 6-9, Orlando, FL.

BASEBALL TRADE SHOW
Mailing Address: P.O. Box A, St. Petersburg, FL 33731. **Telephone:** (866) 926-6452. **FAX; (727) 683-9865.** **Website:** www.baseballtradeshow.com
Contact: Noreen Brantner, Manager, Exhibition Services.
2010 Show: Dec. 6-8, Orlando, FL.

PROFESSIONAL BASEBALL EMPLOYMENT OPPORTUNITIES
Mailing Address: P.O. Box A, St. Petersburg, FL 33731. **Telephone:** (866) 937-7236. **Fax:** (727) 821-5819. **E-Mail Address:** info@pbeo.com. **Website:** www.pbeo.com.
Contact: Scott Kravchuk.

BASEBALL CARD MANUFACTURERS

DONRUSS/PLAYOFF
Mailing Address: 2300 E. Randol Mill, Arlington, TX 76011. **Telephone:** (817) 983-0300. **Fax:** (817) 983-0400. **Website:** www.donruss.com.
Marketing Manager: Scott Prusha.

GRANDSTAND CARDS
Mailing Address: 22647 Ventura Blvd., #192, Woodland Hills, CA 91364. **Telephone:** (818) 992-5642. **Fax:** (818) 348-9122. **E-Mail Address:** gscards1@pacbell.net. **Website:** www.grandstandcards.com.

MULTIAD SPORTS
Mailing Address: 1720 W. Detweiller Dr., Peoria, IL 61615. **Telephone:** (800) 348-6485, ext. **5111. Fax:** (309) 692-8378. **E-Mail Address:** bjeske@multiad.com. **Website:** www.multiad.com/sports.

TOPPS
Mailing Address: One Whitehall St., New York, NY 10004. **Telephone:** (212) 376-0300. **Fax:** (212) 376-0573. **Website:** www.topps.com.

UPPER DECK
Mailing Address: 5909 Sea Otter Place, Carlsbad, CA 92008. **Telephone:** (800) 873-7332. **Fax:** (760) 929-6548. **E-Mail Address:** customer_service@upperdeck.com. **Website:** www.upperdeck.com.

SPRING TRAINING

CACTUS LEAGUE

ARIZONA DIAMONDBACKS

Major League Club
    Complex Address: Tucson Electric Park, 2500 Ajo Way, Tucson, AZ 85713. **Telephone:** (520) 434-1400. **Seating Capacity:** 11,000. **Location:** I-10 to exit 262 (Park Street) or 263 (Kino Street), south to Ajo Way, left (east) on Ajo Way to park.
    Hotel Address: JW Marriott Starr Pass Resort, 3800 W. Starr Pass Blvd., Tucson, AZ 85745. **Telephone:** (520) 792-3500.

Minor League Clubs
    Complex Address: Kino Veterans Memorial Sportspark, 3600 S. Country Club, Tucson, AZ 85713. **Telephone:** (520) 434-1400. **Hotel Address:** The Hotel Arizona, 181 W. Broadway, Tucson, AZ 85701. **Telephone:** (520) 624-8711.

CHICAGO CUBS

Major League Club
    Complex Address: HoHoKam Park, 1235 N. Center St., Mesa, AZ 85201. **Telephone:** (480) 668-0500. **Seating Capacity:** 12,632. **Location:** Main Street (U.S. Highway 60) to Center Street, north 1 ½ miles on Center Street.
    Hotel Address: Best Western Dobson Ranch Inn, 1666 S. Dobson Rd., Mesa, AZ 85202. **Telephone:** (480) 831-7000.

Minor League Clubs
    Complex Address: Fitch Park, 160 E. Sixth Place, Mesa, AZ 85201. **Telephone:** (480) 668-0500. **Fax:** (480) 668-4501. **Hotel Address:** Best Western Mezona, 250 W. Main St., Mesa, AZ 85201. **Telephone:** (480) 834-9233.

CHICAGO WHITE SOX

Major League Club
    Complex Address: Camelback Ranch Glendale, 10710 West Camelback Road, Glendale, AZ 85037. **Telephone:** (623) 302-5000. **Seating Capacity:** 13,000. **Location:** Take the Loop 101 (Agua Fria Loop) to the Camelback Road exit. Turn west to the stadium.
    Hotel Address: Unavailable.

Minor League Clubs
    Complex Address: Same as major league club. **Hotel Address:** Comfort Suites Glendale, 9824 West Camelback Road, Glendale, AZ 85305. **Telephone:** 623-271-9005.

CINCINNATI REDS

Major League Club
    Complex Address: Cincinnati Reds Player Development Complex, 3125 S. Wood Blvd., Goodyear, AZ 85338.
    Telephone: (623) 932-6590. **Hotel Address:** Marriott Residence Inn, 7350 N. Zanjero Blvd., Glendale. AZ 85305. **Telephone:** (623) 772-8900 Fax: (623) 772-8905.

Minor League Clubs
    Complex Address: Same as major league club.

CLEVELAND INDIANS

Major League Club
    Complex Address: Cleveland Indians Player Development Complex, 2601 S. Wood Blvd., Goodyear, AZ 85338. **Telephone:** (623) 302-5678. **Fax:** (623) 302-5670. **Seating Capacity:** 8,000.
    Hotel Address: Quality Inn, 950 North Dysart Road, Goodyear, AZ 85338. **Telephone:** (623) 932-9191. **Telephone:** (863) 294-4451.

Minor League Clubs
    Complex Address/Hotel: Same as major league club.

COLORADO ROCKIES

Major League Club
    Complex Address: Hi Corbett Field, 3400 E. Camino Campestre, Tucson, AZ 85716. **Telephone:** (520) 322-4500. **Seating Capacity:** 8,655. **Location:** I-10 to Broadway exit, east on Broadway to Randolph Park. **Hotel Address:** Hilton Tucson East, 7600 Broadway, Tucson, AZ 85710.

Minor League Clubs
    Complex Address: Same as major league club. **Hotel Address:** Randolph Park Hotel & Suites, 102 N. Alvernon, Tucson, AZ 85711. **Telephone:** (520) 795-0330.

KANSAS CITY ROYALS

Major League Club
    Complex Address (first year): Surprise Stadium (2003), 15946 N. Bullard Ave., Surprise, AZ 85374. **Telephone:** (623) 222-2222. **Seating Capacity:** 10,700. **Location:** I-10 West to Route 101 North, 101 North to Bell Road, left on Bell for five miles, stadium on left.
    Hotel Address: Wingate Inn & Suites, 1188 N. Dysart Rd., Avondale, AZ 85323. **Telephone:** (623) 547-1313.

Minor League Clubs
    Complex: Same as Major League club. **Hotel Address:** Quality Inn, 16741 N. Greasewood St., Surprise, AZ 85374. **Telephone:** (623) 583-3500.

LOS ANGELES ANGELS

Major League Club
    Complex Address (first year): Tempe Diablo Stadium (1993), 2200 W. Alameda, Tempe, AZ 85282. **Telephone:** (480) 858-7500. **Fax:** (480) 438-7583. **Seating Capacity:** 9,785. **Location:** I-10 to exit 153B (48th Street), south one mile on 48th Street to Alameda Drive, left on Alameda.

Minor League Clubs
    Complex Address: Tempe Diablo Minor League Complex, 2225 W. Westcourt Way, Tempe, AZ 85282. **Telephone:** (480) 858-7555.
    Hotel Address: Extended Stay America, 3421 E. Elwood Street, Phoenix, AZ 85040. **Telephone:** (602) 438-2900.

LOS ANGELES DODGERS

Major League Club

Complex Address: Camelback Ranch, 10710 West Camelback Rd., Phoenix, AZ 85037. **Seating Capacity:** 10,000. **Location:** I-10 or I-17 to Loop 101 West or North, Take Exit 5 (Camelback Road West to ballpark. **Telephone:** (623) 877-8585. **Hotel:** Unavailable.

Minor League Clubs

Complex/Hotel Address: Same as major league club.

MILWAUKEE BREWERS

Major League Club

Complex Address: Maryvale Baseball Park, 3600 N. 51st Ave., Phoenix, AZ 85031. **Telephone:** (623) 245-5555. **Seating Capacity:** 9,000. **Location:** I-10 to 51st Ave., north on 51st Ave.

Hotel Address: Staybridge Suites, 9340 West Cabella Drive, Glendale, AZ 85305. **Telephone:** (623) 842-0000

Minor League Teams

Complex Address: Maryvale Baseball Complex, 3805 N. 53rd Ave., Phoenix, AZ 85031. **Telephone:** (623) 245-5600. **Hotel Address:** Same as major league club.

OAKLAND ATHLETICS

Major League Club

Complex Address: Phoenix Municipal Stadium, 5999 E. Van Buren, Phoenix, AZ 85008. **Telephone:** (602) 225-9400. **Seating Capacity:** 8,500. **Location:** I-10 to exit 153 (48th Street), HoHoKam Expressway to Van Buren Street (U.S. Highway 60), right on Van Buren. **Hotel Address:** Doubletree Suites Hotel, 320 N. 44th St., Phoenix, AZ 85008. **Telephone:** (602) 225-0500.

Minor League Clubs

Complex Address: Papago Park Baseball Complex, 1802 N. 64th St., Phoenix, AZ 85008. **Telephone:** (480) 949-5951. **Hotel Address:** Crowne Plaza, 4300 E. Washington, Phoenix, AZ 85034. **Telephone:** (602) 273-7778.

SAN DIEGO PADRES

Major League Club

Complex Address: Peoria Sports Complex 8131 W. Paradise Lane, Peoria, AZ 85382. **Telephone:** (623) 486-7000. **Fax:** (623) 486-7154. **Seating Capacity:** 10,000. **Location:** I-17 to Bell Road exit, west on Bell to 83rd Ave.

Hotel Address: La Quinta Inns and Suites, 16321 N. 83rd Avenue Peoria, AZ 85382. **Telephone:** (623) 487-1900.

Minor League Clubs

Complex/Hotel: Same as major league club.

SAN FRANCISCO GIANTS

Major League Club

Complex Address: Scottsdale Stadium, 7408 E. Osborn Rd., Scottsdale, AZ 85251. **Telephone:** (480) 990-7972. **Fax:** (480) 990-2643. **Seating Capacity:** 11,500. **Location:** Scottsdale Road to Osborne Road, east on Osborne ½ mile.

Hotel Address: Hilton Garden Inn Scottsdale Old Town, 7324 East Indian School Rd., Scottsdale, AZ 85251. **Telephone:** (480) 481-0400.

Minor League Clubs

Complex Address: Giants Minor League Complex 8045 E. Camelback Road, Scottsdale, AZ 85251. **Telephone:** (480) 990-0052. **Fax:** (480) 990-2349.

SEATTLE MARINERS

Major League Club

Complex Address: Peoria Sports Complex, 15707 N. 83rd Ave., Peoria, AZ 85382. **Telephone:** (623) 776-4800. **Fax:** (623) 776-4829. **Seating Capacity:** 11,000. **Location:** I-17 to Bell Road exit, west on Bell to 83rd Ave.

Hotel Address: LaQuinta Inn & Suites, 16321 N. 83rd Ave., Peoria, AZ 85382. **Telephone:** (623) 487-1900.

Minor League Clubs

Complex Address: Peoria Sports Complex, 15707 N. 83rd Ave., Peoria, AZ 85382. **Telephone:** (623) 776-4800. **Fax:** (623) 776-4828. **Hotel Address:** Hampton Inn, 8408 W. Paradise Lane, Peoria, AZ 85382. **Telephone:** (623) 486-9918.

TEXAS RANGERS

Major League Club

Complex Address: Surprise Stadium, 15754 N. Bullard Ave., Surprise, AZ 85374. **Telephone:** (623) 266-8100. **Seating Capacity:** 10,714. **Location:** I-10 West to Route 101 North, 101 North to Bell Road, left at Bell for seven miles, stadium on left. **Hotel Address:** Windmill Suites at Sun City West, 12545 W. Bell Rd., Surprise, AZ 85374. **Telephone:** (623) 583-0133.

Minor League Clubs

Complex Address: Same as major league club.

Hotel Address: Hampton Inn, 2000 N. Litchfield Rd., Goodyear, AZ 85338. **Telephone:** (623) 536-1313; Holiday Inn Express, 1313 N. Litchfield Rd., Goodyear, AZ 85338.

GRAPEFRUIT LEAGUE

ATLANTA BRAVES

Major League Club
Stadium Address: The Ballpark at ESPN Wide World of Sports Complex, 700 S. Victory Way, Kissimmee, FL 34747. **Telephone:** (407) 939-2200. **Seating Capacity:** 9,500. **Location:** I-4 to exit 25B (Highway 192 West), follow signs to Magic Kingdom/Wide World of Sports Complex, right on Victory Way. **Hotel Address:** World Center Marriott, World Center Drive, Orlando, FL 32821. **Telephone:** (407) 239-4200.

Minor League Clubs
Complex Address: Same as major league club. **Telephone:** (407) 939-2232. **Fax:** (407) 939-2225. **Hotel Address:** Marriot Village at Lake Buena Vista, 8623 Vineland Ave., Orlando, FL 32821. **Telephone:** (407) 938-9001.

BALTIMORE ORIOLES

Major League Club
Complex Address (first year): Ed Smith Stadium (2010), 2700 12th Street, Sarasota, FL 34237. **Telephone:** (941) 954-4101 Fax: (941) 365-1587. **Seating Capacity:** 7,500. **Location:** I-75 to exit 39, West on Route 780, right on Tuttle. **Hotel Address:** Hilton Homewood Suites, 3470 Fruitville Road, Sarasota, FL 34237. **Telephone:** (941) 365-7300.

Minor League Clubs
Complex Address: Twin Lakes Park, 6700 Clark Rd., Sarasota, FL 34241. **Telephone:** (941) 923-1996. **Hotel Address:** Days Inn, 5774 Clark Rd., Sarasota, FL 34233. **Telephone:** (941) 921-7812; Americinn, 5931 Fruitville Rd., Sarasota, FL 34232. **Telephone:** (941) 342-8778.

BOSTON RED SOX

Major League Club
Complex Address: City of Palms Park (1993), 2201 Edison Ave., Fort Myers, FL 33901. **Telephone:** (239) 334-4799. **Fax:** (239) 332-8105. **Seating Capacity:** 6,850. **Location:** I-75 to exit 138, four miles west to Fowler St., left on Fowler to Edison Ave., right on Edison Ave., park on right. **Hotel Address:** Homewood Suites Hotel, 5255 Big Pine Way, Fort Myers, FL 33907. **Telephone:** (239) 275-6000.

Minor League Clubs
Complex Address: Red Sox Player Development Complex, 4301 Edison Ave., Fort Myers, FL 33916. **Telephone:** (239) 334-4799. **Hotel Address:** Holiday Inn Historic District, 2431 Cleveland Ave., Fort Myers, FL 33901. **Telephone:** (239) 332-3232.

DETROIT TIGERS

Major League Club
Complex Address: Joker Marchant Stadium, 2301 Lakeland Hills Blvd., Lakeland, FL 33805. **Telephone:** (863) 686-8075. **Seating Capacity:** 9,000. **Location:** I-4 to exit 19 (Lakeland Hills Boulevard). **Hotel Address:** Unavailable.

Minor League Clubs
Complex/Hotel Address: Tigertown, 2125 N. Lake Ave., Lakeland, FL 33805. **Telephone:** (863) 686-8075.

FLORIDA MARLINS

Major League Club
Complex Address: Roger Dean Stadium, 4751 Main St., Jupiter, FL 33458. **Telephone:** (561) 775-1818. **Marlins' Offices:** 561-799-1346.
Seating Capacity: 7,000.
Location: I-95 to exit 83, east on Donald Ross Road for one mile to Central Blvd, left at light, follow Central Boulevard to circle and take Main Street to Roger Dean Stadium.
Hotel Address: Hilton Garden Inn, 3505 Kyoto Gardens Dr., Palm Beach Gardens, FL 33410. **Telephone:** (561) 694-5833. **Fax:** (561) 694-5829.

Minor League Clubs
Complex Address: Same as Major League Club. **Hotel Address:** Same as Major League Club.

HOUSTON ASTROS

Major League Club
Complex Address: Osceola County Stadium, 631 Heritage Park Way, Kissimmee, FL 34744. **Telephone:** (321) 697-3150. **Fax:** (321) 697-3199. **Seating Capacity:** 5,300. **Location:** From Florida Turnpike South, take exit 244, west on U.S. 192, right on Bill Beck Blvd.
Hotel Address: Reunion Resort & Club, 1000 Reunion Way, Reunion, Florida 34747. **Telephone:** 407-662-1000.

Minor League Clubs
Complex Address: 1000 Bill Beck Blvd., Kissimmee, FL 34744. **Telephone:** (321) 697-3100.
Hotel Address: Holiday Inn Hotel Main Gate East, 5711 W. Irlo Bronson Memorial Highway, U.S. 192, Kissimmee, Florida 34746. **Telephone:** 407-396-4222. **Fax:** 407-396-0570.

MINNESOTA TWINS

Major League Club
Complex Address (first year): Lee County Sports Complex/Hammond Stadium (1991), 14100 Six Mile Cypress Pkwy., Fort Myers, FL 33912. **Telephone:** (239) 533-7610. **Seating Capacity:** 7,905. **Location:** Exit 21 off I-75, west on Daniels Parkway, left on Six Mile Cypress Parkway.
Hotel Address: Hilton Garden Inn, 12600 University Drive, Fort Myers, FL 33907. **Telephone:** (239) 790-3500.

Minor League Clubs
Complex Address/Hotel: Same as major league club.

NEW YORK METS

Major League Club
Complex Address: St. Lucie Sports Complex/Tradition Field, 525 NW Peacock Blvd., Port St. Lucie, FL 34986. **Telephone:** (772) 871-2100. **Seating Capacity:** 7,000. **Location:** Exit 121C (St. Lucie West Blvd) off I-95 , east 1/4 mile, left onto NW Peacock.
Hotel Address: Spring Hill Suites, 2000 NW Courtyard Circle, Port St. Lucie, FL 34986. **Telephone:** (772) 871-2929.

Minor League Clubs
Complex Address: Same as major league club. **Hotel Address:** Holiday Inn, 10120 South Federal Hwy., Port St. Lucie, FL 34952. **Telephone:** (772) 337-2200.

NEW YORK YANKEES

Complex Address: George M. Steinbrenner Field, One Steinbrenner Dr., Tampa, FL 33614. **Telephone:** (813) 879-2244. **Seating Capacity:** 11,076. **Hotel:** Unavailable.

Minor League Clubs

Complex Address: Yankees Player Development/Scouting Complex, 3102 N. Himes Ave., Tampa, FL 33607. **Telephone:** (813) 875-7569. **Hotel:** Unavailable.

PHILADELPHIA PHILLIES

Major League Club

Complex Address: Bright House Networks Field, 601 N. Old Coachman Rd., Clearwater, FL 33765. **Telephone:** (727) 467-4457. **Fax:** (727) 712-4498. **Seating Capacity:** 8,500. **Location:** Route 60 West, right on Old Coachman Road, ballpark on right after Drew Street.

Hotels: Holiday Inn Express, 2580 Gulf to Bay Blvd., Clearwater, FL 33765. **Telephone:** (727) 797-6300. La Quinta Inn, 21338 US 19 North, Clearwater, FL 33765. **Telephone:** (727) 799-1565.

Minor League Clubs

Complex Address: Carpenter Complex, 651 N. Old Coachman Rd., Clearwater, FL 33765. **Telephone:** (727) 799-0503. **Fax:** (727) 726-1793. **Hotel Addresses:** Hampton Inn, 21030 U.S. Highway 19 North, Clearwater, FL 34625. **Telephone:** (727) 797-8173; Econolodge, 21252 U.S. Hwy. 19, Clearwater, FL 34625. **Telephone:** (727) 799-1569.

PITTSBURGH PIRATES

Major League Club

Stadium Address: McKechnie Field, 17th Ave. West and Ninth Street West, Bradenton, FL 34205. **Seating Capacity:** 6,562. **Location:** U.S. 41 to 17th Ave, west to 9th Street.

Complex/Hotel Address: Pirate City, 1701 27th St. E., Bradenton, FL 34208. **Telephone:** (941) 747-3031. **Fax:** (941) 747-9549.

Minor League Clubs

Complex/Hotel Address: Same as major league club.

ST. LOUIS CARDINALS

Major League Club

Complex Address: Roger Dean Stadium, 4795 University Dr., Jupiter, FL 33458. **Telephone:** (561) 775-1818. **Fax:** (561) 799-1380. **Seating Capacity:** 6,864. **Location:** I-95 to exit 58, east on Donald Ross Road for 1/4 mile.

Hotel Address: Embassy Suites, 4350 PGA Blvd., Palm Beach Gardens, FL 33410. **Telephone:** (561) 622-1000.

Minor League Clubs

Complex: Same as major league club. **Hotel:** Double Tree Palm Beach Gardens.

TAMPA BAY RAYS

Major League Club

Stadium Address: Charlotte Sports Park, 2300 El Jobean Road, Port Charlotte, FL, 33948. **Telephone:** (888) 326-7297. **Seating Capacity:** 6,823. **Location:** I-75 to US-17 to US-41, turn left onto El Jobean Rd. **Hotel Address:** Unavailable.

Minor League Clubs

Complex/Hotel Address: Same as major league club.

TORONTO BLUE JAYS

Major League Club

Stadium Address: Knology Park, 373 Douglas Ave., Dunedin, FL 34698. **Telephone:** (727) 734-8007. **Seating Capacity:** 5,509. **Location:** From I-275, north on Highway 19, left on Sunset Point Road for 4 miles, right on Douglas Avenue, stadium one mile on right.

Minor League Clubs

Complex Address: Bobby Mattick Training Center at Englebert Complex, 1700 Solon Ave., Dunedin, FL 34698. **Telephone:** (727) 743-8007. **Hotel Address:** Comfort Inn. 26508 U.S. 19 North, Clearwater, FL 33761. **Telephone:** (727) 796-1234.

WASHINGTON NATIONALS

Major League Club

Complex Address (first year): Space Coast Stadium (2003), 5800 Stadium Pkwy., Viera, FL 32940. **Telephone:** (321) 633-9200. **Seating Capacity:** 8,100. **Location:** I-95 southbound to Fiske Blvd. (exit 74), south on Fiske/Stadium Parkway to stadium; I-95 northbound to State Road #509/Wickham Road (exit 73), left off exit, right on Lake Andrew Drive; turn right on Stadium Parkway, stadium is 1/2 mile on left.

Hotel Address: Melbourne Airport Hilton, 200 Rialto Place, Melbourne, FL 32901. **Telephone:** (321) 768-0200.

Minor League Clubs

Complex Address: Carl Barger Complex, 5600 Stadium Pkwy., Viera, FL 32940. **Telephone:** (321) 633-8119. **Hotel Address:** Imperial Hotel & Conference Center, 8298 N. Wickman Rd., Viera, FL 32940. **Telephone:** (321) 255-0077.

SPRING TRAINING SCHEDULES

ARIZONA

MARCH
4	Colorado
5	at Chicago (NL)
6	at San Francisco
7	Colorado
8	Cleveland
9	at Cincinnati
10	at Los Angeles (NL)
11	Los Angeles (AL)
12	Oakland
13	Los Angeles (NL)
14	Colorado
14	at Texas
15	Seattle
16	Cincinnati
17	at Los Angeles (AL)
18	at Oakland
19	Kansas City
20	at Seattle
21	San Francisco
22	San Diego
24	at Chicago (AL)
25	Chicago (NL)
26	Chicago (AL)
27	at Cleveland
28	Milwaukee
29	at San Diego
30	Texas
31	at Colorado

APRIL
1	at Kansas City
1	at Milwaukee
2-3	Chicago (NL)

ATLANTA

MARCH
2	at New York (NL)
3	New York (NL)
4	Pittsburgh
5	Washington
6	at Houston
7	Houston
8	at Detroit
9	Philadelphia
10	New York (NL)
11	at New York (AL)
12	Pittsburgh
13	Toronto
14	at Houston
14	at Toronto
15	at Washington
16	Florida
17	at Florida
18	at St. Louis
19	Detroit
20	at Toronto
21	St. Louis
23	at New York (NL)
24	Philadelphia
25	at Pittsburgh
26	Detroit
27	Washington
28	at Washington
29	at Philadelphia
30	New York (AL)
31	Houston

APRIL
1	at Detroit
2-3	Chicago (AL)

BALTIMORE

MARCH
3	Tampa Bay
4	at Tampa Bay
5	Pittsburgh
6	at Detroit
7	Boston
8	Minnesota
9	Tampa Bay
10	at Pittsburgh
11	at Minnesota
12	Florida
13	at New York (AL)
14	Philadelphia
15	at Boston
16	at Minnesota
17	Toronto
18	at Toronto
19	at Philadelphia
20	at Boston
20	Pittsburgh
21	at Philadelphia
23	at Florida
24	at St. Louis
25	New York (AL)
26	Minnesota
27	Boston
28	at Toronto
29	New York (AL)
30	Detroit
31	Boston

APRIL
1	at Tampa Bay
2	at New York (AL)
3	New York (NL)

BOSTON

MARCH
3	Boston College Eagles
3	Northeastern University
4	Minnesota
5	at Minnesota
6	Minnesota
6	at Tampa Bay
7	at Baltimore
8	St. Louis
9	at Florida
10	Tampa Bay
11	at New York (NL)
12	at St. Louis
13	Pittsburgh
14	at Minnesota
15	Baltimore
16	at Houston
16	at Tampa Bay
17	New York (NL)
19	at Pittsburgh
20	Baltimore
21	Houston
21	at Toronto
22	Tampa Bay

CHICAGO (AL)

(continued top)
23	at Minnesota
24	at Pittsburgh
25	Florida
26	Toronto
27	at Baltimore
28	Minnesota
29	Tampa Bay

APRIL
1	Minnesota
2	Washington
3	at Washington

CHICAGO (AL)

MARCH
5	Los Angeles (NL)
6	at Chicago (NL)
6	at Los Angeles (NL)
7	Chicago (NL)
8	Seattle
9	at San Francisco
10	at Oakland
11	Cleveland
12	at Chicago (NL)
12	at Los Angeles (AL)
13	Chicago (NL)
13	Milwaukee
14	at Cincinnati
15	Kansas City
16	Colorado
17	at Los Angeles (NL)
19	Chicago (NL)
20	San Diego
21	at Milwaukee
22	at Kansas City
23	San Francisco
24	Arizona
25	at San Diego
26	at Arizona
27	at Colorado
28	Kansas City
28	at Texas
29	Los Angeles (AL)
30	Oakland
31	at Cleveland

APRIL
1	at Charlotte
1	at Seattle
2-3	at Atlanta

CHICAGO (NL)

MARCH
4	Oakland
5	Arizona
6	Chicago (AL)
7	at Chicago (AL)
7	Los Angeles (NL)
8	at Oakland
9	Milwaukee
10	San Francisco
11	at San Diego
12	Chicago (AL)
12	at Milwaukee
13	at Chicago (AL)
13	Cincinnati
14	at Los Angeles (AL)
15	at Colorado
16	Texas
18	at Los Angeles (NL)
19	at Chicago (AL)
20	Kansas City
20	at Oakland
21	at Cincinnati
22	Cleveland
23	at Kansas City
24	at Texas
25	at Arizona
26	Oakland
27	San Diego
28	at Seattle
29	Cincinnati
30	at San Francisco
31	Los Angeles (NL)
31	at Milwaukee

APRIL
1	Colorado
2-3	at Arizona

CINCINNATI

MARCH
5	Cleveland
6	at Cleveland
7	at Milwaukee
8	Kansas City
9	Arizona
10	at Los Angeles (AL)
11	Los Angeles (NL)
12	at Los Angeles (NL)
13	at Chicago (NL)
14	Chicago (AL)
15	Oakland
16	at Arizona
17	Cleveland
17	Milwaukee
18	at Cleveland
19	Seattle
20	at San Francisco
21	Chicago (NL)
21	at Oakland
22	Colorado
24	San Francisco
25	at Colorado
26	at Seattle
27	at San Diego
28	Los Angeles (NL)
29	at Chicago (NL)
30	San Diego
31	at Oakland

APRIL
1	Texas
2	at Cleveland
3	Cleveland

CLEVELAND

MARCH
5	at Cincinnati
6	Cincinnati
7	Texas
8	at Arizona
9	at Seattle

10	San Diego
11	at Chicago (AL)
12	Los Angeles (AL)
13	Texas
14	at San Diego
15	at Milwaukee
16	San Francisco
17	at Cincinnati
17	at Colorado
18	Cincinnati
19	at San Francisco
19	at Texas
20	Oakland
21	at Los Angeles (NL)
22	at Chicago (NL)

COLORADO

MARCH

4	at Arizona	19	Oakland
5	at Los Angeles (AL)	20	Los Angeles (AL)
5	at San Francisco	21	at Kansas City
6	Milwaukee	22	at Cincinnati
7	at Arizona	23	San Diego
8	at San Diego	25	Cincinnati
9	at Los Angeles (NL)	26	at Cleveland
10	Kansas City	27	Chicago (AL)
11	Texas	28	at Oakland
12	San Francisco	29	at Texas
13	at Milwaukee	30	Los Angeles (NL)
14	at Arizona	31	Arizona
14	Seattle		

APRIL

15	Chicago (NL)	1	at Chicago (NL)
16	at Chicago (AL)	2	Seattle
17	Cleveland	3	at Seattle
18	at Seattle		

DETROIT

MARCH

2	Florida Southern College	19	at Atlanta
3	at Toronto	19	at New York (AL)
4	Toronto	20	Philadelphia
5	Houston	21	at New York (AL)
6	Baltimore	22	at Toronto
7	at Toronto	23	Washington
8	Atlanta	25	Toronto
9	at Washington	25	at Washington
10	New York (AL)	26	at Atlanta
11	at Philadelphia	27	New York (AL)
12	Philadelphia	28	at New York (AL)
13	New York (AL)	29	at Toronto
13	at New York (NL)	30	at Baltimore
14	Tampa Bay	31	Pittsburgh
15	Toronto		

APRIL

16	at Philadelphia	1	Atlanta
17	at Pittsburgh	1	at Houston
18	Houston	2-3	at Milwaukee

FLORIDA

MARCH

3	University of Miami	18	New York (NL)
4	Washington	19	St. Louis
5	at New York (NL)	20	at Washington
6	St. Louis	21	Washington
7	at St. Louis	23	Baltimore
8	New York (NL)	24	at Minnesota
8	at Washington	25	at Boston
9	Boston	26	New York (NL)
10	at Houston	27	at St. Louis
11	St. Louis	28	Houston
12	at Baltimore	29	at New York (NL)
13	at Tampa Bay	30	Washington
14	New York (NL)	31	at New York (NL)
15	Minnesota		

APRIL

16	at Atlanta	1	at St. Louis
16	at Washington	2	at Jacksonville
17	Atlanta	3	at Greensboro

HOUSTON

MARCH

4	Washington	20	New York (AL)
5	at Detroit	21	at Boston
6	Atlanta	21	New York (NL)
7	at Atlanta	22	St. Louis
8	Toronto	23	at Pittsburgh
9	at New York (NL)	24	at New York (NL)
10	Florida	25	at Philadelphia
11	at Washington	26	Pittsburgh
12	at Toronto	27	Tampa Bay
13	at St. Louis	28	at Florida
13	Washington	29	at Pittsburgh
14	Atlanta	30	Philadelphia
16	Boston	31	at Atlanta
16	at New York (AL)		

APRIL

17	Washington	1	Detroit
18	at Detroit	2-3	Toronto
19	Toronto		

KANSAS CITY

MARCH

4-5	Texas	20	at Milwaukee
6	at Texas	21	Colorado
7	San Francisco	22	Chicago (AL)
8	at Cincinnati	23	Chicago (NL)
9	Oakland	24	at Los Angeles (AL)
10	at Colorado	25	Seattle
11	Los Angeles (NL)	26	at Los Angeles (NL)
12	at Seattle	27	Oakland
13	Los Angeles (AL)	28	at Chicago (AL)
14	at Oakland	29	at Los Angeles (AL)
15	at Chicago (AL)	30	Cleveland
16	Milwaukee	31	at San Diego
17	San Diego		

APRIL

19	at Arizona	1	Arizona
20	at Chicago (NL)	2-3	at Texas

LOS ANGELES (AL)

MARCH

5	Colorado	22	at Los Angeles (NL)
6	at Oakland	23	at Seattle
7	Oakland	24	Kansas City
8	at Texas	25	Texas
9	San Diego	26	at San Francisco
10	Cincinnati	27	San Francisco
11	at Arizona	28	Cleveland
12	Chicago (AL)	29	at Chicago (AL)
12	at Cleveland	29	Kansas City
13	at Kansas City	30	Milwaukee
14	Chicago (NL)	31	at Chicago (NL)
15	Los Angeles (NL)		

APRIL

16	at San Diego	1	Cleveland
17	Arizona	1	San Diego
19	at Milwaukee	2	Los Angeles (NL)
20	at Colorado	3	at Los Angeles (NL)
21	Seattle		

LOS ANGELES (NL)

MARCH

5	at Chicago (AL)	19	at San Diego
6	Chicago (AL)	20	San Diego
7	at Chicago (NL)	20	at Texas
8	at San Francisco	21	Cleveland
9	Colorado	22	Los Angeles (AL)
10	Arizona	22	at Milwaukee
11	at Cincinnati	24	at Oakland
11	at Kansas City	25	Milwaukee
12	Cincinnati	26	Kansas City
13	at Arizona	27	Seattle
14	Texas	28	at Cincinnati
15	at Los Angeles (AL)	29	at Cleveland
17	Chicago (AL)	30	at Colorado
18	Chicago (NL)	31	San Francisco

APRIL
1 . . . . Cleveland

MILWAUKEE

MARCH
4 . . . . . at San Francisco
5 . . . . at Oakland
6 . . . . at Colorado
6 . . . . . . San Francisco
7 . . . . Cincinnati
8 . . . . Seattle
9 . . . . . at Chicago (NL)
10 . . . . at San Diego
11 . . . . Oakland
12 . . . . . Chicago (NL)
13 . . . . at Chicago (AL)
13 . . . . Colorado
14 . . . . at San Francisco
15 . . . . Cleveland
16 . . . . at Kansas City
17 . . . . . at Cincinnati

MINNESOTA

MARCH
4 . . . . at Boston
5 . . . . Boston
6 . . . . at Boston
7 . . . . New York (AL)
7 . . . . . at Pittsburgh
8 . . . . . at Baltimore
9 . . . . St. Louis
11 . . . . . . Baltimore
12 . . . . New York (NL)
13 . . . . at Philadelphia
14 . . . . Boston
15 . . . . . at Florida
16 . . . . Boston
17 . . . . at Tampa Bay
18 . . . . . . Pittsburgh
19 . . at New York (NL)

NEW YORK (AL)

MARCH
3 . . . . Pittsburgh
4 . . . . . at Philadelphia
5 . . . . . Tampa Bay
6 . . . . Toronto
7 . . . . . at Minnesota
8 . . . . . Philadelphia
8 . . . . . at Pittsburgh
9 . . . . Pittsburgh
10 . . . . . . at Detroit
11 . . . . Atlanta
12 . . . . at Washington
13 . . . . . . Baltimore
13 . . . . . at Detroit
14 . . . . at Pittsburgh
16 . . . . Houston
17 . . . . at Philadelphia
18 . . . . . Tampa Bay
19 . . . . Detroit

NEW YORK (NL)

MARCH
2 . . . . Atlanta
3 . . . . at Atlanta
4 . . . . St. Louis
5 . . . . Florida
5 . . . . . . at St. Louis
6 . . . . at Washington
7 . . . . . Washington
8 . . . . . . at Florida
9 . . . . Houston
10 . . . . . . at Atlanta

2 . . . . at Los Angeles (AL)
3 . . . . Los Angeles (AL)

MARCH
18 . . . . at Texas
19 . . . Los Angeles (AL)
20 . . . . . Kansas City
21 . . . . Chicago (AL)
22 . . . Los Angeles (NL)
23 . . . . . at Cleveland
25 . . at Los Angeles (NL)
26 . . . . . San Diego
27 . . . . Texas
28 . . . . . at Arizona
29 . . . . San Francisco
30 . . at Los Angeles (AL)
31 . . . . Chicago (AL)

APRIL
1 . . . . Arizona
2-3 . . . . Detroit

20 . . . . . at Tampa Bay
21 . . . . . . Tampa Bay
23 . . . . Boston
24 . . . . Florida
25 . . . . at Tampa Bay
26 . . . . . at Baltimore
27 . . . . . Philadelphia
28 . . . . . . at Boston
29 . . . . . at St. Louis
30 . . . . . . Pittsburgh
31 . . . . at New York (AL)
31 . . . . . . Tampa Bay

APRIL
1 . . . . at Boston
2-3 . . . . St. Louis

19 . . . . . at Tampa Bay
20 . . . . . at Houston
21 . . . . Detroit
22 . . . . . at Philadelphia
24 . . . . . Washington
25 . . . . . at Baltimore
26 . . . . . Philadelphia
27 . . . . . at Detroit
28 . . . . . . at Detroit
29 . . . . . at Baltimore
30 . . . . . . at Atlanta
30 . . . . Toronto
31 . . . . . . Minnesota

APRIL
1 . . . . at Toronto
2 . . . . Baltimore
3 . . New York (AL) Futures

11 . . . . Boston
12 . . . . at Minnesota
13 . . . . Detroit
14 . . . . . . at Florida
15 . . . . . . St. Louis
17 . . . . . . at Boston
18 . . . . . . at Florida
19 . . . . . Minnesota
20 . . . . . at St. Louis
21 . . . . . at Houston
21 . University of Michigan

22 . . . . . at Washington
23 . . . . Atlanta
24 . . . . Houston
25 . . . . . . at St. Louis
26 . . . . at Florida
27 . . . . . Washington
28 . . . . St. Louis
29 . . . . Florida

OAKLAND

MARCH
4 . . . . . at Chicago (NL)
5 . . . . Milwaukee
6 . . . Los Angeles (AL)
7 . . . at Los Angeles (AL)
8 . . . . . Chicago (AL)
9 . . . . at Kansas City
9 . . . . Texas
10 . . . . . Chicago (AL)
11 . . at Milwaukee
12 . . . . . at Arizona
13 . . . . . San Diego
13 . . at San Francisco
14 . . . . . Kansas City
15 . . . . at Cincinnati
17 . . . . San Francisco
18 . . . . Arizona

PHILADELPHIA

MARCH
3 . Florida State University
4 . . . . . New York (AL)
5 . . . . . . at Toronto
6 . . . . . at Pittsburgh
7 . . . . . . Tampa Bay
8 . . at New York (AL)
9 . . . . . . at Atlanta
10 . . . . . at Toronto
11 . . . . Detroit
12 . . . . . . at Detroit
12 . . . . at Tampa Bay
13 . . . . . Minnesota
14 . . . . . at Baltimore
15 . . . . at Pittsburgh
16 . . . . Detroit
17 . . . New York (AL)

PITTSBURGH

MARCH
2 State College of Florida
3 . . . . at New York (AL)
4 . . . . at Atlanta
5 . . . . . at Baltimore
6 . . . . . Philadelphia
7 . . . . . . Minnesota
8 . . . . New York (AL)
8 . . . at Tampa Bay
9 . at New York (AL)
10 . . . . . Baltimore
11 . . . . . Tampa Bay
12 . . . . . at Atlanta
13 . . . . . at Boston
14 . . New York (AL)
15 . . . . Philadelphia
17 . . . . Detroit

SAN DIEGO

MARCH
4-5 . . . . . . at Seattle
6 . . . . Seattle
7 . . . . . . at Seattle
8 . . . . Colorado
9 . . . at Los Angeles (AL)
10 . . . . . at Cleveland
10 . . . . . . Milwaukee

29 . . . . . at Washington
30 . . . . St. Louis
31 . . . . Florida

APRIL
1 . . . . Washington
2 . . . . . at Tampa Bay
3 . . . . . at Baltimore

19 . . . . . . at Colorado
20 . . . . . Chicago (NL)
20 . . . . at Cleveland
21 . . . . . Cincinnati
22 . . . . . at Seattle
24 . . . Los Angeles (NL)
25 . . at San Francisco
26 . . at Chicago (NL)
26 . . . . . . at Texas
27 . . . at Kansas City
28 . . . . . . Colorado
29 . . . . Seattle
30 . . . at Chicago (AL)
31 . . . . . Cincinnati

APRIL
1-3 . . . . at San Francisco

19 . . . . . . Baltimore
20 . . . . . at Detroit
21 . . . . . Baltimore
22 . . . New York (AL)
23 . . . . . Tampa Bay
24 . . . . . at Atlanta
25 . . . . . . Houston
26 . . . at New York (AL)
27 . . . . at Minnesota
28 . . . . . Pittsburgh
29 . . . . . . Atlanta
30 . . . . at Houston
31 . . . . . . Toronto

APRIL
1-3 . . . . . . Pittsburgh

18 . . . . . at Minnesota
19 . . . . Boston
20 . . . . at Baltimore
21 . . . . . Tampa Bay
23 . . . . . . Houston
24 . . . . Boston
25 . . . . . . Atlanta
26 . . . . . at Houston
27 . . . . . . Toronto
28 . . at Philadelphia
28 . . at Tampa Bay
29 . . . . . . Houston
30 . . . at Minnesota
31 . . . . . at Detroit

APRIL
1-3 . . . . . . Pittsburgh

11 . . . . Chicago (NL)
12 . . . . . . at Texas
13 . . . . . at Oakland
14 . . . . . Cleveland
15 . . . . San Francisco
16 . . . Los Angeles (AL)
17 . . . at Kansas City
19 . . . Los Angeles (NL)

20 . . . . . at Chicago (AL)
20 . . at Los Angeles (NL)
21 . . . . Texas
22 . . . . at Arizona
23 . . . . at Colorado
24 . . . . Seattle
25 . . . . . Chicago (AL)
26 . . . . . at Milwaukee
27 . . . at Chicago (NL)

SAN FRANCISCO

MARCH	
3 . . . . . . at Seattle	16 . . . . . . at Cleveland
4 . . . . Milwaukee	17 . . . . at Oakland
5 . . . . Colorado	18 . . . . Cleveland
6 . . . . Arizona	20 . . . . Cincinnati
6 . . . . . at Milwaukee	21 . . . . . . at Arizona
7 . . . . . at Kansas City	22 . . . . Texas
8 . . Los Angeles (NL)	23 . . at Chicago (AL)
9 . . . . . Chicago (AL)	24 . . . . . at Cincinnati
10 . . . . at Chicago (NL)	25 . . . . Oakland
11 . . . . . . Seattle	26 . . Los Angeles (AL)
12 . . . . . at Colorado	27 . . at Los Angeles (AL)
13 . . . . . . Oakland	28 . . . . San Diego
13 . . . . . at Seattle	29 . . . . . at Milwaukee
14 . . . . . Milwaukee	30 . . . . . Chicago (NL)
15 . . . . . at San Diego	31 . . at Los Angeles (NL)
15 . . . . . . at Texas	APRIL
	1-3 . . . . Oakland

SEATTLE

MARCH	
3 . . . . . . San Francisco	20 . . . . Arizona
4-5 . . . . . San Diego	21 . . at Los Angeles (AL)
6 . . . . at San Diego	22 . . . . Oakland
7 . . . . . San Diego	23 . . . Los Angeles (AL)
8 . . at Chicago (AL)	24 . . . . . at San Diego
8 . . . at Milwaukee	25 . . . . . at Cleveland
9 . . . . . Cleveland	25 . . . . at Kansas City
10 . . . . . . at Texas	26 . . . . Cincinnati
11 . . . at San Francisco	27 . . at Los Angeles (NL)
12 . . . . Kansas City	28 . . . . . Chicago (NL)
13 . . . . San Francisco	29 . . . . . at Oakland
14 . . . . . at Colorado	31 . . . . at Texas
15 . . . . . at Arizona	APRIL
17 . . . . Texas	1 . . . . . . Chicago (AL)
18 . . . . . Colorado	2 . . . . . . at Colorado
19 . . . . . at Cincinnati	3 . . . . Colorado

ST. LOUIS

MARCH	
4 . . . . . at New York (NL)	19 . . . . . at Washington
5 . . . . . New York (NL)	20 . . . . . New York (NL)
6 . . . . . at Florida	21 . . . . . at Atlanta
7 . . . . Florida	22 . . . . . at Houston
8 . . . . . at Boston	24 . . . . . . Baltimore
9 . . . . at Minnesota	25 . . . . . New York (NL)
10 . . . Washington	26 . . . at Washington
11 . . . . at Florida	27 . . . . Florida
12 . . . . . . Boston	28 . . at New York (NL)
13 . . . . . Houston	29 . . . . . Minnesota
14 . . . at Washington	30 . . at New York (NL)
15 . . . at New York (NL)	31 . . . Washington
16 . . . . Washington	APRIL
18 . . . . . . Atlanta	1 . . . . Florida
19 . . . . at Florida	2-3 . . . . at Minnesota

TAMPA BAY

MARCH	
3 . . . . . at Baltimore	9 . . . . . at Baltimore
4 . . . . . . Baltimore	10 . . . . . . at Boston
5 . . at New York (AL)	11 . . . . at Pittsburgh
6 . . . . Boston	11 . . . . . . Toronto
7 . . at Philadelphia	12 . . . Philadelphia
8 . . . . . . Pittsburgh	13 . . . . Florida
	14 . . . . . at Detroit

---

16 . . . . Boston
17 . . . . . . Minnesota
18 . . at New York (AL)
19 . . . New York (AL)
20 . . . . . Minnesota
21 . . . . at Minnesota
21 . . . . at Pittsburgh
22 . . . . . at Boston
23 . . at Philadelphia
24 . . . . . . Toronto
25 . . . . . Minnesota

TEXAS

MARCH	
4-5 . . . . at Kansas City	19 . . . . . . Cleveland
6 . . . . . Kansas City	20 . . . Los Angeles (NL)
7 . . . . at Cleveland	21 . . . at San Diego
8 . . . Los Angeles (AL)	22 . . at San Francisco
9 . . . . . at Oakland	24 . . . . Chicago (AL)
10 . . . . Seattle	25 . . at Los Angeles (AL)
11 . . . at Colorado	26 . . . . Oakland
12 . . . San Diego	27 . . . at Milwaukee
13 . . . at Cleveland	28 . . . . . Chicago (AL)
14 . . . . . Arizona	29 . . . . . . Colorado
14 . at Los Angeles (NL)	30 . . . . . at Arizona
15 . . . San Francisco	31 . . . . Seattle
16 . . . at Chicago (NL)	APRIL
17 . . . . at Seattle	1 . . . . . . at Cincinnati
18 . . . . . Milwaukee	2-3 . . . . . Kansas City

TORONTO

MARCH	
3 . . . . Detroit	20 . . . . Atlanta
4 . . . . . at Detroit	21 . . . . Boston
5 . . . . . Philadelphia	22 . . . . Detroit
6 . . at New York (AL)	24 . . at Tampa Bay
7 . . . . Detroit	25 . . . . . at Detroit
8 . . . . . at Houston	26 . . . . . . at Boston
10 . . . . Philadelphia	26 . . . . Tampa Bay
11 . . . . at Tampa Bay	27 . . at Pittsburgh
12 . . . . . Houston	28 . . . . . Baltimore
13 . . . . at Atlanta	29 . . . . . . Detroit
14 . . . . . Atlanta	30 . . at New York (AL)
15 . . . . . at Detroit	31 . . . at Philadelphia
17 . . . at Baltimore	APRIL
18 . . . . Baltimore	1 . . . . New York (AL)
19 . . . . at Houston	2-3 . . . . . at Houston

WASHINGTON

MARCH	
4 . . . . at Florida	20 . . . . Florida
4 . . . . . at Houston	21 . . . . . . at Florida
5 . . . . . at Atlanta	22 . . . New York (NL)
6 . . . . New York (NL)	23 . . . . . at Detroit
7 . at New York (NL)	24 . . at New York (AL)
8 . . . . . . Florida	25 . . . . . . Detroit
9 . . . . . . Detroit	26 . . . . . St. Louis
10 . . . at St. Louis	27 . . . . . at Atlanta
11 . . . . Houston	27 . . at New York (NL)
12 . . New York (NL)	28 . . . . . . Atlanta
13 . . . at Houston	29 . . . New York (NL)
14 . . . St. Louis	30 . . . . . at Florida
15 . . . . Atlanta	31 . . . . at St. Louis
16 . . . . . . Florida	APRIL
16 . . at St. Louis	1 . . . . at New York (NL)
17 . . . at Houston	2 . . . . . at Boston
19 . . . . . . St. Louis	3 . . . . Boston

MINOR LEAGUES

MINOR LEAGUE BASEBALL

NATIONAL ASSOCIATION OF PROFESSIONAL BASEBALL LEAGUES

MINOR LEAGUE BASEBALL

Office Address: 9550 16th Street North, St. Petersburg, FL 33716.
Mailing Address: P.O. Box A, St. Petersburg, FL 33731. **Telephone:** (727) 822-6937.
Fax: (727) 821-5819. **Website:** www.milb.com.
Year Founded: 1901.
President, Chief Executive Officer: Pat O'Conner.
Vice President: Stan Brand (Washington, D.C.).
Executive VP/Chief Operating Officer: Tim Purpura.
Manager, Baseball Operations/Executive Assistant to President: Mary Wooters.

Pat O'Conner

Senior Vice President, Business Operations: John Cook. **Vice President, MiLB Vero Beach:** Craig Callan. **Vice President Legal Affairs/General Counsel:** D. Scott Poley. **Assistant Director, Legal Affairs:** Sandie Hebert. **Special Counsel:** George Yund (Cincinnati, OH). **Executive Director, Baseball Operations:** Tim Brunswick.

Director, Media Relations: Steve Densa. **Director, Accounting:** Jonathan Shipman. **Director, Security/Facility Operations:** John Skinner. **Assistant Director, Accounting:** James Dispanet. **Manager, Accounting:** Jeff Carrier. **Director, Information Technology:** Rob Colamarino. **Official Statistician:** Major League Baseball Advanced Media, 75 Ninth Ave., New York, NY 10011. **Telephone:** (212) 485-3444.

2010 Winter Meetings: Walt Disney World Swan and Dolphin Resort, December 6-9.

AFFILIATED MEMBERS/COUNCIL OF LEAGUE PRESIDENTS

Triple-A

League	President	Telephone	Fax Number
International	Randy Mobley	(614) 791-9300	(614) 791-9009
Mexican	Plinio Escalante	011-52-555-557-1007	011-52-555-557-1007
Pacific Coast	Branch Rickey	(719) 636-3399	(719) 636-1199

Double-A

League	President	Telephone	Fax Number
Eastern	Joe McEacharn	(207) 761-2700	(207) 761-7064
Southern	Don Mincher	(770) 321-0400	(770) 321-0037
Texas	Tom Kayser	(210) 545-5297	(210) 545-5298

High Class A

League	President	Telephone	Fax Number
California	Charlie Blaney	(805) 985-8585	(805) 985-8580
Carolina	John Hopkins	(336) 691-9030	(336) 691-9070
Florida State	Chuck Murphy	(386) 252-7479	(386) 252-7495

Low Class A

League	President	Telephone	Fax Number
Midwest	George Spelius	(608) 364-1188	(608) 364-1913
South Atlantic	Eric Krupa	(727) 456-1420	(727) 499-6853

Short-Season

League	President	Telephone	Fax Number
New York-Penn	Ben Hayes	(727) 821-7000	(727) 822-3768
Northwest	Bob Richmond	(208) 429-1511	(208) 429-1525

Rookie Advanced

League	President	Telephone	Fax Number
Appalachian	Lee Landers	(704) 873-5300	(704) 873-4333
Pioneer	Jim McCurdy	(509) 456-7615	(509) 456-0136

Rookie

League	President	Telephone	Fax Number
Arizona	Bob Richmond	(208) 429-1511	(208) 429-1525
Dominican Summer	Orlando Diaz	(809) 532-3619	(809) 532-3619
Gulf Coast	Operated by MILB	(727) 456-1734	(727) 821-5819
Venezuela Summer	Saul Gonzalez	011-58-41-24-0321	011-58-41-24-0705

NATIONAL ASSOCIATION BOARD OF TRUSTEES

TRIPLE-A
At-large: Ken Young (Norfolk). **International League:** Mike Tamburro (Pawtucket). **Pacific Coast League:** Sam Bernabe, Chairman (Iowa). **Mexican League:** Cuauhtemoc Rodriguez (Quintana Roo).

DOUBLE-A
Eastern League: Joe Finley, (Trenton). **Southern League:** Frank Burke (Chattanooga). **Texas League:** Bill Valentine (Arkansas).

CLASS A
California League: Tom Volpe (Stockton). **Carolina League:** Chuck Greenberg (Myrtle Beach). **Florida State League:** Ken Carson, secretary (Dunedin). **Midwest League:** Dave Walker (Burlington). **South Atlantic League:** Chip Moore (Rome).

SHORT-SEASON
New York-Penn League: Bill Gladstone (Tri-City). **Northwest League:** Bob Beban (Eugene).

ROOKIE
Appalachian League: Mitch Lukevics (Princeton). **Pioneer League:** Dave Baggott, vice chairman (Ogden). **Gulf Coast League:** Bill Smith (Twins).

PROFESSIONAL BASEBALL PROMOTION CORPORATION
Office Address: 9550 16th Street North, St. Petersburg, FL 33716. **Mailing Address:** P.O. Box A, St. Petersburg, FL 33731. **Telephone:** (727) 822-6937. **Fax/Marketing:** (727) 894-4227. **Fax/Licensing:** (727) 825-3785.
President: Pat O'Conner.
Executive VP/Chief Operating Officer: Tim Purpura.
Senior Vice President, Business Operations: John Cook. **Vice President, MiLB Vero Beach:** Craig Callan. **Vice President, Legal Affairs/General Counsel:** D. Scott Poley. **Executive Director, Baseball Operations:** Tim Brunswick. **Executive Director, Branded Properties:** Brian Earle. **Executive Director, Sales/Marketing:** Rod Meadows. **Director, Athletics/Marketing, MiLB Vero Beach:** Jeff Biddle. **Director, Information Technology:** Rob Colamarino. **Director, Media Relations:** Steve Densa. **Director, Licensing:** Tina Gust. **Director, Accounting:** Jonathan Shipman. **Director, Security/Facility Operations:** John Skinner. **Senior Assistant Director, Special Operations:** Kelly Butler. **Assistant Director, Licensing:** Carrie Adams. **Assistant Director, Accounting:** James Dispanet. **Assistant Director, Special Operations:** Scott Kravchuk. **Senior Manager, Sales/Marketing Operations:** Melissa Agee. **Manager, Exhibition Services:** Noreen Brantner. **Manager, Baseball Operations/Legal Affairs:** Lou Brown, Esq. **Manager, Accounting:** Jeff Carrier. **Manager, Sponsor Relations:** Nicole Ferro. **Manager, Contracts:** Jeannette Machicote. **Manager, Team Relations:** Mary Marandi. **DAP Manager, Durham Operations/Alumni Association/Charities:** Jill Rusinko. **Manager, Trademarks:** Bryan Sayre. **Manager, Special Operations:** Shanelle Slaughter. **Asst. to the Vice President, MiLB Vero Beach:** Nancy Gollnick. **Assistant/Special Operations:** Darryl Henderson. **Assistant to Marketing Director, Sponsorship Development:** Heather Raburn. **Assistant/Baseball Operations:** Andy Shultz.

PROFESSIONAL BASEBALL UMPIRE CORPORATION
Office Address: 9550 16th Street North, St. Petersburg, FL 33716. **Mailing Address:** P.O. Box A, St. Petersburg, FL 33731. **Telephone:** (727) 822-6937. **Fax:** (727) 821-5819.
President: Pat O'Conner. **Treasurer/Vice President Administration:** Tim Purpura. **Secretary/Vice President, Legal Affairs/General Counsel:** D. Scott Poley. **Executive Director, PBUC:** Justin Klemm (Branchburg, NJ). **Chief, Instruction/Field Evaluator:** Mike Felt (Lansing, MI).
Field Evaluators/Instructors: Jorge Bauza (San Juan, PR), Larry Reveal (Chesapeake, VA). **Evaluator:** Dusty Dellinger (China Grove, NC). **Special Assistant, PBUC:** Lillian Patterson.

GENERAL INFORMATION

	Regular Season				All-Star Games		
	Teams	Games	Opening Day	Closing Day	Date	Host	
International	14	144	April 8	Sept. 6	*July 14	Lehigh Valley	
Pacific Coast	16	144	April 8	Sept. 6	*July 14	Lehigh Valley	
Eastern	12	142	April 8	Sept. 6	July 14	Harrisburg	
Southern	10	140	April 8	Sept. 6	July 12	Huntsville	
Texas	8	140	April 8	Sept. 6	June 30	Midland	
California	10	140	April 8	Sept. 6	#June 22	Myrtle Beach	
Carolina	8	140	April 8	Sept. 6	#June 22	Myrtle Beach	
Florida State	12	140	April 8	Sept. 5	June 12	Brevard County	
Midwest	16	140	April 8	Sept. 6	June 22	Fort Wayne	
South Atlantic	14	140	April 8	Sept. 6	June 22	Greenville	
New York-Penn	14	76	June 18	Sept. 5	Aug. 17	Staten Island	
Northwest	8	76	June 18	Sept. 5	None		
Appalachian	10	68	June 22	Aug. 31	None		
Pioneer	8	76	June 21	Sept. 9	None		
Arizona	12	56	June 21	Aug. 29	None		
Gulf Coast	15	56/60	June 21	Aug. 29	None		

*Triple-A All-Star Game. #California League vs. Carolina League

INTERNATIONAL LEAGUE

TRIPLE-A

Office Address: 55 South High St., Suite 202, Dublin, Ohio 43017.
Telephone: (614) 791-9300. **Fax:** (614) 791-9009.
E-Mail Address: office@ilbaseball.com. **Website:** www.ilbaseball.com.
Years League Active: 1884-
President/Treasurer: Randy Mobley
Vice Presidents: Harold Cooper, Dave Rosenfield, Tex Simone.
Assistant to the President: Chris Sprague. **Corporate Secretary:** Max Schumacher.
Directors: Bruce Baldwin (Gwinnett), Don Beaver (Charlotte), Joe Finley (Lehigh Valley), George Habel (Durham), Joe Napoli (Toledo), Bob Rich Jr. (Buffalo), Dave Rosenfield (Norfolk), Jeremy Ruby (Scranton/Wilkes-Barre), Ken Schnacke (Columbus), Max Schumacher (Indianapolis), Naomi Silver (Rochester), John Simone (Syracuse), Mike Tamburro (Pawtucket), Gary Ulmer (Louisville).
Office Manager: Gretchen Addison.
Division Structure: North-Buffalo, Lehigh Valley, Pawtucket, Rochester, Scranton/Wilkes-Barre, Syracuse. **West-**Columbus, Indianapolis, Louisville, Toledo. **South-**Charlotte, Durham, Gwinnett, Norfolk.
Regular Season: 144 games. **2010 Opening Date:** April 8. **Closing Date:** Sept. 6.
All-Star Game: July 14 at Lehigh Valley (IL vs. Pacific Coast League).
Playoff Format: South winner meets West winner in best of five series; wild card (non-division winner with best winning percentage) meets North winner in best of five series. Winners meet in best of five series for Governors' Cup championship.
Triple-A Baseball National Championship Game: Sept. 21, Oklahoma City (IL vs. Pacific Coast League).
Roster Limit: 24. **Player Eligibility:** No restrictions.
Official Baseball: Rawlings ROM-INT.
Umpires: Chris Bakke (Menahga, MN), Lance Barrett (Burleson, TX), Scott Barry (Quincy, MI), Toby Basner (Snellville, GA), Damien Beal (Tampa, FL), Jason Bradley (Blackshear, GA), Fran Burke, (Ridgewood, NJ), Victor Carapazza (Franklin, TN), John Conrad (Meriden, CT), Chris Conroy (North Adams, MA), Derek Crabill (Wonder Lake, IL), Mike Estabrook (Boynton Beach, FL), Chad Fairchild (Parrish, FL), Manny Gonzalez (Venezuela), James Hoye (North Royalton, OH), Adrian Johnson (Houston, TX), Mark Lollo (New Lexington, OH), Jon Merry (Dahlonega, GA), Alan Porter (Warminster, PA), Bobby Price (Marlton, NJ), David Rackley (League City, TX), Art Thigpen (Lakeland, FL), David Uyl (Shorewood, IL), Justin Vogel (Jacksonville, FL), Christopher Ward (Ashland, KY).

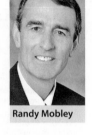

Randy Mobley

STADIUM INFORMATION

Club	Stadium	Opened	Dimensions			Capacity	2009 Att.
			LF	CF	RF		
Buffalo	Coca-Cola Field	1988	325	404	325	18,150	529,789
Charlotte	Knights Stadium	1990	325	400	325	10,002	320,427
Columbus	Huntington Park	2009	325	400	330	15,000	666,797
Durham	Durham Bulls Athletic Park	1995	305	400	327	10,000	488,385
Gwinnett	Gwinnett Stadium	2009	325	400	325	10,000	423,556
Indianapolis	Victory Field	1996	320	402	320	14,500	549,552
Lehigh Valley	Coca-Cola Park	2008	336	400	325	10,000	641,335
Louisville	Louisville Slugger Field	2000	325	400	340	13,131	612,525
Norfolk	Harbor Park	1993	333	410	338	12,067	387,153
Pawtucket	McCoy Stadium	1946	325	400	325	10,031	625,561
Rochester	Frontier Field	1997	335	402	325	10,840	461,946
Scranton/WB	PNC Field	1989	330	408	330	10,982	358,888
Syracuse	Alliance Bank Stadium	1997	330	400	330	11,671	392,518
Toledo	Fifth Third Field	2002	320	412	315	8,943	559,037

BUFFALO BISONS

Office Address: Coca-Cola Field, One James D. Griffin Plaza, Buffalo, NY 14203.
Telephone: (716) 846-2000. **Fax:** (716) 852-6530.
E-Mail address: info@bisons.com. **Website:** www.bisons.com.
Affiliation (first year): New York Mets (2009). **Years in League:** 1886-90, 1912-70, 1998-.

OWNERSHIP, MANAGEMENT

Operated By: Rich Products Corp.
Principal Owner/President: Robert Rich Jr. **President, Rich Entertainment Group:** Melinda Rich. **President, Rich Baseball Operations:** Jon Dandes. **Vice President/Treasurer:** David Rich. **VP/Secretary:** William Gisel.
VP/General Manager: Mike Buczkowski. **VP, Finance:** Joseph Segarra. **Corporate Counsel:** Jill Bond, William

Grieshober. **Director, Sales:** Christopher Hill. **Director, Stadium Operations:** Tom Sciarrino. **Controller:** Kevin Parkinson. **Senior Accountants:** Rita Clark, Nicole Winiarski. **Accountant:** Amy Delaney. **Director, Ticket Operations:** Mike Poreda. **Director, Public Relations:** Brad Bisbing. **Director, Game Day Entertainment/Promotions Coordinator:** Matt LaSota. **Sales Coordinator:** Cindy Smith. **Account Executives:** Mark Gordon, Jim Harrington, Robert Kates, Amanda Kolin, Geoff Lundquist, Burt Mirti, Frank Mooney, Anthony Sprague. **Manager, Merchandise:** Kathleen Wind. **Manager, Office Services:** Margaret Russo. **Executive Assistant:** Tina Lesher. **Community Relations:** Gail Hodges. **Director, Food Services:** Robert Free. **Assistant Concessions Manager:** Roger Buczek. **Head Groundskeeper:** Dan Blank. **Chief Engineer:** Pat Chella. **Home Clubhouse/Baseball Operations Coordinator:** Scott Lesher. **Visiting Clubhouse Manager:** Dan Brick.

FIELD STAFF
   Manager: Ken Oberkfell. **Coach:** Jack Voigt. **Pitching Coach:** Ricky Bones. **Trainer:** Brian Chicklo.

GAME INFORMATION
   Radio Announcers: Ben Wagner, Duke McGuire. **No of Games Broadcast:** Home-72, Road-72. **Flagship Station:** WWKB-1520.
   PA Announcer: Jason Mollica. **Official Scorers:** Kevin Lester, Jon Dare.
   Stadium Name: Coca-Cola Field. **Location:** From north, take I-190 to Elm Street exit, left onto Swan Street. From east, take I-190 West to exit 51 (Route 33) to end, exit at Oak Street, right onto Swan Street. From west, take I-190 East, exit 53 to I-90 North, exit at Elm Street, left onto Swan Street. **Standard Game Times:** 7:05 p.m., 1:05 Sunday Ticket Price Range: $5-18.
   Visiting Club Hotel: Adams Mark Hotel, 120 Church St, Buffalo, NY 14202. **Telephone:** (716) 845-5100. Hyatt Hotel, 2 Fountain Plaza, Buffalo, NY 14202. **Telephone:** (716) 856-1234.

CHARLOTTE KNIGHTS

   Office Address: 2280 Deerfield Dr., Fort Mill, SC 29715.
   Telephone: (704) 357-8071. **Fax:** (704) 329-2155.
   E-Mail address: knights@charlotteknights.com. **Website:** www.charlotteknights.com.
   Affiliation (first year): Chicago White Sox (1999). **Years in League:** 1993-

OWNERSHIP, MANAGEMENT
   Operated by: Knights Baseball, LLC.
   Principal Owners: Don Beaver, Bill Allen.
   Vice President/General Manager: Dan Rajkowski. **Assistant General Manager:** Danny Tetzlaff. **Director, Media Relations:** John Agresti. **Vice President, Marketing/Development:** Mike Riviello. **Director, Broadcasting/Team Travel:** Matt Swierad. **Vice President, Sales:** Chris Semmens. **Operations Manager:** Mark McKinnon. **Business Manager:** Michael Sanger. **Sales Executive:** Heath Dillard. **Ticket Sales Representatives:** Jacob Giles, Tony Furr Jr., Dave LaCroix, Matt Willward. **Box Office Coordinator:** Meredith Storrie. **Director, Merchandise:** Becka Leveille. **Head Groundskeeper:** Eddie Busque. **Clubhouse Manager:** Dan Morphis. **Manager, Media Relations:** Patrick Starck. **Coordinator, Community/Team Relations:** Sarah Szabo. **Corporate Sales Account Executive:** Brett Butler. **Executive Assistant to General Manager:** Julie Clark.

FIELD STAFF
   Manager: Chris Chambliss. **Coach:** Gary Ward. **Pitching Coach:** Richard Dotson. **Trainer:** Scott Johnson. **Strength/Conditioning:** Chad Efron.

GAME INFORMATION
   Radio Announcer: Mike Pacheco, Matt Swierad. **No. of Games Broadcast:** Home-72 Road-72. **Flagship Station:** WRHI 1340-AM/94.3-FM.
   PA Announcer: Ken Conrad. **Official Scorers:** Sam Copeland, Bill Walker.
   Stadium Name: Knights Stadium. **Location:** Exit 88 off I-77, east on Gold Hill Road. **Ticket Price Range:** $8-13.
   Visiting Club Hotel: Comfort Suites, 10415 Centrum Parkway, Pineville, NC 28134. **Telephone:** 704-540-0559.

COLUMBUS CLIPPERS

   Office Address: 330 Huntington Park Lane, Columbus, OH 43215.
   Telephone: (614) 462-5250. **Fax:** (614) 462-3271. Tickets: (614) 462-2757.
   E-Mail address: info@clippersbaseball.com. **Website:** www.clippersbaseball.com.
   Affiliation (first year): Cleveland Indians (2009). **Years in League:** 1955-70, 1977-

OWNERSHIP, MANAGEMENT
   Operated By: Columbus Baseball Team Inc.
   Principal Owner: Franklin County, Ohio. **Board of Directors:** Steven Francis, Tom Fries, Wayne Harer, Thomas Katzenmeyer, David Leland, Cathy Lyttle, Richard Smith, McCullough Williams.
   President/General Manager: Ken Schnacke. **Assistant GM:** Mark Warren. **Director, Ballpark Operations:** Steve Dalin. **Assistant Director, Ballpark Operations:** Phil Collila. **Director, Ticket Operations:** Scott Ziegler. **Assistant Director, Ticket Operations:** Eddie Langhenry. **Director, Marketing/Sales:** Mark Galuska. **Assistant Director, Marketing:** Ty Debevoise. **Assistant Director, Sales:** Kyle Blizzard, Brittany McKittrick. **Director, Communications/**

Media/Team Historian: Joe Santry. **Assistant Director, Media Relations:** Anthony Slosser. **Assistant Director, Communications:** Ben Leland. **Assistant Director, Communications/Webcast Operations:** Paul Loper. **Director, Broadcasting:** Scott Leo. **Assistant Director, Broadcasting:** Ryan Mitchell. **Director, Merchandising:** Krista Oberlander. **Assistant Director, Merchandising:** Brittany White. **Director, Group Sales:** Ben Keller. **Assistant Director, Group Sales:** Brett Patton, Gabe Norris, Jay Schlater. **Director, Multimedia:** Jim Grogan. **Assistant Directors, Multimedia:** Yoshi Ando, Josh Glenn. **Director, Finance:** Bonnie Badgley. **Executive Assistant to the President/GM:** Ashley Alexander. **Office Manager:** Kelly Ryther. **Director, Sponsor Relationships:** Joyce Martin. **Director, Event Planning:** Micki Shier. **Assistant Director, Event Planning:** Arielle Miller, Sara Rudolph. **Director, Clubhouse Operations:** George Robinson. **Clubhouse Manager:** Matt Pruzinsky. **Ballpark Superintendent:** Gary Delozier. **Head Groundskeeper:** Colin Lattimer. **Assistant Groundskeeper:** Cliff Biegler.

FIELD STAFF

Manager: Torey Lovullo. **Hitting Coach:** Jon Nunnally. **Pitching Coach:** Scott Radinsky. **Trainer:** Jeff Desjardins. **Strength/Conditioning Coach:** Brendan Verner.

GAME INFORMATION

Radio Announcer: Scott Leo. **No of Games Broadcast:** Home-72, Road-72. **Flagship Station:** WMNI 920AM.
PA Announcer: Colin Smith. **Official Scorer:** Jim Habermehl.
Stadium Name: Huntington Park. **Location: From north:** South on I-71 to I-670 west. Exit at Neil Avenue. Turn left at intersection onto Neil Avenue. **From south:** North on I-71. Exit at Front St. (#100A). Turn left at intersection onto Front Street. Turn left onto Nationwide Blvd. **From east:** West on I-70. Exit at Fourth Street. Continue on Fulton Street to Front Street. Turn right onto Front Street. Turn left onto Nationwide Blvd. **From west:** East on I-70. Exit at Fourth Street. Continue on Fulton Street to Front Street. Turn right onto Front Street. Turn left onto Nationwide Blvd.
Ticket Price Range: $6-15.
Visiting Club Hotel: Crowne Plaza, 33 E. Nationwide Blvd., Columbus, OH 43215. **Telephone:** 877-348-2424. Drury Hotels Columbus Convention Center, 88 E. Nationwide Blvd., Columbus, OH 43215. **Telephone:** 614-221-7008. Hyatt Regency Downtown, 350 N. High St., Columbus, OH 43215. **Telephone:** 614-463-1234.

DURHAM BULLS

Office Address: 409 Blackwell St., Durham, NC 27701.
Mailing Address: P.O. Box 507, Durham, NC 27702.
Telephone: (919) 687-6500. **Fax:** (919) 687-6560.
Website: www.durhambulls.com
Affiliation (first year): Tampa Bay Rays (1998). **Years in League:** 1998-

OWNERSHIP, MANAGEMENT

Operated By: Capitol Broadcasting Company, Inc.
President, CEO: Jim Goodmon.
Vice President: George Habel.
General Manager: Mike Birling. **Assistant GM:** Jon Bishop. **Director, Corporate Partnerships:** Chris Overby. **Account Executives, Sponsorship:** Rich Brady, Ashley Giovenco, Neil Solondz. **Coordinators, Sponsorship Services:** Allison Phillips, Molly Boyce. **Director, Media Relations/Promotions:** Matt DeMargel. **Coordinator, Multimedia:** John Blotzer Jr. **Coordinator, Mascot/Community Relations:** Nicholas Tennant. **Assistant, Media Relations:** Andrew Zelinsky. **Director, Ticket Operations:** Tim Season. **Business Development Coordinators:** Jonathan Feldman, Mike Miller, Brian Simorka, Ryan Tuttle, Mary Beth Warfford. **Box Office Sales:** Jerry Mach. **Director, Stadium Operations:** Josh Nance. **GM, Concessions:** Tammy Scott. **Assistant GM, Concessions:** Ralph Orona. **Head Groundskeeper:** Scott Strickland. **Manager, Business:** Rhonda Carlile. **Supervisor, Accounting:** Theresa Stocking. **Accountant:** Emily Farlow. **Manager, Home Clubhouse:** Colin Saunders. **Manager, Visiting/Umpires Clubhouses:** Aaron Kuehner. **Team Ambassador:** Bill Law.

FIELD STAFF

Manager: Charlie Montoyo. **Coach:** Dave Myers. **Pitching Coach:** Xavier Hernandez. **Trainer:** Rodger Fleming.

GAME INFORMATION

Radio Announcers: Steve Barnes, Neil Solondz, Ken Tanner. **No. of Games Broadcast:** Home-72, Road-72. **Flagship Station:** 620-AM The Buzz, 99.9 FM the Fan.
PA Announcer: Tony Riggsbee. **Official Scorer:** Brent Belvin.
Stadium Name: Durham Bulls Athletic Park. **Location:** From Raleigh, I-40 West to Highway 147 North, exit 12B to Willard, two blocks on Willard to stadium. From I-85, Gregson Street exit to downtown, left on Chapel Hill Street, right on Mangum Street. **Standard Game Times:** 7 p.m., Sunday 5 p.m. **Ticket Price Range:** $6-9.
Visiting Club Hotel: Durham Marriot at the Civic Center, 201 Foster St., Durham, NC 27701. **Telephone:** (919) 768-6000.

GWINNETT BRAVES

Office Address: One Braves Ave, Lawrenceville, GA 30043.
Mailing Address: PO Box 490310, Lawrenceville, GA 30049.
Telephone: (678) 277-0300. **Fax:** (678) 277-0338

E-Mail Address: gwinnettinfo@braves.com. **Website:** www.gwinnettbraves.com
Affiliation (first year): Atlanta Braves (1966). **Years in League:** 1884, 1915-17, 1954-64, 1966-

OWNERSHIP, MANAGEMENT

General Manager: North Johnson. **Assistant General Managers:** Bill Blackwell, Toby Wyman. **Office Manager:** Deanne Proud. **Manager, Stadium Operations:** Ryan Stoltenberg. **Manager, Field Maintenance:** Gerry Huppman. **Manager, Public/Community Affairs:** Courtney Lawson. **Manager, Corporate/Group Sales:** Samantha Dunn. **Manager, Ticket Operations:** Mike Castle. **Manager, Marketing/Promotions:** Unavailable. **Manager, Merchandise:** Michele Jones. **Coordinator, Marketing/Promotions:** Travis Orton. **Coordinator, Public Affairs:** Nick Margiasso. **Coordinator, Stadium Operations:** Jonathan Blair. **Ticket/Corporate Sales Representatives:** Jerry Pennington, Lindsay Harmon, Kerry Pritchard, Paige Fleckenstien.

FIELD STAFF

Manager: Dave Brundage. **Coach:** Jamie Dismuke. **Pitching Coach:** Derek Botelho. **Trainer:** Mike Graus.

GAME INFORMATION

Radio Announcers: Tony Schiavone, Judd Hickinbotham. **No of Games Broadcast:** Home-72 Road-72. **Flagship Station:** WDUN 550-AM.
PA Announcer: Jeff Bergmann. **Official Scorers:** Tim Gaines, Frank Barnett, James Roberts, Jamie Britt.
Stadium Name: Gwinnett Stadium. **Location:** I-85 (at Exit 115, S.R. 20 West) and I-985 (at Exit 4), follow signs to park. **Ticket Price Range:** $5-30.
Visiting Club Hotel: Courtyard by Marriott Buford/Mall of Georgia, 1405 Mall of Georgia Boulevard, Buford, GA 30519. **Telephone:** (678) 215-8007.

INDIANAPOLIS INDIANS

Office Address: 501 W. Maryland Street, Indianapolis, IN 46225.
Telephone: (317) 269-3542. **Fax:** (317) 269-3541.
E-Mail address: indians@indyindians.com. **Website:** www.indyindians.com.
Affiliation (first year): Pittsburgh Pirates (2005). **Years in League:** 1963, 1998-

OWNERSHIP, MANAGEMENT

Operated By: Indians Inc.
President/Chairman of the Board: Max Schumacher.
Vice President/General Manager: Cal Burleson. **Assistant General Manager:** Randy Lewandowski. **Director, Marketing/Communications:** Chris Herndon. **Director, Facilities:** Tim Hughes. **Director, Business Operations:** Brad Morris. **Director, Tickets:** Matt Guay. **Director, Corporate Partnerships:** Joel Zawacki. **Director, Special Projects:** Bruce Schumacher. **Director, Merchandising:** Mark Schumacher. **Director, Broadcasting:** Howard Kellman. **Event Operations Manager:** Mark Anderson. **Stadium Operations Manager:** Steve Bray. **Stadium Maintenance Manager:** Allan Danehy. **Office Manager:** Julie Fischer. **Administrative Assistant:** Angela Kendall. **Assistant Director, Facilities:** Bill Sampson. **Marketing Manager:** Diana Biette. **Media Relations Manager:** Brian Bosma. **Manager, Community Relations/Promotions:** Ryan Bowman. **Promotions Coordinator:** Brian McLaughlin. **Merchandising Assistant:** Stu Tobias. **Sponsorship Sales Coordinator:** Laura Gaybrick. **Sponsorship Services Coordinator:** Keri Oberting. **Sponsorship Sales Executive:** Bob Woelfel. **Senior Ticket/Premium Services Manager:** Kerry Vick. **Ticket Sales Manager:** Chad Bohm. **Ticket Services Manager:** Bryan Spisak. **Ticket Sales Executives:** Ryan Barrett, Kyle Fisher, Hannah Guess, Jonathan Howard, Scott McCauley. **Ticket Services Assistants:** Lauren Davis, Terri Martin, Zach Wogtech. **Media Relations Assistant:** Chris Binnall. **Community Relations Assistant:** Even DePotter. **Merchandise Assistant:** Missy Weaver. **Promotions Assistant:** Chris Marcum. **Operations Assistant:** Marc Porter. **Head Groundskeeper:** Joey Stevenson. **Assistant Groundskeeper:** Evan Buckley. **Home Clubhouse Manager:** Bob Martin. **Visiting Clubhouse Manager:** Jeremy Martin.

FIELD STAFF

Manager: Frank Kremblas. **Hitting Coach:** Jeff Branson. **Pitching Coach:** Dean Treanor. **Trainer:** Thomas Pribyl. **Strength/Conditioning Coach:** Mubarak Malik.

GAME INFORMATION

Radio Announcer: Howard Kellman, Scott McCauley. **No. of Games Broadcast:** Home-72, Road-72. **Flagship Station:** WXLW 950-AM.
PA Announcer: Bruce Schumacher. **Official Scorers:** Bill McAfee, Gary Johnson, Kim Rogers, Bill Potter.
Stadium Name: Victory Field. **Location:** I-70 to West Street exit, north on West Street to ballpark. I-65 to Martin Luther King and West Street exit, south on West Street to ballpark. **Standard Game Times:** 7 p.m. on Mon/Tues/Thur/Sat., 1 p.m. on Wed., 7:15 p.m. on Fri., 2 p.m. on Sun. **Ticket Price Range:** $9-14.
Visiting Club Hotels: Courtyard by Marriott, 601 West Washington, Indianapolis, IN 46204. **Telephone:** (317) 822-9054. SpringHill Suites, 601 West Washington, Indianapolis, IN 46204. **Telephone:** (317) 972-7293.
Fairfield Inn & Suites, 501 West Washington, Indianapolis, IN 46204. **Telephone:** (317) 636-7678.

LEHIGH VALLEY IRONPIGS

Office Address: 1050 IronPigs Way, Allentown, PA 18109.
Telephone: (610) 841-7447. **Fax:** (610) 841-1509.
E-Mail address: info@ironpigsbaseball.com. **Website:** www.ironpigsbaseball.com.
Affiliation (first year): Philadelphia Phillies (2008). **Years in League:** 2008-

OWNERSHIP, MANAGEMENT

Ownership: Gracie Baseball LP,
President: Chuck Domino.
General Manager: Kurt Landes. **Assistant GM:** Howard Scharf. **Director, Media Relations:** Matt Provence. **Manager, Media Relations:** Jon Schaeffer. **Director, Community Relations:** Sarah Marten. **Director, Merchandise:** Adam Fondl. **Director, Ticket Sales:** Scott Hodge. **Director, Ticket Operations:** Amy Schoch. **Director, Group Sales:** Don Wilson. **Director, Marketing:** Ron Rushe. **Marketing Services Managers:** Corey Bugno, Erin Holt. **Director, Creative Services:** Matt Zidik. **Director, Promotions:** Lindsey Knupp. **Director, Special Events/Catering:** Mary Nixon. **Manager, Special Events/Catering:** Nicole Barela. **Director, Concessions:** Alex Rivera. **Manager, Concessions:** Brock Hartranft. **Executive Chef:** John Ponist. **Director, Finance:** Deb Landes. **Manager, Finance:** Michelle Perl. **Stadium Operations Managers:** Paul Cashin, Jason Kiesel. **Marketing Managers:** Scott Evans, Brandon Greene, Rick Polster. **Manager, Ticket Operations:** Erin Owens. **Tickets/Group Representatives:** Mark Anderson, Brad Ludwig, Alicia Rohrbach, Justin Scariato, Brandon Smith, Katie Ward. **Director, Field Operations:** Bill Butler. **Receptionist:** Ashley Bielec.

FIELD STAFF

Manager: Dave Huppert. **Hitting Coach:** Greg Gross. **Pitching Coach:** Rod Nichols. **Trainer:** Jason Kirkman. **Strength/Conditioning:** Justin Zabrosky.

GAME INFORMATION

Radio Announcers: Matt Provence, Jon Schaeffer. **No. Games Broadcast:** 144 (72 Home; 72 Away). **Flagship Radio Station:** ESPN 1240/1320 AM. **Television Station:** TV2. **Television Announcers:** Mike Zambelli, Steve Degler, Matt Provence. **No. Games Televised:** 72 Home. **PA Announcer:** Tim Chorones. **Official Scorers:** Jack Logic, David Sheriff.
Stadium Name: Coca-Cola Park.
Location: Take U.S. 22 to exit for Airport Road South. Head south, make right on American Parkway. Left into stadium. **Standard Game Times:** 7:05 p.m.; Sat. 6:35 p.m., Sun. 1:35 p.m. (April-May), 5:35 p.m. (June-August).
Visiting Club Hotel: Hotel Bethlehem, 437 Main Street, Bethlehem, PA 18018. **Telephone:** (610) 625-5000.

LOUISVILLE BATS

Office Address: 401 E. Main St, Louisville, KY 40202.
Telephone: (502) 212-2287. **Fax:** (502) 515-2255.
E-Mail address: info@batsbaseball.com. **Website:** www.batsbaseball.com.
Affiliation (first year): Cincinnati Reds (2000). **Years in League:** 1998-

OWNERSHIP, MANAGEMENT

Chariman: Dan Ulmer Jr. **Board of Directors:** Edward Glasscock, Gary Ulmer, Roberts Stallings, Kenny Huber, Steve Trager, J. **Michael Brown.**
President/CEO: Gary Ulmer. **Vice President/General Manager:** Dale Owens. **Assistant GM/Director, Marketing:** Greg Galiette. **Director, Stadium Operations:** Scott Shoemaker. **Director, Ticket Sales:** James Breeding. **Director, Baseball Operations:** Earl Stubblefield. **Controller:** Michele Anderson. **Manager, Tickets:** George Veith. **Director, Ticket Operations:** Kyle Reh. **Director, Public Relations:** Megan Dimond. **Director, Group Sales:** Bryan McBride. **Director, Broadcasting:** Matt Andrews. **Director, Suite Level Services:** Kerri Ferrell. **Senior Account Executives:** Hal Norwood, Jason Abraham, Josh Hargreaves, Curtis Cunningham. **Community Relations Director/Assistant Director, Public Relations:** Nick Evans. **Assistant Director, Stadium Operations:** Randy Williams. **Account Executives:** Evan Patrick, Sarah Nordman, Tony Brown, Patrick Crush. **Groundskeeper:** Tom Nielsen.

FIELD STAFF

Manager: Rick Sweet. **Hitting Coach:** Adrian "Smokey" Garrett. **Pitching Coach:** Ted Power. **Trainer:** Tomas Vera.

GAME INFORMATION

Radio Announcers: Jim Kelch, Matt Andrews. **No. of Games Broadcast:** Home-72, Road-72. **Flagship Station:** WKRD 790-AM.
PA Announcer: Charles Gazaway. **Official Scorer:** Ken Horn. **Organist:** Bob Ramsey.
Stadium Name: Louisville Slugger Field. **Location:** I-64 and I-71 to I-65 South/North to Brook Street exit, right on Market Street, left on Jackson Street; stadium on Main Street between Jackson and Preston. **Ticket Price Range:** $6-11.
Visiting Club Hotel: Galt House Hotel, 140 North Fourth Street, Louisville, KY 40202. **Telephone:** (502) 589-5200.

NORFOLK TIDES

Office Address: 150 Park Ave, Norfolk, VA 23510.
Telephone: (757) 622-2222. **Fax:** (757) 624-9090.
E-Mail Address: receptionist@norfolktides.com. **Website:** www.norfolktides.com.
Affiliation (first year): Baltimore Orioles (2007). **Years in League:** 1969-

OWNERSHIP, MANAGEMENT

Operated By: Tides Baseball Club Inc.
President: Ken Young.
General Manager: Dave Rosenfield. **Assistant GM:** Ben Giancola. **Business Manager:** Mike Giedlin. **Director, Media Relations:** Ian Locke. **Director, Community Relations:** Heather McKeating. **Director, Ticket Operations:** Gretchen Todd. **Business Manager:** Mike Giedlin. **Director, Group Sales:** Stephanie Brammer. **Director, Stadium Operations:** Mike Zeman. **Manager, Merchandising:** Ann Marie Piddisi. **Corporate Sponsorships, Promotions:** Jonathan Mensink, Mike Watkins. **Director, Corporate Development/Military Affairs:** H.M. "Bones" Reynolds. **Assistant Director, Stadium Operations:** Mike Cardwell. **Box Office Manager:** Linda Waisanen. **Event Staff Manager:** Kayla Seil. **Ticket Office Assistant:** Sze Fong. **Administrative Assistant:** Lisa Cox. **Group Sales Assistants:** Sara Keyzers, Christina Dewey. **Head Groundskeeper:** Kenny Magner. **Assistant Groundskeeper:** Keith Collins. Home **Clubhouse Manager:** Kevin Casey. **Visiting Clubhouse Manager:** Mark Bunge.

FIELD STAFF

Manager: Gary Allenson. **Coach:** Richie Hebner. **Pitching Coach:** Mike Griffin. **Trainer:** Mark Shires.

GAME INFORMATION

Radio Announcers: Bob Socci, Pete Michaud. **No. of Games Broadcast:** Home-72, Road-72. **Flagship Station:** ESPN 94.1 FM.
PA Announcers: John Lewis, Jack Ankerson. **Official Scorers:** Dave Lewis, Mike Holtzclaw.
Stadium Name: Harbor Park. **Location:** Exit 9, 11A or 11B off I-264, adjacent to the Elizabeth River in downtown Norfolk. **Ticket Price Range:** $9.50-11.
Visiting Club Hotel: Sheraton Waterside, 777 Waterside Dr, Norfolk, VA 23510. **Telephone:** (757) 622-6664.

PAWTUCKET RED SOX

Office Address: One Ben Mondor Way, Pawtucket, RI 02860.
Mailing Address: P.O. Box 2365, Pawtucket, RI 02861.
Telephone: (401) 724-7300. **Fax:** (401) 724-2140.
E-Mail Address: info@pawsox.com. **Website:** www.pawsox.com.
Affiliation (first year): Boston Red Sox (1973). **Years in League:** 1973-

OWNERSHIP, MANAGEMENT

Operated by: Pawtucket Red Sox Baseball Club, Inc.
Chairman: Ben Mondor. **President:** Mike Tamburro.
Vice President/General Manager: Lou Schwechheimer. **VP, Chief Financial Officer:** Matt White. **VP, Sales/Marketing:** Michael Gwynn. **VP, Stadium Operations:** Mick Tedesco. **VP, Public Relations:** Bill Wanless. **Director, Community Relations:** Jeff Bradley. **Manager, Sales:** Augusto Rojas. **Manager, Finance:** Kathryn Tingley. **Director, Merchandising:** Eric Petterson. **Director, Media Creation:** Kevin Galligan. **Director, Concession Services:** Jim Hogan. **Director, Corporate Sales:** Mike Abramson. **Director, Warehouse Operations:** Dave Johnson. **Director, Group Sales:** Bill Crawford. **Assistant Director, Community Relations:** Becky Berta. **Director, Ticket Operations:** Kelly Bongiovanni. **Account Executives:** Kelsey Albair, Ben Bradley. **Field Superintendant:** Matt McKinnon. **Assistant Groundskeeper:** Kyle Carney. **Director, Security:** Rick Medeiros. **Director, Clubhouse Operations:** Carl Goodreau. **Executive Chef:** Ken Bowdish.

FIELD STAFF

Manager: Torey Lovullo. Hitting Coach: Gerald Perry. **Pitching Coach:** Rich Sauveur. **Trainer:** Jon Jochim.

GAME INFORMATION

Radio Announcer: Dan Hoard, Steve Hyder. **No. of Games Broadcast:** Home-72, Away-72. **Flagship Station:** WHJJ 920-AM.
PA Announcer: Jim Martin. **Official Scorer:** Bruce Guindon.
Stadium Name: McCoy Stadium. **Location:** From north, 95 South to exit 2A in Massachusetts (Newport Ave.), follow Newport Ave. for 2 miles, right on Columbus Ave., follow one mile, stadium on right. From south, 95 North to exit 28 (School Street), right at bottom of exit ramp, through two sets of lights, left onto Pond Street, right on Columbus Ave., stadium entrance on left. From west (Worcester), 295 North to 95 South and follow directions from north. From east (Fall River), 195 West to 95 North and follow directions from south. **Standard Game Times:** 7 p.m.; Sat. 6, Sun. 1. **Ticket Price Range:** $6-10.
Visiting Club Hotel: Comfort Inn, 2 George St., Pawtucket, RI 02860. **Telephone:** (401) 723-6700.

ROCHESTER RED WINGS

Office Address: One Morrie Silver Way, Rochester, NY 14608.
Telephone: (585) 454-1001. **Fax:** (585) 454-1056, (585) 454-1057.
E-Mail Address: info@redwingsbaseball.com. **Website:** www.redwingsbaseball.com.
Affiliation (first year): Minnesota Twins (2003). **Years in League:** 1885-89, 1891-92, 1895-

OWNERSHIP, MANAGEMENT

Operated by: Rochester Community Baseball.
CEO, President: Naomi Silver. **Chairman:** Gary Larder.
General Manager: Dan Mason. **Assistant GM:** Will Rumbold. **Controller:** Darlene Giardina. **Head Groundskeeper:** Gene Buonomo. **Director, Media/Public Relations:** Chuck Hinkel. **Director, Corporate Development:** Nick Sciarratta. **Group/Picnic Director:** Parker Allen. **Director, Promotions:** Matt Cipro. **Director, Ticket Operations:** Rob Dermody. **Director, Production:** Jeff Coltoniak. **Director, Merchandising:** Barbara Moore. **Director, Human Resources:** Paula LoVerde. **Account Executive:** Danielle Barone, Bob Craig. **Executive Secretary:** Ginny Colbert. **Director, Food Services:** Jeff Dodge. **Manager, Catering:** Courtney Trawitz. **Manager, Concessions:** Jeff DeSantis. **Business Manager, Concessions:** Dave Bills. **Clubhouse Operations:** Terry Costello.

FIELD STAFF

Manager: Tom Nieto. **Coach:** Floyd Rayford. **Pitching Coach:** Bobby Cuellar. **Trainer:** Tony Leo.

GAME INFORMATION

Radio Announcers: Josh Whetzel. **No. of Games Broadcast:** Home-72, Away-72. **Flagship Stations:** WHTK 1280-AM, WYSL 1040-AM.
PA Announcer: Kevin Spears. **Official Scorer:** Warren Kozereski.
Stadium Name: Frontier Field. **Location:** I-490 East to exit 12 (Brown/Broad Street) and follow signs. I-490 West to exit 14 (Plymouth Ave.) and follow signs. **Standard Game Times:** 7:05 p.m., Sun 1:35. **Ticket Price Range:** $6.50-10.50
Visiting Club Hotel: Crown Plaza, 70 State St., Rochester, NY 14608. **Telephone:** (585) 546-3450.

SCRANTON/WILKES-BARRE YANKEES

Office Address: 235 Montage Mountain Rd, Moosic, PA 18507.
Telephone: (570) 969-2255. **Fax:** (570) 963-6564.
E-Mail address: info@swbyankees.com. **Website:** www.swbyankees.com.
Affiliation (first year): New York Yankees (2007). **Years in League:** 1989-

OWNERSHIP, MANAGEMENT

Owned By: The Multi-Purpose Stadium Authority of Lackawanna County
Operated By: SWB Yankees, LLC
President: Kristen Rose. **Executive Vice President/GM:** Jeremy Ruby.
Vice President, Marketing Services: Jon Stephenson. **Senior Sponsor Service Manager:** Kristina Knight. **Manager, Sponsor Service/Play Ball:** Mike Cummings. **Sponsor Service Manager:** Amy Ott. **Manager, Marketing/Community Relations:** Brian Bonner. **Vice President, Ticket Sales:** Doug Augis. **Director, Ticket Operations:** Benjamin DuGoff. **Coordinator, Ticket Operations/Sales:** Mark Cole. **Managers, Corporate Marketing:** Jared Gigli, Chris Wallace. **Customer Account Managers:** Ellen Howanitz, Stephen Vasilenko, Jake Winowich. **Group Sales Coordinators:** Allison Baldsare, Tom Baxter, Jessica Cioffi, Bob Mclane. **Director, Corporate Partnerships:** Mike Trudnak. **Vice President, Stadium Operations:** Curt Comoni. **Director, Facility Operations:** Joe Villano. **Director, Field Operations:** Steve Horne. **Operations Manager:** Rob Galdieri. **Director, Game Entertainment:** Barry Snyder. **Vice President, Accounting/Finance:** Paul Chilek. **Staff Accountant:** William Steiner. **Office Manager:** Kelly Byron. **Director, Merchandise:** Sarah Phillips. **Director, Media Relations/Broadcasting:** Mike Vander Woude.

FIELD STAFF

Manager: Dave Miley. **Coach:** Butch Wynegar. **Pitching Coach:** Scott Aldred. **Coach:** Aaron Ledesma. **Trainer:** Darren London. **Strength/Conditioning Coach:** Lee Tressel.

GAME INFORMATION

Radio Announcer: Mike Vander Woude. **No of Games Broadcast:** Home-72 Road-72. **Flagship Station:** WICK 1340-1400 AM.
PA Announcer: John Davies. **Official Scorers:** Dave Lauriha, Armand Rosamila.
Stadium Name: PNC Field. **Location:** I-81 to exit 182 (Davis Street/Montage Mountain Road), take Montage Mountain Road one mile to stadium. **Ticket Price Range:** $8-10.
Visiting Club Hotel: Radisson at Lackawanna Stadium, 700 Lackawanna Ave, Scranton, PA 18503. **Telephone:** (570) 342-8300.

SYRACUSE CHIEFS

Office Address: One Tex Simone Dr., Syracuse, NY 13208.
Telephone: (315) 474-7833. **Fax:** (315) 474-2658.
E-Mail Address: baseball@syracusechiefs.com. **Website:** www.syracusechiefs.com
Affiliation (first year): Washington Nationals (2009). **Years in League:**
1885-89, 1891-92, 1894-1901, 1918, 1920-27, 1934-55, 1961-

OWNERSHIP, MANAGEMENT

Operated by: Community Owned Baseball Club of Central New York, Inc.
Chairman: Charles Rich. **President:** Ron Gersbacher. **Executive Vice President/COO:** Anthony "Tex" Simone. **General Manager:** John Simone. **Assistant General Manager/Director, Marketing/Promotions:** Mike Voutsinas. **Assistant General Manager, Business:** Don Lehtonen. **Director, Sales:** Paul Fairbanks. **Director, Group Sales:** Victor Gallucci. **Director, Broadcasting/Public Relations:** Jason Benetti. **Director, Merchandising:** Wendy Shoen. **Director, Ticket Office:** Erin Shappell. **Administrative Assistant:** Priscilla Venditti. **Turf Manager:** Wes Ganobcik. **Team Historian:** Ron Gersbacher.

FIELD STAFF

Manager: Trent Jewett. **Hitting Coach:** Jerry Browne. **Pitching Coach:** Greg Booker. **Trainer:** Beth Jarrett.

GAME INFORMATION

Radio Announcer: Jason Benetti. **No. of Games Broadcast:** Home-72, Away-72.
Flagship Station: WHEN Sportsradio 620-AM, NOVA 105.1-FM.
PA Announcer: Brent Axe. **Official Scorer:** Tom Leo.
Stadium Name: Alliance Bank Stadium. **Location:** New York State Thruway to exit 36 (I-81 South), to 7th North Street exit, left on 7th North, right on Hiawatha Boulevard. **Standard Game Times:** 7 p.m., Sun. 6. **Ticket Price Range:** $6-10.
Visiting Club Hotel: Ramada Inn, 1305 Buckley Rd., Syracuse, NY 13212. **Telephone:** (315) 457-8670.

TOLEDO MUD HENS

Office Address: 406 Washington St, Toledo, OH 43604.
Telephone: (419) 725-4367. **Fax:** (419) 725-4368.
E-Mail address: mudhens@mudhens.com. **Website:** www.mudhens.com.
Affiliation (first year): Detroit Tigers (1987). **Years in League:** 1889, 1965-

OWNERSHIP, MANAGEMENT

Operated By: Toledo Mud Hens Baseball Club, Inc.
Chairman of the Board: Michael Miller.
Vice President: David Huey. **Secretary/Treasurer:** Charles Bracken.
President/General Manager: Joseph Napoli.
Assistant GM/Director, Marketing, Advertising, Sales: Scott Jeffer. **Assistant GM/Director, Corporate Partnerships:** Neil Neukam. **Assistant GM, Ticket Sales/Operations:** Erik Ibsen. **CFO:** Pam Alspach. **Manager, Promotions:** JaMay Edwards. **Director, Media/Public Relations:** Jason Griffin. **Director, Ticket Sales/Services:** Thomas Townley. **Accounting:** Sheri Kelly, Brian Leverenz. **Manager, Gameday Operations:** Greg Setola. **Manager, Box Office Sales:** Justin Morelli. **Manager, Community Relations:** Cheri Pastula. **Corporate Sales Associate:** Ed Sintic, Todd Yunker. **Season Ticket/Group Sales Associates:** Chris Hole, Mike Keedy, Frank Kristie, Kyle Moll, John Mulka, Eric Tomaszewski. **Manager, Online Marketing:** Nathan Steinmetz. **Season Ticket Service Coordinator:** Jessica Aten. **Manager, Video Board Operations:** Mike Ramirez. **Graphic Designer:** Dan Royer. **Manager, Souvenir Sales:** Craig Katz. **Assistant Manager, Souvenir Sales:** Heidi Srock. **Manager, Ballpark Operations:** Ken Westenkirchner. **Office Manager:** Carol Hamilton. **Executive Assistant:** Tracy Evans. **Turf Manager:** Jake Tyler. **Assistant Turf Manager:** Kyle Leppelmeier. **Clubhouse Manager:** Joe Sarkisian. **Team Historian:** John Husman.

FIELD STAFF

Manager: Larry Parrish. **Coach:** Leon Durham. **Pitching Coach:** A.J. Sager. **Trainer:** Matt Rankin.

GAME INFORMATION

Radio Announcers: Frank Gilhooley, Jim Weber, Jason Griffin. **No of Games Broadcast:** Home-72 Road-72. **Flagship Station:** WCWA 1230 AM
PA Announcer: Kevin Mullan. **Official Scorers:** Jeff Businger, Ron Klenfelter, Guy Lammers, Jay Wagner.
Stadium Name: Fifth Third Field. **Location:** From Ohio Turnpike 80/90, exit 54 (4A) to I-75 North, follow I-75 North to exit 201-B, left onto Erie Street, right onto Washington Street. From Detroit, I-75 South to exit 202-A, right onto Washington Street. From Dayton, I-75 North to exit 201-B, left onto Erie Street, right on Washington Street. From Ann Arbor, Route 23 South to I-475 East, I-475 east to I-75 South, I-75 South to exit 202-A, right onto Washington Street. **Ticket Price Range:** $9.
Visiting Club Hotel: Park Inn, 101 North Summit, Toledo, OH 43604. **Telephone:** (419) 241-3000.

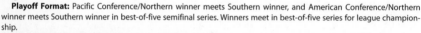

PACIFIC COAST LEAGUE

TRIPLE-A

PACIFIC COAST LEAGUE

Mailing Address: 630 Southpointe Court, Suite 106, Colorado Springs, CO 80906. **Telephone:** (719) 636-3399. **Fax:** (719) 636-1199.

E-Mail Address: office@pclbaseball.com. **Website:** www.pclbaseball.com.

President: Branch B. Rickey.

Vice President: Don Logan (Las Vegas).

Directors: Don Beaver (New Orleans), Sam Bernabe (Iowa), John Pontius (Memphis), Chris Cummings (Fresno), Dave Elmore (Colorado Springs), Kirby Schlegel (Tacoma), Don Logan (Las Vegas), Jay Miller (Round Rock), Greg Miller (Salt Lake), Bill Shea (Omaha), Scott Pruitt (Oklahoma), Merritt Paulson (Portland), TBA (Sacramento), John Traub (Albuquerque), Frank Ward (Nashville), Stuart Katzoff (Reno).

Director, Administration: Melanie Fiore. **Director, Baseball Operations:** Dwight Hall. **Media/Operations Assistant:** Mike Feigen.

Division Structure: American Conference—Northern: Iowa, Memphis, Nashville, Omaha. **Southern:** Albuquerque, New Orleans, Oklahoma, Round Rock. **Pacific Conference—Northern:** Colorado Springs, Portland, Salt Lake, Tacoma. **Southern:** Fresno, Las Vegas, Sacramento, Reno.

Branch Rickey

Regular Season: 144 games. **2010 Opening Date:** April 8. **Closing Date:** Sept. 6.

All-Star Game: July 14 at Lehigh Valley Iron Pigs, Allentown, PA (PCL vs. International League).

Playoff Format: Pacific Conference/Northern winner meets Southern winner, and American Conference/Northern winner meets Southern winner in best-of-five semifinal series. Winners meet in best-of-five series for league championship.

Triple-A Championship Game: Sept. 21, Oklahoma City (PCL vs. International League).

Roster Limit: 24. **Player Eligibility Rule:** No restrictions.

Brand of Baseball: Rawlings ROM.

Umpires: Dan Bellino (Crystal Lake, IL), Cory Blaser (Westminster, CO), John Brammer (Benbrook, TX), Mark Buchanan (Phoenix, AZ), Darren Budahn (Milwaukee, WI), Angel Campos (San Bernadino, CA), Robert Drake (Mesa, AZ), Jason Dunn (Savannah, TN), Clint Fagan (Tomball, TX), Shaun Francis (Cohoes, NY), Tyler Funneman (Wildwood, IL), Take Hirabayashi (Edogawa, Tokyo, Japan), Mike Jarboe (La Crescenta, CA), Brian Knight (Helena, MT), Barry Larson (Hayden, ID), Jeff Latter (Gresham, OR), Eric Loveless (Layton, UT), Mike Lusky (Baldwin Park, CA), Jason Millsap (Bryan, TX), Casey Moser (Iowa Park, TX), Michael Muchlinski (Ephrata, WA), D.J. Reyburn (Nashville, TN), Mark Ripperger (Carlsbad, CA), Will Robinson (Savannah, GA), Dixon Stureman (Morgan Hill, CA), Todd Tichenor (Holcomb, KS), Chris Tiller (Bullard, TX), John Tumpane (Oak Lawn, IL).

Club	Stadium	Opened	Dimensions LF	CF	RF	Capacity	2009 Att.
Albuquerque	Isotopes Park	2003	340	400	340	13,279	602,129
Colorado Springs	Security Service Field	1988	350	410	350	8,400	300,185
Fresno	Chukchansi Park	2002	324	402	335	12,500	480,627
Iowa	Principal Park	1992	335	400	335	11,000	536,872
Las Vegas	Cashman Field	1983	328	433	328	9,334	337,388
Memphis	AutoZone Park	2000	319	400	322	14,200	474,764
Nashville	Herschel Greer Stadium	1978	327	400	327	10,700	305,434
New Orleans	Zephyr Field	1997	333	405	332	10,000	362,771
Oklahoma City	AT&T Bricktown Ballpark	1998	325	400	325	13,066	397,219
Omaha	Johnny Rosenblatt Stadium	1948	332	408	332	24,000	371,046
Portland	PGE Park	1926	319	405	321	19,810	369,580
Reno	Aces Ballpark	2009	339	410	340	9,000	466,606
Round Rock	The Dell Diamond	2000	330	400	325	10,000	626,899
Sacramento	Raley Field	2000	330	405	325	14,111	657,095
Salt Lake	Franklin Covey Field	1994	345	420	315	15,500	492,321
Tacoma	Cheney Stadium	1960	325	425	325	9,600	352,450

ALBUQUERQUE ISOTOPES

Office Address: 1601 Avenida Cesar Chavez SE, Albuquerque, NM 87106.

Telephone: (505) 924-2255. **Fax:** (505) 242-8899.

E-Mail address: info@albuquerquebaseball.com.

Website: www.albuquerquebaseball.com.

Affiliation (first year): Los Angeles Dodgers (2009). **Years in League:** 1972-2000, 2003-

OWNERSHIP, MANAGEMENT

President: Ken Young. **Secretary/Treasurer:** Emmett Hammond. **General Manager:** John Traub. **Assistant General Manager, Sales/Marketing:** Nick LoBue. **Director, Box Office/Retail Operations:** Chrissy Baines. **Director, Sales/**

Promotions: Adam Beggs. **Director, Media Relations:** Steve Hurlbert. **Director, Stadium Operations:** Bobby Atencio. **Manager, Promotions/Marketing:** Chris Holland. **Manager, Suite Relations:** Paul Hartenberger. **Creative Services Manager:** Kris Shepard. **Season Ticket/Group Sales Representatives:** Eddie Enriquez, Jason Buchta, Quentin Andes. **Director, Accounting:** Cynthia DiFrancesco. **Assistant Director, Retail Operations:** Kara Hayes. **Assistant Director, Box Office Operations:** Ben Zalewski. **Director, Field Operations:** Shawn Moore. **Assistant Director, Field Operations:** Casey Griffin. **Visiting Clubhouse Manager:** Rick Pollack. **Office Manager:** Susan Martindale. **General Manager, Ovations Foodservice:** Jay Satenspiel. **Catering Manager, Ovations Foodservice:** Sheryl Duran. **Purchasing/Warehouse Director, Ovations Foodservice:** Matt Butler. **Executive Chef:** Raul Blanco. **Office Manager, Ovations Foodservice:** Jamie Yoder.

FIELD STAFF

Manager: Tim Wallach. **Coach:** John Moses. **Pitching Coach:** Jim Slaton. **Trainer:** Greg Harrel.

GAME INFORMATION

Radio Announcer: Robert Portnoy. **No. of Games Broadcast:** Home-72 Road-72. **Flagship Station:** KNML 610-AM. **PA Announcer:** Stu Walker. **Official Scorers:** Glen Rosales, Gary Herron.
Stadium Name: Isotopes Park. **Location:** From 1-25, exit east on Avenida Cesar Chavez SE to University Boulevard. From I-40, exit south on University Boulevard SE to Avenida Cesar Chavez. **Standard Game Times:** 7:05 p.m., 6:05 Sunday. **Ticket Price Range:** $6-24.
Visiting Club Hotel: MCM Elegante, 2020 Menaul NE, Albuquerque, NM 87107. **Telephone:** (505) 884-2511.

COLORADO SPRINGS
SKY SOX

Office Address: 4385 Tutt Blvd, Colorado Springs, CO 80922.
Telephone: (719) 597-1449. **Fax:** (719) 597-2491.
E-Mail address: info@skysox.com. **Website:** www.skysox.com.
Affiliation (first year): Colorado Rockies (1993). **Years in League:** 1988-

OWNERSHIP, MANAGEMENT

Operated By: Colorado Springs Sky Sox Inc.
Principal Owner: David Elmore.
President/General Manager: Tony Ensor. **Senior Vice President, Marketing:** Rai Henniger. **Assistant GM/Director, Public Relations:** Mike Hobson. **Asst. GM/Director, Corporate Sponsorships/Marketing:** Matt Person. **Director, Broadcast Operations:** Dan Karcher. **Accountant:** Kelly Hanlon. **Director, Ticket Sales:** Whitney Shellem. **Director, Stadium Operations:** Matt Pribbernow. **Director, Group Sales:** Keith Hodges. **Director, Promotions:** Matt Glass. **Assistant Director, Group Sales:** Phil McMullen. **Groups Sales Manager:** Ryan Stos. **Special Event Manager:** Brien Smith. **General Manager/Diamond Creations:** Don Giuliano. **Director, Catering:** Roberto Gutierrez. **Community Relations Coordinator:** Jon Eddy. **Graphics Manager:** Erin Eads. **Head Groundskeeper:** Steve DeLeon. **Administrative Assistant:** Marianne Paine. **Home Clubhouse Manager:** Ricky Grima. **Visiting Clubhouse Manager:** Steve Martin.

FIELD STAFF

Manager: Stu Cole. **Hitting Coach:** Rene Lachemann. **Pitching Coach:** Unavailable. **Trainer:** Heath Townsend.

GAME INFORMATION

Radio Announcer: Dan Karcher. **No. of Games Broadcast:** Home-72 Road-72. **Flagship Station:** AM 1300 "The Sports Animal."
PA Announcer: Josh Howe. **Official Scorer:** Marty Grantz, Rich Wastler.
Stadium Name: Security Service Field. **Location:** I-25 South to Woodmen Road exit, east on Woodmen to Powers Boulevard, right on Powers to Barnes Road. **Standard Game Times:** 7:05 p.m.; Sun. 1:05. **Ticket Price Range:** $5-11.
Visiting Club Hotel: La Quinta Inn, Garden of the Gods, 4385 Sinton Rd., Colorado Springs, CO 80907. **Telephone:** (719) 528-5060.

FRESNO GRIZZLIES

Office Address: 1800 Tulare St, Fresno, CA 93721.
Telephone: (559) 320-4487. **Fax:** (559) 264-0795.
E-Mail address: info@fresnogrizzlies.com. **Website:** www.fresnogrizzlies.com.
Affiliation (first year): San Francisco Giants (1998). **Years in League:** 1998-

OWNERSHIP, MANAGEMENT

Operated By: Fresno Baseball Club, LLC.
Executive Vice President/General Manager: Andrew Stuebner. **Senior VP, Operations:** Garret Fahrmann. **Senior VP, Marketing:** Scott Carter. **VP, Tickets:** Shaun Northup. **VP, Corporate Partnerships:** Josh Phanco. **VP, Finance:** SuSin Correa. **Director, Media/Public Relations:** Noah Frank. **Director, Entertainment/Publications:** Krista Boyd. **Director,**

Marketing: Walmer Medina. **Director, Mascot Relations:** Brad Collins. **Director, Merchandise:** Stephanie Hawkins. **Director, Community Relations:** Danielle Witt. **Community Relations Coordinator:** Daniel Newman. **Director, Client Services:** Andrew Melrose. **Corporate Partnerships Manager:** Ray Ortiz. **Client Services Executives:** Laura Pimentel, Taylor Woods. **Director, Sales:** Derek Franks. **Director, Tickets:** Jason Hannold. **Group Sales Manager:** Freddie Dominguez, Jr. **Ticket Office Manager:** Pat Wallach. **Group Sales Account Executives:** Jonathan Gilbert, Adam Gleich. **Account Executive:** Andrew Milios. **Director, Stadium Operations:** Harvey Kawasaki. **Director, Event Operations:** Matt Studwell. **Manager, Operations:** Ira Calvin. **Head Groundskeeper:** David Jacinto. **Director, Human Resources:** Ashley Tennell. **Finance Managers:** Monica De La Cerda, Becky DeOchoa. **Receptionist:** DeeAnn Hernandez. **GM, Ovations Concessions:** Jim Stearley.

FIELD STAFF

Manager: Steve Decker. **Hitting Coach:** Ken Joyce. **Pitching Coach:** Pat Rice. **Athletic Trainer:** Anthony Reyes.

GAME INFORMATION

Radio Announcers: Doug Greenwald, Guy Haberman. **No. of Games Broadcast:** Home-72 Road-72. **Flagship Station:** ESPN Radio 790-AM.

Official Scorer: Darrell Copeland. **MLBAM Stringer:** Jim Nelson

Stadium Name: Chukchansi Park. **Location:** 1800 Tulare St, Fresno, CA 93721. **Directions:** From 99 North, take Fresno Street exit, left on Fresno Street, left on Inyo or Tulare to stadium. From 99 South, take Fresno Street exit, left on Fresno Street, right on Broadway to H Street. From 41 North, take Van Ness exit toward Fresno, left on Van Ness, left on Inyo or Tulare, stadium is straight ahead. From 41 South, take Tulare exit, stadium is located at Tulare and H Streets, or take Van Ness exit, right on Van Ness, left on Inyo or Tulare, stadium is straight ahead. **Ticket Price Range:** $8-18.

Visiting Club Hotel: Radisson Hotel Fresno, 2233 Ventura St, Fresno, CA 93721. **Telephone:** (559) 441-2931.

IOWA CUBS

Office Address: One Line Dr, Des Moines, IA 50309.
Telephone: (515) 243-6111. **Fax:** (515) 243-5152.
E-Mail address: info@iowacubs.com. **Website:** www.iowacubs.com
Affiliation (first year): Chicago Cubs (1981). **Years in League:** 1969-

OWNERSHIP, MANAGEMENT

Operated By: Raccoon Baseball Inc.
Chairman, Principal Owner: Michael Gartner. **Executive Vice President:** Michael Giudicessi.
President/General Manager: Sam Bernabe. **Shareholder:** Mike C. Gartner. **Vice President/Assistant GM:** Jim Nahas. **VP/CFO:** Sue Tollefson. **VP/Director, Stadium Operations:** Tom Greene. **VP/Director, Broadcast Operations:** Deene Ehlis. **Media Relations Manager:** Andrea Breen. **Director, Logistics:** Scott Sailor. **Group Sales Coordinator:** Kenny Houser. **Director, Sales:** Rich Gilman. **Director, Luxury Suites:** Brent Conkel. **Ticket Office Manager:** Katie Moorhead. **Assistant Ticket Manager:** Mark Dempsey. **Manager, Stadium Operations:** Jeff Tilley. **Assistant Manager, Stadium Operations:** Janelle Stevens. **Corporate Sales Executives:** Melanie Doser, Nate Teut, Randy Wehofer. **Corporate Relations:** Red Hollis. **Head Groundskeeper:** Chris Schlosser. **Director, Merchandise:** Rick Giudicessi. **Coordinator, Merchandise:** Amber Gartner. **Accountant:** Lori Auten. **Manager, Cub Club:** John Gordon. **Director, Information Systems:** Larry Schunk. **Director, Video Operations:** Aaron Johnson. **Office Manager:** Betsy Duncan. **Landscape Coordinator:** Shari Kramer.

FIELD STAFF

Manager: Ryne Sandberg. **Hitting Coach:** Von Joshua. **Pitching Coach:** Mike Mason. **Trainer:** Matt Johnson.

GAME INFORMATION

Radio Announcers: Deene Ehlis, Randy Wehofer. **No. of Games Broadcast:** Home-72 Road-72. **Flagship Station:** AM 940 KPSZ.

PA Announcers: Geoff Conn, Mark Pierce, Corey Coon. **Official Scorers:** Dirk Brinkmeyer, Brian Gibson, Mike Mahon.

Stadium Name: Principal Park. **Location:** I-80 or I-35 to I-235, to Third Street exit, south on Third Street, left on Line Drive. **Standard Game Times:** 7:05 p.m.; 12:05; 1:05 Sundays. **Ticket Price Range:** $6-11.

Visiting Club Hotel: Embassy Suites. 101 East Locust Street. Des Moines, IA 50309. **Telephone:** (515) 244-1700.

LAS VEGAS 51S

Office Address: 850 Las Vegas Blvd. North, Las Vegas, NV 89101.
Telephone: (702) 386-7200. **Fax:** (702) 386-7214.
E-Mail address: info@lv51.com. **Website:** http://www.lv51.com.
Affiliation (second year): Toronto Blue Jays (2009). **Years in League:** 1983-.

OWNERSHIP, MANAGEMENT

Operated By: Stevens Family Trust.
President/General Manager: Don Logan. **Assistant GM/Vice President, Marketing:** Chuck Johnson. **VP, Sales/Marketing:** Mike Hollister. **VP, Ticket Operations:** Mike Rodriguez. **VP, Operations/Security:** Nick Fitzenreider. **Special Assistant to GM:** Bob Blum. **Controller:** Araxi Demirjian. **Director, Business Development:** Derek Eige. **Director,**

Broadcasting: Russ Langer. **Manager, Community Relations:** Larry Brown. **Manager, Baseball Administration:** Denise Korach. **Media Relations Director:** Jim Gemma. **Ticket Operations Assistant:** Michelle Taggart. **Administrative Assistants:** Jan Dillard, Pat Dressel. **Managers, Corporate Marketing:** Erik Eisenberg, Melissa Harkavy, Bruce Simons. **Merchandise Coordinator:** Jason Weber. **Sponsorship Services Manager:** William Graham. **Operations Manager:** Chip Vespe. **Interns:** Justin Dunbar, Dana Pappas, Frank Parish.

FIELD STAFF

Manager: Dan Rohn. **Hitting Coach:** Chad Mottola. **Pitching Coach:** Dave LaRoche. **Trainer:** Voon Chong. **Strength/Conditioning Coach:** Rob Helmick.

GAME INFORMATION

Radio Announcer: Russ Langer. **No. of Games Broadcast:** Home-72 Road-72. **Flagship Station:** Fox Sports Radio 920-AM.

PA Announcer: Dan Bickmore. **Official Scorers:** Mark Wasik, Gary Arlitz.

Stadium Name: Cashman Field. **Location:** I-15 to U.S. 95 exit (downtown), east to Las Vegas Boulevard North exit, one-half mile north to stadium. **Standard Game Time:** 7:05 p.m. **Ticket Price Range:** $9-14.

Visiting Club Hotel: Golden Nugget Hotel & Casino, 129 Fremont Street, Las Vegas, NV 89101. **Telephone:** (702) 385-7111.

MEMPHIS REDBIRDS

Office Address: 175 Toyota Plaza, Suite 300, Memphis, TN 38103.
Telephone: (901) 721-6000. **Fax:** (901) 842-1222.
Website: www.memphisredbirds.com
Affiliation (first year): St. Louis Cardinals (1998). **Years in League:** 1998-

OWNERSHIP, MANAGEMENT

Operated By: Memphis Redbirds Baseball Foundation, Inc.

General Manager: Ben Weiss. **Assistant GM/Director, Sales:** Derek Goldfarb. **Director, Baseball Operations/PR:** Kyle Parkinson. **Director, Operations:** Mark Anderson. **Director, Finance:** Art Davis. **Director, Marketing:** Adam Goldberg. **PR Manager, Community Relations:** Harrison Lampley. **Ticket Operations Manager:** Nick Harvey. **Ticket Sales Manager:** Jason Mott. **Group Sales Coordinator:** Devyn Parkinson. **Graphics Coordinator/Team Photographer:** Allison Rhoades. **Coordinator, Premium Seats/Foundation Services:** Kela Jones. **Programs Coordinator:** Corey Gillum. **Special Event Coordinator:** Kellie Grabert. **Corporate Sales Executives:** Ben White, Dan Hostetter, Jody Sellers. **Corporate Sales Coordinator:** Leigh Eisenberg. **Ticket Sales Executives:** Bryan Gore, Jonathan Hawks, Valerie Hight, Phillip Riley. **Executive Assistant:** Cindy Compton. **Staff Accountant:** Cindy Neal. **Office Coordinator:** Linda Smith. **Head Groundskeeper:** Ed Collins. **Chief Engineer:** Danny Abbott. **Maintenance:** Spencer Shields.

FIELD STAFF

Manager: Chris Maloney. **Hitting Coach:** Mark Budaska. **Pitching Coach:** Derek Lilliquist. **Trainer:** Chris Conroy.

GAME INFORMATION

Radio Announcer: Steve Selby. **No. of Games Broadcast:** Home-72 Road-72. **Flagship Station:** WHBQ 560-AM. **PA Announcer:** Unavailable. **Official Scorer:** J.J. Guinozzo. **Stadium Name:** AutoZone Park. **Location:** North on I-240, exit at Union Avenue West, one and half mile to park. **Standard Game Times:** 7:05 p.m.; **Saturday** 6:05; Sunday 1:35. **Ticket Price Range:** $5-17.

Visiting Club Hotel: Sleep Inn at Court Square, 40 N. Front, Memphis, TN 38103. **Telephone:** (901) 522-9700.

NASHVILLE SOUNDS

Office Address: 534 Chestnut Street, Nashville, TN 37203.
Telephone: (615) 690-HITS. **Fax:** (615) 256-5684.
E-Mail address: info@nashvillesounds.com. **Website:** www.nashvillesounds.com
Affiliation (first year): Milwaukee Brewers (2005). **Years in League:** 1998-

OWNERSHIP, MANAGEMENT

Operated By: MFP Baseball.

Owners: Frank Ward, Steve Posner, Masahiro Honzawa.

Vice President/General Manager: George King. **Vice President, Sales/Marketing:** Brad Tammen. **Director, Operations/Communications:** Doug Scopel. **Director, Accounting:** Barb Walker. **Director, Community Relations:** Heather Colvin. **Manager, Sales/Sports Marketing:** Drew Himsworth. **Manager, Stadium Operations:** Steven McKinney. **Manager, Community Relations:** Buddy Yelton. **Manager, Sales:** Dustin Skilbred. **Manager, Ticketing:** Eric Laue. **Manager, Media Relations:** Michael Whitty. **Manager, Advertising/Promotions:** Jeffrey Young. **Manager, Merchandise:** Erin Rescigno. **Senior Corporate Account Executives:** Darren Feller, Mike Gregory. **Coordinator, Community Relations:** Mindon Whalen. **Coordinator, Stadium Operations:** Elliott Sweitzer. **Coordinator, Accounts:** Brandon Yerger. **Office Manager:** Sharon Ridley. **Head Groundskeeper:** Thomas Trotter. **Assistant Groundskeeper:** Nick Vikstrom. **Clubhouse Managers:** J.R. Rinaldi, Thomas Miller.

FIELD STAFF

Manager: Don Money. **Coach:** Sandy Guerrero. **Pitching Coach:** Rich Gale. **Trainer:** Jeff Paxson. **Trainer:** David Yeager. **Strength/Conditioning Coach:** Andrew Emmick.

GAME INFORMATION

Radio Announcer: Stu Paul. **No of Games Broadcast:** Home-72 Road-72. **Flagship Station:** WGFX 104.5 FM. **PA Announcers:** Eric Berner, Jim Kiser. **Official Scorers:** Eric Jones, Trevor Garrett.
Stadium Name: Herschel Greer Stadium. **Location:** I-65 to Wedgewood exit, west to Eighth Avenue, right on Eighth to Chestnut Street, right on Chestnut. **Standard Game Times:** Mon-Fri (7:05 p.m.), Sat (6:35 p.m.), Sun (2:05 p.m. Apr-Jun 20, 6:35 p.m. Jun 27-Sept). Ticket Price Range: $8-14.
Visiting Club Hotel: Holiday Inn Vanderbilt, 2613 West End Ave, Nashville, TN 37203. Telephone: (615) 327-4707.

NEW ORLEANS ZEPHYRS

Office Address: 6000 Airline Dr, Metairie, LA 70003.
Telephone: (504) 734-5155. **Fax:** (504) 734-5118.
E-Mail address: zephyrs@zephyrsbaseball.com. **Website:** www.zephyrsbaseball.com.
Affiliation (first year): Florida Marlins (2009). **Years in League:** 1998-

OWNERSHIP, MANAGEMENT

Managing Partner/President: Don Beaver.
Executive Director/COO: Ron Maestri.
Minority Owner/VP/General Counsel: Walter Leger.
General Manager: Mike Schline. **VP, Sales/Marketing/Community Relations:** Jeff Booker. **Director, Finance/Accounting:** Donna Light. **Director, Broadcasting/Team Travel:** Tim Grubbs. **Color Analyst/Speakers Bureau:** Ron Swoboda. **Director, Media Relations:** Dave Sachs. **Director, Marketing/Suite Sales:** Katie DeVries. **Director, Promotions/Merchandise:** Jessica De Oro. **Director, Ticket Operations:** Kathy Kaleta. **Director, Community Relations:** Leah Rigby. **Assistant, Community Relations:** Brandon Puls. **Director, Stadium Operations:** Todd Wilson. **Assistant, Stadium Operations:** Chris Taylor. **Director, Clubhouse:** Brett Hebert. **Corporate Sales Executive:** Scott Dietrich. **Group Sales Representatives:** Katie Bonaccorso, Jack Craig, Kevin Ferguson, Jordan Price, Trey Shields. **Head Groundskeeper:** Thomas Marks. **Assistant Groundskeeper:** Corey Cazaubon. **Maintenance Coordinator:** Craig Shaffer. **Receptionist:** Susan Hihar. Director, Operations, Messina's Inc.: George Messina. **Administrative Assistant, Messina's Inc.:** Priscilla Arbello. **Concessions Manager, Messina's Inc.:** Curtis Jacobs. **Catering Manager, Messina's Inc.:** Darin Yuratich.

FIELD STAFF

Manager: Edwin Rodriguez. **Coach:** Steve Phillips. **Pitching Coach:** Scott Mitchell. **Trainer:** Steve Miller. **Strength/Conditioning:** Gary McCoy.

GAME INFORMATION

Radio Announcers: Tim Grubbs, Ron Swoboda. **Color Analyst/Speakers Bureau:** Ron Swoboda. **No. of Games Broadcast:** Home-72 Road-72. **Flagship Station:** WMTI 106.7 FM.
PA Announcer: Doug Moreau. **Official Scorer:** J.L. Vangilder.
Stadium Name: Zephyr Field. **Location:** I-10 West toward Baton Rouge, exit at Clearview Pkwy (exit 226) and continues south, right on Airline Drive (U.S. 61 North) for 1 mile, stadium on left. From airport, take Airline Drive (U.S. 61) east for 4 miles, stadium on right. **Standard Game Times:** 7 p.m.; Sat. 6; Sun. 2 (April-May), 6 (June-Sept.). Ticket Price Range: $6-10.
Visiting Club Hotel: Best Western-St. Christopher, 114 Magazine St., New Orleans, LA 70130. **Telephone:** (504) 648-0444.

OKLAHOMA CITY REDHAWKS

Office Address: 2 S. Mickey Mantle Dr, Oklahoma City, OK 73104.
Telephone: (405) 218-1000. **Fax:** (405) 218-1001.
E-Mail address: info@okcredhawks.com. **Website:** www.okcredhawks.com.
Affiliation (first year): Texas Rangers (1983). **Years in League:** 1963-1968, 1998-

OWNERSHIP, MANAGEMENT

Operated By: Oklahoma Baseball Club LLC.
Principal Owner: Robert Funk. **Managing General Partner:** Scott Pruitt.
Executive Director: John Allgood. **CFO:** Steve McEwen. **Director, Public Relations/Assistant to Managing General Partner:** Holly McGowen. **Director, Facility Operations:** Harlan Budde. **Director, Operations:** Mike Prange. **Director, Sponsorships:** Mark Pritchard. **Director, Multimedia Sales:** David Patterson. **Director, Special Events:** Mary Ramsey. **Senior Accountant:** Nicole Wise. **Corporate Sponsorship:** Brandon Baker. **Ticket Operations Manager:** Armando Reyes. **Director, Ticket Sales:** Jason Black, Account Executives: Jeff Hawkins. **Group Sales Account Executives:** Courtney White. **Office Manager/Administrative Coordinator:** Kellie Mayberry. **Clubhouse Manager:** Russ Oliver. **Head Groundskeeper:** Monte McCoy.

FIELD STAFF

Manager: Bobby Jones. **Pitching Coach:** Terry Clark. **Coach:** Scott Coolbaugh. **Trainer:** Unavailable.

GAME INFORMATION

Radio Announcer: Jim Byers. **No of Games Broadcast:** Home-72 Road-72. **Flagship Station:** KEBC 1340 AM.
PA Announcer: Matt Gierat. **Official Scorers:** Mike Treps, Justin Tinder.
Stadium Name: AT&T Bricktown Ballpark. **Location:** Near interchange of I-235 and I-40, take Lincoln exit off I-40 to Reno, west on Reno to ballpark. **Standard Game Times:** 7:05 p.m.; Sunday 2:05 (April-May), 7:05 (June-August). **Ticket Price Range:** $6-15.
Visiting Club Hotel: Courtyard Oklahoma City Downtown/Bricktown, 2 West Reno Ave., Oklahoma City, OK 73102. **Telephone:** (405) 235-2780.

OMAHA ROYALS

Office Address: Rosenblatt Stadium, 1202 Bert Murphy Ave., Omaha, NE 68107.
Administrative Office Phone: (402) 734-2550. **Ticket Office Phone:** (402) 738-5100.
Fax: (402) 734-7166. **E-Mail Address:** info@oroyals.com. **Website:** www.oroyals.com.
Affiliation (first year): Kansas City Royals (1969). **Years in League:** 1998-.

OWNERSHIP, MANAGEMENT

Operated by: Omaha Royals Limited Partnership.
Principal Owners: William Shea, Warren Buffett, Walter Scott.
President: Alan M. Stein.
Vice President/General Manager: Martie J. Cordaro. **Vice President/Baseball Operations:** Kyle R. Fisher. **Assistant General Manager:** Rob Crain. **Controller:** Laurie Schlender. **Director, Broadcasting:** Mark Nasser. **Director, Media Relations:** Kevin McNabb. **Director, Merchandise:** Jason Kinney. **Director, Business Development:** Dave Endress. **Ticket Operations Manager:** Paul Hammes. **Community Relations Manager:** Diann Spataro. **Creative Services Manager:** Eldon Lindsay. **Promotions Manager:** Ben Hemmen. **Group Sales Manager:** Danny Dunbar. **Corporate Sales Executive:** James Jensen. **Ticket Sales Executives:** Andrea Stava, Rustin Buysse. **Administrative Assistants:** Kay Besta, Lois Biggs. **IT Technician:** Rich Bumann. **Finance Intern:** Drew Stauder. **Group Sales Intern:** Matthew Bradwell. **Ticket Operations Intern:** Kaci Long. Head Groundskeeper: Jesse Cuevas. General Manager, Centerplate (concessions): Ryan Slane.

Field Staff

Manager: Mike Jirschele. **Pitching Coach:** Doug Henry. **Hitting Coach:** Tommy Gregg. **Trainer:** Drew Van Dam. **Strength Coach:** Garrett Sherrill.

GAME INFORMATION

Radio Announcers: Mark Nasser, Kevin McNabb.
No. of Games Broadcast: Home-72, Away-72. **Flagship Station:** KOIL-AM 1180.
PA Announcer: Bill Jensen, Paul Cohen, Craig Evans, Jake Ryan.
Official Scorers: Frank Adkisson, Steve Pivovar, Ryan White.
Stadium Name (year opened): Rosenblatt Stadium (1948) Location: south of I-80 on 13th St.
Standard Game Times: 6:35 p.m. Mon-Thu. (April-May); 7:05 p.m. Mon.-Thu. (June-August); 7:05 p.m. Fri. and Sat.; 1:35 p.m. Sun.; (11:05 a.m. and 12:05 p.m. selected weekdays)
Visiting Club Hotel: Holiday Inn at Ameristar, 2202 River Road, Council Bluffs, IA 51501. **Phone:** (712) 322-5050. **Fax:** (712) 322-9232.

PORTLAND BEAVERS

Office Address: 1844 SW Morrison, Portland, OR 97205.
Telephone: (503) 553-5400. **Fax:** (505) 553-5405.
E-Mail address: info@pgepark.com. **Website:** www.portlandbeavers.com.
Affiliation (first year): San Diego Padres (2001). **Years in League:** 1903-1917, 1919-72, 1978-1993, 2001-

OWNERSHIP, MANAGEMENT

Operated By: Shortstop, LLC.
President/General Manager: Merritt Paulson. **Senior Vice President, Business Development/Broadcasting:** Ryan Brach. **Sr. VP, Operations:** Ken Puckett. **VP, Ticket Sales:** Joe Cote. **VP, Business Operations/Marketing:** Cory Dolich. **VP, Baseball Operations/Communications:** Chris Metz. **Senior Advisor:** Jack Cain. **Finance/Human Resources:** Martin Harvey. **Director, Group Sales:** Ashley Bedford. **Director, Ticket Operations:** Ben Hoel. **Director, Partner Services:** Suzy Stride. **Sr. Manager, Creative Services:** Ryan Wantland. **Sr. Manager, Season Ticket Accounts:** Dan Zusman. **Manager, Partner Services:** Rachel Faires. **Managers, Corporate Partnerships:** Matt Kolasinski, Nate Liberman. **Manager, Housekeeping:** Brian Kennedy. **Manager, Media Relations:** Marc Kostic. **Manager, Community Outreach:** Sierra Smith. **Manager, Promotions:** Jennifer Smoral. **Manager, Facility Maintenance:** Dave Tankersley. **Manager, Guest Services:** Andrea Tolonen. **Sr. Coordinator, Marketing:** Emily Berlin. **Coordinator, Ticket Sales/Executive Assistant:** Patti Peters. **Corporate Ticket Sales Account Executives:** Tim Hagerty, Neil Moore, Brian Pollard, Sara Wiggins. **Account Executives,**

Group Ticket Sales: Katie Hoffner, Alison Mathes, Kyle Veach. **Accounts Receivable:** Penny Bishop. **Accounts Payable:** Mary Cate Preston. **Receptionist/Office Manager:** Jeanne Nichols. **Head Groundskeeper:** Jesse Smith. **Home Clubhouse Manager:** Shane Hickenbottom. **Visiting Clubhouse Manager:** Tyler Neves. **Supervisor, Maintenance:** Ryan Utterback. **Operations/Systems Coordinator:** John Burchim.

FIELD STAFF
Manager: Randy Ready. **Coach:** Max Venable. **Pitching Coach:** Glenn Abbott. **Trainer:** Wade Yamasaki.

GAME INFORMATION
Radio Announcers: Rich Burk, Tim Hagerty. **No. of Games Broadcast:** Home-72 Road-72. **Flagship Station:** KKAD 1550-AM.

PA Announcer: Kevin Flink. **Official Scorer:** Blair Cash.

Stadium Name: PGE Park. **Location:** I-450 to West Burnside exit, SW 20th Street to park. **Standard Game Times:** 7:05 p.m.; Sun. 2:05. **Ticket Price Range:** $5-14.50.

Visiting Club Hotel: Doubletree Hotel-Portland Lloyd Center, 1000 NE Multnomah, Portland, OR 97232. **Telephone:** (503) 281-6111.

RENO ACES

Office Address: 250 Evans Ave., Reno, NV 89501
Telephone: (775) 334-4700. **Fax:** (775) 334-4701. **Website:** www.renoaces.com
Affiliation (second year): Arizona Diamondbacks (2009). **Years in League:** 2009-.

OWNERSHIP, MANAGEMENT
President/Managing Partner: Stuart Katzoff.

Partners: Jerry Katzoff, Herb Simon.

Chief Financial Officer: Bill Minner. **General Counsel:** Brett Beecham.

General Manager: Rick Parr. **Vice President, Baseball Operations/Communications:** T.J. Lasita. **Vice President, Special Projects:** Tracy Berrey. **Director, Broadcasting:** Ryan Radtke. **Coordinator, Media Relations:** Zak Basch. **Vice President, Sales/Marketing:** Justin Piper. **Executive Director, Manhattan Capital Sports:** Lou Scheinfeld. **Director, Marketing Partnerships:** Dwight Dortch. **Manager, Marketing Partnerships:** Karrie Sells. **Account Executive, Marketing Partnerships:** Brady Raggio. **Director, Ticketing:** Brian Moss. **Account Executive, Hospitality:** Dan Izzo. **Account Executive, Group Tickets:** Jeff Kaminski. **Manager, Client Services:** Andrei Losche. **Client Services/Tickets:** Adam Kincaid. **Director, Ticket Operations:** Charles Lucas. **Manager, Ticket Operations:** Brooke Noel. **Director, Marketing:** Brett McGinness. **Coordinator, Promotions:** Amanda Alling. **Coordinator, Mascot:** Bartholomew Piegdon. Vice President, Operations: David Avila. **Director, Ballpark Operations:** Tara O'Connor. **Manager, Grounds:** Eric Blanton. **Director, Merchandise:** Jessica Berry. **Controller:** Jerry Meyer. **Staff Accountant:** Matthew Molinari.

FIELD STAFF
Manager: Brett Butler. **Coach:** Rick Burleson. **Pitching Coach:** Mike Parrott. **Trainer:** James Ready. **Strength/Conditioning Coordinator:** Josh Cuffe.

GAME INFORMATION
Radio Announcer: Ryan Radtke. **No. of Games Broadcast:** Home-72, Away-72. **Flagship Station:** Fox Sports 1450 AM.

PA Announcer: Mike Murray. **Official Scorers:** Steve Widmer, Chad Hartley, Jack Kuestermeyer.

Stadium Name: Aces Ballpark.

Location: From Carson City (south of Reno): 395 North to exit 66 (Mill Street), left at Mill Street, right at S. Park Street, left at Kuenzll Street, right at East 2nd Street to ballpark. **From East:** I-80 West to exit 14 (Wells Avenue), left on Wells, right on Kuenzll, right at East 2nd Street.

Standard Game Times: 7:05 pm/ 6:05 pm; Sun., 1:05 pm/5:05 pm. **Ticket Price Range:** $7-29.

Visiting Club Hotel: Silver Legacy Hotel. **Telephone:** 775-325-7401.

ROUND ROCK EXPRESS

Office Address: 3400 East Palm Valley Blvd., Round Rock, TX 78665.
Telephone: (512) 255-2255. **Fax:** (512) 255-1558.
E-Mail Address: info@rrexpress.com. **Website:** www.roundrockexpress.com
Affiliation (first year): Houston Astros (2005). **Year in League:** 2005-

OWNERSHIP, MANAGEMENT
Operated By: Ryan Sanders Baseball, LP.

Principal Owners: Nolan Ryan, Reid Ryan, Reese Ryan, Don Sanders, Jay Miller, Eddie Maloney, Brad Sanders, Bret Sanders. **Executive VP, Ryan-Sanders Baseball:** J.J. Gottsch. **Executive Assistants, Ryan-Sanders Baseball:** Debbie Bowman, Kelly Looman.

President/COO: Jay Miller. **Senior Vice President/General Manager:** Dave Fendrick. **Vice President, Sales:** Henry Green. **Vice President, Tickets:** Gary Franke. **Vice President, Marketing Development:** Gregg Miller. **Controller:** Debbie Coughlin. **Director, Communications:** Larry Little. **Director, Entertainment/Promotions:** Clint Musslewhite. **Director, Merchandising (Ryan Sanders Baseball):** Brooke Milam. **Director, Ticket Operations:** Ross

Scott. **Director, United Heritage Center:** Scott Allen. **Director, Marketing/Events:** Laura Fragoso. **Senior Account Executive:** Chris Almendarez. **Account Executives:** David Allen, Luke Crum, Trey Epich, Neil Moore, Lloyd Ricketson. **Receptionist:** Wendy Abrahamsen. **Field Superintendent:** Garrett Reddehase. **Director, Broadcasting:** Mike Capps. **Clubhouse Manager:** Kenny Bufton. **Assistant Manager, The Railyard Retail Store:** Debbie Goodman. **Director, Stadium Operations:** Khalil Coltrain. **Director, Stadium Maintenance:** Aurelio Martinez. **Housekeeping:** Ofelia Gonzalez.

FIELD STAFF
Manager: Marc Bombard. **Pitching Coach:** Burt Hooton. **Coach:** Keith Bodie. **Trainer:** Mike Freer.

GAME INFORMATION
Radio Announcer: Mike Capps. **No. of Games Broadcast:** Home-72 Road-72. **Flagship Station:** 1530 AM. **PA Announcer:** Clint Musslewhite. **Official Scorer:** Tommy Tate.
Stadium Name: The Dell Diamond. **Location:** Take I-35 North to Exit 253 (Highway 79 East/Taylor). Highway 79 east for 3½ miles. Stadium on left. **Standard Game Times:** 7:05 p.m., 2:05. **Ticket Price Range:** $5-12.
Visiting Club Hotel: Hilton Garden Inn, 2310 N IH-35, Round Rock, TX 78681. **Telephone:** (512) 341-8200.

SACRAMENTO RIVER CATS

Office Address: 400 Ballpark Dr, West Sacramento, CA 95691.
Telephone: (916) 376-4700. **Fax:** (916) 376-4710.
E-Mail address: info@rivercats.com. **Website:** www.rivercats.com.
Affiliation (first year): Oakland Athletics (2000). **Years in League:** 1903, 1909-11, 1918-60, 1974-76, 2000-

OWNERSHIP, MANAGEMENT
Operated By: Sacramento River Cats Baseball Club, LLC.
Chief Executive Officer: Susan Savage. **President/General Manager/COO:** Alan Ledford. **Vice President, Finance/Project Development:** Jeff Savage. **General Counsel:** Matthew Re. **Senior Manager, Administrative Services:** Gay Caputo. **Executive VP/CFO:** Dan Vistica. **Director, Finance:** Jess Olivares. **Accounting Clerk:** Madeline Forma. **Vice President, Media Relations/Assistant GM:** Gabe Ross. **Senior Vice President, Business Development:** Darrin Gross. **Director, Corporate Partnerships:** Jennifer Maiwald. **Manager, Luxury Suites:** Ryan Von Sossan. **VP, Ticket Sales:** Ripper Hatch. **Director, Business Development:** Chad Collins. **Vice President, Community Relations:** Tony Asaro. **Senior Director, Operations:** Matt Thomas. **Director, Ticket Operations:** Steve Hill. **Senior Manager, Ticket Operations:** Jennifer Tokuyama. **Manager, Group Sales:** Creighton Kahoalii. **Manager, Inside Sales:** Chris Dreesman. **Managers, Ticket Packages:** Scott Kemp, Christi Lorenson, Matt Togami. **Seninor Account Executive, Corporate Sales:** Bryan Iredell. **Account Executive, Corporate Sales:** Steve Gracio. **Senior Group Event Executives:** Melanie Levy, Ross Johnson. **Group Event Executives:** Karen Jackson, Megan Sterling. **Coordinator, Inside Sales:** Kelly Patterson. **Senior Manager, Marketing:** Danna Bubalo. **Coordinator, Website/Research:** Brent Savage. **Graphic Artist, Creative Department:** Mike Villareal. **Head Groundskeeper:** Chris Ralston. **Coordinator, Grounds:** Marcello Clamar. **Manager, Operations:** Mario Constancio. **Manager, Merchandise:** Rose Holland.

FIELD STAFF
Manager: Tony DeFrancesco. **Hitting Coach:** Brian McArn. **Pitching Coach:** Rick Rodriguez. **Trainer:** Brad LaRosa.

GAME INFORMATION
Radio Announcers: Johnny Doskow. **No. of Games Broadcast:** Home-72 Road-72. **Flagship Station:** Unavailable.
PA Announcer: Mark Standriff. **Official Scorers:** Brian Berger, Brian Bjork, Mark Honbo.
Stadium Name: Raley Field. **Location:** I-5 to Business-80 West, exit at Jefferson Boulevard. **Standard Game Time:** 7:05 p.m. **Ticket Price Range:** $5-18.
Visiting Club Hotel: Unavailable.

SALT LAKE BEES

Office Address: 77 W. 1300 South, Salt Lake City, UT 84115.
Mailing Address: P.O. Box 4108, Salt Lake City, UT 84110.
Telephone: (801) 325-2337. **Fax:** (801) 485-6818.
E-Mail Address: info@slbees.com. **Website:** www.slbees.com.
Affiliation (first year): Los Angeles Angels (2001). **Years in League:** 1915-25, 1958-65, 1970-84, 1994-.

OWNERSHIP, MANAGEMENT
Operated by: Larry H. Miller Baseball Inc.
Principal Owner: Gail Miller.
CEO, Larry H. Miller Group of Companies: Greg Miller.
President: Randy Rigby. **Executive Vice President/CFO:** Robert Hyde. **Senior VP:** Jim Olson. **VP/General Manager:** Mark Amicone. **Senior VP, Broadcasting:** Chris Baum. **General Counsel:** Robert Tingey. **Controller:**

McKay Smith. **Director, Corporate Travel:** Judy Adams. **Senior VP, Communications:** Linda Luchetti. **Director, Broadcasting:** Steve Klauke. **Communications Coordinator:** Hannah Lee. **Senior VP, Strategic Partnerships:** Mike Snarr. **VP, Corporate Partnerships:** Greg Tanner. **VP, Marketing:** Eric Schulz. **Director, Local Corporate Partnerships:** Brian Devir. **Director, National Corporate Partnerships:** Ted Roberts. **Senior National Account Executive:** Peter Bland. **Senior Local Account Executive:** Steve Johnson. **Vice President, Ticket Sales:** Clay Jensen. **Director, Ticket Sales/Services:** Casey Patterson. Box Office Manager: Laura Russell. Ticket/Group Sales Manager: Brad Jacoway. Vice President, Public Safety: Jim Bell. **Director, Public Safety:** Al Higham. **Vice President Food Services:** Mark Stedman. **Director, Food Services:** Dave Dalton. **Youth Programs Coordinator:** Nate Martinez. **Head Groundskeeper:** Ryan Kaspitzke. **Clubhouse Manager:** Eli Rice.

FIELD STAFF
Manager: Bobby Mitchell. **Hitting Coach:** Jim Eppard. **Pitching Coach:** Eric Bennett. **Trainer:** Brian Reinker.

GAME INFORMATION
Radio Announcer: Steve Klauke. **No. of Games Broadcast:** Home-72, Away-72. **Flagship Station:** ESPN 1230-AM.
PA Announcer: Unavailable. **Official Scorers:** Unavailable. **Stadium name:** Franklin Covey Field. **Location:** I-15 North/South to 1300 South exit, east to ballpark at West Temple. **Standard Game Times:** 7 p.m., 6:30 (April-May); Sun. 2. **Ticket Price Range:** $7-22.
Visiting Club Hotel: Sheraton City Centre, 150 W. 500 South, Salt Lake City, UT 84101. **Telephone:** (801) 401-2000.

TACOMA RAINIERS

Stadium Address: 2502 South Tyler St., Tacoma, WA 98405.
Office Address: 1804 West Union Ste. 101, Tacoma, WA 98405.
Telephone: (253) 752-7707. **Fax:** (253) 752-7135.
Website: www.tacomarainiers.com
Affiliation: Seattle Mariners (1995). **Years in League:** 1904-1905, 1960-

OWNERSHIP, MANAGEMENT
Owners: Bob Schlegel, Kirby Schlegel, Nick Lachey.
President: Aaron Artman.
Vice President: Jocelyn Hill. **Vice President, Corporate Partnerships:** Mike Shields. **Vice President, Ticket Sales:** Chip Maxson. **General Manager, Food and Beverage:** Corey Brandt. **Director, Corporate Partner Services:** Audrey Berglund. **Director, Marketing/Community Development:** Annie Shultz.Director, Media Development/Events: Alyson Jones. **Director, Game Entertainment:** Jessica McDaniel. **Director, Facilities/Head Groundskeeper:** Ryan Schutt. **Director, Ticket Sales:** Shane Santman. **Director, Merchandise:** Kacy Roe. **Director, Operations:** Ashley Roth. **Director, Administration:** Patti Stacy. **Customer Service Manager:** Mallory Beckingham. **Media Development Manager:** Drew Samuelson. **Controller:** Jacquie Sonnenfeld. **Accounting:** Elise Schorr. **Corporate Sales Managers:** Adam Baker, Matt Barron, Brett Breece, Sergio Magallanes, Jim Flavin. **Group Sales Managers:** Melissa Dingler, Nicole Eaton, Sarah Yelenich, Ryan Latham. **Visitor's Clubhouse Manager:** Alex Muller. **Home Clubhouse Manager:** Eddie Romprey.

FIELD STAFF
Manager: Daren Brown. **Coach:** Alonzo Powell. **Pitching Coach:** Jaime Navarro. **Trainer:** Tom Newberg. **Assistant Trainer:** Jeremy Clipperton.

GAME INFORMATION
Radio Broadcaster: Mike Curto. **No. of Games Broadcast:** Home-72, Away-72. **Flagship Station:** KHHO 850-AM.
PA Announcer: Steve Manning. **Official Scorekeepers:** Gary Brooks, Micahel Jessee.
Stadium Name: Cheney Stadium. **Location:** From I-5, take exit 132 (Highway 16 West) for 1.2 miles to 19th Street East exit, right on Tyler St for 1/3 mile. **Standard Game Times:** 7 p.m.; Sun., 1:35. **Ticket Price Range:** $7-$25.
Visiting Club Hotel: Hotel Murano. 1320 Broadway Plaza Tacoma, WA 98402. **Telephone:** (253) 238-8000.

EASTERN LEAGUE

DOUBLE-A

Office Address: 30 Danforth St., Suite 208, Portland, ME 04101.
Telephone: (207) 761-2700. **Fax:** (207) 761-7064.
E-Mail Address: elpb@easternleague.com. **Website:** www.easternleague.com.
Years League Active: 1923-.
President, Treasurer: Joe McEacharn.
Vice President, Secretary: Charles Eshbach. **Vice President:** Chuck Domino. **Assistant to President:** Bill Rosario.
Directors: Greg Agganis (Akron), Rick Brenner (New Hampshire), Lou DiBella (Richmond), Bill Dowling (New Britain), Charles Eshbach (Portland), Joe Finley (Trenton), Bob Lozinak (Altoona), Art Matin (Erie), Michael Reinsdorf (Harrisburg), Brian Shallcross (Bowie), Craig Stein (Reading), Mike Urda (Binghamton).
Division Structure: Eastern—Binghamton, New Britain, New Hampshire, Portland, Reading, Trenton. **Western**—Akron, Altoona, Bowie, Erie, Harrisburg, Richmond.
Regular Season: 142 games. **2010 Opening Date:** April 8. **Closing Date:** Sept. 7.
All-Star Game: July 14 at Harrisburg.
Playoff Format: Top two teams in each division meet in best-of-five series. Winners meet in best-of-five series for league championship.

Joe McEacharn

Roster Limit: 24. **Player Eligibility Rule:** No restrictions. **Brand of Baseball:** Rawlings .
Umpires: Matthew Abbott (New Concord, OH), Jason Arends (Cedar Rapids, IA), William Best (Richmond, VA), Jon Byrne (Thornlie, Australia), Andrew Dudones (Uniontown, OH), Timothy Eastman (Davison, MI), Adam Hamari (Marquette, MI), Chris Hamner (Richmond, VA), Travis Hatch (Balcatta, Australia), Cory Hinga (Kalamazoo, MI), Thomas Honec (Harrisonburg, VA), Joel Hospodka (Omaha, NE), Doug Levy (Sharon, MA), Scott Mahoney (Pleasant Hill, CA), Brad Purdom (Bend, OR), Jonathan Saphire (Centerville, OH), David Soucy (Brighton, MA), Chad Whitson (Dublin, OH).

STADIUM INFORMATION

			Dimensions				
Club	Stadium	Opened	LF	CF	RF	Capacity	2009 Att.
Akron	Canal Park	1997	331	400	337	9,447	316,836
Altoona	Blair County Ballpark	1999	325	405	325	7,210	275,945
Binghamton	NYSEG Stadium	1992	330	400	330	6,012	210,526
Bowie	Prince George's Stadium	1993	309	405	309	10,000	247,660
Erie	Jerry Uht Park	1995	312	400	328	6,000	220,909
Harrisburg	Commerce Bank Park	1987	335	400	335	6,000	228,741
New Britain	New Britain Stadium	1996	330	400	330	6,146	366,682
New Hampshire	MerchantsAuto.com Stadium	2005	326	400	306	6,500	386,991
Portland	Hadlock Field	1994	315	400	330	7,368	404,709
Reading	FirstEnergy Stadium	1951	330	400	330	9,000	460,791
*Richmond	The Diamond	1985	330	402	330	12,134	N/A
Trenton	Mercer County Waterfront Park	1994	330	407	330	6,440	371,602

* Team played in Connecticut in 2009

AKRON AEROS

Office Address: 300 S Main St, Akron, OH 44308.
Telephone: (330) 253-5151. **Fax:** (330) 253-3300.
E-Mail address: info@akronaeros.com. **Website:** www.akronaeros.com.
Affiliation (first year): Cleveland Indians (1989). **Years in League:** 1989-

OWNERSHIP, MANAGEMENT

Operated By: Akron Professional Baseball, Inc.
Principal Owners: Mike Agganis, Greg Agganis.
Executive Vice President/General Manager: Jeff Auman. **Assistant General Manager:** Ken Fogel. **Director, Corporate/Suite Sales:** Calvin Funkhouser. **Director, Media Relations/Creative Services:** Jeff Holtke. **Director, Community Development:** Mike Link. **Director, Ticket Operations:** Ross Swaldo. **Senior Account Representative, Ticket Sales:** Chris Muhlberg. **Account Representatives, Ticket Sales:** Nori Wieder. Brett Joyce. **Box Office Manager:** Travis Trumitch. **Director, Field/Facility Operations:** Matt Duncan. **Merchandise Coordinator:** Ginger Hubbell. **Office Manager:** Arlene Spahn. **General Manager, Aerofare:** Brad Hooser. **Suites/Picnics Coordinator, Aerofare:** Molly Taylor. **Concessions/Warehouse Coordinator, Aerofare:** Nate Michel.

FIELD STAFF

Manager: Joel Skinner. **Coach:** Jim Rickon. **Pitching Coach:** Greg Hibbard. **Trainer:** Chad Wolfe.

GAME INFORMATION
Radio Announcers: Jim Clark. **No of Games Broadcast:** Home-71 Road-71. **Flagship Station:** Sports Radio 1350-AM. **PA Announcer:** Joe Jastrzemski, Leonard Grabowski. **Official Scorer:** Eric Stasiowski, Bob Scott. **Stadium Name:** Canal Park. **Location:** From I-76 East or I-77 South, exit onto Route 59 East, exit at Exchange/Cedar, right onto Cedar, left at Main Street. From I-76 West or I-77 North, exit at Main Street/Downtown, follow exit onto Broadway Street, left onto Exchange Street, right at Main Street. **Ticket Price Range:** $8-10.
Visiting Club Hotel: Radisson Hotel Akron Centre, 20 W. Mill St, Akron, OH 44308. **Telephone:** (330) 384-1500

ALTOONA CURVE

Office Address: Blair County Ballpark, 1000 Park Avenue, Altoona, PA 16602. **Telephone:** (814) 943-5400. **Fax:** (814) 942-9132. **E-Mail Address:** frontoffice@altoonacurve.com. **Website:** www.altoonacurve. com.
Affiliation (first year): Pittsburgh Pirates (1999). **Years in League:** 1999-

OWNERSHIP, MANAGEMENT
Operated By: Lozinak Professional Baseball.
Managing Member: Bob Lozinak. **COO:** David Lozinak. **CFO:** Mike Lozinak. **Chief Administrative Officer:** Steve Lozinak. **General Manager:** Rob Egan. **Senior Advisor:** Sal Baglieri. **Director, Broadcasting/Communications:** Dan Zangrilli. **Director, Community Relations:** Elsie Zengel. **Director, Merchandising:** Claire Martin. **Director, Ballpark Operations:** Kirk Stiffler. **Director, Ticketing/Promotions:** Matt Hoover. **Director, Creative Services:** John Foreman. **Ticket Sales Associates:** Chris Keefer, Mike Pence, A.J. Palazzi, Cassie Stroup. **Administrative Assistant:** Carol Schmittle. **Sponsorship Sales Account Executive:** Chuck Griswold. **Director, Catering/Concessions:** Barbara Rogier. **Assistant Director, Catering/Concessions:** Glenn McComas.

FIELD STAFF
Manager: Matt Walbeck. **Coach:** Ryan Long. **Pitching Coach:** Tom Filer. **Trainer:** Bryan Housand. **Strength/ Conditioning:** Brandon McDaniel.

GAME INFORMATION
Radio Announcer: Dan Zangrilli. **No. of Games Broadcast:** Home-71 Road-71. **Flagship Station:** ESPN Radio 1430 (WVAM-AM).
PA Announcer: Rich DeLeo. **Official Scorer:** Ted Beam, Dick Wagner. **Stadium Name:** Blair County Ballpark. **Location:** Located just off the Frankstown Road Exit of I-99. **Standard Game Times:** 7 p.m., 6:30 (April-May); Sun. 6, 2 (April-May). **Ticket Price Range:** $5-12.
Visiting Club Hotel: Ramada Altoona, Route 220 and Plank Road, Altoona, PA 16602. **Telephone:** (814) 946-1631.

BINGHAMTON METS

Office Address: 211 Henry St, Binghamton, NY 13901. **Mailing Address:** P.O. Box 598, Binghamton, NY 13902. **Telephone:** (607) 723-6387. **Fax:** (607) 723-7779. **E-Mail address:** bmets@bmets.com. **Website:** www.bmets.com. **Affiliation (first year):** New York Mets (1992). **Years in League:** 1923-37, 1940-63, 1966-68, 1992-

OWNERSHIP, MANAGEMENT
Principal Owners: Bill Maines, David Maines, George Scherer, Michael Urda.
General Manager: Scott Brown. **Assistant GM:** Jim Weed. **Director, Stadium Operations:** Richard Tylicki. **Director, Ticket Operations:** Casey Both. **Director, Video Productions:** Jon Cofer. **Director, Marketing:** Heith Tracy. **Special Event Coordinators:** Connor Gates, Erica Mincher, Bob Urda. **Scholastic Programs Coordinator:** Lou Ferraro. **Community Relations Coordinator:** Amy Fancher. **Office Manager:** Rebecca Brown. **Merchandising Manager:** Lisa Shattuck. **Broadcasting Director:** Robert Ford. **Sports Turf Manager:** Stephen Wiseman. **Home Clubhouse Manager:** Pete Stasio. **Visiting Clubhouse Manager:** Jim Coughlin.

FIELD STAFF
Manager: Tim Teufel. **Coach:** Luis Natera . **Pitching Coach:** Mark Brewer.

GAME INFORMATION
Radio Announcer: Matt McCabe. **No. of Games Broadcast:** Home-71 Road-71. **Flagship Station:** WNBF 1290-AM.
PA Announcer: Unavailable. **Official Scorer:** Steve Kraly. **Stadium Name:** NYSEG Stadium. **Location:** I-81 to exit 4S (Binghamton), Route 11 exit to Henry Street. **Standard Game Times:** 6:35 (Sun-Thur), 7:05 (Fri-Sat); Day Games 1:05. **Ticket Price Range:** $9-10.
Visiting Club Hotel: Best Western, 569 Harry L Drive, Johnson City, NY 13790. **Telephone:** (607) 729-9194.

BOWIE BAYSOX

Office Address: Prince George's Stadium, 4101 NE Crain Hwy, Bowie, MD 20716.
Telephone: (301) 805-6000. Fax: (301) 464-4911.
E-Mail address: info@baysox.com. Website: www.baysox.com.
Affiliation (first year): Baltimore Orioles (1993). Years in League: 1993-

OWNERSHIP, MANAGEMENT
Owned By: Bowie Baysox Baseball Club LLC.
President: Ken Young.
General Manager: Brian Shallcross. Assistant GM: Phil Wrye. Director, Marketing: Brandan Kaiser. Director, Field/Facility Operations: Matt Parrott. Director, Ticket Operations: Charlene Fewer. Director, Sponsorships: Matt McLaughlin. Director, Promotions: Lauren Phillips. Promotions Manager: Chris Rogers. Communications Manager: Tom Sedlacek. Communications Assistant: Robert Bartlett. Community Programs Manager: Dana DeFilippo. Marketing Assistant/Mascot Operations: Henry Gomez. Account Executive: Aaron Gunter. Group Events Managers: Vince Riggs, Janna Green. Manager, Stadium Operations: Rick Wade. Director, Gameday Personnel: Darlene Mingioli. Clubhouse Manager: Andy Maalouf. Visiting Clubhouse Manager: Unavailable. Office Manager: Karen Marcher. Bookkeeper: Carol Terwilliger.

FIELD STAFF
Manager: Brad Komminsk. Coach: Moe Hill. Pitching Coach: Kennie Steenstra. Trainer: Joe Benge.

GAME INFORMATION
Radio Announcer: Unavailable. No. of Games Broadcast: Unavailable. Flagship Station: Unavailable.
PA Announcer: Adrienne Roberson. Official Scorer: Bill Hay, Carl Smith, Peter O'Reilly.
Stadium Name: Prince George's Stadium. Location: ¼ mile south of U.S. 50/RT. 301 Interchange in Bowie.
Standard Game Times: 7:05 p.m; Sun. 2:05 (April-May), 6:05 (June-Sept.). Ticket Price Range: $6-14.
Visiting Club Hotel: Best Western Annapolis, 2520 Riva Rd, Annapolis, MD 21401. Telephone: (410) 224-2800.

ERIE SEA WOLVES

Office Address: 110 E. 10th St, Erie, PA 16501.
Telephone: (814) 456-1300. Fax: (814) 456-7520.
E-Mail address: seawolves@seawolves.com. Website: www.seawolves.com.
Affiliation (first year): Detroit Tigers (2001). Years in League: 1999-

OWNERSHIP, MANAGEMENT
Principal Owners: Mandalay Baseball Properties, LLC.
General Manager: John Frey. Assistant GM, Sales: Mike Uden. Director, Finance: Boyd Armstrong. Director, Ticket Sales: Becky Obradovic. Director, Media Relations/Broadcaster: Greg Gania. Director, Corporate Marketing: Mark Pirrello. Director, Operations/Concessions: Brad Strobl. Operations Manager: Ryan Stephenson. Ticket Operations Manager: Cody Herrick. Director, Special Events/Client Services: Jason Vaughan.

FIELD STAFF
Manager: Phil Nevin. Coach: Glen Adams. Pitching Coach: Ray Burris. Trainer: Chris McDonald.

GAME INFORMATION
Radio Announcer: Greg Gania. No. of Games Broadcast: Home-71 Road-71. Flagship Station: Fox Sports Radio WFNN 1330-AM.
PA Announcer: Bob Shreve. Official Scorer: Les Caldwell.
Stadium Name: Jerry Uht Park. Location: U.S. 79 North to East 12th Street exit, left on State Street, right on 10th Street. Standard Game Times: 7:05 p.m., 6:35 (April-May); Sun. 1:05. Ticket Price Range: $5-12.
Visiting Club Hotel: Unavailable.

HARRISBURG SENATORS

Office Address: Metro Bank Park, City Island, Harrisburg, PA 17101.
Mailing Address: P.O. Box 15757, Harrisburg, PA 17105.
Telephone: (717) 231-4444. Fax: (717) 231-4445.
E-Mail address: information@senatorsbaseball.com. Website: www.senatorsbaseball.com.
Affiliation (first year): Washington Nationals (2005). Years in League: 1924-35, 1987-

OWNERSHIP, MANAGEMENT
Operated By: Senators Partners, LLC.
Chairman: Michael Reinsdorf. CEO: Bill Davidson. President: Kevin Kulp.
General Manager: Randy Whitaker. Director, Broadcasting/Media Relations: Terry Byrom; Director, Stadium Operations: Tim Foreman; Director, Game Entertainment: Aaron Margolis. Director, Group Sales: Mac Simmons.

Director, Community Relations: Emily Winslow. **Director, Electronic Media:** Andy Brooks. **Director, Merchandising:** Ann Marie Naumes. **Ticket Sales Manager:** Jon Tapper. **Box Office Manager:** David Simpson. **Senior Executive, Ticket Sales:** Scott Moudry. **Senior Corporate Sales Executive:** Todd Matthews. **Corporate Sales Executive:** Jessica Snader. **Ticket Sales Executives:** Jon Boles, Jessica Kauffman. **Head Groundskeeper:** Brandon Forsburg. **Bookkeeper:** Donna Demczak. **Interns:** Ryan Miller, Gwen Wiscount, Ashley Ford, Ashley Grotte, Chris French, Matt Tymann, Daniel Haubert, Terrence Breen.

FIELD STAFF
Manager: Randy Knorr. **Coach:** Tony Gingrich. **Pitching Coach:** Randy Tomlin. **Trainer:** Atsushi Toriida.

GAME INFORMATION
Radio Announcer: Terry Byrom, Matt Tymann. **No. of Games Broadcast:** Home-71 Road-71. **Flagship Station:** 1460-AM.
PA Announcer: Chris Andre. **Official Scorer:** Terry Walters, Bruce Bashore.
Stadium Name: Metro Bank Park. **Location:** I-83, exit 23 (Second Street) to Market Street, bridge to City Island. **Ticket Price Range:** $5-12.50
Visiting Club Hotel: Holiday Inn West, 5401 Carlisle Pike, Mechanicsburg, PA 17050. **Telephone:** (800) 772-7829.

NEW BRITAIN ROCK CATS

Office Address: 230 John Karbonic Way, New Britain, CT 06051.
Mailing Address: P.O. Box 1718, New Britain, CT 06050.
Telephone: (860) 224-8383. **Fax:** (860) 225-6267.
E-Mail address: rockcats@rockcats.com. **Website:** www.rockcats.com.
Affiliation (first year): Minnesota Twins (1995). **Years in League:** 1983-

OWNERSHIP, MANAGEMENT
Operated By: New Britain Baseball Club Inc.
Principal Owners: Bill Dowling, Coleman Levy. **President/CEO:** Bill Dowling. **Chairman of the Board:** Coleman Levy.
Vice President/General Manager: John Willi. **Vice President:** Evan Levy. **Assistant GM/Sales:** Ricky Ferrell. **Director, Broadcasting:** Jeff Dooley. **Director, Ticket Operations:** Mike DiMartini. **Director, Group Sales:** Jonathan Lissitchuck. **Director, Promotions:** Kim Pizighelli. **Director, Media Relations:** Robert Dowling. **Director, Corporate Sales:** Andres Levy. **Group Sales Manager:** Evan Paradis. **Marketing Coordinator:** Lori Soltis. **Corporate Sales Manager:** Kate Baumann. **Director, Community Relations:** Amy Helbling. **Corporate Sales:** Nikki Bowey. **Controller:** Paula Perdelwitz. **On-site Manager, Concessionaire Centerplate:** Sheila Fagan.

FIELD STAFF
Manager: Jeff Smith. **Coach:** Rudy Hernandez. **Pitching Coach:** Stu Cliburn. **Trainer:** Chad Jackson.

GAME INFORMATION
Radio Announcer: Jeff Dooley, Joe D'Ambrosio. **No. of Games Broadcast:** Home-71 Road-71. **Flagship Station:** WTIC 1080-AM/96.5-FM, WMRD 1150-AM.
PA Announcer: Don Steele. **Official Scorer:** Ed Smith.
Stadium Name: New Britain Stadium. **Location:** From I-84, take Route 72 East (exit 35 of Route 9 South (exit 39A), left at Ellis Street (exit 25), left at South Main Street, stadium one mile on right. From Route 91 or Route 5, take Route 9 North to Route 71 (exit 24), first exit. **Ticket Price Range:** $5-12.
Visiting Club Hotel: Holiday Inn Express, 120 Laning St, Southington, CT 06489. **Telephone:** (860) 276-0736.

NEW HAMPSHIRE
FISHER CATS

Office Address: 1 Line Dr., Manchester, NH 03101.
Telephone: (603) 641-2005. **Fax:** (603) 641-2055.
E-Mail address: info@nhfishercats.com. **Website:** www.nhfishercats.com.
Affiliation (first year): Toronto Blue Jays (2004). **Years in League:** 2004-

OWNERSHIP, MANAGEMENT
Operated By: Triple Play LLC.
Owner: Art Solomon.
President/General Manager: Rick Brenner. **Vice President, Business Operations:** Tim Restall. **VP, Sales:** Mike Ramshaw. **VP, Marketing:** Loren Foxx. **Corporate Controller:** Cindy Garron. **Director, Public Affairs:** Danielle Matteau. **Director, Media Relations:** Mike Murphy. **Director, Sales:** Istvan Ats. **Director, Group Sales:** Erik Lesniak. **Director, Merchandise/Ticket Operations:** Kaitlyn Tomasello. **Head Turf Manager:** Shaun Meredith. **Manager, Stadium Operations:** Matt Moore. **Community Relations/Office Manager:** Kathryn Mitchell. **Promotional Manager:** Morgan Crandall. **Marketing Manager:** Liam Roberge. **Production Manager:** Jake Dodge. **Box Office Manager:** Tim Hough.

Ticket Sales Account Executives: John Costa, Josh Hubbard, Joel Leroy, Gregg Tadgell. **Assistant Turf Manager:** Brian Schools.

FIELD STAFF

Manager: Luis Rivera. **Hitting Coach:** Ralph Dickenson. **Pitching Coach:** Tom Signore. **Trainer:** Bob Tarpey.

GAME INFORMATION

Radio Announcers: Mike Murphy, Bob Lipman. **No of Games Broadcast:** Home-71 Road-71. **Flagship Station:** WGIR 610-AM.

PA Announcer: Alex James. **Official Scorers:** Chick Smith, Lenny Parker, Greg Royce, Pete Dupuis.

Stadium Name: Merchantsauto.com Stadium. **Location:** From I-93 North, take I-293 North to exit 5 (Granite Street), right on Granite Street, right on South Commercial Street, right on Line Drive. **Ticket Price Range:** $6-12.

Visiting Club Hotel: Comfort Inn, 298 Queen City Ave, Manchester, NH 03102. **Telephone:** (603) 668-2600.

PORTLAND SEA DOGS

Office Address: 271 Park Ave, Portland, ME 04102.
Mailing Address: P.O. Box 636, Portland, ME 04104.
Telephone: (207) 874-9300. **Fax:** (207) 780-0317.
E-Mail address: seadogs@seadogs.com. **Website:** www.seadogs.com.
Affiliation (first year): Boston Red Sox (2003). **Years in League:** 1994-

OWNERSHIP, MANAGEMENT

Operated By: Portland, Maine Baseball, Inc.

Principal Owner, Chairman: Daniel Burke.

President, General Manager: Charles Eshbach. **Executive Vice President:** John Kameisha. **VP:** Jim Heffley. **Assistant GM, Media Relations:** Chris Cameron. **Assistant GM, Sales/Promotions:** Geoff Iacuessa. **Director, Group Sales:** Liz Riley. **Director, Ticketing:** Dave Strong. **Assistant Director, Ticketing:** Sarah Connolly. **Sales/Marketing Administrator:** Brian Murphy. **Director, Broadcasting:** Mike Antonellis. **Director, Food Services:** Mike Scorza. **Assistant Director, Food Services:** Greg Moyes. **Clubhouse Managers:** Craig Candage Sr., Mike Mestieri, Nick Fox. **Head Groundskeeper:** Rick Anderson.

FIELD STAFF

Manager: Arnie Beyeler. **Coach:** Dave Joppie. **Pitching Coach:** Bob Kipper. **Trainer:** Paul Buchheit.

GAME INFORMATION

Radio Announcer: Mike Antonellis. **No. of Games Broadcast:** Home-71 Road-71. **Flagship Station:** WBAE 1490-AM.

PA Announcer: Dean Rogers. **Official Scorer:** Thom Hinton.

Stadium Name: Hadlock Field. **Location:** From South, I-295 to exit 5, merge onto Congress Street, left at St. John Street, merge right onto Park Ave. From North, I-295 to exit 6A, right onto Park Ave. **Ticket Price Range:** $4-9.

Visiting Club Hotel: Wyndham Hotel, 363 Maine Mall Rd, South Portland, ME 04106. **Telephone:** (207) 775-6161.

READING PHILLIES

Office Address: Route 61 South/1900 Centre Ave., Reading, PA 19605.
Mailing Address: P.O. Box 15050, Reading, PA 19612.
Telephone: (610) 375-8469. **Fax:** (610) 373-5868.
E-Mail Address: info@readingphillies.com. **Website:** www.readingphillies.com.
Affiliation (first year): Philadelphia Phillies (1967). **Years in League:** 1933-35, 1952-61, 1963-65, 1967-.

OWNERSHIP, MANAGEMENT

Operated By: E&J Baseball Club, Inc.

Principal Owner: Reading Baseball LP

Managing Partner: Craig Stein.

General Manager: Scott Hunsicker. **Assistant GM:** Ashley Forlini. **Director, Stadium Operations/Concessions:** Andy Bortz. **Director, Sales:** Joe Bialek. **Director, Baseball Operations/Merchandise:** Kevin Sklenarik. **Director, PR/Media Relations:** Tommy Viola. **Director, Ticket Operations:** Mike Becker. **Director, Group Sales:** Mike Robinson. **Director, Fan Development:** Chris McConney. **Controller:** Kristyne Haver. **Corporate Sales/Graphic Artist/Game Entertainment:** Matt Jackson. **Assistant Director, Groups:** Holly Frymyer. **Director, Community Relations:** Matt Hoffmaster. **Video Director:** Andy Kauffman. **Client Relationship Managers:** Curtis Burns, Ryan Contento, Jon Muldowney. **Assistant Director, Tickets:** Tim McGee. **Operations/Concessions Assistant:** Tim Martino. **Head Groundskeeper:** Dan Douglas. **Office Manager:** Deneen Giesen.

FIELD STAFF

Manager: Steve Roadcap. **Coach:** Frank Cacciatore. **Pitching Coach:** Bob Milacki. **Trainer:** Chris Mudd.

GAME INFORMATION

Radio Announcers: Unavailable. **No. of Games Broadcast:** Home-71, Away-71. **Flagship Station:** ESPN 1240-AM.

PA Announcer: Dave Bauman. **Official Scorers:** Paul Jones, Brian Kopetsky, Josh Leiboff, Dick Shute.

Stadium Name: FirstEnergy Stadium. **Location:** From east, take Pennsylvania Turnpike West to Morgantown exit, to 176 North, to 422 West, to Route 12 East, to Route 61 South exit. From west, take 422 East to Route 12 East, to Route 61 South exit. From north, take 222 South to Route 12 exit, to Route 61 South exit. From south, take 222 North to 422 West, to Route 12 East exit at Route 61 South. **Standard Game Times:** 7:05 p.m., Mon.-Thurs. (April-May) 6:35; Sun. 1:05. **Ticket Price Range:** $6-11

Visiting Club Hotel: Days Inn, 910 Woodland Ave., Wyomissing PA 19610. **Telephone:** (610) 375-1500.

RICHMOND
FLYING SQUIRRELS

Office Address: 3001 N. Boulevard, Richmond, VA 23230.
Telephone: (804) 359-3866. **Fax:** (804) 359-1373.
E-Mail address: info@squirrelsbaseball.com. **Website:** www.squirrelsbaseball.com.
Affiliation (first year): San Francisco Giants (2009). **Years in League:** 2009-

OWNERSHIP, MANAGEMENT

Operated By: Navigators Baseball LP.

President/Managing Partner: Lou DiBella.

CEM: Chuck Domino. **Vice President/COO:** Todd Parnell.

General Manager: Bill Papierniak. **Controller:** Faith Casey. **Director, Corporate Sales:** Ben Terry. **Corporate Sales Executives:** Amanda Ayers, Lisa Washington. **Director, Tickets:** Brendon Porter. **Box Office Manager:** Ben Snyder. **Director, Broadcasting:** Jon Laaser. **Director, Media:** Anthony Oppermann. **Director, Community Relations/Promotions:** Christina Shisler. **Director, Group Sales:** Randy Atkinson. **Assistant Director, Group Sales:** Laura Kenny. **Director, Merchandise:** Ben Rothrock. **Director, Food/Beverage:** Justin Rink. **Director, Field Operations:** Steve Ruckman. **Director, Stadium Operations:** Tom White.

FIELD STAFF

Manager: Andy Skeels. **Hitting Coach:** Russ Morman. **Pitching Coach:** Ross Grimsley. **Trainer:** Eric Ortega.

GAME INFORMATION

Radio Announcers: Jon Laaser, Anthony Oppermann. **No. of Games Broadcast:** Home-71 Road-71. **Flagship Station:** Sports Radio 910 WRNL-AM. **PA Announcer:** Unavailable. **Official Scorer:** Unavailable. **Stadium Name:** The Diamond. **Capacity:** 10,500.

Location: Right off I-64 at the Boulevard exit.

Standard Game Times: 7:05 p.m. (M-F), 6:35 p.m. (Sat.), 5:05 (Sun.).

Ticket Price Range: $6-10.

Visiting Club Hotel: Holiday Inn I-64 West End, 2000 Staples Mill Road, Richmond, VA 23230. **Telephone:** (804) 359-6061.

TRENTON THUNDER

Office Address: One Thunder Road, Trenton, NJ 08611.
Telephone: (609) 394-3300. **Fax:** (609) 394-9666.
E-Mail address: fun@trentonthunder.com. **Website:** www.trentonthunder.com.
Affiliation (first year): New York Yankees (2003). **Years in League:** 1994-

OWNERSHIP, MANAGEMENT

Operated By: Garden State Baseball, LLP.
General Manager/COO: Will Smith.
Senior Vice President, Corporate Sales/Sponsorships: Eric Lipsman. **Director, Ticket Operations:** Matt Pentima. **Director, Public Relations:** Bill Cook. **Director, Merchandising:** Joe Pappalardo. **Vice President, Ticket Revenue:** Bob Capewell. **Director, Stadium Operations:** Ryan Crammer. **Director, Food/Beverage:** Kevin O'Byrne. **Assistant Director, Food/Beverage:** Chris Champion. **Director, Community Relations:** Patience Purdy. **Director, Finance:** Catherine Gallagher. **Director, Business Development:** C.J. Johnson. **Office Manager:** Susanna Hall. **Production Manager:** Greg Lavin. **Corporate Partnerships Manager:** Marty Teller. **Baseball Operations/Accounting Manager:** Jeff Hurley. **Stadium Operations Manager:** Steve Brokowsky. **Group Sales Account Executives:** Krysten Hardifer, Chad Heidel, Mike Elser, Lauren Bilardo. **Account Representatives, Ticket Sales/Group Sales:** Anna Rosenblatt, T.J. Jahn, Bobby Picardo. **Ticket Sales Account Executive:** Erin Leigh. **Marketing/Promotions Manager:** Rachel Wolf. **Media Relations/Broadcasting Assistant:** Justin Shackil. **Merchandise Assistant:** Megan Donovan. **Building Superintendent:** Scott Ribsam. **Home Clubhouse Manager:** Tom Kackley. Visiting **Clubhouse Manager:** Jim Billington. **Head Groundskeeper:** Ryan Hills.

FIELD STAFF

Manager: Tony Franklin. **Hitting Coach:** Frank Menechino. **Pitching Coach:** Tommy Phelps. **Coach:** Vic Valencia. **Trainer:** Tim Lentych. Strength/Conditioning Coach: Jason Meredith.

GAME INFORMATION

Radio Announcer: Justin Shackil. **No. of Games Broadcast:** Home-71 Road 71. **Flagship Station:** 107.7 FM The Bronc.
PA Announcer: Bill Bromberg. **Official Scorers:** Jay Dunn, Greg Zak.
Stadium Name: Samuel L. Plumeri Sr. Field at Mercer County Waterfront Park. **Location:** From I-95, take Route 1 North to Route 29 South, stadium entrance just before tunnel. From NJ Turnpike, take Exit 7A and follow I-195 West. Road will become Rte. 29. Follow through tunnel and ballpark is on left. **Standard Game Times:** 7:05 p.m.; Sat. 1:05 (April); Sun 1:05. **Ticket Price Range:** $9-12.
Visiting Club Hotel: Trenton Marriott, 1 West Lafayette Street, Trenton, NJ 08608. **Telephone:** (609) 421-4000.

SOUTHERN LEAGUE

DOUBLE-A

Mailing Address: 2551 Roswell Rd., Suite 330, Marietta, GA 30062. **Telephone:** (770) 321-0400. **Fax:** (770) 321-0037.

E-Mail Address: office@southernleague.com. **Website:** www.southernleague.com.

Years League Active: 1964-.

President: Don Mincher. **Vice President:** Steve DeSalvo.

Directors: Peter Bragan Jr. (Jacksonville), Steve Bryant (Carolina), Frank Burke (Chattanooga), Steve DeSalvo (Mississippi), Tom Dickson (Montgomery), Doug Kirchhofer (Tennessee), Jonathan Nelson (Birmingham), Miles Prentice (Huntsville), Bill Shanahan (Mobile), Reese Smith (West Tenn).

Vice President, Operations: Lori Webb. **Media Relations Director:** Peter Webb.

Division Structure: North—Carolina, Chattanooga, Huntsville, Tennessee, West Tenn. **South**—Birmingham, Jacksonville, Mississippi, Mobile, Montgomery.

Regular Season: 140 games (split schedule). **2010 Opening Date:** April 8. **Closing Date:** Sept. 6.

All-Star Game: July 12 in Huntsville.

Playoff Format: First-half division winners meet second-half division winners in best-of-five series. Winners meet in best-of-five series for league championship.

Roster Limit: 24. **Player Eligibility Rule:** No restrictions.

Brand of Baseball: Rawlings.

Umpires: Gerard Ascani, Nick Bailey, Jordan Baker, Sean Barber, Craig Barron, Travis Brown, Travis Carlson, Jason Cooksey, Tripp Gibson, Will Little, Brent Rice, Matt Schaufert, Chris Segal, Anthony West, Quinn Wolcott.

Don Mincher

STADIUM INFORMATION

Club	Stadium	Opened	LF	CF	RF	Capacity	2009 Att.
Birmingham	Regions Park	1988	340	405	340	10,800	287,185
Carolina	Five County Stadium	1991	330	400	330	6,500	263,175
Chattanooga	AT&T Field	2000	325	400	330	6,362	224,157
Huntsville	Joe W. Davis Municipal Stadium	1985	345	405	330	10,200	93,845
Jacksonville	Baseball Grounds of Jacksonville	2003	321	420	317	11,000	354,553
Mississippi	Trustmark Park	2005	335	402	332	7,416	194,795
Mobile	Hank Aaron Stadium	1997	325	400	310	6,000	209,742
Montgomery	Montgomery Riverwalk Stadium	2004	314	380	332	7,000	266,818
Tennessee	Smokies Park	2000	330	400	330	6,000	260,153
West Tenn	Pringles Park	1998	310	395	320	6,000	129,778

BIRMINGHAM BARONS

Office Address: 100 Ben Chapman Dr., Hoover, AL 35244.
Mailing Address: P.O. Box 360007, Birmingham, AL 35236.
Telephone: (205) 988-3200. **Fax:** (205) 988-9698.
E-Mail Address: barons@barons.com. **Website:** www.barons.com
Affiliation (first year): Chicago White Sox (1986). **Years in League:** 1964-65, 1967-75, 1981-

OWNERSHIP, MANAGEMENT

Principal Owners: Don Logan, Jeff Logan, Stan Logan. **General Manager:** Jonathan Nelson. **Director, Stadium Operations:** James Young. **Director, Broadcasting:** Curt Bloom. **Director, Media Relations:** Justin Rosenberg. **Director, Sales:** Charles Jourdan. **Director, Tickets:** Charlie Santiago. **Director, Group Sales:** Brad Hudson. **Director, Promotions:** Kyle Krebs. **Director, Community Relations:** Shawn Pharo. **Director, Production:** Zane Davitz. **Manager, Operations:** David Madison. **Corporate Event Planners:** Dusty Lewis, Elizabeth Taylor. **General Manager, Grand Slam Catering:** Eric Crook. **Director, Catering:** Taylor Youngson. **Office Manager:** Jennifer Dillard. **Accountant:** Jo Ann Bragan. **Accountant:** Sammy Schillaci. **Head Groundskeeper:** Daniel Ruggiero. **Assistant Groundskeeper:** Caleb Adams. **Interns:** Will Edge, Brandon Harms, Chris Holmes, Zak Blakeney.

FIELD STAFF

Manager: Ever Magallanes. **Hitting Coach:** Andy Tomberlin. **Pitching Coach:** J.R. Pedrew. **Trainer:** Joe Geck. **Strength/Conditioning:** Raymond Smith.

GAME INFORMATION

Radio Announcer: Curt Bloom. **No of Games Broadcast:** Home-70 Road-70. **Flagship Station:** Unavailable. **PA Announcer:** Eddie Layne, Derek Scudder. **Official Scorer:** Grant Martin. **Stadium Name:** Regions Park. **Location:** I-459 to Highway 150 (exit 10) in Hoover. **Standard Game Times:** 7:05 p.m.; Sat. 6:30; Sun. 2:05 (First Half), 5:05 (Second Half). **Ticket Price Range:** $7-12.

Visiting Club Hotel: Days Inn at the Galleria, 1800 Riverchase Dr, Birmingham, AL 35244. **Telephone:** (205) 985-7500.

CAROLINA MUDCATS

Office Address: 1501 N.C. Hwy. 39, Zebulon, NC 27597.
Mailing Address: P.O. Drawer 1218, Zebulon, NC 27597.
Telephone: (919) 269-2287. **Fax:** (919) 269-4910.
E-Mail Address: muddy@gomudcats.com. **Website:** www.gomudcats.com.
Affiliation (first year): Cincinnati Reds (2009). **Years in League:** 1991-

OWNERSHIP, MANAGEMENT

Operated by: Carolina Mudcats Professional Baseball Club Inc.
Principal Owner: Steve Bryant.
General Manager: Joe Kremer. **Assistant GM:** Eric Gardner. **Office Manager:** Jackie DiPrimo. **Directors, Stadium Operations:** Stephen Newsome, Daniel Spence. **Director, Marketing:** Alexandra Briley. **Director, Food/Beverage:** Zia Torabian. **Director, Community Relations:** Lindsay Wiener. **Director, Merchandise:** Anne Allen. **Director, Video Operations/Multimedia Productions/Website:** Aaron Bayles. **Director, Tickets:** Jon Clemmons. **Director, Corporate Sales:** Ricky Ray. **Director, Group Sales:** Haig Lea. **Group Sales Associates:** Chris Signorelli, Joshua Bridges. **Director, Fundraising/Luxury Suites:** Macy Dykema. **Director, Field Operations:** John Packer. **Director, Special Events:** Nathan Priddy.

FIELD STAFF

Manager: David Bell. **Coach:** Ryan Jackson. **Pitching Coach:** Tom Brown. **Trainer:** Jimmy Mattocks.

GAME INFORMATION

Radio Announcers: Patrick Kinas, Joe Bourdow. **No. of Games Broadcast:** Home-70, Away-70. **Flagship Stations:** WDOX-AM 570, WDWG-FM 98.5.
PA Announcer: Dave Slade. **Official Scorer:** Unavailable.
Stadium Name: Five County Stadium. **Location:** From Raleigh, U.S. 64 East to 264 East, exit at Highway 39 in Zebulon. **Standard Game Times:** 7:15 p.m.; Sat. 6:15; Sun. 2. **Ticket Price Range:** $6-11.
Visiting Club Hotel: Unavailable.

CHATTANOOGA LOOKOUTS

Office Address: 201 Power Alley, Chattanooga, TN 37402.
Mailing Address: P.O. Box 11002, Chattanooga, TN 37401.
Telephone: (423) 267-2208. **Fax:** (423) 267-4258.
E-Mail Address: lookouts@lookouts.com. **Website:** www.lookouts.com.
Affiliation (first year): Los Angeles Dodgers (2009). **Years in League:** 1964-65, 1976-

OWNERSHIP, MANAGEMENT

Operated By: Scenic City Baseball LLC.
Principal Owner: Daniel Burke, Frank Burke, Charles Eshbach.
President/General Manager: Frank Burke. **Vice President/Assistant GM:** John Maedel. **Director, Business Administration/Executive Assistant:** Debby Kennedy. **Director, Group Sales:** Bill Wheeler. **Director, Merchandising/Marketing:** Chrysta Jorgensen. **Director, Media Relations:** Peter Intza. **Director, Ticketing Operations:** Luis Gonzalez. **Director, Concessions:** Steve Sullivan. **Director, Broadcasting:** Larry Ward. **Head Groundskeeper:** Bo Henley. **Director, Stadium Operations/Assistant Director, Broadcasting:** Will Poindexter. **Director, Business Administration/Accounting:** Brian Eshbach. **Assistant Director, Concessions:** John Quirk. **Ticketing Assistant:** Gavin Cox. **Ticketing Assistant:** Matt St. Charles.

FIELD STAFF

Manager: Carlos Subero. **Hitting Coach:** John Valentin. **Pitching Coach:** Danny Darwin.

GAME INFORMATION

Radio Announcers: Larry Ward, Will Poindexter. **No. of Games Broadcast:** Home-70 Road-70. **Flagship Station:** WDOD 1310-AM.
PA Announcer: John Maedel. **Official Scorers:** Wirt Gammon, Andy Paul, Laird Leathers .
Stadium Name: AT&T Field. **Location:** From I-24, take U.S. 27 North to exit 1C (4th Street), first left onto Chestnut Street, left onto Third Street. **Ticket Price Range:** $4-8.
Visiting Club Hotel: Clarion Inn & Suites , 2345 Shallowford Rd, Chattanooga, TN 37412. **Telephone:** (423) 855-2898.

HUNTSVILLE STARS

Office Address: 3125 Leeman Ferry Rd., Huntsville, AL 35801.
Telephone: (256) 882-2562. **Fax:** (256) 880-0801.
E-Mail Address: info@huntsvillestars.com. **Website:** www.huntsvillestars.com.
Affiliation (first year): Milwaukee Brewers (1999). **Years in League:** 1985-

OWNERSHIP, MANAGEMENT

Operated By: Huntsville Stars LLC.
President: Miles Prentice.
General Manager: Buck Rogers. **Office Manager:** Earl Grilliot. **Head Groundskeeper:** Jamie Hill. **Director, Media/Public Relations:** Brian Massey. **Director, Merchandising:** Kylee Hanish. **Director, Ticketing/Group Sales:** Babs Rogers. **Director, Concessions:** Scott Tolmach. **Sales Associate:** Matthew Edgeworth.

FIELD STAFF

Manager: Mike Guerrero. **Coach:** Al LeBoeuf. **Pitching Coach:** John Curtis. **Athletic Trainer:** Aaron Hoback.

GAME INFORMATION

Radio Announcer: Brett Pollock. **Flagship station:** All games webcast only.
PA Announcers: Todd Blass, J.J. Lewis. **Official Scorer:** Don Rizzardi.
Stadium Name: Joe W. Davis Municipal Stadium. **Location:** I-65 to I-565 East, south on Memorial Parkway to Drake Avenue exit, right on Don Mincher Drive. **Ticket Price Range:** $8-$20. **Visiting Club Hotel:** Microtel Inn & Suites, 1820 Chase Creek Row, Huntsville, AL 35811. **Telephone:** 256-859-6655.

JACKSONVILLE SUNS

Office Address: 301 A. Philip Randolph Blvd., Jacksonville, FL 32202.
Mailing Address: P.O. Box 4756, Jacksonville, FL 32201.
Telephone: (904) 358-2846. **Fax:** (904) 358-2845.
E-Mail Address: info@jaxsuns.com. **Website:** www.jaxsuns.com.
Affiliation (first year): Florida Marlins (2009). **Years In League:** 1970-

OWNERSHIP, MANAGEMENT

Operated by: Baseball Jax Inc.
Principal Owner/Chairman of the Board: Peter Bragan Sr. **Madame Chairman:** Mary Frances Bragan.
President/General Manager: Peter Bragan Jr. **Senior Assistant GM:** Brad Rodriguez. **Assistant GM, Sales:** Chris Peters. **Director, Field Operations:** Ed Attalla. **Director, Merchandise:** Victoria Eure. **Director, Sales/Promotions:** Casey Nichols. **Director, Stadium Operations:** Matt Glancy. **Director, Business Administration:** Barbara O'Berry. **Director, Video Services:** David Scheldorf. **Ticket Manager:** Amy Delettre. **Manager, Stadium Operations:** J.D. Metrie. **Manager, Community Relations:** Sarah Foster. **Ticket Sales/Media Relations:** Wesley Mitchell. **General Manager, Ballpark Foods:** Jamie Davis. **Assistant GM, Ballpark Foods/Finance:** Mitch Buska. **Administrative Assistants:** Lindsey Weeks, Robert Mousa. **Executive Assistant:** Theresa Viets.

FIELD STAFF

Manager: Tim Leiper. **Hitting Coach:** Corey Hart. **Pitching Coach:** John Duffy. **Trainer:** Dustin Luepker.

GAME INFORMATION

Radio Announcer: J.P. Shadrick. **No. of Games Broadcast:** Home-70, Away-70. **Flagship Station:** WFXJ 930-AM.
PA Announcer: John Leard. **Official Scorer:** Jason Eliopulos. **Press Box Assistant:** Brian DeLettre
Stadium Name: The Baseball Grounds of Jacksonville. **Location:** I-95 South to Martin Luther King Parkway exit, follow Gator Bowl Blvd. around Alltel Stadium; I-95 North to Exit 347 (Emerson Street), go right to Hart Bridge Expressway, take Sports Complex exit, left at light to stop sign, take left and follow around Alltel Stadium; From Mathews Bridge, take A. Philip Randolph exit, right on A. Philip Randolph, straight to stadium. **Standard Game Times:** 7:05 p.m., Wed. 1:05, Sun. 3:05/5:05. **Ticket Price Range:** $5.50-19.50.
Visiting Club Hotel: Hyatt Regency Jacksonville Riverfront, 225 Coastline Dr., Jacksonville, FL 32202. **Telephone:** (904) 633-9095.

MISSISSIPPI BRAVES

Office Address: Trustmark Park, 1 Braves Way, Pearl, MS 39208.
Mailing Address: P.O. Box 97389, Pearl, MS 39288.
Telephone: (601) 932-8788. **Fax:** (601) 936-3567.
E-Mail Address: mississippi.braves@braves.com. **Website:** www.mississippibraves.com.
Affiliation (first year): Atlanta Braves (2005). **Years in League:** 2005-

OWNERSHIP, MANAGEMENT

Operated By: Atlanta National League Baseball Club Inc.

General Manager: Steve DeSalvo. Assistant GM: Jim Bishop. Ticket Manager: Nick Anderson. Merchandise Manager: Sarah Banta. Advertising/Design Manager: Brian Byrd. Sales Associate: Matt McCoy. Head Chef: Tina Funches. Suites/Catering Manager: Debbie Herrington. Stadium Operations Manager: Brian Parker. Assistant Restaurant Manager: Jack McGill. Promotions/Entertainment Manager: Sean Guillotte. Concessions Manager: Felicia Thompson. Office Administrator: Christy Shaw. Restaurant Manager: Gene Slaughter. Director, Field/Facility Operations: Matt Taylor.

FIELD STAFF
Manager: Phillip Wellman. Coach: Garey Ingram. Pitching Coach: Marty Reed. Trainer: Ricky Alcantara.

GAME INFORMATION
Radio Announcer: Ben Ingram. No. of Games Broadcast: Home-70 Road-70. Flagship Station: WYAB 103.9 FM. PA Announcer: Derrel Palmer. Official Scorer: Butch Raley. Stadium Name: Trustmark Park. Location: I-20 to exit 48/Pearl (Pearson Road). Ticket Price Range: $5-12. Visiting Club Hotel: Holiday Inn Trustmark Park, 110 Bass Pro Drive, Pearl, MS 39208. Telephone: (601) 939-5238.

MOBILE BAYBEARS

Office Address: Hank Aaron Stadium, 755 Bolling Bros. Blvd., Mobile, AL 36606. Telephone: (251) 479-2327. Fax: (251) 476-1147. E-Mail Address: baybears@mobilebaybears.com. Website: www.mobilebaybears.com Affiliation (first year): Arizona Diamondbacks (2007). Years in League: 1966, 1970, 1997-

OWNERSHIP, MANAGEMENT
Operated by: HWS Baseball Group. Principal Owner: Mike Savit. President/COO: Bill Shanahan. General Sales Manager: Jeff Long. Assistant General Manager, Finance: Betty Adams. Assistant GM, Promotions/Corporate Sales: Mike Callahan. Assistant GM, Stadium Operations: John Hilliard. Assistant GM, Sales/Concessions: Kyle Schoonover. Director, Community Relations/ Director, Audio/Visual: Ari Rosenbaum. Director, Media Relations (team related): Wayne Randazzo. Director, Youth Programs/Media Relations (non-team related): J.R. Wittner. Box Office Manager: Timothy McCarthy. Director, Stadium Operations: Jason Wilford. Director, Group Sales: Garrett Wolf. Sales Representative: John Golz. Clubhouse Manager: Rick Schweitzer. Stadium Operations Assistant: Wade Vadakin. Internet Liaison/Team Chaplain: Lorin Barr.

FIELD STAFF
Manager: Rico Brogna. Coach: Turner Ward. Pitching Coach: Dan Carlson. Trainer: Ryan DiPanfilo.

GAME INFORMATION
Radio Announcer: Wayne Randazzo. No. of Games Broadcast: Home-70, Away-70. Flagship Station: Comcast Channel 19, www.baybearsradio.com. PA Announcer: Mike Callahan. Official Scorers: Ari Rosenbaum/J.R. Wittner. Stadium Name: Hank Aaron Stadium. Location: I-65 to exit 1 (Government Blvd. East), right at Satchel Paige Drive, right at Bolling Bros. Boulevard. Standard Game Times: 7:05 p.m.; Sun. 6:05, 2:05. Ticket Price Range: $5-15. Visiting Club Hotel: Riverview Plaza, 64 S. Water St., Mobile, AL 36602. Telephone: (251) 438-4000.

MONTGOMERY BISCUITS

Office Address: 200 Coosa St., Montgomery, AL 36104. Telephone: (334) 323-2255. Fax: (334) 323-2225. E-Mail address: info@biscuitsbaseball.com. Website: www.biscuitsbaseball.com. Affiliation (first year): Tampa Bay Rays (2004). Years in League: 1965-1980, 2004-

OWNERSHIP, MANAGEMENT
Operated By: Montgomery Professional Baseball LLC. Principal Owners: Tom Dickson, Sherrie Myers. General Manager: Greg Rauch. Assistant GM: Marla Terranova. Director, Sales: Tyson Smith. Corporate Sales Executive: Scott Trible. Corporate Sales Coordinator: Matt Blagburn. Group Sales Representative: Ben Trombly. Group Sales Intern: Dan Boyd. Marketing Assistant: Jackie Kampf. Season Ticket Concierge: Bob Rabon. Sponsorship Service Representatives: Alison Davis, Erin Tracy. Box Office Manager: Jordan Mandelkorn. Retail Manager: Monte Meyers. Director, Operations: Steve Blackwell. Head Groundskeeper: Lee Murray. Director, Food Service: Travis Johnson. Concessions Manager: Craig Phillips. Kitchen Manager: Mike Smith. Business Manager: Linda Fast. Assistant Business Manager: Dewanna Croy. Office Administrator: Bill Sisk.

FIELD STAFF
Manager: Billy Gardner Jr. Coach: Ozzie Timmons. Pitching Coach: Bill Moloney. Trainer: Lea Slagle.

GAME INFORMATION
Radio Announcer: Joe Davis. No of Games Broadcast: Home-70 Road-70. Flagship Station: WLWI 1440-AM. PA Announcer: Rick Hendrick. Official Scorer: Unavailable. Stadium Name: Montgomery Riverwalk Stadium. Location: I-65 to exit 172, east on Herron Street, left on Coosa

Street. **Ticket Price Range:** $8-12.
Visiting Club Hotel: Unavailable.

TENNESSEE SMOKIES

Office Address: 3540 Line Drive, Kodak, TN 37764.
Telephone: (865) 286-2300. **Fax:** (865) 523-9913.
E-Mail Address: info@smokiesbaseball.com. **Website:** www.smokiesbaseball.com.
Affiliation (first year): Chicago Cubs (2007). **Years in League:** 1964-67, 1972-

OWNERSHIP, MANAGEMENT
Operated By: SPBC LLC.
President: Doug Kirchhofer.
General Manager: Brian Cox. **Assistant GM:** Jeff Shoaf. **Director, Stadium Operations:** Bryan Webster. **Director, Community Relations:** Lauren Chesney. **Director, Food/Beverage:** Tony DaSilveira. **Director, Marketing/Communications:** Rennie Leon. **Director, Entertainment/Client Services:** Ryan Cox. **Director, Ticket/Retail Operations:** Robby Scheuermann. **Director, Field Operations:** Stuart Morris. **Director, Group Sales:** Andy Kroeger. **Corporate Sales Executive:** Dan Blue. **Video Production/Graphic Design Manager:** Tim Avery. **Client Services Manager:** Adam Kline. **Group Sales Representatives:** Matt Strutner, Tim Volk, Rey Regenstreif-Harms, Shea Maple. **Business Manager:** Suzanne French. **Administrative Assistant:** Tolena Trout.

FIELD STAFF
Manager: Bill Dancy. **Hitting Coach:** Tom Beyers. **Pitching Coach:** Dennis Lewallyn. **Trainer:** Nick Frangella.

GAME INFORMATION
Radio Announcer: Mick Gillispie. **No. of Games Broadcast:** Home-70 Road-70. **Flagship Station:** WNML 99.1-FM/990-AM.
PA Announcer: George Yardley. **Official Scorers:** Jeff Muir, Jack Tate, Bernie Reimer, Dave Simpson, Brian Trent.
Stadium Name: Smokies Park. **Location:** I-40 to exit 407, Highway 66 North. **Standard Game Times:** 7:15 p.m., Sun. 2 or 5. **Ticket Price Range:** $5-10.
Visiting Club Hotel: Days Inn-Exit 407, 3402 Winfield Dunn Pkwy, Kodak, TN 37764. **Telephone:** (865) 933-4500.

WEST TENN DIAMOND JAXX

Office Address: 4 Fun Place, Jackson, TN 38305.
Telephone: (731) 988-5299. **Fax:** (731) 988-5246.
E-Mail Address: fun@diamondjaxx.com. **Website:** www.diamondjaxx.com.
Affiliation (third year): Seattle Mariners (2007). **Years in League:** 1998-

OWNERSHIP, MANAGEMENT
Operated by: Diamond Jaxx Baseball Club LLC.
Chairman: David Freeman. **President:** Reese Smith.
General Manager: Tom Hanson. **Assistant General Manager:** Jason Compton. **Director, Security/Stadium Operations:** Robert Jones. **Accounting Manager:** Theresa Barnett. **Manager, Media Relations/Broadcasting:** Chris Harris. **Manager, Tickets/Merchandise:** Andrew Lambert. **Turf Manager:** Tyler Brewer. **Manager, Catering/Concessions:** Kurt Brown. **Customer Service Representative:** Brandy Marshall. **Director, Clubhouse Operations:** Bradley Arnold. **Manager, Home Clubhouse:** C.J. Fedewa. **Customer Service Rep/Community Relations:** Whitney Strawn. **Tickets/Merchandise Intern:** Jonna Sampson. **Media Relations/Publications Intern:** Michael Young. **Sales/Gameday Intern:** Alex Sides.

FIELD STAFF
Manager: Tim Laker. **Hitting Coach:** Andy Fox. **Pitching Coach:** Lance Painter. **Trainer:** Matt Toth .

GAME INFORMATION
Radio Announcer: Chris Harris. **No. of Games Broadcast:** Home-70, Away-70. **Flagship Station:** WNWS 101.5 FM.
PA Announcer: Dan Reeves. **Official Scorer:** Unavailable.
Stadium Name: Pringles Park. **Location:** From I-40, take exit 85 South on F.E. Wright Drive, left onto Ridgecrest Road. **Standard Game Times:** 7:05 p.m.; Sun 2:05. **Ticket Price Range:** $6-10.
Visiting Club Hotel: Doubletree Hotel, 1770 Hwy. 45 Bypass, Jackson, TN 38305. **Telephone:** (731) 664-6900.

TEXAS LEAGUE

DOUBLE-A

Mailing Address: 2442 Facet Oak, San Antonio, TX 78232.
Telephone: (210) 545-5297. **Fax:** (210) 545-5298.
E-Mail Address: texasleague@sbcglobal.net. **Website:** www.texas-league.com.
Years League Active: 1888-1890, 1892, 1895-1899, 1902-1942, 1946-.
President, Treasurer: Tom Kayser.
Vice President: Pete Laven. **Corporate Secretary:** Monty Hoppel. **Assistant to the President:** Ross Bagienski.
Directors: Jon Dandes (Northwest Arkansas), Ken Schrom (Corpus Christi), William DeWitt III (Springfield), Chuck Lamson (Tulsa), Scott Sonju (Frisco), Miles Prentice (Midland), Russ Meeks (Arkansas), Burl Yarbrough (San Antonio).
Division Structure: North—Arkansas, Northwest Arkansas, Springfield, Tulsa. South— Corpus Christi, Frisco, Midland, San Antonio.
Regular Season: 140 games (split schedule). **2010 Opening Date:** April 8. **Closing Date:** Sept. 6. **All-Star Game:** June 30 at Midland.
Playoff Format: First-half division winners play second-half division winners in best-of-five series. Winners meet in best-of-five series for league championship.
Roster Limit: 24. **Player Eligibility Rule:** No restrictions.
Brand of Baseball: Rawlings.
Umpires: Stephen Barga (Castle Rock, CO), Kelvin Bultron (Canovanas, PR), Jeff Gosney (Newark, OH), Brian Hertzog (Lake Stevens, WA), Kellen Levy (Mesa, AZ), Brad Myers (Holland, OH), Dan Oliver (Seattle, WA), Alex Ortiz (Los Angeles, CA), Brett Robson (Cannington, West Australia, Australia), Stu Scheurwater (Regina, Saskatchewan, Canada), Brian Sinclair (San Antonio, TX), Jimmy Volpi (Aurora, CO)

Tom Kayser

STADIUM INFORMATION

Club	Stadium	Opened	LF	CF	RF	Capacity	2009 Att.
Arkansas	Dickey-Stephens Park	2007	332	413	330	10,000	346,635
Corpus Christi	Whataburger Field	2005	325	400	315	5,338	443,628
Frisco	Dr Pepper Ballpark	2003	335	405	355	10,000	553,916
Midland	Citibank Ballpark	2002	330	410	322	4,669	282,283
NW Arkansas	Arvest Ballpark	2008	325	400	325	6,500	318,056
San Antonio	Nelson Wolff Municipal Stadium	1994	310	402	340	6,200	300,669
Springfield	John Q. Hammons Field	2003	315	400	330	6,750	402,618
Tulsa	ONEOK Field	2010	330	400	307	6,200	316,365

Dimensions (over LF, CF, RF columns)

ARKANSAS TRAVELERS

Office Address: Dickey-Stephens Park, 400 West Broadway, North Little Rock, AR 72114.
Mailing Address: P.O. Box 55066, Little Rock, AR 72215.
Telephone: (501) 664-1555. **Fax:** (501) 664-1834.
E-Mail address: travs@travs.com. **Website:** www.travs.com.
Affiliation (first year): Los Angeles Angels (2001). **Years in League:** 1966-

OWNERSHIP, MANAGEMENT

President: Bert Parke.
General Manager: Pete Laven. **Assistant GM, Sales:** Paul Allen. **Assistant GM, Tickets:** David Kay. **Director, Broadcasting/Media Relations:** Phil Elson. **Director, Food/Beverage:** Billy Stinnette. **Director, In-Game Entertainment:** Tommy Adam. **Director, Promotions:** Jeremy Neisser. **Director, Suite Operations:** Heather Massey. **Director, Merchandise:** Debra Wingfield. **Park Superintendent:** Greg Johnston. **Assistant Park Superintendent:** Reggie Temple. **Assistant Groundskeeper:** Brian Lyter. **Bookkeeper:** Nena Valentine. **Office Manager:** Jared Schein. **Sales Associates:** Melissa Jones.

FIELD STAFF

Manager: Bobby Magallanes. **Batting Coach:** Francisco Matos. **Pitching Coach:** Ken Patterson. **Trainer:** Eric Munson.

GAME INFORMATION

Radio Announcer: Phil Elson. **No. of Games Broadcast:** Home-70 Road-70. **Flagship Station:** KARN 920 AM.
PA Announcer: Unavailable. **Official Scorers:** Tim Cooper, Mike Garrity.
Stadium Name: Dickey-Stephens Park. **Location:** I-30 to Broadway exit. Proceed west to ballpark, located at Broadway Avenue and the Broadway Bridge. **Standard Game Time:** 7:10 p.m. **Ticket Price Range:** $3-12.
Visiting Club Hotel: Hilton Little Rock, 925 S. University Avenue, Little Rock, AR 72204. **Telephone:** (501) 664-5020. **Fax:** (501) 614-3803.

CORPUS CHRISTI HOOKS

Office Address: 734 East Port Ave, Corpus Christi, TX 78401.
Telephone: (361) 561-4665. **Fax:** (361) 561-4666.
E-Mail Address: info@cchooks.com. **Website:** www.cchooks.com.
Affiliation (first year): Houston Astros (2005). **Years in League:** 1958-59, 2005-

OWNERSHIP, MANAGEMENT

Operated By: Ryan-Sanders Baseball.
Principal Owners: Eddie Maloney, Reese Ryan, Reid Ryan, Nolan Ryan, Brad Sanders, Bret Sanders, Don Sanders. **CEO:** Reid Ryan. **CFO:** Reese Ryan. **COO:** Jay Miller.
Executive Vice President: JJ Gottsch. **President:** Ken Schrom. **General Manager:** Michael Wood. **Vice President, Sales:** Adam Nuse. **Director, Sponsor Services:** Elisa Macias. **Director, Retail:** Brooke Milam. **Controller:** Christy Lockard. **Director, Communications:** Matt Rogers. **Director, Broadcasting:** Matt Hicks. **Director, Stadium Operations:** Tina Athans. **Director, Group Sales:** Andy Steavens. **Director, Ballpark Entertainment:** Steve Richards. **Box Office Manager:** Spencer Moore. **Director, Season Ticket Services:** Bryan Mayhood. **Field Superintendent:** Izzy Hinojosa. **Community Relations Coordinator:** Gil Perez. **Media Relations Coordinator:** Michael Coffin. **Receptionists:** Jacqueline Hernandez, Amanda Smith.

FIELD STAFF

Manager: Wes Clements. **Hitting Coach:** Mark Bailey. **Pitching Coach:** Travis Driskill. **Athletic Trainer:** Jamey Snodgrass.

GAME INFORMATION

Radio Announcers: Matt Hicks , Michael Coffin, Gene Kasprzyk. **No. of Games Broadcast:** Home-70 Road-70. **Flagship Station:** KKTX-AM 1360.
PA Announcer: Scott Johnson. **Official Scorer:** Unavailable.
Stadium Name: Whataburger Field. **Location:** I-37 to end of interstate, left at Chaparral, left at Hirsh Ave. **Ticket Price Range:** $5-12.
Visiting Club Hotel: Omni Hotel, 900 N. Shoreline Dr., Corpus Christi, TX 78401. **Telephone:** (361) 886-3553.

FRISCO ROUGHRIDERS

Office Address: 7300 RoughRiders Trail, Frisco, TX 75034.
Telephone: (972) 731-9200. **Fax:** (972) 731-5355.
E-Mail Address: info@ridersbaseball.com. **Website:** www.ridersbaseball.com.
Affiliation (first year): Texas Rangers (2003). **Years in League:** 2003-

OWNERSHIP, MANAGEMENT

Operated by: Mandalay Sports Entertainment.
President/General Manager: Scott Sonju. **Accounting/HR Manager:** Dustin Alban. **Senior Vice President:** Michael Byrnes. **Director, Corporate Partnerships:** Steven Nelson. **Director, Business Development:** Katie Maguffee. **Senior Director, Partner Services:** Scott Burchett. **Partner/Event Services Coordinator:** Kristin Russell. **Graphic Design Coordinator:** Erik Davila. **Partner Services Coordinator:** Matt Ratliff. **Director, Community Development:** Mara Simon-Meyer. **VP, Ticket Sales:** Billy Widner. **VP, Ticket Sales:** Billy Widner. **Senior Director, Group Sales:** Jenna Byrnes. **Director, Ticket Sales:** Justin Ramquist. **Ticket Operations Managers:** Mac Amin, Shannon Muller. **Sales/Marketing Coordinator:** Morgan Denton. **Director, Inside Sales/Customer Service:** Jay Lockett. **Senior Corporate Marketing Manager:** Mark Playko. **Director, Game Entertainment:** Gabriel Wilhelm. **VP, Operations:** Michael Poole. **Director, Operations:** Scott Arnold. **Directors, Maintenance:** Alfonso Bailon, Gustavo Bailon. **Head Groundskeeper:** David Bicknell.

FIELD STAFF

Manager: Steve Buechele. **Coach:** Brant Brown. **Pitching Coach:** Jeff Andrews. **Trainer:** Chris Gorosics. **Strength/Conditioning:** Luke Chichetto

GAME INFORMATION

Broadcaster: Aaron Goldsmith. **No. of Games Broadcast:** Home-70, Away-70. **Flagship Station:** Unavailable.
PA Announcer: John Clemens. **Official Scorers:** Kenny King, Larry Bump.
Stadium Name: Dr Pepper Ballpark. **Location:** Dallas North Tollway to State Highway 121. **Standard Game Times:** 7 p.m., Sun. 6.
Visiting Club Hotel: ExtendedStay Deluxe Plano, 2900 North Dallas Tollway. **Telephone:** (972) 378-9978.

MIDLAND ROCKHOUNDS

Office Address: 5514 Champions Dr., Midland, TX 79706.
Telephone: (432) 520-2255. **Fax:** (432) 520-8326.
Website: www.midlandrockhounds.org.

Affiliation (first year): Oakland Athletics (1999). **Years in League:** 1972-

OWNERSHIP, MANAGEMENT

Operated By: Midland Sports, Inc.
Principal Owners: Miles Prentice, Bob Richmond. **President:** Miles Prentice.
Executive Vice President: Bob Richmond. **General Manager:** Monty Hoppel. **Assistant GM:** Jeff VonHolle. **Assistant GM, Marketing/Tickets:** Jamie Richardson. **Assistant GM, Merchandise/Facilities:** Ray Fieldhouse. **Assistant GM, Media Relations:** Greg Bergman. **Director, Broadcasting/Publications:** Bob Hards. **Director, Business Operations:** Eloisa Galvan. **Director, Ticket Operations:** Michael Richardson. **Director, Group Sales:** Jeremy Lukas. **Head Groundskeeper:** Eric Ferland. **Director, Promotions/Game Entertainment:** Jon Conners. **Director, Community Relations/Advertising:** Sara Rader. **Director, Stadium Operations:** Wren Nance. **Office Manager:** Frances Warner. **Marketing/Sales Executive:** Anthony Orlando. **Assistant Groundskeeper:** Eric Campbell. **Administrative Assistant:** Ginny Gotcher. **Assistant Concessions Manager:** Reggie Donald. **Clubhouse Manager:** Rob Pelliccia. **Operations Assistant:** Manabu Beppu. **Administrative Assistant:** Brian Smith. **Administrative Assistant:** Jessica Ng.

FIELD STAFF

Manager: Darren Bush. **Hitting Coach:** Webster Garrison. **Pitching Coach:** Scott Emerson. **Trainer:** Justin Whitehouse.

GAME INFORMATION

Radio Announcer: Bob Hards. **No. of Games Broadcast:** Home-70, Away-70. **Flagship Station:** Unavailable.
PA Announcer: Wes Coles. **Official Scorers:** Paul Burnett, Steve Marcum.
Stadium Name: Citibank Ballpark. **Location:** From I-20, exit Loop 250 North to Highway 191 intersection. **Standard Game Times:** 7 p.m., 6:30 (April-May, August); Sun. 6 (June-Aug.). **Ticket Price Range:** $5-9.
Visiting Club Hotel: Sleep Inn and Suites, 5612 Deauville Blvd, Midland, TX 79706. **Telephone:** (432) 694-4200.

NORTHWEST ARKANSAS
NATURALS

Office Address: 3000 S. 56th Street, Springdale, AR 72762.
Telephone: (479) 927-4900. **Fax:** (479) 756-8088.
E-Mail Address: info@nwanaturals.com. **Website:** www.nwanaturals.com.
Affiliation (first year): Kansas City Royals (1995). **Years in League:** 1987-

OWNERSHIP, MANAGEMENT

Principal Owner: Rich Products Corp.
Chairman: Robert Rich Jr. **President, Rich Entertainment:** Melinda Rich. **President, Rich Baseball:** Jon Dandes.
General Manager: Eric Edelstein. **Assistant GM:** Justin Cole. **Business Manager:** Morgan Smith. **Marketing/PR Manager:** Frank Novak. **Stadium Operations Director:** George Sisson. **Field Turf Manager:** Monty Sowell. **Ticket Office Coordinator:** Andrea Blann. **Special Events Manager:** Kendra Carlson. **Broadcaster/Baseball Operations Coordinator:** Steven Davis. **Sales Coordinator/Community Relations:** Amanda Potter. **Ticket Sales Coordinator:** Dustin Dethlefs. **Entertainment Coordinator:** Douglas Webb. **Account Executives:** Matt Price, Andrew Thaxton, Chantelle Abbott, Mark Zaiger. **Stadium Operations Assistant/Equipment Manager:** Danny Helmer.

FIELD STAFF

Manager: Brian Poldberg. **Hitting Coach:** Terry Bradshaw. **Pitching Coach:** Larry Carter. **Trainer:** Tony Medina.

GAME INFORMATION

Radio Announcers: Steven Davis. **No. of Games Broadcast:** Home-70, Away-70. **Flagship:** ESPN 92.1 The Ticket (KQSM-FM).
PA Announcer: Bill Rogers. **Official Scorer:** Chris Ledeker.
Stadium Name: Arvest Ballpark. **Location:** I-540 to U.S. 412 West (Sunset Ave). Left on 56th St. **Ticket Price Range:** $6-12. **Standard Game Times:** 7 p.m.; Sun. 2 (April/May), 6 (June-Sept.).
Visiting Club Hotel: Holiday Inn Springdale; 1500 S. 48th St., Springdale, AR 72762. **Telephone:** (479) 751-8300.

SAN ANTONIO MISSIONS

Office Address: 5757 Hwy. 90 W, San Antonio, TX 78227.
Telephone: (210) 675-7275. **Fax:** (210) 670-0001.
E-Mail address: sainfo@samissions.com. **Website:** www.samissions.com.
Affiliation (first year): San Diego Padres (2007). **Years in League:** 1888, 1892, 1895-99, 1907-42, 1946-64, 1968-

OWNERSHIP, MANAGEMENT

Operated By: Elmore Sports Group.
Principal Owner: David Elmore.
President: Burl Yarbrough. **General Manager:** David Gasaway. **Assistant GMs:** Mickey Holt, Jeff Long, Bill Gerlt. **Director, Accounting:** Ivan Molina. **Field Superintendent:** Karsten Blackwelder. **Director, Corporate Sales:** Gary Taylor. **Director, Box Office:** Tiffany Johnson.

FIELD STAFF

Manager: Doug Dascenzo. Coach: Max Venable. Pitching Coach: Glenn Abbott. Trainer: JoJo Tarantino.

GAME INFORMATION

Radio Announcer: Roy Acuff. No of Games Broadcast: Home-70 Road-70. Flagship Station: KKYX 680-AM. PA Announcer: Stan Kelly. Official Scorer: David Humphrey.

Stadium Name: Nelson W. Wolff Municipal Stadium. Location: From I-10, I-35, or I-37, take U.S. 90 West to Callaghan Road exit, stadium on right. Ticket Price Range: $5-10.

Visiting Club Hotel: Holiday Inn Northwest/SeaWorld, 10135 State Highway 151, San Antonio, TX 78251. Telephone: (210) 520-2508.

SPRINGFIELD CARDINALS

Office Address: 955 East Trafficway, Springfield, MO 65802.
Telephone: (417) 863-0395. Fax: (417) 863-0388.
E-Mail address: springfield@stlcardinals.com. Website: www.springfieldcardinals.com.
Affiliation (first year): St. Louis Cardinals (2005). Years in League: 2005-

OWNERSHIP, MANAGEMENT

Operated By: St. Louis Cardinals.

Vice President/General Manager: Matt Gifford. VP, Baseball/Business Operations: Scott Smulczenski. VP, Sales: Kim Inman. VP, Facility Operations: Bill Fischer. Director, Ticket Operations: Angela Deke. Manager, Corporate Partnerships: Dan Reiter. Manager, Promotions/Productions: Jacob Neimeyer. Manager, Market Development: Scott Bailes. Manager, Business Sales: Marty Diebold. Manager, Stadium/Game Day Operations: Aaron Lowrey. Office/Guest Services Coordinator: Christine Weyler. Account Executives: Ryan Cullen, Rob Gay, Kyle Snodgrass. Ticket Sales: Jared Nevins. Head Groundskeeper: Brock Phipps. Assistant Groundskeeper: Derek Edwards.

FIELD STAFF

Manager: Ron Warner. Hitting Coach: Derrick May. Pitching Coach: Dennis Martinez. Trainer: Jay Pierson.

GAME INFORMATION

Radio Announcer: Rob Evans. No of Games Broadcast: Home-70 Road-70. Flagship Station: JOCK 98.7-FM. PA Announcer: Kevin Howard. Official Scorers: Mark Stillwell, Tim Tourville.

Stadium Name: Hammons Field. Location: Highway 65 to Chestnut Expressway exit, west to National, south on National, west on Trafficway. Standard Game Time: 7:10 p.m. Ticket Price Range: $6-24.50.

Visiting Club Hotel: University Plaza Hotel, 333 John Q. Hammons Parkway, Springfield, MO 65806. Telephone: (417) 864-7333.

TULSA DRILLERS

Office Address: Office Address: 201 N. Elgin, Tulsa, OK 74120.
Telephone: (918) 744-5998. Fax: (918) 747-3267.
E-Mail Address: mail@tulsadrillers.com. Website: www.tulsadrillers.com.
Affiliation (first year): Colorado Rockies (2003). Years in League: 1933-42, 1946-65, 1977-

OWNERSHIP, MANAGEMENT

Operated By: Tulsa Baseball Inc.

Principal Owner/President: Chuck Lamson. Vice President: Went Hubbard.

General Manager: Mike Melega. Assistant GM: Jason George. Bookkeeper: Cheryll Couey. Director, Ticket Operations: Mark Hilliard. Director, Operations: Peter McAdams. Director, Media/Public Relations: Brian Carroll. Manager, Merchandise: Tom Jones. Manager, Ticket Sales/Marketing: Rob Gardenhire. Manager, Group Ticket Sales: Brandon Shiers. Manager, Promotions: Michael Taranto. Manager, Operations: Shane Lokken. Assistant Manager, Group Sales: Geoff Beaty. Video Production Coordinator: David Ruckman. Ticket Operations Assistant: Kevin Butcher. Promotions Assistant: Justin Gorski. Group Ticket Sales Assistant: Matt Larson. Merchandise Assistant: Baylor Love. Marketing Assistant: Rob Peters. Media/PR Assistant: Matt Watson. Video Production Assistant: Darin McDermott. Video Production Assistant: Troy Machir. Head Groundskeeper: Gary Shepherd. Assistant Groundskeeper: Logan Medlock.

FIELD STAFF

Manager: Ron Gideon. Coach: Dave Hajek. Pitching Coach: Bryan Harvey. Trainer: Austin O'Shea.

GAME INFORMATION

Radio Announcer: Dennis Higgins. No. of Games Broadcast: Home-70 Road-70. Flagship Station: KTBZ 1430-AM. PA Announcer: Kirk McAnany. Official Scorers: Bruce Howard, Duane DaPron, Larry Lewis.

Stadium Name: ONEOK Field. Location: Take I-244 to the Cincinnati/Detroit Exit (#6A); Go south on Cincinnati Ave. to Brady St.; go east two blocks to Elgin Ave. Standard Game Times: 7:05 p.m.; Sun. 2:05 (April-June 6); Sun. 6:05 (June13-August).

Visiting Club Hotel: Southern Hills Marriott, 1902 E. 71st St., Tulsa, OK 74136. Telephone: (918) 493-7000.

CALIFORNIA LEAGUE

Office Address: 709 W Channel Islands Blvd, #321, Port Hueneme, CA 93041
Telephone: 805.985.8585. **Fax:** 805.985.8580.
Website: www.californialeague.com. **E-Mail:** info@californialeague.com.
Years League Active: 1941-1942, 1946-
President: Charlie Blaney.

Vice President: Tom Volpe.

Directors: Bobby Brett (High Desert), Bobby Brett (Rancho Cucamonga), Pete Carfagna (Lancaster), David Elmore (Inland Empire), D.G. Elmore (Bakersfield), Gary Jacobs (Lake Elsinore), Michael Savit (Modesto), Tom Seidler (Visalia), Tom Volpe (Stockton), Jim Weyermann (San Jose).

Director, Operations: Matt Blaney. **Legal Counsel:** Jonathan Light.

Division Structure: North—Bakersfield, Modesto, San Jose, Stockton, Visalia. **South**—High Desert, Inland Empire, Lake Elsinore, Lancaster, Rancho Cucamonga.

Regular Season: 140 games (split schedule).

2010 Opening Date: April 8. **Closing Date:** Sept 6.

Playoff Format: Six teams. First-half winners in each division earn first-round bye; second-half winners meet wild cards with next best overall records in best-of-three quarterfinals. Winners meet first-half champions in best-of-five semifinals. Winners meet in best-of-five series for league championship.

All-Star Game: vs Carolina League, June 22 at Myrtle Beach.

Roster Limit: 25 active (35 under control).

Player Eligibility: No more than two players and one player/coach on active list may have more than six years experience.

Brand of Baseball: Rawlings.

Umpires: Matt Benham (Spokane, WA), Charles Billington (Carnation, WA), Ryan Blakney (Wenatchee, WA), Seth Buckminster (Fort Worth, TX), Spencer Flynn (Temecula, CA), Mike Goebel (Hoquiam, WA), Justin Sassaman (Lewisville, TX), Greg Stanzak (Surprise, AZ), Adam Schwarz (Riverside, CA), Nate Thompson (Attica, MI).

Charlie Blaney

STADIUM INFORMATION

Club	Stadium	Opened	LF	CF	RF	Capacity	2009 Att.
Bakersfield	Sam Lynn Ballpark	1941	328	354	328	4,200	65,656
High Desert	Mavericks Stadium	1991	340	401	340	3,808	112,470
Inland Empire	Arrowhead Credit Union Park	1996	330	410	330	5,000	202,728
Lake Elsinore	The Diamond	1994	330	400	310	7,866	235,174
Lancaster	Clear Channel Stadium	1996	350	410	350	4,500	150,970
Modesto	John Thurman Field	1952	312	400	319	4,000	167,722
R. Cucamonga	The Epicenter	1993	335	400	335	6,615	266,773
San Jose	Municipal Stadium	1942	340	390	340	4,000	211,054
Stockton	Banner Island Ballpark	2005	300	399	326	5,200	203,327
Visalia	Recreation Park	1946	320	405	320	1,647	105,405

BAKERSFIELD BLAZE

Office Address: 4009 Chester Ave., Bakersfield, CA 93301.
Mailing Address: P.O. Box 10031, Bakersfield, CA 93389.
Telephone: (661) 716-4487. **Fax:** (661) 322-6199.
E-Mail Address: blaze@bakersfieldblaze.com. **Website:** www.bakersfieldblaze.com.
Affiliation: Texas Rangers (2005). **Years In League:** 1941-42, 1946-75, 1978-79, 1982-

OWNERSHIP, MANAGEMENT

Principal Owner: Bakersfield Baseball Club LLC.
President: D.G. Elmore.
General Manager: Shawn Schoolcraft. **Director, Food/Beverage:** Ryan Bigler. **Director, Community Relations:** Jill Vawter. **Director, Field Operations:** Bill Gentry. **Clubhouse Manager:** Kevin Johnson.

FIELD STAFF

Manager: Bill Haselman. **Coach:** Jason Wood. **Pitching Coach:** Dave Chavarria. **Trainer:** Jacob Newburn.

GAME INFORMATION

Radio: None.
PA Announcer: Mike Cushine. **Official Scorer:** Tim Wheeler.
Stadium Name: Sam Lynn Ballpark. **Location:** Highway 99 to California Avenue, east three miles to Chester Avenue, north two miles to stadium. **Standard Game Time:** 7:30 p.m. **Ticket Price Range:** $6-10.
Visiting Club Hotel: Four Points, 5101 California Ave Bakersfield, CA 93309. **Telephone:** (661) 862-7423.

HIGH DESERT MAVERICKS

Stadium/Office Address: 12000 Stadium Way, Adelanto, CA 92301.
Telephone: (760) 246-6287. **Fax:** (760) 246-3197.
Website: www.hdmavs.com.
Affiliation (first year): Seattle Mariners (2007). **Years in League:** 1991-

OWNERSHIP, MANAGEMENT
Operated By: High Desert Mavericks Inc.
Principal Owner: Bobby Brett. **Brett Sports COO:** Andy Billig. **President:** Brent Miles. **General Manager:** Tim Altier. **Assistant General Manager:** Eric Jensen. **Sponsorship Coordinator:** Jesse Zumbro. **Account Executive:** Dan O'Neill. **Controller:** Robin Buckles.

FIELD STAFF
Manager: Jim Horner. **Hitting Coach:** Tommy Cruz. **Pitching Coach:** Tom Dettore. **Athletic Trainer:** Eduardo Tamez.

GAME INFORMATION
Radio Announcer: Unavailable. **No. of Games Broadcast:** Home-70 Road-70. **Flagship Station:** KIXW 960 AM.
PA Announcer: Ernie Escajeda. **Official Scorer:** Bob Witt.
Stadium Name: Stater Bros. **Stadium. Location:** I-15 North to Highway 395 to Adelanto Road. **Ticket Price Range:** $6-8.
Visiting Club Hotel: Motel 6, 9757 Cataba Rd. Hesperia, CA 92395. **Telephone:** (760) 947-0094.

INLAND EMPIRE 66ERS

Office Address: 280 South E St., San Bernardino, CA 92401.
Telephone: (909) 888-9922. **Fax:** (909) 888-5251.
Website: www.ie66ers.com.
Affiliation (first year): Los Angeles Dodgers (2007). **Years in League:** 1941, 1987-

OWNERSHIP, MANAGEMENT
Operated by: Inland Empire 66ers Baseball Club of San Bernardino.
Principal Owners: David Elmore, Donna Tuttle.
Owner/President: Dave Elmore. **Owner/Chairman:** Donna Tuttle. **Executive Vice President, Sales:** Mike Gullo. **CFO:** John Fonseca. **Director, Broadcasting/Media Relations:** Mike Saeger. **Director, Food/Beverage:** Joe Hudson. **Manager, Stadium Operations:** Ryan English. **Director, Group Sales:** Steve Pelle. **Community Groups/Merchandise Manager:** Laura Landry. **Director, Ticketing:** Joe Fargnoli. **Corporate Group Managers:** Danny Alvarez, Joe Rugo. **Promotions Manager:** Matt Kowallis. **Administrative Assistant:** Angie Rodriguez. **Head Groundskeeper:** Jason Hilderbrand.

FIELD STAFF
Manager: Jeff Carter. **Hitting Coach:** Franklin Stubbs. **Pitching Coach:** Charlie Hough.

GAME INFORMATION
Radio Announcer: Mike Saeger. **Flagship Station:** KCAA 1050-AM.
PA Announcer: J.J. Gould. **Official Scorer:** Les Canterbury.
Stadium Name: Arrowhead Credit Union Park. **Location:** From south, I-215 to 2nd Street exit, east on 2nd, right on G Street; from north, I-215 to 3rd Street exit, left on Rialto, right on G Street. **Standard Game Times:** 7:05 p.m.; Sun. 1:05 (April-June), 6:05 (July-Aug). **Ticket Price Range:** $5-10.
Visiting Club Hotel: Hilton San Bernardino, 285 East Hospitality Lane, San Bernardino, CA 92408. **Telephone:** (909) 889-0133.

LAKE ELSINORE STORM

Office Address: 500 Diamond Dr, Lake Elsinore, CA 92530.
Mailing Address: P.O. Box 535, Lake Elsinore, CA 92531.
Telephone: (951) 245-4487. **Fax:** (951) 245-0305.
E-Mail Address: info@stormbaseball.com. **Website:** www.stormbaseball.com.
Affiliation (first year): San Diego Padres (2001). **Years in League:** 1994-

OWNERSHIP, MANAGEMENT
Operated By: Lake Elsinore Storm LP.
Owner: Gary Jacobs, Len Simon.
President: Dave Oster. **Vice President/General Manager:** Bruce Kessman. **Assistant GM, Community Relations:** Tracy Kessman. **Assistant GM, Corporate Sales:** Allan Benavides. **Director, Broadcasting:** Sean McCall. **Director, Merchandising:** Donna Grunow. **Graphic Designer:** Mark Beskid. **Director, Food/Beverage:** Arjun Suresh. **Executive Chef:** Steve Bearse. **Director, Ticket Operations:** Ruli Garcia. **Director, Mascot Operations:** Patrick Gardenier. **Director, Finance:** Rick Riegler. **Account Executives:** Dave McCrory, Bob Gillett. **Finance Director:** Christina Conlon. **Head**

Groundskeeper: Peter Hayes. **Maintenance Supervisor:** Roberto Cabrera. **Director, Media Relations:** Steve Smaldone. **Assistant Director, Marketing:** Courtney Kessler. **Assistant Director, Food/Beverage:** Mark Labban. **Assistant Director, Ticket Operations:** J.T. Onyett. **Assistant Director, Stadium Operations:** Colin Cook.

FIELD STAFF
Manager: Carlos Lezcano. **Coach:** Bob Skube. **Pitching Coach:** Dave Rajsich. **Trainer:** Will Sinon.

GAME INFORMATION
Radio Announcer: Sean McCall. **No. of Games Broadcast:** Home-70 Road-70. **Flagship Station:** San Diego 1700-AM.
PA Announcer: Joe Martinez. **Official Scorer:** Lloyd Nixon.
Stadium Name: The Diamond. **Location:** From I-15, exit at Diamond Drive, west one mile to stadium. **Standard Game Times:** 7:05 p.m.; Wed. 6:05; Sun. 2:08 (first half), 6:08 (second half). **Ticket Price Range:** $7-10.
Visiting Club Hotel: Lake Elsinore Hotel and Casino, 20930 Malaga St, Lake Elsniore, CA 92530. **Telephone:** (951) 674-3101.

LANCASTER JETHAWKS

Office Address: 45116 Valley Central Way, Lancaster, CA 93536.
Telephone: (661) 726-5400. **Fax:** (661) 726-5406.
E-Mail Address: info@jethawks.com. **Website:** www.jethawks.com.
Affiliation (first year): Houston Astros (2009). **Years in League:** 1996-

OWNERSHIP, MANAGEMENT
Operated By: Hawks Nest LLC.
President: Peter Carfagna. **Senior Vice President:** Pete Carfagna.
Vice President/General Manager: Larry Thornhill. **Assistant GM:** Derek Sharp. **Director, Stadium Operations:** John Laferney. **Director, Promotions/General Sales Manager:** Jeremy Castillo. **Director, Broadcasting/Media Relations:** Jeff Lasky. **Director, Community Relations:** Will Murphy. **Director, Food/Beverage:** Brandi Casas. **Director, Ticket Operations:** Trent Wondra. **Media Manager/Program Director for CSN:** Will Thornhill. **Account Executive:** Albert Villalobos.

FIELD STAFF
Manager: Tom Lawless. **Coach:** Darryl Robinson. **Pitching Coach:** Don Alexander. **Trainer:** Eric Montague.

GAME INFORMATION
Radio Announcer: Jeff Lasky. **No. of Games Broadcast:** Home-70, Away-70. **Flagship Station:** Unavailable.
PA Announcer: Fred Jaramillo. **Official Scorer:** David Guenther.
Stadium Name: Clear Channel Stadium. **Location:** Highway 14 in Lancaster to Avenue I exit, west one block to stadium. **Standard Game Times:** 7 p.m.; Sun. 5 (April–June), 5 (July-Sept.). **Ticket Price Range:** $6-12.
Visiting Club Hotel: Best Western Antelope Valley Inn, 44055 North Sierra Hwy., Lancaster, CA 93534. **Telephone:** (661) 948-4651.

MODESTO NUTS

Office Address: 601 Neece Dr., Modesto, CA 95351.
Mailing Address: P.O. Box 883, Modesto, CA 95353.
Telephone: (209) 572-4487. **Fax:** (209) 572-4490.
E-Mail Address: fun@modestonuts.com. **Website:** www.modestonuts.com.
Affiliation (first year): Colorado Rockies (2005). **Years in League:** 1946-64, 1966-

OWNERSHIP, MANAGEMENT
Operated by: HWS Group IV.
Principal Owner: Mike Savit.
President: Bill Shanahan. **Vice President/GM:** Michael Gorrasi. **Assistant GM, Marketing:** Joe Wagoner. **Assistant GM, Operations:** Ed Mack. **Director, Tickets:** Zach Brockman. **Director, Community Affairs:** Scott Hoard. **Director, Business Development:** Tyler Richardson. **Director, Group Sales:** Eric Rauber. **Director, Stadium Operations:** Ryan Thomas.

FIELD STAFF
Manager: Jerry Weinstein. **Coach:** Duane Espy. **Pitching Coach:** Darryl Scott. **Trainer:** Chris Dovey.

GAME INFORMATION
Radio Announcer: Greg Young. **No. of Games Broadcast:** Home-50, Away-50. **Flagship Station:** KESP 970-AM.
PA Announcer: Unavailable. **Official Scorer:** Unavailable.
Stadium Name: John Thurman Field. **Location:** Highway 99 in southwest Modesto to Tuolomne Boulevard exit, west on Tuolomne for one block to Neece Drive, left for 1/4 mile to stadium. **Standard Game Times:** 7:05 p.m.; Sun. 1:05 p.m.
Ticket Price Range: $5-10.
Visiting Club Hotel: Clarion Inn, 1612 Sisk Rd., Modesto, CA 95350. **Telephone:** (209) 521-1612.

RANCHO CUCAMONGA
QUAKES

Office Address: 8408 Rochester Ave., Rancho Cucamonga, CA 91730.
Mailing Address: P.O. Box 4139, Rancho Cucamonga, CA 91729.
Telephone: (909) 481-5000. Fax: (909) 481-5005.
E-Mail Address: info@rcquakes.com. Website: www.rcquakes.com.
Affiliation (first year): Los Angeles Angels (2001). Years in League: 1993-

OWNERSHIP, MANAGEMENT
Operated By: Brett Sports & Entertainment.
Principal Owner: Bobby Brett.
President: Brent Miles.
Vice President/General Manager: Grant Riddle. Vice President, Tickets: Monica Ortega. Director, Group Sales: Linda Rathfon. Sports Marketing Consultants: Ryan Millard, Andrew Zamarripa. Director, Promotions: AutumnRose Saenz. Ticket Office Manager: Rachel Barker. Director, Season Tickets: Jesse Robinson. Group Sales Account Executives: Rose Ann A'Jontue, Kyle Burleson, Anthony Cali, Nick Rhodes. Accounting Manager: Amara McClellan. Public Relations Manager/Voice of the Quakes: Mike Lindskog. Office Manager: Shelley Scebbi.

FIELD STAFF
Manager: Keith Johnson. Coach: Damon Mashore. Pitching Coach: Dan Ricabal. Trainer: Mike Metcalfe.

GAME INFORMATION
Radio Announcer: Mike Lindskog.
PA Announcer: Unavailable. Official Scorer: Unavailable.
Stadium Name: The Epicenter. Location: I-10 to I-15 North, exit at Foothill Boulevard, left on Foothill, left on Rochester to Stadium. Standard Game Times: 7:05 p.m.; 7:35 (home Fridays), Sun. 2:05 (April-July), 5:05 (July-Sept.). Ticket Price Range: $8-12.
Visiting Club Hotel: Best Western Heritage Inn, 8179 Spruce Ave, Rancho Cucamonga, CA 91730. Telephone: (909) 466-1111.

SAN JOSE GIANTS

Office Address: 588 E. Alma Ave., San Jose, CA 95112.
Mailing Address: P.O. Box 21727, San Jose, CA 95151.
Telephone: (408) 297-1435. Fax: (408) 297-1453.
E-Mail Address: info@sjgiants.com. Website: www.sjgiants.com.
Affiliation (first year): San Francisco Giants (1988). Years in League: 1942, 1947-58, 1962-76, 1979-

OWNERSHIP, MANAGEMENT
Operated by: Progress Sports Management.
Principal Owners: Heidi Stamas, Richard Beahrs, Rich Kelley, San Francisco Giants.
President/CEO: Jim Weyermann.
Chief Operating Officer/General Manager: Mark Wilson. Chief Marketing Officer: Juliana Paoli. VP, Operations/Assistant General Manager: Zach Walter. VP, Sales: Ainslie Reynolds. VP, Finance/Executive Director San Jose Giants Community Fund: Cami Yuasa. VP, Field Operations/Capital Projects: Lance Motch. Director, Player Personnel: Linda Pereira. Assistant to the President/CEO: Katherine Krassilnikoff. Director, Marketing: Mandy Stone. Director, Sales: Taylor Haynes. Director, Food/Beverage: Will O'Sullivan. Director, Broadcasting: Joe Ritzo. Finance/HR Manager: Renee Ramirez. Sales Manager: Tyson Lamp. Ticket Services Manager: Kellen Minteer. Operations Assistant: Tyler Weyermann. Marketing/Merchandise Assistant: Brad Brown. Marketing Assistant: Ben Guerrero.

FIELD STAFF
Manager: Brian Harper. Hitting Coach: Gary Davenport. Pitching Coach: Jerry Cram. Trainer: James Petra.

GAME INFORMATION
Radio Announcer: Joe Ritzo. No. of Games Broadcast: Home-70, Away-70. Flagship: www.sjgiants.com.
PA Announcer: Russ Call. Official Scorers: Brian Burkett, Michael Mike Hohler, Melligan, Michael Duca.
Stadium Name: Municipal Stadium. Location: South on I-280, Take 10th/11th Street Exit. Turn right on 10th Street. Turn left on Alma Ave. North on I-280: Take the 10th/11th Street Exit. Turn left on 10th Street. Turn Left on Alma Ave. Standard Game Times: 7 p.m.; Sat. 6 p.m.; Sun. 2 p.m. (5 p.m. after June 27). Ticket Price Range: $7-15.
Visiting Club Hotel: Pruneyard Plaza, 1995 S. Bascom Ave., Campbell, CA 95008. Telephone: (408) 559-4300.

STOCKTON PORTS

Office Address: 404 W. Fremont St, Stockton, CA 95203.
Telephone: (209) 644-1900. **Fax:** (209) 644-1931.
E-Mail Address: info@stocktonports.com. **Website:** www.stocktonports.com.
Affiliation (first year): Oakland Athletics (2005). **Years in League:** 1941, 1946-72, 1978-

OWNERSHIP, MANAGEMENT
Operated By: 7th Inning Stretch LLC.
President/General Manager: Pat Filippone. **Assistant GM:** Luke Reiff. **Manager, Media Relations:** Kristin Pratt. **Director, Marketing/Special Events:** Justin Gray. **Director, Group Sales:** Ben Carr. **Director, Finance:** Terri Bailey. **Director, Corporate Sales:** Zach Sharkey. **Senior Account Executive:** John Watts. **Stadium Operations Manager:** Ethan Bagen. **Box Office Manager:** Kyle Osgood. **Account Executives:** Darlene Betz, Sam Harold, Tim Pasisz. **Corporate Sponsorships Account Executive:** Mark Mendes. **Food/Beverage Service Provider:** Ovations. **Front Desk:** Deborah Auditor.

FIELD STAFF
Manager: Steve Scarsone. **Coach:** Tim Garland. **Pitching Coach:** Don Schulze. **Trainer:** Nathan Brooks.

GAME INFORMATION
Radio Announcer: Zack Bayrouty. **No of Games Broadcast:** Home-70, Away-70. **Flagship Station:** KWSX 1280 AM. **PA Announcer:** Mike Conway. **Official Scorer:** Paul Muyskens.
Stadium Name: Banner Island Ballpark. **Location:** From I-5/99, take Crosstown Freeway (Highway 4) exit El Dorado Street, north on El Dorado to Freemont Street, left on Freemont. **Standard Game Times:** 7:05 p.m.; Sun. 2:05 first half, 6:05 second half. **Ticket Price Range:** $7-21.
Visiting Club Hotel: Clarion Inn, 4219 East Waterloo Road, Stockton CA 95215. **Telephone:** (209) 931-3131.

VISALIA RAWHIDE

Office Address: 300 N. Giddings St, Visalia, CA 93291.
Telephone: (559) 732-4433. **Fax:** (559) 739-7732.
E-Mail Address: info@rawhidebaseball.com. **Website:** www.rawhide-baseball.com.
Affiliation (first year): Arizona Diamondbacks (2007). **Years in League:** 1946-62, 1968-75, 1977-

OWNERSHIP, MANAGEMENT
Operated By: Top of the Third Inc.
Principal Owners: Kevin O'Malley, Tom Seidler.
President/General Manager: Tom Seidler. **Assistant GM:** Jennifer Pendergraft. **Assistant GM/Legal Counsel:** Liz Martin. **Director, Ticketing:** Mike Candela. **Director, Broadcasting:** Donny Baarns. **Manager, Media Relations:** Mark Freeman. **Marketing Consultant:** Chris Henstra. **Head Groundskeeper:** Brandon Benson. **Ballpark Operations Manager:** Chris Jones. **Ballpark Operations:** Dan Hargey. **Client Servicing Manager:** Adam Martin. **Client Servicing Coordinator:** Marissa Smith. **Group Coordinator:** Sarah Twiggs. **Community Relations Manager:** Brittany Sackmann. **Executive Assistant:** Kacey Conley. **Clubhouse Manager:** Brad Chang.

FIELD STAFF
Manager: Audo Vicente. **Coach:** Alan Zinter. **Pitching Coach:** Erik Sabel. **Trainer:** Nick Oldroyd. **Strength/Conditioning:** Jason Mitchell.

GAME INFORMATION
Radio Announcers: Donny Baarns, Mark Freeman. **No. of Games Broadcast:** Home-70, Away-70. **Flagship Station:** KJUG 1270-AM.
PA Announcer: Bryan Anthony. **Official Scorers:** Harry Kargenian, Chuck Knox.
Stadium Name: Recreation Ballpark. **Location:** From Highway 99, take 198 East to Mooney Boulevard exit, left at second signal on Giddings; four blocks to ballpark. **Standard Game Times:** Mon.-Sat. 7:00 p.m.; Sun. 2:00 (first half), 6:00 (second half). **Ticket Price Range:** $6-20.
Visiting Club Hotel: Lamp Liter Inn, 3300 W Mineral King Ave, Visalia, CA 93291. **Telephone:** (559) 732-4511.

CAROLINA LEAGUE

HIGH CLASS A

Office Address: 1806 Pembroke Rd., Suite 2-B, Greensboro, NC 27408.
Mailing Address: P.O. Box 9503, Greensboro, NC 27429.
Telephone: (336) 691-9030. **Fax:** (336) 691-9070.
E-Mail Address: office@carolinaleague.com.
Website: www.carolinaleague.com
Years League Active: 1945-.
President/Treasurer: John Hopkins.
Vice Presidents: Art Silber (Potomac), Cam McRae (Kinston). **Corporate Secretary:** Ken Young (Frederick). **Directors:** Tim Zue (Salem), Calvin Falwell (Lynchburg), Chuck Greenberg (Myrtle Beach), Dave Ziedelis (Frederick), Cam McRae (Kinston), Jack Minker (Wilmington), Billy Prim (Winston-Salem), Art Silber (Potomac).
Administrative Assistant: Marnee Larkins.
Division Structure: North—Frederick, Lynchburg, Potomac, Wilmington. **South**—Kinston, Myrtle Beach, Salem, Winston-Salem.
Regular Season: 140 games (split schedule). **2010 Opening Date:** April 8. **Closing Date:** Sept. 6.
All-Star Game: June 22 at Myrtle Beach. (Carolina League vs. California League).
Playoff Format: First-half division winners play second-half division winners in best-of-five series; if a team wins both halves, it plays a wild card (team with next-best second-half record). Division series winners meet in best-of-five series for Mills Cup.
Roster Limit: 25 active. **Player Eligibility Rule:** No age limit. No more than two players and one player/coach on active list may have six or more years of prior minor league service.
Brand of Baseball: Rawlings.
Umpires: Joey Amaral (Baltimore, MD),Drew Ashcraft (Lexington, KY), Jeremy Crowe (Hartford, KY), Matt Cumbee (Raleigh, NC),Chris Graham (Brampton, ON),Kolin Kline (Arvada, CO), Shaylor Smith (Colleyville, TX), Doug Vines (Kennesaw, GA).

John Hopkins

STADIUM INFORMATION

Club	Stadium	Opened	Dimensions			Capacity	2009 Att.
			LF	CF	RF		
Frederick	Harry Grove Stadium	1990	325	400	325	5,400	293,438
Kinston	Grainger Stadium	1949	335	390	335	4,100	133,049
Lynchburg	City Stadium	1939	325	390	325	4,000	164,328
Myrtle Beach	BB&T Coastal Federal Field	1999	325	405	328	5,200	238,287
Potomac	Pfitzner Stadium	1984	315	400	315	6,000	180,541
Salem	Salem Memorial Stadium	1995	325	401	325	6,300	231,186
Wilmington	Frawley Stadium	1993	325	400	325	6,532	288,094
Winston-Salem	Winston-Salem Downtown Ballpark	1956	325	400	325	6,000	57,665

FREDERICK KEYS

Office Address: 21 Stadium Dr, Frederick, MD 21703.
Telephone: (301) 662-0013. **Fax:** (301) 662-0018.
E-Mail address: info@frederickkeys.com. **Website:** www.frederickkeys.com.
Affiliation (first year): Baltimore Orioles (1989). **Years in League:** 1989–

OWNERSHIP, MANAGEMENT

Ownership: Maryland Baseball Holding LLC.
President: Ken Young. **General Manager:** Dave Ziedelis. **Assistant General Manager:** Branden McGee. **Director, Sponsorships:** Christian Amorosi. **Director, Public Relations:** Adam Pohl. **Director, Ticket Operations:** Adam Weaver. **Director, Marketing:** Katy Fincham. **Director, Group Sales:** Quinn Williams. **Director, Ticket Sales:** Jeff Wiggins. **Finance Manager:** Tami Hetrick. **Office Manager:** Barb Freund. **Account Managers:** Dave Burdette, Tyler Schlatter, Matt Cherry. **Head Groundskeeper:** Kyle Slaton. **Stadium Operations Manager:** Nick Kefauver. **Clubhouse Operations Manager:** Mitch Strakonsky. **Public Relations Assistant:** Tim Murray. **Marketing Assistants:** Lauren Gaudreau, Brian Tardif. **Group Sales Assistant:** Matt Miller. **Sponsorship Sales Assistant:** Dan Goodman. **Box Office Assistant:** Sadie Portman. **Ovations General Manager:** Anita Clarke.

FIELD STAFF

Manager: Orlando Goodman. **Coach:** Denny Hocking. **Pitching Coach:** Blaine Beatty. **Trainer:** Patrick Wesley.

GAME INFORMATION

Radio Announcers: Adam Pohl, Tim Murray.
PA Announcer: Andy Redmond. **Official Scorers:** Bob Roberson, Dennis Hetrick, Dave Musil.
Stadium Name: Harry Grove Stadium. **Location:** From I-70, take exit 54 (Market Street), left at light. From I-270, take

exit 32 (I-70 Baltimore/Hagerstown) towards Baltimore (I-70), to exit 54 at Market Street. **Ticket Price Range:** $8-11.
Visiting Club Hotel: Comfort Inn, 7300 Executive Way, Frederick, MD 21701. **Telephone:** (301) 668-7272.

KINSTON INDIANS

Office Address: 400 East Grainger Avenue, Kinston, NC 28501.
Mailing Address: P.O. Box 3542, Kinston, NC 28502.
Telephone: (252) 527-9111. **Fax:** (252) 527-0498.
E-Mail Address: info@kinstonindians.com. **Website:** www.kinstonindians.com.
Affiliation (first year): Cleveland Indians (1987). **Years in League:** 1956-57, 1962-74, 1978-

OWNERSHIP, MANAGEMENT
Operated by: Slugger Partners LP.
Principal Owner/Chairman: Cam McRae.
General Manager: Shari Massengill. **Assistant GM:** Janell Bullock. **Director, Broadcasting/Public Relations:** Chris Hemeyer. **Director, Food/Beverage:** Tony Patterson. **Head Groundskeeper:** Steven Watson. **Team Photographer:** Carl Kline.

FIELD STAFF
Manager: Aaron Holbert. **Coach:** Rouglas Odor. **Pitching Coach:** Tony Arnold. **Trainer:** Jeremy Heller.

GAME INFORMATION
Radio Announcer: Chris Hemeyer. **No. of Games Broadcast:** Home-70, Away-70. **Flagship Station:** WWNB 1490 AM.
PA Announcer: Matt Friedman. **Official Scorer:** Steve Oliver.
Stadium Name: Grainger Stadium. **Location:** From west, take U.S. 70 Business (Vernon Avenue), left on East Street; from east, take U.S. 70 West, right on Highway 58, right on Vernon Avenue, right on East Street. **Standard Game Times:** 7 p.m., Sun. 2. **Ticket Price Range:** $5-7.
Visiting Club Hotel: Hampton Inn, Highway 70 Bypass, Kinston NC 28504. **Telephone:** (252) 523-1400.

LYNCHBURG HILLCATS

Office Address: Lynchburg City Stadium, 3180 Fort Ave, Lynchburg, VA 24501.
Mailing Address: P.O. Box 10213, Lynchburg, VA 24506.
Telephone: (434) 528-1144. **Fax:** (434) 846-0768.
E-Mail address: info@lynchburg-hillcats.com. **Website:** www.lynchburg-hillcats.com.
Affiliation (first year): Cincinnati Reds (2010). **Years in League:** 1966-

OWNERSHIP, MANAGEMENT
Operated By: Lynchburg Baseball Corp.
Chairman of the Board: Calvin Falwell.
President: C Rex Angel.
General Manager: Paul Sunwall. **Assistant GM:** Ronnie Roberts. **Head Groundskeeper/Sales:** Darren Johnson.
Director, Broadcasting/Publications: Scott Bacon. **Director, Food/Beverage:** Tyree Kim. **Ticket Manager:** Zach Willis.
Director, Information Technology: Andrew Chesser. **Office Manager:** Diane Tucker.

FIELD STAFF
Manager: Pat Kelly. **Coach:** Tony Jaramillo. **Pitching Coach:** Rigo Beltran. **Trainer:** Dale Nitzel. **Strength/Condition Coach:** Jake Dyskin.

GAME INFORMATION
Radio Announcer: Scott Bacon. **No. of Games Broadcast:** Home-70 Road-70. **Flagship Station:** WKDE 105.5-FM.
PA Announcer: Chuck Young. **Official Scorers:** Malcolm Haley, Chuck Young.
Stadium Name: Calvin Falwell Field at Lynchburg City Stadium. **Location:** U.S. 29 Business South to Lynchburg City Stadium (exit 6). U.S. 29 Business North to Lynchburg City Stadium (exit 4). **Ticket Price Range:** $5-9.
Visiting Club Hotel: Best Western, 2815 Candlers Mountain Rd, Lynchburg, VA 24502. **Telephone:** (434) 237-2986.

MYRTLE BEACH PELICANS

Office Address: 1251 21st Ave. N, Myrtle Beach, SC 29577.
Telephone: (843) 918-6002. **Fax:** (843) 918-6001.
E-Mail Address: info@myrtlebeachpelicans.com. **Website:** www.myrtlebeachpelicans.com.
Affiliation (first year): Atlanta Braves (1999). **Years in League:** 1999-

OWNERSHIP, MANAGEMENT
Operated By: Myrtle Beach Pelicans LP.
Managing Partner: Chuck Greenberg.

General Manager: Scott Brown. **Senior Director, Business Development:** Guy Schuman. **Senior Director, Finance:** Anne Frost. **Senior Director, Sports Turf Management/Ballpark Operations:** Chris Ball. **Director, Ticketing:** Josh Holley. **Corporate Sales Manager:** Denny Watson. **Box Office Manager:** Justin Cartor. **Group Sales Manager, Tourism:** Brian Stefan. **Group Sales Managers:** Stewart Comer, Matt Dedeluk. **Director, Broadcasting/Media Relations:** Tyler Maun. **Assistant Director, Broadcasting/Media Relations:** Anthony Masterson. **Director, Marketing/Promotions:** Maggie Neil. **Director, Community Relations:** Julie Borshak. **Executive Producer, In-Game Entertainment:** Jake White. **Facility Operations Manager:** Mike Snow. **Director, Merchandising:** Dan Bailey. **GM/Ovations Catering:** Brad Leininger. **Clubhouse Manager:** Stan Hunter. **Visiting Clubhouse Manager:** Bob Leber. **Administrative Assistant:** Beth Freitas. **Accounting Assistant:** Karen Ulyicsni.

FIELD STAFF

Manager: Rocket Wheeler. **Hitting Coach:** Rick Albert. **Pitching Coach:** Kent Willis. **Trainer:** Chas Miller.

GAME INFORMATION

Radio Announcers: Tyler Maun, Anthony Masterson. **No. of Games Broadcast:** Home-70, Road-70. **Flagship Station:** ESPN Radio The Team 93.9-FM/93.7-FM/1050-AM.

PA Announcer: Ryan Ibbotson. **Official Scorer:** Steve Walsch.

Stadium Name: BB&T Coastal Federal Field. **Location:** U.S. Highway 17 Bypass to 21st Avenue North, 1/2 mile to stadium. **Standard Game Times:** 7:05 p.m.; Sun. 3:05/6:05. **Ticket Price Range:** $7-11.

Visiting Club Hotel: Hampton Inn-Broadway at the Beach, 1140 Celebrity Circle, Myrtle Beach, SC 29577. **Telephone:** (843) 916-0600.

POTOMAC NATIONALS

Office Address: 7 County Complex Ct., Woodbridge, VA 22192.
Mailing Address: P.O. Box 2148, Woodbridge, VA 22195.
Telephone: (703) 590-2311. **Fax:** (703) 590-5716.
E-Mail Address: info@potomacnationals.com. **Website:** www.potomacnationals.com.
Affiliation (first year): Washington Nationals (2005). **Years in League:** 1978-

OWNERSHIP, MANAGEMENT

Operated By: Potomac Baseball LLC.

Principal Owner: Art Silber. **President:** Lani Silber Weiss.

Vice President/General Manager: Jonathan Griffith. **Assistant GM, Stadium Operations:** Carter Buschman. **Director, Ticket Operations:** Michelle Metzgar. **Director, Corporate Sales:** Libby Huguley. **Director, Food Services:** Jim Johnson. **Director, Media Relations:** Tripp Miller. **Group Sales Account Executives:** Andrew Stinson, Bill Kenney. **Corporate Sales Executive:** Travis Painter.

FIELD STAFF

Manager: Gary Cathcart. **Hitting Coach:** Matt Nokes. **Pitching Coach:** Paul Menhart. **Trainer:** Jeff Allred.

GAME INFORMATION

Radio Announcer: Will Flemming. **No. of Games Broadcast:** Home-70 Road-70. **Flagship:** www.potomacnationals.com.

Official Scorer: David Vincent, Ben Trittipoe.

Stadium Name: G. Richard Pfitzner Stadium. **Location:** From I-95, take exit 158B and continue on Prince William Parkway for five miles, right into County Complex Court. **Standard Game Times:** 7:03 p.m.; Sat. 6:35; Sun. 1:05. **Ticket Price Range:** $7-14.

Visiting Club Hotel: Hampton Inn Gainesville-Haymarket, 7300 Atlas Walk Way, Gainesville, VA 22155. **Telephone:** (703) 753-1500.

SALEM RED SOX

Office Address: 1004 Texas St., Salem, VA 24153.
Mailing Address: P.O. Box 842, Salem, VA 24153.
Telephone: (540) 389-3333. **Fax:** (540) 389-9710.
E-Mail Address: info@salemsox.com. **Website:** www.salemsox.com.
Affiliation (first year): Boston Red Sox (2009). **Years in League:** 1968-

OWNERSHIP, MANAGEMENT

Operated By: Carolina Baseball LLC/Fenway Sports Group.

President: Sam Kennedy.

Vice President/General Manager: Todd Stephenson. **Senior Assistant GM:** Allen Lawrence. **Director, Sales:** Dennis Robarge. **Director, Food/Beverage:** Rick Mosher. **Head Groundskeeper:** Tracy Schneweis. **Director, Ticket Operations/Special Events:** Jeanne Boester. **Assistant Director, Group Sales:** Jeremy Long. **Food Service Manager:** Giles Cochran. **Director, Broadcasting:** Evan Lepler. **Media/Community Relations Manager:** Dave Cawley. **Ticket Manager:** Steven Elovich. **Merchandise Manager:** Erin Hanson. **Publishing/Marketing Coordinator:** Andrew Goetz. **Clubhouse Manager:** Tom Wagner.

FIELD STAFF

Manager: Kevin Boles. **Coach:** Carlos Febles. **Pitching Coach:** Dick Such. **Trainer:** Brandon Henry.

GAME INFORMATION
Radio Announcer: Evan Lepler. **No. of Games Broadcast:** Home-70 Road-70. **Flagship Station:** WFIR 960-AM. **PA Announcer:** Travis Jenkins. **Official Scorer:** Billy Wells.

Stadium Name: Lewis-Gale Field at Salem Memorial Ballpark. **Location:** I-81 to exit 141 (Route 419), follow signs to Salem Civic Center Complex. **Standard Game Times:** 7:05 p.m.; Sat. 6:05; Sun. 4:05. **Ticket Price Range:** $7. 50-9.

Visiting Club Hotel: Comfort Inn Airport, 5070 Valley View Blvd, Roanoke, VA 24012. **Telephone:** (540) 527-2020.

WILMINGTON BLUE ROCKS

Office Address: 801 Shipyard Dr., Wilmington, DE 19801.
Telephone: (302) 888-2015. **Fax:** (302) 888-2032.
E-Mail Address: info@bluerocks.com. **Website:** www.bluerocks.com.
Affiliation (first year): Kansas City Royals (1993-2004, 2007-Present). **Years in League:** 1993-Present

OWNERSHIP, MANAGEMENT
Operated by: Wilmington Blue Rocks LP.

Honorary President: Matt Minker. **President:** Tom Palmer. **General Manager:** Chris Kemple. **Assistant GM:** Andrew Layman. **Director, Broadcasting/Media Relations:** John Sadak. **Assistant Director, Broadcasting/Media Relations:** Matt Janus. **Director, Merchandise:** Jim Beck. **Merchandise Assistant:** Tim Dinan. **Director, Promotions:** Kevin Linton. **Director, Video Production/Game Entertainment:** Kyle Love. **Production/Promotions Assistant:** Jake Schrum. **Director, Marketing:** Mark VanderHaar. **Marketing Assistant:** Brandon Apter. **Director, Community Relations:** Dave Arthur. **Community Relations Assistant:** Jacob Dukes. **Director, Sales/Ticket Operations:** Jared Forma. **Ticket Manager:** Mike Miller. **Group Sales Associates:** Stefani DiChiara-Rash, Joe Valenti. **Group Sales Assistant:** Greg Mathews. **Ticket Office Assistants:** Jared Lineweaver, Ira Luke III. **Director, Field Operations:** Steve Gold. **Director, Finance:** Denis Weigert. **Office Manager:** Elizabeth Kolodziej.

FIELD STAFF
Manager: Brian Rupp. **Coach:** Justin Gemoll. **Pitching Coach:** Steve Luebber. **Athletic Trainer:** Dave Iannicca.

GAME INFORMATION
Radio Announcers: John Sadak, Matt Janus. **No. of Games Broadcast:** Home-70, Away-70. **Flagship Station:** WWTX 1290-AM.

PA Announcer: Kevin Linton. **Official Scorers:** Dick Shute, Adam Kamras.

Stadium Name: Judy Johnson Field at Daniel S. Frawley Stadium. **Location:** I-95 North to Maryland Ave. (exit 6), right on Maryland Ave., and through traffic light onto Martin Luther King Blvd., right at traffic light on Justison St., follow to Shipyard Dr.; I-95 South to Maryland Ave. (exit 6), left at fourth light on Martin Luther King Blvd., right at fourth light on Justison St., follow to Shipyard Dr. **Standard Game Times:** 7:05 p.m., 6:35 (April-May); Sat. 6:05; Sun. 1:35. **Ticket Price Range:** $4-10.

Visiting Club Hotel: Quality Inn-Skyways, 147 N. DuPont Hwy., New Castle, DE 19720. **Telephone:** (302) 328-6666.

WIINSTON-SALEM DASH

Office Address: 926 Brookstown Ave., Winston-Salem, NC 27101.
Stadium Address: 951 Ballpark Way, Winston-Salem, NC 27101.
Telephone: (336) 714-2287. **Fax:** (336) 714-2288
Website: www.wsdash.com. **E-Mail Address:** info@wsdash.com.
Affiliation (first year): Chicago White Sox (1997). **Years in League:** 1945-present

OWNERSHIP, MANAGEMENT
Operated by: Sports Menagerie LLC. **Principal Owner:** Billy Prim. **President:** Geoff Lassiter. **CFO:** Kurt Gehsmann. **VP, Baseball Operations:** Ryan Manuel. **VP, Sponsorship Services:** Angie Lynde. **Director, Entertainment:** Trey Kalny. **Staff Accountant:** Anita Jasso. **Sponsor Services Director:** Gerri Brommer. **Marketing Manager, Sponsor Services:** Jill Heller. **Creative Manager:** Caleb Pardick. **Box Office Manager:** Steve Young. **Sales Coordinator:** Brandy Jamison. **Corporate Marketing Managers:** Jeremy Boler, Avery Robbins, Chris Wood. **Inside Sales Representatives:** Jenna Anderson, Kristen Farley, Russell Parmele, Michael Smith. **Group Sales Coordinators:** Brent Beam, Pat Riley. **Head Groundskeeper:** Doug Tanis. **MVP Education Program Coordinator:** Tielor Robinson.

FIELD STAFF
Manager: Joe McEwing. **Hitting Coach:** Robert Sasser. **Pitching Coach:** Bobby Thigpen. **Athletic Trainer:** Josh Fallin. **Strength Coach:** Adam Tischler.

GAME INFORMATION
Radio Announcer: Unavailaable. **No. of Games Broadcast:** Home-70, Away-70. **Flagship Station:** www.wsdash.com. **PA Announcer:** Cabell Philpott. **Official Scorer:** Unavailable.

Stadium Name: Winston-Salem Downtown Ballpark.

Stadium Location: I-40 Business to Peters Creek Parkway exit (exit 5A). **Standard Game Times:** Monday-Saturday: 7 p.m.; **Sunday:** 2 p.m.

Visiting Club Hotel: Quality Inn at Hanes Mall, 2008 S Hawthorne Rd, Winston-Salem, NC 27103. **Telephone:** (336) 765-6670.

FLORIDA STATE LEAGUE

HIGH CLASS A

Office Address: 115 E. Orange Ave., Daytona Beach, FL 32114.
Mailing Address: P.O. Box 349, Daytona Beach, FL 32115.
Telephone: (386) 252-7479. **Fax:** (386) 252-7495.
E-Mail Address: fslbaseball@cfl.rr.com. **Website:** www.floridastateleague.com.
Years League Active: 1919-1927, 1936-1941, 1946-.
President/Treasurer: Chuck Murphy.
Vice Presidents: Ken Carson (Dunedin), Paul Taglieri (St. Lucie).
Corporate Secretary: C. David Hood.
Directors: Joe Pinto(Jupiter/Palm Beach), Ken Carson (Dunedin), Jeff Eiseman (Port Charlotte), Marvin Goldklang (Fort Myers), Trevor Gooby (Bradenton), Ron Myers (Lakeland), Brady Ballard (Daytona), Kyle Smith (Brevard County), C.Vance Smith (Tampa), Paul Taglieri (St. Lucie), John Timberlake (Clearwater).
Office Manager: Laura LeCras.
Division Structure: North—Brevard County, Clearwater, Daytona, Dunedin, Lakeland, Tampa. **South**—Fort Myers, Jupiter, Palm Beach, Port Charlotte, St. Lucie, Bradenton.
Regular Season: 140 games (split schedule). **2010 Opening Date:** April 8. **Closing Date:** Sept. 5.
All-Star Game: June 12 at Brevard County.
Playoff Format: First-half division winners meet second-half winners in best-of-three series. Winners meet in best-of-five series for league championship.
Roster Limit: 25. **Player Eligibility Rule:** No age limit. No more than two players and one player-coach on active list may have six or more years of prior minor league service.
Brand of Baseball: Rawlings.
Umpires: Matthew A. Cunningham (Indianapolis, IN), Ian R. Fazio (Tavernier, FL), Jordan S. Ferrell (Clarksville, TN.), James M. Guyll (Ft. Wayne, IN), Joseph M. Hannigan (Westmont, IL.), Brandon K. Henson (Gowrie, IA),Anthony A. Johnson (McComb, MS), Benjamin J. May (Racine, WI),Roberto M. Medina (Toa Baja, PR), Brandon A. Misun (Edmond, OK), Ross K. Nickel(Seattle, WA), Eric G. Underwood (Powder Springs, GA).

Chuck Murphy

STADIUM INFORMATION

Club	Stadium	Opened	LF	CF	RF	Capacity	2009 Att.
*Bradenton	McKechnie Field	1923	335	400	335	6,602	N/A
Brevard County	Space Coast Stadium	1994	340	404	340	7,500	68,596
Clearwater	Bright House Networks Field	2004	330	400	330	8,500	169,559
Charlotte	Charlotte Sports Park	2009	343	413	343	5,028	171,314
Daytona	Jackie Robinson Ballpark	1930	317	400	325	4,000	147,921
Dunedin	Dunedin Stadium	1977	335	400	315	5,509	35,683
Fort Myers	Hammond Stadium	1991	330	405	330	7,500	115,361
Jupiter	Roger Dean Stadium	1998	330	400	325	6,871	68,741
Lakeland	Joker Marchant Stadium	1966	340	420	340	7,100	49,569
Palm Beach	Roger Dean Stadium	1998	330	400	325	6,871	68,562
St. Lucie	Tradition Field	1988	338	410	338	7,500	95,598
Tampa	Steinbrenner Field	1996	318	408	314	10,386	92,670

* Played in Sarasota in 2009

BRADENTON MARAUDERS

Mailing Address: 1701 27th Street East, Bradenton, FL 34208.
Telephone: (941) 747-3031. **Fax:** (941) 747-9442.
E-Mail Address: MaraudersInfo@pirates.com. **Website:** www.BradentonMarauders.com
Affiliation (first year): Pittsburgh Pirates (2010). **Years in League (Bradenton):** 1919-20, 1923-24, 1926

OWNERSHIP, MANAGEMENT
Operated By: Pittsburgh Associates.
General Manager: Dan Wolfert. **Coordinator, Stadium Operations:** Darren Smith. **Coordinator, Sales/Marketing:** Stacy Morgan. **Coordinator, Ticket Operations:** Rich Morris. **Head Groundskeeper:** Victor Madrigal.

FIELD STAFF
Manager: P.J. Forbes. **Coach:** Dave Howard. **Coach:** Wally Whitehurst. **Athletic Trainer:** Keito Homma. **Strength/Conditioning Coach:** Brendan Verner.

GAME INFORMATION
Radio: None.

PA Announcer: Unavailable. Official Scorer: Unavailable.
Stadium Name: McKechnie Field. Location: I-75 to exit 220 (220B from I-75N) to SR 64 West/Manatee Ave. Left onto 9th St. West. McKechnie Field on the left. Standard Game Times: 7 p.m.; Sat. 6; Sun. 1. Ticket Price Range: $4-$6.
Visiting Club Hotel: Courtyard by Marriott Bradenton Sarasota Waterfront, 100 Riverfront Drive West, Bradenton, FL 34205. Telephone: (941) 747-3727.

BREVARD COUNTY MANATEES

Office Address: 5800 Stadium Pkwy., Suite 101, Viera, FL 32940.
Telephone: (321) 633-9200. Fax: (321) 633-4418.
E-Mail Address: info@spacecoaststadium.com. Website: www.manateesbaseball.com.
Affiliation (first year): Milwaukee Brewers (2005). Years in League: 1994-

OWNERSHIP, MANAGEMENT
Operated By: Central Florida Baseball Group LLC.
Chairman: Dr. Tom Winters. Vice Chairman: Dwight Titus. President: Charlie Baumann.
General Manager: Kyle Smith. Business Operations Manager: Kelley Wheeler. Director, Group Sales: Meghan Cornett. Director, Ticketing: Katy Bubeck.

FIELD STAFF
Manager: Bob Miscik. Hitting Coach: Dwayne Hosey. Pitching Coach: Fred Dabney. Trainer: Tommy Craig. Strength/Conditioning: Chris Gavranic.

GAME INFORMATION
PA Announcer: J.C. Meyerholz. Radio: None.
Official Scorer: Eric Valenstein.
Stadium Name: Space Coast Stadium. Location: I-95 North to Wickham Rd. (exit 191), left onto Wickham, right at traffic circle onto Lake Andrew Drive for 1 1/2 miles through the Brevard County government office complex to the four-way stop, right on Stadium Parkway. Space Coast Stadium 1/2 mile on the left. I-95 South to Rockledge exit (exit 195), left onto Stadium Parkway. Space Coast Stadium is 3 miles on right. Standard Game Times: 7 pm.; Sat. 7; Sun. 1. Ticket Price Range: $7.
Visiting Club Hotel: Holiday Inn Hotel & Conference Center, 8928 N. Wickham Rd, Viera, FL 32940. Telephone: (321) 255-0077.

CHARLOTTE STONE CRABS

Office Address: 2300 El Jobean Rd., Port Charlotte, FL 33948.
Mailing Address: 2300 El Jobean Rd., Building A, Port Charlotte, FL 33948.
Telephone: (941) 206-4487. Fax: (941) 206-3599.
E-Mail Address: info@stonecrabsbaseball.com. Website: www.stonecrabsbaseball.com.
Affiliation (first year): Tampa Bay Rays (2009). Years in League: 2009-

OWNERSHIP, MANAGEMENT
Operated By: Ripken Baseball.
General Manager: Joe Hart. Marketing Manager: Jonathan Gantt. Director/Assistant GM, Food/Beverage/Operations: Nick Barkley. Director, Operations: Sean Sawyer. Director, Ticket Sales: Adam English. Box Office Manager: Chris Sprunger. Assistant GM, Sales: Patrick McMaster. Bookkeeper: Tamera Figueroa. Account Executives: Jill Baksa, Peter Walsifer, Rob Coons, Joe Mandele.

FIELD STAFF
Manager: Jim Morrison. Coach: Joe Szekely. Pitching Coach: Neil Allen. Trainer: Chris Tomashoff.

GAME INFORMATION
PA Announcer: Josh Grant. Official Scorer: Not Available.
Stadium Name: Charlotte Sports Park. Location: I-75 to Exit 179, turn left onto Toldeo Blade Blvd. then right on El Jobean Rd. Ticket Price Range: $6-11.
Visiting Club Hotel: Days Inn, 1941 Tamiami Trail, Port Charlotte, FL 33948. Telephone: 941-627-8900.

CLEARWATER THRESHERS

Office Address: 601 N. Old Coachman Rd, Clearwater, FL 33765.
Telephone: (727) 712-4300. Fax: (727) 712-4498.
Website: www.threshersbaseball.com.
Affiliation (first year): Philadelphia Phillies (1985). Years in League: 1985-

OWNERSHIP, MANAGEMENT
Operated by: Philadelphia Phillies.

Chairman: Bill Giles. **President:** David Montgomery.

Director, Florida Operations/General Manager: John Timberlake. **Assistant Director, Minor League Operations:** Lee McDaniel. **Business Manager:** Dianne Gonzalez. **Assistant GM/Director, Sales:** Dan McDonough. **Assistant GM/Ticketing:** Jason Adams. **Office Administration:** DeDe Angelillis. **Manager, Group Sales:** Dan Madden. **Assistant Manager, Group Sales:** Bobby Mitchell. **Manager, Ballpark Operations:** Jerry Warren. **Coordinator, Facility Maintenance:** Cory Sipe. **Manager, Special Events:** Doug Kemp. **Manager, Community Relations/Promotions:** Amanda Warner. **Clubhouse Manager:** Mark Meschede. **Manager,** Food/Beverage: Brad Dudash. **Assistant, Food/ Beverage:** Craig Glover. **Ticket Office Manager:** Mike Nash. **Group Sales Assistant:** Maria Spesia. **Operations Assistant:** Jim Boros. **Coordinator, Audio/Video:** Nic Repper. **Interns:** Sean McCarthy, Tony Penna, Vince Grasso.

FIELD STAFF

Manager: Dusty Wathan. **Coach:** Kevin Jordan. **Pitching Coach:** Dave Lundquist.

GAME INFORMATION

Radio: None.

PA Announcer: Don Guckian. **Official Scorer:** Larry Wiederecht.

Stadium Name: Bright House Field. **Location:** U.S. 19 North and Drew Street in Clearwater. **Standard Game Times:** 7 p.m.; Sun. 1. **Ticket Price Range:** $4-9.

Visiting Club Hotel: Unavailable.

DAYTONA CUBS

Office Address: 105 E. Orange Ave, Daytona Beach, FL 32114.
Telephone: (386) 257-3172. **Fax:** (386) 257-3382.
E-Mail Address: info@daytonacubs.com. **Website:** www.daytonacubs.com.
Affiliation (first year): Chicago Cubs (1993). **Years in League:** 1920-24, 1928, 1936-41, 1946-73, 1977-87, 1993-

OWNERSHIP, MANAGEMENT

Operated By: Big Game Florida LLC.

Principal Owner/President: Andrew Rayburn.

General Manager: Brady Ballard. **Assistant GMs:** Jamie Jarrett, Josh Lawther. **Director, Broadcasting/Media Relations:** Christian Bruey. **Director, Stadium Operations:** J.R. Laub. **Director, Tickets:** Amanda Earnest. **Director, Groups:** Clint Cure. **Director, Food/Beverage:** Eric Freeman. **Manager, Special Events/Merchandise:** Ashley Allphin. **Manager, Tickets/Group Sales:** Jim Jaworski. **Office Manager:** Tammy Devine.

FIELD STAFF

Manager: Buddy Bailey. **Coach:** Richie Zisk. **Pitching Coach:** Tom Pratt. **Trainer:** Bob Grimes.

GAME INFORMATION

Radio Announcer: Christian Bruey. **No. of Games Broadcast:** Home-70, Road-70. **Flagship Station:** AM-1340 WROD.

PA Announcer: Tim Lecras. **Official Scorer:** Don Roberts.

Stadium Name: Jackie Robinson Ballpark. **Location:** I-95 to International Speedway Blvd. Exit (Route 92), east to Beach Street, south to Magnolia Ave., east to ballpark; A1A North/South to Orange Ave., west to ballpark. **Standard Game Time:** 7:05 p.m. **Ticket Price Range:** $6-12.

Visiting Club Hotel: Acapulco Hotel & Resort, 2505 S. Atlantic Ave., Daytona Beach Shores, FL 32218. **Telephone:** (386) 761-2210.

DUNEDIN BLUE JAYS

Office Address: 373-A Douglas Ave., Dunedin, FL 34698.
Telephone: (727) 733-9302. **Fax:** (727) 734-7661.
E-Mail Address: feedback@dunedinbluejays.com. **Website:** www.dunedinbluejays.com.
Affiliation (first year): Toronto Blue Jays (1987). **Years in League:** 1978-79, 1987-

OWNERSHIP, MANAGEMENT

Operated by: Toronto Blue Jays.

General Manager: Shelby Nelson. **Assistant GM:** Janette Donoghue. **Senior Consultant:** Ken Carson. **Supervisor, Ticket Operations:** Garrett Konrad. **Account Manager, Ticket/Corporate Sales:** Kevin Schildt. **Sports Turf Superintendent:** Patrick Skunda. **Coordinator, Communications:** Tim Livingston. **Coordinator, Community Relations:** Tony Penna. **Sales Coordinator:** Andrew Johnson. **Administrative Assistant:** Cile Fullerton. **Account Executives:** Kevin Schildt, Kathi Wiegand. **Office Manager:** Karen Howell. **Clubhouse Managers:** Freddy Mcdina.

FIELD STAFF

Manager: Clayton McCullough. **Hitting Coach:** Justin Mashore. **Pitching Coach:** Darold Knowles. **Trainer:** Dan McIntosh.

GAME INFORMATION

Radio: None.

PA Announcer: Alan Wilcox. **Official Scorer:** Josh Huff.

Stadium Name: Dunedin Stadium. **Location:** From I-275, north on Highway 19, left on Sunset Point Rd. for 4 1/2 miles, right on Douglas Ave., stadium is 1/2 mile on right. **Standard Game Times:** 7 p.m.; Sun. 1. **Ticket Price Range:** $6.
Visiting Club Hotel: Comfort Inn Countryside, 26508 U.S. 19 N., Clearwater, FL 33761. **Telephone:** (727) 796-1234.

FORT MYERS MIRACLE

Office Address: 14400 Six Mile Cypress Pkwy, Fort Myers, FL 33912.
Telephone: (239) 768-4210. **Fax:** (239) 768-4211.
E-Mail Address: miracle@miraclebaseball.com. **Website:** www.miraclebaseball.com.
Affiliation (first year): Minnesota Twins (1993). **Years in League:** 1926, 1978-87, 1991-

OWNERSHIP, MANAGEMENT
Operated By: Greater Miami Baseball Club LP.
Principal Owner/Chairman: Marvin Goldklang. **Vice Chairman:** Mike Veeck. **Executive Vice President/General Manager:** Steve Gliner. **Assistant General Manager:** Kris Koch. **Director, Business Operations:** Suzanne Reaves. **Senior Director, Corporate Sales/Marketing:** Terry Simon. **Director, Media Relations/Promotions:** Gary Sharp. **Director, Food/Beverage:** Rory Broome. **Assistant, Food/Beverage:** Phillip Bush. **Manager, Tickets:** Ryan Dimmitt. **Community Relations Coordinator:** Joy Donahue. **Account Executives:** Travis Easton, Sean Kelly. **Administrative Assistants:** Matt McLaughlin, Amanda Simat. **Customer Relations Associates:** Nikki Greer, Sue Pinola. **Head Groundskeeper:** Keith Blasingim.

FIELD STAFF
Manager: Jake Mauer. **Coach:** Jim Dwyer. **Pitching Coach:** Steve Mintz. **Trainer:** Larry Bennese.

GAME INFORMATION
Radio Announcer: Alex Margulies. **No. of Games Broadcast:** Home-70, Road-70. **Internet Broadcasts:** www.miracle-baseball.com.
PA Announcer: Gary Sharp. **Official Scorer:** Scott Pedersen.
Stadium Name: William H. Hammond Stadium. **Location:** Exit 131 off I-75, west on Daniels Parkway, left on Six Mile Cypress Parkway. **Standard Game Times:** 7:05 p.m.; Sun. 1:05. **Ticket Price Range:** $5-8.50.
Visiting Club Hotel: Fairfield Inn by Marriot, 7090 Cypress Terrace, Fort Myers, FL 33907. **Telephone:** (239) 437-5600.

JUPITER HAMMERHEADS

Office Address: 4751 Main Street, Jupiter, FL 33458.
Telephone: (561) 775-1818. **Fax:** (561) 691-6886.
E-Mail Address: f.desk@rogerdeanstadium.com. **Website:** www.jupiterhammerheads.com.
Affiliation (first year): Florida Marlins (2002). **Years in League:** 1998-

OWNERSHIP, MANAGEMENT
Owned By: St. Louis Cardinals. **Operated By:** Jupiter Stadium LLC.
General Manager, Jupiter Stadium, LLC: Joe Pinto. **Executive Assistant:** Carol McAteer.
GM, Jupiter Hammerheads: Unavailable. **Assistant GM:** Marshall Jennings. **Corporate Partnership Director:** Melissa Kuper. **Corporate Partnership Manager:** Stephanie Glavin. **Merchandise Manager:** Lauren Gurley. **Ticket Manager:** Noel Ruiz-Castaneda. **Ticket Sales/Promotions Manager:** Lisa Fegley. **Stadium/Event Operations Manager:** Bryan Knapp. **Stadium Building Manager:** Jorge Toro. **Assistant Facility Operations Managers:** Matt Eggerman, Jordan Treadway. **Assistant Ticket Manager:** Amanda Avila. **Ticket Sales Representative:** Alex Inman. **Office Manager:** Monica West.

FIELD STAFF
Manager: Ron Hassey. **Coach:** Robert Bell. **Pitching Coach:** Steve Doc Watson.

GAME INFORMATION
Radio: None.
PA Announcers: John Frost, Dick Sanford. **Official Scorer:** Brennan McDonald.
Stadium Name: Roger Dean Stadium. **Location:** I-95 to exit 83, east on Donald Ross Road for 1/4 mile. **Standard Game Times:** 7:05 p.m.; Sat. 6:05; Sun. 5:05. **Ticket Price Range:** $6.50-8.50.
Visiting Club Hotel: Comfort Inn & Suites Jupiter, 6752 West Indiantown Rd, Jupiter, FL 33458. **Telephone:** (561) 745-7997.

LAKELAND FLYING TIGERS

Office Address: 2125 N Lake Ave, Lakeland, FL 33805.
Mailing Address: 2125 N Lake Ave, Lakeland, FL 33805.
Telephone: (863) 686-8075. **Fax:** (863) 688-9589.
Website: www.lakelandflyingtigers.com.
Affiliation (first year): Detroit Tigers (1967). **Years in League:** 1919-26, 1953-55, 1960, 1962-64, 1967-.

OWNERSHIP, MANAGEMENT

Owned By: Detroit Tigers, Inc.

Principal Owner: Mike Ilitch. **President:** David Dombrowski. **Director, Florida Operations:** Ron Myers. **General Manager:** Zack Burek. **Manager, Administration/Operations:** Shannon Follett. **Ticket Manager:** Ryan Eason. **Group Sales Manager:** Dan Lauer. **Executive Chef:** Tom Mackinnon. **Receptionist:** Maria Walls.

FIELD STAFF

Manager: Andy Barkett. **Coach:** Larry Herndon. **Pitching Coach:** Joe Coleman.

GAME INFORMATION

Radio: None.

PA Announcers: Shari Szabo. **Official Scorer:** Sandy Shaw. **Stadium Name:** Joker Marchant Stadium. **Location:** Exit 33 on I-4 to 33 South, 1.5 miles on left. **Standard Game Times:** 7 pm; Sat 6; Sun 1. **Ticket Price Range:** $4-6.

Visiting Club Hotel: Holiday Inn Lakeland Hotel & Conference Center, 3260 US Highway 98 North, Lakeland, FL 33805. **Telephone:** (863) 688-8080.

PALM BEACH CARDINALS

Office Address: 4751 Main Street, Jupiter, FL 33458.
Telephone: (561) 775-1818. **Fax:** (561) 691-6886.
E-Mail address: f.desk@rogerdeanstadium.com. **Website:** www.palmbeachcardinals.com.
Affiliation (first year): St. Louis Cardinals (2003). **Years in League:** 2003-

OWNERSHIP, MANAGEMENT

Owned By: St. Louis Cardinals. **Operated By:** Jupiter Stadium LLC

General Manager, Jupiter Stadium, LLC: Joe Pinto. **Executive Assistant:** Carol McAteer. **GM, Palm Beach Cardinals:** Marshall Jennings. **Corporate Partnership Director:** Melissa Kuper. **Corporate Partnership Manager:** Stephanie Glavin. **Merchandise Manager:** Lauren Gurley. **Ticket Manager:** Noel Ruiz-Castaneda. **Manager, Ticket Sales/Promotions:** Lisa Fegley. **Manager, Stadium/Event Operations:** Bryan Knapp. **Stadium Building Manager:** Jorge Toro. **Managers, Assistant Facility Operations:** Matt Eggerman, Jordan Treadway. **Assistant Ticket Manager:** Amanda Avila. **Ticket Sales Representative:** Alex Inman. **Office Manager:** Monica West.

FIELD STAFF

Manager: Luis Aquayo. **Coach:** Jeff Albert. **Pitching Coach:** Bryan Eversgerd.

GAME INFORMATION

Radio: None.

PA Announcers: John Frost, Dick Sanford. **Official Scorer:** Lou Villano. **Stadium Name:** Roger Dean Stadium. **Location:** I-95 to exit 83, east on Donald Ross Road for 1/4 mile. **Standard Game Times:** 7:05 p.m.; Sat. 6:05; Sun. 5:05. **Ticket Price Range:** $6.50-8.50.

Visiting Club Hotel: Comfort Inn & Suites Jupiter, 6752 West Indiantown Rd, Jupiter, FL 33458. **Telephone:** (561) 745-7997.

ST. LUCIE METS

Office Address: 525 NW Peacock Blvd., Port St. Lucie, FL 34986.
Telephone: (772) 871-2100. **Fax:** (772) 878-9802.
Website: www.traditionfield.com.
Affiliation (first year): New York Mets (1988). **Years in League:** 1988-

OWNERSHIP, MANAGEMENT

Operated by: Sterling Mets LP.

Chairman: Fred Wilpon. **President:** Saul Katz. **Senior Executive Vice President/COO:** Jeff Wilpon. **Director, Florida Operations/General Manager:** Paul Taglieri. **Assistant Director, Florida Operations/Assistant General Manager:** Traer Van Allen. **Manager, Food/Beverage Operations:** Brian Paupeck. **Manager, Sales/Ballpark Operations:** Ryan Strickland. **Group Sales/Community Relations Coordinator:** Katie Hatch. **Executive Assistant:** Cynthia Malaspino. **Staff Accountant:** Paula Andreozzi. **Media Relations Manager:** Matt Gagnon. **Ticketing/Merchandise Manager:** Clinton Van Allen. **Head Groundskeeper:** Tommy Bowes. **Clubhouse Manager:** Jack Brenner.

FIELD STAFF

Manager: Edgar Alfonzo. **Coaches:** G. Greer/J. Carreno. **Pitching Coach:** Phil Regan.

GAME INFORMATION

Radio: None.

PA Announcer: Matt Gagnon. **Official Scorer:** Bob Adams.

Stadium Name: Tradition Field. **Location:** Exit 121 (St. Lucie West Blvd.) off I-95, east 1/2 mile, left on NW Peacock Blvd. **Standard Game Times:** 7 p.m.; Sat. 6; Sun. 1. **Ticket Price Range:** $4-6.

Visiting Club Hotel: Springhill Suites, 2000 NW Courtyard Circle., Port St. Lucie, FL 34956. **Telephone:** (772) 879-2929.

TAMPA YANKEES

Office Address: One Steinbrenner Dr., Tampa, FL 33614.
Telephone: (813) 875-7753. **Fax:** (813) 673-3174.
E-Mail Address: vsmith@yankees.com. **Website:** tybaseball.com.
Affiliation (first year): New York Yankees (1994). **Years in League:** 1919-27, 1957-1988, 1994-

OWNERSHIP, MANAGEMENT

Operated by: New York Yankees LP.
Principal Owner: George Steinbrenner.
General Manager: Vance Smith. **Assistant GM:** Julie Kremer. **Director, Sales/Marketing:** Howard Grosswirth. **Director, Ticket Sales:** Brian Valdez. **Head Groundskeeper:** Ritchie Anderson.

FIELD STAFF

Manager: Luis Sojo. **Hitting Coach:** Julius Matos. **Pitching Coach:** Greg Pavlick. **Coach:** Derek Shumpert. **Trainer:** Kris Russell. **Strength/Conditioning:** Jay Signorelli.

GAME INFORMATION

Radio: None.
PA Announcer: Steve Hague. **Official Scorer:** Unavailable.
Stadium Name: Steinbrenner Field. **Location:** I-275 to Martin Luther King, west on Martin Luther King to Dale Mabry. **Standard Game Times:** 7 p.m.; Sun. 1. **Ticket Price Range:** $4-6.

Visiting Club Hotel: Sheraton Suites Tampa Airport, 4400 W. Cypress St., Tampa, FL 33607. **Telephone:** (813) 873-8675.

MIDWEST LEAGUE

LOW CLASS A

Office Address: 1118 Cranston Rd., Beloit, WI 53511.
Mailing Address: P.O. Box 936, Beloit, WI 53512.
Telephone: (608) 364-1188. **Fax:** (608) 364-1913.
E-Mail Address: mwl@midwestleague.com. **Website:** www.midwestleague.com.
Years League Active: 1947-.
President, Treasurer: George H. Spelius.
Vice Presidents: Ed Larson, Richard A. Nussbaum II. **Legal Counsel/Secretary:** Richard A. Nussbaum II.
Directors: Tom Barbee (Cedar Rapids), Peter Carfagna (Lake County), Lew Chamberlin (West Michigan), Dennis Conerton (Beloit), Tom Dickson (Lansing), Jason Freier (Fort Wayne), David Heller (Quad Cities), Joe Kernan (South Bend), Gary Mayse (Dayton), Paul Schnack (Clinton), Art Solomon (Bowling Green), William Stavropoulos (Great Lakes), Rocky Vonachen (Peoria), Dave Walker (Burlington), Mike Woleben (Kane County), Rob Zerjav (Wisconsin).
League Administrator: Holly Voss.
Division Structure: East—Bowling Green, Dayton, Fort Wayne, Lake County, Lansing, South Bend, Great Lakes, West Michigan. **West**—Beloit, Burlington, Cedar Rapids, Clinton, Kane County, Peoria, Quad Cities, Wisconsin.
Regular Season: 140 games (split schedule). **2010 Opening Date:** April 8. **Closing Date:** Sept. 6.
All-Star Game: June 22 at Fort Wayne.
Playoff Format: Eight teams qualify. First-half and second-half division winners and wild-card teams meet in best-of-three quarterfinal series. Winners meet in best-of-three series for division championships. Division champions meet in best-of-five final for league championship.
Roster Limit: 25 active. **Player Eligibility Rule:** No age limit. No more than two players and one player-coach on active list may have more than five years experience.
Brand of Baseball: Rawlings ROM-MID.
Umpires: Unavailable.

George Spelius

STADIUM INFORMATION

Club	Stadium	Opened	Dimensions LF	CF	RF	Capacity	2009 Att.
Beloit	Pohlman Field	1982	325	380	325	3,500	83,480
*Bowling Green	Bowling Green Ballpark	2009	312	401	325	4,559	232,987
Burlington	Community Field	1947	338	403	318	3,200	64,499
Cedar Rapids	Veterans Memorial Stadium	2000	315	400	325	5,300	169,697
Clinton	Alliant Energy Field	1937	335	390	325	4,000	107,665
Dayton	Fifth Third Field	2000	338	402	338	7,230	586,193
Fort Wayne	Parkview Field	2009	336	400	318	8,100	378,529
Great Lakes	Dow Diamond	2007	332	400	325	5,200	271,146
Kane County	Philip B. Elfstrom Stadium	1991	335	400	335	7,400	400,040
*Lake County	Classic Park	2003	320	400	320	7,273	267,895
Lansing	Oldsmobile Park	1996	305	412	305	11,000	346,935
Peoria	O'Brien Field	2002	310	400	310	7,500	219,168
Quad Cities	John O'Donnell Stadium	1931	343	400	318	4,024	236,401
South Bend	Coveleski Regional Stadium	1987	336	405	336	5,000	155,403
West Michigan	Fifth Third Ballpark	1994	317	402	327	10,051	356,642
Wisconsin	Fox Cities Stadium	1995	325	400	325	5,500	253,240

*Played in South Atlantic League in 2009

BELOIT SNAPPERS

Office Address: 2301 Skyline Dr., Beloit, WI 53511.
Mailing Address: P.O. Box 855, Beloit, WI 53512.
Telephone: (608) 362-2272. **Fax:** (608) 362-0418.
E-Mail Address: snappy@snappersbaseball.com. **Website:** www.snappersbaseball.com.
Affiliation (first year): Minnesota Twins (2005). **Years in League:** 1982-.

OWNERSHIP, MANAGEMENT

Operated by: Beloit Professional Baseball Association Inc.
Chairman: Dennis Conerton. **President:** Perry Folts.
General Manager: Jeff Vohs. **Assistant General Manager, Corporate Sales/Promotions:** Riley Gostisha. **Director, Media/Community Relations/Marketing:** Marcus Jacobs. **Director, Ticket Operations/Merchandise:** Matt Bosen. **Director, Food/Beverage:** Tom Gross. **Head Groundskeeper:** Eric Williams.

FIELD STAFF

Manager: Nelson Prada. **Hitting Coach:** Tommy Watkins. **Pitching Coach:** Gary Lucas. **Trainer:** Alan Rail.

GAME INFORMATION

Radio Announcer: Andrew Liebetrau. **No. of Games Broadcast:** 21. **Flagship Station:** 1380-AM ESPN.
PA Announcer: Marcus Jacobs. **Official Scorer:** Unavailable.
Stadium Name: Pohlman Field. **Location:** I-90 to exit 185-A, right at Cranston Road for 1 1/2 miles; I-43 to Wisconsin 81 to Cranston Road, right at Cranston for 1 1/2 miles.
Standard Game Times: 7 p.m., 6:30 (April-May); Sun. 2. **Ticket Price Range:** $6-8.
Visiting Club Hotel: Econo Lodge, 2956 Milwaukee Rd., Beloit, WI 53511. **Telephone:** (608) 364-4000.

BOWLING GREEN HOT RODS

Office Address: Bowling Green Ballpark, 300 8th Avenue, Bowling Green, KY 42104.
Telephone: (270) 901-2121. **Fax:** (270) 901-2165.
E-Mail Address: fun@bghotrods.com. **Website:** www.bghotrods.com.
Affiliation (first year): Tampa Bay Rays (2009). **Years in League:** 2010-

OWNERSHIP, MANAGEMENT

Operated By: Triple Play, LLC.
Owner: Art Solomon.
President: Rick Brenner. **General Manager/CEO:** Brad Taylor. **Assistant General Manager/Sales:** Greg Coleman. **Assistant General Manager, Operations:** Ken Clary. **Controller:** Sally Lancaster. **Director, Ticket Sales:** John Neeley. **Director, Broadcast/Media Relations:** Tom Gauthier. **Director, Merchandise:** Kyle Hanrahan. **Head Turf Manager:** Ray Sayre. **Stadium Operations Assistant:** Chase Elliott. **Production Manager:** Atlee McHeffey. **Ticket Operations Manager:** Julie Harrigan. **Account Executives:** Keith Hetzer, Adam Smedberg. **Marketing/Sales Assistant:** Shari Krakauer.

FIELD STAFF

Manager: Brady Williams. **Coach:** Manny Castillo. **Pitching Coach:** RC Lichtenstein. **Trainer:** Scott Thurston.

GAME INFORMATION

Radio Announcer: Tom Gauthier. **No. of Games Broadcast:** Home-70, Away-70. **Flagship Station:** WBGN 1340-AM.
PA Announcer: Unavailable. **Official Scorer:** Unavailable.
Stadium Name: Bowling Green Ballpark. **Location:** From I-65, take Exit 26 (KY-234/Cemetery Road) into Bowling Green for 3.2 miles, Left onto South Kentucky Street for 0.2 miles, Left onto 8th Avenue. **Standard Game Times:** Mon.-Thurs.: 6:35 PM (April, Aug.), 7:05 (May-July); Fri. 7:05; Sat. 5:05 (April), 7:05 (May-Aug.); Sun. 2:05. **Ticket Prices:** $5-10.
Visiting Club Hotel: Candlewood Suites, 540 Wall Street, Bowling Green, KY 42104. **Telephone:** (270) 843-5505.

BURLINGTON BEES

Office Address: 2712 Mt. Pleasant St, Burlington, IA 52601.
Mailing Address: P.O. Box 824, Burlington, IA 52601.
Telephone: (319) 754-5705. **Fax:** (319) 754-5882. **E-Mail Address:** staff@gobees. com. **Website:** www.gobees.com.
Affiliation (first year): Kansas City Royals (2001). **Years in League:** 1962-

OWNERSHIP, MANAGEMENT

Operated By: Burlington Baseball Association Inc.
President: Dave Walker.
General Manager: Chuck Brockett. **Assistant GM, Sales/Marketing:** Jared Schjei. **Director, Media Relations/Broadcaster:** Nick Devlin. **Director, Group Outings:** Whitney Henderson. **Groundskeeper:** T.J. Brewer.

FIELD STAFF

Manager: Jim Gabella. **Coach:** Omar Rameriz. **Pitching Coach:** Jerry Nyman. **Athletic Trainer:** Mark Stubblefield.

GAME INFORMATION

Radio Announcer: Nick Devlin. **No. of Games Broadcast:** Home-70, Away-70. **Flagship Station:** NewsRadio KBUR 1490-AM.
PA Announcer: Nathan McCoy. **Official Scorer:** Ted Gutman.
Stadium Name: Community Field. **Location:** From U.S. 34, take U.S. 61 North to Mt. Pleasant Street, east 1/8 mile. **Standard Game Times:** 6:30 p.m., Sun. 2. **Ticket Price Range:** $4-7.
Visiting Club Hotel: Pzazz Best Western FunCity, 3001 Winegard Dr, Burlington, IA 52601. **Telephone:** (319) 753-2223.

CEDAR RAPIDS KERNELS

Office Address: 950 Rockford Rd. SW, Cedar Rapids, IA 52404.
Mailing Address: P.O. Box 2001, Cedar Rapids, IA 52406.
Telephone: (319) 363-3887. **Fax:** (319) 363-5631. **E-Mail Address:** kernels@kernels.com. **Website:** www.kernels.com.
Affiliation (first year): Los Angeles Angels (1993). **Years in League:** 1962-

OWNERSHIP, MANAGEMENT
Operated by: Cedar Rapids Ball Club Inc.
President: Tom Barbee.
General Manager: Jack Roeder. **CFO:** Doug Nelson. **Assistant General Manager:** Scott Wilson. **Director, Broadcasting:** John Rodgers. **Director, Communications:** Andrew Pantini. **Sports Turf Manager:** Jesse Roeder. **Director, Ticket/Group Sales:** Andrea Murphy. **Director, Finance/Human Resources:** Charlie Patrick. **Director, Entertainment:** Sonya Masse. **Stadium Operations Manager:** Seth Dohrn. **Director, Marketing/Community Relations:** Jessica Fergesen. **Director, Food/Beverage:** Dave Soper. **Receptionist:** Marcia Moran.

FIELD STAFF
Manager: Bill Mosiello. **Hitting Coach:** Brent Del Chiaro. **Pitching Coach:** Brandon Emanuel. **Trainer:** Dan Nichols.

GAME INFORMATION
Radio Announcer: John Rodgers. **No. of Games Broadcast:** Home-70, Away-70. **Flagship Station:** KMRY 1450-AM.
PA Announcer: Dale Brodt. **Official Scorers:** Al Gruwell, Eric Olson.
Stadium Name: Veterans Memorial Stadium. **Location:** From I-380 North, take the Wilson Ave. exit, turn left on Wilson Ave. After the railroad tracks, turn right on Rockford Road. Proceed .8 miles, stadium is on left. From I-380 South, exit at First Avenue. Proceed to Eighth Avenue (first stop sign) and turn left. Stadium entrance is .1 miles on right (before tennis courts). **Standard Game Times:** 6:35 p.m., Sat.-Sun.: 2:05. **Ticket Price Range:** $7-10.
Visiting Club Hotel: Best Western Cooper's Mill, 100 F Ave. NW, Cedar Rapids, IA 52405. **Telephone:** (319) 366-5323.

CLINTON LUMBERKINGS

Office Address: Alliant Energy Field, 537 Ball Park Drive, Clinton, IA 52732.
Mailing Address: P.O. Box 1295, Clinton, IA 52733.
Telephone: (563) 242-0727. **Fax:** (563) 242-1433.
E-Mail Address: lumberkings@lumberkings.com. **Website:** www.lumberkings.com.
Affiliation (first year): Seattle Mariners (2009). **Years in League:** 1956-

OWNERSHIP, MANAGEMENT
Operated By: Clinton Baseball Club Inc.
Chairman: Don Roode. **President:** Paul Schnack. **General Manager:** Ted Tornow. **Assistant GM:** Nate Kreinbrink. **Director, Operations:** Mitch Butz. **Director, Broadcasting/Media Relations:** Dave Lezotte. **Assistant Director, Operations:** Morty Kreiner.

FIELD STAFF
Manager: John Tamargo. **Coach:** Terry Pollreisz. **Pitching Coach:** Dwight Bernard. **Trainer:** B.J. Downie. **Equipment Manager:** Tyler Hildreth.

GAME INFORMATION
Radio Announcer: Dave Lezotte. **No. of Games Broadcast:** Home-70, Away-70. **Flagship Station:** KCLN 1390-AM.
PA Announcer: Brad Seward. **Official Scorers:** Tom Whaley, J. Robert Willey.
Stadium Name: Alliant Energy Field. **Location:** Highway 67 North to Sixth Avenue North, right on Sixth, cross railroad tracks, stadium on right. **Standard Game Times:** 6:30 p.m. (April-May, Aug. 21-Sept.), 7:00 (June 1-Aug. 13); Sun. 2:00. **Ticket Price Range:** $5-7.
Visiting Club Hotel: Unavailable.

DAYTON DRAGONS

Office Address: Fifth Third Field, 220 N. Patterson Blvd, Dayton, OH 45402.
Mailing Address: P.O. 2107, Dayton, OH 45401.
Telephone: (937) 228-2287. **Fax:** (937) 228-2284.
E-Mail Address: dragons@daytondragons.com. **Website:** www.daytondragons.com.
Affiliation (first year): Cincinnati Reds (2000). **Years in League:** 2000-

OWNERSHIP, MANAGEMENT
Operated By: Dayton Professional Baseball Club LLC/Mandalay Baseball Properties, LLC. **Owners:** Mandalay Baseball Properties, LLC, Earvin "Magic" Johnson, Archie Griffin.
President: Robert Murphy. **Executive Vice President:** Eric Deutsch. **Executive VP/General Manager:** Gary Mayse. **VP,**

Accounting/Finance: Mark Schlein. **VP, Sponsorships:** Jeff Webb. **VP, Ticket Sales:** Jeff Stewart. **VP, Sponsor Services:** Brad Eaton. **Director, Entertainment:** Kaitlin Murphy. **Director, Marketing:** Jim Francis. **Director, Media Relations:** Tom Nichols. **Senior Ticketing Agent:** Sally Ledford. **Senior Marketing Managers:** Brandy Abney, Laura Rose. **Marketing Managers:** Nicole Becker, Brian Botos, Chris Hart, Clint Taylor. **Senior Ticket Sales Managers:** Andrew Aldenderfer, Mike Vujea. **Corporate Marketing Managers:** Viterio Jones, Phil Salwan, Ryan York. **Event Operations Manager:** Chad Adams. **Senior Operations Director:** Joe Eaglowski. **Facilities Operations Manager:** Joe Elking. **Baseball Operations Manager:** John Wallace. **Director, Operations:** Andrew Ottmar. **Office Manager:** Leslie Stuck. **Staff Accountant:** Dorothy Day. **Administrative Assistant:** Lisa Rike. **Administrative Secretary:** Barbara Van Schaik.

FIELD STAFF
Manager: Todd Benzinger. **Hitting Coach:** Ken Griffey. **Pitching Coach:** Tony Fossas. **Trainer:** Tyler Steele.

GAME INFORMATION
Radio Announcer: Tom Nichols. **No. of Games Broadcast:** Home-70, Away-70. **Flagship Station:** WING 1410-AM ESPN Radio.
PA Announcers: Ben Oburn, Kim Parker. **Official Scorers:** Roy Cassidy, Matt Lindsay.
Stadium Name: Fifth Third Field. **Location:** I-75 South to downtown Dayton, left at First Street; I-75 North, right at First Street exit. **Ticket Price Range:** $7-13.25.
Visiting Club Hotel: Unavailable.

FORT WAYNE TINCAPS

Office Address: 1301 Ewing St. Fort Wayne, IN 46802.
Telephone: (260) 482-6400. **Fax:** (260) 471-4678.
E-Mail Address: info@tincaps.com. **Website:** www.tincaps.com.
Affiliation (first year): San Diego Padres (1999). **Years in League:** 1993-.

OWNERSHIP, MANAGEMENT
Operated By: Hardball Capital.
Owners: Jason Freier, Chris Schoen.
President/General Manager: Mike Nutter. **Vice President/Assistant GM, Sales/Finance:** Brian Schackow. **VP/Senior Assistant GM, Corporate Partnerships:** David Lorenz. **VP/Assistant GM, Marketing/Entertainment/Promotions:** Michael Limmer. **Director, Group Sales:** Brad Shank. **Assistant Director, Group Sales:** Jared Parcell. **Director, Ticketing:** Pat Ventura. **Director, Concessions:** Bill Lehn. **Culinary Director:** Scott Kammerer. **Manager, Catering:** Brandon Tinkle. **Director, Facilities:** Tim Burkhart. **Assistant Director, Facilities:** Chris Watson. **Director, Field Maintenance:** Mitch McClary. **Creative Director:** Tony DesPlaines. **Manager, Video Production:** Allen Wertheimer. **Managers, Ticket Sales:** Tyler Baker, Brent Harring, Penny Wascovich, Justin Shurley. **Manager, Corporate Partnerships:** Chris Snyder. **Director, Broadcasting:** Dan Watson. **Office Manager:** Cathy Tinney. **Manager, Merchandise:** Karen Schieber. **Manager, Promotions:** Abigail Naas.

FIELD STAFF
Manager: Jose Flores. **Hitting Coach:** Tom Tornincasa. **Pitching Coach:** Bronswell Patrick. **Trainer:** Nate Stewart.

GAME INFORMATION
Radio Announcers: Dan Watson, Mike Maahs. **No. of Games Broadcast:** Home-70, Away-70. **Flagship Station:** WKJG 1380-AM.
PA Announcers: Jared Parcell, Jim Shovlin. **Official Scorer:** Unavailable.
Stadium Name: Parkview Field. **Location:** Downtown Fort Wayne off of Jefferson Blvd.
Ticket Price Range: $5-12.50.
Visiting Club Hotel: Quality Inn, 1734 W. Washington Center Road, Fort Wayne, IN 46818. **Telephone:** (260) 489-5554.

GREAT LAKES LOONS

Office Address: 825 East Main St., Midland, MI 48640.
Mailing Address: P.O. Box 365, Midland, MI 48640.
Telephone: (989) 837-2255. **Fax:** (989) 837-8780.
E-Mail Address: info@loons.com. **Website:** www.loons.com.
Affiliation (first year): Los Angeles Dodgers (2007). **Years in League:** 2007-.

OWNERSHIP, MANAGEMENT
Operated By: Michigan Baseball Operations.
Stadium Ownership: Michigan Baseball Foundation.
Founder/Foundation President: William Stavropoulos.
President/General Manager: Paul Barbeau.
Vice President, Corporate Partnerships/Event Operations: Scott Litle. **Vice President, Facilities/Operations:** Matt McQuaid. **VP, Finance:** Tammy Brinkman. **VP, Marketing/Entertainment:** Chris Mundhenk. **GM, ESPN 100.9-FM:** Jerry O'Donnell. **Assistant GM, Business Operations (Loons)/Director, Programs/Fund Development (MBF):** Patti Tuma. **Assistant GM, Production/Entertainment:** Chris Lones. **Assistant GM, Retail Operations/Guest Services:** Ann Craig.

Assistant GM, Ticket Sales: Lance LeFevre. **Director, Accounting:** Jamie Start. **Director, Corporate Partnerships:** Emily Schafer. **Director, Food/Beverage:** Nick Kavalauskas. **Director, Group Sales:** Tiffany Seward. **Director, Programming (ESPN 100.9-FM):** Brad Golder. **Director, Promotions:** Linda Uliano. **Director, Sales (ESPN 100.9-FM):** Jay Arons. **Director, Special Events:** Dave Gomola. **Director, Ticket Operations:** Heather Jones. **Director, Ticket Package Sales:** Korrey Shoup. **Assistant Director, Food, Beverage/Catering:** Alyson Schafer. **Assistant to MBF President:** Marge Parker. **Concessions Manager:** Nick Barton. **Corporate Account Executive:** Kevin Schunk. **Executive Chef:** Jenny Coleman. **Groundscrew Supervisor:** Dan Jennings. **Group Sales Coordinator:** Jessica Olpere. **Retail Manager:** Jenean Clarkson.

FIELD STAFF

Manager: Juan Bustabad. **Hitting Coach:** Michael Boughton. **Pitching Coach:** Chuck Crim. **Trainer:** Unavailable.

GAME INFORMATION

Radio Announcer: Brad Golder. **No. of Games Broadcast:** Home-70, Away-70. **Flagship Station:** ESPN 100.9-FM WLUN.

PA Announcer: Jerry O'Donnell. **Official Scorers:** Terry Wilczek, Larry Loiselle.

Stadium Name: Dow Diamond. **Location:** I-75 to US-10 W. Take the M-20/US10 Business exit on the left toward downtown Midland. Merge onto US-10 W/MI-20 W (also known as Indian Street). Turn left onto State Street. The entrance to the stadium is at the intersection of Ellsworth and State Streets.

Standard Game Times: 6:05 p.m. (April), 7:05 (May-Sept.), Sun. 3:05.

Ticket Price Range: $6-9.

Visiting Club Hotel: Holiday Inn, 810 Cinema Dr., Midland, MI 48642. **Telephone:** (989) 794-8500.

KANE COUNTY COUGARS

Office Address: 34W002 Cherry Lane, Geneva, IL 60134.
Telephone: (630) 232-8811. **Fax:** (630) 232-8815.
E-Mail Address: info@kanecountycougars.com. **Website:** www.kccougars.com.
Affiliation (first year): Oakland Athletics (2003). **Years in League:** 1991-

OWNERSHIP, MANAGEMENT

Operated By: Cougars Baseball Partnership/American Sports Enterprises, Inc.
President: Mike Woleben.
Vice President: Mike Murtaugh. **Vice President/General Manager:** Jeff Sedivy. **Assistant GM/Sales Director:** Curtis Haug. **Assistant GM, Media/Promotions:** Jeff Ney. **Special Assistant to GM:** Rich Essegian. **Director, Food/Beverage:** Mike Klafehn. **Catering Manager:** Sheila Savage. **Concessions Supervisor:** Jon Williams. **Personnel Manager:** Robin Newlin. **Senior Ticket Sales Representatives:** Alex Miller, Patti Savage. **Director, Ticket Operations:** Erin Wiencek. **Box Office Manager:** Rob Koskosky. **Director, Community Relation Programming:** Amy Mason. **Media Relations Coordinator:** Shawn Touney. **Manager, Advertising Placement:** Bill Baker. **Design/Graphics:** Emmet Broderick, Nick Braglia. **Webmaster/PA Announcer:** Kevin Sullivan. **Business Manager:** Mary Almlie. **Controller:** Doug Czurylo. **Finance/Accounting Manager:** Lance Buhmann. **Director, Security:** Dan Klinkhamer. **Stadium Operations/Account Executive:** David Edison. **Stadium Maintenance Supervisor:** Jeff Snyder. **Head Groundskeeper:** Matt Ramirez.

FIELD STAFF

Manager: Aaron Nieckula. **Hitting Coach:** Haas Pratt. **Pitching Coach:** Jimmy Escalante. **Trainer:** Doc Thorson.

GAME INFORMATION

Radio Announcer: Jeff Hem. **No. of Games Broadcast:** Home-70, Away-70. **Flagship Station:** WBIG 1280-AM.
PA Announcer: Kevin Sullivan. **Official Scorer:** Bill Baker.
Stadium Name: Philip B. Elfstrom Stadium. **Location:** From east or west, I-88 (Ronald Reagan Memorial Tollway) to Farnsworth Avenue North exit, north five miles to Cherry Lane, left into stadium complex; from northwest, I-90 (Jane Addams Memorial Tollway) to Randall Road South exit, south to Fabyan Parkway, east to Kirk Road, north to Cherry Lane, left into stadium complex. **Standard Game Times:** 6:30 p.m.; Sat. 6; Sun. 2. **Ticket Price Range:** $8-14.
Visiting Club Hotel: Best Western Naperville, 1617 Naperville Rd., Naperville, IL 60563. **Telephone:** (630) 505-0200.

LAKE COUNTY CAPTAINS

Office Address: Classic Park, 35300 Vine Street, Eastlake, OH 44095-3142.
Telephone: (440) 975-8085. **Fax:** (440) 975-8958.
E-Mail Address: bseymour@captainsbaseball.com. **Website:** www.captainsbaseball.com.
Affiliation (first year): Cleveland Indians (2003). **Years in League:** 2010-

OWNERSHIP, MANAGEMENT

Operated By: Cascia, LLC.
Owners: Peter & Rita Carfagna, Ray & Katie Murphy.
Chairman/Secretary/Treasurer: Peter Carfagna. **Vice Chairman:** Rita Carfagna. **Vice President:** Ray Murphy. **Senior Vice President:** Pete E. Carfagna. **Vice President, General Manager:** Brad Seymour. **Assistant General Manager, Sales:** Neil Stein. **Senior Director, Media/Community Relations:** Craig Deas. **Director, Promotions:** Jonathan Levey. **Director,**

Captains Concessions: John Klein. **Manager, Stadium Operations:** Joe Engel. **Director, Turf Management/Stadium Operations:** Jared Olson. **Director, Finance:** Rob Demko. **Manager, Ticket Operations/Merchandise:** Jen Yorko. **Manager, Group Sales:** Amy Gladieux. **Account Representatives, Group Sales:** Jeff Gates, Andrew Grover, Shannon O'Boyle. **Office Assistant:** Jim Carfagna.

FIELD STAFF
Manager: Ted Kubiak. **Coach:** Phil Clark. **Pitching Coach:** Mickey Callaway. **Trainer:** Issei Kamada.

GAME INFORMATION
Radio Announcer: Craig Deas. **No. of Games Broadcast:** Home-70, Away-70. **Flagship Station:** WREO 97.1-FM. **PA Announcer:** Ray Milavec. **Official Scorer:** Unavailable.
Stadium Name: Classic Park. **Location:** From Ohio State Route 2 East, exit at Ohio 91, go left and the stadium is 1/4 mile north on your right. From Ohio State Route 90 East, exit at Ohio 91, go right and the stadium in approximately five miles north on your right. **Standard Game Times:** 6:30 p.m. (April-May), 7 (June-Sept.); Sat.: 1 (April-May); 7 (June-Sept); Sun. 1.
Visiting Club Hotel: Comfort Inn & Suites, 7701 Reynolds Road, Mentor, OH 44060. **Telephone:** (440) 951-7333.

LANSING LUGNUTS

Office Address: 505 E. Michigan Ave, Lansing, MI 48912.
Telephone: (517) 485-4500. **Fax:** (517) 485-4518.
E-Mail Address: info@lansinglugnuts.com. **Website:** www.lansinglug-nuts.com.
Affiliation (first year): Toronto Blue Jays (2005). **Years in League:** 1996-

OWNERSHIP, MANAGEMENT
Operated By: Take Me Out to the Ballgame LLC.
Principal Owners: Tom Dickson, Sherrie Myers.
General Manager: Pat Day. **Assistant GM:** Nick Grueser. **Corporate Sales Manager:** Nick Brzezinski. **Corporate Account Executive:** Scott Tenney. **Group Sales Manager:** Greg Kruger. **Senior Group Sales Representative:** Kohl Tyrrell. **Group Sales Representative:** Chris Arth. **Box Office Manager:** Brian Burita. **Retail Manager:** Matt Hicks. **Director, Stadium Operations:** Matt Anderson. **Stadium Operations Supervisor:** Dennis Busse. **Director, Food/Beverage:** Brett Telder. **Assistant Director, Food/Beverage:** Mike Koski. **Director, Marketing:** Julia Janssen. **Marketing Assistant:** Lauren Truax. **Sponsorship Service Representatives:** Michaela McAnany, Jill Niemi. **Business Manager:** Heather Viele. **Assistant Business Manager:** Rebekah Butler. **Administrative Assistant:** Angela Sees.

FIELD STAFF
Manager: Sal Fasano. **Hitting Coach:** John Tamargo, Jr. **Pitching Coach:** Antonio Caceres. **Trainer:** James Gardiner.

GAME INFORMATION
Radio Announcer: Jesse Goldberg-Strassler. **No of Games Broadcast:** Home-70, Away-70. **Flagship Station:** WQTX 92.1-FM.
PA Announcer: Unavailable. **Official Scorers:** Seth Van Hoven, Dave Schaberg.
Stadium Name: Oldsmobile Park. **Location:** I-96 East/West to U.S. 496, exit at Larch Street, north of Larch, stadium on left. **Ticket Price Range:** $8-10.
Visiting Club Hotel: Lexington Lansing Grand Hotel, 925 South Creyts Road, Lansing MI 48917. **Telephone:** (517) 323-7100.

PEORIA CHIEFS

Office Address: 730 SW Jefferson, Peoria, IL 61602.
Telephone: (309) 680-4000. **Fax:** (309) 680-4080.
E-Mail Address: feedback@chiefsnet.com. **Website:** www.peoriachiefs.com.
Affiliation (first year): Chicago Cubs (2005). **Years in League:** 1983-

OWNERSHIP, MANAGEMENT
Operated By: Peoria Chiefs Community Baseball Club LLC.
President: Rocky Vonachen. **Vice President/General Manager:** Ralph Converse. **Director, Ticket Sales:** Eric Obalil. **Broadcast/Media Manager:** Nathan Baliva. **Manager, Box Office:** Ryan Sivori. **Entertainment/Events Manager:** Lucas Smith. **Director, Guest Services/Account Executive:** Howard Yates. **Account Executives:** Luke Cross, Amanda Curtis, Joel Merrill, Jack Schmitz, Kyle Wicks. **Head Groundskeeper:** Noel Brusius.

FIELD STAFF
Manager: Casey Kopitzke. **Hitting Coach:** Barbaro Garbey. **Pitching Coach:** David Rosario. **Trainer:** Dan Golden.

GAME INFORMATION
Radio Announcer: Nathan Baliva. **No. of Games Broadcast:** Home-70, Away-70. **Flagship Station:** 96.5-FM ESPN Radio.
PA Announcer: Unavailable. **Official Scorer:** Unavailable.
Stadium Name: O'Brien Field. **Location:** From South/East, I-74 to exit 93 (Jefferson Street), continue one mile, stadium

is one block on left. From North/West, I-74 to Glen Oak Exit. Turn right on Glendale which turns into Kumpf Blvd. Turn right on Jefferson, stadium on left. **Standard Game Times:** 7 p.m., 6:30 (April-May, after Aug. 19); Sat. 6:30; Sun. 1. **Ticket Price Range:** $6-10.

Visiting Club Hotel: Jameson Inn & Suites, 4112 N. Brandywine Drive, Peoria, IL 61614. **Telephone:** 309-685-5226.

QUAD CITIES RIVER BANDITS

Office Address: 209 S. Gaines St., Davenport, IA 52802.
Telephone: (563) 322-6348. **Fax:** (563) 324-3109.
E-Mail Address: bandit@riverbandits.com. **Website:** www.riverbandits.com.
Affiliation (first year): St. Louis Cardinals (2005). **Years in League:** 1960-.

OWNERSHIP, MANAGEMENT

Operated by: Main Street Iowa.
Vice President/General Manager: Kirk Goodman. **Assistant GMs:** Stefanie Brown. **Executive Director, Corporate Partnerships:** Shawn Brown. **Director, Media Relations:** Tommy Thrall. **Director, Baseball Operations:** Bob Evans. **Head Groundskeeper/Stadium Operations:** Ben Kratz. **Director, Ticket Operations:** Blake Huckaby. **Manager, Production:** Shane Huff. **Graphic Designer:** Chris Read. **Manager, Community Relations/Client Relations:** Maggie McCoy. **Manager, Special Events:** Andrea Nolan. **Manager, Stadium Operations/Assistant Groundskeeper:** Kyle Brudos. **Account Executives:** Justin Jacobs, Matt Tangen. **Director, Food/Beverage:** Ben Blankenship.

FIELD STAFF

Manager: Johnny Rodriguez. **Hitting Coach:** Unavailable. **Pitching Coach:** Tim Leveque. **Trainer:** Manabu Kuwauru.

GAME INFORMATION

Radio: None.
PA Announcer: Unavailable. **Official Scorer:** Jim Tappa.
Stadium Name: Modern Woodmen Park. **Location:** From I-74, take Grant Street exit left, west onto River Drive, left on South Gaines Street; from I-80, take Brady Street exit south, right on River Drive, left on South Gaines Street. **Standard Game Times:** 7 p.m., Sat.: 6., Sun.: 1 (April-May, Aug.-Sept.), 5 (June-July). **Ticket Price Range:** $5-12.
Visiting Club Hotel: Clarion Hotel, 5202 Brady St., Davenport, IA 52806. **Telephone:** (563) 391-1230.

SOUTH BEND
SILVER HAWKS

Office Address: 501 W. South St, South Bend, IN 46601.
Mailing Address: P.O. Box 4218, South Bend, IN 46634.
Telephone: (574) 235-9988. **Fax:** (574) 235-9950.
E-Mail Address: hawks@silverhawks.com. **Website:** www.silverhawks.com.
Affiliation (first year): Arizona Diamondbacks (1997). **Years in League:** 1988-.

OWNERSHIP, MANAGEMENT

Operated By: South Bend Professional Baseball Club LLC.
President: Joe Kernan.
Vice President/General Manager: Lynn Kachmarik. **Vice President, Baseball Operations:** John Baxter. **Director, Finance:** Cheryl Carlson. **Director, Sales/Marketing:** Amy Hill. **Director, Stadium Operations:** Peter Argueta. **Marketing Manager:** Jeff Scholfield. **Group Sales Manager:** James McAvoy. **Box Office Manager:** Kirk Venderlic. **Sales Manager:** Terry Coleman. **Senior Account Executive:** Jon Lies. **Account Executive:** Jackie Batteast. **Corporate Sales:** Rita Baxter. **Head Groundskeeper:** Joel Reinebold.

FIELD STAFF

Manager: Mark Haley. **Hitting Coach:** Francisco Morales. **Pitching Coach:** Wellington Cepeda. **Trainer:** Brian Czachowski. **Strength Coach:** Jordan Wolf.

GAME INFORMATION

Radio: ESPN Radio 1620 AM.
Stadium Name: Stanley Coveleski Regional Stadium. **Location:** I-80/90 toll road to exit 77, take US 31/33 south to South Bend to downtown (Main Street), to Western Avenue, right on Western, left on Taylor. **Ticket Price Range:** $6-8.
Visiting Club Hotel: Quality Inn, 515 Dixie Way North, South Bend, IN 46637. **Telephone:** (574) 272-6600.

WEST MICHIGAN
WHITECAPS

Office Address: 4500 West River Dr., Comstock Park, MI 49321.
Mailing Address: P.O. Box 428, Comstock Park, MI 49321.
Telephone: (616) 784-4131. **Fax:** (616) 784-4911.
E-Mail Address: playball@whitecaps-baseball.com. **Website:** www.whitecapsbaseball.com.
Affiliation (first year): Detroit Tigers (1997). **Years in League:** 1994-

OWNERSHIP, MANAGEMENT
Operated By: Whitecaps Professional Baseball Corp.
Principal Owners: Denny Baxter, Lew Chamberlin.
President: Scott Lane. **Vice President, Whitecaps Professional Baseball:** Jim Jarecki. **VP, Sales:** Steve McCarthy.
Manager, Facility Events: Dan Glowinski. **Manager, Operations:** Craig Yust. **Director, Food/Beverage:** Matt Timon.
Director, New Business Development: Dan McCrath. **Community Relations Coordinator:** Anna Peterson. **Manager, Marketing/Media:** Mickey Graham. **Promotions Coordinator:** Brian Oropallo. **Box Office Manager:** Meghan Brennan.
Groundskeeper: Greg Salyer. **Manager, Facility Maintenance:** John Passarelli. **Director, Ticket Sales:** Chad Sayen.

FIELD STAFF
Manager: Joe DePastino. **Hitting Coach:** Luis Quinones. **Pitching Coach:** Mark Johnson. **Trainer:** Corey Tremble.

GAME INFORMATION
Radio Announcer: Unavailable. **No. of Games Broadcast:** Home-70, Away-70. **Flagship Station:** WBBL 107.3-FM.
PA Announcers: Mike Newell, Bob Wells. **Official Scorers:** Mike Dean, Don Thomas.
Stadium Name: Fifth Third Ballpark. **Location:** U.S. 131 North from Grand Rapids to exit 91 (West River Drive). **Ticket Price Range:** $5-13.
Visiting Club Hotel: Holiday Inn Express-GR North, 358 River Ridge Dr. NW, Walker, MI 49544. **Telephone:** (616) 647-4100.

WISCONSIN TIMBER RATTLERS

Office Address: 2400 N. Casaloma Dr, Appleton, WI 54913.
Mailing Address: P.O. Box 7464, Appleton, WI 54912.
Telephone: (920) 733-4152. **Fax:** (920) 733-8032.
E-Mail Address: info@timberrattlers.com. **Website:** www.timberrattlers.com.
Affiliation (first year): Milwaukee Brewers (2009). **Years in League:** 1962-

OWNERSHIP, MANAGEMENT
Operated By: Appleton Baseball Club, Inc.
Chairman: Alan Stewart.
President, General Manager: Rob Zerjav. **Assistant GM/Director, Ticket Sales:** Aaron Hahn. **Controller:** Cathy Spanbauer. **Vice President, Marketing:** Angie Ceranski. **Director, Media Relations:** Chris Mehring. **Director, Food/Beverage:** Ryan Grossman. **Director, Stadium Operations:** Ron Kaiser. **Director, Corporate Marketing/Community Relations:** Sarah Heth. **Corporate Partnerships:** Ryan Cunniff. **Merchandise Manager:** Jay Gruszinski. **Box Office Manager:** Darren Shimanski. **Group Sales:** Isaac Bray, Brandon Goebel, Dayna Haddock. **Production Manager/Marketing Assistant:** Cameron Wengrzyn. **Team Operations/Clubhouse Manager:** Bob Estes. **Office Manager:** Mary Robinson. **Groundskeeper:** Eddie Warczak. **Assistant Groundskeeper:** Daniel Crockett.

FIELD STAFF
Manager: Jeff Isom. **Hitting Coach:** Matt Erickson. **Pitching Coach:** Chris Hook. **Trainer:** Jeff Paxson.

GAME INFORMATION
Radio Announcer: Chris Mehring. **No. of Games Broadcast:** Home-70, Away-70. **Flagship Station:** WNAM 1280-AM.
PA Announcer: Joe Dotterweich. **Official Scorer:** Jay Gruszinski.
Stadium Name: Time Warner Cable Field Fox Cities Stadium. **Location:** Highway 41 to Highway 15 (00) exit, west to Casaloma Drive, left to stadium. **Standard Game Times:** 7:05 p.m., 6:35 (April-May); Sat. 6:35; Sun. **1:**05. **Ticket Price Range:** $5-8.50.
Visiting Club Hotel: Microtel Inn & Suites, 321 Metro Dr, Appleton, WI 54913. **Telephone:** (920) 997-3121.

SOUTH ATLANTIC LEAGUE

SOUTH ATLANTIC LEAGUE
"THE LEAGUE OF CHOICE"

LOW CLASS A

Office Address: 111 Second Avenue NE, Suite 335, St. Petersburg, FL 33701.
Telephone: (727) 456-1240. **Fax:** (727) 499-6853.
E-Mail Address: office@saloffice.com. **Website:** www.southatlanticleague.com.
Years League Active: 1904-1964, 1979-.
President/Secretary-Treasurer: Eric Krupa.
First Vice President: Chip Moore (Rome). **Second Vice President:** Craig Brown (Greenville).
Directors: Don Beaver (Hickory), Cooper Brantley (Greensboro), Craig Brown (Greenville), Joseph Finley (Lakewood), Marvin Goldklang (Charleston), Alan Ostfield (Asheville), Alan Levin (West Virginia), Tom Volpe (Delmarva), Chip Moore (Rome), Art Matin (Hagerstown), Chris Flannery (Augusta), Jason Freier (Savannah), Brad Smith (Kannapolis), Alan Stein (Lexington).
Division Structure: North—Delmarva, Greensboro, Hagerstown, Hickory, Kannapolis, Lakewood, West Virginia. **South**—Asheville, Augusta, Charleston, Greenville, Lexington, Rome, Savannah.
Regular Season: 140 games (split schedule). **2010 Opening Date:** April 8. **Closing Date:** Sept. 6.
All-Star Game: June 22 at Greenville.
Playoff Format: First-half and second-half division winners meet in best-of-three semifinal series. Winners meet in best-of-five series for league championship.
Roster Limit: 25 active. **Player Eligibility Rule:** No age limit. No more than two players and one player-coach on active list may have more than five years of experience.
Brand of Baseball: Rawlings.
Umpires: Unavailable.

Eric Krupa

STADIUM INFORMATION

Club	Stadium	Opened	Dimensions LF	CF	RF	Capacity	2009 Att.
Asheville	McCormick Field	1992	326	373	297	4,000	146,353
Augusta	Lake Olmstead Stadium	1995	330	400	330	4,322	194,437
Charleston	Joseph P. Riley Jr. Ballpark	1997	306	386	336	5,800	268,985
Delmarva	Arthur W. Perdue Stadium	1996	309	402	309	5,200	214,575
Greensboro	NewBridge Bank Park	2005	322	400	320	7,599	406,549
Greenville	West End Field	2006	310	400	302	5,000	335,159
Hagerstown	Municipal Stadium	1931	335	400	330	4,600	126,166
Hickory	L.P. Frans Stadium	1993	330	401	330	5,062	131,414
Kannapolis	Fieldcrest Cannon Stadium	1995	330	400	310	4,700	132,342
Lakewood	FirstEnergy Park	2001	325	400	325	6,588	429,221
Lexington	Applebee's Park	2001	320	401	318	6,033	332,588
Rome	State Mutual Stadium	2003	335	400	330	5,100	183,750
Savannah	Historic Grayson Stadium	1941	290	410	310	8,000	110,846
West Virginia	Appalachian Power Park	2005	330	400	320	4,300	177,691

ASHEVILLE TOURISTS

Office Address: McCormick Field, 30 Buchanan Place, Asheville, NC 28801.
Telephone: (828) 258-0428. **Fax:** (828) 258-0320.
E-Mail Address: info@theashevilletourists.com. **Website:** www.theashevilletourists.com.
Affiliation (first year): Colorado Rockies (1994). **Years in League:** 1976-

OWNERSHIP, MANAGEMENT

Operated By: DeWine Seeds Silver Dollar Baseball LLC.
President: Brian DeWine.
Executive Director: Mike Bauer. **General Manager:** Larry Hawkins. **Assistant GMs:** Jodee Ciszewski, Chris Smith.
Box Office Manager: Patrick Spence. **Office Manager:** Ryan Doyle. **Director, Broadcasting:** Jay Burnham. **Group Sales Managers:** Mike Kish, Ryan Koehler. **Outside Sales Representatives:** Bob Jones, Matt Riley. **Publications/Website:** Bill Ballew.

FIELD STAFF

Manager: Joe Mikulik. **Coach:** Kevin Riggs. **Pitching Coach:** Dave Schuler. **Trainer:** Billy Whitehead.

GAME INFORMATION

Radio Announcer: Jay Burnham. **No. of Games Broadcast:** Home-70 Road-70. **Flagship Station:** WRES 100.7 FM.

PA Announcer: Rick Diggler. **Official Scorer:** Mike Gore.
Stadium Name: McCormick Field. **Location:** I-240 to Charlotte Street South exit, south one mile on Charlotte, left on McCormick Place. **Ticket Price Range:** $6-10.
Visiting Club Hotel: Quality Inn, 1 Skyline Drive, Arden, NC 28704. **Telephone:** (828) 684-6688.

AUGUSTA GREENJACKETS

Office Address: 78 Milledge Rd., Augusta, GA 30904.
Mailing Address: P.O. Box 3746 Hill Station, Augusta, GA 30914.
Telephone: (706) 736-7889. **Fax:** (706) 736-1122.
E-Mail Address: info@greenjacketsbaseball.com. **Website:** www.greenjacketsbaseball.com.
Affiliation (first year): San Francisco Giants (2005). **Years in League:** 1988-.

OWNERSHIP, MANAGEMENT

Owners: Baseball Enterprises, LCC.
Operated By: Ripken Professional Baseball.
General Manager: Nick Brown. **Director, Stadium Operations:** David Ryther, Jr. **Ticket Sales Manager:** Jonathan Pribble. **Corporate Partnership Manager:** Brian Colopy. **Assistant Manager, Corporate/Ticket Sales:** Andy Beuster. **Marketing Manager:** Lauren Christie. **Box Office Manager:** Brian Marshall. **Account Executives:** Adam Schmansky, Emily McDonald, Joe Reeder, Dan Szatkowski. **Bookkeeper:** Stephanie Smith.

FIELD STAFF

Manager: Dave Machemer. **Hitting Coach:** Lipso Nava. **Pitching Coach:** Steve Kline. **Trainer:** David Getsoff.

GAME INFORMATION

Radio Announcer: Eric Little. **No. of Games Broadcast:** Home-70 Road-70. **Flagship Station:** WRDW 1630-AM.
PA Announcer: Scott Skadan. **Official Scorer:** Ted Miller.
Stadium Name: Lake Olmstead Stadium. **Location:** I-20 to Washington Road exit, east to Broad Street exit, left on Milledge Road. **Standard Game Times:** Mon.-Sat.: 7:05 p.m.; Sun. 2:05/5:35. **Ticket Price Range:** $7-12.
Visiting Club Hotel: Baymont Inn & Suites, 629 Northwest Frontage Road, Augusta, GA 30907. **Telephone:** (706) 855-6060.

CHARLESTON RIVERDOGS

Office Address: 360 Fishburne St., Charleston, SC 29403.
Mailing Address: P.O. Box 20849, Charleston, SC 29413.
Telephone: (843) 723-7241. **Fax:** (843) 723-2641.
E-Mail Address: admin@riverdogs.com. **Website:** www.riverdogs.com.
Affiliation (first year): New York Yankees (2005). **Years in League:** 1973-78, 1980-.

OWNERSHIP, MANAGEMENT

Operated by: The Goldklang Group/South Carolina Baseball Club LP.
Chairman: Marv Goldklang. **President:** Mike Veeck. **Director of Fun:** Bill Murray. **Co-Owner:** Dr. Gene Budig.
Executive Vice President/General Manager: Dave Echols. **Assistant GMs:** Andy Lange, Jim Pfander. **Director, Sales/Operations:** Harold Craw. **Director, Media Relations:** Andy Solomon. **Business Manager:** Dale Stickney. **Director, Special Events:** Melissa McCants. **Sales Managers:** Jake Terrell, Mike Petrini. **Office Manager:** Kristal Lessington. **Director, Community Relations/Mascot Development:** Jamie Ballentine. **Director, Merchandise:** Mike DeAntonio. **Box Office Manager:** Noel Blaha. **Head Groundskeeper:** Mike Williams. **Clubhouse Manager:** Vinnie Colangelo.

FIELD STAFF

Manager: Torre Tyson. **Hitting Coach:** Greg Colbrunn. **Pitching Coach:** Jeff Ware. **First-Base Coach:** Carlos Mendoza. **Trainer:** Scott DiFrancesco.

GAME INFORMATION

Radio Announcer: Danny Reed. **No. of Games Broadcast:** Home-70, Away-70. **Flagship Station:** WTMZ 910-AM.
PA Announcer: Ken Carrington. **Official Scorer:** Chuck Manka.
Stadium Name: Joseph P. Riley Jr. Ballpark. **Location:** From U.S. 17, take Lockwood Drive North, right on Fishburne Street. **Standard Game Times:** 7:05 p.m., Sun. 5:05. **Ticket Price Range:** $5-14.
Visiting Club Hotel: Best Western, 146 Lockwood Dr., Charleston, SC 29403.
Telephone: (843) 722-4000.

DELMARVA SHOREBIRDS

Office Address: 6400 Hobbs Rd, Salisbury, MD 21804.
Mailing Address: P.O. Box 1557, Salisbury, MD 21802.
Telephone: (410) 219-3112. **Fax:** (410) 219-9164.
E-Mail Address: information@theshorebirds.com. **Website:** www.theshorebirds.com.
Affiliation (first year): Baltimore Orioles (1997). **Years in League:** 1996-.

OWNERSHIP, MANAGEMENT

Operated By: 7th Inning Stretch, LLP.
Directors: Tom Volpe, Pat Filippone.
General Manager: Chris Bitters. **Assistant GM/Director, Corporate Sales:** Jimmy Sweet. **Director, Community Relations:** Emily Horlacher. **Director, Ticket Sales:** Evan Wagner. **Ticket Sales Account Executive:** Lindsay Carroll. **Director, Stadium Operations:** Aaron Becker. **Head Groundskeeper:** Dave Super. **Marketing Manager:** Brandon Berns. **Marketing Associate:** Bret Lasky. **Group Sales Manager:** David Bledsoe. **Corporate Sales Account Executive:** Adrian Urbanski. **Accounting Manager:** Gail Potts. **Office Manager:** Audrey Vane.

FIELD STAFF

Manager: Ryan Minor. **Coach:** Mike Devereaux. **Pitching Coach:** Troy Mattes. **Trainer:** Aaron Scott.

GAME INFORMATION

Radio Announcer: Bret Lasky. **No of Games Broadcast:** Home-70 Road-70. **Flagship Station:** WTGM 960-AM.
PA Announcer: Unavailable. **Official Scorer:** Gary Hicks.
Stadium Name: Arthur W. Perdue Stadium. **Location:** From U.S. 50 East, right on Hobbs Road; From U.S. 50 West, left on Hobbs Road. **Standard Game Times:** 7:05 p.m. **Ticket Price Range:** $4-12.
Visiting Club Hotel: Hampton Inn & Suites, 304 Prosperity Lane, Fruitland, MD 21826. **Telephone:** (410) 548-1282.

GREENSBORO GRASSHOPPERS

Office Address: 408 Bellemeade St., Greensboro, NC 27401.
Telephone: (336) 268-2255. **Fax:** (336) 273-7350.
E-Mail Address: info@gsohoppers.com. **Website:** www.gsohoppers.com.
Affiliation (first year): Florida Marlins (2003). **Years in League:** 1979-.

OWNERSHIP, MANAGEMENT

Operated By: Greensboro Baseball LLC.
Principal Owners: Cooper Brantley, Wes Elingburg, Len White.
President/General Manager: Donald Moore. **Vice President, Baseball Operations:** Katie Dannemiller. **CFO:** Jimmy Kesler. **Assistant GM/Head Groundskeeper:** Jake Holloway. **Assistant GM, Sales/Marketing:** Tim Vangel. **Director, Ticketing:** Kate Barnhill. **Executive Assistant:** Rosalee Brewer. **Director, Community Relations/Promotions:** Laura Damico. **Assistant Director, Stadium Operations:** Chad Green. **Assistant Groundskeeper:** Kaid Musgrave. **Director, Merchandise:** Yunhui Harris. **Director, Group Sales:** Brian Lee. **Group Sales Associates:** Travis Kerstetter, Todd Olson. **Director, Special Events/Hoppin' Fun:** Allison Moore. **Director, Creative Services:** Amanda Williams.

FIELD STAFF

Manager: Andy Haines. **Hitting Coach:** Kevin Randel. **Pitching Coach:** Charlie Corbell. **Trainer:** Julio Hernandez.

GAME INFORMATION

Radio Announcer: Andy Durham. **No. of Games Broadcast:** Home-70, Away-0. **Flagship Station:** WPET 950-AM.
PA Announcer: Jim Scott. **Official Scorer:** Unavailable.
Stadium Name: NewBridge Bank Park. **Location:** From I-85, take Highway 220 South (exit 36) to Coliseum Blvd, continue on Edgeworth Street, ballpark at corner of Edgeworth and Bellemeade Streets. **Ticket Price Range:** $6-9.
Visiting Club Hotel: Country Hearth Inn & Suites 6102 Landmark Center Boulevard, Greensboro, NC 27407. **Telephone:** (336) 553.2763.

GREENVILLE DRIVE

Office Address: 945 South Main St, Greenville, SC 29601.
Telephone: (864) 240-4500. **Fax:** (864) 240-4501.
E-Mail Address: info@greenvilledrive.com. **Website:** www.greenvilledrive.com.
Affiliation (first year): Boston Red Sox (2005). **Years in League:** 2005-

OWNERSHIP, MANAGEMENT
Operated By: RB3 LLC.
Co-Owner/President: Craig Brown.
Co-Owners: Roy Bostock, Paul Raether.
General Manager: Mike deMaine. **Senior Vice President:** Nate Lipscomb. **Vice President, Finance:** Cathy Boortz. **Senior Director, Marketing/Media Servces:** Eric Jarinko. **Director, Ticket Operations:** Paul Ortenzo. **Director, Group/Inside Sales:** Andy Paul. **Director, Outside Sales:** Stacy Morgan. **Director, Ballpark Operations:** Blake Wilson. **Operations Manager:** Justin Miller. **Director, Food/Beverage:** Jeff Cirelli. **Spinx 500 Club/Events Manager:** Ashley Greene. **Producer, Game Entertainment:** Jeremiah Dew. **Entertainment Production Manager:** Jon Eckert. **Special Projects Manager:** Jennifer Brown. **Account Executives:** Jeff Chiappini, Ashleigh Cox, Brendan Jones. **Head Groundskeeper:** Greg Burgess. **Assistant Groundskeeper:** Ross Groenevelt.

FIELD STAFF
Manager: Billy McMillon. **Hitting Coach:** Luis Lopez. **Pitching Coach:** Kevin Walker.

GAME INFORMATION
Radio: None.
PA Announcer: Chris Lee. **Official Scorer:** Sanford Rogers.
Stadium Name: Fluor Field. **Location:** From south: I-85N to exit 42 toward downtown Greenville, turn left onto Augusta Road, stadium is two miles on the left. **From north:** I-85S to I-385 toward Greenville, turn left onto Church Street, turn right onto University Ridge. **Standard Game Times:** 7 p.m.; Sun. 2. **Ticket Price Range:** $5-8.
Visiting Club Hotel: Hampton Inn Greenville-Haywood, 246 Congaree Road, Greenville, SC 29607. **Telephone:** (864) 288-1200.

HAGERSTOWN SUNS

HAGERSTOWN SUNS

Office Address: 274 E. Memorial Blvd., Hagerstown, MD 21740.
Telephone: (301) 791-6266. **Fax:** (301) 791-6066.
E-Mail Address: info@hagerstownsuns.com. **Website:** www.hagerstownsuns.com.
Affiliation (first year): Washington Nationals (2007). **Years in League:** 1993-

OWNERSHIP, MANAGEMENT
Principal Owner/Operated by: Mandalay Baseball Properties LLC.
President: Bob Flannery. **Assistant General Manager:** Joel Pagliaro. **Senior Director, Ticket Sales:** Ben Burnett. **Director, Business Operations:** Carol Gehr. **Director, Media Relations/Broadcasting:** Ryan Mock. **Director, Entertainment:** Reed Hunley. **Director, Operations:** Nick Bilski. **Director, Ticketing Operations:** Karl Micka-Foos. **Head Groundskeeper:** Brandon Dougan. **Clubhouse Manager:** Michael Jech.

FIELD STAFF
Manager: Matt LeCroy. **Hitting Coach:** Tony Tarasco. **Pitching Coach:** Chris Michalak.

GAME INFORMATION
Radio Announcer: Ryan Mock. **No. of Games Broadcast:** Home-70, Away-70. **Flagship Station:** Unavailable.
PA Announcer: Karl Micka-Foos. **Official Scorer:** Chris Spaid.
Stadium Name: Municipal Stadium. **Location:** Exit 32B (U.S. 40 West) on I-70 West, left at Eastern Boulevard; Exit 6A (U.S. 40 East) on I-81, right at Eastern Boulevard. **Standard Game Times:** 7:05 p.m., 6:35 (April-May); Sun. 1:35, 5:35 (July-Sept.). **Ticket Price Range:** $5-13.
Visiting Club Hotel: Unavailable.

HICKORY CRAWDADS

Office Address: 2500 Clement Blvd. NW, Hickory, NC 28601.
Mailing Address: P.O. Box 1268, Hickory, NC 28603.
Telephone: (828) 322-3000. Fax: (828) 322-6137.
E-Mail Address: crawdad@hickorycrawdads.com. Website: www.hickorycrawdads.com.
Affiliation (first year): Texas Rangers (2009). Years in League: 1952, 1960, 1993-

OWNERSHIP, MANAGEMENT

Operated by: Hickory Baseball Inc.
Principal Owners: Don Beaver, Luther Beaver, Charles Young.
President: Don Beaver. General Manager: Mark Seaman. Assistant GM: Charlie Downs. Director, Promotions: Brett Koch. Director, Broadcasting/Media Relations: Andrew Buchbinder. Business Manager: Donna White. Head Groundskeeper: Andrew Tallent. Clubhouse Manager: Tony Iliano. Co-Directors, Group Sales: Kathryn Bobel, Kim Scercy. Director, Catering: Rosie Caldwell. Interim Director, Ticket Operations: Josh Blackwell. Group Sales Assistant: Gregor Walz. Concessions Assistant: Vince Chow. Promotions Assistant: Michael Johnson. Stadium Operations Assistant: Jeff Baltusnik.

FIELD STAFF

Manager: Bill Richardson. Hitting Coach: Jason Hart. Pitching Coach: Brad Holman. Trainer: Jeff Bodenheimer. Strength/Conditioning: Ryan McNeal.

GAME INFORMATION

Radio Announcer: Andrew Buchbinder. No. of Games Broadcast: Home-70, Away-70. Flagship Station: WMNC 92.1-FM.
PA Announcers: JuJu Phillips, Ralph Mangum, Jason Savage. Official Scorer: Gary Olinger.
Stadium Name: L.P. Frans Stadium. Location: I-40 to exit 123 (Lenoir North), 321 North to Clement Blvd., left for 1/2 mile. Standard Game Times: 7 p.m.; Sun. 5.
Visiting Club Hotel: Crowne Plaza, 1385 Lenior-Rhyne Boulevard SE, Hickory, NC 28602. Telephone: (828) 323-1000.

KANNAPOLIS INTIMIDATORS

Office Address: 2888 Moose Rd., Kannapolis, NC 28083.
Mailing Address: P.O. Box 64, Kannapolis, NC 28082.
Telephone: (704) 932-3267. Fax: (704) 938-7040.
E-Mail Address: info@intimidatorsbaseball.com. Website: www.intimidatorsbaseball.com.
Affiliation (first year): Chicago White Sox (2001). Years in League: 1995-

OWNERSHIP, MANAGEMENT

Operated by: Smith Family Baseball Inc.
President: Brad Smith.
Vice President: Tim Mueller. General Manager: Randy Long. Director, Head Groundskeeper/Stadium Operations: Billy Ball. Director, Ticket Sales: Jason Bright. Director, Group Sales: Greg Pizzuto. Director, Operations/Sales Executive: Michael Childers. Group Sales Executive: Kaitlyn Murphy. Group Sales Executive: Sean Salemme. Director, Broadcasting/Media Relations: Josh Ellis. Interns: Sam Griscom, Andrew Bridgham, Kelly Tyson, Angela Kutach, Scott Rendell.

FIELD STAFF

Manager: Ernie Young. Hitting Coach: Greg Briley. Pitching Coach: Larry Owens. Trainer: Kevin Pillifant. Strength/Conditioning Coach: Jeremie Imbus.

GAME INFORMATION

Radio Announcer: Josh Ellis. No. of Games Broadcast: Home-70, Away-70. Flagship Station: www.intimidators-baseball.com.
PA Announcer: Shea Griffin. Official Scorer: Unavailable.
Stadium Name: Fieldcrest Cannon Stadium. Location: Exit 63 on I-85, west on Lane Street to Stadium Drive. Standard Game Times: 7:05 p.m., Sun. 5:05. Ticket Price Range: $3-8.
Visiting Club Hotel: Fairfield Inn by Marriott, 3033 Cloverleaf Pkwy., Kannapolis, NC 28083. Telephone: (704) 795-4888.

LAKEWOOD BLUECLAWS

Office Address: 2 Stadium Way, Lakewood, NJ 08701.
Telephone: (732) 901-7000. **Fax:** (732) 901-3967.
Email Address: info@blueclaws.com. **Website:** www.blueclaws.com.
Affiliation (first year): Philadelphia Phillies (2001). **Years in League:** 2001-

OWNERSHIP, MANAGEMENT

Operated By: American Baseball Company, LLC.
President: Joseph Finley. **Partners:** Joseph Caruso, Lewis Eisenberg, Joseph Plumeri, Craig Stein.
General Manager: Geoff Brown. **Assistant General Manager, Operations:** Brandon Marano. **Assistant General Manager, Sales:** Rich Mozingo. **Controller:** Bob Halsey. **Director, Marketing:** Mike Ryan. **Director, Promotions:** Hal Hansen. **Director, Community Relations:** Jim DeAngelis. **Director, Business Development:** Dan DeYoung. **Director, Group Sales:** Jim McNamara. **Director, New Client Development:** Mike Van Hise. **Director, Ticket Operations:** Rebecca Ramos. **Director, Ticket Sales:** Joe Harrington. **Director, Special Events:** Steve Farago. **Director, Inside Sales:** Lisa Carone. **Director, Food/Beverage Services:** Chris Tafrow. **Assistant Director, Sponsorships:** Zack Rosenberg. **Executive Chef:** Sandy Cohen. **Front Office Manager:** Jaimie Smith. **Group Sales Manager:** Tracy Davis. **Group Sales Manager:** Ross Pibal. **Ticket Sales Managers:** Ryan Strzalka, Tom Frye. **Regional Sales Managers:** Casey Coppinger, Josh Feinberg, Kevin Fenstermacher. **Corporate Sales Manager:** Joe Pilon. **Merchandise Manager:** Garret Streisel. **Media/Public Relations Manager:** Greg Giombarrese. **Concessions Manager:** Brendan Geary. **Clubhouse Manager:** Russ Schaffer. **Head Groundskeeper:** Ryan Radcliffe. **Assistants:** Felicia Adamus, Dave Bochanski, Nicholas Cataldi, Amy DeMichele, David Foley, Whitney Goulish, James Hambrick, Danielle Hanula, Greg Heroy, Kevin Kay, Charles Keller, Jason Lefkowitz, Ignacio Munoz, Kristopher Neild, Doug Rowan, Geoffrey Siddons, David Terreros.

FIELD STAFF

Manager: Mark Parent. **Hitting Coach:** Greg Legg. **Pitching Coach:** Steve Schrenk. **Trainer:** Mickey Kozack.

GAME INFORMATION

Radio Announcers: Greg Giombarrese, Josh Ellis. **No. of Games Broadcast:** Home-70, Road-70. **Flagship Station:** WOBM 1160-AM.
PA Announcers: Kevin Clark, Mike Gavin. **Official Scorer:** Joe Bellina.
Stadium Name: FirstEnergy Park. **Location:** Route 70 to New Hampshire Ave., north on New Hampshire for 2 1/2 miles to ballpark. **Standard Game Times:** 7:05 p.m., 6:35 (April-May); Sun. 1:05, 5:05 (July-Aug.). **Ticket Prices:** $7-11.
Visiting Team Hotel: Quality Inn of Toms River, 815 Route 37 West, Toms River, NJ 08755. **Telephone:** (732) 341-3400.

LEXINGTON LEGENDS

Office Address: 207 Legends Lane, Lexington, KY 40505.
Telephone: (859) 252-4487. **Fax:** (859) 252-0747.
E-Mail Address: webmaster@lexingtonlegends.com. **Website:** www.lexington-legends.com.
Affiliation (first year): Houston Astros (2001). **Years in League:** 2001-

OWNERSHIP, MANAGEMENT

Operated By: Ivy Walls Management Co.
Principal Owner: Bill Shea. **President/COO:** Alan Stein.
General Manager: Andy Shea. **Assistant GM:** Luke Kuboushek. **Vice President, Facilities:** Gary Durbin. **Director, Stadium Operations/Human Resource Manager:** Shannon Kidd. **Business Manager:** Jeff Black. **Staff Accountant:** Tina Wright. **Director, Marketing:** Seth Poteat. **Box Office Manager:** David Barry. **Director, Broadcasting/Media Relations:** Keith Elkins. **Account Executive:** Ron Borkowski. **Senior Sales Executives:** Justin Ball, Scott Tenney. **Office Manager/Community Relations:** Stephanie Fish. **Promotions Coordinator:** Mario Anderson. **Head Groundskeeper:** Chris Pearl. **Facility Specialist:** Steve Moore.

FIELD STAFF

Manager: Rodney Linares. **Coach:** Stubby Clapp. **Pitching Coach:** Travis Driskoll. **Trainer:** Jon Patton.

GAME INFORMATION

Radio Announcer: Keith Elkins. **No of Games Broadcast:** Home-70 Road-70. **Flagship Station:** WLXG 1300-AM.
PA Announcer: Unavailable. **Official Scorer:** Travis Weber.
Stadium Name: Applebee's Park. **Location:** From I-64/75, take exit 113, right onto North Broadway toward downtown Lexington for 1.2 miles, past New Circle Road (Highway 4), right into stadium, located adjacent to Northland Shopping Center. **Standard Game Times:** 7:05 p.m., 6:35 (April-May); Sun. 2:05 (April-May), 6:05 (June-Aug.). **Ticket Price Range:** $4-16.50.
Visiting Club Hotel: Ramada Inn and Conference Center, 2143 N. Broadway, Lexington, KY 40505. **Telephone:** (859) 299-1261.

ROME BRAVES

Office Address: State Mutual Stadium, 755 Braves Blvd., Rome, GA 30161.
Mailing Address: P.O. Box 1915, Rome, GA 30162-1915.
Telephone: (706) 368-9388. **Fax:** (706) 368-6525.
E-Mail Address: rome.braves@braves.com. **Website:** www.romebraves.com.
Affiliation (first year): Atlanta Braves (2003). **Years in League:** 2003-.

OWNERSHIP, MANAGEMENT

Operated By: Atlanta National League Baseball Club Inc.
General Manager: Michael Dunn. **Assistant GM:** Jim Jones. **Director, Stadium Operations:** Eric Allman. **Director, Ticket Manager:** Doug Bryller. **Director, Food/Beverage:** Dave Atwood. **Manager, Special Projects:** Erin White. **Administrative Manager:** Libby Simonds. **Account Representatives:** John Layng, David Lembeck. **Head Groundskeeper:** Mike Geiger. **Retail Manager:** Starla Roden. **Warehouse Operations Manager:** Terry Morgan. **Neighborhood Outreach Coordinator:** Laura Harrison.

FIELD STAFF

Manager: Randy Ingle. **Coach:** Bobby Moore. **Pitching Coach:** Jim Czajkowski. **Trainer:** Allan Chase.

GAME INFORMATION

Radio Announcer: JB Smith. **No. of Games Broadcast:** Home-70, Away-70. **Flagship Station:** WLAQ 1410-AM.
PA Announcer: Eddie Brock. **Official Scorers:** Jim O'Hara, Lyndon Huckaby.
Stadium Name: State Mutual Stadium. **Location:** I-75 North to exit 190 (Rome/Canton), left off exit and follow Highway 411/Highway 20 to Rome, right at intersection on Highway 411 and Highway 1 (Veterans Memorial Highway), stadium is at intersection of Veterans Memorial Highway and Riverside Parkway. **Ticket Price Range:** $4-10.
Visiting Club Hotel: Days Inn, 840 Turner McCall Blvd., Rome, GA 30161. **Telephone:** (706) 295-0400.

SAVANNAH SAND GNATS

Office Address: 1401 E. Victory Dr., Savannah, GA 31404.
Mailing Address: P.O. Box 3783, Savannah, GA 31414.
Telephone: (912) 351-9150. **Fax:** (912) 352-9722.
E-Mail Address: info@sandgnats.com. **Website:** www.sandgnats.com.
Affiliation (firt year): New York Mets (2007). **Years in League:** 1904-1915, 1936-1960, 1962, 1984-

OWNERSHIP, MANAGEMENT

Operated By: Savannah Professional Baseball, LLC.
President: John Katz.
Vice President, Business Operations: Jeremy Auker. **Vice President, Food/Beverage:** Scott Burton. **Director, Sales:** Ric Sisler. **Director, Broadcasting/Communications:** Toby Hyde. **Public Affairs, Special Events/Merchandise Manager:** Ryan Kirwan. **Stadium Operations Manager:** Evan Christian. **Ticketing Manager:** Terry McMurtry. **Account Executive:** Chase Polhemus. **Head Groundskeeper:** Andy Rock.

FIELD STAFF

Manager: Pedro Lopez. **Coach:** Ryan Ellis. **Pitching Coach:** Marc Valdez. Trainer: Brad Hudson.

GAME INFORMATION

Radio Announcer: Toby Hyde. **No. of Games Broadcast:** Home-70, Away-0. **Flagship Station:** The Ticket AM-900.
PA Announcer: Unavailable. **Official Scorer:** Michael MacEachern.
Stadium Name: Historic Grayson Stadium. **Location:** I-16 to 37th Street exit, left on 37th, right on Abercorn Street, left on Victory Drive; From I-95 to exit 16, east on 204, right on Victory Drive, Stadium is on right in Daffin Park. **Standard Game Times:** 7 p.m., Sun. 2. **Ticket Price Range:** $7-10.
Visiting Club Hotel: Unavailable.

WEST VIRGINIA POWER

Office Address: 601 Morris St, Suite 201, Charlestown, WV 25301.
Telephone: (304) 344-2287. **Fax:** (304) 344-0083.
E-Mail Address: team@wvpower.com. **Website:** www.wvpower.com.
Affiliation (first year): Pittsburgh Pirates (2009). **Years in League:** 1987-

OWNERSHIP, MANAGEMENT

Operated By: Palisades Baseball.
Principal Owner: Alan Levin.
Executive Vice President: Andy Milovich. **Director, Operations:** Jeremy Taylor. **Director, Marketing:** Kristin Call. **Director, Promotions:** Dan Helm. **Director, Food/Beverage:** Jeff Meehan. **Assistant Director, Food/Beverage:** Keegan McDonalds. **General Counsel/Special Assistant:** Stacey Chesser. **Accountant:** Kim Hill. **Box Office Manager:** Dan Cudoc. **Groundskeeper:** Brian Eiche. **Stadium Maintenance:** Julio Silva. **Stadium Maintenance:** Brent Szarka. **Receptionist:** Terri Byrd.

FIELD STAFF

Manager: Gary Green. **Coach:** Edgar Varela. **Pitching Coach:** Jeff Johnson.

GAME INFORMATION

Radio Announcer: Unavailable. **No. of Games Broadcast:** Home-70, Away-70. **Flagship Station:** WSWW 1490-AM.
PA Announcer: Unavailable. **Official Scorer:** Unavailable.
Stadium Name: Appalachian Power Park. **Location:** I-77 South to Capitol Street exit, left on Lee Street, left on Brooks Street. **Standard Game Times:** 7:05 p.m., Sun. 2:05 (April-May); 5:05 (June-Sept.). **Ticket Price Range:** $6-8.
Visiting Club Hotel: Ramada Charleston, 400 Second Avenue SW, South Charleston, WV 25303. **Telephone:** (304) 744-4641.

NEW YORK-PENN LEAGUE

SHORT-SEASON

Mailing Address: 6161 MLK Street North, Suite 205, St. Petersburg, FL 33703.
Telephone: (727) 289-7112. **Fax:** (727) 683-9691.

Website: www.newyork-pennleague.com.
Years League Active: 1939–
President: Ben J. Hayes.
President Emeritus: Robert F. Julian. **Treasurer:** Jon Dandes (Jamestown).

Ben Hayes

Directors: Tim Bawmann (Lowell), Steve Cohen (Brooklyn), Jon Dandes (Jamestown), Jeff Eiseman (Aberdeen), Tom Ganey (Auburn), Bill Gladstone (Tri-City), Jeff Goldklang (Hudson Valley), Chuck Greenberg (State College), CJ Knudsen (Vermont), Michael Savit (Mahoning Valley), E. Miles Prentice (Oneonta), Naomi Silver (Batavia), Art Matin (Staten Island), Paul Velte (Williamsport).

League Historian: Charles Wride.

Division Structure: McNamara—Aberdeen, Brooklyn, Hudson Valley, Staten Island. **Pinckney**—Auburn, Batavia, Jamestown, Mahoning Valley, State College, Williamsport. **Stedler**—Lowell, Oneonta, Tri-City, Vermont.

Regular Season: 76 games. **2010 Opening Date:** June 18. **Closing Date:** Sept. 5. **All-Star Game:** Aug. 17 at Lowell. **Hall of Fame Game:** Tri-City vs. Oneonta, July 24, in Cooperstown.

Playoff Format: Division winners and wild-card team meet in best-of-three semifinals. Winners meet in best-of-three series for league championship.

Roster Limit: 30 active, but only 25 may be in uniform and eligible to play in any given game. **Player Eligibility Rule:** No more than four players 23 or older; no more than three players on active list may have four or more years of prior service. **Brand of Baseball:** Rawlings. **Umpires:** Unavailable.

STADIUM INFORMATION

			Dimensions				
Club	**Stadium**	**Opened**	**LF**	**CF**	**RF**	**Capacity**	**2009 Att.**
Aberdeen	Ripken Stadium	2002	310	400	310	6,000	247,061
Auburn	Falcon Park	1995	330	400	330	2,800	55,804
Batavia	Dwyer Stadium	1996	325	400	325	2,600	35,620
Brooklyn	KeySpan Park	2001	315	412	325	7,500	264,102
Hudson Valley	Dutchess Stadium	1994	325	400	325	4,494	161,332
Jamestown	Russell E. Diethrick Jr. Park	1941	335	410	353	3,324	45,095
Lowell	Edward LeLacheur Park	1998	337	400	302	5,000	186,522
Mahoning Valley	Eastwood Field	1999	335	405	335	6,000	120,755
Oneonta	Damaschke Field	1906	350	406	350	4,200	23,521
State College	Medlar Field at Lubrano Park	2006	328	403	322	5,412	142,068
Staten Island	Richmond County Bank Ballpark	2001	325	400	325	6,500	206,635
Tri-City	Joseph L. Bruno Stadium	2002	325	400	325	5,000	145,976
Vermont	Centennial Field	1922	330	405	323	4,400	84,114
Williamsport	Bowman Field	1923	345	405	350	4,200	68,130

ABERDEEN IRONBIRDS

Office Address: 873 Long Drive, Aberdeen, MD 21001.
Telephone: (410) 297-9292. **Fax:** (410) 297-6653.
E-Mail Address: info@ironbirdsbaseball.com. **Website:** www.ironbirdsbaseball.com.
Affiliation (eighth year): Baltimore Orioles (2002). **Years in League:** 2002-

OWNERSHIP, MANAGEMENT

Operated By: Ripken Professional Baseball LLC.
Principal Owner: Cal Ripken Jr. **Co-Owner/Executive Vice President:** Bill Ripken. **VP:** Jeff Eiseman.
General Manager: Aaron Moszer. **Sales Managers:** Jenna Raglani, Chris Savio. **Director, Ticket Operations:** Brad Cox. **Director, Retail Merchandising:** Don Eney. **Manager, Facilities:** Dino Profili. **Head Groundskeeper:** Chris Walsh.

FIELD STAFF

Manager: Gary Kendall. **Coach:** Cesar Devarez. **Pitching Coach:** Scott McGregor.

GAME INFORMATION

Radio Announcer: Unavailable. **No. of Games Broadcast:** Home-38, Away-38. **Flagship Station:** Unavailable. **PA Announcer:** Jay Szech. **Official Scorer:** Joe Stetka.
Stadium Name: Ripken Stadium. **Location:** I-95 to exit 85 (Route 22), west on 22 West, right onto Long Drive. **Ticket Price Range:** $6-15.
Visiting Club Hotel: Marriott Courtyard Aberdeen at Ripken Stadium. **Telephone:** 410-272-0440.

AUBURN DOUBLEDAYS

Office Address: 130 N. Division St., Auburn, NY 13021.
Telephone: (315) 255-2489. **Fax:** (315) 255-2675.
E-Mail Address: ddays@auburndoubledays.com. **Website:** www.auburndoubledays.com.
Affiliation (first year): Toronto Blue Jays (2001). **Years in League:** 1958-80, 1982-

OWNERSHIP, MANAGEMENT

Operated by: Auburn Community Non-Profit Baseball Association Inc.
CEO: Tom Ganey.
General Manager: Carl Gutelius. **Assistant GM:** Chris Reed.

FIELD STAFF

Manager: Dennis Holmberg. **Coach:** Kenny Graham. **Pitching Coach:** Vince Horsman. **Trainer:** Shawn McDermott.

GAME INFORMATION

Radio Announcer: Unavailable. **No of Games Broadcast:** Home-38 Away-38. **Flagship Station:** WIN 89.1 FM.
PA Announcer: Mike Deforrest. **Official Scorer:** Unavailable.
Stadium Name: Falcon Park. **Location:** I-90 to exit 40, right on Route 34 for 8 miles to York Street, right on York, left on North Division Street. **Standard Game Times:** 7 p.m.; Sun. 6. **Ticket Price Range:** $4-7.
Visiting Club Hotel: Inn at the Fingerlakes, 12 Seminary Ave., Auburn, NY 13021. **Telephone:** (315) 253-5000.

BATAVIA MUCKDOGS

Office Address: Dwyer Stadium, 299 Bank St, Batavia, NY 14020.
Telephone: (585) 343-5454. **Fax:** (585) 343-5620.
E-Mail Address: info@muckdogs.com. **Website:** www.muckdogs.com.
Affiliation (first year): St. Louis Cardinals (2007). **Years in League:** 1939-53, 1957-59, 1961-

OWNERSHIP, MANAGEMENT

Operated By: Red Wings Management, LLC.
General Manager: Travis Sick. **Clubhouse Operations:** Tony Pecora.

FIELD STAFF

Manager: Dann Bilardelo. **Hitting Coach:** Joe Kruzel. **Pitching Coach:** Arthur "Ace" Adams. **Trainer:** Eric Bauer.

GAME INFORMATION

Radio Announcer: Pat Melacaro. **No. of Games Broadcast:** Home-38 Away-20.
Flagship Station: WBTA 1490-AM. **PA Announcer:** Unavailable. **Official Scorer:** Unavailable. **Stadium Name:** Dwyer Stadium.
Location: I-90 to exit 48, left on Route 98 South, left on Richmond Avenue, left on Bank Street.
Standard Game Times: 7:05 p.m.; Sun. 1:05, 5:05. **Ticket Price Range:** $5-7.
Visiting Club Hotel: Days Inn of Batavia, 200 Oak St., Batavia, NY 14020. **Telephone:** (585) 343-1440.

BROOKLYN CYCLONES

Office Address: 1904 Surf Ave, Brooklyn, NY 11224.
Telephone: (718) 449-8497. **Fax:** (718) 449-6368.
E-Mail Address: info@brooklyncyclones.com. **Website:** www.brooklyncyclones.com.
Affiliation (first year): New York Mets (2001). **Years in League:** 2001-

OWNERSHIP, MANAGEMENT

Chairman, CEO: Fred Wilpon.
President: Saul Katz. **COO:** Jeff Wilpon.
General Manager: Steve Cohen. **Assistant General Manager:** Kevin Mahoney. **Director, Communications:** Dave Campanaro. **Director, New Business Development:** Gary J. Perone. **Director, Ticket Operations:** Chris Nervegna. **Director, Ticket Sales:** Matt Slatus. **Marketing Assistant/Promotions Manager:** Alexa Atria. **Graphics Manager:** Kevin Jimenez. **Operations Manager:** Vladimir Lipsman. **Community Relations Manager:** Elizabeth Lombardi. **Head

 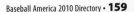

Groundskeeper: Kevin Ponte. **Senior Accountant:** Sharif Soliman. **Account Executives:** Brian Berman, Katie Grenda, John Haley, Ricky Viola. **Staff Accountant:** Tatiana Isdith. **Administrative Assistant, Community Relations:** Sharon Lundy-Ross.

FIELD STAFF

   Manager: Wally Backman. **Hitting Coach:** Benny Distefano. **Pitching Coach:** Rick Tomlin.

GAME INFORMATION

   Radio Announcer: Warner Fusselle. **No. of Games Broadcast:** Home-38, Away-38. **Flagship Station:** WKRB 90.3-FM. **PA Announcer:** Unavailable. **Official Scorer:** Unavailable.
   Stadium Name: KeySpan Park. **Location:** Belt Parkway to Cropsey Ave. South, continue on Cropsey until it becomes West 17th St.; continue to Surf Ave., stadium on south side of Surf Ave. By subway, west/south to Stillwell Ave./Coney Island station. **Ticket Price Range:** $8-17.
   Visiting Club Hotel: Holiday Inn Express, 279 Butler Street, Brooklyn, NY 11217. **Telephone:** (718) 855-9600.

HUDSON VALLEY RENEGADES

   Office Address: Dutchess Stadium, Route 9D, Wappingers Falls, NY 12590.
   Mailing Address: P.O. Box 661, Fishkill, NY 12524.
   Telephone: (845) 838-0094. **Fax:** (845) 838-0014.
   E-Mail Address: gadesinfo@hvrenegades.com. **Website:** www.hvrenegades.com.
   Affiliation (first year): Tampa Bay Rays (1996). **Years in League:** 1994-.

OWNERSHIP, MANAGEMENT

   Operated by: Keystone Professional Baseball Club Inc.
   Principal Owner: Marv Goldklang. **President:** Jeff Goldklang.
   General Manager: Eben Yager. **Assistant GM:** Corey Whitted. **Sales Manager:** Joe Ausanio. **Director, Media Relations:** Rick Kubitschek. **Director, Community Relations:** Annie Rapalje. **Director, Ticket Sales:** Kristen Huss. **Group Sales Manager:** Kaitlin Lambert. **Sales Account Executive:** Sean Kammerer. **New Media Manager:** Megan Ogulnick. **Community Relations Specialist:** Bob Outer. **Director, Business Operations:** Vicky DeFreese. **Director, Pitch for Kids:** Rick Zolzer. **Director, Promotions:** Andy Wilmert. **Director, Stadium Operations:** Tom Hubmaster.

FIELD STAFF

   Manager: Jared Sandberg. **Coach:** Reinaldo Ruiz. **Pitching Coach:** Jack Giese. **Trainer:** Andrew Hauser.

GAME INFORMATION

   Radio Announcer: Unavailable. **No. of Games Broadcast:** Home-38, Away-38. **Flagship Stations:** WBNR 1260-AM/WLNA 1420-AM.
   PA Announcer: Rick Zolzer. **Official Scorers:** Unavailable.
   Stadium Name: Dutchess Stadium. **Location:** I-84 to exit 11 (Route 9D North), north one mile to stadium. **Standard Game Times:** 7:05 p.m.; Sun. 5:05.
   Visiting Club Hotel: Ramada Inn, 20 Schuyler Blvd. and Route 9, Fishkill, NY 12524. **Telephone:** (845) 896-4995.

JAMESTOWN JAMMERS

   Office Address: 485 Falconer St, Jamestown, NY 14701.
   Mailing Address: P.O. Box 638, Jamestown, NY 14702.
   Telephone: (716) 664-0915. **Fax:** (716) 664-4175.
   E-Mail Address: email@jamestownjammers.com. **Website:** www.jamestownjammers.com.
   Affiliation (first year): Florida Marlins (2002). **Years in League:** 1939-57, 1961-73, 1977-.

OWNERSHIP, MANAGEMENT

   Operated By: Rich Baseball Operations.
   President: Robert Rich Jr. **Chief Operating Officer:** Jonathon Dandes.
   General Manager: Matthew Drayer. **Sales/Operations Manager:** John Pogorzelski. **Director, Head Groundskeeper:** Jamie Bloomquist.

FIELD STAFF

   Manager: David Berg. **Coach:** Frank Moore. **Pitching Coach:** Steve Watson. **Trainer:** Patrick Amorelli.

GAME INFORMATION

   Radio: Unavailable.
   PA Announcer: Unavailable. **Official Scorer:** Rim Riggs, Scott Eddy.
   Stadium Name: Russell E. Diethrick Jr Park. **Location:** From I-90, south on Route 60, left on Buffalo Street, left on Falconer Street. **Standard Game Times:** 7:05 p.m.; Sun. 6:05. **Ticket Price Range:** $4.50-7.
   Visiting Club Hotel: Red Roof Inn, 1980 Main St., Falconer, NY 14733. **Telephone:** (716) 665-3670.

LOWELL SPINNERS

Office Address: 450 Aiken St, Lowell, MA 01854.
Telephone: (978) 459-2255. **Fax:** (978) 459-1674.
E-Mail Address: generalinfo@lowellspinners.com. **Website:** www.lowellspinners.com.
Affiliation (first year): Boston Red Sox (1996). **Years in League:** 1996-

OWNERSHIP, MANAGEMENT

Operated By: Diamond Action Inc.
Owner/CEO: Drew Weber.
Vice President/General Manager: Tim Bawmann. **VP, Business Operations:** Brian Lindsay. **Corporate Controller:** Patricia Harbour. **VP, Corporate Communications:** Jon Goode. **Director, Stadium Operations:** Dan Beaulieu. **Director, Facility Management:** Gareth Markey. **Media Relations Manager:** Jon Boswell. **Director, Merchandising:** Jeff Cohen. **Director, Ticket Group Sales:** Jon Healy. **Director, Ticket Operations:** Justin Williams. **Director, Game Day Entertainment:** Matt Steinberg. **Administrative Assistant:** Kyle Coffman. **Head Groundskeeper:** Jeff Paolino. **Clubhouse Manager:** Del Christman.

FIELD STAFF

Manager: Gary DiSarcina. **Hitting Coach:** Luis Lopez. **Pitching Coach:** Kevin Walker. **Trainer:** David Herrera

GAME INFORMATION

Radio Announcer: Ken Cail. **No. of Games Broadcast:** Home-38 Away-38. **Flagship Station:** WCAP 980-AM.
PA Announcer: George Brown. **Official Scorers:** David Rourke.
Stadium Name: Edward A. LeLacheur Park. **Location:** From Route 495 and 3, take exit 35C (Lowell Connector), follow connector to exit 5B (Thorndike Street) onto Dutton Street, left onto Father Morrissette Boulevard, right on Aiken Street.
Standard Game Times: 7:05 p.m.; Sat.-Sun. 5:05. **Ticket Price Range:** $5-10.
Visiting Club Hotel: Doubletree Inn, 50 Warren St, Lowell, MA 01852. **Telephone:** (978) 452-1200.

MAHONING VALLEY SCRAPPERS

Office Address: 111 Eastwood Mall Blvd, Niles, OH 44446.
Mailing Address: 111 Eastwood Mall Blvd, Niles, OH 44446.
Telephone: (330) 505-0000. **Fax:** (303) 505-9696.
E-Mail Address: info@mvscrappers.com. **Website:** www.mvscrappers.com.
Affiliation (first year): Cleveland Indians (1999). **Years in League:** 1999-

OWNERSHIP, MANAGEMENT

Operated By: HWS Baseball Group.
Managing General Partner: Michael Savit.
General Manager: Dave Smith. **Assistant GM:** Jordan Taylor. **Director, Finance:** Debbie Primmer. **Director, Corporate Sales:** Matt Thompson. **Box Office Manager:** Stephanie Fife. **Director, Stadium Operations:** Dan Stricko. **Director, Entertainment:** Heather Sahli. **Director, Group Sales:** Mark Libs.

FIELD STAFF

Manager: Travis Fryman. **Pitching Coach:** Ken Rowe. **Coach:** Dennis Malave.

GAME INFORMATION

Radio Announcer: Unavailable. **No. of Games Broadcast:** Home-38, Away-38. **Flagship Station:** WNIO 1390-AM.
PA Announcer: Unavailable. **Official Scorer:** Craig Antush.
Stadium Name: Eastwood Field. **Location:** I-80 to 11 North to 82 West to 46 South; stadium located behind Eastwood Mall. **Ticket Price Range:** $7-9.
Visiting Club Hotel: Days Inn & Suites, 1615 Liberty St., Girard, OH 44429. **Telephone:** (330) 759-9820

ONEONTA TIGERS

Office Address: 15 James Georgeson Ave., Oneonta, NY 13820.
Mailing Address: PO Box 1070, Oneonta, NY 13820
Telephone: (607) 432-6326. **Fax:** (607) 432-1965.
E-Mail Address: info@oneontatigers.com. **Website:** www.oneontatigers.com.
Affiliation (first year): Detroit Tigers (1999). **Years in League:** 1966-

OWNERSHIP, MANAGEMENT

Operated By: Oneonta Athletic Corp.
President: Miles Prenctice. **Executive Vice Presidents:** John Gleason, Stephen Long, Bill Larkin. **General Manager:**

Andrew Weber. **Assistant General Manager:** Eric Knighton. **Director, Community Relations:** Steve Pindor. **Director, Concessions:** Kris German.

FIELD STAFF
Manager: Howard Bushong. **Hitting Coach:** Luis Quinones. **Pitching Coach:** Jorge Cordova. **Trainer:** Aron Low. **Strength Coach:** Kyle Bergman.

GAME INFORMATION
Radio: Eric Knighton.
PA Announcer: John Horne. **Official Scorer:** Tom Heitz.
Stadium Name: Damaschke Field. **Location:** Exit 15 off I-88. **Standard Game Times:** 7 p.m.; Sun. 6 p.m. **Ticket Price Range:** $5-10.
Visiting Club Hotel: Super 8 Motel, 4973 St Hwy 23, Oneonta, NY 13820. **Telephone:** (607) 432-9505.

STATE COLLEGE SPIKES

Office Address: 112 Medlar Field, Lubrano Park, University Park, PA 16802.
Telephone: (814) 272-1711. **Fax:** (814) 272-1718.
Website: www.statecollegespikes.com
Affiliation (first year): Pittsburgh Pirates (2007). **Years in League:** 2006-.

OWNERSHIP, MANAGEMENT
Operated By: Spikes Baseball LP.
Chairman/Managing Partner: Chuck Greenberg. **Executive Vice President:** Rick Janac. **General Manager:** Jason Dambach. **Assistant General Manager:** Katie Beekman. **Director, Premium Sales:** Chris Phillips. **Director, Group Sales:** Scott Walker. **Director, Promotions/Community Relations:** Jen Orlando. **Director, Ballpark Operations:** Dan Petrazzolo. **Accounting Manager:** Karen Mahon. **Accounting/Administrative Assistant:** Rani Poague. **Concessions Manager:** Cody Begg. **Premium Sales Manager:** Greg Huff. **Group Sales Managers:** Jon Musselman, Devin Smith.

FIELD STAFF
Manager: Gary Robinson. **Hitting Coach:** Brandon Moore. **Pitching Coach:** Mike Steele. **Trainer:** Mike Zalno.

GAME INFORMATION
Radio Announcers: Steve Jones. **No of Games Broadcast:** Home-38 Road-38. **Flagship Station:** WZWW 95.3-FM.
PA Announcer: Jeff Brown. **Official Scorer:** Dave Baker, John Dixon.
Stadium Name: Medlar Field at Lubrano Park. **Location:** From west, U.S. 322 to Mount Nittany Expressway, I-80 to exit 158 (old exit 23/Milesburg), follow Route 150 South to Route 26 South. From east, I-80 to exit 161 (old exit 24/Bellefonte) to Route 26 South or U.S. 220/I-99 South. **Standard Game Times:** 7:05 p.m., Sun. 6:05. **Ticket Price Range:** $6-14.
Visiting Club Hotel: Ramada Conference Center State College, 1450 Atherton St., State College, PA 16801. **Telephone:** (814) 238-3001.

STATEN ISLAND YANKEES

Stadium Address: 75 Richmond Terrace, Staten Island, NY 10301.
Telephone: (718) 720-9265. **Fax:** (718) 273-5763.
Website: www.siyanks.com.
Affiliation (first year): New York Yankees (1999). **Years in League:** 1999-.

OWNERSHIP, MANAGEMENT
Operated by: Mandalay Baseball Properties.
Principal Owners: Staten Island Minor League Holdings LLC.
President: Joseph Ricciutti.
Executive Vice President/General Manager: Jane Rogers. **VP, Ticket Sales:** Jason Cohen. **Finance Manager:** Wayne Seguin. **Director, Ticket Operations:** Matt Gulino. **Director, Entertainment:** Mike d'Amboise. **Director, Sponsor Services:** Heidi Silber. **Manager, Sponsor Services:** Tak Mihara. **Marketing Coordinator:** John McCutchan. **Senior Corporate Marketing Manager:** Domenick Loccisano. **Group Sales Coordinators:** Tom Kurtz, Joe Kronander, Matt Schulman, Thomas Sheridan. **Customer Account Managers:** Tom Conway, Nicole Carballeira. **Director, Stadium Operations:** Robert Brown. **Groundskeeper:** Ryan Woodley.

FIELD STAFF
Manager: Josh Paul. **Hitting Coach:** Ty Hawkins. **Pitching Coach:** Pat Daneker. **Coach:** Justin Pope. **Trainer:** Lee Myers.

GAME INFORMATION
Radio Announcer: Unavailable. **No. of Games Broadcast:** Home-38, Away-38. **Flagship Station:** Unavailable.
PA Announcer: Unavailable. **Official Scorer:** Unavailable.
Stadium Name: Richmond County Bank Ballpark at St. George. **Location:** From I-95, take exit 13E (1-278 and Staten

Island), cross Goethals Bridge, stay on I-278 East and take last exit before Verrazano Narrows Bridge, north on Father Cappodanno Boulevard, which turns into Bay Street, which goes to ferry terminal; ballpark next to Staten Island Ferry Terminal. **Standard Game Times:** 7 p.m.; Sun 2. **Ticket Price Range:** $9-11.

Visiting Club Hotel: The Navy Lodge, 408 North Path Rd., Staten Island, NY 10305. **Telephone:** (718) 442-0413.

TRI-CITY VALLEYCATS

Office Address: Joseph L. Bruno Stadium, 80 Vandenburg Ave, Troy, NY 12180.
Mailing Address: P.O. Box 694, Troy, NY 12181.
Telephone: (518) 629-2287. **Fax:** (518) 629-2299.
E-Mail Address: info@tcvalleycats.com. **Website:** www.tcvalleycats.com.
Affiliation (first year): Houston Astros (2001). **Years in League:** 2002-

OWNERSHIP, MANAGEMENT

Operated By: Tri-City ValleyCats Inc.
Principal Owners: Martin Barr, John Burton, William Gladstone, Rick Murphy, Alfred Roberts, Stephen Siegel.
President: William Gladstone.
Vice President/General Manager: Rick Murphy. **Assistant GM:** Vic Christopher. **Director, Fan Development:** Heather LaVine. **Stadium Operations Manager:** Keith Sweeney. **Community Relations Manager:** Ryan Burke. **Media Relations Manager:** Matt Van Pelt. **Business Development Manager:** Matt Callahan. **Account Executives:** Chris Dawson. **Food/Beverage Coordinator:** Gian Rafaniello. **Administrative Assistant:** Michelle Skinner. **Senior Advisor:** Buddy Caruso. **Bookkeeper:** Gene Gleason.

FIELD STAFF

Manager: Jim Pankovits. **Coach:** Joel Chimelis. **Pitching Coach:** Gary Ruby. **Trainer:** Brian Baca.

GAME INFORMATION

Radio Announcer:. No. of Games Broadcast: Home-38, Away-38. **Flagship Station:** Unavailable.
PA Announcer: Anthony Pettograsso. **Official Scorer:** Unavailable.
Stadium Name: Joseph L. Bruno Stadium. **Location:** From north, I-87 to exit 7 (Route 7), go east 1½ miles to I-787 South, to Route 378 East, go over bridge to Route 4, right to Route 4 South, one mile to Hudson Valley Community College campus on left. From south, I-87 to exit 23 (I-787), I-787 north six miles to exit for Route 378 east, over bridge to Route 4, right to Route 4 South, one mile to campus on left. From east, Massachusetts Turnpike to exit B-1 (I-90), nine miles to Exit 8 (Defreestville), left off ramp to Route 4 North, five miles to campus on right. From west, I-90 to exit 24 (I-90 East), I-90 East for six miles to I-787 North (Troy), 2.2 miles to exit for Route 378 East, over bridge to Route 4, right to Route 4 south for one mile to campus on left. **Standard Game Times:** 7 p.m.; Sun. 5. **Ticket Price Range:** $5-10.
Visiting Club Hotel: Unavailable.

VERMONT LAKE MONSTERS

Office Address: 1 King Street Ferry Dock, Burlington, VT 05401.
Telephone: (802) 655-4200. **Fax:** (802) 655-5660.
E-Mail Address: info@vermontlakemonsters.com. **Website:** www.vermontlakemonsters.com.
Affiliation (first year): Washington Nationals (2005). **Years in League:** 1994-

OWNERSHIP, MANAGEMENT

Operated by: Vermont Expos Inc.
Principal Owner/President: Ray Pecor.
General Manager: Nate Cloutier. **Director, Ticket Operations:** Steve Hennessey. **Director, Finance/Merchandise:** Kate Echo. **Director, Marketing/Promotions:** Shelby Sorrentino. **Director, Media Relations:** Paul Stanfield. **Director, Stadium Operations:** Jim O'Brien. **Director, Special Projects:** Onnie Matthews. **Clubhouse Operations:** Phil Schelzo.

FIELD STAFF

Manager: Jeff Garber. **Hitting Coach:** Paul Sanagorski. **Pitching Coach:** Franklyn Bravo.

GAME INFORMATION

Radio Announcers: Rob Ryan, George Commo. **No. of Games Broadcast:** Home-38, Away-38. **Flagship Station:** The Zone 960-AM (delete 96.7 FM).
PA Announcer: Rich Haskell. **Official Scorer:** Ev Smith, Bruce Bosley.
Stadium Name: Centennial Field. **Location:** I-89 to exit 14W, right on East Avenue for one mile, right at Colchester Avenue. **Standard Game Times:** 7:05 p.m.; Sat. 6:05, Sun. 1:05.
Ticket Price Range: $5-8.
Visiting Club Hotel: Comfort Inn & Suites, 5 Dorset St., South Burlington, VT 05403. **Telephone:** (802) 863-5541.

WILLIAMSPORT
CROSSCUTTERS

Office Address: Bowman Field, 1700 W. Fourth St, Williamsport, PA 17701.
Mailing Address: P.O. Box 3173, Williamsport, PA 17701.
Telephone: (570) 326-3389. **Fax:** (570) 326-3494.
E-Mail Address: mail@crosscutters.com. **Website:** www.crosscutters.com.
Affiliation (first year): Philadelphia Phillies (2007). **Years in League:** 1968-72, 1994-

OWNERSHIP, MANAGEMENT

Operated By: Geneva Cubs Baseball Inc.
Principal Owners: Paul Velte, John Schreyer.
President: Paul Velte. **Executive Vice President:** John Schreyer.
Vice President/General Manager: Doug Estes. **Vice President, Marketing/Public Relations:** Gabe Sinicropi. **Director, Concessions:** Bill Gehron. **Director, Ticket Operations/Community Relations:** Sarah Budd. **Head Groundskeeper:** Brian McLaughlin.

FIELD STAFF

Manager: Chris Truby. **Coach:** Jorge Velandia. **Pitching Coach:** Lance Carter.

GAME INFORMATION

Radio Announcer: Todd Bartley. **No. of Games Broadcast:** Home-38, Away-38. **Flagship Station:** WLYC 1050-AM., 104.1-FM.
PA Announcer: Rob Thomas. **Official Scorer:** Ken Myers.
Stadium Name: Bowman Field. **Location:** From south, Route 15 to Maynard Street, right on Maynard, left on Fourth Street for one mile. From north, Route 15 to Fourth Street, left on Fourth. **Ticket Price Range:** $4.50-7.25
Visiting Club Hotel: Best Western, 1840 E. Third St, Williamsport, PA 17701. **Telephone:** (570) 326-1981.

NORTHWEST LEAGUE

SHORT-SEASON

Office Address: 620 W. Franklin St., Boise, ID 83702.
Mailing Address: P.O. Box 1645, Boise, ID 83701.
Telephone: (208) 429-1511. **Fax:** (208) 429-1525.
E-Mail Address: bobrichmond@qwestoffice.net. **Website:** www.northwestleague.com.
Years League Active: 1954-.
President/Treasurer: Bob Richmond.
Vice President: Brent Miles. **Corporate Secretary:** Jerry Walker (Salem-Keizer).
Directors: Bob Beban (Eugene), Bobby Brett (Spokane), Tom Volpe (Everett), Jake Kerr (Vancouver), Mike McMurray (Yakima), Brent Miles (Tri-City), Jerry Walker (Salem-Keizer), Neil Leibman (Boise). **Administrative Assistant:** Rob Richmond.
Division Structure: East—Boise, Spokane, Tri-City, Yakima. **West**—Eugene, Everett, Salem-Keizer, Vancouver.
Regular Season: 76 games. **2010 Opening Date:** June 20. **Closing Date:** Sept. 6.
Playoff Format: Division winners meet in best-of-five series for league championship.
All-Star Game: None.
Roster Limit: 30 active, 35 under control. **Player Eligibility Rule:** No more than three players on active list may have four or more years of prior service.
Brand of Baseball: Rawlings.
Umpires: Unavailable.

Bob Richmond

STADIUM INFORMATION

| Club | Stadium | Opened | Dimensions | | | Capacity | 2009 Att. |
			LF	CF	RF		
Boise	Memorial Stadium	1989	335	405	335	4,500	103,783
Eugene	PK Park	2010	335	400	325	2,000	125,475
Everett	Everett Memorial Stadium	1984	330	395	330	3,682	89,929
Salem-Keizer	Volcanoes Stadium	1997	325	400	325	4,100	106,590
Spokane	Avista Stadium	1958	335	398	335	7,162	174,941
Tri-City	Dust Devils Stadium	1995	335	400	335	3,730	84,198
Vancouver	Nat Bailey Stadium	1951	335	395	335	6,500	149,297
Yakima	Yakima County Stadium	1993	295	406	295	3,000	72,881

BOISE HAWKS

Office Address: 5600 N. Glenwood St., Boise, ID 83714.
Telephone: (208) 322-5000. **Fax:** (208) 322-6846.
Website: www.boisehawks.com.
Affiliation (first year): Chicago Cubs (2001). **Years in League:** 1975-76, 1978, 1987-

OWNERSHIP, MANAGEMENT

Operated by: Boise Baseball LLC.
CEO: Neil Leibman.
President/General Manager: Todd Rahr. **Assistant GM/Director, Business Operations:** Dina Duncan. **Director, Sales:** Andy Simon. **Director, Stadium Operations:** Jeff Israel. **Manager, Brand/ Merchandise:** Kelly Kerkvliet. **Marketing Manager:** Kristen Nimmo. **Ticket Sales Manager:** Bryan McMartin. **Group Sales Coordinator:** Greg Marconi. **Web/Digital Content:** Ken Hyde.

FIELD STAFF

Manager: Jody Davis. **Hitting Coach:** Ricardo Medina. **Pitching Coach:** Jeff Fassaro. **Trainer:** Aaron Larsen.

GAME INFORMATION

Radio Announcer: Mike Safford. **No. of Games Broadcast:** Home-38, Away-38. **Flagship Station:** KTIK 1350-AM.
PA Announcer: Unavailable. **Official Scorer:** Unavailable.
Stadium Name: Memorial Stadium. **Location:** I-84 to Cole Road, north to Western Idaho Fairgrounds at 5600 North Glenwood Street. **Standard Game Time:** 7:15 p.m. **Ticket Price Range:** $6-11.
Visiting Club Hotel: Owyhee Plaza Hotel, 1109 Main St., Boise, ID 83702. **Telephone:** (208) 343-4611.

EUGENE EMERALDS

Office Address: 2077 Willamette St, Eugene, OR 97405.
Mailing Address: P.O. Box 5566, Eugene, OR 97405.
Telephone: (541) 342-5367. **Fax:** (541) 342-6089.
E-Mail Address: ems@go-ems.com. **Website:** www.go-ems.com.
Affiliation (first year): San Diego Padres (2001). **Years in League:** 1955-68, 1974-

OWNERSHIP, MANAGEMENT

Operated By: Elmore Sports Group Ltd.
Principal Owner: David Elmore.
President/General Manager: Bob Beban. **Assistant GMs:** Bryan Beban, Nathan Skalsky. **Director, Business Operations:** Eileen Beban. **Director, Food Services:** Phil Bopp. **Directors, Tickets/Special Events:** Koo Yul Kim, Travis Anderson. **Director, Stadium Operations:** David Puente. **Director, Media Relations:** Bryan Beban. **Grounds Superintendent:** Brian Burroughs.

FIELD STAFF

Manager: Greg Riddoch. **Coach:** Eric Payton. **Pitching Coach:** Tom Bradley. **Trainer:** Nate Stewart.

GAME INFORMATION

Radio Announcer: Chris Fisher. **No. of Games Broadcast:** Home-38, Away-38. **Flagship Station:** KPNW 1120-AM.
PA Announcer: Grant McHill. **Official Scorer:** George McPherson.
Stadium Name: PK Park. **Ticket Price Range:** $5.50-9.
Visiting Club Hotel: Shilo Inn Eugene/Springfield, 3350 Gateway Street, Springfield, OR 97477. **Telephone:** (541) 747-0332.

EVERETT AQUASOX

Mailing Address: 3802 Broadway, Everett, WA 98201.
Telephone: (425) 258-3673. **Fax:** (425) 258-3675.
E-Mail Address: aquasox@aquasox.com. **Website:** www.aquasox.com.
Affiliation (first year): Seattle Mariners (1995). **Years in League:** 1984-

OWNERSHIP, MANAGEMENT

Operated by: 7th Inning Stretch, LLC
Directors: Tom Volpe, Pat Filippone.
Executive Vice President: Tom Backemeyer. **General Manager:** Brian Sloan. **Director, Broadcasting/Corporate Sales:** Pat Dillon. **Director, Food/Beverage:** Todd Holterhoff. **Director, Accounting:** Teresa Sarsted. **Director, Tickets:** Rick Dooley. **Manager, Community Relations:** Katie Crawford. **Account Executives:** Troy Sherry, Chris Kelley, Ryan Pearman. **Head Groundskeeper:** Brian Burroughs.

FIELD STAFF

Manager: Jose Moreno. **Coach:** Scott Steinmann. **Pitching Coach:** Rich Dorman.

GAME INFORMATION

Radio Announcer: Pat Dillon. **No. of Games Broadcast:** Home-38, Away-38. **Flagship Station:** KRKO 1380-AM.
PA Announcer: Tom Lafferty. **Official Scorer:** Pat Castro.
Stadium Name: Everett Memorial Stadium. **Location:** I-5, exit 192. **Standard Game Times:** 7:05 p.m., Sun. 1:05. **Ticket Price Range:** $7-15.
Visiting Club Hotel: Holiday Inn, Downtown Everett, 3105 Pine St., Everett, WA 98201. **Telephone:** (425) 339-2000.

SALEM-KEIZER VOLCANOES

Street Address: 6700 Field of Dreams Way NE, Keizer, OR 97303.
Mailing Address: P.O. Box 20936, Keizer, OR 97307.
Telephone: (503) 390-2225. **Fax:** (503) 390-2227.
E-Mail Address: probasebal@aol.com. **Website:** www.volcanoesbaseball.com.
Affiliation (first year): San Francisco Giants (1997). **Years in League:** 1997-

OWNERSHIP, MANAGEMENT

Operated By: Sports Enterprises Inc.
Principal Owners: Jerry Walker, Bill Tucker.
President/General Manager: Jerry Walker. **Vice President, Operations:** Rick Nelson. **Corporate Sponsorships:** Jerry Howard. **Media Relations:** Rick Nelson. **Director, Merchandising/Ticket Office Operations:** Bea Howard.

FIELD STAFF

Manager: Tom Trebelhorn. **Coach:** Ricky Ward. **Pitching Coach:** Brian Cooper. **Trainer:** Chris McKenna.

GAME INFORMATION

Radio Announcer: Mark Gilman. **No. of Games Broadcast:** Home-38, Away-38. **Flagship Station:** KBZY AM-1490. **PA Announcer:** Bill Post. **Official Scorer:** Scott Sepich.

Stadium Name: Volcanoes Stadium. **Location:** I-5 to exit 260 (Chemawa Road), west one block to Stadium Way NE, north six blocks to stadium. **Standard Game Times:** 6:35 p.m.; Fri-Sat. 7:05; Sun. 5:05. **Ticket Price Range:** $7-11.

Visiting Club Hotel: Comfort Suites, 630 Hawthorne Ave. SE, Salem, OR 97301. **Telephone:** (503) 585-9705.

SPOKANE INDIANS

Office Address: Avista Stadium, 602 N. Havana, Spokane, WA 99202.

Mailing Address: P.O. Box 4758, Spokane, WA 99220.

Telephone: (509) 535-2922. **Fax:** (509) 534-5368.

E-Mail Address: mail@spokaneindiansbaseball.com. **Website:** www.spokaneindiansbaseball.com.

Affiliation (first year): Texas Rangers (2003). **Years in League:** 1972, 1983-

OWNERSHIP, MANAGEMENT

Operated By: Longball Inc.

Principal Owner: Bobby Brett. **President:** Andrew Billig.

Vice President/General Manager: Chris Duff. **Senior VP:** Otto Klein. **VP, Tickets:** Josh Roys. **Assistant GM:** Lesley DeHart. **Assistant GM, Promotions:** Sarah Travis. **Director, Sponsorships/Operations:** Kyle Erwert. **Director, Promotions:** Dimitri Perera. **Director, Group Sales:** Sheldon Weddle. **Group Sales Coordinator:** Briana K'Burg. **Director, Concessions/Hospitality:** Ryan Jordan. **Director, Stadium Operations:** Seth Moir. **CFO:** Greg Sloan. **Accounting:** Dawnelle Shaw. **Head Groundskeeper:** Brennan Prestley. **Assistant Director, Stadium Operations:** Larry Blumer.

FIELD STAFF

Manager: Tim Hulett. **Coach:** Josue Perez, Brian Dayette. **Pitching Coach:** Justin Thompson.

GAME INFORMATION

Radio Announcer: Bob Robertson. **No. of Games Broadcast:** Home-38, Away-38. **Flagship Station:** 1510 KGA. **PA Announcer:** Unavailable. **Official Scorer:** Unavailable.

Stadium Name: Avista Stadium at the Spokane Fair and Expo Center. **Location:** From west, I-90 to exit 283B (Thor/Freya), east on Third Avenue, left onto Havana. From east, I-90 to Broadway exit, right onto Broadway, left onto Havana. **Standard Game Time:** 6:30 p.m. **Ticket Price Range:** $4-9.

Visiting Club Hotel: Mirabeau Park Hotel & Convention Center, N. 1100 Sullivan Rd, Spokane, WA 99037. **Telephone:** (509) 924-9000.

TRI-CITY DUST DEVILS

Office Address: 6200 Burden Blvd., Pasco, WA 99301.

Telephone: (509) 544-8789. **Fax:** (509) 547-9570.

E-Mail Address: info@dustdevilsbaseball.com. **Website:** www.dustdevilsbaseball.com.

Affiliation (first year): Colorado Rockies (2001). **Years in League:** 1955-1974, 1983-1986, 2001-.

OWNERSHIP, MANAGEMENT

Operated by: Northwest Baseball Ventures.

Principal Owners: George Brett, Hoshino Dreams Corp., Brent Miles.

President: Brent Miles. **Vice President/General Manager:** Derrel Ebert. **VP, Business Operations:** Tim Gittel. **Director, Season Tickets:** Matt Nash. **Director, Sponsorships:** Kelli Foos. **Director, Group Sales:** Dennis da Silva. **Director, Stadium Operations:** Jeff Volaski. **Account Executive:** Erik Roach. **Sponsorships Coordinator:** Molly Klippert. **Head Groundskeeper:** Michael Angel.

FIELD STAFF

Manager: Freddie Ocasio. **Coach:** Anthony Sanders. **Pitching Coach:** Joey Eischen. **Trainer:** Andy Stover.

GAME INFORMATION

Radio Announcer: Mike Boyle. **No. of Games Broadcast:** Home-38, Away-38. **Flagship Station:** Newstalk 870 AM KFLD.

PA Announcer: Patrick Harvey. **Official Scorers:** Tony Wise, Scott Tylinski.

Stadium Name: Gesa Stadium. **Location:** I-182 to exit 9 (Road 68), north to Burden Blvd., right to stadium. **Standard Game Time:** 7:15 p.m. **Ticket Price Range:** $5-9.

Visiting Club Hotel: Red Lion Hotel-Columbia Center, 1101 N. Columbia Center Blvd., Kennewick, WA 99336. **Telephone:** (509) 783-0611.

VANCOUVER CANADIANS

Office Address: Nat Bailey Stadium, 4601 Ontario St., Vancouver, British Columbia V5V 3H4.
Telephone: (604) 872-5232. **Fax:** (604) 872-1714.
E-Mail Address: staff@canadiansbaseball.com. **Website:** www.canadiansbaseball.com.
Affiliation (first year): Oakland Athletics (2000). **Years in League:** 2000-

OWNERSHIP, MANAGEMENT
Operated by: Vancouver Canadians Professional Baseball LLP.
Principal Owners: Jake Kerr, Jeff Mooney. **President:** Andy Dunn.
General Manager: Jason Takefman. **Assistant General Managers:** Rob Fai, JC Fraser. **VP, Sales/Marketing:** Graham Wall. **Director, Sales:** Scott Masse. **Manager, Sales/Marketing Services:** Cynthia Wildman. **Director, Ticket Operations:** Allan Bailey. **Director, Group Sales/Community Relations:** Spiro Khouri. **Groundskeepers:** Tom Archibald, Trevor Sheffield.

FIELD STAFF
Manager: Rick Magnante. **Coach:** Casey Myers. **Pitching Coach:** Craig Lefferts. **Trainer:** Travis Tims.

GAME INFORMATION
Radio Announcer: Rob Fai. **No. of Games Broadcast:** Home-38, Away-38. **Flagship Station:** The Team 1040-AM.
PA Announcer: Don Andrews. **Official Scorer:** Pat Karl.
Stadium Name: Nat Bailey Stadium. **Location:** From downtown, take Cambie Street Bridge, left on East 25th Ave./King Edward Ave., right on Main Street, right on 33rd Ave., right on Ontario St. to stadium. From south, take Highway 99 to Oak Street, right on 41st Ave., left on Main Street to 33rd Ave., right on Ontario St. to stadium. **Standard Game Times:** 7:05 p.m., Sun. 1:05. **Ticket Price Range:** $9-20.
Visiting Club Hotel: Accent Inns, 10551 Edwards Dr., Richmond, B.C. V6X 3L8. **Telephone:** (604) 273-3311.

YAKIMA BEARS

Office Address: 17 N. 3rd Street, Suite 101, Yakima, WA 98901.
Mailing Address: P.O. Box 483, Yakima, WA 98907.
Telephone: (509) 457-5151. **Fax:** (509) 457-9909.
E-Mail Address: info@yakimabears.com. **Website:** www.yakimabears.com.
Affiliation (first year): Arizona Diamondbacks (2001). **Years in League:** 1955-66, 1990-

OWNERSHIP, MANAGEMENT
Operated by: Short Season LLC.
Managing Partners: Mike McMurray, Mike Ellis, Josh Weinman, Myron Levin, Mike Ormsby.
President: Mike McMurray.
General Manager: K.L. Wombacher. **Assistant GM, Sales:** Aaron Arndt. **Director, Ballpark Operations:** Jared Jacobs. **Director, Ticket Operations:** Ryan Coffey. **Director, Group Sales:** Ricky Torres. **Director, Merchandise:** Lauren Wombacher. **Office Assistant/Reception:** Andrea Russell. **Head Groundskeeper:** Ronnie Ross. **Director, Media Relations/Broadcasting:** Drew Bontadelli. **Administrative Assistants:** Lukas Moedritzer.

FIELD STAFF
Manager: Bob Didier. **Hitting Coach:** Andy Abad. **Pitching Coach:** Doug Drabek. **Trainer:** Ben Fraser.

GAME INFORMATION
Radio Announcer: Drew Bontadelli. **No. of Games Broadcast:** Home-38, Away-38. **Flagship Station:** KUTI 1460-AM.
PA Announcer: Todd Lyons. **Official Scorer:** Unavailable.
Stadium Name: Yakima County Stadium. **Location:** 1301 S. Fair Avenue. I-82 to exit 34 (Nob Hill Boulevard), west to Fair Avenue, right on Fair, right on Pacific Avenue. **Standard Game Times:** 7:05 p.m., Sun. 5:35 p.m. **Ticket Price Range:** $4.50-$9.50.
Visiting Club Hotel: Best Western Ahtanum Inn, 2408 Rudkin Rd., Union Gap, WA 98903. **Telephone:** (509) 248-9700.

APPALACHIAN LEAGUE

APPALACHIAN LEAGUE
of professional baseball clubs

ROOKIE ADVANCED

Mailing Address: 283 Deerchase Circle, Statesville, NC 28625.
Telephone: (704) 873-5300. **Fax:** (704) 873-4333.
E-Mail Address: appylg@hughes.net. **Website:** www.appyleague.com.
Years League Active: 1921-25, 1937-55, 1957-.
President/Treasurer: Lee Landers. **Corporate Secretary:** Jim Holland (Princeton).
Directors: Ricky Bennett (Greeneville), Pedro Grifol (Pulaski), Mitch Lukevics (Princeton), Scott Sharp (Burlington), Buddy Bell (Bristol), Len Johnston (Bluefield), Jeff Luhnow (Johnson City), Kurt Kemp (Danville), Adam Wogan (Kingsport), Jim Rantz (Elizabethton).
League Administrator: Bobbi Landers.
Division Structure: East—Bluefield, Burlington, Danville, Princeton, Pulaski. **West**—Bristol, Elizabethton, Greeneville, Johnson City, Kingsport.
Regular Season: 68 games. **2010 Opening Date:** June 22. **Closing Date:** Aug. 31.
All-Star Game: None.
Playoff Format: First round (best of three): East winner versus West 2nd place; West winner versus East 2nd place. Winners meet in best of three for league championship.
Roster Limit: 30 active, 35 under control. **Player Eligibility Rule:** No more than two years of prior minor league service.
Brand of Baseball: Rawlings.
Umpires: Unavailable

Lee Landers

STADIUM INFORMATION

| Club | Stadium | Opened | Dimensions | | | Capacity | 2009 Att. |
			LF	CF	RF		
Bluefield	Bowen Field	1939	335	400	335	2,250	34,510
Bristol	DeVault Memorial Stadium	1969	325	400	310	2,000	19,390
Burlington	Burlington Athletic Stadium	1960	335	410	335	3,000	29,621
Danville	Dan Daniel Memorial Park	1993	330	400	330	2,588	35,743
Elizabethton	Joe O'Brien Field	1974	335	414	326	1,500	27,767
Greeneville	Pioneer Park	2004	331	400	331	2,400	49,293
Johnson City	Howard Johnson Field	1956	320	410	320	2,500	23,639
Kingsport	Hunter Wright Stadium	1995	330	410	330	2,500	33,691
Princeton	Hunnicutt Field	1988	330	396	330	1,950	25,944
Pulaski	Calfee Park	1935	335	405	310	2,500	30,526

BLUEFIELD ORIOLES

Office Address: Stadium Drive, Bluefield, WV 24701.
Mailing Address: P.O. Box 356, Bluefield, WV 24701.
Telephone: (276) 326-1326. **Fax:** (276) 326-1318.
E-Mail Address: babybirds1@comcast.net. **Website:** www.bluefieldorioles.com.
Affiliation (first year): Baltimore Orioles (1958). **Years in League:** 1946-55, 1957-

OWNERSHIP, MANAGEMENT
Operated By: Adam Shaffer.
Director: Len Johnston (Baltimore Orioles).
Vice President: Cecil Smith. **Secretary:** M.K. Burton. **Counsel:** David Kersey.
President: George McGonagle. **General Manager:** Michael Showe. **Director, Creative Services:** Katherine Ward. **Director, Stadium Services:** Aaron Showe. **Director, Field Operations/Grounds:** Mike White. **Director, Concessions:** Gary Halsey.

FIELD STAFF
Manager: Einar Diaz. **Coach:** Jim Saul. **Pitching Coach:** Troy Mattes. **Trainer:** T.D. Swinford.

GAME INFORMATION
Radio Announcer: Buford Early. **No. of Games Broadcast:** Home-34 Road-34. **Flagship Station:** WHIS 1440-AM/WTZE 1470-AM.
PA Announcer: Buford Early. **Official Scorer:** Unavailable.
Stadium Name: Bowen Field. **Location:** I-77 to Bluefield exit 1, Route 290 to Route 460 West, fourth light right onto Leatherwood Lane, left at first light, past Chevron station and turn right, stadium 1/4 mile on left. **Ticket Price Range:** $3.50.
Visiting Club Hotel: Holiday Inn Bluefield, 3350 Big Laurel Highway. U.S. 460, Bluefield, WV 24701. **Telephone:** (304) 325-6170.

BRISTOL WHITE SOX

Ballpark Location: 1501 Euclid Ave., Bristol, VA 24201.
Mailing Address: P.O. Box 1434, Bristol, VA 24203.
Telephone: (276) 206-9946. **Fax:** (276) 669-7686.
E-Mail Address: brisox@btes.tv. **Website:** www.bristolsox.com.
Affiliation (first year): Chicago White Sox (1995-). **Years in League:** 1921-25, 1940-55, 1969-

OWNERSHIP, MANAGEMENT
Owned by: Chicago White Sox.
Operated by: Bristol Baseball Inc.
Director: Buddy Bell (Chicago White Sox).
President: Mahlon Luttrell. **Vice Presidents:** Lynn Armstrong, Perry Hustad.
General Manager: Mahlon Luttrell. **Treasurer:** Dorothy Cox. **Secretary:** Bentley Hudgins.

FIELD STAFF
Manager: Ryan Newman. **Hitting Coach:** Jerry Hairston. **Pitching Coach:** Curt Hasler. **Trainer:** Cory Barton. **Conditioning Coach:** Ibrahim Rivera.

GAME INFORMATION
Radio: None.
PA Announcer: Chuck Necessary. **Official Scorer:** Perry Hustad.
Stadium Name: DeVault Memorial Stadium. **Location:** I-81 to exit 3 onto Commonwealth Ave., right on Euclid Ave. for ½ mile. **Standard Game Time:** 7 p.m. **Ticket Price Range:** $3-5.
Visiting Club Hotel: Holiday Inn, 3005 Linden Drive Bristol VA 24202. **Telephone:** (276) 466-4100.

BURLINGTON ROYALS

Office Address: 1450 Graham St., Burlington, NC 27217.
Mailing Address: P.O. Box 1143, Burlington, NC 27216.
Telephone: (336) 222-0223. **Fax:** (336) 226-2498.
E-Mail Address: info@burlingtonroyals.com. **Website:** www.burlingtonroyals.com.
Affiliation (first year): Kansas City Royals (2007). **Years in League:** 1986-

OWNERSHIP, MANAGEMENT
Operated by: Burlington Baseball Club Inc.
Director: Scott Sharp (Kansas City Royals).
President: Miles Wolff. **Vice President:** Dan Moushon.
General Manager: Steve Brice. **Director, Marketing/Promotions:** Molly Butler. **Director, Stadium Operations:** Mike Thompson.

FIELD STAFF
Manager: Nelson Liriano. **Hitting Coach:** Unavailable. **Pitching Coach:** Bobby St. Pierre.

GAME INFORMATION
Radio Announcer: Unavailable. **No. of Games Broadcast:** Home-34, Away-34. **Flagship:** www.burlingtonroyals.com.
PA Announcer: Unavailable. **Official Scorer:** Wes Gullett, Andrew Keever, Jon Cole.
Stadium Name: Burlington Athletic Stadium. **Location:** I-40/85 to exit 145, north on Route 100 (Maple Avenue) for 1½ miles, right on Mebane Street for 1½ miles, right on Beaumont, left on Graham. **Standard Game Time:** 7 p.m. **Ticket Price Range:** $3-8.

DANVILLE BRAVES

Office Address: Dan Daniel Memorial Park, 302 River Park Dr., Danville, VA 24540.
Mailing Address: P.O. Box 378, Danville, VA 24543.
Telephone: (434) 797-3792. **Fax:** (434) 797-3799.
E-Mail Address: info@dbraves.com. **Website:** www.dbraves.com.
Affiliation (first year): Atlanta Braves (1993). **Years in League:** 1993-

OWNERSHIP, MANAGEMENT
Operated by: Atlanta National League Baseball Club Inc. **Director:** Kurt Kemp (Atlanta Braves). **General Manager:** David Cross. **Assistant GM:** Bob Kitzmiller. **Operations Manager:** Kyle Mikesell. **Head Groundskeeper:** Jon Hall.

FIELD STAFF
Manager: Paul Runge. **Hitting Coach:** Carlos Mendez. **Pitching Coach:** Derrick Lewis. **Athletic Trainer:** Colin Myers.

GAME INFORMATION

Radio Announcer: Nick Pierce. **No. of Games Broadcast:** Home-Unavailable, Away-Unavailable. **Flagship Station:** WMNA 106.3-FM.

PA Announcer: Jay Stephens. **Official Scorer:** Mark Bowman.

Stadium Name: American Legion Field Post 325 Field at Dan Daniel Memorial Park. **Location:** U.S. 29 Bypass to River Park Drive/Dan Daniel Memorial Park exit; follow signs to park. **Standard Game Times:** 7 p.m., Sun. 4. **Ticket Price Range:** $4-7.

Visiting Club Hotel: Innkeeper-West, 3020 Riverside Dr., Danville, VA 24541. **Telephone:** (434) 799-1202.

ELIZABETHTON TWINS

Office Address: 300 West Mill Street, Elizabethton, TN 37643
Stadium Address: 208 N. Holly Lane, Elizabethton, TN 37643.
Mailing Address: 136 S. Sycamore St., Elizabethton, TN 37643.
Telephone: (423) 547-6441. **Fax:** (423) 547-6442.
E-Mail Address: etwins@charterinternet.com. **Website:** www.elizabethtontwins.com.
Affiliation (first year): Minnesota Twins (1974). **Years in League:** 1937-42, 1945-51, 1974-

OWNERSHIP, MANAGEMENT

Operator: City of Elizabethton.
Director: Jim Rantz (Minnesota Twins).
President: Harold Mains.
General Manager: Mike Mains. **Clubhouse Operations/Head Groundskeeper:** David McQueen.

FIELD STAFF

Manager: Ray Smith. **Coach:** Jeff Reed. **Pitching Coach:** Jim Shellenback. **Trainer:** Ryan Headwall.

GAME INFORMATION

Radio Announcer: Unavailable. **No. of Games Broadcast:** Home-34, Away-6. **Flagship Station:** WBEJ 1240-AM.
PA Announcer: Tom Banks. **Official Scorer:** Bill Crow.
Stadium Name: Joe O'Brien Field. **Location:** I-81 to Highway I-26, exit at Highway 321/67, left on Holly Lane. **Standard Game Time:** 7 p.m. **Ticket Price Range:** $3-5.
Visiting Club Hotel: Holiday Inn, 101 W. Springbrook Dr., Johnson City, TN 37601. **Telephone:** (423) 282-4611.

GREENEVILLE ASTROS

Office Address: 135 Shiloh Road., Greeneville, TN 37743.
Mailing Address: P.O. Box 5192, Greeneville, TN 37743.
Telephone: (423) 638-0411. **Fax:** (423) 638-9450.
E-Mail Address: info@greenevilleastros.com. **Website:** www.greenevilleastros.com.
Affiliation (first year): Houston Astros (2004). **Years in League:** 2004-

OWNERSHIP, MANAGEMENT

Operated by: Houston Astros Baseball Club.
Director: Ricky Bennett (Houston Astros).
General Manager: David Lane. **Assistant GM:** Hunter Reed. **Head Groundskeeper:** Blake Anderson. **Clubhouse Operations:** Unavailable.

FIELD STAFF

Manager: Ed Romero. **Pitching Coach:** Unavailable. **Hitting Coach:** Pete Rancont. **Trainer:** Grant Hufford.

GAME INFORMATION

Radio: None.
PA Announcer: Bobby Rader. **Official Scorer:** Johnny Painter.
Stadium Name: Howard Johnson Field at Cardinal Park. **Location:** I-181 to exit 32, left on East Main, through light onto Legion Street. **Standard Game Time:** 7 p.m. **Ticket Price Range:** $3-5.
Visiting Club Hotel: Unavailable.

JOHNSON CITY CARDINALS

Office Address: 111 Legion St., Johnson City, TN 37601.
Mailing Address: P.O. Box 179, Johnson City, TN 37605.
Telephone: (423) 461-4866. **Fax:** (423) 461-4864.
E-Mail Address: info@jccardinals.com. **Website:** www.jccardinals.com.
Affiliation (first year): St. Louis Cardinals (1975). **Years in League:** 1911-13, 1921-24, 1937-55, 1957-61, 1964-

OWNERSHIP, MANAGEMENT
Operated by: Johnson City Sports Foundation Inc.
President: Mark Fox.
Director: John Vuch (St. Louis Cardinals).
General Manager: Chuck Arnold.

FIELD STAFF
Manager: Mike Shildt. **Coach:** Ramon Ortiz. **Pitching Coach:** Doug White.

GAME INFORMATION
Radio: None.
PA Announcer: Unavailable. **Official Scorer:** Unavailable.
Stadium Name: Howard Johnson Field at Cardinal Park. **Location:** I-26 to exit 23, left on East Main, through light onto Legion Street. **Standard Game Time:** 7 p.m. **Ticket Price Range:** $3-5.
Visiting Club Hotel: Holiday Inn, 101 W. Springbrook Dr., Johnson City, TN 37601. **Telephone:** (423) 282-4611.

KINGSPORT METS

Office Address: 800 Granby Rd, Kingsport, TN 37660.
Mailing Address: P.O. Box 1128, Kingsport, TN 37662.
Telephone: (423) 378-3744. **Fax:** (423) 392-8538.
E-Mail Address: info@kmets.com. **Website:** www.kmets.com.
Affiliation (first year): New York Mets (1980). **Years in League:** 1921-25, 1938-52, 1957, 1960-63, 1969-82, 1984-

OWNERSHIP, MANAGEMENT
Operated By: S&H Baseball LLC.
Director: Adam Wogan (New York Mets).
President: Rick Spivey. **Vice President:** Steve Harville. **VP/General Manager:** Roman Stout. **Accountant:** Bob Dingus.
Director, Concessions: Teresa Haywood. **Head Groundskeeper:** Josh Warner. **Clubhouse Attendant:** Travis Baker.

FiELD STAFF
Manager: Mike DiFelice. **Hitting Coach:** Bobby Malek. **Pitching Coach:** Jonathan Hurst.

GAME INFORMATION
Radio: None.
PA Announcer: Don Spivey. **Official Scorer:** Eddie Durham.
Stadium Name: Hunter Wright Stadium. **Location:** I-81 to I-181 North, exit 1 (Stone Drive), left on West Stone Drive (U.S. 11W), right on Granby Road. **Ticket Price Range:** $3-5.
Visiting Club Hotel: The Jameson Inn, 3004 Bays Mountain Plaza, Kingsport, TN 37660. **Telephone:** (423) 282-4611.

PRINCETON RAYS

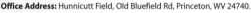

Office Address: Hunnicutt Field, Old Bluefield Rd, Princeton, WV 24740.
Mailing Address: P.O. Box 5646, Princeton, WV 24740.
Telephone: (304) 487-2000. **Fax:** (304) 487-8762.
E-Mail Address: raysball@sunlitsurf.com. **Website:** www.princetonrays.net.
Affiliation (first year): Tampa Bay Rays (1997). **Years in League:** 1988-

OWNERSHIP, MANAGEMENT
Operated By: Princeton Baseball Association Inc.
Director: Mitch Lukevics (Tampa Bay Rays). **President:** Mori Williams.
General Manager: Jim Holland. **Director, Stadium Operations:** Mick Bayle. **Official Scorer:** Bob Redd. **Head, Security/Ticket Sales:** Ken Wallace. **Photographers:** Bo Bowman, Samantha Craig. **Audio Engineer:** David Craig. **Graphic Designer:** Warren Hypes. **Administrative Assistant:** Tommy Thomason. **Transportation:** Everette Bailey. **Adopt-A-Player Coordinator:** Daniella Hatfeld. **Chaplain:** Craig Stout.

FIELD STAFF
Manager: Michael Johns. **Hitting Coach:** Wuarnner Rincones. **Pitching Coach:** Marty DeMerritt. **Coach:** Dan DeMent. **Trainer:** Nick Medina.

GAME INFORMATION

Radio Announcer: Kyle Cooper. **No. of Games Broadcast:** Home-34, Away-34. **Flagship Station:** WAEY 1490-AM.
PA Announcer: Jordan Pruett. **Official Scorer:** Bob Redd.
Stadium Name: Hunnicutt Field. **Location:** Exit 9 off I-77, U.S. 460 West to downtown exit, left on Stafford Drive, stadium located behind Mercer County Technical Education Center. **Standard Game Times:** 7 p.m., Sun 4. **Ticket Price Range:** $3-5.
Visiting Club Hotel: Days Inn, I-77 and Ambrose Lane, Princeton, WV 24740. **Telephone:** (304) 425-8100.

PULASKI MARINERS

Mailing Address: P.O. Box 676, Pulaski, VA 24301.
Telephone: (540) 980-1070. **Fax:** (540) 980-1850.
E-Mail Address: info@pulaskimariners.net
Affiliation (first year): Seattle Mariners (2008). **Years in League:** 1946-50, 1952-55, 1957-58, 1969-77, 1982-92, 1997-2006, 2008-

OWNERSHIP, MANAGEMENT

Operated By: Pulaski Baseball Inc.
Director: Pedro Grifol (Seattle Mariners).
President/General Manager: Tom Compton.

FIELD STAFF

Manager: Eriberto Menchaca. **Hitting Coach:** Rafael Santo Domingo. **Pitching Coach:** Unavailable.

GAME INFORMATION

Radio: None.
PA Announcer: Unavailable. **Official Scorer:** Charles Altizer.
Stadium Name: Calfee Park. **Location:** Interstate 81 to Exit 89-B (Route
11), north to Pulaski, right on Pierce Avenue. **Standard Game Times:** 7 p.m.
Ticket Price Range: $4-6.
Visiting Club Hotel: Comfort Inn, 4424 Cleburne Blvd, Dublin, Virginia. **Telephone:** (540) 674-1100.

PIONEER LEAGUE

ROOKIE LEAGUE

Office Address: 157 S. Lincoln Ave., Spokane, WA 99201.
Mailing Address: P.O. Box 2564, Spokane, WA 99220.
Telephone: (509) 456-7615. **Fax:** (509) 456-0136.
E-Mail Address: fanmail@pioneerleague.com. **Website:** www.pioneerleague.com.
Years League Active: 1939-42, 1946-.
President/Secretary-Treasurer: Jim McCurdy.
Vice President: Mike Ellis (Missoula).
Directors: Dave Baggott (Ogden), Mike Ellis (Missoula), D.G. Elmore (Helena), Kevin Greene (Idaho Falls), Kevin Haughian (Casper), Jeff Katofsky (Orem), Vinny Purpura (Great Falls), Jim Iverson (Billings).
Administrative Assistant: Teryl MacDonald.
Division Structure: North—Billings, Great Falls, Helena, Missoula. **South**—Casper, Idaho Falls, Ogden, Orem.
Regular Season: 76 games (split schedule). **2010 Opening Date:** June 21. **Closing Date:** Sept. 9.
Playoff Format: First-half division winners meet second-half division winners in best-of-three series. Winners meet in best-of-three series for league championship.
All-Star Game: None.
Roster Limit: 35 active, 30 dressed for each game. **Player Eligibility Rule:** No more than 17 players 21 and older, provided that no more than two are 23 or older. No player on active list may have three or more years of prior minor league service.
Brand of Baseball: Rawlings.
Umpires: Unavailable.

Jim McCurdy

STADIUM INFORMATION

Club	Stadium	Opened	Dimensions LF	CF	RF	Capacity	2009 Att.
Billings	Dehler Park	2008	329	410	350	3,071	105,173
Casper	Mike Lansing Field	2002	355	400	345	2,500	56,680
Great Falls	Centene Stadium at Legion Park	1956	335	414	335	3,800	103,909
Helena	Kindrick Field	1939	335	400	325	1,700	33,478
Idaho Falls	Melaleuca Field	1976	340	400	350	3,400	94,674
Missoula	Ogren Park at Allegiance Field	2004	309	398	287	3,500	85,034
Ogden	Lindquist Field	1997	335	396	334	5,000	146,068
Orem	Home of the Owlz	2005	305	408	312	4,500	96,926

BILLINGS MUSTANGS

Office Address: Dehler Park, 2611 Ninth Avenue North, Billings, MT 59101.
Mailing Address: P.O. Box 1553, Billings, MT 59103.
Telephone: (406) 252-1241. **Fax:** (406) 252-2968.
E-Mail Address: mustangs@billingsmustangs.com. **Website:** www.billingsmustangs.com.
Affiliation (first year): Cincinnati Reds (1974). **Years in League:** 1948-63, 1969-

OWNERSHIP, MANAGEMENT

Operated By: Billings Pioneer Baseball Club Inc.
President: Woody Hahn.
General Manager: Gary Roller. **Assistant GM:** Matt Bender. **Director, Stadium Operations:** Chris Marshall. **Director, Food/Beverage:** Curt Prchal. **Director, Broadcasting:** Ed Cohen. **Director, Field Maintenance:** John Barta.

FIELD STAFF

Manager: Delino DeShields. **Coach:** Alex Pelaez. **Pitching Coach:** Bob Forsch. **Trainer:** Charles Leddon.

GAME INFORMATION

Radio Announcer: Unavailable. **No. of Games Broadcast:** Home-38, Away-38. **Flagship Station:** KBUL 970-AM.
PA Announcer: Kyle Riley. **Official Scorer:** Phil Sites.
Stadium Name: Dehler Park. **Location:** I-90 to North 27th Street exit, north to Ninth Avenue North. **Standard Game Times:** 7:05 p.m.; Sun. 4:05. **Ticket Price Range:** $3-9.
Visiting Club Hotel: Rimrock Inn, 1203 North 27th Street, Billings, MT 59101. **Telephone:** (406) 252-7107.

CASPER GHOSTS

Office Address: 330 Kati Lane, Casper, WY 82601.
Mailing Address: P.O. Box 1293, Casper, WY 82602.
Telephone: (307) 232-1111. **Fax:** (307) 265-7867.
E-Mail Address: homerun@ghostsbaseball.com. **Website:** www.ghostsbaseball.com.
Affiliation (first year): Colorado Rockies (2001). **Years in League:** 2001-

OWNERSHIP, MANAGEMENT
Operated by: Casper Professional Baseball Club LLC.
Principal Owner, CEO: Kevin Haughian.
General Manager: Mike Sandler. **Office Manager:** Marlyn Black. **Assistant General Manager:** Chris Maxwell.
Director, Operations: Phil Choler.

FIELD STAFF
Manager: Tony Diaz. **Hitting Coach:** Jonathan Stone. **Pitching Coach:** Craig Bjornson. **Trainer:** Josh Guterman.

GAME INFORMATION
Radio Announcer: Tim Ray. **No. of Games Broadcast:** Home-38, Away-38. **Flagship Station:** Unavailable.
PA Announcer: Unavailable. **Official Scorer:** Unavailable.
Stadium Name: Mike Lansing Field. **Location:** I-25 to Poplar Street exit, north on Poplar Street, right into Crossroads Park. **Standard Game Times:** 7:05 p.m., Sun. 4:05. **Ticket Price Range:** $7.50-9.
Visiting Club Hotel: Parkway Plaza, 123 West E St., Casper, WY 82601. **Telephone:** (307) 235-1777.

GREAT FALLS VOYAGERS

Office Address: 1015 25th St. N, Great Falls, MT 59401.
Mailing Address: P.O. Box 1621, Great Falls, MT 59403.
Telephone: (406) 452-5311. **Fax:** (406) 454-0811.
E-Mail Address: voyagers@gfvoyagers.com. **Website:** www.gfvoyagers.com .
Affiliation (first year): Chicago White Sox (2003). **Years in League:** 1948-1963, 1969-

OWNERSHIP, MANAGEMENT
Operated By: Great Falls Baseball Club, Inc.
President: Vinney Purpura. **General Manager:** Jim Keough. **Head Groundskeeper:** Billy Chafin. **Office Manager:** Karen Skolrud. **Director, Marketing/Community Affairs:** Lorie Harris.

FIELD STAFF
Manager: Chris Cron. **Hitting Coach:** Eric Hollis. **Pitching Coach:** Brian Drahman.

GAME INFORMATION
Radio Announcer: Unavailable. **No. of Games Broadcast:** Home-38, Away-38. **Flagship Station:** KMON 560-AM.
PA Announcer: Tim Paul. **Official Scorer:** Mike Lewis.
Stadium Name: Centene Stadium located at Legion Park. **Location:** From I-15 to exit 281 (10th Ave. S), left on 26th, left on Eighth Ave. North, right on 25th, ballpark on right, past railroad tracks. **Ticket Price Range:** $5-8.
Visiting Club Hotel: Mid Town Motel, 526 Second Ave. N, Great Falls, MT 59401. **Telephone:** (406) 453-2411.

HELENA BREWERS

Office Address: 1300 N. Ewing, Helena, MT 59601.
Mailing Address: P.O. Box 6756, Helena, MT 59604.
Telephone: (406) 495-0500. **Fax:** (406) 495-0900.
E-Mail Address: info@helenabrewers.net. **Website:** www.helenabrewers.net.
Affiliation (first year): Milwaukee Brewers (2003). **Years in League:** 1978-2000, 2003-

OWNERSHIP, MANAGEMENT
Operated by: Helena Baseball Club LLC.
Principal Owner: D.G. Elmore.
General Manager: Paul Fetz. **Assistant GM:** Nick Bowsher. **Director, Hospitality:** Emma Moore. **Director, Broadcasting/Media Relations:** Steve Wendt.

FIELD STAFF
Manager: Joe Ayrault. **Coach:** Ned Yost IV. **Pitching Coach:** Elvin Nina. **Trainer:** Jimmy Gentry.

GAME INFORMATION
Radio Announcer: Unavailable. **No. of Games Broadcast:** Home-38, Away-38. **Flagship Station:** KCAP 1340-AM.
PA Announcer: Randy Bowsher. **Official Scorers:** Kevin Higgens, Craig Struble, Jim Shope.

Stadium Name: Kindrick Field. Location: Cedar Street exit off I-15, west to Last Chance Gulch, left at Memorial Park. Standard Game Time: 7:05 p.m. Sun. 4:05. Ticket Price Range: $6-9.
Visiting Club Hotel: Colonial Red Lion Hotel. Telephone: 406-443-2100.

IDAHO FALLS CHUKARS

Office Address: 568 W. Elva, Idaho Falls, ID 83402.
Mailing Address: P.O. 2183, Idaho, ID 83403.
Telephone: (208) 522-8363. Fax: (208) 522-9858.
E-Mail Address: chukars@ifchukars.com. Website: www.ifchukars.com.
Affiliation (first year): Kansas City Royals (2004). Years in League: 1940-42, 1946-

OWNERSHIP, MANAGEMENT
Operated By: The Elmore Group. Principal Owner: David Elmore.
President/General Manager: Kevin Greene. Assistant GM, Merchandise: Andrew Daugherty. Associate Director, Stadium Operations: Jon Clark. Account Manager/Food Service Specialist: Paul Henderson. Food Service Manager: Kira Walker. Clubhouse Manager: Jared Troescher.

FIELD STAFF
Manager: Brian Buchanan. Coach: Julio Bruno. Pitching Coach: Carlos Martinez. Trainer: Masa Koyanagi.

GAME INFORMATION
Radio Announcers: John Balginy, Jim Garshow. No. of Games Broadcast: Home-38 Road-38. Flagship Station: KUPI 980-AM.
Official Scorer: John Balginy.
Stadium Name: Melaleuca Field. Location: I-15 to West Broadway exit, left onto Memorial Drive, right on Mound Avenue, ¼ mile to stadium. Standard Game Times: 7:15 p.m., Sun. 4. Ticket Price Range: $6-9.
Visiting Club Hotel: Guesthouse Inn & Suites, 850 Lindsay Blvd, Idaho Falls, ID 83402. Telephone: (208) 522-6260.

MISSOULA OSPREY

Office Address: 412 W. Alder St, Missoula, MT 59802.
Telephone: (406) 543-3300. Fax: (406) 543-9463.
E-Mail Address: info@missoulaosprey.com. Website: www.missoulaosprey.com.
Affiliation (first year): Arizona Diamondbacks (1999). Years in League: 1956-60, 1999-

OWNERSHIP, MANAGEMENT
Operated By: Mountain Baseball LLC.
President: Mike Ellis. Vice President: Judy Ellis.
Executive Vice President: Matt Ellis. VP, Finance/Merchandising: Shelly Ellis. General Manager/Operations: Jared Amoss. General Manager, Sales/Marketing: Jeff Griffin. Director, Stadium Operations: Byron Dike. Director, Ticket Operations: Nola Hunter. Account Executive: Jake Boggs.

FIELD STAFF
Manager: Hector De La Cruz. Coach: Jason Hardtke. Pitching Coach: Gil Heredia. Trainer: Joe Metz.

GAME INFORMATION
Radio Announcer: Ben Catley. No. of Games Broadcast: Home-38, Away-38. Flagship Station: KMPT 930-AM.
PA Announcer: Unavailable. Official Scorer: David Kinsey.
Stadium Name: Ogren Park at Allegiance Field. Location: 700 Cregg Lane. Directions: Take Orange Street to Cregg Lane, west on Cregg Lane, stadium west of McCormick Park. Standard Game Times: 7:05 p.m.; Sun 5:05 p.m. Ticket Price Range: $5-10.
Visiting Club Hotel: Mountain Valley Inn, 420 W. Broadway, Missoula, Mt. 59802. Telephone: (406) 728-4500

OGDEN RAPTORS

Office Address: 2330 Lincoln Ave, Ogden, UT 84401.
Telephone: (801) 393-2400. Fax: (801) 393-2473.
E-Mail Address: homerun@ogden-raptors.com. Website: www.ogden-raptors.com.
Affiliation (first year): Los Angeles Dodgers (2003). Years in League: 1939-42, 1946-55, 1966-74, 1994-

OWNERSHIP, MANAGEMENT
Operated By: Ogden Professional Baseball, Inc.
Principal Owners: Dave Baggott, John Lindquist. Chairman, President: Dave Baggott.
General Manager: Joey Stein. VP/Director, Marketing: John Stein. Broadcaster/Media Relations: Eric Knighton.
Director, Merchandise: Gerri Kopinski. Public Relations: Pete Diamond. Groundskeeper: Kenny Kopinski. Assistant

Groundkeeper: Bob Richardson. **Assistant Food Director:** Louise Hillard. **Clubhouse Manager:** Kirby Hoover. **Director, Press Box:** Brandon Kunimura.

FIELD STAFF

Manager: Damon Berryhill. **Coach:** Juhnny Washington. **Pitching Coach:** Chuck Crim. **Trainer:** Robert Dyson. **Strength/Conditioning:** Adam Wagner.

GAME INFORMATION

Radio Announcer: Jake Kelman. **No. of Games Broadcast:** Home-38, Away-38. **Flagship Station:** 1490 AM KOGN. **PA Announcer:** Pete Diamond. **Official Scorer:** Dennis Kunimura.
Stadium Name: Lindquist Field. **Location:** I-15 North to 21th Street exit, east to Lincoln Avenue, south three blocks to park. **Standard Game Times:** 7 p.m ., Sun. 1. **Ticket Price Range:** $6-9.
Visiting Club Hotel: Hotel Ben Lomond, 2510 Washington Blvd., Ogden, UT 84401. **Telephone:** (801) 627-1900.

OREM OWLZ

Office Address: 970 W. University Parkway, Orem, UT 84058.
Telephone: (801) 377-2255. **Fax:** (801) 377-2345.
E-Mail Address: fan@oremowlz.com. **Website:** www.oremowlz.com.
Affiliation (first year): Los Angeles Angels (2001). **Years in League:** 2001-

OWNERSHIP, MANAGEMENT

Operated By: Bery Bery Gud To Me LLC.
Principal Owner: Jeff Katofsky.
General Manager: Aaron Wells. **Assistant GM/Sales:** Blake Buswell. **Director, Baseball Operations/Clubhouse Manager:** Brett Crane. **Director, Ticketing:** Andrew Scott. **IT Manager:** Julie Hatch. **Assistant Clubhouse Manager:** Casey Brallsford.

FIELD STAFF

Manager: Tom Kotchman. **Coach:** Mike Eylward. **Pitching Coach:** Zeke Zimmerman. **Trainer:** Mike Dart.

GAME INFORMATION

Radio Announcer: Matt Gittins. **No. of Games Broadcast:** Home-38, Away-38. **Flagship Station:** Unavailable.
PA Announcer: Lincoln Fillmore. **Official Scorer:** Unavailable.
Stadium Name: Home of the Owlz. **Location:** Exit 269 (University Parkway) off I-15 at Utah Valley University campus. **Ticket Price Range:** $4-9.
Visiting Club Hotel: Provo Days Inn, 1675 N. 200 West, Provo, UT 84604. **Telephone:** (801) 375-8600.

ARIZONA LEAGUE

ROOKIE

Office Address: 620 W. Franklin St., Boise, ID 83702.
Mailing Address: P.O. Box 1645, Boise, ID 83701.
Telephone: (208) 429-1511. **Fax:** (208) 429-1525. **E-Mail Address:** bobrichmond@qwestoffice.net
Years League Active: 1988-.
President/Treasurer: Bob Richmond.
Vice President: Oneri Fleita (Cubs). **Corporate Secretary:** Ted Polakowski (Athletics).
Administrative Assistant: Rob Richmond.
Division Structure: East/Central/West divisions.
Regular Season: 56 games. Aug. 30 semifinal games; Aug. 31 championship. **2010 Opening Date:** June 21. **Closing Date:** Aug. 31.
Standard Game Times: 7 p.m.
Playoff Format: Team with best record plays wildcard in one-game playoff on Aug. 30; other two divisions play one-game playoff. Winners play for League championship on Aug. 31.
All-Star Game: None.
Roster Limit: 35 active. **Player Eligibility Rule:** No player may have three or more years of prior Minor League Service.
Brand of Baseball: Rawlings.

Clubs	Playing Site	Manager	Coach	Pitching Coach(es)
Angels	Angels complex, Tempe	Ty Boykin	Dick Schofield	Trevor Wilson
Athletics	Papago Park Baseball Complex, Phoenix	Marcus Jensen	Juan Dilone	Ariel Prieto
Brewers	Maryvale Baseball Complex, Phoenix	Tony Diggs	Kenny Dominguez	Steve Cline
Cubs	Fitch Park, Mesa	Juan Cabreja	Desi Wilson	Rick Tronerud
Dodgers	Camelback Ranch, Glendale	Lorenzo Bundy	Leo Garcia	Glen Dishman
Giants	Giants complex, Scottsdale	Mike Goff	Victor Torres	M. Caldwell/M. Garcia
Indians	Goodyear Ballpark	Chris Tremie	Anthony Medrano	Jeff Harris
Mariners	Peoria Sports Complex	Jesus Azuaje	Andy Bottin	Gary Wheelock
Padres	Peoria Sports Complex	Ivan Cruz	Kory Dehaan	Jimmy Jones
Rangers	Surprise Recreation Campus	Jayce Tingler	H. Ortiz/O. Bernard	R. O'Malley/J. Jaimes
Reds	Goodyear Ballpark	Julio Garcia	Jorge Orta	Tom Browning
Royals	Surprise Recreation Campus	Darryl Kennedy	A. David/J. Williams	C. Reyes/M. Davis

GULF COAST LEAGUE

ROOKIE

Operated By: Minor League Baseball.
Office Address: 9550 16th Street North, St. Petersburg, FL 33716.
Telephone: 727-456-1734. **FAX:** 727-821-5819.
Website: www.milb.com. **E-mail Address:** gcl@milb.com.
Executive Vice President/COO: Tim Purpura. **Executive Director, Baseball Operations:** Tim Brunswick. **Baseball Operations Assistant:** Andy Shultz.
2010 Opening Date: June 21. **Closing Date:** August 29. **Regular Season:** 56/60 games.
Divisional Alignment: East—Astros, Cardinals, Marlins, Mets, Nationals. **North**—Blue Jays, Braves, Phillies, Pirates, Tigers, Yankees. **South**—Orioles, Rays, Red Sox, Twins.
Playoff Format: The division winner with the best record plays the wild card; the other two division winners meet in a one-game playoff. The winners meet in a best-of-three series.
All-Star Game: None. **Roster Limit:** 35 active, only 30 of whom may be in uniform and eligible to play in any given game. At least 10 must be pitchers as of July 1.
Player Eligibility Rule: No player may have three or more years of prior minor league service.
Brand of Baseball: Rawlings. **Statistician:** Major League Baseball Advanced Media

Clubs	Playing Site	Manager	Coach(es)	Pitching Coach
Astros	Astros complex, Kissimmee	Omar Lopez	D.J. Boston	unavailable
Blue Jays	Mattick Training Center, Dunedin	John Schneider	D. Pano/D. Solano	Vince Horsman
Braves	Disney's Wide World of Sports, Orlando	Luis Ortiz	Sixto Lezcano	Gabe Luckert
Cardinals	Cardinals complex, Jupiter	Steve Turco	Unavailable	Henderson Lugo
Marlins	Roger Dean complex, Jupiter	Jorge Hernandez	Angel Espada	Jeff Schwarz
Mets	St. Lucie Sports Complex, St. Lucie	Edgar Alfonzo	Donovan Mitchell	Hector Berrios
Nationals	Carl Barger Baseball Complex, Melbourne	Bobby Williams	S. Mendez/B. Popper	Joel Sanchez
Orioles	Twin Lakes Park, Sarasota	Ramon Sambo	Milt May	Calvin Maduro
Phillies	Carpenter Complex, Clearwater	Roly DeArmas	Donnie Sadler	Chuck Hernandez
Pirates	Pirate City Complex, Bradenton	Tom Prince	R. Pena/W. Huyke/M. Lum	Miguel Bonilla
Rays	Charlotte County Complex, Port Charlotte	Joe Alvarez	D. DeMent/H. Torres	Darwin Peguero
Red Sox	Red Sox complex	Dave Tomlin	U.L. Washington	Walter Miranda
Tigers	Tigertown, Lakeland	Basilio Cabrera	Andrew Graham	Greg Sabat
Twins	Lee County Complex, Fort Myers	Chris Heintz	M. Cuyler/R. Borrego	Ivan Arteaga
Yankees	Yankee complex, Tampa	Tom Slater	Unavailable	Carlos Chantres

INDEPENDENT
LEAGUES

AMERICAN ASSOCIATION

Office Address: 1415 Hwy. 54 West, Suite 210, Durham, NC 27707.
Telephone: (919) 401-8150. **FAX:** (919) 401-8152. **Website:** www.americanassociationbaseball.com.
Year Founded: 2005.
Commissioner: Miles Wolff. **President:** Dan Moushon.
Administrative Assistant: Jason Deans. **Director of Umpires:** Kevin Winn.
Division Structure: North—Lincoln, St. Paul, Sioux City, Sioux Falls, Wichita. **South**—El Paso, Fort Worth, Grand Prairie, Pensacola, Shreveport-Bossier.
Regular Season: 96 games (split schedule). **2010 Opening Date:** May 13. **2010 Closing Date:** August 29.
All-Star Game: July 27 at Wichita (North Division vs. South Division).
Playoff Format: First-half division winners and second-half division winners in best-of-five series. Winners meet in best-of-five series for league championship.
Roster Limit: 22. **Player Eligibility Rule:** Minimum of five first-year players, maximum of four veterans with at least four years of professional experience.
Brand of Baseball: Rawlings.
Statistician: STATS LLC, 2775 Shermer Road, Northbrook, IL 60062.

STADIUM INFORMATION

Club	Stadium	Opened	LF	CF	RF	Capacity	2009 Att.
El Paso	Cohen Stadium	1990	340	410	340	9,725	200,323
Fort Worth	LaGrave Field	2002	325	400	335	5,100	177,807
Grand Prairie	QuikTrip Park at Grand Prairie	2008	330	400	330	5,445	141,132
Lincoln	Haymarket Park	2001	335	395	325	4,500	172,445
Pensacola	Pelican Park	1991	320	390	320	2,500	71,797
St. Paul	Midway Stadium	1982	320	400	320	6,069	267,398
Shreveport-Bossier	Fair Grounds Field	1986	330	400	330	4,500	86,635
Sioux City	Lewis and Clark Park	1993	330	400	330	3,630	70,978
Sioux Falls	Sioux Falls Stadium	1964	312	410	312	4,029	132,529
Wichita	Lawrence-Dumont Stadium	1934	344	401	312	6,055	161,170

EL PASO DIABLOS

Office Address: 9700 Gateway North Blvd., El Paso, TX 79924.
Telephone: (915) 755-2000. **Fax:** (915) 757-0681.
E-mail Address: info@diablos.com. **Website:** www.diablos.com.
Managing Partner: Mark Schuster, Ventura Sports Group, LLC.
General Manager: Matt LaBranche. **Director, Sponsorships:** Bernie Ricono. **Director, Media/Community Relations:** Adriana Ruiz. **Director, Group Sales:** Rachael Ross. **Box Office Manager:** Steve Martinez.
Account Executives: Donna Blair, Henry Quintana III, Lizette Espinosa. **Business Manager:** Pat Hofman.
Manager: Butch Henry. **Coach:** Ryan Medrano.

GAME INFORMATION
Radio Announcer: Nick Vlietstra. **Games Broadcast:** 96. **Flagship Station:** ESPN Radio 1380-AM. **Webcast Address:** www.diablos.com.
Stadium Name: Cohen Stadium. **Location:** I-10 to U.S. 54 (Patriot Freeway), east to Diana exit to Gateway North Boulevard.
Standard Game Times: Monday-Saturday, 7:05 p.m.; Sunday, 6:05 p.m.
Visiting Club Hotel: Holiday Inn Airport, 6655 Gateway West, El Paso, TX 79925. **Telephone:** (915) 342-5330.

FORT WORTH CATS

Office Address: 301 NE Sixth St., Fort Worth, TX 76164.
Telephone: (817) 332-2287. **Fax:** (817) 386-5524.
E-Mail Address: info@fwcats.com. **Website:** www.fwcats.com.
Principal Owner/CEO: Carl Bell.
General Manager: Dick Smith. **Director, Sales/Marketing:** Bob Flanagan.
Director, Player Personnel/Manager: Chad Tredaway.

GAME INFORMATION
Stadium Name: LaGrave Field. **Location:** From I-30, take I-35 North to North Side Drive exit, left (west) off exit to Main Street, left (south) on Main, left (east) onto NE Sixth Street.
Standard Game Times: Monday – Saturday, 7:05 p.m.; Sunday (May/June), 2:05 p.m.
Visiting Club Hotel: Unavailable.

GRAND PRAIRIE AIRHOGS

Office Address: 1600 Lone Star Parkway, Grand Prairie, TX 75050.
Telephone: (972) 504-9383. **Fax:** (972) 504-2288.
Website: www.airhogsbaseball.com.
Operated By: Ventura Sports Group, LLC.
Executive VP/General Manager: Dave Burke. **VP, Sales:** Andrew Seymour. **Assistant General Manager:** Matt Barry. **Ticket Sales Manager:** J Willms. **Group Sales Executive:** Karissa Hookstadt. **Finance Manager:** Trista Earlston. **Box Office Manager:** Sam Ward. **Director, Communications:** Cassie Cullins. **Director, Food/Beverage:** Sodexo. **CFO:** Greg Engeldinger.
Manager: Pete Incaviglia. **Coach:** Curtis Wilkerson.

GAME INFORMATION

Stadium Name: QuikTrip Park at Grand Prairie. **Location:** From I-30, take Beltline Road exit going north. Once on Beltline Road (1/2 mile), take Lone Star Park entrance (gate #2) towards the stadium.
Standard Game Times: Monday – Saturday, 7:05 p.m.; Sundays, 6:05 p.m.
Visiting Club Hotel: Elegante Hotel and Suites, 2330 West Northwest Highway, Dallas, TX 75220. **Telephone:** (214)351-4477.

LINCOLN SALTDOGS

Office Address: 403 Line Drive Circle, Suite A, Lincoln, NE 68508.
Telephone: (402) 474-2255. **Fax:** (402) 474-2254.
E-Mail Address: info@saltdogs.com. **Website:** www.saltdogs.com.
Owner: Jim Abel. **President:** Charlie Meyer.
Vice President/General Manager: Tim Utrup. **Assistant GM/Director, Sales/Marketing:** Bret Beer. **Director, Broadcasting/Communications:** Jason Van Arkel. **Director, Merchandising/Promotions:** Anne Duchek. **Director, Season Tickets/Ticket Packages:** Toby Antonson. **Director, Group Sales:** Jeff Koncaba. **Director, Stadium Operations:** Dave Aschwege. **Assistant Director, Stadium Operations:** Brett Myers. **Office Manager:** Alicia Oakeson. **Athletic Turf Manager:** Josh Klute. **Assistant Turf Managers:** J.J. Borecky, Jen Roeber.
Manager: Marty Scott. **Coaches:** Chris Miyake.

GAME INFORMATION

Radio Announcer: Jason Van Arkel. **No. of Games Broadcast:** 96. **Flagship Station:** KFOR 1240-AM. **Webcast Address:** www.kfor1240.com.
Stadium Name: Haymarket Park. **Location:** I-80 to Cornhusker Highway West, left on First Street, right on Sun Valley Boulevard, left on Line Drive.
Standard Game Times: Monday – Saturday, 7:05 p.m.; Sunday, 6:05 p.m.
Visiting Club Hotel: Unavailable.

PENSACOLA PELICANS

Office Address: 41 North Jefferson Street, Suite 300 Pensacola, FL 32502.
Telephone: (850) 934-8444. **Fax:** (850) 791-6256.
E-Mail Address: info@pensacolapelicans.com. **Website:** www.pensacolapelicans.com.
Owners: Quint Studer, Rishy Studer. **President:** Rishy Studer. **CEO:** Quint Studer.
General Manager: Talmadge Nunnari. **Assistant General Manager:** Jason Libbert.
Chief Financial Officer: Bess Abernathy. **Ticketing Director:** Shelley Welch. **Community Relations Director:** Carrie Smith. **Sales Executives:** Paul Chestnutt, Gary Colon. **Finance Assistant:** Theresa Waggoner.
Manager: Talmadge Nunnari. **Pitching Coach:** Justin Lord. **Player Procurement:** James Gamble.

GAME INFORMATION

Radio Announcer: Unavailable. **No. of Games Broadcast:** 96. **Flagship Station:** WNRP 1620-AM. **Webcast Address:** www.pensacolapelicans.com.
Stadium Name: Jim Spooner Field at Pelican Park. **Location:** On the campus of University of West Florida. From I-10 West, north on Davis Highway (SR 291) to exit 13, left on University Parkway, right on Campus Drive, stadium 1/2 mile on right.
Standard Game Times: 6:45 p.m.; Sunday, 6:05.
Visiting Club Hotel: Unavailable.

ST. PAUL SAINTS

Office Address: 1771 Energy Park Dr., St. Paul, MN 55108.
Telephone: (651) 644-3517. **Fax:** (651) 644-1627.
E-Mail Address: funsgood@saintsbaseball.com. **Website:** www.saintsbaseball.com.

Principal Owners: Marv Goldklang, Mike Veeck, Bill Murray. **Chairman:** Marv Goldklang. **President:** Mike Veeck.
Executive Vice President/General Manager: Derek Sharrer. **Executive Vice President:** Tom Whaley. **Assistant GM:** Dan Lehv. **Vice President, Customer Service/Community Partnerships:** Annie Huidekoper. **Director, Ticket Sales:** Matt Teske. **Manager, Group/Season Ticket Sales:** Erin Luethi. **Manager, Technology/Group Ticket Sales:** Jeremy Loosbrock. **Ticket Sales Representative:** Chuck Richards. **Director, Broadcast/Communications:** Sean Aronson. **Coordinator, Special Events/Corporate Sales Coordinator:** Erin Kohles. **Director, Food/Beverage:** Curtis Nachtsheim. **Business Manager:** Leesa Anderson. **Office Manager:** Gina Kray. **Stadium Operations:** Bob Klepperich. **Groundskeeper:** Connie Rudolph.
Manager: George Tsamis. **Coaches:** Lamarr Rogers, Jason Verdugo, TJ Wiesner.

GAME INFORMATION

Radio Announcer: Sean Aronson. **No. of Games Broadcast:** 96. **Flagship Station:** Relevant Radio 1330-AM. **Webcast Address:** www.saintsbaseball.com.
Stadium Name: Midway Stadium. **Location:** From I-94, take Snelling Avenue North exit, west onto Energy Park Drive.
Standard Game Times: Monday – Saturday, 7:05 p.m.; Sunday, 1:05 p.m.
Visiting Club Hotel: Sheraton St. Paul Woodbury. 676 Bielenberg Drive, Woodbury, MN 55125. **Telephone:** (651)209-3280.

SHREVEPORT-BOSSIER CAPTAINS

Office Address: 2901 Pershing Blvd, Shreveport, LA 71109.
Telephone: (318) 636-5555. **Fax:** (318) 636-5670.
Website: www.sbcaptains.com.
Owner: Gary Elliston. **President:** Scott Berry.
Vice President/General Manager: Craig Brasfield. **Assistant General Manager:** Chet Carey. **Director, Stadium Operations:** Bobby Entrekin. **Director, Group Sales, Food/Beverage:** Rob Gusick. **Director, Broadcasting/Media Relations:** Josh Hirsch. **Business Manager/Director, Merchandise:** Carrie Brasfield. **Head Groundskeeper:** Josh Keith. **Assistant, Stadium Operations/Group Sales:** Lane Smith. **Manager:** Ricky VanAsselberg. **Coaches:** Darien Dukes, John Harris, B.J. Litchfield.

GAME INFORMATION

Radio Announcer: Josh Hirsch. **No. of Games Broadcast:** 96. **Flagship Station:** Supertalk 1340/ESPN Radio, 1340 KRMD-AM. **Webcast Address:** www.sbcaptains.com.
Stadium Name: Fair Grounds Field. **Location:** Hearne Avenue (U.S. 171) exit off I-20 at Louisiana State Fairgrounds.
Standard Game Times: Monday-Saturday, 7:05 p.m.; Sunday, 6:05 p.m.
Visiting Club Hotel: Holiday Inn Shreveport West, 5555 Financial Plaza, Shreveport, LA 71129. **Telephone:** (318) 688-3000.

SIOUX CITY EXPLORERS

Office Address: 3400 Line Drive, Sioux City, IA 51106.
Telephone: (712) 277-9467. **Fax:** (712) 277-9406.
E-Mail Address: promotions@xsbaseball.com. **Website:** www.xsbaseball.com.
President: John Roost.
General Manager: Shane M. **Tritz. Assistant GM:** Ashley Schoenrock. **Office Manager:** Julie Stringer.
Field Manager/Player Procurement Director: Les Lancaster.

GAME INFORMATION

Radio Announcer: Dave Nitz. **No. of Games Broadcast:** 96. **Flagship Station:** KSCJ 1360-AM. **Webcast Address:** www.xsbaseball.com.
Stadium Name: Lewis and Clark Park. **Location:** I-29 to Singing Hills Blvd. North, right on Line Drive.
Standard Game Times: 7:05 p.m.; Sunday, 2:05 (May/June); 6:05 (July/August).
Visiting Club Hotel: Unavailable.

SIOUX FALLS CANARIES

Office Address: 1001 N. West Ave., Sioux Falls, SD 57104.
Telephone: (605) 333-0179. **Fax:** (605) 333-0139.
E-Mail Address: olander@sfstampede.com. **Website:** www.canariesbaseball.com.
Operated by: Sioux Falls Sports, LLC.
Assistant GM/Groundskeeper: Larry McKenney. **Assistant GM:** Chris Schwab. **Senior VP, Corporate Partnerships:** Jim Loria. **Office/Ticketing Manager:** Wendy Loria. **VP, Media/Public Relations:** Jim Olander.
Manager: Steve Shirley.

GAME INFORMATION

Stadium Name: Sioux Falls Stadium. **Location:** I-29 to Russell Street, east one mile, right on West Avenue.
Standard Game Times: 7:05 p.m.; Sunday, 5:05.
Visiting Club Hotel: Unavailable.

WICHITA WINGNUTS

Office Address: 300 South Sycamore, Wichita, KS 67213.
Telephone: (316) 264-6887. **Fax:** (316) 264-2129.
Website: www.wichitawingnuts.com.
Owners: Steve Ruud, Dan Waller, Gary Austerman, Nick Easter, Nate Robertson.
President/General Manager: Josh Robertson. **Assistant General Manager/Director, Corporate Sales:** Ben Keiter. **Assistant General Manager/Director, Ticket Sales:** Jeremy Mock. **Special Assistant to General Manager:** Brian Holman. **Director, Broadcasting:** Steve Schuster. **Director, Finance:** Kay Brown. **Director, Stadium Operations:** Jeff Kline. **Crew Chief, Stadium Operations:** Scott Taylor. **Tournament Director, NBC World Series:** Jerry Taylor. **Operations Manager, NBC World Series:** Casey Walkup. **Group Sales Manager:** Brian Turner. **Game Day Personnel/Merchandise Manager:** Caitlin Smith. **Clubhouse Manager:** Brad Brungardt. **Assistant Clubhouse Manager:** Bill "Sarge" Cook.
Manager: Kevin Hooper. **Pitching Coach:** Luke Robertson.

GAME INFORMATION

Radio Announcer: Steve Schuster. **Games Broadcast:** KGSO 1410-AM. **Webcast Address:** www.wichitawingnuts.com, www.kgso.com.
Stadium Name: Lawrence-Dumont Stadium. **Location:** 135 North to Kellogg (54) West. Take Seneca Street exit North to Maple. Go East on Maple to Sycamore. Stadium is located on corner of Maple and Sycamore.
Standard Game Times: 7:05 p.m.; Sunday, 5:05.
Visiting Club Hotel: North Rock Suites, 7856 E. 36th St. N., Wichita, KS, 67226. **Telephone:** (316) 634-2303.

ATLANTIC LEAGUE

Mailing Address: 401 N. Delaware Ave. Camden, NJ 08102.
Telephone: (856) 541-9400. **FAX:** (856) 541-9410.
E-Mail Address: info@atlanticleague.com. **Website:** www.atlanticleague.com.
Year Founded: 1998.
Chief Executive Officer/Founder: Frank Boulton. **Vice Presidents:** Peter Kirk, Steven Kalafer.
Executive Director: Joe Klein.
Directors: Frank Boulton (Long Island , Bridgeport, Newark),Steve Kalafer (Somerset), Peter Kirk (Lancaster, York, Southern Maryland). Frank Boulton/Peter Kirk (Camden)
League Operations Latin Coordinator: Ellie Rodriguez. **Director, Baseball Administration:** Patty MacLuckie.
Division Structure: Liberty—Bridgeport, Camden, Long Island, Southern Maryland **Freedom**—Lancaster, Newark, Somerset, York.
Regular Season: 140 games (split-schedule).
2010 Opening Date: April 22. **Closing Date:** Sept. 19.
All-Star Game: July 6 at Long Island.
Playoff Format: First-half division winners meet second-half winners in best of five series. Winners meet in best-of-five final for league championship.
Roster Limit: 25. Teams may keep 27 players from start of season until May 31, 2010.
Eligibility Rule: No restrictions.
Brand of Baseball: Rawlings.
Statistician: STATS, LLC 2775 Shermer Rd Northbrook, Ill 60062

STADIUM INFORMATION

Club	Stadium	Opened	LF	CF	RF	Capacity	2009 Att.
Bridgeport	The Ballpark at Harbor Yard	1998	325	405	325	5,300	162,121
Camden	Campbell's Field	2001	325	405	325	6,425	234,519
Lancaster	Clipper Magazine Stadium	2005	372	400	300	6,000	314,228
Long Island	Citibank Park	2000	325	400	325	6,002	414,973
Newark	Bears & Eagles Riverfront Stadium	1999	302	394	323	6,201	163,736
Somerset	Commerce Bank Ballpark	1999	317	402	315	6,100	355,429
So. Maryland	Regency Stadium	2008	305	400	320	6,000	239,541
York	Sovereign Bank Stadium	2007	300	400	325	5,000	276,446

BRIDGEPORT BLUEFISH

Office Address: 500 Main St., Bridgeport, CT 06604. **Telephone:** (203) 345-4800. **FAX:** (203) 345-4830. **Website:** www.bridgeportbluefish.com.
Operated by: Past Time Partners, LLC.
Principal Owner/CEO, Past Time Partners: Frank Boulton. **Senior VP, Past Time Partners:** Mike Pfaff. **Partners, Past Time Partners:** Tony Rosenthal, Fred Heyman, Jeff Serkes.
General Manager: Robert Goughan. **Business Manager:** Mary Jayne Wells. **Ticket Sales Manager:** Rob Finn. **Public Relations Director:** Paul Herrmann. **Community Relations Coordinator:** Marilyn Guarino. **Facilities Coordinator:** Tom Yario. **Promotions Coordinator:** Tim Carr. **Head Groundskeeper:** Mike Larson.
Manager: Willie Upshaw. **Coach:** Unavailable. **Pitching Coach:** Unavailable. **Trainer:** Unavailable.

GAME INFORMATION

Radio Announcer: Perry Miles. **No. of Games Broadcast:** 140 (webcast). **Flagship Station:** Unavailable. **PA Announcer:** Bill Jensen. **Official Scorer:** Chuck Sadowski.
Stadium Name: The Ballpark at Harbor Yard. **Location:** I-95 to exit 27, Route 8/25 to exit 1. **Standard Game Times:** 7:05 p.m.; Saturday, 6:05 p.m.; Sunday, 2:05 p.m.
Visiting Club Hotel: Holiday Inn Bridgeport, 1070 Main St., Bridgeport, CT 06604. **Telephone:** (203) 334-1234.

CAMDEN RIVERSHARKS

Office Address: 401 N. Delaware Ave., Camden, NJ 08102. **Telephone:** (856) 963-2600. **FAX:** (856) 963-8534. **E-Mail Address:** riversharks@riversharks.com. **Website:** www.river-sharks.com. **Operated by:** Camden Baseball, LLC
Principal Owners: Frank Boulton, Peter Kirk. **President:** Jon Danos. **Controller:** Emily Merrill. **General Manager:** Adam Lorber. **Assistant General Manager:** Joel Seiden. **Director, Ticket Operations:** Jeremy VanEtten. **Director, Finance/Ticketing:** Michael Plunkett. **Director, Marketing:** Nikki Varoutsos. **Director, Group Events:** Bob Nehring. **Corporate Partnerships Manager:** Nate Parkyn. **Group Account Manager:** Mark Schieber. **Partnership Marketing Manager:** Poorya Nayerahmadi. **Box Office Manager:** Aaron Moss. **Group Sales Manager:** Lindsay Rosenberg. **Corporate Partnerships**

Coordinator: Drew Nelson. **Public Relations Assistant:** Gina DiDomenicis. **Group Sales Assistant:** Brian Frankowski. **Group Sales Assistant:** Jason Taylor. **Ticket Office Assistant:** Sean Maher. **Groundskeeper:** Scott Wilkinson. **Stadium Operations Manager:** Frank Slavinkski. **Centerplate General Manager:** Joe Hammer. **Centerplate Assistant General Manager:** Harry Smith. **Office Manager:** Dolores Rozier.
Director of Baseball Operations: Jeff Scott. **Manager:** Von Hayes. **Pitching Coach:** Jeff Scott. **Trainer:** Jason Kopec

GAME INFORMATION

Radio: www.riversharks.com. **Riversharks Broadcaster:** Tim Saunders. **PA Announcer:** Kevin Casey. **Official Scorer:** Dick Shute
Stadium Name: Campbell's Field
Location: From Philadelphia, right on Sixth Street, right after Ben Franklin Bridge toll booth, right on Cooper Street until it ends at Delaware Ave. From Camden, I-676 to exit 5B, follow signs to field. **Standard Game Times:** 7:05 p.m., 5:05 (Saturday), 1:05 (Sunday). Gates open one hour prior to game time.
Visiting Club Hotels: Holiday Inn, Route 70 and Sayer Avenue, Cherry Hill, NJ 08002. **Telephone:** (856) 663-5300. Extended Stay America, 1653 E State Highway 70, Cherry Hill, NJ 08002. **Telephone:** (856) 616-1200.

LANCASTER BARNSTORMERS

Office Address: 650 North Prince St., Lancaster, PA 17603.
Telephone: (717) 509-4487. **FAX:** (717) 509-4486.
E-Mail Address: info@lancasterbarnstormers.com. **Website:** www.lancasterbarnstormers.com.
Operated by: Lancaster Barnstormers Baseball Club, LLC.
Principal Owners: Opening Day Partners.
President: Jon Danos.
Vice President, Business Development: Mark Wilson. **Controller:** Emily Merrill. **General Manager:** Vince Bulik. **Assistant GM:** Kristen Simon. **Director, Stadium Operations:** Don Pryer. **Director, Finance:** Barbara Wert. **Director, Premium Account Services:** Kaye Willis. **Creative Services Manager:** Tom Gorman. **Ticket Operations Manager:** Maureen Wheeler. **Stadium Operations Manager:** Ed Snyder. **Marketing/Public Relations Manager:** Pamela Denlinger. **Manager, Marketing/Community Relations:** Emily Reinbold. **Corporate Partnerships Executives:** Robert Ford, Brian Radle. **Group Events Coordinators:** Christopher Burton, Josh Kirchner, John Warnick. **Administrative Assistant:** Liz Welch.
Manager: Tom Herr. **Pitching Coach:** Danny Cox. **Hitting Coach:** Lance Burkhart. **Trainer:** Unavailable.

GAME INFORMATION

Radio Announcer: Dave Collins. **No. of Games Broadcast:** Home-70, Away-70. **Flagship Station:** WLPA 1490-AM. **PA Announcer:** John Witwer. **Official Scorer:** Joel Schreiner.
Stadium Name: Clipper Magazine Stadium. **Location:** From Route 30, take Fruitville Pike or Harrisburg Pike toward downtown Lancaster, stadium at intersection of Prince Street and Harrisburg Pike. **Standard Game Times:** Mon. through Thurs. 7:00 p.m.; Sat. 6:30 p.m.; Sun. 1:30 p.m.
Visiting Team Hotel: Unavailable.

LONG ISLAND DUCKS

Mailing Address: 3 Court House Dr., Central Islip, NY 11722.
Telephone: (631) 940-3825. **FAX:** (631) 940-3800.
E-Mail Address: info@liducks.com. **Website:** www.liducks.com.
Operated by: Long Island Ducks Professional Baseball, LLC.
Principal Owner/CEO: Frank Boulton. **Owner/Senior Vice President, Baseball Operations:** Bud Harrelson.
General Manager: Michael Pfaff. **Assistant GMs:** Doug Cohen, Alex Scannella. **Manager, Group Sales:** John Wolff. **Director, Administration:** Gerry Anderson. **Director, Merchandise/Operations:** Anthony Barberio. **Manager, Box Office:** Ben Harper. **Manager, Promotions/Sponsorship:** Rob Lyons. **Manager, Media Relations:** Casey Lynn. **Operations Coordinator:** Tim LaMare. **Manager, Ticket Sales:** Brad Kallman. **Manager, Community Relations:** Katie Capria. **Coordinator, Administration:** Missy Lumas. **Account Executives:** Jay Randle, Chris Rufle. **Head Groundskeeper:** Brad Keith. **Clubhouse Manager:** Rich Jensen. **Ticket Assistants:** Joe Devlin, Christopher Stellato.
Manager: Dave LaPoint. **Coaches:** Bud Harrelson, Kevin Baez. **Trainers:** Tony Amin, Adam Lewis, Dorothy Pitchford.

GAME INFORMATION

Radio Announcers: Chris King, Casey Lynn, David Weiss. **No. of Games Broadcast:** 140 on www.liducks.com. **Flagship Station:** Unavailable. **PA Announcer:** Bob Ottone. **Official Scorers:** Joe Donnelly
Stadium Name: Citibank Park. **Location:** Southern State Parkway east to Carleton Avenue North (exit 43 A), right onto Courthouse Drive, stadium behind federal courthouse complex. **Standard Game Times:** 7:05 p.m.; 1:35/5:05 (Sun).
Visiting Club Hotel: Holiday Inn. Long Island Islip Airport, 3845 Veterans Memorial Highway, Ronkonkoma NY 11779. **Telephone:** (631) 585-9500

NEWARK BEARS

Office Address: 450 Broad St., Newark, NJ 07102.
Telephone: (973) 848-1000. **FAX:** (973) 621-0095.
Website: www.newarkbears.com.
Operated by: Bears Baseball, LLC.
General Manager: RC Reuteman. **Assistant General Manager/Ticketing:** Adam Sciorsci.
Business Manager/Comptroller: Tom Phillips. **Corporate Sales Manager:** Stephen Bauer. **Manager, Media Relations/Broadcasting:** David Greenwald. **Community Relations Manager:** Sakinah Abdul-Hakeem.
Manager: Tim Raines. **Coach:** Ron Karkovice.

GAME INFORMATION

Radio Announcer: David Greenwald. **No. of Games Broadcast:** Home-70, Away-70. **Flagship Station:** All-In Internet Broadcasting. **Official Scorer:** Unavailable.
Stadium Name: Bears & Eagles Riverfront Stadium. **Location:** Garden State Parkway North/South to exit 145 (280 East), to exit 15; New Jersey Turnpike North/South to 280 West, to exit 15A. **Standard Game Times:** 11:05 a.m. **(Mon/Tues)**, 6:35 p.m. **(Wed/Thurs)**, 7:05 p.m. **(Fri/Sat)**, 1:35 (Sun). (April-June, September), 1:35 p.m. (July/August).
Visiting Club Hotel: Unavailable.

SOMERSET PATRIOTS

Office Address: One Patriots Park, Bridgewater, NJ 08807. **Telephone:** (908) 252-0700. **FAX:** (908) 252-0776. **Website:** www.somersetpatriots.com.
Operated by: Somerset Patriots Baseball Club, LLC.
Principal Owners: Steve Kalafer, Jack Cust, Byron Brisby, Don Miller. **Chairman:** Steve Kalafer.
President/General Manager: Patrick McVerry. **Senior Vice President, Marketing:** Dave Marek. **VP/Assistant GM:** Rob Lukachyk. **VP, Public Relations:** Marc Russinoff. **VP, Ticketing:** Bryan Iwicki. **Head Groundskeeper:** Ray Cipperly. **Director, Group Sales:** Matt Kopas. **Director, Sales:** Kevin Forrester. **Director, Operations:** Tim Ur. **Corporate Marketing Manager:** Mike Burnett. **Community Relations Manager:** Brian Cahill. **Account Executives:** Robert Crossman, Tom Gibat, Anthony Lugara. **Ticket Sales Manager:** Adam Shakour. **Executive Assistant to GM:** Michele DaCosta. **Controller:** Ron Schulz. **Accountants:** Stephanie Diez, Tom Unchester. **Receptionist:** Lorraine Ott. **GM, Centerplate:** Mike McDermott. **Groundskeeper:** Dan Purner.
Manager: Sparky Lyle. **Director, Player Procurement/Pitching Coach:** Brett Jodie. **Hitting Coach:** Travis Anderson. **Trainer:** Ryan McMahon.

GAME INFORMATION

Radio Announcer: Brian Bender. **No. of Games Broadcast:** Home-70, Away-70. **Flagship Station:** WCTC 1450-AM. **PA Announcer:** Paul Spychala. **Official Scorer:** John Nolan.
Stadium Name: TD Bank Ballpark. **Location:** Route 287 North to exit 13B/Route 287 South to exit 13 (Somerville Route 28 West); follow signs to ballpark. **Standard Game Times:** 7:05 p.m.; Sunday, 1:35
Visiting Club Hotel: Unavailable.

SOUTHERN MARYLAND
BLUE CRABS

Office Address: 11765 St. Linus Dr., Waldorf, MD 20602.
Telephone: 301-638-9788. **Fax:** 301-638-9788.
E-Mail address: info@somdbluecrabs.com. **Website:** www.somdbluecrabs.com.
Principal Owners: Opening Day Partners LLC, Brooks Robinson.
Chairman: Peter Kirk. **President:** Jon Danos. **Controller:** Emily Merrill.
General Manager: Chris Allen. **Director, Finance:** Sheree Ebron. **Director, Ticket Sales:** Kyle Knichel. **Group Sales Executive:** John Watson. **Group Sales Executive:** Jace Gonnerman. **Corporate Sales Executive:** Bill Snitcher. **Corporate Sales Executive:** Candace Gick. **Director, Creative Services:** Chris Deines. **Marketing Manager:** Courtney Freeland. **Director, Media Relations/Broadcasting:** Paul Braverman. **Box Office Manager:** Josh Cockerham. **Box Office Executive/Office Manager:** Tricia Aoki. **Stadium Operations:** Matt Myers. **GM, Centerplate Concessions/Merchandise:** Darren Hubbard. **Centerplate Office Manager/Fundraising Coordinator:** Theresa Thomas. **Centerplate Chef:** Scott Fowler. **Head Groundskeeper:** Tyler Thaler.
Manager: Butch Hobson. **Pitching Coach:** Marty Janzen. **Hitting Coach:** Jeremy Owens (player/coach). **Trainer:** Mia Del Hierro.

GAME INFORMATION

Radio: 140 games, www.somdbluecrabs.com. **Radio Announcer:** Paul Braverman. **Stadium:** Regency Furniture Stadium. **Standard Game Times:** 7:05 p.m., 6:35 p.m.**(Sat)** 2:05/5:05 (Sun).

YORK REVOLUTION

Office Address: 5 Brooks Robinson Way, York, PA 17401.
Telephone: (717) 801-4487. **FAX:** (717) 801-4499.
E-mail Address: info@yorkrevolution.com. **Website:** www.yorkrevolution.com.
Operated by: York Professional Baseball Club, LLC.
Principal Owners: Opening Day Partners.
President: Jon Danos. **Controller:** Emily Merrill.
General Manager: Matt O'Brien. **Assistant GM:** Neil Fortier. **Finance Manager:** Lori Brunson. **Ticketing Director:** Megan Hendon. **Marketing/Promotions Director:** Tim Beckwith. **Corporate Sales Managers:** John Gibson, Mary Beth Ching. **Client Services Associate:** Scott Youcheff. **Facility Operations Manager:** Josh Brown. **Group Events Manager:** Michelle Gemmill. **Group Events Coordinators:** Stephen Barber. **Box Office Manager:** Cindy Burkholder. **Head Groundskeeper:** Brandon Putman. **Centerplate General Manager (Concessions/Merchandise):** Mike Wilson.
Baseball Operations Director: Michael Kirk. **Manager:** Andy Etchebarren. **Pitching Coach:** Mark Mason.

GAME INFORMATION

Radio Announcer: Darrell Henry. **No. of Games Broadcast:** 140. **Flagship Station:** WOYK 1350 AM. **PA Announcer:** Unavailable. **Official Scorer:** Brian Wisler.
Stadium Name: Sovereign Bank Stadium. **Location:** Take Route 30 West to North George Street. Turn left onto North George Street. Follow that straight for four lights, Sovereign Bank Stadium is on left. **Standard Game Times:** TBA
Visiting Club Hotel: The Yorktowne Hotel, 48 E Market St. York, PA 17401. **Telephone:** 717-848-1111.

CAN-AM LEAGUE

Office Address: 1415 Hwy. 54 West, Suite 210, Durham, NC 27707.
Telephone: (919) 401-8150. **Fax:** (919) 401-8152. **Website:** www.canamleague.com.
Year Founded: 2004.
Commissioner: Miles Wolff. **President:** Dan Moushon.
Administrative Assistant: Jason Deans. **Director of Umpires:** Kevin Winn.
Division Structure: None.
Regular Season: 94 games (split schedule).
2010 Opening Date: May 27. **2010 Closing Date:** September 6.
Playoff Format: First and second-half winners meet two teams with best overall records in best-of-five series. Winners meet in best-of-five series for league championship.
Roster Limit: 22. **Eligibility Rule:** Minimum of five first-year players; maximum of four veterans with at least four years of professional experience.
Brand of Baseball: Rawlings.
Statistician: STATS LLC, 2775 Shermer Road, Northbrook, IL 60062.

STADIUM INFORMATION

Club	Stadium	Opened	LF	CF	RF	Capacity	2009 Att.
Brockton	Campanelli Stadium	2002	340	404	320	4,750	112,343
New Jersey	Yogi Berra Stadium	1998	308	398	308	3,784	88,658
Pittsfield	Wahconah Park	1919	334	374	333	4,500	N/A
Quebec	Stade Municipal de Quebec	1938	315	385	315	4,800	164,009
Sussex	Skylands Park	1994	330	392	330	4,300	79,663
Worcester	Hanover Insurance Park-Fitton Field	1905	361	417	307	3,000	78,174

BROCKTON ROX

Office Address: One Feinberg Way, Brockton, MA 02301.
Telephone: (508) 559-7000. **Fax:** (508) 587-2802.
E-Mail: roxfun@brocktonrox.com. **Website:** www.brocktonrox.com.
Principal Owner: Van Schley. **President:** Chris Carminucci. **Executive Vice President:** Michael Canina. **Legal Counsel:** Jack Yunits.
General Manager: Brian Voelkel. **Director, Communications:** Hoffman Wolff. **Groundskeeper:** Tom Hassett.
Manager: Chris Carminucci. **Coach:** Ed Nottle.

GAME INFORMATION

Stadium Name: Campanelli Stadium. **Location:** Route 24 North/South to Route 123 east, stadium is two miles on right.
Standard Game Times: Monday/Tuesday/Saturday, 6:05 p.m.; Wednesday-Friday, 7:05 p.m.; Sunday (May/June), 1:05 p.m. (July/August), 5:05 p.m.
Visiting Club Hotel: Unavailable.

PITTSFIELD

Office Address: 2 South Street, Pittsfield, MA 01201.
Operated By: Baseball All-Stars, LLC.
Principal Owner: Buddy Lewis.
Baseball Operations: Dan Duquette.
Manager: Unavailable.

GAME INFORMATION

Stadium Name: Wahconah Park. **Location: From the west:** 295-E to 41-N to 20-E to Pittsfield, left on Route 7, right on North Street, left on Wahconah Street. **From the east:** Massachusetts Turnpike exit 2 to Route 7, right on North Street, left on Wahconah Street.

NEW JERSEY JACKALS

Office Address: One Hall Dr., Little Falls, NJ 07424.
Telephone: (973) 746-7434. **Fax:** (973) 655-8006.
E-Mail Address: info@jackals.com. **Website:** www.jackals.com.
Operated by: Floyd Hall Enterprises, LLC.
Chairman: Floyd Hall. **President:** Greg Lockard.
General Manager: Larry Hall. **Business Manager:** Jennifer Fertig. **Director, Operations:** Pierson Van Raalte. **Director,**

Sales: Sue Beck. **Facilities Manager:** Aldo Licitra. **Concessions Manager:** Michelle Guarino. **Clubhouse Manager:** Wally Brackett.

Manager: Joe Calfapietra. **Coaches:** Ed Ott, Ani Ramos.

GAME INFORMATION

Announcer (Webcast): Joey Whelan. **No. of Games Broadcast:** 94. **Webcast Address:** www.jackals.com.

Stadium Name: Yogi Berra Stadium. **Location:** Route 80 or Garden State Parkway to Route 46, take Valley Road exit to Montclair State University. **Standard Game Times:** 7:05 p.m.; Sunday, 2:05.

Visiting Club Hotel: Ramada Inn, 130 Rte. 10 West, East Hanover, NJ 07936. **Telephone:** (973) 386-5622.

QUEBEC CAPITALES

Office Address: 100 Rue du Cardinal Maurice-Roy, Quebec City, QC G1K8Z1.

Telephone: (418) 521-2255. **Fax:** (418) 521-2266.

E-Mail Address: baseball@capitalesdequebec.com. **Website:** www.capitalesdequebec.com.

Owner/President: Miles Wolff.

General Manager: Alex Harvey. **Vice Presidents:** Michel Laplante, Stephane Dionne. **Sales Director:** Maxime Lamarche. **Promotions Director:** Jean-Phillip Auger. **Media Relations Director:** Pier-Luc Nappert. **Sales Representative:** Jean Marois.

Manager: Michel Laplante. **Coaches:** Patrick Scalabrini.

GAME INFORMATION

Radio Announcers: Jacques Doucet, Francois Paquet. **No. of Games Broadcast:** 94. **Flagship Station:** Quebec 800-AM. **Webcast Address:** www.info800.ca.

Stadium Name: Stade Municipal de Quebec. **Location:** Highway 40 to Highway 173 (Centre-Ville) exit 2 to Parc Victoria.

Standard Game Times: 7:05 p.m.; Sunday, 1:05 p.m.

Visiting Club Hotel: Hotel du Nord, 640 St. Vallier Ouest, Quebec City, QC G1N1C5. **Telephone:** (418) 522-1554.

SUSSEX SKYHAWKS

Office Address: 94 Championship Place Suite 11, Augusta, NJ 07822.

Telephone: (973) 300-1000. **Fax:** (973) 300-9000.

E-Mail Address: info@sussexskyhawks.com. **Website:** www.sussexskyhawks.com.

Operated By: Sussex Professional Baseball, LLC.

President: Larry Hall.

General Manager: Ben Wittkowski. **Director, Corporate Sales:** Laura Temple-Brockmann. **Director, Ticket Sales/Operations:** Matt Myers. **Concessions Manager:** Michelle Guarino. **Facility Manager:** Aldo Licitra.

Manager: Unavailable.

GAME INFORMATION

Stadium Name: Skylands Park. **Location:** From New Jersey, I-80 to exit 34B (Rt. 15 N) to Route 565; From Pennsylvania, I-84 to Route 6 to Route 206 North to Route 565 East.

Standard Game Times: 7:05 p.m.; 5:05 (Sat); 2:05 (Sun).

Visiting Club Hotel: Ramada Inn, 130 Rte. 10 West, East Hanover, NJ 07936. **Telephone:** (973) 386-5622.

WORCESTER TORNADOES

Office Address: 303 Main St., Worcester, MA 01613.

Telephone: (508) 792-2288. **Fax:** (506) 926-3662.

E-Mail Address: info@worcestertornadoes.com. **Website:** www.worcestertornadoes.com.

General Manager: Jorg Bassiacos. **VP/Director, Sales:** Dave Peterson. **Director, Broadcasting:** Pete Sachs. **Director, Communications:** Mike Tetler. **Director, Group Sales:** Miriam Hyder. **Ticket Manager:** Alise Wales. **Director, Stadium Operations:** Chris Leach. **Senior Account Executive:** Sarah Farley. **Account Executives:** Chase Milanese, Jonathan Way.

Manager: Rich Gedman. **Coaches:** Roger LaFrancois and Ed Gallagher. **Director, Player Personnel:** Brad Michals.

GAME INFORMATION

Radio Announcer: Pete Sachs. **No. of Games Broadcast:** 94. **Flagship Station:** WTAG 580-AM. **Webcast Address:** www.worcestertornadoes.com.

Stadium Name: Hanover Insurance Park at Fitton Field. **Location:** I-290 to exit 11 College Square, right on College Street, left on Fitton Avenue.

Standard Game Times: 7:05 p.m.; 2:05 (Sun).

Visiting Club Hotel: Quality Inn & Suites, 50 Oriol Drive, Worcester, MA 01605. **Telephone:** 508-852-2800. **Fax:** 508-852-4605.

FRONTIER LEAGUE

Office Address: 2041 Goose Lake Rd. Suite 2A, Sauget, Il. 62206.
Mailing Address: Same as above.
Telephone: (618) 215-4134. **FAX:** (618) 332-2115.
E-Mail Address: office@frontierleague.com. **Website:** www.frontierleague.com.
Year Founded: 1993.
Commissioner: Bill Lee.
Chairman: Dr. Chris Hanners.
President: Rich Sauget (Gateway). **Vice Presidents:** Clint Brown (Florence) Mike Stranczek (Windy City).
Corporate Secretary/Treasurer: Bob Wolfe.
Deputy Commissioner: Steve Tahsler.
Directors: Clint Brown (Florence), Bill Bussing (Evansville), Steven Edelson (Lake Erie), Erik Haag (Southern Illinois), Rob Hilliard (Oakland County), Steve Malliet (River City/Normal), Bill Wright (Kalamazoo), Rich Sauget (Gateway), Mike Stranczek (Windy City), Stu Williams (Washington), Leslye Wuerfel (Traverse City).
Division Structure: East— Kalamazoo, Lake Erie, Oakland County, Traverse City, Washington, Windy City **West—** Evansville, Florence, Gateway, River City, Rockford, Southern Illinois.
Regular Season: 96 games. **2010 Opening Date:** May 20. **Closing Date:** Sept. 5.
All-Star Game: July 14 at Southern Illinois.
Playoff Format: Top 2 teams in each Division will meet in best-of-five semifinal series. Winners meet in best-of-five series for league championship.
Roster Limit: 24. **Eligibility Rule:** Minimum of eleven Rookie 1 or Rookie 2 players; maximum of seven players with one year of professional experience, maximum of three players with two years of experience and maximum of three players with three or more years of experience. No player may be 27 prior to Jan. 1 of current season with the exeption of one player that may not be 30 years of age prior to Jan. 1 of the current season.
Brand of Baseball: Wilson.
Statistician: SportsTicker, 55 Reality Drive, Suite 200, Cheshire, CT 06410.

STADIUM INFORMATION

Club	Stadium	Opened	Dimensions			Capacity	2009 Att.
			LF	CF	RF		
Evansville	Bosse Field	1915	315	415	315	5,181	104,829
Florence	Champion Window Field	2004	325	395	325	4,200	102,086
Gateway	GCS Ballpark	2002	318	395	325	5,500	175,720
Kalamazoo	Homer Stryker Field	1995	306	400	330	4,806	70,499
Lake Erie	All-Pro Freight	2009	325	400	325	5,000	153,654
Midwest	Unavailable	2010	N/A	N/A	N/A	N/A	20,252
Oakland County	Diamond at The Summit	2010	N/A	N/A	N/A	N/A	N/A
River City	T.R. Hughes Ballpark	1999	320	382	299	4,989	106,114
So. Illinois	Rent One Park	2007	325	400	330	4,500	218,191
Traverse City	Wuerfel Park	2006	320	400	320	4,600	193,724
Washington	Consol Energy Park	2002	325	400	325	3,200	154,444
Windy City	Standard Bank Stadium	1999	335	390	335	4,000	90,616

EVANSVILLE OTTERS

Mailing Address: 1701 N. Main St., Evansville, IN 47711.
Telephone: (812) 435-8686.
Operated by: Evansville Baseball, LLC.
President: Bill Bussing.
Senior Vice President: Pat Rayburn. **General Manager:** Liam Miller. **Assistant GM:** Casie Williams. **Operations Manager/Account Executive:** Brandon McClish. Manager/Director, Baseball Operations: Wayne Krenchicki. Coaches: Steve Foucault, Ryan Jones.

GAME INFORMATION
Radio Announcer: Unavailable. **No. of Games Broadcast:** Home-48, Away-48. **Flagship Station:** WUEV 91.5-FM. **PA Announcer:** Unavailable. **Official Scorer:** Unavailable.
Stadium Name: Bosse Field. **Location:** U.S. 41 to Lloyd Expressway West (IN-62), Main St. Exit, Right on Main St., ahead 1 mile to Bosse Field. **Standard Game Times:** 7:05 p.m.; Sunday, 6:05 p.m.
Visiting Club Hotel: Unavailable.

FLORENCE FREEDOM

Office Address: 7950 Freedom Way, Florence, KY 41042.
Telephone: (859) 594-4487. **FAX:** (859) 594-3194.

E-Mail Address: info@florencefreedom.com. **Website:** www.florencefreedom.com.
Operated by: Canterbury Baseball, LLC.
President: Clint Brown. **General Manager:** Kari Rumfield. **Director, Community Relations:** Kim Brown. **Box Office Manager:** Sarah Straughn. **Stadium Operations Manager:** Stephen Mace. **Director, Ticket Sales:** Elizabeth Quatman. **Promotions Manager:** Alyssa Meyer.
Baseball Operations/Manager: Toby Rumfield. **Coach:** Greg Stone. **Pitching Coach:** James Frisbie. **Trainer:** Chris Unkraut.

GAME INFORMATION
Flagship Station: 106.7 WNKR. **Radio Broadcaster:** Josh Anderson. **PA Announcer:** Kevin Schwab. **Official Scorer:** Unavailable.
Stadium: Champion Window Field. **Location:** I-71/75 South to exit 180, left onto US 42, right on Freedom Way; I-71/75 North to exit 180. **Standard Game Times:** 7:05 p.m.; 6:05 (Sat); 2:05/6:05 (Sun)
Visiting Club Hotel: Wildwood Inn.

GATEWAY GRIZZLIES

Mailing Address: 2301 Grizzlie Bear Blvd., Sauget, IL 62206.
Telephone: (618) 337-3000. **FAX:** (618) 332-3625.
E-Mail Address: grizzlies@accessus.net. **Website:** www.gatewaygrizzlies.com.
Operated by: Gateway Baseball, LLC.
Managing Officer: Richard Sauget.
General Manager: Steven Gomric. **Director, Group Sales:** Jason Murphy. **Ticket Operations:** Brent Pownall. **Media Relations Director/Events Coordinator:** Jeff O'Neill. **Director, Sales:** C.J. Hendrickson. **Director, Stadium Operations:** Josh LeMasters. **Director, Promotions:** Craig Dohm. **Ticket Sales Associates:** Jeremy Thorpe, Steven Gonzalez. **Director, Merchandise:** Lauren Jones.
Manager: Phil Warren. **Pitching Coach:** Randy Martz. **Bench Coach:** Darin Kinsolving. **Trainer:** Geof Manzo. **Clubhouse Manager:** Chris Majerchin.

GAME INFORMATION
Radio Announcer: Joe Pott. **No of Games Broadcast:** Home-48, Away-48. **Flagship Station:** 590-AM KFNS. **PA Announcer:** Tom Calhoun. **Official Scorer:** Matthew Frey.
Stadium Name: GCS Ballpark. **Location:** I-255 at exit 15 (Mousette Lane). **Standard Game Times:** 7:05 p.m.; 6:05/3:05 (Sun).
Visiting Club Hotel: Ramada Inn, 6900 N. Illinois St., Fairview Heights, IL 62208. **Telephone:** (618) 632-4747.

KALAMAZOO KINGS

Mailing Address: 251 Mills St., Kalamazoo, MI 49048.
Telephone: (269) 388-8326. **FAX:** (269) 388-8333.
Website: www.kalamazookings.com.
Operated by: Team Kalamazoo, LLC. **Owners:** Bill Wright, Mike Seelye, Pat Seelye, Joe Rosenhagen, Ed Bernard, Scott Hocevar. **President/Managing Partner:** Bill Wright. **Assistant GM:** Ryan LaPorte. **Director, Community Relations:** Chris Peake. **VP, Baseball Operations:** Eric Volann. **Director, Sales/Game Day Operations:** Dan Wiener. **Account Executive:** Matt Holden. **Ticket Office Manager:** Gary Watson.
Field Manager/Director, Player Personnel: Jamie Keefe. **Groundskeeper:** Jim Greene. **Clubhouse Manager:** Jason Sulen.

GAME INFORMATION
Radio Announcers: Unavailable. **No. of Games Broadcast:** Home-48, Away-48. **Flagship Station:** Unavailable. **PA Announcer:** Unavailable. **Official Scorer:** Unavailable.
Stadium Name: Homer Stryker Field. **Location:** I-94 to Sprinkle Road (exit 80), north on Sprinkle Road, left on Business Loop I-94, left on Kings Highway, right on Mills Street.
Standard Game Times: 7:05 p.m.; Sunday, 2:05 p.m.
Visiting Club Hotel: Unavailable.

LAKE ERIE CRUSHERS

Mailing Address: 2009 Baseball Blvd., Avon, OH, 44011.
Telephone: (440) 934-3636. **FAX:** (440) 934-2458.
E-Mail Address: info@lakeeriecrushers.com. **Website:** www.lakeeriecrushers.com.
Operated by: Avon Pro Baseball LLC.
Managing Officer: Steven Edelson.
General Manager: Ryan Gates. **Assistant GM, Operations:** Paul Siegwarth. **Business Manager:** Jen Doan. **Box Office Manager:** Kelly Dolan. **Director, Creative Services:** Nicolle Meyer. **Director, Sales:** Randy Newell. **Account Executives:**

Derek Stapinski, Zack Krantz. **Director, Merchandise:** Dan Helm.
Manager: John Massarelli. **Pitching Coach:** Chris Steinborn. **Hitting Coach:** Dave Schaub.

GAME INFORMATION
Stadium Name: All Pro Freight Stadium. **Location:** Intersection of I-90 and Colorado Ave. in Avon, OH. **Standard Game Times:** 7:05 p.m.; 5:05 (Sun).

NORMAL CORNBELTERS

Mailing Address:1000 West RAAB Road, Normal, IL 61761.
Telephone: 309-454-2255(BALL). **Fax:** 309- 454-2287(BATS).
Ownership: Normal Baseball Group.
President: Steve Malliet. **Director, Ticket Sales:** Zach Ziller. **Ticket Operations Manager:** Mchael Schulte. **Ticket Sales Managers:** Joe Rejc, Bradley Vitale. **Business Manager:** Heather Manint. **Community Relations Manager:** Jon Young.
Field Manager: Hal Lanier. **Pitching Coach:** Brook Casey. **Hitting Coach:** Josh Patton.
Radio Announcer: Unavailable. **Flagship Station:** WTRX 93.7FM The Oldies Channel. **No. of Games Broadcast:** Home—48, Away—48.
Standard Game Times: 7 p.m. 5 (Sun). **Stadium Name:** The Corn Crib. **Location:** From I-55 North, Go South on I-55 and take the 165 exit (Heartland College). Turn Left at light. Turn right on Raab road to ballpark on right; From South, go north on I-55 and take the 165 exit (Heartland). Turn right on Route 51 (Main street). Turn right on Raab road to ballpark on right.
Visiting Team Hotel: The Chateau.

OAKLAND COUNTY CRUISERS

Mailing Address: P.O. Box 981408, Ypsilanti MI 48198.
E-mail Address: info@cruisersbaseball.com. **Website:** www.midwestsliders.com.
Operated By: Baseball Heroes of Oakland County, LP.
President/Director, Team Personnel: Rob Hilliard. **Executive Vice President, Business Development:** Tim Birtsas. **Senior Vice President, Merchandising:** Tim Nick. **Vice President, Operations:** Bob Vita. **Director, Sales/Customer Relations:** Jerry Garland. **Manager, OC Cruisers Baseball Academy:** Matt Dillard. **Director, Transportation:** George Hamilton.

RIVER CITY RASCALS

Office Address: 900 T.R. Hughes Blvd., O'Fallon, MO 63366.
Telephone: (636) 240-2287. **FAX:** (636) 240-7313.
E-Mail Address: info@rivercityrascals.com. **Website:** www.rivercityrascals.com.
Operated by: PS and J Professional Baseball Club LLC. **Owners:** Tim Hoeksema, Jan Hoeksema, Fred Stratton, Anne Stratton, Pam Malliet, Steve Malliet, Michael Veeck.
Vice President/General Manager: Chris Franklin. **Business Manager:** Michelle Stuckey. **Senior Director, Ticket Sales:** Zach Prehn. **GM, Aramark Sports/Entertainment Services:** Mark Duffy.
Team Manager: Unavailable. **Pitching Coach:** Unavailable. **Bench Coach:** Steve Brook.

GAME INFORMATION
Radio Announcer: Unavailable. **No. of Games Broadcast:** Home-48, Away-48. **Flagship Station:** 590 The FAN KFNS. **PA Announcer:** Unavailable. **Official Scorer:** Unavailable.
Stadium Name: T.R. Hughes Ballpark. **Location:** I-70 to exit 219, north on T.R. Hughes Road, follow signs to ballpark.
Standard Game Times: 7:05 p.m.; 6:05 (Sun).
Visiting Club Hotel: Hilton Garden Inn, 2310 Technology Drive, O'Fallon, MO 63368, (636) 625-2700

SOUTHERN ILLINOIS MINERS

Office Address: Rent One Park, 1000 Miners Drive, Marion, IL 62959.
Telephone: (618) 998-8499. **Fax:** (618) 969-8550.
E-Mail Address: info@southernillinoisminers.com. **Website:** www.southernillinoisminers.com.
Operated by: Southern Illinois Baseball Group.
Vice President: Erik Haag. **General Manager:** Tim Arseneau. **Assistant GM:** Billy Richards. **Director, Ticket Operations:** Kyle Bass. **Manager, Client Services:** Sarah Chamness. **Director, Media Relations/Broadcasting:** Scott Gierman. **Team Merchandise:** Justin Moore. **Director, Finance:** Cathy Perry. **Director, Stadium Operations:** Billy Peterman. **Operations/Clubhouse Manager:** Jeff Pink. **Account Executives:** Jennifer Wade, Dennis Watson.
Manager: Mike Pinto. **Pitching Coach:** Bart Zeller. **Hitting Coach:** Ralph Santana. **Coach:** Ron Biga.

GAME INFORMATION

Radio Announcer: Scott Gierman. **No. of Games Broadcast:** 96. **Flagship Station:** 97.7 WQUL-FM. **Stadium Name:** Rent One Park. **Location:** US 57 to Route 13 East, right at Halfway Road to Fairmont Dr. **Standard Game Times:** 7:05 p.m.; Sunday, 5:05 p.m.

Visiting Club Hotel: Econo Lodge, 1806 Bittle Place, Marion, IL 62959.

TRAVERSE CITY BEACH BUMS

Office Address: 333 Stadium Dr., Traverse City, MI 49684.
Telephone: (231) 943-0100. **FAX:** (231) 943-0900.
E-Mail Address: info@tcbeachbums.com. **Website:** www.traversecitybeachbums.com.
Operated by: Traverse City Beach Bums, LLC.
Managing Partners: John Wuerfel, Leslye Wuerfel, Jason Wuerfel.
President/CEO: John Wuerfel. **General Manager:** Leslye Wuerfel. **Vice President:** Jason Wuerfel. **Director, Sales/ Marketing:** Jeremy Crum. **Director, Concessions:** Tom Goethel III. **Director, Merchandise:** Scott McDowell. **Director, Ticketing:** Stephen Toth. **Director, Broadcasting:** Tim Calderwood.
Manager: Gregg Langbehn. **Hitting Coach:** Unavailable. **Pitching Coach:** Unavailable. **Clubhouse Manager:** Denny Dame. **Trainer:** Unavailable.

GAME INFORMATION

Radio Announcer: Tim Calderwood. **No. of Games Broadcast:** Home-48, Away-48. **Flagship Stations:** WFCX 94.3-FM; WFDX 92.5-FM. **PA. Announcer:** Tim Moeggenberg. **Official Scorer:** Greg Rosinski.
Stadium Name: Wuerfel Park. **Location:** 3 miles south of the Grand Traverse Mall just off US-31 and M-37 in Chums Village. Stadium is visible from the highway (Or north of US 31 and M-37 Chums Corner intersection). Turn-west on Chums Village Drive, north on Village Park Drive, right on Stadium Drive. **Standard Game Times:** 7:05 p.m.; 5:35 (Sun).
Visiting Club Hotel: Days Inn & Suites of Traverse City.

WASHINGTON WILD THINGS

Office Address: One Washington Federal Way, Washington, PA 15301.
Telephone: (724) 250-9555. **FAX:** (724) 250-2333.
E-Mail Address: info@washingtonwildthings.com . **Website:** www.washingtonwildthings.com.
Owned by: Sports Facility, LLC. **Operated by:** Washington Frontier League Baseball, LLC.
Managing Partner: John Swiatek.
President/Chief Executive Officer: John Swiatek.
General Manager: Ross Vecchio. **Director, Marketing:** Christine Blaine. **Director. Stadium Operations:** Steve Zavacky. **Sponsorship Account Executive:** Rick Minetti. **Box Office Manager:** Geoff Nilsen. **Merchandise Manager:** Ashley Nichol. **Ticket Account Executives:** Phil Dillon, Carissa Diethorn, Dave Wojtkowski, Greg Smith, Tammy Pirone.
Manager: Unavailable. **Coach:** Bob Bozzuto. **Hitting Coach:** Jon Cahill.

GAME INFORMATION

Radio Announcer: Unavailable. **No. of Games Broadcast:** Home-50, Away-45. **Flagship Station:** WJPA 95.3-FM . **PA Announcer:** Unavailable. **Official Scorer:** Unavailable.
Stadium Name: CONSOL Energy Park. **Location:** I-70 to exit 15 (Chestnut Street), right on Chestnut Street to Washington Crown Center Mall, right at mall entrance, right on to Mall Drive to stadium. **Standard Game Times:** 7:05 p.m.; 6:35 (Sun).
Visiting Club Hotel: Unavailable.

WINDY CITY THUNDERBOLTS

Office Address: 14011 South Kenton Ave., Crestwood, IL 60445-2252.
Telephone: (708) 489-2255. **FAX:** (708) 489-2999.
E-Mail Address: info@wcthunderbolts.com. **Website:** www.wcthunderbolts.com.
Owned by: Crestwood Professional Baseball, LLC.
General Manager: Mike Lucas. **Diretor Food/Beverage:** Adam Gorniak. **Director, Community Relations:** Kathy Jermal. **Director, Fundraising/Head Groundskeeper:** Mike VerSchave.
Field Manager: Mike Kashirsky. **Pitching Coach:** Billy Bryk. **Hitting Coach:** Marcus Nettles. **Bench Coach:** Pascual Santiago.

GAME INFORMATION

Radio Announcers: Unavailable. **No. of Games Broadcast:** 96. **Flagship Station:** WXAV, 88.3 FM. **PA Announcer:** Unavailable. **Official Scorer:** Unavailable.
Stadium Name: Standard Bank Stadium. **Location:** I-294 to S. Cicero Ave., exit (Route 50), south for 1 1/2 miles, left at Midlothian Turnpike, right on Kenton Ave.; I-57 to 147th Street, west on 147th to Cicero, north on Cicero, right on Midlothian Turnpike, right on Kenton. **Standard Game Times:** 7:05 p.m.; 6:05 (Sun).
Visiting Club Hotel: Georgio's Comfort Inn, 8800 W. 159th St., Orland Park, IL 60462. **Telephone:** (708) 403-1100. **Fax:** (708) 403-1105.

GOLDEN LEAGUE

Office Address: 6111 Bollinger Canyon Road, Suite 580, San Ramon, CA 94583.
Telephone: (925) 302-7378. **FAX:** (925) 302-7375.
E-mail Address: info@goldenbaseball.com. **Website:** www.goldenbaseball.com.
Founded: 2005.
CEO/President: David Kaval.
Commissioner/COO: Kevin Outcalt. **Vice President/Operations:** Curt Jacey. **Director, Administration:** Stephen Bedford. **League Historian/Secretary:** Bill Weiss. **Supervisor, Officials:** Dan Perugini.
Division Structure: North—Edmonton, Calgary, Chico, Victoria, St. George. South—Tucson, Tijuana, Orange County, Maui, Yuma.
Regular Season: 90 games.
2010 Opening Date: May 21. **Closing Date:** Sep. 6.
Playoff Format: First- and second-half division winners meet in best-of-five semifinals; winners meet in championship series.
Roster Limit: 22. **Eligibility Rules:** No minimum number of rookies, age limit of 28 as of Jan. 1 unless player has major league, Triple-A, Double-A, top foreign or former GBL experience.
Brand of Baseball: Rawlings
Statistician: Pointstreak, www.pointstreak.com.

STADIUM INFORMATION

Club	Stadium	Opened	LF	CF	RF	Capacity	2009 Att.
Calgary	Foothills Stadium	1966	345	400	325	8,000	54,910
Chico	Nettleton Stadium	1997	330	405	330	4,400	89,276
Edmonton	TELUS Field	1995	340	420	420	9,200	484,813
*Maui	Iron Maehara Stadium	1973	330	400	330	3,500	N/A
Orange County	Goodwin Field	1992	330	400	330	3,500	28,344
*Tijuana	Calimax Stadium	1976	340	395	340	14,000	N/A
Tucson	Hi Corbett Field	1937	366	392	348	9,500	139,149
St.George	Bruce Hurst Field	1994	340	390	335	3,000	44,417
Victoria Royal	Athletic Park	1967	320	415	335	9,247	93,691
Yuma	Desert Sun Stadium	1969	335	410	335	7,100	41,578

*New franchises for 2010.

CALGARY VIPERS

Address: 2255 Crowchild Trail NW, Calgary, Alberta, Canada T2M4S7.
Telephone: (403) 277-2255
E-Mail Address: johnconrad@calgaryvipers.com. **Website:** www.calgaryvipers.com.
President/Chief Operating Officer: John Conrad. **Facilities Director:** Rick enner. **Senior Accountant:** John Kirkbride. **Director, Absolute Baseball Academy:** Neil Gidney. **Media Relations:** Patrich Haas. **Administrative Assistance:** Jaylene Church
Manager: Morgan Burkhart. **Coach:** Boots Day. **Pitching Coach:** Unavailable.

GAME INFORMATION

Radio Announcer: Patrick Haas. **No. of Games Broadcast:** Home-45 Away-45. **Flagship Station:** AM 770 CHQR. **PA Announcer:** Kramer. **Official Scorer:** Darcy Leitz/Gord Siminon.
Stadium Name: Foothills Athletic Park. **Standard Game Times:** 7:05 p.m., Sat. 5:05, Sun. 1:35.
Visiting Club Hotel: Unavailable.

CHICO OUTLAWS

Office Address: 313 Walnut Street, Suite 110, Chico, CA. 95928
Telephone: (530) 345-3210.
E-Mail Address: cjacey@goldenbaseball.com. **Website:** www.chicooutlawsbaseball.com.
Owner: Diamond Sports & Entertainment. **General Manager:** Curt Jacey.
Manager: Garry Templeton.

GAME INFORMATION

Radio Announcer: Unavailable. **No. of Games Broadcast:** Home-45, Away-45. **Flagship Station:** Unavailable.
PA Announcer: Unavailable. **Official Scorer:** Unavailable.
Stadium Name: Nettleton Stadium. **Location:** California 99 North to California 32 West/East Eighth Street, right on Main Street, left on West First Street; stadium at 400 West First Street. **Standard Game Times:** 7:05 p.m., Sun. 1:05.
Visiting Club Hotel: Unavailable.

EDMONTON CRACKER CATS

Address: 10233-96 Avenue, Edmonton, Alberta, Canada T5K0A5.
Telephone: (780) 423-2255.
E-Mail Address: teaminfo@crackercats.ca. **Website:** www.crackercats.ca
Owner: Katz Baseball Corporation.
General Manager: Craig Tkachuk
Manager: Brent Bowers. **Coach:** Unavailable. **Pitching Coach:** Unavailable.

GAME INFORMATION

Radio Announcer: N/A. **No. of Games Broadcast:** Home-45 Away-45. **Flagship Station:** Unavailable.
PA Announcer: Unavailable. **Official Scorer:** Unavailable.
Stadium Name: Telus Field. **From North:** 101st Street to 96th Ave. Left on 96th, 1 block East. **From South:** Take Calgary Trail North to Queen Elizabeth Hill, make a right across Walterdale Bridge, and then a right on 96th Avenue.
Standard Game Times: 7:05 p.m., Sun. 1:35.
Visiting Club Hotel: Sutton Place Hotel, 10235-101st Street, Edmonton, Alberta, Canada T5J3E9 (780) 428-7111.

NA IKAIKA KOA MAUI

Address: 700 Halia Nakoa Street, Wailuku, Maui, HI
Telephone: (808)270-7389
Owners: XnE, Inc.
E-Mail Address: rberry@goldenbaseball.com. **Website:** N/A.
President: Michael Cummings. **General Manager:** Rick Berry.
Manager: Cory Snyder. **Coach:** Unavailable. **Pitching Coach:** Unavailable.

GAME INFORMATION

Radio Announcer: Unavailable. **No. of Games Broadcast:** Away-44. **Flagship Station:** KBLU 560-AM. **PA Announcer:** Virgil Tudor. **Official Scorer:** Greg Abbott.
Stadium Name: Iron Maehara Stadium. **Location:** 700 Halia Nakoa Street, Wailuku, HI. Maui.
Standard Game Times: 7:05 p.m., Sun. 1:05.
Visiting Club Hotel: N/A.

ORANGE COUNTY FLYERS

Office Address: 2461 E. Orangethorpe, Suite 102, Fullerton, CA 92831.
Telephone: (714) 526-8326.
E-Mail Address: amintz@orangecountyflyers.com. **Website:** www.orangecountyflyers.
com
President/GM: Dan MacLeith. **Director, Player Personnel:** Harris Tulchin.
Manager: Paul Abbott. **Coach:** Unavailable. **Pitching Coach:** Unavailable.

GAME INFORMATION

Radio: FM 90.1 KBPK; www.SportsNetUSA.net. **PA Announcer:** Unavailable. **Official Scorer:** Unavailable.
Stadium Name: Goodwin Field. **Location:** From Orange Freeway, take Yorba Linda Blvd. Exit, west on Yorba Linda, left on Associated Road to parking lot G. **Standard Game Times:** 7:05 p.m.; Sunday, 1:05 p.m.
Visiting Club Hotel: Holiday Inn Express, Placentia, 118 E Orangethorpe Ave, Placentia, CA 92870 714-528-7778.

TUCSON TOROS

Office Address: 2919 E. Broadway, Suite 200, Tucson, AZ 85716.
Telephone: (520) 322-6989.
E-Mail Address: jay@tucsontoros.com . **Website:** www.tucsontoros.com
Owner: Jay Zucker.
General Manager: Sean Smock. **Media Contact:** Landon Q. Vincent.
Manager: Tim Johnson. **Coach:** Unavailable. **Pitching Coach:** Unavailable.

GAME INFORMATION

Radio: COOL 1450 AM. **PA Announcer:** Dale Lopez. **Official Scorer:** Unavailable.
Stadium Name: Hi Corbett Field. **Standard Game Times:** 7:05 p.m.; Sunday, 1:05 p.m.
Visiting Club Hotel: Unavailable

ST. GEORGE ROAD RUNNERS

Office Address: 216 W. St. George Blvd, Suite A, St. George, Utah 84770.
Telephone: (435) 673-5333.
E-Mail Address: rberry@goldenbaseball.com. **Website:** www.stgeorgeroadrunners.com.
Owner: Hot Corner Baseball, LLC
General Manager: Rick Berry.
Manager: Unavailable. **Pitching Coach:** Unavailable. **Hitting Coach:** Unavailable

GAME INFORMATION
Radio Announcer: John Potter. **No. of Games Broadcast:** Home-45, Away-45. **Flagship Station:** 1210 AM ESPN. **PA Announcer:** Ed Rogers. **Official Scorer:** Jeff Clough.
Stadium Name: Bruce Hurst Field. **Location:** 225 South 700 East Saint George, UT. **Standard Game Times:** 7:05 p.m.
Visiting Club Hotels: Budget Inn & Suites, Comfort Suites, Holiday Inn, Ramada Inn, and Hilton Garden Inn all in St. George, Utah.

TIJUANA CIMARRONES

Address: Unavailable.
Telephone: Unavailable
E-Mail Address: Unavailable. **Website:** Unavailable.
Owner/General Manager: Florention Rosas
Manager: Unavailable. **Coach:** Unavailable. **Pitching Coach:** Unavailable.

GAME INFORMATION
Radio Announcer: Unavailable. **No. of Games Broadcast:** Away-45, Home - 45. **Flagship Station:** Unavailable. **PA Announcer:** Unavailable. **Official Scorer:** Unavailable.
Stadium Name: Calimax Stadium. **Location:** Standard Game Times: 7:05 p.m., Sun. 1:05.
Visiting Club Hotel: Unavailable

VICTORIA SEALS

Address: 1014 Caledonia Avenue, Victoria, BC, CAN V8T1G1.
Telephone: (250)480-4487.
E-Mail Address: darren@victoriaseals.ca. **Website:** www.victoriaseals.ca.
Owner: Darren Parker, Russ Parker.
General Manager: Roxann Bury.
Manager: Darrell Evans. **Coach:** Unavailable. **Pitching Coach:** Unavailable.

GAME INFORMATION
Radio Announcer: Unavailable. **No. of Games Broadcast:** Away-45. **Flagship Station:** Unavailable. **PA Announcer:** Unavailable. **Official Scorer:** Unavailable.
Stadium Name: Royal Athletic Park. **Standard Game Times:** 7:05 p.m., Sun. 1:05.
Visiting Club Hotel: Unavailable.

YUMA SCORPIONS

Address: 1280 W. Desert Sun Dr., Yuma, AZ 85366.
Telephone: (928) 257-4700.
E-Mail Address: mmarshall@goldenbaseball.com. **Website:** www.yumascorpions.com.
General Manager: Mike Marshall. **Director, Operations:** Mary Marshall.
Manager: Mike Marshall. **Coach:** Unavailable. **Pitching Coach:** Unavailable.

GAME INFORMATION
Radio Announcer: Unavailable. **No. of Games Broadcast:** Away-44. **Flagship Station:** KBLU 560-AM. **PA Announcer:** Virgil Tudor. **Official Scorer:** Greg Abbott.
Stadium Name: Desert Sun Stadium. **Location:** From I-8, take Fourth Avenue or 16th Street exit to Avenue A. **Standard Game Times:** 7:05 p.m., Sun. 1:05.
Visiting Club Hotel: Ramada Inn. 300 East 32nd Street. Yuma, AZ 85364. 928-344-1050.

NORTHERN LEAGUE

Office Addresses: 80 South Eighth Street, Suite 4920, Minneapolis, MN 55402 (Commissioner); One Mayor Art Schultz Dr, Joliet, IL 60432 (Treasurer); PO Box 1588, Soquel, CA 95073 (Director, Baseball Operations). **Telephone:** (612) 338-9097. **Fax:** (612) 338-9098. **Email:** commissioner@northernleague.com, baseballoperations@northernleague.com. **Website:** www.northern-league.com
Founded: 1993
Commissioner: Clark Griffith. **Director, Baseball Operations:** Harry Stavrenos.
Directors: John Ehlert (Kansas City), Rich Ehrenreich (Schaumburg/Lake County), John Costello (Joliet), Sam Katz (Winnipeg), Pat Salvi (Gary), Bruce Thom (Fargo) Kurt Carlson/Dave Ciarrachi (Rockford).
Regular Season: 100 games.
2010 Opening Date: May 20. **Closing Date:** Sept. 6.
All-Star Game: July 14 at Hi Corbett Field, Tucson, Ariz. vs Golden Baseball League.
Playoff Format: Top four teams meet in best-of-five semifinal series. Winners meet in best-of-five championship.
Brand of Baseball: Rawlings
Statistician: Stats, LLC.

STADIUM INFORMATION

| Club | Stadium | Opened | Dimensions | | | Capacity | 2009 Att. |
			LF	CF	RF		
Gary	Newman Outfoor Field	1996	318	400	318	4,513	166,334
Fargo-Moorhead	U.S. Steel Yard	2003	320	400	335	6,139	181,872
Joliet	Silver Cross Field	2002	330	400	327	4,616	146,258
Kansas City	Community America Ballpark	2003	300	396	328	4,365	245,625
Lake County	Fielders Stadium	2010	325	400	330	8,000	N/A
Schaumburg	Alexian Field	1999	355	400	353	7,048	202,112
Winnipeg	CanWest Global Park	1999	325	400	325	7,481	278,099

FARGO-MOORHEAD REDHAWKS

Office Address: 1515 15th Ave. N., Fargo, ND 58102.
Telephone: (701) 235-6161. **FAX:** (701) 297-9247.
E-Mail Address: redhawks@fmredhawks.com. **Website:** www.fmredhawks.com.
Operated by: Fargo Baseball LLC.
President: Bruce Thom. **Chief Executive Officer:** Brad Thom.
General Manager: Josh Buchholz. **Assistant GM/Promotions:** Megan Salic. **Senior Accountant:** Sue Wild. **Director, Stadium Operations:** Eric Jorgenson. **Director, Ticket Sales:** Michael Larson. **Director, Group Sales:** Karl Hoium. **Director, Food/Beverage:** Sean Kiernan. **Head Sports Turf Manager:** Matt Wallace.
Manager/Director, Player Procurement: Doug Simunic. **Player Procurement Consultant:** Jeff Bittiger. **Pitching Coach:** Steve Montgomery. **Coaches:** Bucky Burgau, Robbie Lopez. **Trainer:** Mike Bogenreif. **Clubhouse Operations:** Matt Gastecki.

GAME INFORMATION
Radio Announcer: Unavailable. **No. of Games Broadcast:** Home-50, Away-50. **Flagship Station:** 740 AM The FAN. **PA Announcer:** Unavailable. **Official Scorer:** Rob Olson.
Stadium Name: Newman Outdoor Field. **Location:** I-29 North to exit 67, right on 19th Ave. North, right on Albrecht Boulevard. **Standard Game Times:** 7:02 p.m.; Saturday 6 p.m.; Sunday, 1 p.m.
Visiting Club Hotel: Unavailable.

GARY SOUTHSHORE RAILCATS

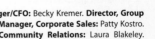

Office Address: One Stadium Plaza, Gary, IN 46402.
Telephone: (219) 882-2255. **FAX:** (219) 882-2259.
E-Mail Address: info@railcatsbaseball.com. **Website:** www.railcatsbaseball.com.
Operated by: SouthShore Baseball, LLC.
Owner/CEO: Pat Salvi. **Owner:** Lindy Salvi.
President/General Manager: Roger Wexelberg. **Assistant General Manager/CFO:** Becky Kremer. **Director, Group Sales:** Alan Bowman. **Director, Media Relations/Broadcasting:** Andy Viano. **Manager, Corporate Sales:** Patty Kostro. **Manager, Advertising/Promotions:** Dave Salvi. **Manager, Merchandise/Community Relations:** Laura Blakeley. **Manager, Stadium Operations:** Nick Lampasona. **Head Groundskeeper:** Blake Bostelman. **Account Executives:** Adam Harris, Radley Robinson, Patrick Galvin. **Assistant Manager Merchandise/Community Relations:** Nikki Kimbrough. **Media/Advertising Assistant:** Ed McCaskey. **Manager, Stadium Maintenance:** Jim Kerr. **Executive Assistant:** Arcella

Moxley. **Stadium Maintenance:** Stephanie Tavorn.
    Manager: Greg Tagert. **Coaches:** Jamie Bennett, Joe Gates.

GAME INFORMATION
    Radio Announcer: Andy Viano. **No. of Games Broadcast:** Home-50, Away-50. **Flagship Station:** WLPR 89.1-FM.
    Stadium Name: U.S. Steel Yard. **Location:** I-80/94 to Broadway Exit (Exit 10). North on Broadway to Fifth Avenue. East one block to stadium. **Standard Game Times:** 7 p.m.; Tuesday/Saturday, 6; Sunday, 2.
    Visiting Club Hotel: Radisson Hotel at Star Plaza, 800 E 81st Ave., Merrillville, IN 46410. **Telephone:** (219) 769-6311.

JOLIET JACKHAMMERS

Office Address: 1 Mayor Art Schultz Dr., Joliet, IL 60432.
Telephone: (815) 726-2255. **Fax:** (815) 726-9223.
E-Mail Address: info@jackhammersbaseball.com. **Website:** www.jackhammerbaseball.com.
Operated by: Joliet Professional Baseball Club, LLC.
Chairman: Peter Ferro. **Executive Vice President/General Manager:** Jamie Toole. **Executive Vice President/CFO:** John Costello. **Vice President, Operations/Marketing:** Kelly Sufka. **Special Assistant to GM/Baseball Operations:** John Cangelosi. **Director, Promotions/Community Relations:** Sean Keegan. **Corporate Opportunites Executive:** Matthew Mendes. **Group Sales Manager:** Jim Rice. **Outside Sales Representative:** Lisa Pierson. **Marketing/Community Relations Coordinator:** Kelli Drechsel. **Director, Field/Stadium Operations:** Nick Hill. **Internship Coordinator:** Margaret Dixon. **Box Office Manager:** Patrick Spellman. **Corporate Opportunites Manager:** Stephanie Cuba. **Administrative Coordinator:** Courtney Schuster.
    Manager: Chad Parker. **Pitching Coach:** Bryce Florie.

GAME INFORMATION
    Radio Announcer: Jason Lamar. **No. of Games Broadcast:** Home-48, Away-48. **Flagship Station:** WJOL, 1340-AM.
    Stadium Name: Silver Cross Field. **Location:** I-80 to Chicago Street/Route 53 North exit, go 1/2 mile on Chicago Street, right on Washington Street to Jefferson Street/U.S. 52, right on Jefferson, ballpark on left. **Standard Game Times:** 7:05 p.m. 6:10 (Tues), 2:10 (Sun).

KANSAS CITY T-BONES

Office Address: 1800 Village West Parkway Kansas City, KS 66111.
Telephone: (913) 328-2255. **Fax:** (913) 328-5652.
E-mail Address: batterup@tbonesbaseball.com. **Website:** www.tbonesbaseball.com.
Operated By: T-Bones Baseball Club, LLC; Ehlert Development.
Owner, President: John Ehlert. **Vice President:** Adam Ehlert.
    Vice President/General Manager: Chris Browne. **VP/Corporate Partnerships:** Scott Steckly. **Assistant GM/Group Sales:** Eric Marshall. **Director, Merchandise:** Laura Hayes. **Director, Media Relations/Press Box:** Stan Duitsman. **Director, Promotions:** Emily Hoskins. **Director, Ticket Operations/Box Office Manager:** Kurt Sieker. **Head Groundskeeper/Facilities Manager:** Joey Fitzgerald. **Operations Manager:** Rylan D. **Brody. Bookkeeper:** Sherrie Stover. **Account Executive:** Jason Young.
    Manager: Tim Doherty. **Coach:** Unavailable. **Pitching Coach:** Caleb Balbuena. **Trainer:** Josh Adams.

GAME INFORMATION
    Radio Announcer: Unavailable. **No. of Games Broadcast:** Home-50, Away-50. **Flagship Station:** WDAF 1660 AM. **Official Scorer:** Louis Spry. **PA Announcer:** Dan Roberts.
    Stadium Name: CommunityAmerica Ballpark. **Location:** State Avenue West off I-435 and State Avenue. **Standard Game Times:** 7:05 p.m.; 5:05 (Sun).
    Visiting Club Hotel: Hyatt Regency Crown Center.

LAKE COUNTY FIELDERS

Office Address: 850 Green Bay Road, Zion, IL 60099.
Telephone: (847) 731-8000. **Website:** www.fieldersbaseball.com.
Operated by: Grand Slam Sports & Entertainment, LLC.
Owner: Kevin Costner.
Managing Partner/President: Rich Ehrenreich.
    Executive VP: Rick Rungaitis. **VP, Sales:** Mike Beauvais. **Director, Group Sales:** Bobby Mengler. **Corporate Sales Manager:** Kevin Dooley. **Ticket Manager:** Keenan Bigg. **Graphics/Publications Manager:** Dan Garwood. **Marketing/Sponsorship Coordinator:** Shannon Myers. **Manager, Community Relations/Promotions:** Beth Alderson. **Inside Sales Representatives:** Ryan Anderskow, Charlie Hogan, Dan Zarzynski. **Group Sales Account Executive:** Nicholas Suydam. **Field Agent:** Scott Murphy.
    Manager: Fran Riordan. **Coach:** Unavailable. **Pitching Coach:** Unavailable.

GAME INFORMATION

    Radio Announcer: Les Grobstein. **No. of Games broadcast:** Home-50, Away-50. **Flagship Station:** WKRS 1220-AM. **Stadium Name:** Fielders Stadium.

    Location: From the North (Wisconsin): Green Bay Rd (Rt 131) South, past Russell Rd. to NW corner of Green Bay & 9th St.; **From the South:** I-94N or US41(Skokie Hwy) N to Rt 173 (Rosecrans), East on Rt. 173 to Green Bay Rd. (Rt. 131), Turn Left (North) on Green Bay Rd 1/2 Mile to NW corner of Green Bay Rd & 9th Street; **From the East:** Rt. 173 West to Green Bay Rd. (Rt. 131), Turn Right (North) on Green Bay Rd., 1/2 Mile to NW corner of Green Bay Rd. & 9th Street; **From the West:** Rt. 173 (Rosecrans) East to Green Bay Rd. (Rt 131), Turn Left (North) on Green Bay Rd., 1/2 Mile to NW corner of Green Bay & 9th Street.

    Standard Game Times: 7:00 p.m.; Sat. 6; Sun. 1.

ROCKFORD RIVERHAWKS

    Office Address: 4503 Interstate Blvd., Loves Park, IL 61111.

    Telephone: (815) 885-2255. **Fax:** (815) 885-2204.

    Website: www.rockfordriverhawks.com.

    Owners: Dennis Arouca, Kurt Carlson, Dave Ciarrachi, Brian McClure. **Managing Partner:** Dave Ciarrachi.

    General Manager: Josh Olerud. **Assistant GM/Baseball Operations:** Todd Fulk. **Director, Broadcasting/Media Relations:** Bill Czaja. **Director, Tickets/Finance:** Brad Sholes. **Director, Operations:** Chris Daleo. **Director, Group Sales:** Jeff Olerud.

    Manager: Bob Koopmann. **Coaches:** J.D. Arndt, Sam Knaack, Spiro Lempesis, Richard Austin. **Trainer:** Rockford Orthopedic Associates.

GAME INFORMATION

    Radio Announcer: Bill Czaja. **No. of Games Broadcast:** Home-50, Away-50. **Flagship Station:** WTJK1380-AM. **PA Announcer:** CJ Finn. **Official Scorer:** Kevin Hoos.

    Stadium Name: Road Ranger Stadium. **Location:** I-90 (Jane Addams Tollway) to Riverside Boulevard exit (automatic toll booth), east to Interstate Drive, left on Interstate Drive. **Standard Game Times:** 7:05 p.m.; Sat. 6:05; Sun. 4:05.

    Visiting Club Hotel: Clock Tower Resort, 7801 East State Street, Rockford, IL 61108. **Telephone:** (815) 398-6000

SCHAUMBURG FLYERS

    Office Address: 1999 S. Springinsguth Rd., Schaumburg, IL 60193.

    Telephone: (847) 891-2255. **Fax:** (847) 891-6441.

    E-Mail Address: info@flyersbaseball.com. **Website:** www.flyersbaseball.com.

    Principal Owners: Richard Ehrenreich, John Hughes, Mike Conley. **Managing Partner:** Richard Ehrenreich.

    General Manager: Ben Burke. **Assistant GM/Director, Ticket Operations:** Scott Boor. **Assistant GM/Director, Operations:** Aaron Studebaker. **Director, Corporate Partnerships:** Bill Foss. **Ticket Manager:** Dave Lesch. **Promotions/ Merchandise Manager:** Liz Hamilton. **Community Relations Manager/Group Sales Assistant:** Kelly Hopkins. **Graphics Manager:** Matt Dunlap. **Group Sales Associate:** Ray Gross. **Medical Director:** Tony Garofalo.

    Manager: Michael Busch.

GAME INFORMATION

    Radio Announcer: Unavailable. **No. of Games Broadcast:** Home-50, Away-50. **Flagship Station:** WRMN 1410AM. **PA Announcer:** Unavailable. **Official Scorer:** Mark Madorin.

    Stadium Name: Alexian Field. **Location:** From north, I-290 to Elgin-O'Hare Expressway (Thorndale), west on expressway to Irving Park Road exit, left on Springinsguth under expressway, stadium on left; From south, U.S. 20 West (Lake Street) to Elgin-O'Hare Expressway (Thorndale), east on expressway, south on Springinsguth Road. **Standard Game Times:** 7:05 p.m.; Fri. 6:45; Sat. 6:05; Sun. 1:20.

    Visiting Club Hotel: Country Inn and Suites/Hotel Indigo.

WINNIPEG GOLDEYES

    Office Address: One Portage Ave. E., Winnipeg, Manitoba R3B 3N3.

    Telephone: (204) 982-2273. **Fax:** (204) 982-2274.

    E-Mail Address: goldeyes@goldeyes.com. **Website:** www.goldeyes.com.

    Operated by: Winnipeg Goldeyes Baseball Club Inc.

    Principal Owner/President: Sam Katz.

    General Manager: Andrew Collier. **Assistant GM:** Regan Katz. **Director, Communications:** Jonathan Green. **Administrative Assistant:** Bonnie Benson. **Chief Financial Officer:** Jason McRae-King. **Controller:** Judy Jones. **Director, Sales/Marketing:** Dan Chase. **Sales/Marketing Coordinator:** Angela Sanche. **Account Representatives:** Paul Duque, Paul Edmonds, Sarah Kyrylchuk, Dennis McLean, Scott Taylor. **Promotions Coordinator:** Sarah Kyrylchuk. **Retail Manager:** Megan Tucker. **Facility Manager/Head Groundskeeper:** Don Ferguson.

    Manager/Director, Player Procurement: Rick Forney. **Coaches:** Rudy Arias, Tom Vaeth. **Trainer:** Andrew Wautier.

Clubhouse Manager: Jamie Samson.

GAME INFORMATION

Radio Announcer: Paul Edmonds. **No. of Games Broadcast:** Home-50, Road-50. **Flagship Station:** CFRW 1290-AM. **Television Announcers:** Scott Taylor, Ken Wiebe, Jamie Bettens. **No. of Games Telecast:** Home-24, Away-0. **Station:** Shaw TV Channel 9.

PA Announcer: Ron Arnst. **Official Scorer:** Steve Eitzen.

Stadium Name: Canwest Park. **Location:** North on Pembina Highway to Broadway. East on Broadway to Main Street. North on Main Street to Water Avenue. East on Water Avenue to Westbrook Street. North on Westbrook Street to Lombard Avenue. East on Lombard Avenue to Mill Street. South on Mill Street to ballpark. **Standard Game Times:** 7 p.m.; Sat. 6; Sun. 1:30.

Visiting Club Hotel: The Radisson, 288 Portage Ave., Winnipeg, Manitoba R3C 0B8. **Telephone:** (204) 956-0410.

UNITED LEAGUE

Office Address: 920 North Sugar Road, Suite #10, Edinburg, Texas 78541. **Telephone:** (800) 930-8189 Ext. 100. **Fax:** (888) 803-6517.

E-mail Address: info@unitedleague.org. **Website:** www.unitedleague.org

Founded: 2006.

Owners: John Bryant, Byron Pierce.

President: Byron Pierce.

Regular Season: 200 games. **2010 Opening Date:** Unavailable. **Closing Date:** Unavailable.

Playoff Format: Top four teams meet in best of three series. Winners meet in best of three championship series.

AMARILLO DILLAS

Office Address: 801 S Polk St., Amarillo, TX 79106.

Telephone: (806) 342-0400. **Fax:** (806) 342-0407.

E-mail Address: mlee@unitedleague.org. **Website:** www.myamarillodillas.com.

General Manager: Mark Lee. **Assistant GM:** Dave Kost. **Office/Ticket Manager:** Jaylin Henderson.

GAME INFORMATION

Radio Announcer: Unavailable. **PA Announcer:** Joe Frank Wheeler. **Official Scorer:** Unavailable.

COASTAL BEND THUNDER

Office Address: 1011 Texas Yes Blvd Robstown, TX 78380.

Telephone: (361) 933-1120. **Fax:** (361) 933-1129.

E-mail Address: rahunt@hotmail.com. **Website:** www.coastalbendthunder.com.

General Manager: Unavailable. **Assistant General Manager, Stadium Operations:** Ray Hunt. **Assistant General Manager, Sales/Marketing:** Javier Limon. **Manager:** Al Gallagher.

GAME INFORMATION

Radio Announcer: Unavailable. **No. of Games Broadcast:** 44. **PA Announcer:** Unavailable. **Official Scorer:** Unavailable.

Standard Game Time: 7:05 p.m. **Visiting Club Hotel:** Red Roof Inn, 3030 Buffalo St. Corpus Christi, TX 78408. **Telephone:** (361) 888-7663.

EDINBURG ROADRUNNERS

Office Address: 920 North Sugar Road, Edinburg, TX 78541.

Telephone: 956-380-4446. **Fax:** 956-380-4344.

E-Mail Address: roadrunners2009@gmail.com. **Website:** www.roadrunnerball.com.

General Manager: Doug Leary. **Director, Sales/Marketing:** Jeremy Martin. **Ticket Manager:** Jesse Gonzalez. **Account Executive:** Rudy Rodriguez. **Office Manager:** Alejandra Cobos. **Stadium Opertations:** Estella De La Cruz. **Merchandise Manager:** Elva Garza. **Manager/Director, Player Personnel:** Vince Moore.

GAME INFORMATION

Radio Announcer: Danny Elizondo. **No. of Games Broadcast:** 90. **Website:** www.roadrunnerball.com. **PA Announcer:** Seve Lara. **Official Scorer:** Rey Silva.

Stadium: Edinburg Stadium. **Standard Game Time:** 7:05 p.m.; 6:05 (Sun).

LAREDO BRONCOS

Office Address: 2200 Santa Maria, Laredo, TX 78040. **Mailing Address:** P.O. Box 2836, Laredo, TX 78044. **Telephone:** (956) 723-2273 Fax: (956) 723-3491.
E-mail Address: jose@laredobroncos.com. **Website:** www.laredobroncos.com.
General Manager: Jose Melendez. **Assistant General Manager, Sales:** Arnold Cantu. **Manager, Director Player Personnel:** Dan Firova.

GAME INFORMATION
Radio Announcer: Unavailable. **No. of Games Broadcast:** 90 . **Website:** www.laredobroncos.com.
PA Announcer: Chema Guevara. **Official Scorer:** Dan Lathey.
Stadium: Veterans Field. **Standard Game Time:** 7:35 p.m.

RIO GRANDE VALLEY
WHITEWINGS

Office Address: 1216 Fair Park Blvd, Harlingen, TX 78550. **Telephone:** (956) 423-WING (9464). **Fax:** (956) 423-9466.
E-mail Address: cdirksen@whitewingsbaseball.com. **Website:** www.whitewingsbaseball.com.
General Manager: Cory Dirksen. **Director, Ticket Operations:** Dan Ramirez. **Office Mamager:** Beverly Woodward. **Manager:** Eddie Dennis.

GAME INFORMATION
Radio Announcer: Jonah Goldberg. **No. of Games Broadcast:** 90 . **Website:** www.whitewingsbaseball.com.
Stadium: Harlingen Field. **Standard Game Time:** 7:05 p.m.

SAN ANGELO COLTS

Office Address: 1600 University, San Angelo, TX 76951.
Telephone: (325) 942-6587. **Fax:** (325) 947-9480.
E-mail Address: mbabcock@sanangelocolts.com. **Website:** www.sanangelocolts.com.
General Manager: Mike Babcock. **Assistant General Manager:** Ken Franz. **Head Groundskeeper:** Drew Caraway. **Director, Sales:** Mike Clark. **Director, Media Operations/Broadcasting:** Ira Liebman. **Office Manager/Director, Ticketing:** Lea Self.
Manager/Director, Player Personnel: Doc Edwards. **Trainer:** Randy Matthews.
GAME INFORMATION
Radio Announcer: Ira Liebman. **No. of Games Broadcast:** 100. **Flagship Station:** KCLL-100.1 FM. **PA Announcer:** Jeremy Bryant. **Official Scorer:** Bill Mahr. **Standard Game Time:** 7:05 p.m. **Visiting Club Hotel:** Inn of the Conchos.

CONTINENTAL LEAGUE

Office Address: 16633 Dallas Parkway, Suite 600, Addison, TX.
Telephone: (214) 234-0018. **Fax:** (972) 588-3363.
Website: www.cblproball.com
CEO/President: Ron Baron. **Director, League Operations/Communications:** Bob Ibach.
Year Founded: 2007.
Regular Season: 60 games.
2010 Opening Date: Unavailable.
Member Clubs: Alexandria Aces (Alexandria, La.), Big Bend Cowboys (Alpine, Texas), East Texas Roadhogs, Las Cruces Vaqueroes, West Texas Pavement Crushers.
All-Star Game: Unavailable.
Playoff Format: Unavailable.
Roster Limit: 25.
Official Baseball: Unavailable. **Statistician:** Unavailable.

INTERNATIONAL

AMERICAS

MEXICO

MEXICAN LEAGUE

Member, National Association
NOTE: The Mexican League is a member of the National Association of Professional Baseball Leagues and has a Triple-A classification. However, its member clubs operate largely independent of the 30 major league teams, and for that reason the league is listed in the international section.
Mailing Address: Angel Pola No. 16 Col. Periodista. Mexico, D.F. CP 11220, Del. Miguel Hidalgo. **Telephone:** 52-55-5557-1007. **Fax:** 52-55-5395-2454. **E-Mail Address:** oficina@lmb.com.mx. **Website:** www.lmb.com.mx.
Years League Active: 1955-.
President: Plinio Escalante Bolio. **Operations Manager:** Nestor Alba Brito.
Division Structure: North—Chihuahua, Laguna, Mexico, Monclova, Monterrey, Nuevo Laredo, Reynosa, Saltillo. South—Campeche, Minatitlan, Oaxaca, Puebla, Quintana Roo, Tabasco, Veracruz, Yucatan.
Regular Season: 110 games (split-schedule). **2010 Opening Date:** March 25. **Closing Date:** July 30.
All-Star Game: June 7, site unavailable.
Playoff Format: Eight teams qualify, including first- and second-half division winners plus wild-card teams with best overall records. Quarterfinals, semifinals and finals are all best of seven series.
Roster Limit: 28. **Roster Limit, Imports:** 6.

CAMPECHE PIRATES
Office Address: Calle Filiberto Qui Farfan No. 2, Col. Camino Real, CP 24020, Campeche, Campeche. **Telephone:** (52) 981-827-4759. **Fax:** (52) 981-8274767. **E-Mail Address:** piratas@prodigy.net.mx. **Website:** www.piratasdecampeche.com.mx.
President: Gabriel Escalante Castillo. **General Manager:** Maria del Socorro Morales.
Manager: Hector Estrada.

CHIHUAHUA GOLDENS
Office Address: Blvd. Juan Pablo II No. 4506, Col. Aeropuerto CP 31380. **Telephone:** (52) 614-459-0317. **Fax:** (52) 614-459-0336. **E-Mail Address:** icampos@doradoslmb.com. **Website:** www.doradoslmb.com.
President: Mario Rodriguez. **General Manager:** Iram Campos Lara.
Manager: Arturo de Freitas.

LAGUNA COWBOYS
Office Address: Juan Gutenberg s/n, Col. Centro, CP 27000, Torreon, Coahuila. **Telephone:** (52) 871-718-5515. **Fax:** (52) 871-717-4335. **E-Mail Address:** unionlag@prodigy.net.mx. **Website:** www.clubvaqueroslaguna.com.
President: Carlos Gomez del Campo. **General Manager:** Carlos de la Garza.
Manager: Derek Bryant.

MEXICO CITY RED DEVILS
Office Address: Av. Cuauhtemoc #451-101, Col. Narvarte, CP 03020, Mexico DF. **Telephone:** (52) 555-639-8722. **Fax:** (52) 555-639-9722. **E-Mail Address:** diablos@sportsya.com. **Website:** www.diablos.com.mx.
President: Roberto Mansur Galán. **General Manager:** Eduardo de la Cerda.
Manager: Daniel Fernandez.

MONCLOVA STEELERS
Office Address: Cuauhtemoc #299, Col. Ciudad Deportiva, CP 25750, Monclova, Coahuila. **Telephone:** (52) 866-636-2650. **Fax:** (52) 866-636-2688. **E-Mail Address:** acererosdelnorte@prodigy.net.mx. **Website:** www.acereros.com.mx.
President: Donaciano Garza Gutierrez. **General Manager:** Victor Favela Lopez.
Manager: Francisco Rodriguez.

MONTERREY SULTANS
Office Address: Av. Manuel Barragan s/n, Estadio Monterrey, Apartado Postal 870, Monterrey, Nuevo Leon, CP 66460. **Telephone:** (52) 81-8351-0209. **Fax:** (52) 81-8351-8022. **E-Mail Address:** sultanes@sultanes.com.mx. **Website:** www.sultanes.com.mx.
President: José Maiz García. **General Manager:** Roberto Magdaleno Ramírez.
Manager: Felix Fermin.

NUEVO LAREDO OWLS
Office Address: Av. Santos Degollado 235-G, Col. Independencia, CP 88020, Nuevo Laredo, Tamaulipas. **Telephone:** (52) 867-712-2299. **Fax:** (52) 867-712-0736. **E-Mail Address:** tecolotes@globalpc.net. **Website:** www.tecolotesdenuevolaredo.com.
President: Victor Lozano Rendon. **General Manager:** Ruben Estrada Ordonez.
Manager: Gerardo Sanchez.

OAXACA WARRIORS
Office Address: M. Bravo 417 Col. Centro 68000, Oaxaca, Oaxaca. **Telephone:** (52) 951-515-5522. **Fax:** (52) 951-515-4966. **E-Mail Address:** oaxacaguerreros@gmail.com. **Website:** www.guerrerosdeoaxaca.com.mx.
President: Avellá Villa Vicente Pérez. **General Manager:** Lic Spindola Guillermo Morales.
Manager: Eddy Diaz.

MINATITLAN OILERS
Office Address: Av. Avila Camacho esquina con H. Colegio Militar, Estadio 18 de Marzo de 1938, Col. De los Maestros, CP 96849, Minatitlan, Veracruz. **Telephone:** (52) 951-515-5522. **Fax:** (52) 951-515-4966. **E-Mail Address:** webmaster@petrolerosdeminatitlan.com.mx. **Website:** www.petrolerosdeminatitlan.com.mx.
Manager: Andres Mora.

PUEBLA PARROTS
Office Address: Calz. Zaragoza S/N, Unidad Deportiva 5 de Mayo, Col. Maravillas, CP 72220, Puebla, Puebla. **Telephone:** (52) 222-222-2116. **Fax:** (52) 222-222-2117. **E-Mail Address:** oficina@pericosdepuebla.com.mx. **Website:** www.pericosdepuebla.com.mx.
President: Rafael Moreno Valle Sanchez. **General Manager:** Edgar Ramirez.
Manager: Alfonso Jimenez.

QUINTANA ROO TIGERS
Office Address: Av. Mayapan Mz. 4 Lt. 1 Super Mz. 21, CP 77500, Cancun, Quintana Roo. **Telephone:** (52) 998-887-3108. **Fax:** (52) 998-887-1313. **E-Mail Address:** tigres@tigrescapitalinos.com.mx. **Website:** www.tigresqr.com.
President: Cuauhtémoc Rodriguez. **General Manager:** Francisco Minjarez.
Manager: Matias Carrillo.

SALTILLO SARAPE MAKERS
Office Address: Blvd. Nazario Ortiz Esquina con Blvd. Jesus Sanchez, CP 25280, Saltillo, Coahuila. **Telephone:** (52) 844-416-9455. **Fax:** (52) 844-439-1330. **E-Mail Address:** aley@grupoley.com. **Website:** www.saraperos.com.mx.
President: Alvaro Ley Lopez. **General Manager:**

Eduardo Valenzuela Guajardo.
Manager: Orlando Sanchez.

TABASCO OLMECS

Office Address: Explanada de la Ciudad Deportiva, Parque de Beisbol Centenario del 27 de Febrero, Col. Atasta de Serra, CP 86100, Villahermosa, Tabasco. **Telephone:** (52) 993-352-2787. **Fax:** (52) 993-352-2788. **E-Mail Address:** olmecastab@prodigy.net.mx. **Website:** www.olmecasdetabasco.com.mx.
President: Raul Gonzalez Rodriguez. **General Manager:** Luis Guzman Ramos.
Manager: Luis de los Santos.

REYNOSA BRONCOS

Office Address: Paris 511, Esq. c/ Tiburcio Garza Zamora Altos, Locales 6 y 7, Col Beatty, Reynosa, Tamps. **Telephone:** (52) 922-3462. **Fax:** (52) 925-7118. **E-Mail Address:** broncosdereynosa@gmail.com. **Website:** www.broncosreynosa.com.
Manager: Homar Rojas.

VERACRUZ RED EAGLES

Office Address: Av. Jacarandas S/N, Esquina España, Fraccionamiento Virginia, CP 94294, Boca del Rio, Veracruz. **Telephone:** (52) 229-935-5004. **Fax:** (229) 935-5008. **E-Mail Address:** rojosdelaguila@terra.com.mx. **Website:** www.aguiladeveracruz.com.
President: Jose Antonio Mansur Beltran. **General Manager:** Carlos Nahun Hernandez.
Manager: Enrique Reyes.

YUCATAN LIONS

Office Address: Calle 50 #406-B, Entre 35 y 37, Col. Jesus Carranza, CP 97109, Merida, Yucatán. **Telephone:** (52) 999-926-3022. **Fax:** (52) 999-926-3631. **E-Mail Addresses:** leones@prodigy.net.mx. **Website:** www.leonesdeyucatan.com.mx.
President: Ricalde Gustavo Durán. **General Manager:** Jose Rivero.
Manager: Lino Rivera.

MEXICAN ACADEMY

Rookie Classification
Mailing Address: Angel Pola No. 16, Col. Periodista, CP 11220, Mexico, D.F. **Telephone:** (52) 555-557-1007. **Fax:** (52) 555-395-2454. **E-Mail Address:** mbl@prodigy.net.mx. **Website:** www.academialmb.com.
Member Clubs: Celaya, Guanajuato, Queretaro, Salamanca.
Director General: Raul Martinez. **Administration:** Pela Villalobos.
Regular Season: 50 games. **2008 Opening Date:** Oct. 9. **Closing Date:** Dec. 21.

DOMINICAN REPUBLIC
DOMINICAN SUMMER LEAGUE

Member, National Association
Rookie Classification
Mailing Address: Calle Segunda No. 64, Reparto Antilla, Santo Domingo, Dominican Republic. **Telephone/Fax:** (809) 532-3619. **Website:** www.dominicansummerleague.com. **E-Mail Address:** ligadeverano@codetel.net.do.
Years League Active: 1985-.
President: Orlando Diaz.
Member Clubs/Division Structure: Boca Chica North—Blue Jays, Brewers/Orioles (shared team), Cubs 2, Dodgers, Giants, Marlins, Mets, Pirates, Rays, Red Sox, Royals, Yankees 1. Santo Domingo North—Athletics, Cardinals, Mariners, Phillies. Boca Chica Baseball City—Cubs 1, Diamondbacks, Indians, Nationals, Orioles, Padres, Reds, Rockies, Tigers, Twins, White Sox, Yankees 2. San Pedro de Macoris—Angels, Astros, Braves, Rangers 1, Rangers 2.
Regular Season: 72 games. **2010 Opening Date:** June 3. **Closing Date:** Aug. 20.
Playoff Format: Six teams qualify for playoffs, including four division winners and two wild-card teams. Teams with two best records receive a bye to the semifinals; four other playoff teams play best-of-three series. Winners advance to best-of-three semifinals. Winners advance to best-of-five championship series.
Roster Limit: 35 active. **Player Eligibility Rule:** No player may have four or more years of prior minor league service. Draft-eligible players may not participate in the DSL or VSL, with the exception of two players from Puerto Rico. No age limits apply.

VENEZUELA
VENEZUELAN SUMMER LEAGUE

Member, National Association
Rookie Classification
Mailing Address: Torre Movilnet, Oficina 10, Piso 9, Valencia, Carabobo, Venezuela. **Telephone:** (58) 241-823-8101. **Fax:** (58) 241-824-3340. **Website:** www.vsl.com.ve.
Years League Active: 1997-.
Administrator: Saul Gonzalez. **Coordinator:** Ramon Feriera.
Participating Organizations: Cardinals, Mariners, Mets, Phillies, Pirates, Rays, Tigers.
Regular Season: 70 games. **2010 Opening Date:** May 17. **Closing Date:** Aug. 27.
Playoffs: Best-of-three series between top two teams in regular season.
Roster Limit: 35 active. **Player Eligibility Rule:** No player may have four or more years of prior minor league service. Draft-eligible players may not participate in the DSL or VSL, with the exception of two players from Puerto Rico. No age limits apply.

ASIA

CHINA
CHINA BASEBALL LEAGUE

Mailing Address: 5, Tiyuguan Road, Beijing 100763, China. **Telephone:** (86) 10-6716-9082. **Fax:** (86) 10-6716-2993. **E-Mail Address:** cga_cra@263.net.
Years League Active: 2002-.

Chairman: Hu Jian Guo. **Vice Chairmen:** Tom McCarthy, Shen Wei. **Executive Director:** Yang Jie. **General Manager, Marketing/Promotion:** Lin Xiao Wu.
Member Clubs: Beijing Tigers, Guangdong Leopards, Henan Elephants, Jiangsu Hopestars, Shanghai Golden Eagles, Sichuan Dragons, Tianjin Lions.
Regular Season: 28 games.
Playoff Format: Top two teams meet in one-game championship.

JAPAN

NIPPON PROFESSIONAL BASEBALL

Mailing Address: Imperial Tower, 14F, 1-1-1 Uchisaiwai-cho, Chiyoda-ku, Tokyo 100-0011. **Telephone:** 03-3502-0022. **Fax:** 03-3502-0140. **Website:** www.npb.or.jp, www.npb.or.jp/eng

Commissioner: Ryozo Kato.

Executive Secretary: Kunio Shimoda. **Director, Administration:** Atsushi Ihara. **Director, Baseball Operations:** Nobby Ito. **Directors, Public Relations:** Minoru Hirata, Katsuhisa Matsuzaki.

Director, Central League Operations: Kazunori Ogaki. **Director, Pacific League Operations:** Shiromitsu Hanai.

Japan Series: Best-of-seven series between Central and Pacific League champions, begins Oct. 30 at home of Central League club.

All-Star Series: July 23 at Fukuoka Yahoo Japan Dome; July 24 at Hard-Off Stadium, Niigata.

Roster Limit: 70 per organization (one major league club, one minor league club). Major league club is permitted to register 28 players at a time, though just 25 may be available for each game.

Roster Limit, Imports: Four in majors (no more than three position players or pitchers); unlimited in minors.

CENTRAL LEAGUE

Regular Season: 144 games.

2010 Opening Date: March 26. **Closing Date:** Sept. 23, with makeup games played until Oct. 10.

Playoff Format: Second-place team meets third-place team in best-of-three series. Winner meets first-place team in best-of-seven series to determine representative in Japan Series (first-place team has one-game advantage to begin series).

CHUNICHI DRAGONS

Mailing Address: Chunichi Bldg. 6F, 4-1-1 Sakae, Naka-ku, Nagoya 460-0008. **Telephone:** 052-261-8811. **Fax:** 052-263-7696.

Chairman: Bungo Shirai. **President:** Junnosuke Nishikawa. **General Manager:** Norihito Nishwaki. **Field Manager:** Hiromitsu Ochiai.

2010 Foreign Players: Tony Blanco, Dionys Cesar, Maximo Nelson, Edward Valdez, Chen Wei Yin.

HANSHIN TIGERS

Mailing Address: 2-33 Koshien-cho, Nishinomiya-shi, Hyogo-ken 663-8152. **Telephone:** 0798-46-1515. **Fax:** 0798-46-3555.

Chairman: Shinya Sakai. **President:** Nobuo Minami. **Field Manager:** Akinobu Mayumi.

2010 Foreign Players: Craig Brazell, Casey Fossum, Cheng Kai Un, Randy Messenger, Matt Murton.

HIROSHIMA TOYO CARP

Mailing Address: 2-3-1 Minami Kaniya, Minami-ku, Hiroshima 732-8501. **Telephone:** 082-554-1000. **Fax:** 082-568-1190.

President: Hajime Matsuda. **General Manager:** Kiyoaki Suzuki. **Field Manager:** Kenjiro Nomura.

2010 Foreign Players: Carlo Alvarado, Jeff Fiorentino, Justin Huber, Mike Schultz.

TOKYO YAKULT SWALLOWS

Mailing Address: Shimbashi MCV Bldg. 5F, 5-13-5 Shimbashi, Minato-ku, Tokyo 105-0004. **Telephone:** 03-5470-8915. **Fax:** 03-5470-8916.

Chairman: Sumiya Hori. **President:** Tadashi Suzuki. **General Manager:** Kesanori Kurashima. **Field Manager:** Shigeru Takada.

2010 Foreign Players: Tony Barnette, Jamie D'Antona, Eulo de la Cruz, Aaron Guiel, Lee Hye Chun, Lim Chang Yong.

YOKOHAMA BAYSTARS

Mailing Address: Kannai Arai Bldg, 7F, 1-8 Onoe-cho, Naka-ku, Yokohama 231-0015. **Telephone:** 045-681-0811. **Fax:** 045-661-2500.

Chairman: Kiyoshi Wakabayashi. **President:** Takao Kaji. **Field Manager:** Takao Obana.

2010 Foreign Players: Chris Bootcheck, Jose Castillo, Stephen Randolph, Terrmel Sledge, Wang Yi-zheng.

YOMIURI GIANTS

Mailing Address: Otemachi Nomura Bldg., 7F, 2-1-1 Otemachi, Chiyoda-ku, Tokyo 100-8151. **Telephone:** 03-3246-7733. **Fax:** 03-3246-2726.

Chairman: Takuo Takihana. **President:** Tsunekazu Momoi. **General Manager:** Hidetoshi Kiyotake. **Field Manager:** Tatsunori Hara.

2010 Foreign Players: Dicky Gonzalez, Edgar Gonzalez, Seth Greisinger, Marc Kroon, Wirfin Obispo, Alex Ramirez, Lee Seung Yeop. **Coach:** John Turney.

PACIFIC LEAGUE

Regular Season: 144 games.

2010 Opening Date: March 20. **Closing Date:** Sept. 26, with makeup games played until Oct. 10.

Playoff Format: Second-place team meets third-place team in best-of-three series. Winner meets first-place team in best-of-seven series to determine league's representative in Japan Series (first-place team has one-game advantage to begin series).

CHIBA LOTTE MARINES

Mailing Address: 1 Mihama, Mihama-ku, Chiba-shi, Chiba-ken 261-8587. **Telephone:** 043-296-1450. **Fax:** 043-296-7496.

Chairman: Takeo Shigemitsu. **President:** Ryuzo Setoyama. **Field Manager:** Norifumi Nishimura.

2010 Foreign Players: Bryan Corey, Kim Tae Hyun, Bill Murphy.

FUKUOKA SOFTBANK HAWKS

Mailing Address: Fukuoka Yahoo! Japan Dome, Hawks Town, Chuo-ku, Fukuoka 810-0065. **Telephone:** 092-844-1189. **Fax:** 092-844-4600.

Owner: Masayoshi Son. **Chairman:** Sadaharu Oh. **President:** Kazuhiko Kasai. **Field Manager:** Koji Akiyama.

2010 Foreign Players: Brian Falkenborg, D.J. Houlton, Lee Boem Ho, Jose Ortiz, Yang Yao-hsun.

HOKKAIDO NIPPON HAM FIGHTERS

Mailing Address: 1 Hitsujigaoka, Toyohira-ku, Sapporo 062-8655. **Telephone:** 011-857-3939. **Fax:** 011-857-3900.

Chairman: Hiroji Okoso. **President:** Junichi Fujii. **General Manager:** Masao Yamada. **Field Manager:** Masataka Nashida.

2010 Foreign Players: Buddy Carlyle, Bobby Keppel, Brian Wolfe.

ORIX BUFFALOES

Mailing Address: 3-Kita-2-30 Chiyozaki, Nishi-ku, Osaka 530-0023. **Telephone:** 06-6586-0221. **Fax:** 06-6586-0240.

Chairman: Yoshihiko Miyauchi. **President:** Hiroaki Nishina. **General Manager:** Yoshio Murayama. **Field Manager:** Akinobu Okada.

2010 Foreign Players: Aarom Baldiris, Alex Cabrera, Greg LaRocca, Jon Leicester.

SAITAMA SEIBU LIONS

Mailing Address: 2135 Kami-Yamaguchi, Tokorozawa-shi, Saitama-ken 359-1189. **Telephone:** 04-2924-1155. **Fax:** 04-2928-1919.

President: Shinji Kobayashi. **Field Manager:** Hisanobu Watanabe.

2010 Foreign Players: Dee Brown, Alex Graman, Hsu Ming-chieh, Brian Sikorski.

TOHOKU RAKUTEN GOLDEN EAGLES

Mailing Address: 2-11-6 Miyagino, Miyagino-ku, Sendai-shi, Miyagi-ken 983-0045. **Telephone:** 022-298-5300. **Fax:** 022-298-5360.

Chairman: Hiroshi Mikitani. **President:** Toru Shimada. **Field Manager:** Marty Brown.

2010 Foreign Players: Todd Linden, Juan Morillo, Andy Phillips, Darrell Rasner. **Coaches:** Jeff Livesey, Luis Lopez.

KOREA
KOREA BASEBALL ORGANIZATION

Mailing Address: 946-16 Dokokdong, Kangnam-gu, Seoul, Korea. **Telephone:** (02) 3460-4600. **Fax:** (02) 3460-4639.

Years League Active: 1982-.

Website: www.koreabaseball.com.

Commissioner: Shin Sang-woo. **Secretary General:** Ha Il-sung. **Deputy Secretary General:** Lee Sang-il.

Member Clubs: Doosan Bears, Hanwha Eagles, Kia Tigers, LG Twins, Lotte Giants, Samsung Lions, Seoul Heroes, SK Wyverns.

Regular Season: 133 games. **2010 Opening Date:** April 4.

Playoffs: Third- and fourth-place teams meet in best-of-three series; winner advances to meet second-place team in best-of-five series; winner meets first-place team in best-of-seven Korean Series for league championship.

Roster Limit: 26 active through Sept. 1, when rosters expand to 31. **Imports:** Two active.

TAIWAN
CHINESE PROFESSIONAL BASEBALL LEAGUE

Mailing Address: 2F, No. 32, Pateh Road, Sec. 3, Taipei, Taiwan 10559. **Telephone:** 886-2-2577-6992. **Fax:** 886-2-2577-2606. **Website:** www.cpbl.com.tw.

Years League Active: 1990-.

Commissioner: Shou-Po Chao. **Secretary General:** Wen-pin Lee. **International Affairs:** Richard Wang. **E-Mail Address:** richard.wang@cpbl.com.tw.

Member Clubs: Brother Elephants, Uni Lions, Sinon Bulls, La New Bears.

Regular Season: 100 games. **2010 Opening Date:** March 28.

Playoffs: Second- and third-place teams meet in best-of-five series; winner advances to meet first-place team in best-of-seven championship series.

Import Rule: Only three import players may be active, and only two may be on the field at the same time.

EUROPE

NETHERLANDS
DUTCH MAJOR LEAGUE

Mailing Address: Koninklijke Nederlandse Baseball en Softball Bond (Royal Dutch Baseball and Softball Association), Postbus 2650, 3430 GB Nieuwegein, Holland. **Telephone:** 31-30-751-3650. **FAX:** 31-30-751-3651. **Website:** www.knbsb.nl.

Member Clubs: ADO, Amsterdam, HCAW, Hoofddorp, Kinheim, Neptunus, RCH, Sparta/Feyenoord.

President: Hans Meijer.

ITALY
SERIE A

Mailing Address: Federazione Italiana Baseball Softball, Viale Tiziano 74, 00196 Roma, Italy. **Telephone:** 39-06-36858376. **FAX:** 39-06-36858201. **Website:** www.fibs.it.

Member Clubs: Bologna, Godo, Grosseto, Nettuno, Parma, Reggio Emilia, Rimini, San Marino.

President: Riccardo Fraccari.

WINTER BASEBALL

CARIBBEAN BASEBALL CONFEDERATION

Mailing Address: Frank Feliz Miranda No. 1 Naco, Santo Domingo, Dominican Republic. **Telephone:** (809) 381-2643. **Fax:** (809) 565-4654. **Website:** www.ebeisbol.com.

Commissioner: Juan Francisco Puello. **Secretary:** Benny Agosto.

Member Countries: Colombia, Dominican Republic, Mexico, Nicaragua, Puerto Rico, Venezuela (Colombia and Nicaragua do not play in the Caribbean Series).

2011 Caribbean Series: Dominican Republic, February.

DOMINICAN LEAGUE

Office Address: Estadio Quisqueya, 2da. Planta, Ens. La Fe, Santo Domingo, Dominican Republic. **Telephone:** (809) 567-6371. **Fax:** (809) 567-5720. **E-Mail Address:** ligadom@hotmail.com. **Website:** www.lidom.com.

Years League Active: 1951-.

President: Leonardo Matos Berrido. **Vice President:** Jose Rafael Alvarez Sanchez. **Administrator:** Marcos Rodríguez. **Public Relations Director:** Jorge Torres.

Member Clubs: Aguilas Cibaenas, Estrellas de Oriente, Gigantes del Cibao, Leones del Escogido, Tigres del Licey, Toros del Este.

Regular Season: 50 games. **2010 Opening Date:** Oct. 16.

Playoff Format: Top four teams meet in 18-game round-robin. Top two teams advance to best-of-nine series for league championship. Winner advances to Caribbean Series.

Roster Limit: 30. **Imports:** 7.

MEXICAN PACIFIC LEAGUE

Mailing Address: Blvd. Solidaridad No. 335, Plaza las Palmas, Edificio A, Nivel 1, Local 4, Hermosillo, Sonora, Mexico CP 83246. **Telephone:** (52) 662-310-9714. **Fax:** (52) 662-310-9715. **E-Mail Address:** ligadelpacifico@ligadelpacifico.com.mx. **Website:** www.ligadelpacifico.com.mx.

Years League Active: 1958-.

President: Omar Canizales. **Administration:** Vanessa Palacios. **Sports Manager:** Dennis Gonzalez Oviel.

Member Clubs: Culiacan Tomateros, Guasave Algodoneros, Hermosillo Naranjeros, Los Mochis Caneros, Mazatlan Venados, Mexicali Aguilas, Navojoa Mayos, Obregon Yaquis.

Regular Season: 68 games. **2010 Opening Date:** Oct. 16.

Playoff Format: Six teams advance to best-of-seven quarterfinals. Three winners and losing team with best record advance to best-of-seven semifinals. Winners meet in best-of-seven series for league championship. Winner advances to Caribbean Series.

Roster Limit: 30. **Imports:** 5.

PUERTO RICAN LEAGUE

Office Address: Avenida Munoz Rivera 1056, Edificio First Federal, Suite 501, Rio Piedras, PR 00925. **Mailing Address:** P.O. Box 191852, San Juan, PR 00019. **Telephone:** (787) 765-6285, 765-7285. **Fax:** (787) 767-3028. **Website:** www.puertoricobaseballleague.com.

Years League Active: 1938-2007; 2008-

President: Joaquin Monserrate Matienzo. **Executive Director:** Benny Agosto.

Member Clubs: Arecibo Lobos, Caguas Criollos, Carolina Gigantes, Mayaguez Indios, Ponce Leones.

Regular Season: 42 games. **2010 Opening Date:** Nov. 11.

Playoff Format: Top four teams meet in best-of-seven semifinal series. Winners meet in best-of-nine series for league championship. Winner advances to Caribbean Series.

Roster Limit: 30. **Imports:** 5.

VENEZUELAN LEAGUE

Mailing Address: Avenida Casanova, Centro Comercial "El Recreo," Torre Sur, Piso 3, Oficinas 6 y 7, Sabana Grande, Caracas, Venezuela. **Telephone:** (58) 212-761-6408. **Fax:** (58) 212-761-7661. **Website:** www.lvbp.com.

Years League Active: 1946-.

President: Jose Grasso Vecchio. **Vice Presidents:** Rafael Chaverogazdik, Gustavo Massiani. **General Manager:** Domingo Alvarez.

Member Clubs: Anzoategui Caribes, Aragua Tigres, Caracas Leones, La Guaira Tiburones, Lara Cardenales, Magallanes Navegantes, Margarita Bravos, Zulia Aguilas.

Regular Season: 64 games. **2010 Opening Date:** Oct. 18.

Playoff Format: Top two teams in each division, plus a wild-card team, meet in 16-game round-robin series. Top two finishers meet in best-of-seven series for league championship. Winner advances to Caribbean Series.

Roster Limit: 26. **Imports:** 7.

COLOMBIAN LEAGUE

Office/Mailing Address: Unavailable. **Telephone:** Unavailable. **Website:** www.teamrenteria.com.

Member Clubs: Barranquilla, Cartagena, Monteria, Sincelejo.

Regular season: 65 games. **2010 Opening Date:** Oct. 28.

Playoff Format: Top two teams meet in best-of-seven finals for league championship.

NICARAGUAN LEAGUE

Office Address/Mailing Address: Canal 2 TV, Casa #26, Managua, Nicaragua. **Telephone:** 505-2266-3645. **Website:** www.lnbp.com.ni.

Commissioner: Noel Urcuyo Baez. **General Manager:** Azalea Salmeron. **Marketing Director:** Jessica Market.

Member Clubs: Chinandega, Granada, Leon, Managua.

Regular Season: 40 games. **2010 Opening Date:** Dec. 1.

Playoff Format: Top two teams meet in best-of-seven finals for league championship.

DOMESTIC LEAGUE

ARIZONA FALL LEAGUE

Mailing Address: 2415 E. Camelback Road, Suite 850, Phoenix, AZ 85016. **Telephone:** (602) 281-7250. **Fax:** (602) 281-7313. **E-Mail Address:** afl@mlb.com. **Website:** www.mlb.com.

Years League Active: 1992-.

Operated by: Major League Baseball.

Executive Director: Steve Cobb. **Seasonal Assistant:** Joan McGrath.

Teams: Mesa Solar Sox, Peoria Javelinas, Peoria Saguaros, Phoenix Desert Dogs, Scottsdale Scorpions, Surprise Rafters.

2010 Opening Date: Unavailable. Play usually opens in mid-October.

Playoff Format: Division champions meet in one-game championship.

Roster Limit: 30. Players with less than one year of major league service are eligible, with one foreign player and one player below the Double-A level allowed per team.

MINOR LEAGUE SCHEDULES

TRIPLE-A

INTERNATIONAL LEAGUE

BUFFALO

APRIL		JULY	
8-11	.at Scranton-Wilkes Barre	1-3	Rochester
12-13	at Syracuse	4-7	at Syracuse
14-16	Pawtucket	8-9	Scranton-Wilkes Barre
17-20	Scranton-Wilkes Barre	10-11	at Rochester
21-22	at Rochester	15-18	Gwinnett
23-26	at Pawtucket	19-20	at Rochester
27-30	Durham	21-22	Rochester
		23-26	.at Toledo
MAY		27-30	at Columbus
1-4	Louisville	31	Lehigh Valley
6-9	at Indianapolis		
10-13	.at Louisville	AUGUST	
14-17	Norfolk	1-3	Lehigh Valley
18-21	Charlotte Knights	5-8	Columbus
22-25	at Lehigh Valley	9-10	at Lehigh Valley
27-30	Toledo	11-12	at Scranton-Wilkes Barre
31	Syracuse	13-16	at Pawtucket
		18-20	Rochester
JUNE		21-25	Pawtucket
1-3	Syracuse	26-27	at Syracuse
4-7	at Norfolk	28-29	at Scranton-Wilkes Barre
8-11	.at Durham	30-31	Syracuse
12-15	Lehigh Valley		
17-20	.Indianapolis	SEPTEMBER	
21-24	.at Gwinnett	1-2	Scranton-Wilkes Barre
25-28	at Charlotte Knights	3-4	at Lehigh Valley
29-30	Syracuse		

CHARLOTTE KNIGHTS

APRIL		JULY	
9-11	at Gwinnett	1-3	at Norfolk
12-14	at Norfolk	4-5	.Norfolk
15-18	Gwinnett	6-7	Durham
19-20	Durham	8-11	at Gwinnett
21-22	.at Durham	15-16	.at Durham
23-26	.Norfolk	17-18	Durham
27-30	at Columbus	19-22	Louisville
		23-26	at Indianapolis
MAY		27-30	at Louisville
1-4	.at Toledo	31	Rochester
6-9	Pawtucket		
10-13	Lehigh Valley	AUGUST	
14-17	at Scranton-Wilkes Barre	1-3	Rochester
18-21	at Buffalo	5-8	Toledo
22-25	Columbus	10-12	.at Durham
27-30	.Indianapolis	13-15	at Norfolk
31	at Pawtucket	16-18	Durham
		19-22	Gwinnett
JUNE		23-25	.at Gwinnett
1-3	at Pawtucket	26-27	.Norfolk
4-7	at Lehigh Valley	28-29	Durham
8-11	Scranton-Wilkes Barre	30-31	.at Durham
12-15	Syracuse		
17-20	at Rochester	SEPTEMBER	
21-24	at Syracuse	1	.at Durham
25-28	Buffalo	2-3	at Norfolk
29-30	Norfolk		

COLUMBUS

APRIL		MAY	
9-11	.Indianapolis	1-4	Syracuse
12-13	Louisville	6-9	at Lehigh Valley
14-15	Toledo	10-13	at Scranton-Wilkes Barre
16-19	at Louisville	14-17	Durham
20-24	at Indianapolis	18-21	.at Gwinnett
22-24	.at Toledo	22-25	at Charlotte Knights
25-26	Toledo	27-30	Lehigh Valley
27-30	Charlotte Knights	31	Louisville

JUNE

JUNE			
1-2	Louisville	27-30	Buffalo
4-7	at Indianapolis	31	at Louisville
8-11	Rochester	AUGUST	
12-15	.Norfolk	1	.at Louisville
17-20	at Pawtucket	3-4	Louisville
21-24	at Rochester	5-8	at Buffalo
25-28	Gwinnett	9-12	at Syracuse
29-30	.Indianapolis	13-15	Louisville
		17-20	Scranton-Wilkes Barre
JULY		21-23	Toledo
1-2	at Indianapolis	24-25	.at Toledo
3-5	.at Toledo	26-27	.at Louisville
6-7	Toledo	28-29	.Indianapolis
8-9	.Indianapolis	30-31	at Indianapolis
10-11	at Louisville	SEPTEMBER	
15-18	at Norfolk	1	at Indianapolis
19-22	.at Durham	2-3	Toledo
23-26	Pawtucket		

DURHAM

APRIL		JULY	
9-11	at Norfolk	1-2	Louisville
12-14	at Gwinnett	3-5	Gwinnett
15-18	.Norfolk	6-7	at Charlotte Knights
19-20	at Charlotte Knights	8-9	.Norfolk
21-22	Charlotte Knights	10-11	at Norfolk
23-26	Gwinnett	15-16	Charlotte Knights
27-30	at Buffalo	17-18	at Charlotte Knights
		19-22	Columbus
MAY		23-26	Syracuse
1-4	at Rochester	27-30	at Lehigh Valley
6-9	Scranton-Wilkes Barre	31	at Pawtucket
10-13	Toledo		
14-17	at Columbus	AUGUST	
18-21	.at Toledo	1-3	at Pawtucket
22-25	.Pawtucket	5-8	.Indianapolis
27-30	Rochester	10-12	Charlotte Knights
31	.at Scranton-Wilkes Barre	13-15	.at Gwinnett
		16-18	at Charlotte Knights
JUNE		19-23	Charlotte Knights
1-3	.at Scranton-Wilkes Barre	24-25	.Norfolk
4-7	at Syracuse	26-27	.at Gwinnett
8-11	Buffalo	28-29	at Charlotte Knights
12-13	Gwinnett	30-31	Charlotte Knights
14-15	at Gwinnett		
17-20	at Louisville	SEPTEMBER	
21-24	at Indianapolis	1	Charlotte Knights
25-28	Lehigh Valley	2-3	Gwinnett
29-30	Louisville		

GWINNETT

APRIL			
9-11	Charlotte Knights	8-11	at Norfolk
12-14	Durham	12-13	.at Durham
15-18	at Charlotte Knights	14-15	Durham
19-22	at Norfolk	17-20	Syracuse
23-26	.at Durham	21-24	Buffalo
27-30	.Norfolk	25-28	at Columbus
		29-30	.at Toledo
MAY		JULY	
1-4	.Pawtucket	1-2	.at Toledo
6-9	at Syracuse	3-5	.at Durham
10-13	at Pawtucket	6-7	.Norfolk
14-17	Lehigh Valley	8-11	Charlotte Knights
18-21	Columbus	15-18	at Buffalo
22-25	at Indianapolis	19-22	at Scranton-Wilkes Barre
27-30	.at Louisville	23-26	Louisville
31	.Indianapolis	27-30	Rochester
		31	Toledo
JUNE		AUGUST	
1-3	.Indianapolis	1-3	Toledo
4-7	Scranton-Wilkes Barre		

5-8. . . . . . at Lehigh Valley
9-12. . . . . . . at Rochester
13-15. . . . . Durham
16-17. . . . . .Norfolk
19-22 . at Charlotte Knights
23-25 . . Charlotte Knights
26-27 . . . . Durham

28-30 . . . . .Norfolk
31 . . . . at Norfolk

SEPTEMBER
1. . . . . at Norfolk
2-3. . . . . .at Durham

INDIANAPOLIS

APRIL
9-11 . . . . . . at Columbus
12-13 . . . . .at Toledo
14-15 . . . . at Louisville
16-19 . . . . Toledo
20-21 . . . . . . Columbus
22-24 . . . . . . Louisville
25-26 . . . .at Louisville
27-30 . . . . . at Pawtucket

MAY
1-4. . . . . at Lehigh Valley
6-9. . . . . Buffalo
10-13 . . . . . . Rochester
14-17 . . . . . .at Toledo
18-21 . Scranton-Wilkes Barre
22-25 . . . . . . Gwinnett
27-30 . at Charlotte Knights
31 . . . . .at Gwinnett

JUNE
1-3. . . . . .at Gwinnett
4-7. . . . . Columbus
8-11 . . . . .Pawtucket
12-15at Scranton-Wilkes Barre
17-20 . . . . . . at Buffalo
21-24 . . . . Durham
25-28 . . . . Toledo
29-30 . . . . . at Columbus

JULY
1-2. . . . . Columbus
3 . . . . at Louisville
4-5. . . . . . . Louisville
6-7. . . . . .at Louisville
8-9. . . . . . at Columbus
10-11 . . . . . . .at Toledo
15-18 . . . . at Rochester
19-22 . . . . Lehigh Valley
23-26 . . Charlotte Knights
27-30 . . . . . at Syracuse
31 . . . . at Norfolk

AUGUST
1-3. . . . . at Norfolk
5-8. . . . . .at Durham
9-12. . . . . .Norfolk
13-16 . . . . . . Syracuse
18-20 . . . . . . .at Toledo
21-23 . . . . . . Louisville
24-25 . . . . at Louisville
26-27 . . . . Toledo
28-29 . . . . at Columbus
30-31 . . . . Columbus

SEPTEMBER
1. . . . . Columbus
2-4. . . . . . . Louisville

LEHIGH VALLEY

APRIL
8-11 . . . . . . at Syracuse
12-13 . . . . . at Pawtucket
14-16 . . . . . Rochester
17-20 . . . . . . Syracuse
21-22 . . . . . .Pawtucket
23-26at Scranton-Wilkes Barre
27-30 . . . . . at Rochester

MAY
1-4. . . . . . . .Indianapolis
6-9. . . . . Columbus
10-13 . at Charlotte Knights
14-17 . . . . . .at Gwinnett
18-21 . . . . . Louisville
22-25 . . . . Buffalo
27-30 . . . . at Columbus
31 . . . . .at Toledo

JUNE
1-3. . . . . .at Toledo
4-7. . . . Charlotte Knights
8-11 . . . . Toledo
12-15 . . . . . . at Buffalo
17-20 . Scranton-Wilkes Barre
21-24 . . . . . at Norfolk
25-28 . . . . .at Durham
29-30 . . . . . Rochester

JULY
1-2. . . . . Syracuse
3 . . . . . . at Pawtucket
4-7. . . . . . . .Pawtucket
8-9. . . . . . at Syracuse
10-11at Scranton-Wilkes Barre
15-18 . . . .at Louisville
19-22 . . . . at Indianapolis
23-26 . . . . .Norfolk
27-30 . . . . Durham
31 . . . . at Buffalo

AUGUST
1-3. . . . . at Buffalo
5-8. . . . . Gwinnett
9-10. . . . . Buffalo
11-12 . . . . . . .Pawtucket
13-16 . . . . at Rochester
18-20 . . . . . at Pawtucket
21-23 . . . . . . Rochester
24-25 . . . . . . Syracuse
26-27at Scranton-Wilkes Barre
28-29 . . . . at Syracuse
30-31 . Scranton-Wilkes Barre

SEPTEMBER
1-2. . . . . . . at Pawtucket
3-4. . . . . Buffalo

LOUISVILLE

APRIL
8-11 . . . . .at Toledo
12-13 . . . . at Columbus
14-15 . . . .Indianapolis
16-19 . . . . . . Columbus

MAY
1-4. . . . . at Buffalo
6-9. . . . . Rochester
10-13 . . . . .Buffalo
14-17 . . . . at Rochester
18-21 . . . at Lehigh Valley
22-25 . Scranton-Wilkes Barre
27-30 . . . . . . Gwinnett
31 . . . . . . at Columbus

JUNE
1-2. . . . . . at Columbus
4-7. . . . . . . .Pawtucket
8-11 . . . . . at Syracuse
12-15 . . . . at Pawtucket
17-20 . . . . Durham
21-24 . . . . . . Toledo
25-28 . . . . at Norfolk
29-30 . . . . . .at Durham

JULY
1-2. . . . . .at Durham
3 . . . . .Indianapolis
4-5. . . . . at Indianapolis
6-7. . . . . . . .Indianapolis

NORFOLK

APRIL
9-11 . . . . Durham
12-14 . . Charlotte Knights
15-18 . . . . . .at Durham
19-22 . . . . . . Gwinnett
23-26 . at Charlotte Knights
27-30 . . . . . at Gwinnett

MAY
1-4. . Scranton-Wilkes Barre
6-9. . . . . Toledo
10-13 . . . . at Syracuse
14-17 . . . . . at Buffalo
18-21 . . . . . . .Pawtucket
22-25 . . . . . . Rochester
27-30 . . . . at Pawtucket
31 . . . . at Rochester

JUNE
1-3. . . . . . . at Rochester
4-7. . . . . Buffalo
8-11 . . . . Gwinnett
12-15 . . . . at Columbus
17-20 . . . . . . .at Toledo
21-24 . . . . Lehigh Valley
25-28 . . . . . Louisville
29-30 . at Charlotte Knights

JULY
1-3. . . . . Charlotte Knights
4-5. . . at Charlotte Knights
6-7. . . . . at Gwinnett
8-9. . . . . . . .at Durham
10-11 . . . . . . Durham
15-18 . . . . . . Columbus
19-22 . . . . . . Syracuse
23-26 . . . at Lehigh Valley
27-30at Scranton-Wilkes Barre
31 . . . . .Indianapolis

AUGUST
1-3. . . . . . . .Indianapolis
5-8. . . . . . . .at Louisville
9-12. . . . at Indianapolis
13-15 . . . Charlotte Knights
16-17 . . . . . at Gwinnett
19-23 . . . . Durham
24-25 . . . . .at Durham
26-27 . at Charlotte Knights
28-30 . . . . at Gwinnett
31 . . . . Gwinnett

SEPTEMBER
1 . . . . Gwinnett
2-3. . . . Charlotte Knights

PAWTUCKET

APRIL
9-11 . . . . Rochester
12-13 . . . .Lehigh Valley
14-16 . . . . . . at Buffalo
17-20 . . . . at Rochester
21-22 . . . at Lehigh Valley
23-26 . . . . Buffalo
27-30 . . . . .Indianapolis

MAY
1-4. . . . . .at Gwinnett
6-9. . . at Charlotte Knights
10-13 . . . . . . Gwinnett
14-17 . . . . . Syracuse
18-21 . . . . . at Norfolk
22-25 . . . . . .at Durham
27-30 . . . . .Norfolk
31 . . . Charlotte Knights

JUNE
1-3. . . . Charlotte Knights
4-7. . . . . .at Louisville

8-11 . . . . . at Indianapolis
12-15 . . . . . . Louisville
17-20 . . . . . . Columbus
21-24at Scranton-Wilkes Barre
25-28 . . . . at Syracuse
29-30 . Scranton-Wilkes Barre

JULY
1-2. . Scranton-Wilkes Barre
3 . . . . .Lehigh Valley
4-7. . . . . at Lehigh Valley
8-9. . . . . Rochester
10-11 . . . . . Syracuse
15-18 . . . . at Syracuse
19-22 . . . . Toledo
23-26 . . . . at Columbus
27-30 . . . . . .at Toledo
31 . . . . Durham

AUGUST
1-3. . . . . at Durham
5-8. . . Scranton-Wilkes Barre

9-10 .at Scranton-Wilkes Barre
11-12 . . . . at Lehigh Valley
13-16 . . . . Buffalo
18-20 . . . . . . Lehigh Valley
21-25 . . . . at Buffalo
26-29 . . . . . . at Rochester

30-31 . . . . Rochester

SEPTEMBER
1-2. . . . . . . Lehigh Valley
3-4. .at Scranton-Wilkes Barre

ROCHESTER

APRIL	
9-11 . . . . . . at Pawtucket	
12-13at Scranton-Wilkes Barre	
14-16 . . . . at Lehigh Valley	
17-20 . . . . Pawtucket	
21-22 . . . . Buffalo	
23-26 . . . . . . at Syracuse	
27-30 . . . . . Lehigh Valley	

MAY
1-4. . . . . Durham
6-9. . . . . at Louisville
10-13 . . . . .at Indianapolis
14-17 . . . . Louisville
18-21 . . . . Syracuse
22-25 . . . . . . at Norfolk
27-30 . . . . .at Durham
31 . . . . Norfolk

JUNE
1-3. . . . . Norfolk
4-7. . . . . Toledo
8-11 . . . . . . at Columbus
12-15 . . . . . .at Toledo
17-20 . . . Charlotte Knights
21-24 . . . . Columbus
25-28at Scranton-Wilkes Barre
29-30 . . . . at Lehigh Valley

JULY
1-3. . . . . at Buffalo
4-7. . . Scranton-Wilkes Barre
8-9. . . . . . . at Pawtucket
10-11 . . . . Buffalo
15-18 . . . . . . .Indianapolis
19-20 . . . . Buffalo
21-22 . . . . . . at Buffalo
23-26 . Scranton-Wilkes Barre
27-30 . . . . . .at Gwinnett
31 . . . at Charlotte Knights

AUGUST
1-3. . at Charlotte Knights
5-6. . . . . Syracuse
7-8. . . . . . . at Syracuse
9-12. . . . . Gwinnett
13-16 . . . . . Lehigh Valley
18-20 . . . . . . at Buffalo
21-23 . . . . at Lehigh Valley
24-25at Scranton-Wilkes Barre
26-29 . . . . Pawtucket
30-31 . . . . . at Pawtucket

SEPTEMBER
1-2. . . . . at Syracuse
3-4. . . . . Syracuse

SCRANTON-WILKES BARRE

APRIL	
8-11 . . . . Buffalo	
12-13 . . . . Rochester	
14-16 . . . . Syracuse	
17-20 . . . . . . at Buffalo	
21-22 . . . . . at Syracuse	
23-26 . . . . . Lehigh Valley	
27-30 . . . . Louisville	

MAY
1-4. . . . . at Norfolk
6-9. . . . . .at Durham
10-13 . . . . Columbus
14-17 . . Charlotte Knights
18-21 . . . . at Indianapolis
22-25 . . . . . .at Louisville
27-28 . . . . Syracuse
29-30 . . . . . . at Syracuse
31 . . . . Durham

JUNE
1-3. . . . . Durham
4-7. . . . . at Gwinnett
8-11 . at Charlotte Knights
12-15 . . . . . .Indianapolis
17-20 . . . . at Lehigh Valley
21-24 . . . . Pawtucket
25-28 . . . . . . Rochester
29-30 . . . . . at Pawtucket

JULY
1-2. . . . . . . at Pawtucket
3 . . . . Syracuse
4-7. . . . . . . at Rochester
8-9. . . . . at Buffalo
10-11 . . . . . Lehigh Valley
15-18 . . . . Toledo
19-22 . . . . . . Gwinnett
23-26 . . . . . at Rochester
27-30 . . . . .Norfolk
31 . . . . Syracuse

AUGUST
1 . . . . Syracuse
2-3. . . . . at Syracuse
5-8. . . . . . at Pawtucket
9-10 . . . . .Pawtucket
11-12 . . . . Buffalo
13-16 . . . . . .at Toledo
17-20 . . . . at Columbus
21-22 . . . . . at Syracuse
24-25 . . . . . . Rochester
26-27 . . . . . Lehigh Valley
28-29 . . . . Buffalo
30-31 . . . at Lehigh Valley

SEPTEMBER
1-2. . . . . at Buffalo
3-4. . . . . .Pawtucket

SYRACUSE

APRIL	
8-11 . . . . . . Lehigh Valley	
12-13 . . . . Buffalo	
14-16at Scranton-Wilkes Barre	
17-20 . . . . at Lehigh Valley	
21-22 . Scranton-Wilkes Barre	

23-26 . . . . . . Rochester
27-30 . . . . . . .at Toledo

MAY
1-4. . . . . . . at Columbus
6-9. . . . . Gwinnett

10-13 . . . . .Norfolk
14-17 . . . . . at Pawtucket
18-21 . . . . . at Rochester
22-25 . . . . Toledo
27-28at Scranton-Wilkes Barre
29-30 . Scranton-Wilkes Barre
31 . . . . at Buffalo

JUNE
1-3. . . . . at Buffalo
4-7. . . . . Durham
8-11 . . . . Louisville
12-15 . at Charlotte Knights
17-20 . . . . . . .at Gwinnett
21-24 . . . Charlotte Knights
25-28 . . . . .Pawtucket
29-30 . . . . . . at Buffalo

JULY
1-2. . . . . at Lehigh Valley
3 . . .at Scranton-Wilkes Barre
4-7. . . . . Buffalo
8-9. . . . . . . Lehigh Valley
10-11 . . . . . at Pawtucket

TOLEDO

APRIL	
8-11 . . . . Louisville	
12-13 . . . . . . .Indianapolis	
14-15 . . . . at Columbus	
16-19 . . . at Indianapolis	
20-21 . . . . .at Louisville	
22-24 . . . . Columbus	
25-26 . . . . at Columbus	
27-30 . . . . Syracuse	

MAY
1-4. . . . Charlotte Knights
6-9. . . . . at Norfolk
10-13 . . . . . .at Durham
14-17 . . . . . .Indianapolis
18-21 . . . . Durham
22-25 . . . . . at Syracuse
27-30 . . . . . . at Buffalo
31 . . . . Lehigh Valley

JUNE
1-3. . . . . . . Lehigh Valley
4-7. . . . . . . at Rochester
8-11 . . . . at Lehigh Valley
12-15 . . . . . . Rochester
17-20 . . . . . . .Norfolk
21-24 . . . . .at Louisville
25-28 . . . at Indianapolis
29-30 . . . . . . Gwinnett

JULY
1-2. . . . . Gwinnett
3-5. . . . . Columbus
6-7. . . . . . at Columbus
8-9. . . . . . . at Louisville
10-11 . . . . .Indianapolis
15-18at Scranton-Wilkes Barre
19-22 . . . . at Pawtucket
23-26 . . . . Buffalo
27-30 . . . . . . .Pawtucket
31 . . . . .at Gwinnett

AUGUST
1-3. . . . . at Gwinnett
5-8. . . at Charlotte Knights
9-12. . . . . Louisville
13-16 . Scranton-Wilkes Barre
18-20 . . . . . .Indianapolis
21-23 . . . . at Columbus
24-25 . . . . Columbus
26-27 . . . .at Indianapolis
28-30 . . . . at Louisville
31 . . . . Louisville

SEPTEMBER
1 . . . . Louisville
2-3. . . . . . . at Columbus

10-13 . . . . .Norfolk
14-17 . . . . at Pawtucket
18-21 . . . . . at Rochester
22-25 . . . . Toledo
27-28at Scranton-Wilkes Barre
29-30 . Scranton-Wilkes Barre
31 . . . . at Buffalo

JUNE
1-3. . . . . at Buffalo
4-7. . . . . Durham
8-11 . . . . Louisville
12-15 . at Charlotte Knights
17-20 . . . . . . .at Gwinnett
21-24 . . . Charlotte Knights
25-28 . . . . .Pawtucket
29-30 . . . . . . at Buffalo

JULY
1-2. . . . . at Lehigh Valley
3 . . .at Scranton-Wilkes Barre
4-7. . . . . Buffalo
8-9. . . . . . . Lehigh Valley
10-11 . . . . . at Pawtucket

15-18 . . . . . . .Pawtucket
19-22 . . . . . . at Norfolk
23-26 . . . . . .at Durham
27-30 . . . . . .Indianapolis
31 . .at Scranton-Wilkes Barre

AUGUST
1 . .at Scranton-Wilkes Barre
2-3. . . Scranton-Wilkes Barre
5-6. . . . . . at Rochester
7-8. . . . . Rochester
9-12. . . . . Columbus
13-16 . . . at Indianapolis
17-20 . . . . at Louisville
21-22 . Scranton-Wilkes Barre
24-25 . . . at Lehigh Valley
26-27 . . . . Buffalo
28-29 . . . . . Lehigh Valley
30-31 . . . . . . at Buffalo

SEPTEMBER
1-2. . . . . Rochester
3-4. . . . . . . at Rochester

PACIFIC COAST LEAGUE

ALBUQUERQUE

APRIL	
8-11 . . . . at Oklahoma City	
12-15 . . . . . New Orleans	
16-19 . . . . . . .Omaha	
20-23 . . . .at New Orleans	
24-27 . . . . . . at Omaha	
29-30 . . . . . .Round Rock	

MAY
1-2. . . . . . . .Round Rock
3-6. . . . . . . .at Memphis
7-10. . . . . . . .Nashville
11-14 .at Colorado Springs
15-18 . . . . at Salt Lake
20-23 . . . . Las Vegas
24-27 . . . . Reno
28-31 . . . .at Memphis

JUNE
1-4. . . . . at Nashville
5-8. . . . . Memphis
10-13 . . at Oklahoma City
14-17 . . . . . . .Omaha
18-21 . . . . . .at Iowa
22-25 . . . at Round Rock
26-29 . . . . . . Memphis

JULY
1-3. . . . . Oklahoma City
4-7. . . . . . . .at Iowa
8-11 . . . . . . at Omaha
15-18 . . . . .Round Rock
19-22 . . at Nashville
23-26 . . . . . .Nashville
27-30 . . . . Iowa
31 . . . . . .at New Orleans

AUGUST
1-3 . . . . . .at New Orleans
4-7 . . . . .Sacramento
8-11 . . . . Fresno
13-16 . . at Portland Beavers
17-20 . . . . at Tacoma

COLORADO SPRINGS

APRIL
8-11 . . . . at Tacoma
12-15 . . at Portland Beavers
16-19 . . . . . Las Vegas
20-23 . . . . . . .Tacoma
24-27 . . . . . . .at Reno
29-30 . . . . . .at Las Vegas

MAY
1-2 . . . . . . .at Las Vegas
3-6 . . . . Fresno
7-10 . . . . . at Sacramento
11-14 . . . . . Albuquerque
15-18 . . . . . .Round Rock
20-23 . . . . . . .at Iowa
24-27 . . . . at Omaha
28-31 . . Portland Beavers

JUNE
1-4 . . . . Reno
5-8 . . . . . at Salt Lake
10-13 . . . . .at Las Vegas
14-17 . . . . . .Tacoma
18-21 . . . . Las Vegas
22-25 . . . . .at Reno

FRESNO

APRIL
8-11 . . . . .at Reno
12-15 . . . . . .at Las Vegas
16-19 . . Portland Beavers
20-23 . . . . . . Reno
24-27 . . at Portland Beavers
29-30 . . . . . .Sacramento

MAY
1-2 . . . . . . .Sacramento
3-6 . . . .at Colorado Springs
7-10 . . . . Salt Lake
11-14 . . .at New Orleans
15-18 . . at Oklahoma City
20-23 . . . . . . .Nashville
24-27 . . . . . . Memphis
28-31 . . . . at Salt Lake

JUNE
1-4 . . . . .at Las Vegas
5-8 . . . . . Sacramento
10-13 . . . . . at Tacoma
14-17 . . . Portland Beavers
18-21 . . . . . Reno
22-25 . . at Portland Beavers

IOWA

APRIL
8-11 . . . . . . .Nashville
12-15 . . . . Memphis
16-19 . . . . . at Nashville
20-23 . . . . . .at Memphis
24-27 . . . . . .Round Rock
29-30 . . . . .Omaha

MAY
1-2 . . . . . . .Omaha
3-6 . . . . . .at New Orleans
7-10 . . . .Oklahoma City
11-14 . . . . . .at Las Vegas

21-24 . . . . . . New Orleans
25-29 . . . .Oklahoma City
30-31 . . . . Iowa

SEPTEMBER
1-2 . . . . Iowa

26-29 . . . Portland Beavers

JULY
1-3 . . . . Salt Lake
4-7 . . . . .at Fresno
8-11 . . . . Reno
15-18 . . at Portland Beavers
19-22 . . . . . .Sacramento
23-26 . . . . . at Salt Lake
27-30 . . . . at Sacramento
31 . . . . .at Fresno

AUGUST
1-3 . . . . .at Fresno
4-7 . . . . . . New Orleans
8-11 . . . . .Oklahoma City
13-16 . . . . . .at Memphis
17-20 . . . . . at Nashville
21-24 . . . . Fresno
25-29 . . . . . Salt Lake
30-31 . . . . . . at Tacoma

SEPTEMBER
1-2 . . . . at Tacoma

26-29 . . . . Las Vegas

JULY
1-3 . . . . . . at Sacramento
4-7 . . . . Colorado Springs
8-11 . . . . at Tacoma
15-18 . . . . Las Vegas
19-22 . . . . . . .Salt Lake
23-26 . . . . . . .at Reno
27-30 . . . . .Tacoma
31 . . . . . Colorado Springs

AUGUST
1-3 . . . . Colorado Springs
4-7 . . . . . at Round Rock
8-11 . . . at Albuquerque
13-16 . . . . Iowa
17-20 . . . . .Omaha
21-24 . .at Colorado Springs
25-29 . . . at Sacramento
30-31 . . . . at Salt Lake

SEPTEMBER
1-2 . . . . at Salt Lake

15-18 . . . . .at Reno
20-23 . . . Colorado Springs
24-27 . . . . . . .Salt Lake
28-31 . . . . at Nashville

JUNE
1-4 . . . . . . at Round Rock
5-8 . . . . New Orleans
10-13 . . . . . .at Memphis
14-17 . . . . . .Round Rock
18-21 . . . . . Albuquerque
22-25 . . . . .Omaha
26-29 . . . .at New Orleans

JULY
1-3 . . . . at Omaha
4-7 . . . . . . Albuquerque
8-11 . . . . . New Orleans
15-18 . . at Oklahoma City
19-22 . . . .Oklahoma City
23-26 . . . at Round Rock
27-30 . . . . at Albuquerque
31 . . . . . at Oklahoma City

AUGUST
1-3 . . . at Oklahoma City

LAS VEGAS

APRIL
8-11 . . . . .Salt Lake
12-15 . . . . Fresno
16-19 . .at Colorado Springs
20-23 . . . . at Salt Lake
24-27 . . . . . .Sacramento
29-30 . . . Colorado Springs

MAY
1-2 . . . . Colorado Springs
3-6 . . . . .at Reno
7-10 . . . . at Tacoma
11-14 . . . . Iowa
15-18 . . . . .Omaha
20-23 . . . at Albuquerque
24-27 . . . . at Round Rock
28-31 . . . . . . .Tacoma

JUNE
1-4 . . . . Fresno
5-8 . . . . at Tacoma
10-13 . . . Colorado Springs
14-17 . . . . . . at Salt Lake
18-21 . .at Colorado Springs
22-25 . . . . . . .Sacramento

MEMPHIS

APRIL
8-11 . . . . at Omaha
12-15 . . . . .at Iowa
16-19 . . . .Oklahoma City
20-23 . . . . Iowa
24-27 . . . at Oklahoma City
29-30 . . . at Nashville

MAY
1-2 . . . . at Nashville
3-6 . . . . Albuquerque
7-10 . . . . . at Round Rock
11-14 . . . Portland Beavers
15-18 . . . . .Tacoma
20-23 . . . . at Sacramento
24-27 . . . . . . .at Fresno
28-31 . . . . . Albuquerque

JUNE
1-4 . . . at Oklahoma City
5-8 . . . . . at Albuquerque
10-13 . . . . Iowa
14-17 . . . . at Nashville
18-21 . . . . . New Orleans
22-25 . . . . .Nashville

NASHVILLE

APRIL
8-11 . . . . .at Iowa
12-15 . . . . at Omaha
16-19 . . . . Iowa
20-23 . . . .Oklahoma City
24-27 . . . .at New Orleans
29-30 . . . . Memphis

4-7 . . . . .Tacoma
8-11 . . . Portland Beavers
13-16 . . . . . . .at Fresno
17-20 . . . . at Sacramento
21-24 . . . . .Nashville
25-29 . . . . . at Omaha
30-31 . . . . at Albuquerque

SEPTEMBER
1-2 . . . . . at Albuquerque

26-29 . . . . .at Fresno

JULY
1-3 . . . . Reno
4-7 . . . at Portland Beavers
8-10 . . . . .Salt Lake
15-18 . . . . .at Fresno
19-22 . . . . .Tacoma
23-26 . . . Portland Beavers
27-30 . . . . .at Reno
31 . . . . . at Sacramento

AUGUST
1-3 . . . . . at Sacramento
4-7 . . . . Memphis
8-11 . . . . .Nashville
13-16 . . at Oklahoma City
17-20 . . . at New Orleans
21-24 . . . Portland Beavers
25-29 . . . . Reno
30-31 . . . at Sacramento

SEPTEMBER
1-2 . . . . . . at Sacramento

26-29 . . . . at Albuquerque

JULY
1-3 . . . . .Round Rock
4-7 . . . . . at Round Rock
8-11 . . . . .Nashville
15-18 . . .at New Orleans
19-22 . . . . .Omaha
23-26 . . . .Oklahoma City
27-30 . . .at New Orleans
31 . . . . .Omaha

AUGUST
1-3 . . . . .Omaha
4-7 . . . . .at Las Vegas
8-11 . . . . .at Reno
13-16 . . . Colorado Springs
17-20 . . . . .Salt Lake
21-24 . . . . at Omaha
25-29 . . . . . .Round Rock
30-31 . . . . . New Orleans

SEPTEMBER
1-2 . . . . New Orleans

MAY
1-2 . . . . Memphis
3-6 . . . . . . at Round Rock
7-10 . . . at Albuquerque
11-14 . . . . .Tacoma
15-18 . . . Portland Beavers
20-23 . . . . .at Fresno

24-27 . . . . . at Sacramento
28-31 . . . . Iowa

JUNE
1-4 . . . . Albuquerque
5-8 . . . . . . at Round Rock
10-13 . . . . at Omaha
14-17 . . . . Memphis
18-21 . . . Oklahoma City
22-25 . . . . at Memphis
26-29 . . . Round Rock

JULY
1-3 . . . . New Orleans
4-7 . . . . at Oklahoma City
8-11 . . . . . at Memphis
15-18 . . . . Omaha

NEW ORLEANS

APRIL
8-11 . . . . Round Rock
12-15 . . . . at Albuquerque
16-19 . . . at Round Rock
20-23 . . . . Albuquerque
24-27 . . . . Nashville
29-30 . . at Oklahoma City

MAY
1-2 . . . . at Oklahoma City
3-6 . . . . Iowa
7-10 . . . . . . at Omaha
11-14 . . . . . . Fresno
15-18 . . . . . Sacramento
20-23 . . . . at Tacoma
24-27 . at Portland Beavers
28-31 . . . . Oklahoma City

JUNE
1-4 . . . . Omaha
5-8 . . . . at Iowa
10-13 . . . . . Round Rock
14-17 . . at Oklahoma City
18-21 . . . . . at Memphis

22-25 . . . . Oklahoma City
26-29 . . . . Iowa

JULY
1-3 . . . . at Nashville
4-7 . . . . Omaha
8-11 . . . . at Iowa
15-18 . . . . . . Memphis
19-22 . . . at Round Rock
23-26 . . . . at Omaha
27-30 . . . . Memphis
31 . . . . Albuquerque

AUGUST
1-3 . . . . Albuquerque
4-7 . . . at Colorado Springs
8-11 . . . . . . at Salt Lake
13-16 . . . . . . Reno
17-20 . . . . . Las Vegas
21-24 . . at Albuquerque
25-29 . . . at Nashville
30-31 . . . . at Memphis

SEPTEMBER
1-2 . . . . at Memphis

OKLAHOMA CITY

APRIL
8-11 . . . . . . Albuquerque
12-15 . . . . . . Round Rock
16-19 . . . . . at Memphis
20-23 . . . . at Nashville
24-27 . . . . . . Memphis
29-30 . . . . . New Orleans

MAY
1-2 . . . . . . New Orleans
3-6 . . . . at Omaha
7-10 . . . . at Iowa
11-14 . . . . . Sacramento
15-18 . . . . . Fresno
20-23 . . at Portland Beavers
24-27 . . . . at Tacoma
28-31 . . . . at New Orleans

JUNE
1-4 . . . . Memphis
5-8 . . . . at Omaha
10-13 . . . Albuquerque
14-17 . . . . New Orleans
18-21 . . . . at Nashville

20-23 . . . . at Round Rock
24-27 . . . . . Albuquerque
29-30 . . . . at Iowa

JULY
1-3 . . . . . at Albuquerque
4-7 . . . . Nashville
8-11 . . . . at Round Rock
15-18 . . . . Iowa
19-22 . . . . at Iowa
23-26 . . . at Memphis
27-30 . . . . Round Rock
31 . . . . Iowa

AUGUST
1-3 . . . . Iowa
4-7 . . . . at Salt Lake
8-11 . . at Colorado Springs
13-16 . . . . Las Vegas
17-20 . . . . . . Reno
21-24 . . . at Round Rock
25-29 . . at Albuquerque
30-31 . . . . Nashville

SEPTEMBER
1-2 . . . . Nashville

OMAHA

APRIL
8-11 . . . . Memphis
12-15 . . . . Nashville
16-19 . . . . at Albuquerque

20-23 . . . . at Round Rock
24-27 . . . . . Albuquerque
29-30 . . . . at Iowa

MAY
1-2 . . . . at Iowa
3-6 . . . . . . Oklahoma City
7-10 . . . . New Orleans
11-14 . . . . . at Reno
15-18 . . . . . at Las Vegas
20-23 . . . . . Salt Lake
24-27 . . Colorado Springs
28-31 . . . . Round Rock

JUNE
1-4 . . . at New Orleans
5-8 . . . . Oklahoma City
10-13 . . . . . Nashville
14-17 . . . at Albuquerque
18-21 . . at Round Rock
22-25 . . . . . . at Iowa
26-29 . . . at Oklahoma City

JULY
1-3 . . . . Iowa
4-7 . . . at New Orleans
8-11 . . . . Albuquerque

PORTLAND BEAVERS

APRIL
8-11 . . . . Sacramento
12-15 . . . Colorado Springs
16-19 . . . . at Fresno
20-23 . . . at Sacramento
24-27 . . . . . . Fresno
29-30 . . . . at Salt Lake

MAY
1-2 . . . . . at Salt Lake
3-6 . . . . Tacoma
7-10 . . . . Reno
11-14 . . . . at Memphis
15-18 . . . at Nashville
20-23 . . . Oklahoma City
24-27 . . . New Orleans
28-31 . at Colorado Springs

JUNE
1-4 . . . . Salt Lake
5-8 . . . . at Reno
10-13 . . . . . Sacramento
14-17 . . . . . . at Fresno
18-21 . . . . . . Tacoma
22-25 . . . . Fresno

RENO

APRIL
8-11 . . . . Fresno
12-15 . . . . . Salt Lake
16-19 . . . at Sacramento
20-23 . . . . at Fresno
24-27 . . Colorado Springs
29-30 . . . . at Tacoma

MAY
1-2 . . . . . . at Tacoma
3-6 . . . . . Las Vegas
7-10 . . at Portland Beavers
11-14 . . . . . Omaha
15-18 . . . . Iowa
20-23 . . at Round Rock
24-27 . . at Albuquerque
28-31 . . . . Sacramento

JUNE
1-4 . . . at Colorado Springs
5-8 . . . Portland Beavers
10-13 . . . . . Salt Lake
14-17 . . . at Sacramento
18-21 . . . . . at Fresno

15-18 . . . . . . at Nashville
19-22 . . . . . at Memphis
23-26 . . . . . New Orleans
27-30 . . . . at Nashville
31 . . . . at Memphis

AUGUST
1-3 . . . . at Memphis
4-7 . . . . Portland Beavers
8-11 . . . . Tacoma
13-16 . . . . at Sacramento
17-20 . . . . . at Fresno
21-24 . . . . . Memphis
25-29 . . . . Iowa
30-31 . . . . . Round Rock

SEPTEMBER
1-2 . . . . Round Rock
Pacific Coast League All-Stars

JULY

26-29 . . at Colorado Springs

JULY
1-3 . . . . at Tacoma
4-7 . . . . . Las Vegas
8-11 . . . at Sacramento
15-18 . . . Colorado Springs
19-22 . . . . . . Reno
23-26 . . at Las Vegas
27-30 . . at Salt Lake
31 . . . . Salt Lake

AUGUST
1-3 . . . . Salt Lake
4-7 . . . . . . at Omaha
8-11 . . . . . . at Iowa
13-16 . . . Albuquerque
17-20 . . . Round Rock
21-24 . . at Las Vegas
25-29 . . . at Tacoma
30-31 . . . . at Reno

SEPTEMBER
1-2 . . . . at Reno

22-25 . . . Colorado Springs
26-29 . . . . . at Salt Lake

JULY
1-3 . . . . . . at Las Vegas
4-7 . . . . Sacramento
8-11 . . at Colorado Springs
15-18 . . . . . . Tacoma
19-22 . . at Portland Beavers
23-26 . . . . . . Fresno
27-30 . . . . Las Vegas
31 . . . . at Tacoma

AUGUST
1-3 . . . . . . at Tacoma
4-7 . . . . . . Nashville
8-11 . . . . . . Memphis
13-16 . . at New Orleans
17-20 . . at Oklahoma City
21-24 . . . . . Tacoma
25-29 . . . at Las Vegas
30-31 . . . Portland Beavers

SEPTEMBER
1-2 . . . . . Portland Beavers

ROUND ROCK

APRIL
8-11 . . . . . .at New Orleans
12-15 . . . at Oklahoma City
16-19 . . . . . New Orleans
20-23 . . . . .Omaha
24-27 . . . . .at Iowa
29-30 . . . . at Albuquerque

MAY
1-2. . . . . at Albuquerque
3-6. . . . . .Nashville
7-10 . . . . Memphis
11-14 . . . . . at Salt Lake
15-18 . .at Colorado Springs
20-23 . . . . Reno
24-27 . . . . . . Las Vegas
28-31 . . . . . . at Omaha

JUNE
1-4. . . . . Iowa
5-8. . . . . .Nashville
10-13 . . . .at New Orleans
14-17 . . . . .at Iowa
18-21 . . . . .Omaha

22-25 . . . . . . Albuquerque
26-29 . . . . at Nashville

JULY
1-3. . . . . .at Memphis
4-7. . . . . Memphis
8-11 . . . . . Oklahoma City
15-18 . . . at Albuquerque
19-22 . . . . . New Orleans
23-26 . . . . Iowa
27-30 . . at Oklahoma City
31 . . . . .at Nashville

AUGUST
1-3. . . . . at Nashville
4-7. . . . . Fresno
8-11 . . . . . .Sacramento
13-16 . . . . . . at Tacoma
17-20 . .at Portland Beavers
21-24 . . . . Oklahoma City
25-29 . . . . .at Memphis
30-31 . . . . . . at Omaha

SEPTEMBER
1-2. . . . . at Omaha

SALT LAKE

APRIL
8-11 . . . . .at Las Vegas
12-15 . . . . .at Reno
16-19 . . . . .Tacoma
20-23 . . . . . . Las Vegas
24-27 . . . . . . at Tacoma
29-30 . . . Portland Beavers

MAY
1-2. . . . . Portland Beavers
3-6. . . . . . at Sacramento
7-10 . . . . .at Fresno
11-14 . . . . . . .Round Rock
15-18 . . . . Albuquerque
20-23 . . . . . . at Omaha
24-27 . . . . . . .at Iowa
28-31 . . . . Fresno

JUNE
1-4. . . . at Portland Beavers
5-8. . . . . Colorado Springs
10-13 . . . . .at Reno
14-17 . . . . . Las Vegas
18-21 . . . . . at Sacramento

22-25 . . . . at Tacoma
26-29 . . . . Reno

JULY
1-3. . . . .at Colorado Springs
4-7. . . . . .Tacoma
8-11 . . . . . .at Las Vegas
15-18 . . . . . . .Sacramento
19-22 . . . . .at Fresno
23-26 . . . . Colorado Springs
27-30 . . . Portland Beavers
31 . . . .at Portland Beavers

AUGUST
1-3. . . . .at Portland Beavers
4-7. . . . . . . .Oklahoma City
8-11 . . . . . . New Orleans
13-16 . . . . . at Nashville
17-20 . . . . .at Memphis
21-24 . . . . . .Sacramento
25-29 . .at Colorado Springs
30-31 . . . . Fresno

SEPTEMBER
1-2. . . . . Fresno

SACRAMENTO

APRIL
8-11 . . . at Portland Beavers
12-15 . . . . at Tacoma
16-19 . . . . Reno
20-23 . . . Portland Beavers
24-27 . . . .at Las Vegas
29-30 . . . . .at Fresno

MAY
1-2. . . . . .at Fresno
3-6. . . . . .Salt Lake
7-10 . . . . Colorado Springs
11-14 . . . at Oklahoma City
15-18 . . . .at New Orleans
20-23 . . . . Memphis
24-27 . . . . . . .Nashville
28-31 . . . . .at Reno

JUNE
1-4. . . . . .Tacoma
5-8. . . . . .at Fresno
10-13 . . at Portland Beavers
14-17 . . . . Reno
18-21 . . . . . . .Salt Lake

22-25 . . . . . .at Las Vegas
26-29 . . . . .Tacoma

JULY
1-3. . . . . Fresno
4-7. . . . . .at Reno
8-11 . . . . Portland Beavers
15-18 . . . . . at Salt Lake
19-22 . .at Colorado Springs
23-26 . . . . at Tacoma
27-30 . . . Colorado Springs
31 . . . . Las Vegas

AUGUST
1-3. . . . . Las Vegas
4-7. . . . . at Albuquerque
8-11 . . . . at Round Rock
13-16 . . . . .Omaha
17-20 . . . . Iowa
21-24 . . . . . at Salt Lake
25-29 . . . . Fresno
30-31 . . . . . . Las Vegas

SEPTEMBER
1-2. . . . . Las Vegas

TACOMA

APRIL
8-11 . . . . Colorado Springs
12-15 . . . . . . .Sacramento
16-19 . . . . . at Salt Lake
20-23 . .at Colorado Springs
24-27 . . . . . . .Salt Lake
29-30 . . . . Reno

MAY
1-2. . . . . Reno
3-6. . . .at Portland Beavers
7-10 . . . . Las Vegas
11-14 . . . . . at Nashville
15-18 . . . . .at Memphis
20-23 . . . . . New Orleans
24-27 . . . .Oklahoma City
28-31 . . . . . .at Las Vegas

JUNE
1-4. . . . . . at Sacramento
5-8. . . . . Las Vegas
10-13 . . . . Fresno
14-17 . .at Colorado Springs
18-21 . .at Portland Beavers
22-25 . . . . .Salt Lake

26-29 . . . . . at Sacramento

JULY
1-3. . . . . Portland Beavers
4-7. . . . . . at Salt Lake
8-11 . . . . Fresno
15-18 . . . . .at Reno
19-22 . . . . .at Las Vegas
23-26 . . . . . .Sacramento
27-30 . . . . .at Reno
31 . . . . Reno

AUGUST
1-3. . . . . Reno
4-7. . . . . .at Iowa
8-11 . . . . . . at Omaha
13-16 . . . . . .Round Rock
17-20 . . . . . . Albuquerque
21-24 . . . . .at Reno
25-29 . . . Portland Beavers
30-31 . . . Colorado Springs

SEPTEMBER
1-2. . . . . Colorado Springs

DOUBLE-A

EASTERN LEAGUE

AKRON

APRIL
8-11 . . . . . .at Binghamton
12-14 . . . . at Trenton
15-18 . . . . .Bowie
19-21 . . . . . . Altoona
22-25 . . . . . at Bowie
26-28 . . . . .at Altoona
30 . . . . Binghamton

MAY
1-2. . . . . . Binghamton
3-6. . . . . Trenton
7-9. . . . . .at Reading

10-12 . . . . at Erie
13-16 . . . . Reading
18-20 . . . . . . .at Altoona
21-23 . . . . . .Harrisburg
24-27 . . . . Altoona
28-31 . . . . .at Binghamton

JUNE
1-3. . . . . Erie
4-6. . . . . . .at Harrisburg
8-10 . . . . New Hampshire
11-13 . . Portland Sea Dogs
15-17 . . at New Hampshire

18-20 . .at Portland Sea Dogs
22-24 . . . . . . .Richmond
25-27 . . . . . Binghamton
28-30 . . . . . . at Richmond

JULY
1-4. . . . . at Bowie
5-8. . . . . Trenton
9-12 . . . . at Erie
15-18 . . . . Erie
19-21 . . . . Altoona
22-25 . . . .at Reading
26-28 . . . . . . .Bowie
29-31 . . . . Reading

AUGUST
1 . . . . Reading
3-5. . . . . .at Altoona
6-8. . . . . . at New Britain
10-12 . . . . Reading
13-15 . . . . . . New Britain
17-19 . . . . . .at Reading
20-22 . . . . . .Harrisburg
23-25 . . . . . .at Bowie
26-29 . . . . Erie
30-31 . . . . . .at Trenton

SEPTEMBER
1-2. . . . . at Trenton

ALTOONA

APRIL
8-11	Harrisburg
12-14	Richmond
15-18	at Erie
19-21	at Akron
22-25	Erie
26-28	Akron
30	at Harrisburg

MAY
1-2	at Harrisburg
3-6	at Richmond
7-9	Erie
10-12	Harrisburg
13-16	at Richmond
18-20	Akron
21-23	at Erie
24-27	at Akron
28-31	Reading

JUNE
1-3	at New Britain
4-6	at New Hampshire
8-10	Harrisburg
11-13	New Britain
15-17	at Trenton
18-20	at Richmond

22-24	Portland Sea Dogs
25-27	Bowie
28-30	at Binghamton

JULY
1-4	at Reading
5-8	Binghamton
9-12	Richmond
15-18	at Harrisburg
19-21	at Akron
22-25	Trenton
26-28	at Erie
29-31	at Richmond

AUGUST
1	at Richmond
3-5	Akron
6-8	at Harrisburg
10-12	Trenton
13-15	New Hampshire
17-19	at Portland Sea Dogs
20-22	at Binghamton
23-25	Erie
26-29	Richmond
30-31	at Bowie

SEPTEMBER
1-2	at Bowie

BINGHAMTON

APRIL
8-11	Akron
12-14	Erie
15-18	at New Hampshire
19-21	at Portland Sea Dogs
22-25	New Hampshire
26-28	Portland Sea Dogs
30	at Akron

MAY
1-2	at Akron
3-6	at Erie
7-9	New Hampshire
10-12	at Portland Sea Dogs
13-16	at Trenton
18-20	Bowie
21-23	at New Britain
24-27	Richmond
28-31	Akron

JUNE
1-3	at Bowie
4-6	at New Britain
8-10	Bowie
11-13	at Trenton
15-17	at Richmond
18-20	Trenton
22-24	New Britain

25-27	at Akron
28-30	Altoona

JULY
1-4	Portland Sea Dogs
5-8	at Altoona
9-12	New Hampshire
15-18	at New Hampshire
19-21	at Bowie
22-25	Erie
26-28	Portland Sea Dogs
29-31	at Erie

AUGUST
1	at Erie
3-5	Harrisburg
6-8	at Trenton
10-12	at Harrisburg
13-15	Reading
17-19	at New Hampshire
20-22	Altoona
23-25	New Britain
26-29	at Reading
30-31	at Portland Sea Dogs

SEPTEMBER
1-2	at Portland Sea Dogs

BOWIE

APRIL
8-11	Richmond
12-14	Harrisburg
15-18	at Akron
19-21	at Erie
22-25	Akron
27-29	Erie
30	at Richmond

MAY
1-2	at Richmond
3-6	at Harrisburg
7-9	at Trenton
10-12	Richmond
13-16	Erie

18-20	at Binghamton
21-23	New Hampshire
24-27	at Harrisburg
28-31	at Richmond

JUNE
1-3	Binghamton
4-6	Erie
8-10	at Binghamton
11-13	at Harrisburg
15-17	Reading
18-20	Harrisburg
22-24	at Reading
25-27	at Altoona
28-30	Erie

ERIE

APRIL
8-11	at Trenton
12-14	at Binghamton
15-18	Altoona
19-21	Bowie
22-25	at Altoona
27-29	at Bowie
30	Trenton

MAY
1-2	Trenton
3-6	Binghamton
7-9	at Altoona
10-12	Akron
13-16	at Bowie
18-20	at Richmond
21-23	Altoona
24-27	at Trenton
28-31	Harrisburg

JUNE
1-3	at Akron
4-6	at Bowie
8-10	Portland Sea Dogs
11-13	New Hampshire
15-17	at Portland Sea Dogs
18-20	at New Hampshire
22-24	Trenton

HARRISBURG

APRIL
8-11	at Altoona
12-14	at Bowie
15-18	New Britain
19-21	Reading
22-25	at New Britain
26-28	at Reading
30	Altoona

MAY
1-2	Altoona
3-6	Bowie
7-9	Richmond
10-12	at Altoona
13-16	New Britain
18-20	Reading
21-23	at Akron
24-27	Bowie
28-31	at Erie

JUNE
1-3	at Richmond
4-6	Akron
8-10	at Altoona
11-13	Bowie
15-17	at New Britain
18-20	at Bowie

22-24	New Hampshire
25-27	Reading
28-30	at Portland Sea Dogs

JULY
1-4	at Trenton
5-8	Richmond
9-12	at Reading
15-18	Altoona
19-21	New Britain
22-25	at Portland Sea Dogs
26-28	at New Hampshire
29-31	Portland Sea Dogs

AUGUST
1	Portland Sea Dogs
3-5	at Binghamton
6-8	Altoona
10-12	Binghamton
13-15	at Trenton
17-19	Erie
20-22	at Akron
23-25	Portland Sea Dogs
26-29	Trenton
30-31	at New Hampshire

SEPTEMBER
1-2	at New Hampshire

JULY
3-5	at Portland Sea Dogs
6-8	at New Hampshire
10-12	Portland Sea Dogs
13-15	at Erie
17-19	at Trenton
20-22	Richmond
23-25	Akron
26-29	at New Britain
30-31	Altoona

SEPTEMBER
1-2	Altoona

JULY
1-4	Akron
5-8	at Erie
9-12	Trenton
15-18	at Richmond
19-21	Binghamton
22-25	Richmond
26-28	at Akron
29-31	New Britain

AUGUST
1	New Britain

JULY
1-4	at Richmond
5-8	Bowie
9-12	Akron
15-18	at Akron
19-21	Reading
22-25	at Binghamton
26-28	Altoona
29-31	Binghamton

AUGUST
1	Binghamton
3-5	at New Britain
6-8	at Reading
10-12	New Britain
13-15	Bowie
17-19	at Harrisburg
20-22	Reading
23-25	at Altoona
26-29	at Akron
30-31	Richmond

SEPTEMBER
1-2	Richmond

NEW BRITAIN

APRIL
8-11 . . . . . New Hampshire
12-14 . . Portland Sea Dogs
15-18 . . . . . at Harrisburg
19-21 . . . . . . at Richmond
22-25 . . . . . .Harrisburg
26-28 . . . . . . .Richmond
30 . . .at Portland Sea Dogs

MAY
1-2 .at Portland Sea Dogs
3-6 . . . . at New Hampshire
7-9 . . . Portland Sea Dogs
10-12 . . . . Trenton
13-16 . . . . at Harrisburg
18-20 .at Portland Sea Dogs
21-23 . . . . . Binghamton
24-27 . . . . New Hampshire
28-31 .at Portland Sea Dogs

JUNE
1-3 . . . . Altoona
4-6 . . . . Binghamton
8-10 . . . . at Richmond
11-13 . . . . . . .at Altoona
15-17 . . . . . .Harrisburg
18-20 . . . . . .at Reading

(continued)
22-24 . . . . .at Binghamton
25-27 . . Portland Sea Dogs
28-30 . . . . Trenton

JULY
1-4. . . . at New Hampshire
5-8 . . . . Reading
9-12 . .at Portland Sea Dogs
15-18 . . Portland Sea Dogs
19-21 . . . . . at Harrisburg
22-25 . . . New Hampshire
26-28 . . . . .at Trenton
29-31 . . . . . at Bowie

AUGUST
1 . . . . at Bowie
3-5 . . . . Erie
6-8 . . . . .Akron
10-12 . . . . at Erie
13-15 . . . . . at Akron
17-19 . . . . . . .Richmond
20-22 . . at New Hampshire
23-25 . . . .at Binghamton
26-29 . . . . .Bowie
30-31 . . . . . .at Reading

SEPTEMBER
1-2 . . . . .at Reading

NEW HAMPSHIRE

APRIL
8-11 . . . . . . at New Britain
12-14 . . . . . . .at Reading
15-18 . . . . . Binghamton
19-21 . . . . . . Trenton
22-25 . . . .at Binghamton
27-29 . . . . at Trenton
30 . . . . Reading

MAY
1-2 . . . . Reading
3-6 . . . . New Britain
7-9 . . . . . .at Binghamton
10-12 . . . . . . .at Reading
13-16 . . Portland Sea Dogs
18-20 . . . . Trenton
21-23 . . . . at Bowie
24-27 . . . . at New Britain
28-31 . . . . . . Trenton

JUNE
1-3 . . . . .at Reading
4-6 . . . . Altoona
8-10 . . . . . at Akron
11-13 . . . . . . at Erie
15-17 . . . . .Akron
18-20 . . . . Erie

(continued)
22-24 . . . . . at Harrisburg
25-27 . . . . . . .at Trenton
28-30 . . . . Reading

JULY
1-4 . . . . New Britain
5-8 . . .at Portland Sea Dogs
9-12 . . . . . .at Binghamton
15-18 . . . . . Binghamton
19-21 . . Portland Sea Dogs
22-25 . . . at New Britain
26-28 . . . . . .Harrisburg
29-31 . . . . . . .at Trenton

AUGUST
1 . . . . at Trenton
3-5 . . . . .Richmond
6-8 . . . . .Bowie
10-12 . . . . at Richmond
13-15 . . . . . . .at Altoona
17-19 . . . . . Binghamton
20-22 . . . . . New Britain
23-25 . . . . . at Trenton
26-29 . . Portland Sea Dogs
30-31 . . . . . .Harrisburg

SEPTEMBER
1-2 . . . . .Harrisburg

PORTLAND SEA DOGS

APRIL
8-11 . . . . .at Reading
12-14 . . . at New Britain
15-18 . . . . Trenton
19-21 . . . . . Binghamton
22-25 . . . . . at Trenton
26-28 . . . .at Binghamton
30 . . . . New Britain

MAY
1-2 . . . . New Britain
3-6 . . . . Reading
7-9 . . . . . at New Britain
10-12 . . . . Binghamton
13-16 . . at New Hampshire
18-20 . . . . . . New Britain

(continued)
21-23 . . . . Trenton
24-27 . . . . . . .at Reading
28-31 . . . . . .New Britain

JUNE
1-3 . . . . at Trenton
4-6 . . . . Reading
8-10 . . . . at Erie
11-13 . . . . . at Akron
15-17 . . . . Erie
18-20 . . . . .Akron
22-24 . . . . . . .at Altoona
25-27 . . at New Britain
28-30 . . . . . . .Harrisburg

JULY
1-4 . . . . . .at Binghamton

READING

APRIL
8-11 . . . Portland Sea Dogs
12-14 . . . . New Hampshire
15-18 . . . . at Richmond
19-21 . . . . . at Harrisburg
23-25 . . . . . . .Richmond
26-28 . . . . . .Harrisburg
30 . . . . at New Hampshire

MAY
1-2 . . . at New Hampshire
3-6 . . . at Portland Sea Dogs
7-9 . . . . .Akron
10-12 . . . New Hampshire
13-16 . . . . . . at Akron
18-20 . . . . at Harrisburg
21-23 . . . . . . .Richmond
24-27 . . Portland Sea Dogs
28-31 . . . . .at Altoona

JUNE
1-3 . . . . . New Hampshire
4-6 . . .at Portland Sea Dogs
8-10 . . . . Trenton
11-14 . . . . . . .Richmond
15-17 . . . . . . .at Bowie
18-20 . . . . . New Britain

(continued)
22-24 . . . . .Bowie
25-27 . . . . . at Harrisburg
28-30 . . at New Hampshire

JULY
1-4 . . . . Altoona
5-8 . . . . . at New Britain
9-12 . . . . .Harrisburg
15-18 . . . . .at Trenton
19-21 . . . . at Erie
22-25 . . . . .Akron
26-28 . . . at Richmond
29-31 . . . . . at Akron

AUGUST
1 . . . . at Akron
3-5 . . . . Trenton
6-8 . . . . Erie
10-12 . . . . . . at Akron
13-15 . . . .at Binghamton
17-19 . . . . .Akron
20-22 . . . . at Erie
23-25 . . . at Richmond
26-29 . . . . . Binghamton
30-31 . . . . . New Britain

SEPTEMBER
1-2 . . . . New Britain

RICHMOND

APRIL
8-11 . . . . .at Bowie
12-14 . . . . . . .at Altoona
15-18 . . . . Reading
19-21 . . . . . New Britain
23-25 . . . . . .at Reading
26-28 . . . at New Britain
30 . . . . .Bowie

MAY
1-2 . . . . .Bowie
3-6 . . . . Altoona
7-9 . . . . at Harrisburg
10-12 . . . . . . at Bowie
13-16 . . . . . Altoona
18-20 . . . . Erie
21-23 . . . . . .at Reading
24-27 . . . .at Binghamton
28-31 . . . . .Bowie

JUNE
1-3 . . . . .Harrisburg
4-6 . . . . at Trenton
8-10 . . . . . New Britain
11-14 . . . .at Reading
15-17 . . . . . Binghamton
18-20 . . . . Altoona

(continued)
22-24 . . . . at Akron
25-27 . . . . at Erie
28-30 . . . . .Akron

JULY
1-4 . . . . Erie
5-8 . . . . . at Harrisburg
9-12 . . . . .at Altoona
15-18 . . . . .Bowie
19-21 . . . . . . Trenton
22-25 . . . . . at Bowie
26-28 . . . . . Reading
29-31 . . . . . Altoona

AUGUST
1 . . . . Altoona
3-5 . . . at New Hampshire
6-8 . . .at Portland Sea Dogs
10-12 . . . . New Britain
13-15 . . Portland Sea Dogs
17-19 . . . . at New Britain
20-22 . . . . . . at Bowie
23-25 . . . . Reading
26-29 . . . . . .at Altoona
30-31 . . . . . . at Erie

SEPTEMBER
1-2 . . . . at Erie

TRENTON

APRIL
8-11 . . . . Erie
12-14 . . . . .Akron
15-18 .at Portland Sea Dogs
19-21 . . at New Hampshire
22-25 . . Portland Sea Dogs
27-29 . . . New Hampshire
30 . . . . at Erie

MAY
1-2. . . . . at Erie
3-6. . . . . at Akron
7-9. . . . . .Bowie
10-12 . . . . at New Britain
13-16 . . . . . Binghamton
18-20 . . at New Hampshire
21-23 .at Portland Sea Dogs
24-27 . . . . Erie
28-31 . . at New Hampshire

JUNE
1-3. . . . Portland Sea Dogs
4-6. . . . . .Richmond
8-10 . . . . . . .at Reading
11-13 . . . . . Binghamton
15-17 . . . . Altoona
18-20 . . .at Binghamton

22-24 . . . . at Erie
25-27 . . . . New Hampshire
28-30 . . . . at New Britain

JULY
1-4. . . . . .Harrisburg
5-8. . . . . at Akron
9-12 . . . . at Bowie
15-18 . . . . . . Reading
19-21 . . . . at Richmond
22-25 . . . . . .at Altoona
26-28 . . . . New Britain
29-31 . . . . New Hampshire

AUGUST
1 . . . . New Hampshire
3-5. . . . . .at Reading
6-8. . . . . . . Binghamton
10-12 . . . . . . .at Altoona
13-15 . . . . . . .Harrisburg
17-19 . . . . .Bowie
20-22 .at Portland Sea Dogs
23-25 . . . . New Hampshire
26-29 . . . at Harrisburg
30-31 . . . . .Akron

SEPTEMBER
1-2. . . . . .Akron

SOUTHERN LEAGUE

BIRMINGHAM

APRIL
8-12 . . . . Carolina
14-18 . . . . at Mobile
19-23 . . . . . Jacksonville
24-28 . . . . . at Tennessee
29-30 . . . . . . Huntsville

MAY
1-3. . . . . Huntsville
5-9. . . . . .at Mississippi
10-14 . . . . at Jacksonville
15-19 . . . . . Montgomery
20-23 . . . . Mobile
26-30 . . . . at Huntsville
31 . . . . Tennessee

JUNE
1-4. . . . . Tennessee
5-9. . . . . . . at Mobile
10-14 . . . at Montgomery
16-20 . . . . . Jacksonville
22-27 . . . at Chattanooga

28-30 . . . . . . .Mississippi

JULY
1-3. . . . . .Mississippi
4-6. . . . . at Montgomery
7-10 . . . . . at Mississippi
14-16 . . . . . . West Tenn
17-20 . . . . . . Jacksonville
22-26 . . . . at West Tenn
28-31 . . . . . Chattanooga

AUGUST
1 . . . . Chattanooga
2-6. . . . . . . at Jacksonville
7-11 . . . . .Mississippi
12-16 . . . . . at Mobile
18-22 . . . . . . Huntsville
23-25 . . . . . .at Carolina
26-29 . . . . at Tennessee
31 . . . . Carolina

SEPTEMBER
1-2. . . . . Carolina

CAROLINA

APRIL
8-12 . . . .at Birmingham
14-18 . . . . Montgomery
19-23 . . . . . . .Tennessee
24-28 . . . . at Jacksonville
29-30 . . . . . . at Mobile

MAY
1-3. . . . . at Mobile
5-9. . . . . . . Chattanooga
10-14 . . . . at Tennessee
15-19 . . . . . Jacksonville
20-24 . . . at Chattanooga
26-30 . . . . . West Tenn
31 . . . . . . at Jacksonville

JUNE
1-4. . . . . . at Jacksonville
5-9. . . . . at Chattanooga

10-14 . . . . Huntsville
16-20 . . . . . . .Mississippi
22-27 . . . . at Tennessee
28-30 . . . . . Jacksonville

JULY
1-3. . . . . Jacksonville
4-6. . . . . at Chattanooga
7-10 . . . . at West Tenn
14-16 . . . . . Montgomery
17-20 . . . Chattanooga
22-26 . . . at Montgomery
28-31 . . . . . Jacksonville

AUGUST
1 . . . . .Jacksonville
2-6. . . . . . . at Huntsville
7-11 . . . . Chattanooga
12-16 . . . at Jacksonville

18-22 . . . . Mobile
23-25 . . . . Birmingham
27-30 . . . . . at Mississippi

SEPTEMBER
1-2. . . . . .at Birmingham

CHATTANOOGA

APRIL
8-12 . . . . Huntsville
14-18 . . . at Tennessee
19-23 . . . . Montgomery
24-28 . . . at Huntsville
29-30 . . . . . Tennessee

MAY
1-3. . . . . Tennessee
5-9. . . . . .at Carolina
10-14 . . . . .Mississippi
15-19 . . . . at Mobile
20-24 . . . . . Carolina
26-30 . . . at Jacksonville
31 . . . . West Tenn

JUNE
1-4. . . . . . . West Tenn
5-9. . . . . . . Carolina
10-14 . . . at Mississippi
16-20 . . . at West Tenn
22-27 . . . Birmingham

29-30 . . . . . at Huntsville

JULY
1-3. . . . . at Huntsville
4-6. . . . . Carolina
7-10 . . . . Huntsville
14-16 . . . . at Tennessee
17-20 . . . . .at Carolina
22-26 . . . . . . Mobile
28-31 . . . . .at Birmingham

AUGUST
1 . . . . .at Birmingham
2-6. . . . . .West Tenn
7-11 . . . . . . .at Carolina
12-16 . . . . . . .Tennessee
18-22 . . . . at Montgomery
23-25 . . . . . . Mobile
26-29 . . . . Jacksonville
31 . . . . at Mobile

SEPTEMBER
1-2. . . . . at Mobile

HUNTSVILLE

APRIL
8-12 . . . . . at Chattanooga
14-18 . . . . Jacksonville
19-23 . . . . at West Tenn
24-28 . . . . Chattanooga
29-30 . . .at Birmingham

MAY
1-3. . . . . .at Birmingham
4-8. . . . . . . West Tenn
10-14 . . . at Montgomery
15-19 . . . . . . .Tennessee
20-24 . . . at Mississippi
26-30 . . . . Birmingham
31 . . . . Mobile

JUNE
1-4. . . . . Mobile
5-9. . . . . . at Tennessee
10-14 . . . .at Carolina
16-20 . . . . Montgomery
22-27 . . . . at Jacksonville

29-30 . . . . . Chattanooga

JULY
1-3. . . . . . Chattanooga
4-6. . . . . . at Tennessee
7-10 . . . . at Chattanooga
14-16 . . . . . . .Mississippi
17-20 . . . . . . West Tenn
22-26 . . . . at Jacksonville
28-31 . . . . . .Mississippi

AUGUST
1 . . . . .Mississippi
2-6. . . . . Carolina
7-11 . . . . . at Tennessee
12-16 . . . . . . West Tenn
18-22 . . . . .at Birmingham
23-25 . . . . Montgomery
26-29 . . . . . at Mobile
31 . . . . . . at Montgomery

SEPTEMBER
1-2. . . . . . at Montgomery

JACKSONVILLE

APRIL
8-12 . . . . West Tenn
14-18 . . . . at Huntsville
19-23 . . .at Birmingham
24-28 . . . . Carolina
29-30 . . . . . . .Mississippi

MAY
1-3. . . . . .Mississippi
4-8. . . . . at Montgomery
10-14 . . . . Birmingham
15-19 . . . . .at Carolina
20-24 . . . . at Tennessee
26-30 . . . . Chattanooga
31 . . . . Carolina

JUNE
1-4. . . . . Carolina
5-9. . . . . at Montgomery
10-14 . . . . . Mobile
16-20 . . . .at Birmingham
22-27 . . . . Huntsville

28-30 . . . . . . .at Carolina

JULY
1-3. . . . . .at Carolina
4-6. . . . . Mobile
7-10 . . . . .Tennessee
14-16 . . . . . at Mobile
17-20 . . . .at Birmingham
22-26 . . . . . Huntsville
28-31 . . . . .at Carolina

AUGUST
1 . . . . .at Carolina
2-6. . . . . . . Birmingham
7-11 . . . . . at Mobile
12-16 . . . . . . Carolina
18-22 . . . . . at West Tenn
23-25 . . . at Mississippi
26-29 . . . at Chattanooga
31 . . . . .Tennessee

SEPTEMBER
1-2. . . . . .Tennessee

MISSISSIPPI

APRIL
8-12	Tennessee
14-18	at West Tenn
19-23	Mobile
24-28	at Montgomery
29-30	at Jacksonville

MAY
1-3	at Jacksonville
5-9	Birmingham
10-14	at Chattanooga
15-19	West Tenn
20-24	Huntsville
26-30	at Mobile
31	Montgomery

JUNE
1-4	Montgomery
5-9	at West Tenn
10-14	Chattanooga
16-20	at Carolina
22-27	Mobile

28-30	at Birmingham

JULY
1-3	at Birmingham
4-6	West Tenn
7-10	Birmingham
14-16	at Huntsville
17-20	at Mobile
22-26	Tennessee
28-31	at Huntsville

AUGUST
1	at Huntsville
2-6	Mobile
7-11	at Birmingham
12-16	Montgomery
18-22	at Tennessee
23-25	Jacksonville
27-30	Carolina
31	at West Tenn

SEPTEMBER
1-2	at West Tenn

MOBILE

APRIL
8-12	at Montgomery
14-18	Birmingham
19-23	at Mississippi
24-28	West Tenn
29-30	Carolina

MAY
1-3	Carolina
5-9	at Tennessee
10-14	at West Tenn
15-19	Chattanooga
20-23	at Birmingham
26-30	Mississippi
31	at Huntsville

JUNE
1-4	at Huntsville
5-9	Birmingham
10-14	at Jacksonville
16-20	Tennessee
22-27	at Mississippi

28-30	Montgomery

JULY
1-3	Montgomery
4-6	at Jacksonville
7-10	at Montgomery
14-16	Jacksonville
17-20	Mississippi
22-26	at Chattanooga
28-31	Montgomery

AUGUST
1	Montgomery
2-6	at Mississippi
7-11	Jacksonville
12-16	Birmingham
18-22	at Carolina
23-25	at Chattanooga
26-29	Huntsville
31	Chattanooga

SEPTEMBER
1-2	Chattanooga

MONTGOMERY

APRIL
8-12	Mobile
14-18	at Carolina
19-23	at Chattanooga
24-28	Mississippi
29-30	at West Tenn

MAY
1-3	at West Tenn
4-8	Jacksonville
10-14	Huntsville
15-19	at Birmingham
20-24	at West Tenn
26-30	Tennessee
31	at Mississippi

JUNE
1-4	at Mississippi
5-9	Jacksonville
10-14	Birmingham
16-20	at Huntsville
22-27	West Tenn

28-30	at Mobile

JULY
1-3	at Mobile
4-6	Birmingham
7-10	Mobile
14-16	at Carolina
17-20	at Tennessee
22-26	Carolina
28-31	at Mobile

AUGUST
1	at Mobile
2-6	Tennessee
7-11	at West Tenn
12-16	at Mississippi
18-22	Chattanooga
23-25	Huntsville
26-29	West Tenn
31	Huntsville

SEPTEMBER
1-2	Huntsville

TENNESSEE

APRIL
8-12	at Mississippi
14-18	Chattanooga
19-23	at Carolina
24-28	Birmingham
29-30	at Chattanooga

MAY
1-3	at Chattanooga
5-9	Mobile
10-14	Carolina
15-19	at Huntsville
20-24	Jacksonville
26-30	at Montgomery
31	at Birmingham

JUNE
1-4	at Birmingham
5-9	Huntsville
10-14	West Tenn
16-20	at Mobile
22-27	Carolina

28-30	at West Tenn

JULY
1-3	at West Tenn
4-6	Huntsville
7-10	at Jacksonville
14-16	Chattanooga
17-20	Montgomery
22-26	at Mississippi
28-31	West Tenn

AUGUST
1	West Tenn
2-6	at Montgomery
7-11	Huntsville
12-16	at Chattanooga
18-22	Mississippi
23-25	at West Tenn
26-29	Birmingham
31	at Jacksonville

SEPTEMBER
1-2	at Jacksonville

WEST TENN

APRIL
8-12	at Jacksonville
14-18	Mississippi
19-23	Huntsville
24-28	at Mobile
29-30	Montgomery

MAY
1-3	Montgomery
4-8	at Huntsville
10-14	Mobile
15-19	at Mississippi
20-24	Montgomery
26-30	at Carolina
31	at Chattanooga

JUNE
1-4	at Chattanooga
5-9	Mississippi
10-14	at Tennessee
16-20	Chattanooga
22-27	at Montgomery
28-30	Tennessee

JULY
1-3	Tennessee
4-6	at Mississippi
7-10	Carolina
14-16	at Birmingham
17-20	at Huntsville
22-26	Birmingham
28-31	at Tennessee

AUGUST
1	at Tennessee
2-6	at Chattanooga
7-11	Montgomery
12-16	at Huntsville
18-22	Jacksonville
23-25	Tennessee
26-29	at Montgomery
31	Mississippi

SEPTEMBER
1-2	Mississippi

TEXAS LEAGUE

ARKANSAS

APRIL
8-10	at Midland
11-13	at Frisco
15-17	Midland
18-20	Frisco
22-25	at Northwest Arkansas
26-29	Tulsa
30	Northwest Arkansas

MAY
1-3	Northwest Arkansas
4-7	at Tulsa
8-11	Springfield
13-16	Tulsa
17-20	at Springfield
21-24	at Northwest Arkansas
26-28	San Antonio
29-31	Corpus Christi

JUNE
2-4	at San Antonio
5-7	at Corpus Christi
9-12	Northwest Arkansas

13-16	at Springfield
17-20	at Tulsa
21-24	Springfield
25-28	Northwest Arkansas

JULY
1-3	at Midland
4-6	at Frisco
8-10	Midland
11-13	Frisco
15-18	at Tulsa
19-22	Northwest Arkansas
23-26	at Tulsa
27-29	Springfield
30-31	Tulsa

AUGUST
1-2	Tulsa
3-5	at Springfield
6-9	at Northwest Arkansas
11-13	San Antonio
14-16	Corpus Christi
18-20	at San Antonio

21-23 . . . .at Corpus Christi
24-27 . . . . Tulsa
28-30 . . . . .at Springfield

31 . .at Northwest Arkansas

SEPTEMBER
1-3 . .at Northwest Arkansas

CORPUS CHRISTI

APRIL
8-10 . . . . .at Tulsa
11-13 at Northwest Arkansas
15-17 . . . . Tulsa
18-20 . Northwest Arkansas
22-25 . . . . at Frisco
26-29 . . . . Midland
30 . . . . .Frisco

MAY
1-3 . . . . .Frisco
4-7 . . . . at Midland
8-11 . . . . . . San Antonio
13-16 . . . . at Frisco
17-20 . . . .at San Antonio
21-24 . . . . Midland
26-28 . . .at Springfield
29-31 . . at Arkansas

JUNE
2-4 . . . . Springfield
5-7 . . . . .Arkansas
9-12 . . . . at Midland
13-16 . . . . . San Antonio
17-20 . . . . .Frisco
21-24 . . . .at San Antonio

25-28 . . . . .Frisco

JULY
1-3 . . . . .at Tulsa
4-6 . .at Northwest Arkansas
8-10 . . . . Tulsa
11-13 . Northwest Arkansas
15-18 . . . . at Frisco
19-22 . . . . Midland
23-26 . . . . at Frisco
27-29 . . . .at San Antonio
30-31 . . . . Midland

AUGUST
1-2 . . . . Midland
3-5 . . . . San Antonio
6-9 . . . . at Midland
11-13 . . .at Springfield
14-16 . . . . at Arkansas
18-20 . . . . . Springfield
21-23 . . . . . .Arkansas
24-27 . . . . at Midland
28-30 . . .at San Antonio
31 . . . . .Frisco

SEPTEMBER
1-3 . . . . .Frisco

FRISCO

APRIL
8-10 . . . . Springfield
11-13 . . . . .Arkansas
15-17 . . . . . .at Springfield
18-20 . . . . . at Arkansas
22-25 . . . . Corpus Christi
26-29 . . . . San Antonio
30 . . . . .at Corpus Christi

MAY
1-3 . . . . .at Corpus Christi
4-7 . . . . .at San Antonio
8-11 . . . . Midland
13-16 . . . . Corpus Christi
17-20 . . . . at Midland
21-24 . . . .at San Antonio
26-28 . Northwest Arkansas
29-31 . . . . Tulsa

JUNE
2-4 . .at Northwest Arkansas
5-7 . . . . .at Tulsa
9-12 . . . . San Antonio
13-16 . . . . Midland
17-20 . . .at Corpus Christi
21-24 . . . . . at Midland

25-28 . . . .at Corpus Christi

JULY
1-3 . . . . Springfield
4-6 . . . . .Arkansas
8-10 . . . . . .at Springfield
11-13 . . . . at Arkansas
15-18 . . . . Corpus Christi
19-22 . . .at San Antonio
23-26 . . . . Corpus Christi
27-29 . . . . at Midland
30-31 . . . . . San Antonio

AUGUST
1-2 . . . . San Antonio
3-5 . . . . Midland
6-9 . . . . . .at San Antonio
11-13 . Northwest Arkansas
14-16 . . . . Tulsa
18-20 at Northwest Arkansas
21-23 . . . . .at Tulsa
24-27 . . . . San Antonio
28-30 . . . . . Midland
31 . . . . .at Corpus Christi

SEPTEMBER
1-3 . . . . .at Corpus Christi

MIDLAND

APRIL
8-10 . . . . .Arkansas
11-13 . . . . Springfield
15-17 . . . . . . at Arkansas
18-20 . . . . .at Springfield
22-25 . . . . . San Antonio
26-29 . . .at Corpus Christi
30 . . . . . .at San Antonio

MAY
1-3 . . . . .at San Antonio
4-7 . . . . . . Corpus Christi
8-11 . . . . at Frisco

13-16 . . . . . San Antonio
17-20 . . . . .Frisco
21-24 . . .at Corpus Christi
26-28 . . . . Tulsa
29-31 . Northwest Arkansas

JUNE
2-4 . . . . .at Tulsa
5-7 . .at Northwest Arkansas
9-12 . . . . . Corpus Christi
13-16 . . . . . . at Frisco
17-20 . . . at San Antonio
21-24 . . . . .Frisco

25-28 . . . . at San Antonio

JULY
1-3 . . . . .Springfield
4-6 . . . . .Arkansas
8-10 . . . . . . at Arkansas
11-13 . . . .at Springfield
15-18 . . . . . San Antonio
19-22 . . .at Corpus Christi
23-26 . . . . San Antonio
27-29 . . . . .Frisco
30-31 . . . .at Corpus Christi

AUGUST
1-2 . . . . Midland
3-5 . . . . San Antonio
6-9 . . . . . . at Midland
11-13 . . . .at Springfield
14-16 . . . . at Arkansas
18-20 . . . . . Springfield
21-23 . . . . . .Arkansas
24-27 . . . . at Midland
28-30 . . . .at San Antonio
31 . . . . .Frisco

SEPTEMBER
1-3 . . . . .Frisco

NORTHWEST ARKANSAS

APRIL
8-10 . . . . . . San Antonio
11-13 . . . . Corpus Christi
15-17 . . . .at San Antonio
18-20 . . .at Corpus Christi
22-25 . . . . .Arkansas
26-29 . . . . .at Springfield
30 . . . . . . at Arkansas

MAY
1-3 . . . . at Arkansas
4-7 . . . . Springfield
8-11 . . . . .at Tulsa
13-16 . . . .at Springfield
17-20 . . . . Tulsa
21-24 . . . . . .Arkansas
26-28 . . . . . at Frisco
29-31 . . . . . . at Midland

JUNE
2-4 . . . . .Frisco
5-7 . . . . Midland
9-12 . . . . at Arkansas
13-16 . . . . . . .at Tulsa
17-20 . . . . . Springfield
21-24 . . . . Tulsa

25-28 . . . . . . at Arkansas

JULY
1-3 . . . . San Antonio
4-6 . . . . . . Corpus Christi
8-10 . . . .at San Antonio
11-13 . . .at Corpus Christi
15-18 . . . . . . Springfield
19-22 . . . . . at Arkansas
23-26 . . . . . Springfield
27-29 . . . . .at Tulsa
30-31 . . . . .at Springfield

AUGUST
1-2 . . . . . . .at Springfield
3-5 . . . . Tulsa
6-9 . . . . .Arkansas
11-13 . . . . at Frisco
14-16 . . . . at Midland
18-20 . . . . .Frisco
21-23 . . . . . Midland
24-27 . . . .at Springfield
28-30 . . . . . . .at Tulsa
31 . . . . .Arkansas

SEPTEMBER
1-3 . . . . .Arkansas

SAN ANTONIO

APRIL
8-10 .at Northwest Arkansas
11-13 . . . . .at Tulsa
15-17 . Northwest Arkansas
18-20 . . . . Tulsa
22-25 . . . . at Midland
26-29 . . . . at Frisco
30 . . . . Midland

MAY
1-3 . . . . Midland
4-7 . . . . .Frisco
8-11 . . . .at Corpus Christi
13-16 . . . . at Midland
17-20 . . . . Corpus Christi
21-24 . . . . .Frisco
26-28 . . . . . . at Arkansas
29-31 . . . . .at Springfield

JUNE
2-4 . . . . .Arkansas
5-7 . . . . Springfield
9-12 . . . . . . at Frisco
13-16 . . .at Corpus Christi
17-20 . . . . . Midland
21-24 . . . . . Corpus Christi

25-28 . . . . Midland

JULY
1-3 . .at Northwest Arkansas
4-6 . . . . .at Tulsa
8-10 . . Northwest Arkansas
11-13 . . . . Tulsa
15-18 . . . . . . at Midland
19-22 . . . . .Frisco
23-26 . . . . . at Midland
27-29 . . . . Corpus Christi
30-31 . . . . . at Frisco

AUGUST
1-2 . . . . at Frisco
3-5 . . . .at Corpus Christi
6-9 . . . . .Frisco
11-13 . . . . at Arkansas
14-16 . . . . .at Springfield
18-20 . . . . . .Arkansas
21-23 . . . . . Springfield
24-27 . . . . . at Frisco
28-30 . . . . Corpus Christi
31 . . . . Midland

SEPTEMBER
1-3 . . . . Midland

SPRINGFIELD

APRIL
8-10 . . . . at Frisco
11-13 . . . . . . at Midland
15-17 . . . . Frisco
18-20 . . . . . . Midland
22-25 . . . . .at Tulsa
26-29 . Northwest Arkansas
30 . . . . Tulsa

MAY
1-3 . . . . Tulsa
4-7 . .at Northwest Arkansas
8-11 . . . . . . at Arkansas
13-16 . Northwest Arkansas
17-20 . . . . .Arkansas
21-24 . . . . at Tulsa
26-28 . . . . Corpus Christi
29-31 . . . . . . San Antonio

JUNE
2-4 . . . .at Corpus Christi
5-7 . . . .at San Antonio
9-12 . . . . Tulsa
13-16 . . . . .Arkansas
17-20at Northwest Arkansas
21-24 . . . . . . at Arkansas

25-28 . . . . Tulsa

JULY
1-3 . . . . at Frisco
4-6 . . . . at Midland
8-10 . . . . .Frisco
11-13 . . . . Midland
15-18at Northwest Arkansas
19-22 . . . . Tulsa
23-26at Northwest Arkansas
27-29 . . . . . at Arkansas
30-31 . Northwest Arkansas

AUGUST
1-2 . . . Northwest Arkansas
3-5 . . . . .Arkansas
6-9 . . . . .at Tulsa
11-13 . . . . Corpus Christi
14-16 . . . . . San Antonio
18-20 . . . .at Corpus Christi
21-23 . . . .at San Antonio
24-27 . Northwest Arkansas
28-30 . . . . . . .Arkansas
31 . . . . .at Tulsa

SEPTEMBER
1-3 . . . . .at Tulsa

TULSA

APRIL
8-10 . . . . . Corpus Christi
11-13 . . . . . San Antonio
15-17 . . . .at Corpus Christi
18-20 . . . .at San Antonio
22-25 . . . . . . Springfield
26-29 . . . . . . at Arkansas
30 . . . . . . .at Springfield

MAY
1-3 . . . . . . .at Springfield
4-7 . . . . .Arkansas
8-11 . . Northwest Arkansas
13-16 . . . . . . at Arkansas
17-20at Northwest Arkansas
21-24 . . . . . . Springfield
26-28 . . . . . at Midland
29-31 . . . . at Frisco

JUNE
2-4 . . . . Midland
5-7 . . . . .Frisco
9-12 . . . . . .at Springfield
13-16 . Northwest Arkansas
17-20 . . . . . . .Arkansas
21-24at Northwest Arkansas

25-28 . . . . .at Springfield

JULY
1-3 . . . . . . Corpus Christi
4-6 . . . . . . San Antonio
8-10 . . . .at Corpus Christi
11-13 . . . .at San Antonio
15-18 . . . . . . .Arkansas
19-22 . . . . .at Springfield
23-26 . . . . . . .Arkansas
27-29 . Northwest Arkansas
30-31 . . . . . . at Arkansas

AUGUST
1-2 . . . . at Arkansas
3-5 . .at Northwest Arkansas
6-9 . . . . Springfield
11-13 . . . . . at Midland
14-16 . . . . . . at Frisco
18-20 . . . . . . Midland
21-23 . . . . .Frisco
24-27 . . . . . at Arkansas
28-30 . Northwest Arkansas
31 . . . . Springfield

SEPTEMBER
1-3 . . . . Springfield

HIGH CLASS A

CALIFORNIA LEAGUE

BAKERSFIELD

APRIL
8-11 . . . . Lancaster
12-14 . . . . .Stockton
15-18 . . . . . . at San Jose
19-21 . . . . . at Modesto
22-25 . . . . . . San Jose
26-28 . . . . . .Modesto
29-30 . . . . . . at Stockton

MAY
1-2 . . . . at Stockton
4-6 . . . . .at Visalia
7-10 . . . . .Stockton
11-13 . . . . . .High Desert
14-17 . . . . . . at San Jose
18-20 . . . . . . at Modesto
21-24 . . . . . Lake Elsinore
26-29 . . .at Inland Empire
30-31 . . . . Visalia

JUNE
1 . . . . Visalia
3-6 . . . . San Jose
7-10 . . . . at Stockton
11-13 . . . . . at San Jose
14-16 . . . . .Stockton
17-19 . . . . at Modesto
24-27 . . . . Visalia

28-30 . . . . . . at Stockton

JULY
1-3 . . . . at Modesto
4-6 . . . . San Jose
7-9 . . . . .Modesto
10-12 . . . . . . .at Visalia
14-16 . Rancho Cucamonga
17-19 . . . . Visalia
20-22at Rancho Cucamonga
23-25 . . at Lake Elsinore
27-29 . . . . . . .Modesto
30-31 . . . . . .at Lancaster

AUGUST
1 . . . . .at Lancaster
3-5 . . . . .at Visalia
6-8 . . . . San Jose
10-12 . . at High Desert
13-15 . . . . Visalia
17-20 . . . . . . at Modesto
21-23 . . . . Inland Empire
24-26 . Rancho Cucamonga
27-30 . . . .at Inland Empire
31 . . . . .at Visalia

SEPTEMBER
1-2 . . . . at Visalia

HIGH DESERT

APRIL
8-11 . . . . at Lake Elsinore
12-14 . . . .at Inland Empire
15-18 . . . . . Lake Elsinore
19-21 . . . . Lancaster
22-25 . . at Lake Elsinore
26-28 . . . .at Lancaster
29-30 . Rancho Cucamonga

MAY
1-2 . . . Rancho Cucamonga
4-6 . . . . Lancaster
7-10 . . . . . . at San Jose
11-13 . . . .at Bakersfield
14-17 . . . . .Stockton
18-20 . . . . Inland Empire
21-24 . . . .at Lancaster
26-29 . . . . . . .Modesto
30-31 . . . . at Lake Elsinore

JUNE
1 . . . . at Lake Elsinore
3-6 . . . . .at Inland Empire
7-10 . . Rancho Cucamonga
11-13 . . . . . . .at Visalia
14-16 . . . . . . San Jose
17-19 . . . . . . Lancaster
24-27 . . . . Inland Empire
28-30at Rancho Cucamonga

JULY
1-3 . . . . .at Inland Empire
4-6 . . . Rancho Cucamonga

INLAND EMPIRE

APRIL
8-11 .at Rancho Cucamonga
12-14 . . . . . .High Desert
15-18 . . . . .Modesto
19-21 . . . . . . at Stockton
22-25 . . . . .at Visalia
26-28 . . . . . Lake Elsinore
29-30 . . . . Visalia

MAY
1-2 . . . . Visalia
4-6 . . . . . at Lake Elsinore
7-10 . . . . . . .at Lancaster
11-13 . . . . . Lake Elsinore
7-9 . . . . Visalia
10-12at Rancho Cucamonga
14-16 . . . . San Jose
17-19 . . . . Inland Empire
20-22 . . . . . at Modesto
23-25 . . . . at San Jose
27-29 . . . . Inland Empire
30-31 . Rancho Cucamonga

AUGUST
1 . . . . Rancho Cucamonga
3-5 . . . . at Modesto
6-8 . . . . at Stockton
10-12 . . . . . . Bakersfield
13-15 . . . . . Lake Elsinore
17-20at Rancho Cucamonga
21-23 . . . . Lancaster
24-26 . . . .at Inland Empire
27-30 . . . . Lake Elsinore
31 . .at Rancho Cucamonga

SEPTEMBER
1-2 . .at Rancho Cucamonga

MAY
1-2 . . . Rancho Cucamonga
4-6 . . . . Lancaster
7-10 . . . . . . at San Jose
11-13 . . . .at Bakersfield
14-17 . . . . .Stockton
18-20 . . . . Inland Empire
21-24 . . . .at Lancaster
26-29 . . . . . . .Modesto
30-31 . . . . at Lake Elsinore

JUNE
1 . . . . . . at Lake Elsinore
3-6 . . . . .at Inland Empire
7-10 . . Rancho Cucamonga
11-13 . . . . . . .at Visalia
14-16 . . . . . . San Jose
17-19 . . . . . . Lancaster
24-27 . . . . Inland Empire
28-30at Rancho Cucamonga

JULY
1-3 . . . . .at Inland Empire
4-6 . . . Rancho Cucamonga

14-17 . Rancho Cucamonga
18-20 . . . . . at High Desert
21-24at Rancho Cucamonga
26-29 . . . . . . Bakersfield
30-31 . . . . . .at Lancaster

JUNE
1 . . . . .at Lancaster
3-6 . . . . .High Desert
7-10 . . . . . at Lake Elsinore
11-13 . Rancho Cucamonga
14-16 . . . . . . Lancaster
17-19at Rancho Cucamonga
24-27 . . . . at High Desert

28-30 . . . . . Lake Elsinore	

JULY
1-3 . . . . .High Desert
4-6 . . . . . . .at Lancaster
7-9 . . . . at Lake Elsinore
10-12 . . . . . Lancaster
14-16 . . at Lake Elsinore
17-19 . . at High Desert
20-22 . . . Lake Elsinore
23-25 . Rancho Cucamonga
27-29 . . at High Desert
30-31 . . . . . . .San Jose

AUGUST
1 . . . . San Jose
3-5 . . . . Lancaster
6-8 . .at Rancho Cucamonga
10-12 . . . . .Stockton
13-15 . . . . .at Lancaster
17-20 . . . . . Lake Elsinore
21-23 . . .at Bakersfield
24-26 . . . . . .High Desert
27-30 . . . . . . Bakersfield
31 . . . . at San Jose

SEPTEMBER
1-2 . . . . at San Jose

LAKE ELSINORE

APRIL
8-11 . . . . . . .High Desert
12-14 . . . . .at Lancaster
15-18 . . . . at High Desert
19-21 . Rancho Cucamonga
22-25 . . . . .High Desert
26-28 . . at Inland Empire
29-30 . . . . . .at Lancaster

MAY
1-2 . . . . .at Lancaster
4-6 . . . . . . Inland Empire
7-10 .at Rancho Cucamonga
11-13 . . .at Inland Empire
14-17 . . . . Lancaster
18-20 . . . . .Stockton
21-24 . . . .at Bakersfield
26-29 . . . . . Lancaster
30-31 . . . . . .High Desert

JUNE
1 . . . . .High Desert
3-6 . . . . at Modesto
7-10 . . . . . Inland Empire
11-13 . . . . .at Lancaster
14-16 at Rancho Cucamonga
17-19 . . . . San Jose
24-27 . Rancho Cucamonga

LANCASTER

APRIL
8-11 . . . . . .at Bakersfield
12-14 . . . . . Lake Elsinore
15-18 . Rancho Cucamonga
19-21 . . . at High Desert
22-25 at Bakersfield
26-28 . . . . .High Desert
29-30 . . . . Lake Elsinore

MAY
1-2 . . . . . . Lake Elsinore
4-6 . . . . . at High Desert
7-10 . . . . Inland Empire
11-13 at Rancho Cucamonga
14-17 . . . . at Lake Elsinore
18-20 . Rancho Cucamonga
21-24 . . . . .High Desert
26-29 . . at Lake Elsinore
30-31 . . . . Inland Empire

JUNE
1 . . . . Inland Empire
3-6 . .at Rancho Cucamonga
7-10 . . . . Visalia
11-13 . . . . . Lake Elsinore
14-16 . . .at Inland Empire
17-19 . . . . at High Desert
24-27 . . . . Stockton

28-30 . . . . . . at Modesto

JULY
1-3 . . . . at San Jose
4-6 . . . . . . Inland Empire
7-9 . . . Rancho Cucamonga
10-12 . . .at Inland Empire
14-16 . . . . Modesto
17-19 . . . . San Jose
20-22 . . . . at Visalia
23-25 . . . . at Modesto
27-29 . . . . . . Visalia
30-31 . . . . . Bakersfield

AUGUST
1 . . . . Bakersfield
3-5 . . .at Inland Empire
6-8 . . . . . at Lake Elsinore
9-11 . . . . . . San Jose
13-15 . . . . Inland Empire
17-20 . . . . .at Stockton
21-23 . . at High Desert
24-26 . . at Lake Elsinore
27-30 at Rancho Cucamonga
31 . . . . Lake Elsinore

SEPTEMBER
1-2 . . . . Lake Elsinore

MODESTO

APRIL
8-11 . . . . San Jose
12-14 at Rancho Cucamonga
15-18 . . .at Inland Empire
19-21 . . . . Bakersfield
22-25 . . . . . . .Stockton
26-28 . . at Bakersfield
29-30 . . . at San Jose

MAY
1-2 . . . . . at San Jose
4-6 . . . Rancho Cucamonga
7-10 . . . . Visalia
11-13 . . . . . at Stockton
14-17 . . . . . at Visalia
18-20 . . . . Bakersfield
21-24 . . . . . . San Jose
26-29 . . . . at High Desert
30-31 . . . . .Stockton

JUNE
1 . . . . .Stockton
3-6 . . . . . . Lake Elsinore
7-10 . . . . . at San Jose
11-13 . . . . . at Stockton
14-16 . . . . . . at Visalia
17-19 . . . . . Bakersfield
24-27 . . . at San Jose

28-30 . . . . Lancaster

JULY
1-3 . . . . Bakersfield
4-6 . . . . . . at Stockton
7-9 . . . . . .at Bakersfield
10-12 . . . . . . .Stockton
14-16 . . . .at Lancaster
17-19 . . . at Lake Elsinore
20-22 . . . .High Desert
23-25 . . . . . Lancaster
27-29 . . . at Bakersfield
30-31 . . . . at Stockton

AUGUST
1 . . . . at Stockton
3-5 . . . . . . .High Desert
6-8 . . . . Visalia
10-12 . . . . . . at Visalia
13-15 . . . . at San Jose
17-20 . . . . Bakersfield
21-23 . . . . Visalia
24-26 . . . . at Stockton
27-30 . . . . at Visalia
31 . . . . Stockton

SEPTEMBER
1-2 . . . . .Stockton

RANCHO CUCAMONGA

APRIL
8-11 . . . . . Inland Empire
12-14 . . . . . . Modesto
15-18 . . . . .at Lancaster
19-21 . . at Lake Elsinore
22-25 . . . . . Lancaster
26-28 . . . . . Visalia
29-30 . . . . at High Desert

MAY
1-2 . . . . . . at High Desert
4-6 . . . . at Modesto
7-10 . . . . . Lake Elsinore
11-13 . . . . . Lancaster
14-17 . . . at Inland Empire
18-20 . . . .at Lancaster
21-24 . . . Inland Empire
26-29 . . . . . at Visalia
30-31 . . . . . at San Jose

JUNE
1 . . . . at San Jose
3-6 . . . . Lancaster
7-10 . . . at High Desert
11-13 . . at Inland Empire
14-16 . . . . . Lake Elsinore
17-19 . . . . Inland Empire
24-27 . . at Lake Elsinore

28-30 . . . . .High Desert

JULY
1-3 . . . . Lake Elsinore
4-6 . . . . . at High Desert
7-9 . . . . . . .at Lancaster
10-12 . . . . . . .Stockton
14-16 . . . . .at Bakersfield
17-19 . . . . . at Stockton
20-22 . . . . . Bakersfield
23-25 . . . .at Inland Empire
27-29 . . . . . . San Jose
30-31 . . at High Desert

AUGUST
1 . . . . at High Desert
3-5 . . . . . Lake Elsinore
6-8 . . . . . Inland Empire
10-12 . . at Lake Elsinore
13-15 . . . . . .Stockton
17-20 . . . . .High Desert
21-23 . . . at Lake Elsinore
24-26 . . .at Bakersfield
27-30 . . . . . Lancaster
31 . . . . .High Desert

SEPTEMBER
1-2 . . . . .High Desert

SAN JOSE

APRIL
8-11 . . . . . at Modesto
12-14 . . . . . . Visalia
15-18 . . . . Bakersfield
19-21 . . . . . at Visalia
22-25 . . .at Bakersfield
26-28 . . . . .Stockton
29-30 . . . . . . Modesto

MAY
1-2 . . . . Modesto
4-6 . . . . at San Jose
7-10 . . . . . .High Desert
11-13 . . . . .at Visalia
14-17 . . . . . Bakersfield
18-20 . . . . Visalia
21-24 . . . . at Modesto
26-29 . . . . . at Stockton
30-31 . Rancho Cucamonga

JUNE
1 . . . . Rancho Cucamonga
3-6 . . . . . . at Bakersfield
7-10 . . . . Modesto
11-13 . . . . . Bakersfield
14-16 . . . . at High Desert
17-19 . . at Lake Elsinore
24-27 . . . . . Modesto
28-30 . . . . . . at Visalia

JULY
1-3	Lancaster
4-6	at Bakersfield
7-9	at Stockton
10-12	Lake Elsinore
14-16	at High Desert
17-19	at Lancaster
20-22	Stockton
23-25	High Desert
27-29	at Rancho Cucamonga
30-31	at Inland Empire

AUGUST
1	at Inland Empire
3-5	Stockton
6-8	at Bakersfield
9-11	at Lancaster
13-15	Modesto
17-20	at Visalia
21-23	Stockton
24-26	Visalia
27-30	at Stockton
31	Inland Empire

SEPTEMBER
1-2	Inland Empire

STOCKTON

APRIL
8-11	at Visalia
12-14	at Bakersfield
15-18	Visalia
19-21	Inland Empire
22-25	at Modesto
26-28	at San Jose
29-30	Bakersfield

MAY
1-2	Bakersfield
4-6	San Jose
7-10	at Bakersfield
11-13	Modesto
14-17	at High Desert
18-20	at Lake Elsinore
21-24	Visalia
26-29	San Jose
30-31	at Modesto

JUNE
1	at Modesto
3-6	at Visalia
7-10	Bakersfield
11-13	Modesto
14-16	at Bakersfield
17-19	Visalia
24-27	at Lancaster

28-30	Bakersfield

JULY
1-3	at Visalia
4-6	Modesto
7-9	San Jose
10-12	at Modesto
14-16	Visalia
17-19	Rancho Cucamonga
20-22	at San Jose
23-25	at Visalia
27-29	Lake Elsinore
30-31	Modesto

AUGUST
1	Modesto
3-5	at San Jose
6-8	High Desert
10-12	at Inland Empire
13-15	at Rancho Cucamonga
17-20	Lancaster
21-23	at San Jose
24-26	Modesto
27-30	San Jose
31	at Modesto

SEPTEMBER
1-2	at Modesto

VISALIA

APRIL
8-11	Stockton
12-14	at San Jose
15-18	at Stockton
19-21	San Jose
22-25	Inland Empire
26-28	at Rancho Cucamonga
29-30	at Inland Empire

MAY
1-2	at Inland Empire
4-6	Bakersfield
7-10	at Modesto
11-13	San Jose
14-17	Modesto
18-20	at San Jose
21-24	at Stockton
26-29	Rancho Cucamonga
30-31	at Bakersfield

JUNE
1	at Bakersfield
3-6	Stockton
7-10	at Lancaster
11-13	High Desert
14-16	Modesto
17-19	at Stockton
24-27	at Bakersfield

28-30	San Jose

JULY
1-3	Stockton
4-6	at Lake Elsinore
7-9	at High Desert
10-12	Bakersfield
14-16	at Stockton
17-19	at Bakersfield
20-22	Lancaster
23-25	Stockton
27-29	at Lancaster
30-31	Lake Elsinore

AUGUST
1	Lake Elsinore
3-5	Bakersfield
6-8	at Modesto
10-12	Modesto
13-15	at Bakersfield
17-20	San Jose
21-23	at Modesto
24-26	at San Jose
27-30	Modesto
31	Bakersfield

SEPTEMBER
1-2	Bakersfield

CAROLINA LEAGUE

FREDERICK

APRIL
8-11	at Lynchburg
13-15	Myrtle Beach
16-18	Lynchburg
19-22	at Potomac
23-25	Salem
27-29	at Winston-Salem
30	at Myrtle Beach

MAY
1-2	at Myrtle Beach
3-6	Winston-Salem
7-9	Wilmington
10-13	at Salem
14-16	at Kinston
17-20	Potomac
21-23	Kinston
24-26	at Wilmington
28-30	at Lynchburg
31	Myrtle Beach

JUNE
1-2	Myrtle Beach
3-6	Lynchburg
7-9	at Potomac
10-13	Salem
15-17	at Winston-Salem
18-20	at Myrtle Beach

24-26	Winston-Salem
27-29	Wilmington
30	at Salem

JULY
1-2	at Salem
3-5	at Kinston
7-9	Potomac
10-12	Kinston
14-17	at Wilmington
19-21	at Lynchburg
22-25	Myrtle Beach
26-28	Lynchburg
29-31	at Potomac

AUGUST
2-4	Salem
5-8	at Winston-Salem
9-12	at Myrtle Beach
13-15	Winston-Salem
16-19	Wilmington
20-22	at Salem
23-26	at Kinston
27-29	Potomac
31	Kinston

SEPTEMBER
1-3	Kinston

KINSTON

APRIL
8-11	Winston-Salem
12-14	Wilmington
16-18	at Winston-Salem
19-22	at Wilmington
23-25	Myrtle Beach
27-29	Lynchburg
30	at Salem

MAY
1-2	at Salem
3-6	at Lynchburg
7-9	Potomac
10-13	at Myrtle Beach
14-16	Frederick
17-20	Salem
21-23	at Frederick
24-26	at Potomac
28-30	Winston-Salem
31	Wilmington

JUNE
1-2	Wilmington
3-6	at Winston-Salem
7-9	at Wilmington
10-13	Myrtle Beach
15-17	at Lynchburg
18-20	at Salem

24-26	Lynchburg
27-29	Potomac
30	at Myrtle Beach

JULY
1-2	at Myrtle Beach
3-5	Frederick
7-9	Salem
10-12	at Frederick
14-17	at Potomac
19-21	Winston-Salem
22-25	Wilmington
26-28	at Winston-Salem
29-31	at Wilmington

AUGUST
2-4	Myrtle Beach
5-8	Lynchburg
9-12	at Salem
13-15	at Lynchburg
16-19	Potomac
20-22	at Myrtle Beach
23-26	Frederick
27-29	Salem
31	at Frederick

SEPTEMBER
1-3	at Frederick

LYNCHBURG

APRIL
8-11	Frederick
13-15	Salem
16-18	at Frederick
19-22	at Salem
23-25	at Potomac
27-29	at Kinston
30	Potomac

MAY
1-2	Potomac
3-6	Kinston

7-9	Myrtle Beach
10-13	at Wilmington
14-16	Winston-Salem
17-20	Wilmington
21-23	at Winston-Salem
25-27	at Myrtle Beach
28-30	Frederick
31	Salem

JUNE
1-2	Salem
3-6	at Frederick

7-9 . . . . at Salem
10-13 . . . . Potomac
15-17 . . . . .Kinston
18-20 . . . . . . at Potomac
24-26 . . . . . . at Kinston
27-29 . . . Myrtle Beach
30 . . . . . . at Wilmington

JULY
1-2 . . . . . . at Wilmington
3-5 . . . . . .Winston-Salem
7-9 . . . . .Wilmington
10-12 . . at Winston-Salem
14-17 . . . at Myrtle Beach
19-21 . . . . .Frederick
22-25 . . . . .Salem

26-28 . . . . . . at Frederick
29-31 . . . . . . at Salem

AUGUST
2-4 . . . . .Potomac
5-8 . . . . at Kinston
9-12 . . . . at Potomac
13-15 . . . . .Kinston
16-19 . . . . . . Myrtle Beach
20-22 . . . . at Wilmington
23-26 . . . .Winston-Salem
27-29 . . . . . Wilmington
31 . . . . at Winston-Salem

SEPTEMBER
1-3 . . . . at Winston-Salem

MYRTLE BEACH

APRIL
8-11 . . . . Wilmington
13-15 . . . . . . at Frederick
16-18 . . . . at Salem
19-22 . . . .Winston-Salem
23-25 . . . . at Kinston
27-29 . . . . .Potomac
30 . . . . .Frederick

MAY
1-2 . . . . .Frederick
3-6 . . . . at Potomac
7-9 . . . . . . at Lynchburg
10-13 . . . . .Kinston
14-16 . . . . .Salem
17-20 . . . at Winston-Salem
21-23 . . . . . . at Kinston
25-27 . . . . . . .Lynchburg
28-30 . . . . . . Wilmington
31 . . . . at Frederick

JUNE
1-2 . . . . at Frederick
3-6 . . . . at Salem
7-9 . . . . . .Winston-Salem
10-13 . . . . . . at Kinston
15-17 . . . . .Potomac
18-20 . . . . .Frederick

24-26 . . . . . . at Potomac
27-29 . . . . at Lynchburg
30 . . . . .Kinston

JULY
1-2 . . . . .Kinston
3-6 . . . . .Salem
7-9 . . . at Winston-Salem
10-12 . . . . . at Wilmington
14-17 . . . . . .Lynchburg
19-21 . . . . . . Wilmington
22-25 . . . . . . at Frederick
26-28 . . . . . . at Salem
29-31 . . . .Winston-Salem

AUGUST
2-4 . . . . at Kinston
5-8 . . . . .Potomac
9-12 . . . . .Frederick
13-15 . . . . . . at Potomac
16-19 . . . . . at Lynchburg
20-22 . . . . .Kinston
24-26 . . . . .Salem
27-29 . . . at Winston-Salem
30-31 . . . . at Wilmington

SEPTEMBER
1-2 . . . . . . at Wilmington

POTOMAC

APRIL
8-11 . . . . .Salem
13-15 . . . at Winston-Salem
16-18 . . . . at Wilmington
19-22 . . . . .Frederick
23-25 . . . . . . .Lynchburg
27-29 . . . at Myrtle Beach
30 . . . . at Lynchburg

MAY
1-2 . . . . . . at Lynchburg
3-6 . . . . . . Myrtle Beach
7-9 . . . . at Kinston
10-13 . . . .Winston-Salem
14-16 . . . . . . Wilmington
17-20 . . . . . at Frederick
21-23 . . . . at Salem
24-26 . . . . .Kinston
28-30 . . . . .Salem
31 . . . . . at Winston-Salem

JUNE
1-2 . . . . . .Winston-Salem
3-6 . . . . . . at Wilmington
7-9 . . . . .Frederick
10-13 . . . . at Lynchburg
15-17 . . . at Myrtle Beach
18-20 . . . . . . .Lynchburg

24-26 . . . . . Myrtle Beach
27-29 . . . . . . at Kinston
30 . . . . at Winston-Salem

JULY
1-2 . . . . at Winston-Salem
3-6 . . . . Wilmington
7-9 . . . . at Frederick
10-12 . . . . at Salem
14-17 . . . . .Kinston
19-21 . . . . .Salem
22-25 . . . at Winston-Salem
26-28 . . . . at Wilmington
29-31 . . . . .Frederick

AUGUST
2-4 . . . . at Lynchburg
5-8 . . . . . at Myrtle Beach
9-12 . . . . at Kinston
13-15 . . . . . Myrtle Beach
16-19 . . . . at Kinston
20-22 . . . .Winston-Salem
23-25 . . . . Wilmington
27-29 . . . . . at Frederick
31 . . . . at Salem

SEPTEMBER
1-3 . . . . at Salem

SALEM

APRIL
8-11 . . . . at Potomac
13-15 . . . . . at Lynchburg
16-18 . . . . . Myrtle Beach
19-22 . . . . . .Lynchburg
23-25 . . . . . . at Frederick
26-28 . . . . . . Wilmington
30 . . . . .Kinston

MAY
1-2 . . . . .Kinston
3-6 . . . . . . at Wilmington
7-9 . . . . at Winston-Salem
10-13 . . . . .Frederick
14-16 . . . . at Myrtle Beach
17-20 . . . . . . at Kinston
21-23 . . . . .Potomac
25-27 . . . .Winston-Salem
28-30 . . . . . . at Potomac
31 . . . . at Lynchburg

JUNE
1-2 . . . . . . at Lynchburg
3-6 . . . . . . Myrtle Beach
7-9 . . . . .Lynchburg
10-13 . . . . . . at Frederick
15-17 . . . . . . Wilmington
18-20 . . . . .Kinston

24-26 . . . . . at Wilmington
27-29 . . at Winston-Salem
30 . . . . .Frederick

JULY
1-2 . . . . .Frederick
3-6 . . . . at Myrtle Beach
7-9 . . . . at Kinston
10-12 . . . . .Potomac
14-17 . . . .Winston-Salem
19-21 . . . . . . at Potomac
22-25 . . . . at Lynchburg
26-28 . . . Myrtle Beach
29-31 . . . . . . .Lynchburg

AUGUST
2-4 . . . . at Frederick
5-8 . . . . Wilmington
9-12 . . . . .Kinston
13-15 . . . . at Wilmington
16-19 . . . at Winston-Salem
20-22 . . . . . . .Frederick
24-26 . . . at Myrtle Beach
27-29 . . . . . . at Kinston
31 . . . . .Potomac

SEPTEMBER
1-3 . . . . .Potomac

WILMINGTON

APRIL
8-11 . . . . . at Myrtle Beach
12-14 . . . . at Kinston
16-18 . . . . Potomac
19-22 . . . . .Kinston
23-25 . . at Winston-Salem
26-28 . . . . . . at Salem
30 . . . .Winston-Salem

MAY
1-2 . . . . . .Winston-Salem
3-6 . . . . .Salem
7-9 . . . . . . at Lynchburg
10-13 . . . . . . .Lynchburg
14-16 . . . . . at Potomac
17-20 . . . . at Lynchburg
21-23 . . . . Myrtle Beach
24-26 . . . . . . .Frederick
28-30 . . . at Myrtle Beach
31 . . . . at Kinston

JUNE
1-2 . . . . at Kinston
3-6 . . . . .Potomac
7-9 . . . . .Kinston
10-13 . . . at Winston-Salem
15-17 . . . . . . at Salem
18-20 . . . .Winston-Salem

24-26 . . . . .Salem
27-29 . . . . . at Frederick
30 . . . . .Lynchburg

JULY
1-2 . . . . .Lynchburg
3-6 . . . . at Potomac
7-9 . . . . . . at Lynchburg
10-12 . . . . . Myrtle Beach
14-17 . . . . .Frederick
19-21 . . . at Myrtle Beach
22-25 . . . . at Kinston
26-28 . . . . .Potomac
29-31 . . . . .Kinston

AUGUST
2-4 . . . . . at Winston-Salem
5-8 . . . . at Salem
9-12 . . . . .Winston-Salem
13-15 . . . . .Salem
16-19 . . . . . . at Frederick
20-22 . . . . . . .Lynchburg
23-25 . . . . . . at Potomac
27-29 . . . at Winston-Salem
30-31 . . . . Myrtle Beach

SEPTEMBER
1-2 . . . . Myrtle Beach

WINSTON-SALEM

APRIL
8-11 . . . . at Kinston
13-15 . . . . . . .Potomac
16-18 . . . . .Kinston
19-22 . . . at Myrtle Beach
23-25 . . . . . .Wilmington
27-29 . . . . . .Frederick
30 . . . . . . at Wilmington

MAY
1-2 . . . . at Wilmington
3-6 . . . . at Frederick
7-9 . . . . .Salem

10-13 . . . . . . at Potomac
14-16 . . . . . . at Kinston
17-20 . . . . Myrtle Beach
21-23 . . . . . . .Lynchburg
25-27 . . . . at Salem
28-30 . . . . . . at Kinston
31 . . . . at Potomac

JUNE
1-2 . . . . at Potomac
3-6 . . . . .Kinston
7-9 . . . . at Myrtle Beach
10-13 . . . . . . Wilmington

15-17 . . . . .Frederick	29-31 . . . . at Myrtle Beach
18-20 . . . . . at Wilmington	**AUGUST**
24-26 . . . . . . at Frederick	2-4. . . . . .Wilmington
27-29 . . . . . . .Salem	5-8. . . . . .Frederick
30 . . . . .Potomac	9-12 . . . . at Wilmington
JULY	13-15 . . . . at Frederick
1-2. . . . . . . .Potomac	16-19 . . . . .Salem
3-5. . . . . . at Lynchburg	20-22 . . . . at Potomac
7-9. . . Myrtle Beach	23-26 . . . at Lynchburg
10-12 . . . . . .Lynchburg	27-29 . . . Myrtle Beach
14-17 . . . . . at Salem	31 . . . . .Lynchburg
19-21 . . . . . at Kinston	**SEPTEMBER**
22-25 . . . . . .Potomac	1-3. . . . . .Lynchburg
26-28 . . . . .Kinston	

18-21 . . . . at Palm Beach	15-17 . . . . .Dunedin
22-25 . . . at Fort Myers	18-19 . . . . at Lakeland
27-28 . . . . at St. Lucie	20 . . . . .Lakeland
29-30 . . . . . St. Lucie	21 . . . . at Daytona
31 . . . . Jupiter	22 . . . . Daytona
AUGUST	23 . . . . . . at Daytona
1-3. . . . . Jupiter	24-26 . . . . Tampa
4-7. . . . . . at Bradenton	27-29 . . . . Clearwater
8-10 . . . . at Dunedin	31 . . . . .at Tampa
12 . . . . . . at Lakeland	**SEPTEMBER**
13-14 . . . . .Lakeland	1-2. . . . . .at Tampa

FLORIDA STATE LEAGUE

BRADENTON

APRIL	
8 . . . . .Fort Myers	24-26 . . . . at Jupiter
9-10 . . . . . at Fort Myers	27-28 . . . . . .Fort Myers
12 . . . . . . .Fort Myers	29-30 . . . . at Fort Myers
13-15 . . . . at Jupiter	**JULY**
16-18 . . . . . St. Lucie	1-3. .at Charlotte Stone Crabs
19-21 . . . . . Jupiter	4-6. . . . . Palm Beach
22 . . . . at Fort Myers	7-9. . . Charlotte Stone Crabs
23 . . . . . . .Fort Myers	10-12 . . . . at Palm Beach
24-26 . . . . at St. Lucie	14-17 . . . . . Clearwater
27-29 . . . . Palm Beach	18-21 . . . . .at Tampa
30 . . . Charlotte Stone Crabs	22-25 . . . . Dunedin
MAY	27 . . . . .Lakeland
1-2. . . Charlotte Stone Crabs	28-30 . . . . at Lakeland
3-5. . . . at Palm Beach	31 . . . . at Daytona
6-8. .at Charlotte Stone Crabs	**AUGUST**
10-13 . . . . . . Daytona	1-3. . . . . . . at Daytona
14 . . . . .Fort Myers	4-7. . . . . Brevard County
15 . . . at Fort Myers	9-11 . . . . at Palm Beach
16-19 . . . . at Dunedin	12-14 . . . . Jupiter
20-23 . . .at Clearwater	15-17 . . . . Palm Beach
24-26 . . . . .Fort Myers	18-20 . . . . . . at Jupiter
27-30 . . . . . . Tampa	21-22 . . . . at Fort Myers
JUNE	23 . . . . .Fort Myers
1-3. . . . . .Lakeland	24-26 . . . . St. Lucie
4 . . . . . at Lakeland	27-28 . Charlotte Stone Crabs
5-8. . . . .at Brevard County	30 . . . Charlotte Stone Crabs
9-10 . . . . . at Fort Myers	31 . . . . at St. Lucie
14-16 . . . . . . at St. Lucie	**SEPTEMBER**
17-19 . . . . . Jupiter	1-2. . . . . . . at St. Lucie
21-23 . . . . . . St. Lucie	

BREVARD COUNTY

APRIL	
8 . . . . Daytona	25 . . . . at Daytona
9-10 . . . . at Daytona	26 . . . . Daytona
11 . . . . Daytona	27-30 . . . . . . .Fort Myers
12-14 . . . . .Lakeland	**JUNE**
15-17 . . . . . Dunedin	1-4. . . . . at Jupiter
18-20 . . . . at Lakeland	5-8. . . . . . . .Bradenton
21-23 . . . . at Dunedin	9-10 . . . . at Daytona
24-25 . . . . . Daytona	14-16 . . . .at Clearwater
27-29 . . .at Clearwater	17-19 . . . . . at Lakeland
30 . . . . .at Tampa	21-23 . . . . Clearwater
MAY	24-26 . . . . .Lakeland
1-2. . . . . at Tampa	27 . . . . . at Daytona
3-5. . . . . Clearwater	28 . . . . Daytona
6-8. . . . . . . Tampa	29 . . . . . at Daytona
10-11 . . . at St. Lucie	30 . . . . Daytona
12-13 . . . . at St. Lucie	**JULY**
14 . . . . Daytona	1-3. . . . . at Dunedin
15 . . . . . at Daytona	4-6. . . . . . . Tampa
16-19 . . . . Palm Beach	7-9. . . . . . Dunedin
20-23 at Charlotte Stone Crabs	10-12 . . . . .at Tampa
24 . . . . Daytona	14-17 . Charlotte Stone Crabs

CHARLOTTE STONE CRABS

APRIL	
8-9. . . . . Palm Beach	24-26 . . . . . at Fort Myers
10-11 . . . . at Palm Beach	27-28 . . . . . Palm Beach
13-15 . . . . .Fort Myers	29-30 . . . . at Palm Beach
16-18 . . . . Jupiter	**JULY**
19-21 . . . at Fort Myers	1-3. . . . . .Bradenton
22-23 . . . Palm Beach	4-6. . . . . . . at St. Lucie
24-26 . . . . at Jupiter	7-9. . . . . . . at Bradenton
27-29 . . . . . St. Lucie	10-12 . . . . . St. Lucie
30 . . . . . . at Bradenton	14-17 . . at Brevard County
MAY	18-21 . . . . . . Daytona
1-2. . . . . . . at Bradenton	22-25 . . .at Clearwater
3-5. . . . . . at St. Lucie	27-30 . . . . . .at Tampa
6-8. . . . . . .Bradenton	31 . . . . Dunedin
10-13 . . . . at Lakeland	**AUGUST**
14-15 . . . at Palm Beach	1-3. . . . . Dunedin
16-19 . . . . . Tampa	4-7. . . . . .Lakeland
20-23 . . . Brevard County	9-11 . . . . . at St. Lucie
24-25 . . . Palm Beach	12-14 . . . . .Fort Myers
26 . . . . at Palm Beach	15-17 . . . . . St. Lucie
27-30 . . . . . at Dunedin	18-20 . . . . at Fort Myers
JUNE	21 . . . . at Palm Beach
1-4. . . . . . at Daytona	22-23 . . . . . . Palm Beach
5-8. . . . . Clearwater	24-26 . . . . . . Jupiter
9-10 . . . . at Palm Beach	27-28 . . . at Bradenton
14-16 . . . . at Jupiter	30 . . . . . . at Bradenton
17-19 . . . .Fort Myers	31 . . . . at Jupiter
20-22 . . . . Jupiter	**SEPTEMBER**
	1-2. . . . . at Jupiter

CLEARWATER

APRIL	JUNE
8 . . . . . . at Dunedin	1-4. . . . . Palm Beach
9 . . . . Dunedin	5-8. .at Charlotte Stone Crabs
10 . . . . at Dunedin	9-10 . . . . . . at Dunedin
11 . . . . Dunedin	14-16 . . . . Brevard County
12-14 . . . . . Tampa	17-19 . . . . Tampa
15 . . . . at Lakeland	21-23 . . at Brevard County
16-17 . . . . . .Lakeland	24-26 . . . . . .at Tampa
18-20 . . . . .at Tampa	27-28 . . . . . Dunedin
21 . . . . . . at Lakeland	29 . . . . at Dunedin
22 . . . . .Lakeland	30 . . . . Dunedin
23 . . . . . . at Lakeland	**JULY**
24 . . . . at Dunedin	1-3. . . . . .Lakeland
25 . . . . Dunedin	4-6. . . . . at Daytona
27-29 . . . . Brevard County	7-9. . . . . . . at Lakeland
30 . . . . Daytona	10-12 . . . . . . .at Tampa
MAY	14-17 . . . . . at Bradenton
1-2. . . . . Daytona	18-21 . . . . . . St. Lucie
3-5. . .at Brevard County	22-25 . Charlotte Stone Crabs
6-8. . . . . . . at Daytona	27-30 . . . . . . .at Jupiter
10-13 . . . . . Jupiter	31 . . . . . at Palm Beach
14 . . . . . . at Dunedin	**AUGUST**
15 . . . . .Dunedin	1-3. . . . . at Palm Beach
16-19 . . . . at Fort Myers	4-7. . . . . .Fort Myers
20-23 . . . .Bradenton	9-11 . . . . . . at Lakeland
24 . . . . Dunedin	12 . . . . Tampa
25-26 . . . . at Dunedin	13 . . . . .at Tampa
27-30 . . . . at St. Lucie	14 . . . . Tampa
	15-17 . . . . . . .Lakeland

18 . . . . .at Tampa	24-26 . . . . . . at Daytona
19 . . . . Tampa	27-29 . . .at Brevard County
20 . . . . .at Tampa	31 . . . . Daytona
21 . . . . at Dunedin	**SEPTEMBER**
22-23 . . . . Dunedin	1-2 . . . . Daytona

DAYTONA

APRIL	
8 . . . . .at Brevard County	24-26 . . . . . . at Dunedin
9-10 . . . . Brevard County	27 . . . . . Brevard County
11 . . . .at Brevard County	28 . . . .at Brevard County
12-14 . . . . Dunedin	29 . . . . Brevard County
15-17 . . . . .at Tampa	30 . . . .at Brevard County
18-20 . . . . . . at Dunedin	**JULY**
21-23 . . . . Tampa	1-3 . . . . .at Tampa
24-25 . . .at Brevard County	4-6 . . . . . . Clearwater
27-29 . . . . . . .Lakeland	7-9 . . . . Tampa
30 . . . . at Clearwater	10-12 . . . at Clearwater
MAY	14-17 . . . . . .Fort Myers
1-2 . . . . . . at Clearwater	18-21at Charlotte Stone Crabs
3-5 . . . . at Lakeland	22-25 . . . . . at St. Lucie
6-8 . . . . Clearwater	27-30 . . . Palm Beach
10-13 . . . . . at Bradenton	31 . . . . .Bradenton
14 . . . .at Brevard County	**AUGUST**
15 . . . . Brevard County	1-3 . . . . .Bradenton
16-19 . . . . . St. Lucie	4-7 . . . . . . at Jupiter
20-23 . . . at Fort Myers	9-11 . . . . Tampa
24 . . . .at Brevard County	12-14 . . . . . . Dunedin
25 . . . . Brevard County	15-17 . . . . . .at Tampa
26 . . .at Brevard County	18-20 . . . . at Dunedin
27-30 . . . . Jupiter	21 . . . . . Brevard County
JUNE	22 . . . .at Brevard County
1-4 . . Charlotte Stone Crabs	23 . . . . . Brevard County
5-8 . . . . . . at Palm Beach	24-26 . . . . . Clearwater
9-10 . . . . Brevard County	27-29 . . . . . .Lakeland
14-16 . . . . .Lakeland	31 . . . . . . at Clearwater
17-19 . . . . Dunedin	**SEPTEMBER**
21-23 . . . . . . at Lakeland	1-2 . . . . . .at Clearwater

DUNEDIN

APRIL	
8 . . . . Clearwater	17-19 . . . . . . at Daytona
9 . . . . .at Clearwater	21-23 . . . . Tampa
10 . . . . Clearwater	24-26 . . . . . . Daytona
11 . . . .at Clearwater	27-28 . . . .at Clearwater
12-14 . . . . . at Daytona	29 . . . . Clearwater
15-17 . . .at Brevard County	30 . . . . at Clearwater
18-20 . . . . Daytona	**JULY**
21-23 . . Brevard County	1-3 . . . . . Brevard County
24 . . . . Clearwater	4-6 . . . . at Lakeland
25 . . . . at Clearwater	7-9 . . . .at Brevard County
27-29 . . . . .at Tampa	10-12 . . . . . . .Lakeland
30 . . . . at Lakeland	14-17 . . . . at St. Lucie
MAY	18-21 . . . . Jupiter
1-2 . . . . at Lakeland	22-25 . . . . . at Bradenton
3-5 . . . . Tampa	27-30 . . . . . .Fort Myers
6-8 . . . . .Lakeland	31 . .at Charlotte Stone Crabs
10-13 . . at Palm Beach	**AUGUST**
14 . . . . at Clearwater	1-3 . .at Charlotte Stone Crabs
15 . . . . at Clearwater	4-7 . . . . Palm Beach
16-19 . . . . . .Bradenton	8-10 . . . . Brevard County
20-23 . . . . at Jupiter	12-14 . . . . . . at Daytona
24 . . . . .at Clearwater	15-17 . . .at Brevard County
25-26 . . . . . Clearwater	18-20 . . . . Daytona
27-30 . Charlotte Stone Crabs	21 . . . . Clearwater
JUNE	22-23 . . . .at Clearwater
1-4 . . . . at Fort Myers	24-26 . . . . . . .Lakeland
5-8 . . . . St. Lucie	27-29 . . . . Tampa
9-10 . . . . . . Clearwater	31 . . . . at Lakeland
14-16 . . . . .at Tampa	**SEPTEMBER**
	1-2 . . . . at Lakeland

FORT MYERS

APRIL	
8 . . . . at Bradenton	21-23 . . . . . at Palm Beach
9-10 . . . . . . .Bradenton	24-26 . Charlotte Stone Crabs
12 . . . . at Bradenton	27-28 . . . . at Bradenton
13-15 at Charlotte Stone Crabs	29-30 . . . . . . .Bradenton
16-18 . . . at Palm Beach	**JULY**
19-21 . Charlotte Stone Crabs	1-3 . . . . St. Lucie
22 . . . . .Bradenton	4-6 . . . . at Jupiter
23 . . . . . . at Bradenton	7-9 . . . . . at St. Lucie
24-26 . . . . . . Palm Beach	10-12 . . . . Jupiter
27-29 . . . . . at Jupiter	14-17 . . . . . at Daytona
30 . . . . . . at St. Lucie	18-21 . . . . . . .Lakeland
MAY	22-25 . . . Brevard County
1-2 . . . . . . at St. Lucie	27-30 . . . . . at Dunedin
3-5 . . . . Jupiter	31 . . . . Tampa
6-8 . . . . . . St. Lucie	**AUGUST**
10-13 . . . . . .at Tampa	1-3 . . . . Tampa
14 . . . . . at Bradenton	4-7 . . . . . . .at Clearwater
15 . . . . . . .Bradenton	9-11 . . . . Jupiter
16-19 . . . . Clearwater	12-14 at Charlotte Stone Crabs
20-23 . . . . . . Daytona	15-17 . . . . . at Jupiter
24-26 . . . . at Bradenton	18-20 . Charlotte Stone Crabs
27-30 . . .at Brevard County	21-22 . . . . . . .Bradenton
JUNE	23 . . . . . . at Bradenton
1-4 . . . . Dunedin	24-26 . . . . at Palm Beach
5-8 . . . . . . at Lakeland	27-29 . . . . . St. Lucie
9-10 . . . . . . .Bradenton	31 . . . . . . Palm Beach
14-16 . . . . . Palm Beach	**SEPTEMBER**
17-19 at Charlotte Stone Crabs	1-2 . . . . . . Palm Beach

JUPITER

APRIL	
8-9 . . . . St. Lucie	24-26 . . . . . . .Bradenton
10-11 . . . . at St. Lucie	27-28 . . . . . . St. Lucie
13-15 . . . . . . .Bradenton	29-30 . . . . at St. Lucie
16-18 at Charlotte Stone Crabs	**JULY**
19-21 . . . at Bradenton	1-3 . . . . at Palm Beach
22-23 . . . . . . St. Lucie	4-6 . . . . .Fort Myers
24-26 . Charlotte Stone Crabs	7-9 . . . . . . Palm Beach
27-29 . . . . . .Fort Myers	10-12 . . . at Fort Myers
30 . . . . . at Palm Beach	14-17 . . . . Tampa
MAY	18-21 . . . . . at Dunedin
1 . . . . Palm Beach	22-25 . . . . .at Lakeland
2 . . . . . . at Palm Beach	27-30 . . . . Clearwater
3-5 . . . . . . at Fort Myers	31 . . . . .at Brevard County
6 . . . . . . at Palm Beach	**AUGUST**
7-8 . . . . . . Palm Beach	1-3 . . . . .at Brevard County
10-13 . . . . .at Clearwater	4-7 . . . . Daytona
14-15 . . . . at St. Lucie	9-11 . . . . . at Fort Myers
16-19 . . . . . .Lakeland	12-14 . . . . at Bradenton
20-23 . . . . . Dunedin	15-17 . . . . .Fort Myers
24-25 . . . . . St. Lucie	18-20 . . . . . .Bradenton
26 . . . . . at St. Lucie	21 . . . . at St. Lucie
27-30 . . . . . at Daytona	22-23 . . . . . . St. Lucie
JUNE	24-26at Charlotte Stone Crabs
1-4 . . . . . Brevard County	27 . . . . . at Palm Beach
5-8 . . . . . .at Tampa	28 . . . . . at Palm Beach
9-10 . . . . . . at St. Lucie	29 . . . . . at Palm Beach
14-16 . Charlotte Stone Crabs	31 . . . Charlotte Stone Crabs
17-19 . . . at Bradenton	**SEPTEMBER**
20-22at Charlotte Stone Crabs	1-2 . . . Charlotte Stone Crabs
	3-4 . . . . Palm Beach

LAKELAND

APRIL
8	at Tampa
9	Tampa
10	at Tampa
11	Tampa
12-14	at Brevard County
15	Clearwater
16-17	at Clearwater
18-20	Brevard County
21	Clearwater
22	at Clearwater
23	Clearwater
24	Tampa
25	at Tampa
27-29	at Daytona
30	Dunedin

MAY
1-2	Dunedin
3-5	Daytona
6-8	at Dunedin
10-13	Charlotte Stone Crabs
14	at Tampa
15	Tampa
16-19	at Jupiter
20-23	St. Lucie
24	at Tampa
25	Tampa
26	at Tampa
27-30	at Palm Beach

JUNE
1-3	at Bradenton
4	Bradenton
5-8	Fort Myers
9	Tampa
10	at Tampa
14-16	at Daytona

17-19	Brevard County
21-23	Daytona
24-26	at Brevard County
27	Tampa
28	at Tampa
29	Tampa
30	at Tampa

JULY
1-3	at Clearwater
4-6	Dunedin
7-9	Clearwater
10-12	at Dunedin
14-17	Palm Beach
18-21	at Fort Myers
22-25	Jupiter
27	at Bradenton
28-30	Bradenton
31	at St. Lucie

AUGUST
1-3	at St. Lucie
4-7	at Charlotte Stone Crabs
9-11	Clearwater
12	Brevard County
13-14	at Brevard County
15-17	at Clearwater
18-19	Brevard County
20	at Brevard County
21	Tampa
22	at Tampa
23	Tampa
24-26	at Dunedin
27-29	at Daytona
31	Dunedin

SEPTEMBER
1-2	Dunedin

PALM BEACH

APRIL
8-9	at Charlotte Stone Crabs
10-11	Charlotte Stone Crabs
13-15	at St. Lucie
16-18	Fort Myers
19-21	St. Lucie
22-23	at Charlotte Stone Crabs
24-26	at Fort Myers
27-29	at Bradenton
30	Jupiter

MAY
1	at Jupiter
2	Jupiter
3-5	Bradenton
6	Jupiter
7-8	at Jupiter
10-13	Dunedin
14-15	Charlotte Stone Crabs
16-19	at Brevard County
20-23	at Tampa
24-25	at Charlotte Stone Crabs
26	Charlotte Stone Crabs
27-30	Lakeland

JUNE
1-4	at Clearwater
5-8	Daytona
9-10	Charlotte Stone Crabs
14-16	at Fort Myers
18-20	St. Lucie
21-23	Fort Myers

24-26	at St. Lucie
27-28	at Charlotte Stone Crabs
29-30	Charlotte Stone Crabs

JULY
1-3	Jupiter
4-6	at Bradenton
7-9	at Jupiter
10-12	Bradenton
14-17	at Lakeland
18-21	Brevard County
22-25	Tampa
27-30	at Daytona
31	Clearwater

AUGUST
1-3	Clearwater
4-7	at Dunedin
9-11	Bradenton
12-14	St. Lucie
15-17	at Bradenton
18-20	at St. Lucie
21	Charlotte Stone Crabs
22-23	at Charlotte Stone Crabs
24-26	Fort Myers
27	Jupiter
28	at Jupiter
29	Jupiter
31	at Fort Myers

SEPTEMBER
1-2	at Fort Myers
3-4	at Jupiter

ST. LUCIE

APRIL
8-9	at Jupiter
10-11	Jupiter
13-15	Palm Beach
16-18	at Bradenton
19-21	at Palm Beach
22-23	at Jupiter
24-26	Bradenton
27-29	at Charlotte Stone Crabs
30	Fort Myers

MAY
1-2	Fort Myers
3-5	Charlotte Stone Crabs
6-8	at Fort Myers
10-11	at Brevard County
12-13	Brevard County
14-15	Jupiter
16-19	at Daytona
20-23	at Lakeland
24-25	at Jupiter
26	Jupiter
27-30	Clearwater

JUNE
1-4	Tampa
5-8	at Dunedin
9-10	Jupiter
14-16	Bradenton
18-20	at Palm Beach
21-23	at Bradenton

24-26	Palm Beach
27-28	at Jupiter
29-30	Jupiter

JULY
1-3	at Fort Myers
4-6	Charlotte Stone Crabs
7-9	Fort Myers
10-12	at Charlotte Stone Crabs
14-17	Dunedin
18-21	at Clearwater
22-25	Daytona
27-28	Brevard County
29-30	at Brevard County
31	Lakeland

AUGUST
1-3	Lakeland
4-7	at Tampa
9-11	Charlotte Stone Crabs
12-14	at Palm Beach
15-17	at Charlotte Stone Crabs
18-20	Palm Beach
21	Jupiter
22-23	at Jupiter
24-26	at Bradenton
27-29	at Fort Myers
31	Bradenton

SEPTEMBER
1-2	Bradenton

TAMPA

APRIL
8	Lakeland
9	at Lakeland
10	at Lakeland
11	at Lakeland
12-14	at Clearwater
15-17	Daytona
18-20	Clearwater
21-23	at Daytona
24	at Lakeland
25	Lakeland
27-29	Dunedin
30	Brevard County

MAY
1-2	Brevard County
3-5	at Dunedin
6-8	at Brevard County
10-13	Fort Myers
14	at Lakeland
15	at Lakeland
16-19	at Charlotte Stone Crabs
20-23	Palm Beach
24	Lakeland
25	at Lakeland
26	Lakeland
27-30	at Bradenton

JUNE
1-4	at St. Lucie
5-8	Jupiter
9	at Lakeland
10	Lakeland
14-16	Dunedin
17-19	at Clearwater
21-23	at Dunedin
24-26	Clearwater

27	at Lakeland
28	Lakeland
29	at Lakeland
30	Lakeland

JULY
1-3	Daytona
4-6	at Brevard County
7-9	at Daytona
10-12	Brevard County
14-17	at Jupiter
18-21	Bradenton
22-25	at Palm Beach
27-30	Charlotte Stone Crabs
31	at Fort Myers

AUGUST
1-3	at Fort Myers
4-7	St. Lucie
9-11	at Daytona
12	at Clearwater
13	Clearwater
14	at Clearwater
15-17	Daytona
18	Clearwater
19	at Clearwater
20	Clearwater
21	at Lakeland
22	Lakeland
23	at Lakeland
24-26	at Brevard County
27-29	at Dunedin
31	Brevard County

SEPTEMBER
1-2	Brevard County

LOW CLASS A

MIDWEST LEAGUE

BELOIT

APRIL	
8-10	at Cedar Rapids
11-13	Peoria
14-16	at Kane County
17-19	Clinton
20-22	Quad Cities
23-25	at Wisconsin
26-28	at Burlington Bees
30	Wisconsin

MAY	
1-3	Wisconsin
4-6	at Clinton
7-9	Burlington Bees
10-12	Kane County
13-16	at Wisconsin
18-20	Kane County
21-24	Cedar Rapids
25-27	at Quad Cities
28-31	at Peoria

JUNE	
1-3	at Lake County
4-6	at Fort Wayne
8-10	Dayton
11-13	Bowling Green
15-17	at Cedar Rapids
18-20	Clinton

25-27	at Clinton
28-30	Cedar Rapids

JULY	
1-3	Quad Cities
4-6	at Kane County
7-9	Wisconsin
10-12	at Quad Cities
14-16	Great Lakes
17-19	Lansing
21-23	at South Bend
24-26	at West Michigan
28-30	at Burlington Bees
31	Peoria

AUGUST	
1-2	Peoria
3-6	Burlington Bees
7-10	at Cedar Rapids
11-13	at Peoria
14-16	Clinton
18-20	at Wisconsin
21-24	at Burlington Bees
25-27	Kane County
28-31	Burlington Bees

SEPTEMBER	
1-3	at Clinton

BOWLING GREEN

APRIL	
8-10	at Fort Wayne
11-13	Dayton
14-16	West Michigan
17-19	at Lansing
20-22	at South Bend
23-25	Lake County
27-29	Great Lakes
30	at Dayton

MAY	
1-3	at Dayton
4-6	Fort Wayne
7-9	at West Michigan
10-12	at Lake County
13-16	Lansing
18-20	at Great Lakes
21-24	at Dayton
25-27	South Bend
28-31	Fort Wayne

JUNE	
1-3	Clinton
4-6	Kane County
8-10	at Wisconsin
11-13	at Beloit
15-17	at Lansing
18-20	West Michigan

25-27	at Fort Wayne
28-30	Lansing

JULY	
1-3	Fort Wayne
4-6	at Fort Wayne
7-9	Dayton
10-12	at Lansing
14-16	at Burlington Bees
17-19	at Peoria
21-23	Quad Cities
24-26	Cedar Rapids
28-30	at Dayton
31	Lansing

AUGUST	
1-2	Lansing
3-6	South Bend
7-10	at Fort Wayne
11-13	West Michigan
14-16	Great Lakes
18-20	at Lake County
21-24	at South Bend
25-27	Lake County
28-31	Fort Wayne

SEPTEMBER	
1-3	at Dayton

BURLINGTON BEES

APRIL	
8-10	Quad Cities
11-13	at Kane County
14-16	Wisconsin
17-19	at Peoria
20-22	at Clinton
23-25	Cedar Rapids

26-28	Beloit
30	at Quad Cities

MAY	
1-3	at Quad Cities
4-6	Kane County
7-9	at Beloit
10-12	at Cedar Rapids

13-16	Peoria
18-20	Clinton
21-24	at Wisconsin
25-27	at Clinton
28-31	Quad Cities

JUNE	
1-3	at West Michigan
4-6	at South Bend
8-10	Great Lakes
11-13	Lansing
14-16	Peoria
18-20	at Cedar Rapids
25-27	at Wisconsin
28-30	Peoria

JULY	
1-3	Wisconsin
4-6	at Quad Cities
7-9	Cedar Rapids
10-12	at Wisconsin

CEDAR RAPIDS

APRIL	
8-10	Beloit
11-13	at Quad Cities
14-16	Peoria
17-19	at Kane County
20-22	at Wisconsin
23-25	at Burlington Bees
27-29	Clinton
30	Kane County

MAY	
1-3	Kane County
4-6	at Peoria
7-9	at Wisconsin
10-12	Burlington Bees
13-16	at Clinton
18-20	Quad Cities
21-24	at Beloit
25-27	at Peoria
28-31	Wisconsin

JUNE	
1-3	at Lansing
4-6	at Great Lakes
8-10	West Michigan
11-13	South Bend
15-17	Beloit
18-20	Burlington Bees

25-27	at Peoria
28-30	at Beloit

JULY	
1-3	Clinton
4-6	Wisconsin
7-9	at Burlington Bees
10-12	Peoria
14-16	Fort Wayne
17-19	Lake County
21-23	at Dayton
24-26	at Bowling Green
28-30	at Clinton
31	Quad Cities

AUGUST	
1-2	Quad Cities
3-6	at Kane County
7-10	Beloit
11-13	Kane County
14-16	at Wisconsin
18-20	Kane County
21-24	Wisconsin
25-27	at Peoria
28-31	at Quad Cities

SEPTEMBER	
1-3	Burlington Bees

CLINTON

APRIL	
8-10	Peoria
11-13	at Wisconsin
14-16	Quad Cities
17-19	at Beloit
20-22	Burlington Bees
23-25	Kane County
27-29	at Cedar Rapids
30	at Peoria

MAY	
1-3	at Peoria
4-6	Beloit
7-9	at Quad Cities
10-12	at Peoria
13-16	Cedar Rapids
18-20	at Burlington Bees
21-24	Kane County
25-27	Burlington Bees
28-31	at Kane County

JUNE	
1-3	at Bowling Green
4-6	at Dayton
8-10	Lake County
11-13	Fort Wayne
15-17	Wisconsin
18-20	at Beloit
25-27	Beloit
28-30	Kane County

JULY	
1-3	at Cedar Rapids
4-6	at Peoria
7-9	Quad Cities
10-12	at Kane County
14-16	West Michigan
17-19	South Bend
21-23	at Great Lakes
24-26	at Lansing
28-30	Cedar Rapids

31 . . . . at Wisconsin	18-20 . . . . . at Quad Cities
	21-24 . . . . Peoria
AUGUST	25-27 . . . . Quad Cities
1-2 . . . . at Wisconsin	28-31 . . . . at Peoria
3-6 . . . . . at Quad Cities	
7-10 . . . . Wisconsin	**SEPTEMBER**
11-13 . . . Burlington Bees	1-3 . . . . Beloit
14-16 . . . . at Beloit	

DAYTON

APRIL	25-27 . . . . at Lansing
8-10 . . . . Lansing	28-30 . . . . . Fort Wayne
11-13 . . at Bowling Green	
14-16 . . . . . at Fort Wayne	**JULY**
17-19 . . . . . South Bend	1-3 . . . . Great Lakes
20-22 . . . West Michigan	4-6 . . . . at West Michigan
23-25 . . . . at Lansing	7-9 . . . at Bowling Green
27-29 . . . . Lake County	10-12 . . . . . Great Lakes
30 . . . . . . Bowling Green	14-16 . . . . at Peoria
	17-19 . . at Burlington Bees
MAY	21-23 . . . Cedar Rapids
1-3 . . . . . Bowling Green	24-26 . . . . Quad Cities
4-6 . . . . at Lake County	28-30 . . . . Bowling Green
7-9 . . . at South Bend	31 . . . at West Michigan
10-12 . . . . . . Fort Wayne	
13-16 . . . . at Great Lakes	**AUGUST**
18-20 . . . . Lansing	1-2 . . . . at West Michigan
21-24 . . . . Bowling Green	3-6 . . . . . at Lake County
25-27 . . . at Lake County	7-10 . . . West Michigan
28-31 . . at West Michigan	11-13 . . . . Lansing
	14-16 . . . at Lake County
JUNE	18-20 . . . at Great Lakes
1-3 . . . . Kane County	21-24 . . . . . Lake County
4-6 . . . . Clinton	25-27 . . . . at South Bend
8-10 . . . . at Beloit	28-31 . . . . at Lansing
11-13 . . . . . at Wisconsin	
15-17 . . . . at Fort Wayne	**SEPTEMBER**
18-20 . . . . . . Great Lakes	1-3 . . . . . . Bowling Green

FORT WAYNE

APRIL	25-27 . . . . Bowling Green
8-10 . . . . . Bowling Green	28-30 . . . . . . at Dayton
11-13 . . . at West Michigan	
14-16 . . . . Dayton	**JULY**
17-19 . . . . at Lake County	1-3 . . . . at Bowling Green
20-22 . . . . Lansing	4-6 . . . . . . Bowling Green
23-25 . . . . at Great Lakes	7-9 . . . at Lake County
27-29 . . . . . South Bend	10-12 . . . . . . South Bend
30 . . . . at Lansing	14-16 . . . at Cedar Rapids
	17-19 . . . at Quad Cities
MAY	21-23 . . . . Peoria
1-3 . . . . at Lansing	24-26 . . . Burlington Bees
4-6 . . . at Bowling Green	28-30 . . . . . South Bend
7-9 . . . . Lansing	31 . . . . at Great Lakes
10-12 . . . . . . at Dayton	
13-16 . . . . . Lake County	**AUGUST**
17-19 . . at South Bend	1-2 . . . . . at Great Lakes
21-24 . . . West Michigan	3-6 . . . . at Lansing
25-27 . . . . . Great Lakes	7-10 . . . Bowling Green
28-31 . . at Bowling Green	11-13 . . . . . Lake County
	14-16 . . . . . . at Lansing
JUNE	18-20 . . at West Michigan
1-3 . . . . Wisconsin	21-24 . . . . Lansing
4-6 . . . . Beloit	25-27 . . . . . Great Lakes
8-10 . . . at Kane County	28-31 . . at Bowling Green
11-13 . . . . at Clinton	
15-17 . . . . Dayton	**SEPTEMBER**
18-20 . . . . at South Bend	1-3 . . . . . . at South Bend

GREAT LAKES

APRIL	25-27 . . . . . . South Bend
8-10 . . . . . at South Bend	28-30 . . . . . at Lake County
11-13 . . . . Lansing	
14-16 . . . . . . South Bend	**JULY**
17-19 . . at West Michigan	1-3 . . . . at Dayton
20-22 . . . . at Lake County	4-6 . . . . South Bend
23-25 . . . . . Fort Wayne	7-9 . . . . Lansing
27-29 . . at Bowling Green	10-12 . . . . . . at Dayton
30 . . . . . . at Lake County	14-16 . . . . at Beloit
	17-19 . . . at Wisconsin
MAY	21-23 . . . . Clinton
1-3 . . . . . . at Lake County	24-26 . . . . . Kane County
4-6 . . . . . . West Michigan	28-30 . . . . . at Lansing
7-9 . . . . . . Lake County	31 . . . . . . Fort Wayne
10-12 . . . . at South Bend	
13-16 . . . . Dayton	**AUGUST**
18-20 . . . Bowling Green	1-2 . . . . Fort Wayne
21-24 . . . . . . at Lansing	3-6 . . at West Michigan
25-27 . . . at Fort Wayne	7-10 . . . . Lansing
28-31 . . . Lake County	11-13 . . . . at South Bend
	14-16 . . at Bowling Green
JUNE	18-20 . . . . Dayton
1-3 . . . . Quad Cities	21-24 . . . . West Michigan
4-6 . . . . Cedar Rapids	25-27 . . . . at Fort Wayne
8-10 . . at Burlington Bees	28-31 . . at West Michigan
11-13 . . . at Peoria	
15-17 . . . . . South Bend	**SEPTEMBER**
18-20 . . . . . . at Dayton	1-3 . . . . Lake County

KANE COUNTY

APRIL	25-27 . . . . at Quad Cities
8-10 . . . . . . at Wisconsin	28-30 . . . . at Clinton
11-13 . . . Burlington Bees	
14-16 . . . . Beloit	**JULY**
17-19 . . . Cedar Rapids	1-3 . . . . Peoria
20-22 . . . . . at Peoria	4-6 . . . . Beloit
23-25 . . . . at Clinton	7-9 . . . . . . at Peoria
27-29 . . . . . Quad Cities	10-12 . . . . Clinton
30 . . . . . at Cedar Rapids	14-16 . . . . . . South Bend
	17-19 . . . . West Michigan
MAY	21-23 . . . . . . at Lansing
1-3 . . . . . at Cedar Rapids	24-26 . . . . at Great Lakes
4-6 . . . at Burlington Bees	28-30 . . . at Quad Cities
7-9 . . . . Peoria	31 . . . . Burlington Bees
10-12 . . . . at Beloit	
13-16 . . . . Quad Cities	**AUGUST**
18-20 . . . . . . at Beloit	1-2 . . . . . Burlington Bees
21-24 . . . . at Clinton	3-6 . . . . . Cedar Rapids
25-27 . . . . . Wisconsin	7-10 . . at Burlington Bees
28-31 . . . . Clinton	11-13 . . . . at Cedar Rapids
	14-16 . . . . Peoria
JUNE	18-20 . . . at Cedar Rapids
1-3 . . . . at Dayton	21-24 . . . . Quad Cities
4-6 . . . at Bowling Green	25-27 . . . . . . at Beloit
8-10 . . . . . . Fort Wayne	28-31 . . . . at Wisconsin
11-13 . . . . Lake County	
15-17 . . at Quad Cities	**SEPTEMBER**
18-20 . . . . . . Wisconsin	1-3 . . . . Peoria

LAKE COUNTY

APRIL	10-12 . . . . Bowling Green
8-10 . . . . . West Michigan	13-16 . . . . . at Fort Wayne
11-13 . . . at South Bend	18-20 . . at West Michigan
14-16 . . . . . at Lansing	21-24 . . . South Bend
17-19 . . . Fort Wayne	25-27 . . . . Dayton
20-22 . . . Great Lakes	28-31 . . . . at Great Lakes
23-25 . . . at Bowling Green	
27-29 . . . . at Dayton	**JUNE**
30 . . . . Great Lakes	1-3 . . . . Beloit
	4-6 . . . . Wisconsin
MAY	8-10 . . . . at Clinton
1-3 . . . . Great Lakes	11-13 . . . at Kane County
4-6 . . . . Dayton	15-17 . . at West Michigan
7-9 . . . . . at Great Lakes	18-20 . . . . . Lansing
	25-27 . . at West Michigan

28-30 . . . . . . Great Lakes

JULY
1-3 . . . . . . West Michigan
4-6 . . . . . . .at Lansing
7-9 . . . . Fort Wayne
10-12 . . at West Michigan
14-16 . . . . at Quad Cities
17-19 . . . at Cedar Rapids
21-23 . . . Burlington Bees
24-26 . . . . Peoria
28-30 . . . . West Michigan
31 . . . . at South Bend

LANSING

APRIL
8-10 . . . . at Dayton
11-13 . . . at Great Lakes
14-16 . . . . . Lake County
17-19 . . . Bowling Green
20-22 . . . .at Fort Wayne
23-25 . . . . Dayton
27-29 . . . at West Michigan
30 . . . . Fort Wayne

MAY
1-3 . . . . Fort Wayne
4-6 . . . . South Bend
7-9 . . . . . .at Fort Wayne
10-12 . . . . West Michigan
13-16 . . . at Bowling Green
18-20 . . . . . . at Dayton
21-24 . . . . . Great Lakes
25-27 . . . . . West Michigan
28-31 . . . . at South Bend

JUNE
1-3 . . . . . Cedar Rapids
4-6 . . . . Quad Cities
8-10 . . . . .at Peoria
11-13 . . at Burlington Bees
15-17 . . . Bowling Green
18-20 . . . .at Lake County

PEORIA

APRIL
8-10 . . . . at Clinton
11-13 . . . . . . at Beloit
14-16 . . . . at Cedar Rapids
17-19 . . . Burlington Bees
20-22 . . . . . Kane County
23-25 . . . at Quad Cities
27-29 . . . . . . Wisconsin
30 . . . . Clinton

MAY
1-3 . . . . Clinton
4-6 . . . . Cedar Rapids
7-9 . . . . . at Kane County
10-12 . . . . Clinton
13-16 . . at Burlington Bees
18-20 . . . . . at Wisconsin
21-24 . . . at Quad Cities
25-27 . . . . . Cedar Rapids
28-31 . . . . Beloit

JUNE
1-3 . . . . . . at South Bend
4-6 . . . . at West Michigan
8-10 . . . . Lansing
11-13 . . . . . Great Lakes
14-16 . . Burlington Bees
18-20 . . . . . . Quad Cities

AUGUST
1-2 . . . . . . at South Bend
3-6 . . . . Dayton
7-10 . . . . . at South Bend
11-13 . . . .at Fort Wayne
14-16 . . . . Dayton
18-20 . . . . Bowling Green
21-24 . . . . . . at Dayton
25-27 . . at Bowling Green
28-31 . . . . . . South Bend

SEPTEMBER
1-3 . . . . . . at Great Lakes

25-27 . . . . Dayton
28-30 . . at Bowling Green

JULY
1-3 . . . . . . at South Bend
4-6 . . . . Lake County
7-9 . . . . . . at Great Lakes
10-12 . . . . . Bowling Green
14-16 . . . . . at Wisconsin
17-19 . . . . . . at Beloit
21-23 . . . . . Kane County
24-26 . . . . Clinton
28-30 . . . Great Lakes
31 . . . . at Bowling Green

AUGUST
1-2 . . . . at Bowling Green
3-6 . . . . Fort Wayne
7-10 . . . . . at Great Lakes
11-13 . . . . . at Dayton
14-16 . . . . Fort Wayne
18-20 . . . . . . South Bend
21-24 . . . .at Fort Wayne
25-27 . . at West Michigan
28-31 . . . . Dayton

SEPTEMBER
1-3 . . . . . . West Michigan

25-27 . . . . . Cedar Rapids
28-30 . . at Burlington Bees

JULY
1-3 . . . . . . at Kane County
4-6 . . . . Clinton
7-9 . . . . Kane County
10-12 . . . at Cedar Rapids
14-16 . . . . Dayton
17-19 . . . Bowling Green
21-23 . . . . .at Fort Wayne
24-26 . . . .at Lake County
28-30 . . . . . . Wisconsin
31 . . . . at Beloit

AUGUST
1-2 . . . . at Beloit
3-6 . . . . . . at Wisconsin
7-10 . . . . Quad Cities
11-13 . . . . Beloit
14-16 . . . at Kane County
18-20 . . . Burlington Bees
21-24 . . . . . at Clinton
25-27 . . . . . Cedar Rapids
28-31 . . . . Clinton

SEPTEMBER
1-3 . . . . . at Kane County

QUAD CITIES

APRIL
8-10 . . . at Burlington Bees
11-13 . . . . Cedar Rapids
14-16 . . . . at Clinton
17-19 . . . . . Wisconsin
20-22 . . . . . . at Beloit
23-25 . . . . Peoria
27-29 . . at Kane County
30 . . . . . Burlington Bees

MAY
1-3 . . . . . Burlington Bees
4-6 . . . . at Wisconsin
7-9 . . . . .Clinton
10-12 . . . . Wisconsin
13-16 . . . at Kane County
18-20 . . . at Cedar Rapids
21-24 . . . . Peoria
25-27 . . . . Beloit
28-31 . . at Burlington Bees

JUNE
1-3 . . . . . . at Great Lakes
4-6 . . . . .at Lansing
8-10 . . . . South Bend
11-13 . . . . West Michigan
15-17 . . . . . Kane County
18-20 . . . . .at Peoria

SOUTH BEND

APRIL
8-10 . . . . Great Lakes
11-13 . . . . . Lake County
14-16 . . . at Great Lakes
17-19 . . . . at Dayton
20-22 . . . Bowling Green
23-25 . . at West Michigan
27-29 . . . . .at Fort Wayne
30 . . . . . . West Michigan

MAY
1-3 . . . . West Michigan
4-6 . . . . at Lansing
7-9 . . . . .Dayton
10-12 . . . . . Great Lakes
13-16 . . at West Michigan
17-19 . . . . . Fort Wayne
21-24 . . . .at Lake County
25-27 . . at Bowling Green
28-31 . . . . Lansing

JUNE
1-3 . . . . Peoria
4-6 . . . . Burlington Bees
8-10 . . . . at Quad Cities
11-13 . . at Cedar Rapids
15-17 . . . . at Great Lakes
18-20 . . . . Fort Wayne

WEST MICHIGAN

APRIL
8-10 . . . .at Lake County
11-13 . . . . Fort Wayne
14-16 . . at Bowling Green
17-19 . . . . . Great Lakes
20-22 . . . . . . at Dayton
23-25 . . . . . South Bend
27-29 . . . . Lansing
30 . . . . . . at South Bend

MAY
1-3 . . . . . . at South Bend
4-6 . . . . . at Great Lakes
7-9 . . . . . Bowling Green
10-12 . . . . .at Lansing

25-27 . . . . . Kane County
28-30 . . . . at Wisconsin

JULY
1-3 . . . . at Beloit
4-6 . . . . . Burlington Bees
7-9 . . . . at Clinton
10-12 . . . . .Beloit
14-16 . . . . . Lake County
17-19 . . . . . Fort Wayne
21-23 . . at Bowling Green
24-26 . . . . . . at Dayton
28-30 . . . Kane County
31 . . . . at Cedar Rapids

AUGUST
1-2 . . . . . at Cedar Rapids
3-6 . . . . Clinton
7-10 . . . . .at Peoria
11-13 . . . . Wisconsin
14-16 . . at Burlington Bees
18-20 . . . . Clinton
21-24 . . at Kane County
25-27 . . . . at Clinton
28-31 . . . . Cedar Rapids

SEPTEMBER
1-3 . . . . at Wisconsin

25-27 . . . . at Great Lakes
28-30 . . . .West Michigan

JULY
1-3 . . . . Lansing
4-6 . . . . . at Great Lakes
7-9 . . . . . West Michigan
10-12 . . . .at Fort Wayne
14-16 . . . at Kane County
17-19 . . . . . . at Clinton
21-23 . . . . .Beloit
24-26 . . . . . Wisconsin
28-30 . . . .at Fort Wayne
31 . . . . Lake County

AUGUST
1-2 . . . . Lake County
3-6 . . . . at Bowling Green
7-10 . . . . . Lake County
11-13 . . . . . Great Lakes
14-16 . . at West Michigan
18-20 . . . . . . .at Lansing
21-24 . . . . Bowling Green
25-27 . . . . Dayton
28-31 . . . .at Lake County

SEPTEMBER
1-3 . . . . Fort Wayne

13-16 . . . . . . South Bend
18-20 . . . Lake County
21-24 . . . .at Fort Wayne
25-27 . . . . at Lansing
28-31 . . . . . Dayton

JUNE
1-3 . . . . . Burlington Bees
4-6 . . . . Peoria
8-10 . . . at Cedar Rapids
11-13 . . . . at Quad Cities
15-17 . . . . . Lake County
18-20 . . at Bowling Green
25-27 . . . . . Lake County
28-30 . . . at South Bend

JULY
1-3 . . . . . . at Lake County
4-6 . . . . Dayton
7-9 . . . . . at South Bend
10-12 . . . . . Lake County
14-16 . . . . at Clinton
17-19 . . . at Kane County
21-23 . . . . . Wisconsin
24-26 . . . . Beloit
28-30 . . . . at Lake County
31 . . . . Dayton

AUGUST
1-2 . . . . Dayton
3-6 . . . . Great Lakes
7-10 . . . . at Dayton
11-13 . . at Bowling Green
14-16 . . . . . . South Bend
18-20 . . . . . Fort Wayne
21-24 . . . at Great Lakes
25-27 . . . . Lansing
28-31 . . . . . Great Lakes

SEPTEMBER
1-3 . . . . at Lansing

WISCONSIN

APRIL
8-10 . . . . . . Kane County
11-13 . . . . Clinton
14-16 . . at Burlington Bees
17-19 . . . at Quad Cities
20-22 . . . . Cedar Rapids
23-25 . . . . Beloit
27-29 . . . . . . at Peoria
30 . . . . at Beloit

MAY
1-3 . . . . at Beloit
4-6 . . . . . . Quad Cities
7-9 . . . . Cedar Rapids
10-12 . . . . at Quad Cities
13-16 . . . . Beloit
18-20 . . . . Peoria
21-24 . . Burlington Bees
25-27 . . at Kane County
28-31 . . . at Cedar Rapids

JUNE
1-3 . . . . . at Fort Wayne
4-6 . . . . at Lake County
8-10 . . . . . Bowling Green
11-13 . . . . Dayton
15-17 . . . . at Clinton
18-20 . . . at Kane County

25-27 . . . Burlington Bees
28-30 . . . . . Quad Cities

JULY
1-3 . . . at Burlington Bees
4-6 . . . at Cedar Rapids
7-9 . . . . at Beloit
10-12 . . Burlington Bees
14-16 . . . . . . Lansing
17-19 . . . . . Great Lakes
21-23 . . at West Michigan
24-26 . . . at South Bend
28-30 . . . . at Peoria
31 . . . . Clinton

AUGUST
1-2 . . . . Clinton
3-6 . . . . Peoria
7-10 . . . . . . at Clinton
11-13 . . . at Quad Cities
14-16 . . . Cedar Rapids
18-20 . . . . Beloit
21-24 . . at Cedar Rapids
25-27 . . at Burlington Bees
28-31 . . . . . Kane County

SEPTEMBER
1-3 . . . . . . Quad Cities

SOUTH ATLANTIC LEAGUE

ASHEVILLE

APRIL
8-11 . . . . Lakewood
12-15 . . . . Hickory
16-19 . . . at West Virginia
20-23 . . . . . at Lexington
24-27 . . . . . . Augusta
28-30 . . . . . Delmarva

MAY
1 . . . . Delmarva
3-6 . . . . at Hickory
7-10 . . . . . . at Rome
12-15 . . . . . Lexington
16-19 . . . at Hagerstown
20-23 . . . . . Kannapolis
24-27 . . . . . Greensboro
28-31 . . . . at Augusta

JUNE
1-4 . . . . at Savannah
5-8 . . . . West Virginia
10-12 . . . . at Kannapolis
14-16 . . . . . Hagerstown
17-20 . . . . . Greensboro

24-28 . . . . . at Savannah
29-30 . . . . . Kannapolis

JULY
1-3 . . . . Kannapolis
4-7 . . . . . at Charleston
8-12 . . . . Savannah
14-18 . . at Greensboro
20-23 . . . . Hagerstown
24-27 . . . . at Kannapolis
29-31 . . . . Rome

AUGUST
1 . . . . Rome
2-5 . . . . . at Hickory
6-10 . . . . . at Augusta
12-16 . . . . . Greenville
17-20 . . . at West Virginia
21-24 . . . . . Savannah
26-29 . . . . at Greenville
30-31 . . . . Hickory

SEPTEMBER
1-2 . . . . Hickory

AUGUSTA

APRIL
8-11 . . . at Greensboro
12-15 . . . . at Savannah
16-19 . . . Charleston
20-23 . . . . . Savannah
24-27 . . . at Asheville
28-30 . . . at Hagerstown

MAY
1 . . . . . at Hagerstown
3-6 . . . . . Greenville
7-10 . . . . . . Hagerstown
12-15 . . at Charleston
16-19 . . . . . Savannah
20-23 . . at Greenville
24-27 . . . . Rome
28-31 . . . . . Asheville

JUNE
1-4 . . . . . . at Rome
5-8 . . . . at Greenville
10-12 . . . . Hickory
14-16 . . at Charleston
17-20 . . . Savannah

24-28 . . . . . at Kannapolis
29-30 . . . . . Charleston

JULY
1-3 . . . . Charleston
4-7 . . . . . . at Lexington
8-12 . . . . . Kannapolis
14-18 . . at Charleston
20-23 . . . Greensboro
24-27 . . . . . Hickory
29-31 . . . at Savannah

AUGUST
1 . . . . at Savannah
2-5 . . . . . . Charleston
6-10 . . . . Asheville
12-16 . . . . . at Rome
17-20 . . . at Savannah
21-24 . . . . . Lexington
25-28 . . . . West Virginia
30-31 . . . at Lakewood

SEPTEMBER
1-2 . . . . . . at Lakewood

CHARLESTON

APRIL
8-11 . . . . . . Lexington
12-15 . . . West Virginia
16-19 . . . at Augusta
20-23 . . . at Hickory
24-27 . . . . Rome
28-30 . . . . . . Hickory

MAY
1 . . . . Hickory
3-6 . . . . . . at Lakewood
7-10 . . . at Delmarva
12-15 . . . Augusta
16-19 . . . . . at Rome
20-23 . . . . . Savannah
24-27 . . . at Greenville
28-31 . . . . . at Kannapolis

JUNE
1-4 . . . . Hickory
5-8 . . . . Rome
10-12 . . at Hagerstown
14-16 . . . . . Augusta

17-20 . . . . at Rome
24-28 . . . . . Greenville
29-30 . . . at Augusta

JULY
1-3 . . . . at Augusta
4-7 . . . . Asheville
8-12 . . . . . . at Rome
14-18 . . . . . Augusta
20-23 . . . at Lakewood
24-27 . . at Greensboro
28-31 . . . . Greenville

AUGUST
2-5 . . . . . at Augusta
6-10 . . . . . . Savannah
12-16 . . . . at Hickory
17-20 . . . . . Rome
21-24 . . at Greenville
25-28 . . . at Savannah
30-31 . . . . Greenville

SEPTEMBER
1-2 . . . . Greenville

DELMARVA

APRIL
8-11 . . . . at Greenville
12-15 . . . at Greensboro
16-19 . . . Hagerstown
20-23 . . . Greensboro
24-27 . . at Hagerstown
28-30 . . . at Asheville

MAY
1 . . . . . . at Asheville
3-6 . . . . . Savannah
7-10 . . . . . Charleston
12-15 . . at Kannapolis
16-19 . . at West Virginia
20-23 . . Hagerstown
24-27 . . . at Hickory
28-31 . . . . . Lakewood

JUNE
1-4 . . . at Greensboro
5-8 . . . . Hagerstown
10-12 . . . at Lexington
14-16 . . . Kannapolis
17-20 . . . Lexington

24-28 . . . . . Lakewood
29-30 . . . at West Virginia

JULY
1-3 . . . . at West Virginia
4-7 . . . . Hickory
8-12 . . . at Lakewood
14-18 . . West Virginia
20-23 . . . at Hickory
24-27 . . . . . Lakewood
29-31 . . . at Lexington

AUGUST
1 . . . . . . at Lexington
2-5 . . . . at West Virginia
6-10 . . . . . . Lexington
12-16 . . at Lakewood
17-20 . . . Hagerstown
21-24 . . . at Hickory
25-28 . . at Hagerstown
30-31 . . . . Kannapolis

SEPTEMBER
1-2 . . . . . . Kannapolis

GREENSBORO

APRIL
8-11 . . . . Augusta
12-15 . . . . Delmarva
16-19 . . . . . at Lakewood
20-23 . . . .at Delmarva
24-27 . . . . . .Lakewood
28-30 . . . . .Rome

MAY
1 . . . . .Rome
3-6. . . . . at West Virginia
7-10 . . . . . . at Lexington
12-15 . . . . .Hickory
16-19 . . . . . . .Lakewood
20-23 . . . . . . Lexington
24-27 . . . . at Asheville
28-31 . . . . . at Lexington

JUNE
1-4. . . . . Delmarva
5-8. . . . . at Lakewood
10-12 . . . . Savannah
13-15 . . . . at Greenville
17-20 . . . . at Asheville

24-28 . . . . . West Virginia
29-30 . . . . at Rome

JULY
1-3 . . . . at Rome
4-7 . . . . .Lakewood
8-12 . . . . . at Hickory
14-18 . . . . .Asheville
20-23 . . . . at Augusta
24-27 . . . . . Charleston
29-31 . . . . . .Hagerstown

AUGUST
1 . . . . .Hagerstown
2-5. . . . .at Kannapolis
6-10 . . . . .Hickory
12-16 . . . . at Hagerstown
17-20 . . . . at Lakewood
21-24 . . . . . Kannapolis
25-28 . . . . . at Rome
30-31 . . . . Savannah

SEPTEMBER
1-2. . . . . Savannah

GREENVILLE

APRIL
8-11 . . . . Delmarva
12-15 . . . . .Rome
16-19 . . . . . at Lexington
20-23 . . . . at West Virginia
24-27 . . . . . Lexington
28-30 . . . . West Virginia

MAY
1 . . . . West Virginia
3-6. . . . . at Augusta
7-10 . . . . . . at Hickory
12-15 . . . . . . .Lakewood
16-19 . . . . . Lexington
20-23 . . . . Augusta
24-27 . . . . . Charleston
28-31 . . . . at Hagerstown

JUNE
1-4. . . . . . .at Kannapolis
5-8. . . . . Augusta
10-12 . . . . . . at Rome
13-15 . . . . . Greensboro
17-20 . . . . at Hickory

24-28 . . . . . at Charleston
29-30 . . . . . . Savannah

JULY
1-3 . . . . Savannah
4-7 . . . . . .at Kannapolis
8-12 . . . . . .Hagerstown
14-18 . . . .at Savannah
20-23 . . . . Kannapolis
24-27 . . . . . at Rome
28-31 . . . . at Charleston

AUGUST
2-5. . . . . Lakewood
6-10 . . . . .Rome
12-16 . . . . at Asheville
17-20 . . . . at Lexington
21-24 . . . . . Charleston
26-29 . . . . . .Asheville
30-31 . . . .at Charleston

SEPTEMBER
1-2. . . . . . at Charleston

HAGERSTOWN

APRIL
8-11 . . . . .Hickory
12-15 . . . . . .Lakewood
16-19 . . . . . .at Delmarva
20-23 . . . . at Lakewood
24-27 . . . . . Delmarva
28-30 . . . . . Augusta

MAY
1 . . . . Augusta
3-6. . . . . at Rome
7-10 . . . . . at Augusta
12-15 . . . . . West Virginia
16-19 . . . . . .Asheville
20-23 . . . . at Delmarva
24-27 . . . . at Lakewood
28-31 . . . . . Greenville

JUNE
1-4. . . . . . . .Lakewood
5-8. . . . . . .at Delmarva
10-12 . . . . Charleston
14-16 . . . . at Asheville
17-20 . . . . at West Virginia

24-28 . . . . .Hickory
29-30 . . . . . at Lakewood

JULY
1-3 . . . . . at Lakewood
4-7 . . . . . . West Virginia
8-12 . . . . at Greenville
14-18 . . . . .Rome
20-23 . . . . at Asheville
24-27 . . . . West Virginia
29-31 . . . . at Greensboro

AUGUST
1 . . . . at Greensboro
2-5. . . . . . . Lexington
6-10 . . . . .at Kannapolis
12-16 . . . . . Greensboro
17-20 . . . . .at Delmarva
21-24 . . . .Lakewood
25-28 . . . . Delmarva
30-31 . . . . at Lexington

SEPTEMBER
1-2. . . . . . at Lexington

HICKORY

APRIL
8-11 . . . . . at Hagerstown
12-15 . . . . . at Asheville
16-19 . . . . . Kannapolis
20-23 . . . . . Charleston
24-27 . . . .at Savannah
28-30 . . . . at Charleston

MAY
1 . . . . . . at Charleston
3-6. . . . . . . .Asheville
7-10 . . . . Greenville
12-15 . . . . at Greensboro
16-19 . . . .at Kannapolis
20-23 . . . . . . .Rome
24-27 . . . . . Delmarva
28-31 . . . . at West Virginia

JUNE
1-4. . . . . at Charleston
5-8. . . . . Lexington
10-12 . . . . at Augusta
14-16 . . . . West Virginia
17-20 . . . . . Greenville

24-28 . . . . . at Hagerstown
29-30 . . . . Lexington

JULY
1-3 . . . . Lexington
4-7 . . . . .at Delmarva
8-12 . . . . . Greensboro
14-18 . . . at Lexington
20-23 . . . . Delmarva
24-27 . . . . at Augusta
29-31 . . . . . Kannapolis

AUGUST
1 . . . . Kannapolis
2-5. . . . . .Asheville
6-10 . . . . at Greensboro
12-16 . . . . . Charleston
17-20 . . . .at Kannapolis
21-24 . . . . . Delmarva
25-28 . . . .Lakewood
30-31 . . . . at Asheville

SEPTEMBER
1-2. . . . . . . at Asheville

KANNAPOLIS

APRIL
8-11 . . . . .Rome
12-15 . . . . . . Lexington
16-19 . . . . . at Hickory
20-23 . . . . . at Rome
24-27 . . . . West Virginia
28-30 . . . . . Lakewood

MAY
1 . . . . Lakewood
3-6. . . . . . at Lexington
7-10 . . . . at West Virginia
12-15 . . . . . Delmarva
16-19 . . . . . . .Hickory
20-23 . . . . at Asheville
24-27 . . . .at Savannah
28-31 . . . . Charleston

JUNE
1-4. . . . . . . Greenville
5-8. . . . . . . .at Savannah
10-12 . . . . . . .Asheville
14-16 . . . .at Delmarva
17-20 . . . . . at Lakewood

24-28 . . . . Augusta
29-30 . . . . . at Asheville

JULY
1-3 . . . . at Asheville
4-7 . . . . Greenville
8-12 . . . . at Augusta
14-18 . . . . at Greenville
20-23 . . . . at Greenville
24-27 . . . . . . .Asheville
29-31 . . . . at Hickory

AUGUST
1 . . . . at Hickory
2-5. . . . . . Greensboro
6-10 . . . . .Hagerstown
12-16 . . . .at Savannah
17-20 . . . . . . .Hickory
21-24 . . . . at Greensboro
25-28 . . . . . Lexington
30-31 . . . . .at Delmarva

SEPTEMBER
1-2. . . . . . . .at Delmarva

LAKEWOOD

APRIL
8-11 . . . . at Asheville
12-15 . . . . at Hagerstown
16-19 . . . . . . Greensboro
20-23 . . . . . .Hagerstown
24-27 . . . . at Greensboro
28-30 . . . .at Kannapolis

MAY
1 . . . . . .at Kannapolis
3-6. . . . . . Charleston
7-10 . . . . Savannah
12-15 . . . . at Greenville
16-19 . . . . at Greensboro
20-23 . . . . West Virginia
24-27 . . . . .Hagerstown
28-31 . . . . . .at Delmarva

JUNE
1-4. . . . . at Hagerstown
5-8. . . . . . . Greensboro
10-12 . . . at West Virginia
14-16 . . . . Lexington
17-20 . . . . . . Kannapolis

24-28 . . . . . .at Delmarva
29-30 . . . . . .Hagerstown

JULY
1-3 . . . . .Hagerstown
4-7 . . . . . at Greensboro
8-12 . . . . . Delmarva
14-18 . . . .at Kannapolis
20-23 . . . . . . Charleston
24-27 . . . . . .at Delmarva
28-31 . . . . . West Virginia

AUGUST
2-5. . . . . . . at Greenville
6-10 . . . . at West Virginia
12-16 . . . . . Delmarva
17-20 . . . . . Greensboro
21-24 . . . . at Hagerstown
25-28 . . . . at Hickory
30-31 . . . . Augusta

SEPTEMBER
1-2. . . . . Augusta

LEXINGTON

APRIL
8-11 . . . . . .at Charleston
12-15 . . . . . .at Kannapolis
16-19 . . . . . . Greenville
20-23 . . . . . .Asheville
24-27 . . . . at Greenville
28-30 . . . . . .at Savannah

MAY
1 . . . . . . .at Savannah
3-6 . . . . . . Kannapolis
7-10 . . . . . .Greensboro
12-15 . . . . at Asheville
16-19 . . . . . Greenville
20-23 . . . . at Greensboro
24-27 . . . . at West Virginia
28-31 . . . . . Greensboro

JUNE
1-4 . . . . West Virginia
5-8 . . . . at Hickory
10-12 . . . . . . Delmarva
14-16 . . . . . at Lakewood
17-20 . . . . . .at Delmarva

24-28 . . . . .Rome
29-30 . . . . at Hickory

JULY
1-3 . . . . at Hickory
4-7 . . . . Augusta
8-12 . . . . at West Virginia
14-18 . . . . . . .Hickory
20-23 . . . . at Rome
24-27 . . . . Savannah
29-31 . . . . Delmarva

AUGUST
1 . . . . Delmarva
2-5 . . . . . .at Hagerstown
6-10 . . . . . .at Delmarva
12-16 . . . . . West Virginia
17-20 . . . . . . Greenville
21-24 . . . . . at Augusta
25-28 . . . . .at Kannapolis
30-31 . . . . . .Hagerstown

SEPTEMBER
1-2 . . . . .Hagerstown

ROME

APRIL
8-11 . . . . . . .at Kannapolis
12-15 . . . . at Greenville
16-19 . . . . . . Savannah
20-23 . . . . Kannapolis
24-27 . . . . .at Charleston
28-30 . . . . at Greensboro

MAY
1 . . . . at Greensboro
3-6 . . . . .Hagerstown
7-10 . . . . . . .Asheville
12-15 . . .at Savannah
16-19 . . . . . . Charleston
20-23 . . . . . at Hickory
24-27 . . . . at Augusta
28-31 . . . . Savannah

JUNE
1-4 . . . . Augusta
5-8 . . . . . . .at Charleston
10-12 . . . . Greenville
14-16 . . . . .at Savannah
17-20 . . . . . . Charleston

24-28 . . . . . at Lexington
29-30 . . . . . . Greensboro

JULY
1-3 . . . . .Greensboro
4-7 . . . . .at Savannah
8-12 . . . . Charleston
14-18 . . . . at Hagerstown
20-23 . . . . . Lexington
24-27 . . . . . Greenville
29-31 . . . . at Asheville

AUGUST
1 . . . . at Asheville
2-5 . . . . . . Savannah
6-10 . . . . . at Greenville
12-16 . . . . . . Augusta
17-20 . . . .at Charleston
21-24 . . . . . West Virginia
25-28 . . . . .Greensboro
30-31 . . . . at West Virginia

SEPTEMBER
1-2 . . . . at West Virginia

SAVANNAH

APRIL
8-11 . . . . . . West Virginia
12-15 . . . . Augusta
16-19 . . . . . . at Rome
20-23 . . . . . at Augusta
24-27 . . . . .Hickory
28-30 . . . . . Lexington

MAY
1 . . . . Lexington
3-6 . . . . . .at Delmarva
7-10 . . . . . at Lakewood
12-15 . . . . .Rome
16-19 . . . . . at Augusta
20-23 . . .at Charleston
24-27 . . . . . Kannapolis
28-31 . . . . . at Rome

JUNE
1-4 . . . . .Asheville
5-8 . . . . . . Kannapolis
10-12 . . . . at Greensboro
14-16 . . . . . . .Rome
17-20 . . . . . . at Augusta

24-28 . . . . Asheville
29-30 . . . . at Greenville

JULY
1-3 . . . . . at Greenville
4-7 . . . . .Rome
8-12 . . . . at Asheville
14-18 . . . . . Greenville
20-23 . . . . at West Virginia
24-27 . . at Lexington
29-31 . . . . Augusta

AUGUST
1 . . . . Augusta
2-5 . . . . at Rome
6-10 . . . . .at Charleston
12-16 . . . . . Kannapolis
17-20 . . . . . . Augusta
21-24 . . . . at Asheville
25-28 . . . . . Charleston
30-31 . . . . at Greensboro

SEPTEMBER
1-2 . . . . . . at Greensboro

WEST VIRGINIA

APRIL
8-11 . . . . . . .at Savannah
12-15 . . . . .at Charleston
16-19 . . . . . .Asheville
20-23 . . . . Greenville
24-27 . . .at Kannapolis
28-30 . . . . at Greenville

MAY
1 . . . . at Greenville
3-6 . . . . .Greensboro
7-10 . . . . . . Kannapolis
12-15 . . . . at Hagerstown
16-19 . . . . . . Delmarva
20-23 . . . at Lakewood
24-27 . . . . . Lexington
28-31 . . . . . .Hickory

JUNE
1-4 . . . . at Lexington
5-8 . . . . at Asheville
10-12 . . . . . . .Lakewood
14-16 . . . . . . at Hickory

17-20 . . . . . .Hagerstown
24-28 . . . . at Greensboro
29-30 . . . . Delmarva

JULY
1-3 . . . . Delmarva
4-7 . . . . . . at Hagerstown
8-12 . . . . Lexington
14-18 . . . . .at Delmarva
20-23 . . . . . . Savannah
24-27 . . . at Hagerstown
28-31 . . . . at Lakewood

AUGUST
2-5 . . . . Delmarva
6-10 . . . . .Lakewood
12-16 . . . . at Lexington
17-20 . . . . . .Asheville
21-24 . . . . at Rome
25-28 . . . . at Augusta
30-31 . . . . .Rome

SEPTEMBER
1-2 . . . . .Rome

SHORT SEASON

NORTHWEST LEAGUE

BOISE

JUNE
18-20 . . . . at Yakima
21-25 . . . . . Salem-Keizer
26-30 . . . . . at Eugene

JULY
1-3 . . . . Yakima
4-6 . . . . at Spokane
8-12 . . . . .Eugene
13-17 . . . . at Salem-Keizer
18-20 . . . . Spokane
21-23 . . Tri-City Dust Devils
24-26 . . . . at Yakima
28-31 . . . . . . .Vancouver

AUGUST
1 . . . . .Vancouver
2-4 . . .at Tri-City Dust Devils
5-9 . . . . at Everett
11-13 . . Tri-City Dust Devils
14-18 . . . . Everett
20-24 . . . . . . at Vancouver
25-27 .at Tri-City Dust Devils
28-30 . . . . at Spokane
31 . . . . Spokane

SEPTEMBER
1-2 . . . . Spokane

EUGENE

JUNE
18-20 . . . . . . .Vancouver
21-25 .at Tri-City Dust Devils
26-30 . . . . Boise

JULY
1-3 . . . . at Vancouver
4-6 . . . . Everett
8-12 . . . . at Boise
13-17 . . Tri-City Dust Devils
18-20 . . . . at Everett
21-23 . . . . . at Vancouver
24-26 . . . . . .Vancouver
28-31 . . . . .Spokane

AUGUST
1 . . . . Spokane
2-6 . . . . at Yakima
7-9 . . . . . . Salem-Keizer
11-13 . . . . at Salem-Keizer
14-18 . . . . .Yakima
20-24 . . . . . . at Spokane
25-27 . . . . Everett
28-30 . . . . at Everett
31 . . . . Salem-Keizer

SEPTEMBER
1-2 . . . . Salem-Keizer

EVERETT

JUNE	
18-20	at Salem-Keizer
21-25	Yakima
26-30	at Spokane

JULY	
1-3	Salem-Keizer
4-6	at Eugene
8-12	Spokane
13-17	at Yakima
18-20	Eugene
21-23	at Salem-Keizer
24-26	Salem-Keizer
28-31	at Tri-City Dust Devils

AUGUST	
1 . . .	at Tri-City Dust Devils
2-4	Vancouver
5-9	Boise
11-13	at Vancouver
14-18	at Boise
20-24 . .	Tri-City Dust Devils
25-27	at Eugene
28-30	Eugene
31	Vancouver

SEPTEMBER	
1-2	Vancouver

SALEM-KEIZER

JUNE	
18-20	Everett
21-25	at Boise
26-30 . .	Tri-City Dust Devils

JULY	
1-3	at Everett
4-6	Vancouver
8-12 .	at Tri-City Dust Devils
13-17	Boise
18-20 . . .	at Vancouver
21-23	Everett
24-26	at Everett
28-31	Yakima

AUGUST	
1	Yakima
2-6	at Spokane
7-9	at Eugene
11-13	Eugene
14-18	Spokane
20-24	at Yakima
25-27	Vancouver
28-30	at Vancouver
31	at Eugene

SEPTEMBER	
1-2	at Eugene

SPOKANE

JUNE	
18-20 . .	Tri-City Dust Devils
21-25	at Vancouver
26-30	Everett

JULY	
1-3 . .	at Tri-City Dust Devils
4-6	Boise
8-12	at Everett
13-17	Vancouver
18-20	at Boise
21-23	Yakima
24-26 . .	Tri-City Dust Devils
28-31	at Eugene

AUGUST	
1	at Eugene
2-6	Salem-Keizer
7-9	Yakima
11-13	at Yakima
14-18 . . .	at Salem-Keizer
20-24	Eugene
25-27	at Yakima
28-30	Boise
31	at Boise

SEPTEMBER	
1-2	at Boise

TRI-CITY DUST DEVILS

JUNE	
18-20	at Spokane
21-25	Eugene
26-30 . . .	at Salem-Keizer

JULY	
1-3	Spokane
4-6	at Yakima
8-12 . . .	Salem-Keizer
13-17	at Eugene
18-20	Yakima
21-23	at Boise
24-26 . . .	at Spokane
28-31	Everett

AUGUST	
1	Everett
2-4	Boise
5-9	at Vancouver
11-13	at Boise
14-18	Vancouver
20-24	at Everett
25-27	Boise
28-30	Yakima
31	at Yakima

SEPTEMBER	
1-2	at Yakima

VANCOUVER

JUNE	
18-20	at Eugene
21-25	Spokane
26-30	at Yakima

JULY	
1-3	Eugene
4-6	at Salem-Keizer
8-12	Yakima
13-17	at Spokane
18-20	Salem-Keizer
21-23	Eugene
24-26	at Eugene
28-31	at Boise

AUGUST	
1	at Boise
2-4	at Everett
5-9 . .	Tri-City Dust Devils
11-13	Everett
14-18	at Tri-City Dust Devils
20-24	Boise
25-27 . .	at Salem-Keizer
28-30 . . .	Salem-Keizer
31	at Everett

SEPTEMBER	
1-2	at Everett

YAKIMA

JUNE	
18-20	Boise
21-25	at Everett
26-30	Vancouver

JULY	
1-3	at Boise
4-6 . . .	Tri-City Dust Devils
8-12 . . .	at Vancouver
13-17 . . .	Everett
18-20	at Tri-City Dust Devils
21-23 . . .	at Spokane
24-26	Boise
28-31 . .	at Salem-Keizer

AUGUST	
1	at Salem-Keizer
2-6	Eugene
7-9	at Spokane
11-13	Spokane
14-18 . . .	at Eugene
20-24 . .	Salem-Keizer
25-27	Spokane
28-30	at Tri-City Dust Devils
31 . . .	Tri-City Dust Devils

SEPTEMBER	
1-2 . . .	Tri-City Dust Devils

NEW YORK-PENN LEAGUE

ABERDEEN

JUNE	
18-20	Hudson Valley
21-22	at Brooklyn
23-25 . .	at Staten Island
26-27	Brooklyn
28-30	Staten Island

JULY	
1-3	at Hudson Valley
4-6	Lowell
8-10 . . .	at Williamsport
11-13	Auburn
14-16	at Vermont
17-19	at Lowell
20-22 . .	Tri-City ValleyCats
23-24 . . .	Hudson Valley
25-26 . .	at Hudson Valley
28-30	Brooklyn

31	at Hudson Valley

AUGUST	
1	at Hudson Valley
2-3	Staten Island
4-6	Jamestown
7-9 . .	at Mahoning Valley
10-12	at Batavia
13-15 . . .	State College
18-19 . .	Hudson Valley
20-22 .	at Tri-City ValleyCats
23-24 . .	at Staten Island
25-27 . . .	at Brooklyn
28-30 . . .	Vermont
31	at Oneonta

SEPTEMBER	
1-2	at Oneonta

AUBURN

JUNE	
18	Batavia
19	at Batavia
20	Batavia
21-23 .	at Mahoning Valley
24-25 . .	Williamsport
26-27 .	Mahoning Valley
28-30 . .	at Williamsport

JULY	
1	Batavia
2-3	at Batavia
4-6 . . .	Staten Island
8-10 . .	at Hudson Valley
11-13 . .	at Aberdeen
14-16 .	Tri-City ValleyCats
17-19 . .	State College

20-21 . . .	at Jamestown
22-24 . .	at State College
25-26 . . .	Jamestown
28-29 . . .	Batavia
30	at Batavia
31 . . .	State College

AUGUST	
1	State College
2-3 . . .	at Williamsport
4-6 . . .	at Vermont
7-9	Lowell
10-12 . . .	Brooklyn
13-15 . . .	at Oneonta
18-20 . .	Williamsport
21-23 . .	at Jamestown
24-26 . . .	Jamestown

27-29 . . . .Mahoning Valley
30-31 . . at Mahoning Valley

SEPTEMBER
1-2 . . . . . at State College
3 . . . . at Batavia
4 . . . . Batavia

BATAVIA

JUNE	
18 . . . . at Auburn	30 . . . . .Auburn
19 . . . . .Auburn	31 . . . . Jamestown
20 . . . . at Auburn	**AUGUST**
21-23 . . . at State College	1 . . . . at Jamestown
24-25 . . at Mahoning Valley	2-3 . . . .Mahoning Valley
26-27 . . . . . State College	4-6 . . . . at Brooklyn
28-30 . . . .Mahoning Valley	7-9 . . . . at Vermont
JULY	10-12 . . . . Aberdeen
1 . . . . at Auburn	13-15 . . . Hudson Valley
2-3 . . . . .Auburn	18-20 . . at Mahoning Valley
4-6 . . . at Tri-City ValleyCats	21-23 . . . .at Williamsport
8-10 . . . . .Oneonta	24-26 . . . . Williamsport
11-13 . . at Staten Island	27-28 . . . . at State College
14-16 . . . . Lowell	29-31 . . . . . State College
17-19 . . . . Jamestown	**SEPTEMBER**
20-21 . . . .at Williamsport	1 . . . . at Jamestown
22-24 . . . . . at Jamestown	2 . . . . Jamestown
25-26 . . . . . Williamsport	3 . . . . .Auburn
28-29 . . . . . . at Auburn	4 . . . . at Auburn

BROOKLYN

JUNE	
18 . . . . . at Staten Island	25 . . . . . . Staten Island
19 . . . . . . at Staten Island	26 . . . . . . at Staten Island
20 . . . . . at Staten Island	28-30 . . . . . at Aberdeen
21-22 . . . . Aberdeen	31 . . . . Staten Island
23 . . . . .at Hudson Valley	**AUGUST**
24 . . . . . Hudson Valley	1 . . . . . at Staten Island
25 . . . . .at Hudson Valley	2 . . . . . . Hudson Valley
26-27 . . . at Aberdeen	3 . . . . .at Hudson Valley
28 . . . . . Hudson Valley	4-6 . . . . Batavia
29 . . . . .at Hudson Valley	7-9 . . . . Oneonta
30 . . . . . Hudson Valley	10-12 . . . . . . at Auburn
JULY	13-15 . . . .at Williamsport
1 . . . . . . Staten Island	18 . . . . . . at Staten Island
2 . . . . . . at Staten Island	19 . . . . . at Staten Island
3 . . . . . . Staten Island	20-22 . . . . . . at Vermont
4-6 . . . . . at Jamestown	23 . . . . .at Hudson Valley
8-10 . . . . . State College	24 . . . . . Hudson Valley
11-13 . . . . .at Lowell	25-27 . . . . Aberdeen
14-16 . . . .Mahoning Valley	28-30 . . . . at Oneonta
17-19 . at Tri-City ValleyCats	31 . . . . Vermont
20-22 . . . . Lowell	**SEPTEMBER**
23 . . . . Staten Island	1-2 . . . . .Vermont
24 . . . . . at Staten Island	

HUDSON VALLEY

JUNE	
18-20 . . . . . at Aberdeen	20 . . . . . at Staten Island
21-22 . . . . . Staten Island	21 . . . . . . Staten Island
23 . . . . .Brooklyn	22 . . . . . at Staten Island
24 . . . . . . at Brooklyn	23-24 . . . . . at Aberdeen
25 . . . . .Brooklyn	25-26 . . . . . Aberdeen
26-27 . . . . at Staten Island	28-30 . . . . at Vermont
28 . . . . . . at Brooklyn	31 . . . . Aberdeen
29 . . . . .Brooklyn	**AUGUST**
30 . . . . . . at Brooklyn	1 . . . . Aberdeen
JULY	2 . . . . at Brooklyn
1-3 . . . . Aberdeen	3 . . . . .Brooklyn
4-6 . . . . . at State College	4-6 . . . . at Oneonta
8-10 . . . . .Auburn	7-9 . . . . Jamestown
11-13 . . at Mahoning Valley	10-12 . . . . Vermont
14-16 . . . . . Williamsport	13-15 . . . . . . at Batavia
17-19 . . . . .Oneonta	18-19 . . . at Aberdeen
	20-22 . . . . . . .at Lowell

---

23 . . . . .Brooklyn
24 . . . . at Brooklyn
25-27 . . Tri-City ValleyCats
28-30 . at Tri-City ValleyCats

JAMESTOWN

JUNE	
18-20 . . . .Mahoning Valley	31 . . . . at Batavia
21-23 . . . .at Williamsport	**AUGUST**
24-25 . . . . at State College	1 . . . . Batavia
26-27 . . . . . Williamsport	2-3 . . . . State College
28-30 . . . . . State College	4-6 . . . . at Aberdeen
JULY	7-9 . . . .at Hudson Valley
1-3 . . . at Mahoning Valley	10-12 . . . . .Oneonta
4-6 . . . . .Brooklyn	13-15 . . . . Vermont
8-10 . . . . .at Lowell	18-20 . . at State College
11-13 . at Tri-City ValleyCats	21-23 . . . . .Auburn
14-16 . . . . Staten Island	24-26 . . . . . at Auburn
17-19 . . . . . . at Batavia	27-29 . . . . Williamsport
20-21 . . . . .Auburn	30-31 . . . .at Williamsport
22-24 . . . . Batavia	**SEPTEMBER**
25-26 . . . . . . at Auburn	1 . . . . Batavia
28-30 . . . .Mahoning Valley	2 . . . . at Batavia

LOWELL

JUNE	
18-20 . . . . . . at Vermont	31 . . . . Vermont
21-22 . . Tri-City ValleyCats	**AUGUST**
23-25 . . . . .Oneonta	1 . . . . Vermont
26-27 . at Tri-City ValleyCats	2-3 . . . . at Oneonta
28-30 . . . . . . at Oneonta	4-6 . . . . . .at Williamsport
JULY	7-9 . . . . at Auburn
1-3 . . . . Vermont	10-12 . . . State College
4-6 . . . . at Aberdeen	13-15 . . . .Mahoning Valley
8-10 . . . . Jamestown	18-19 . . . . . at Vermont
11-13 . . . . . . .Brooklyn	20-22 . . . Hudson Valley
14-16 . . . . . . at Batavia	23-24 . . . . . . Vermont
17-19 . . . . Aberdeen	25-27 . . . at Staten Island
20-22 . . . . . at Brooklyn	28-30 . . . Staten Island
23-24 . . . . . at Vermont	31 . . . Tri-City ValleyCats
25-26 . . . . . . .Oneonta	**SEPTEMBER**
28-30 . at Tri-City ValleyCats	1-2 . . . . Tri-City ValleyCats

MAHONING VALLEY

JUNE	
18-20 . . . . at Jamestown	28-30 . . . . at Jamestown
21-23 . . . . .Auburn	31 . . . . . . Williamsport
24-25 . . . . Batavia	**AUGUST**
26-27 . . . . . . at Auburn	1 . . . . Williamsport
28-30 . . . . at Batavia	2-3 . . . . at Batavia
JULY	4-6 . . . . Tri-City ValleyCats
1-3 . . . . Jamestown	7-9 . . . . Aberdeen
4-6 . . . . at Oneonta	10-12 . . . at Staten Island
8-10 . . . . Vermont	13-15 . . . . .at Lowell
11-13 . . . . Hudson Valley	18-20 . . . . Batavia
14-16 . . . . . at Auburn	21-23 . . . at State College
17-19 . . . . Williamsport	24-26 . . . State College
20-21 . . at State College	27-29 . . . . at Auburn
22-24 . . .at Williamsport	30-31 . . . . . . .Auburn
25-26 . . . . . State College	**SEPTEMBER**
	1-2 . . . . . .at Williamsport

---

31 . . . . Staten Island

SEPTEMBER
1 . . . . . . at Staten Island
2 . . . . Staten Island

ONEONTA

JUNE
18-20 . at Tri-City ValleyCats
21-22 . . . . at Vermont
23-25 . . . . .at Lowell
26-27 . . . . Vermont
28-30 . . . . Lowell

JULY
1-3. . . at Tri-City ValleyCats
4-6. . . . . .Mahoning Valley
8-10 . . . . . . at Batavia
11-13 . . . . .at Williamsport
14-16 . . . . . . State College
17-19 . . .at Hudson Valley
20-22 . . . . Vermont
23-24 . . Tri-City ValleyCats
25-26 . . . . . . .at Lowell
28-30 . . . . at Staten Island

31 . . . . . Tri-City ValleyCats

AUGUST
1 . . . . . . Tri-City ValleyCats
2-3 . . . . Lowell
4-6. . . . . . Hudson Valley
7-9. . . . . at Brooklyn
10-12 . . . . . at Jamestown
13-15 . . . . .Auburn
18-19 . . Tri-City ValleyCats
20-22 . . . . . Staten Island
23 . . . . Tri-City ValleyCats
24 . . at Tri-City ValleyCats
25-27 . . . . . . at Vermont
28-30 . . . . . . .Brooklyn
31 . . . . Aberdeen

SEPTEMBER
1-2. . . . . Aberdeen

STATE COLLEGE

JUNE
18 . . . . . .at Williamsport
19 . . . . Williamsport
20 . . . . . .at Williamsport
21-23 . . . . .Batavia
24-25 . . . . . . Jamestown
26-27 . . . . . . at Batavia
28-30 . . . . at Jamestown

JULY
1-2. . . . . . . Williamsport
3 . . . . . .at Williamsport
4-6. . . . . . Hudson Valley
8-10 . . . . . . at Brooklyn
11-13 . . . . Vermont
14-16 . . . . . at Oneonta
17-19 . . . . . . at Auburn
20-21 . . .Mahoning Valley
22-24 . . . . .Auburn
25-26 . . at Mahoning Valley

28 . . . . Williamsport
29 . . . . . .at Williamsport
30 . . . . Williamsport
31 . . . . at Auburn

AUGUST
1 . . . . at Auburn
2-3. . . . . . at Jamestown
4-6. . . . . . Staten Island
7-9. . . . . Tri-City ValleyCats
10-12 . . . . . . .at Lowell
13-15 . . . . . at Aberdeen
18-20 . . . . . Jamestown
21-23 . . .Mahoning Valley
24-26 . . at Mahoning Valley
27-28 . . . . .Batavia
29-31 . . . . . . at Batavia

SEPTEMBER
1-2. . . . . .Auburn
3-4. . . . . . .at Williamsport

STATEN ISLAND

JUNE
18 . . . . .Brooklyn
19 . . . . at Brooklyn
20 . . . . .Brooklyn
21-22 . . .at Hudson Valley
23-25 . . . . . . Aberdeen
26-27 . . . . . Hudson Valley
28-30 . . . . . at Aberdeen

JULY
1 . . . . at Brooklyn
2 . . . . .Brooklyn
3 . . . . at Brooklyn
4-6. . . . . at Auburn
8-10 . . . . Tri-City ValleyCats
11-13 . . . . .Batavia
14-16 . . . . . at Jamestown
17-19 . . . . . at Vermont
20 . . . . . . .at Hudson Valley
21 . . . . .at Hudson Valley
22 . . . . Hudson Valley
23 . . . . at Brooklyn
24 . . . . .Brooklyn

25 . . . . at Brooklyn
26 . . . . .Brooklyn
28-30 . . . . Oneonta
31 . . . . at Brooklyn

AUGUST
1 . . . . .Brooklyn
2-3. . . . . . . at Aberdeen
4-6. . . . . . at State College
7-9. . . . . . . Williamsport
10-12 . . .Mahoning Valley
13-15 . at Tri-City ValleyCats
18 . . . . at Brooklyn
19 . . . . .Brooklyn
20-22 . . . . . . at Oneonta
23-24 . . . . . . Aberdeen
25-27 . . . . Lowell
28-30 . . . . . . .at Lowell
31 . . . . .at Hudson Valley

SEPTEMBER
1 . . . . Hudson Valley
2 . . . . . .at Hudson Valley

TRI-CITY VALLEYCATS

JUNE
18-20 . . . . .Oneonta
21-22 . . . . .at Lowell
23-25 . . . . Vermont
26-27 . . . . Lowell
28-30 . . . . . . at Vermont

JULY
1-3. . . . . .Oneonta
4-6. . . . . Batavia
8-10 . . . . . at Staten Island
11-13 . . . . . Jamestown
14-16 . . . . . . at Auburn
17-19 . . . . . . .Brooklyn
20-22 . . . . at Aberdeen
23-24 . . . . . at Oneonta
25-26 . . . . . . at Vermont
28-30 . . . . Lowell

31 . . . . at Oneonta

AUGUST
1 . . . . at Oneonta
2-3. . . . . Vermont
4-6. . . . at Mahoning Valley
7-9. . . . . . at State College
10-12 . . . . . . Williamsport
13-15 . . . . . Staten Island
18-19 . . . . . at Oneonta
20-22 . . . . . . Aberdeen
23 . . . . at Oneonta
24 . . . . .Oneonta
25-27 . . .at Hudson Valley
28-30 . . . Hudson Valley
31 . . . . .at Lowell

SEPTEMBER
1-2. . . . . .at Lowell

VERMONT

JUNE
18-20 . . . . Lowell
21-22 . . . . .Oneonta
23-25 . at Tri-City ValleyCats
26-27 . . . . . at Oneonta
28-30 . . . Tri-City ValleyCats

JULY
1-3. . . . . .at Lowell
4-6. . . . . . . Williamsport
8-10 . . at Mahoning Valley
11-13 . . . at State College
14-16 . . . . Aberdeen
17-19 . . . . . Staten Island
20-22 . . . . . at Oneonta
23-24 . . . . Lowell
25-26 . . Tri-City ValleyCats
28-30 . . . . . Hudson Valley

31 . . . . .at Lowell

AUGUST
1 . . . . .at Lowell
2-3. . . at Tri-City ValleyCats
4-6. . . . . .Auburn
7-9. . . . . Batavia
10-12 . . .at Hudson Valley
13-15 . . . . . at Jamestown
18-19 . . . . Lowell
20-22 . . . . . . .Brooklyn
23-24 . . . . . . .at Lowell
25-27 . . . . .Oneonta
28-30 . . . . at Aberdeen
31 . . . . at Brooklyn

SEPTEMBER
1-2. . . . . . . at Brooklyn

WILLIAMSPORT

JUNE
18 . . . . State College
19 . . . . . at State College
20 . . . . . State College
21-23 . . . . . . Jamestown
24-25 . . . . at Auburn
26-27 . . at Jamestown
28-30 . . . . .Auburn

JULY
1-2. . . . . at State College
3 . . . . . State College
4-6. . . . . . . at Vermont
8-10 . . . . Aberdeen
11-13 . . . . . .Oneonta
14-16 . . .at Hudson Valley
17-19 . . at Mahoning Valley
20-21 . . . . .Batavia
22-24 . . .Mahoning Valley
25-26 . . . . at Batavia

28 . . . . . at State College
29 . . . . . at State College
30 . . . . . at State College
31 . . .at Mahoning Valley

AUGUST
1 . . . . . at Mahoning Valley
2-3. . . . . .Auburn
4-6. . . . . Lowell
7-9. . . . . . at Staten Island
10-12 . at Tri-City ValleyCats
13-15 . . . . . . .Brooklyn
18-20 . . . . . . at Auburn
21-23 . . . . .Batavia
24-26 . . . . . at Batavia
27-29 . . . . at Jamestown
30-31 . . . . . . Jamestown

SEPTEMBER
1-2. . . . . .Mahoning Valley
3-4. . . . . . . State College

ROOKIE

APPALACHIAN LEAGUE

BLUEFIELD

JUNE	
22-24	at Pulaski
25-27	Danville
28-30	at Burlington Royals
JULY	
1-3	Burlington Royals
4-6	at Princeton
7-9	Johnson City
10-12	Greeneville
14-16	Kingsport
17-19	at Greeneville
20-22	at Kingsport
23-25	Princeton
26-28	Pulaski
29-31	at Burlington Royals
AUGUST	
1-3	at Danville
5-7	at Elizabethton
8	at Princeton
9-11	Pulaski
12-14	Danville
15-17	at Princeton
19-21	Bristol
22-24	Elizabethton
25-27	at Bristol
28-30	at Johnson City

BRISTOL

JUNE	
22-24	Elizabethton
25-27	Princeton
28-30	at Johnson City
JULY	
1-3	Greeneville
4-6	at Pulaski
7-9	Kingsport
10-12	at Elizabethton
14-16	at Princeton
17-19	Elizabethton
20-22	at Greeneville
23-25	Pulaski
26-28	Danville
29-31	at Greeneville
AUGUST	
1-3	Burlington Royals
5-7	Johnson City
8	at Pulaski
9-11	at Danville
12-14	at Burlington Royals
15-17	at Kingsport
19-21	at Bluefield
22-24	Johnson City
25-27	Bluefield
28	Pulaski

BURLINGTON

JUNE	
22-24	Greeneville
25-27	at Pulaski
28-30	Bluefield
JULY	
1-3	at Bluefield
4-6	Elizabethton
7-9	at Danville
10-12	Princeton
14-16	at Greeneville
17-19	at Princeton
20-22	Princeton
23-25	at Elizabethton
26-28	Johnson City
29-31	Bluefield
AUGUST	
1-3	at Bristol
5-7	Pulaski
8	Danville
9-11	at Johnson City
12-14	Bristol
15-16	at Danville
17	Danville
19-21	Kingsport
22-24	at Pulaski
25-27	at Kingsport
28-29	Danville
Danville	

DANVILLE

JUNE	
22-24	at Princeton
25-27	at Bluefield
28-30	Elizabethton
JULY	
1-3	Princeton
4-6	at Johnson City
7-9	Burlington Royals
10-12	Pulaski
14-16	at Elizabethton
17-19	at Pulaski
20-22	Pulaski
23-25	Johnson City
26-28	at Bristol
29-31	at Princeton
AUGUST	
1-3	Bluefield
5-7	at Kingsport
8	at Burlington Royals
9-11	Bristol
12-14	at Bluefield
15-16	Burlington Royals
17	at Burlington Royals
19-21	Greeneville
22-24	Kingsport
25-27	at Greeneville
28-29	at Burlington Royals

ELIZABETHTON

JUNE	
22-24	at Bristol
25-27	Kingsport
28-30	at Danville
JULY	
1-2	Johnson City
3	at Johnson City
4-6	at Burlington Royals
7-9	at Princeton
10-12	Bristol
14-16	Danville
17-19	at Bristol
20	Johnson City
21-22	at Johnson City
23-25	Burlington Royals
26-28	Greeneville
29-31	at Johnson City
AUGUST	
1-3	at Kingsport
5-7	Bluefield
8	Johnson City
9-11	at Greeneville
12-14	Kingsport
15-17	Greeneville
19-21	at Pulaski
22-24	at Bluefield
25-27	Pulaski
28-30	Princeton

GREENEVILLE

JUNE	
22-24	at Burlington Royals
25-27	Johnson City
28-30	at Kingsport
JULY	
1-3	at Bristol
4-6	Kingsport
7-9	Pulaski
10-12	at Bluefield
14-16	Burlington Royals
17-19	Bluefield
20-22	Bristol
23-25	at Kingsport
26-28	at Elizabethton
29-31	Bristol
AUGUST	
1-3	Johnson City
5-7	at Princeton
8	at Kingsport
9-11	Elizabethton
12-14	at Johnson City
15-17	at Elizabethton
19-21	at Danville
22-24	Princeton
25-27	Danville
28	Kingsport

JOHNSON CITY

JUNE	
22-23	Kingsport
24	at Kingsport
25-27	at Greeneville
28-30	Bristol
JULY	
1-2	at Elizabethton
3	Elizabethton
4-6	Danville
7-9	at Bluefield
10-11	at Kingsport
12	Kingsport
14-16	at Pulaski
17-19	Kingsport
20	at Elizabethton
21-22	Elizabethton
23-25	at Danville
26-28	at Burlington Royals
29-31	Elizabethton
AUGUST	
1-3	at Greeneville
5-7	at Bristol
8	at Elizabethton
9-11	Burlington Royals
12-14	Greeneville
15-17	Pulaski
19-21	at Princeton
22-24	at Bristol
25-27	Princeton
28-30	Bluefield

KINGSPORT

JUNE	
22-23	at Johnson City
24	Johnson City
25-27	at Elizabethton
28-30	Greeneville
JULY	
1-3	Pulaski
4-6	at Greeneville
7-9	at Bristol
10-11	Johnson City
12	at Johnson City
14-16	at Bluefield
17-19	at Johnson City
20-22	Bluefield
23-25	Greeneville
26-28	at Princeton
29-31	at Pulaski
AUGUST	
1-3	Elizabethton
5-7	Danville
8	Greeneville
9-11	Princeton
12-14	at Elizabethton
15-17	Bristol
19-21	at Burlington Royals
22-24	at Danville
25-27	Burlington Royals
28	at Greeneville

PRINCETON

JUNE	
22-24	Danville
25-27	at Bristol
28-30	Pulaski

JULY	
1-3	at Danville
4-6	Bluefield
7-9	Elizabethton
10-12	at Burlington Royals
14-16	Bristol
17-19	Burlington Royals
20-22	at Burlington Royals
23-25	at Bluefield

26-28	Kingsport
29-31	Danville

AUGUST	
1-3	at Pulaski
5-7	Greeneville
8	Bluefield
9-11	at Kingsport
12-14	at Pulaski
15-17	Bluefield
19-21	Johnson City
22-24	at Greeneville
25-27	at Johnson City
28-30	at Elizabethton

PULASKI

JUNE	
22-24	Bluefield
25-27	Burlington Royals
28-30	at Princeton

JULY	
1-3	at Kingsport
4-6	Bristol
7-9	at Greeneville
10-12	at Danville
14-16	Johnson City
17-19	Danville
20-22	at Danville
23-25	at Bristol

26-28	at Bluefield
29-31	Kingsport

AUGUST	
1-3	Princeton
5-7	at Burlington Royals
8	Bristol
9-11	at Bluefield
12-14	Princeton
15-17	at Johnson City
19-21	Elizabethton
22-24	Burlington Royals
25-27	at Elizabethton
28	at Bristol

PIONEER LEAGUE

BILLINGS

JUNE	
21-24	Great Falls
25-27	at Missoula
28-30	at Helena

JULY	
1-2	Helena
3-6	at Great Falls
7-9	Missoula
10-12	Helena
14-16	at Idaho Falls
17-20	at Casper
21-24	Idaho Falls
25-27	Casper
29-30	at Missoula
31	at Helena

AUGUST	
1-2	at Helena
3-5	Helena
6-8	Missoula
9-10	at Helena
11-12	at Great Falls
13-14	Great Falls
16-19	at Ogden
20-22	at Orem
24-26	Ogden
27-30	Orem

SEPTEMBER	
1-3	at Missoula
4-5	at Great Falls
6-7	Missoula

CASPER

JUNE	
21-23	Ogden
24-25	at Idaho Falls
26-28	at Ogden
29-30	Idaho Falls

JULY	
1-2	Idaho Falls
3-5	Orem
6-7	at Idaho Falls
8-9	at Ogden
10-12	at Orem
14-16	Great Falls
17-20	Billings
21-24	at Great Falls
25-27	at Billings

29-30	Orem
31	Ogden

AUGUST	
1	Ogden
2-4	at Orem
5-7	Ogden
9-12	at Idaho Falls
13-15	Orem
16-19	at Helena
20-22	at Missoula
24-26	Helena
27-30	Missoula

SEPTEMBER	
1-2	at Orem
3-5	at Ogden

GREAT FALLS

JUNE	
21-24	at Billings
25-27	Helena
28-30	at Missoula

JULY	
1-2	Missoula
3-6	Billings
7-9	at Helena
10-12	Missoula
14-16	at Casper
17-20	at Idaho Falls
21-24	Casper
25-27	Idaho Falls
29-30	at Helena
31	at Missoula

AUGUST	
1-2	at Missoula
3-5	Missoula
6-8	Helena
9-10	at Missoula
11-12	Billings
13-14	at Billings
16-19	at Orem
20-22	at Ogden
24-26	Orem
27-30	Ogden

SEPTEMBER	
1-3	at Helena
4-5	Billings
6-7	Helena

HELENA

JUNE	
21-24	Missoula
25-27	at Great Falls
28-30	Billings

JULY	
1-2	at Billings
3-6	at Missoula
7-9	Great Falls
10-12	at Billings
14-16	Ogden
17-20	Orem
21-24	at Ogden
25-27	at Orem
29-30	Great Falls
31	Billings

AUGUST	
1-2	Billings
3-5	at Billings
6-8	at Great Falls
9-10	Billings
11-12	at Missoula
13-14	Missoula
16-19	Casper
20-22	Idaho Falls
24-26	at Casper
27-30	at Idaho Falls

SEPTEMBER	
1-3	Great Falls
4-5	at Missoula
6-7	at Great Falls

IDAHO FALLS

JUNE	
21-23	Orem
24-25	Casper
26-28	at Orem
29-30	at Casper

JULY	
1-2	at Casper
3-5	Ogden
6-7	Casper
8-9	at Orem
10-12	at Ogden
14-16	Orem
17-20	Great Falls
21-24	at Billings
25-27	at Great Falls

29-30	Ogden
31	Orem

AUGUST	
1	Orem
2-4	at Ogden
5-7	at Orem
9-12	Casper
13-15	Ogden
16-19	at Missoula
20-22	at Helena
24-26	Missoula
27-30	Helena

SEPTEMBER	
1-2	at Ogden
3-5	Orem

MISSOULA

JUNE	
21-24	at Helena
25-27	Billings
28-30	Great Falls

JULY	
1-2	at Great Falls
3-6	Helena
7-9	at Billings
10-12	at Great Falls
14-16	Orem
17-20	Ogden
21-24	at Orem
25-27	at Ogden
29-30	Billings
31	Great Falls

AUGUST	
1-2	Great Falls
3-5	at Great Falls
6-8	at Billings
9-10	Great Falls
11-12	Helena
13-14	at Helena
16-19	Idaho Falls
20-22	Casper
24-26	at Idaho Falls
27-30	at Casper

SEPTEMBER	
1-3	Billings
4-5	Helena
6-7	at Billings

OGDEN

JUNE	
21-23 . . . . at Casper	31 . . . . at Casper
24-25 . . . . Orem	**AUGUST**
26-28 . . . . Casper	1 . . . . at Casper
29-30 . . . . at Orem	2-4 . . . . .Idaho Falls
JULY	5-7 . . . . at Casper
1-2 . . . . at Orem	9-10 . . . . at Orem
3-5 . . . . . . at Idaho Falls	11-12 . . . . Orem
6-7 . . . . Orem	13-15 . . . . at Idaho Falls
8-9 . . . . Casper	16-19 . . . . Billings
10-12 . . . . . .Idaho Falls	20-22 . . . . . . Great Falls
14-16 . . . . . . at Helena	24-26 . . . . . . at Billings
17-20 . . . . . . at Missoula	27-30 . . . . at Great Falls
21-24 . . . . Helena	**SEPTEMBER**
25-27 . . . . Missoula	1-2 . . . . .Idaho Falls
29-30 . . . . . at Idaho Falls	3-5 . . . . Casper
	6-7 . . . . at Orem

OREM

JUNE	AUGUST
21-23 . . . . . at Idaho Falls	1 . . . . at Idaho Falls
24-25 . . . . at Ogden	2-4 . . . . Casper
26-28 . . . . . .Idaho Falls	5-7 . . . . .Idaho Falls
29-30 . . . . Ogden	9-10 . . . . Ogden
JULY	11-12 . . . . . . at Ogden
1-2 . . . . Ogden	13-15 . . . . . . at Casper
3-5 . . . . at Casper	16-19 . . . . . Great Falls
6-7 . . . . at Ogden	20-22 . . . . Billings
8-9 . . . . .Idaho Falls	24-26 . . . . at Great Falls
10-12 . . . . Casper	27-30 . . . . . . at Billings
14-16 . . . . . . at Missoula	**SEPTEMBER**
17-20 . . . . . . at Helena	1-2 . . . . Casper
21-24 . . . . Missoula	3-5 . . . . . . at Idaho Falls
25-27 . . . . Helena	6-7 . . . . Ogden
29-30 . . . . at Casper	
31 . . . . . . at Idaho Falls	

ARIZONA LEAGUE

ROYALS   HOME GAMES ONLY

JUNE	
21 . . . . Padres	26 . . . . Athletics
24 . . . . Mariners	29 . . . . Padres
26 . . . . Indians	30 . . . . Cubs
28 . . . . Cubs	**AUGUST**
JULY	4 . . . . Angels
1 . . . . Athletics	5 . . . . .Indians
3 . . . . Rangers	8 . . . . Giants
4 . . . . Padres	10 . . . . Dodgers
9 . . . . Reds	13 . . . . Reds
10 . . . . Mariners	15 . . . . Brewers
15 . . . . Giants	18 . . . . Mariners
16 . . . . Angels	19 . . . . Rangers
18 . . . . Brewers	22 . . . . Rangers
20 . . . . Dodgers	25 . . . . Padres
24 . . . . Mariners	27 . . . . Rangers

RANGERS

JUNE	
21 . . . . Mariners	11 . . . . Brewers
23 . . . . Royals	14 . . . . Cubs
25 . . . . Dodgers	15 . . . . Athletics
28 . . . . Reds	19 . . . . Giants
30 . . . . Padres	20 . . . . Padres
JULY	23 . . . . Royals
4 . . . . Angels	25 . . . . Dodgers
5 . . . . Mariners	29 . . . . Angels
8 . . . . .Indians	30 . . . . Brewers

AUGUST (continued top right)

AUGUST	
2 . . . . Royals	14 . . . . Giants
3 . . . . Mariners	17 . . . . Royals
7 . . . . Reds	18 . . . . Athletics
9 . . . . Cubs	23 . . . . Padres
13 . . . . Padres	24 . . . . Mariners
	28 . . . . .Indians

PADRES

JUNE	25 . . . . Royals
22 . . . . Mariners	30 . . . . Dodgers
24 . . . . Rangers	**AUGUST**
25 . . . . Royals	1 . . . . Giants
JULY	4 . . . . Mariners
1 . . . . .Indians	6 . . . . Reds
2 . . . . Athletics	8 . . . . Cubs
5 . . . . Cubs	11 . . . . Athletics
6 . . . . Angels	14 . . . . Royals
10 . . . . Rangers	16 . . . . Brewers
11 . . . . .Indians	20 . . . . Rangers
16 . . . . Brewers	21 . . . . Mariners
17 . . . . Dodgers	24 . . . . Royals
19 . . . . Angels	26 . . . . Mariners
22 . . . . Giants	28 . . . . Reds
24 . . . . Rangers	

MARINERS

JUNE	27 . . . . Athletics
25 . . . . Brewers	29 . . . . .Indians
26 . . . . Angels	**AUGUST**
29 . . . . Padres	1 . . . . Reds
30 . . . . Royals	5 . . . . Angels
JULY	6 . . . . .Indians
6 . . . . Dodgers	8 . . . . Rangers
7 . . . . Giants	10 . . . . Rangers
9 . . . . Rangers	14 . . . . Cubs
12 . . . . Athletics	16 . . . . Dodgers
14 . . . . Reds	19 . . . . Padres
15 . . . . Padres	20 . . . . Royals
20 . . . . Cubs	23 . . . . Giants
21 . . . . Royals	25 . . . . Rangers
25 . . . . Brewers	28 . . . . Royals
	29 . . . . Padres

DODGERS

JUNE	26 . . . . Mariners
21 . . . . Reds	28 . . . . Rangers
23 . . . . .Indians	**AUGUST**
26 . . . . Rangers	1 . . . . .Indians
27 . . . . Mariners	4 . . . . Cubs
30 . . . . Brewers	5 . . . . Padres
JULY	9 . . . . Brewers
3 . . . . Giants	11 . . . . Angels
7 . . . . Athletics	14 . . . . Athletics
8 . . . . Cubs	15 . . . . Reds
11 . . . . Angels	19 . . . . Giants
13 . . . . Royals	22 . . . . .Indians
16 . . . . Reds	26 . . . . Reds
18 . . . . .Indians	27 . . . . Brewers
21 . . . . Padres	29 . . . . Royals
23 . . . . Brewers	

BREWERS

JUNE	5 . . . . Giants
22 . . . . .Indians	8 . . . . Royals
26 . . . . Padres	10 . . . . Dodgers
27 . . . . .Indians	12 . . . . .Indians
JULY	15 . . . . Cubs
1 . . . . Mariners	17 . . . . Athletics
2 . . . . Reds	21 . . . . Rangers
	22 . . . . Mariners

26 . . . . Reds	11 . . . . Cubs
28 . . . . Royals	14 . . . . Angels
31 . . . . .Dodgers	17 . . . . .Indians
AUGUST	20 . . . . Reds
1 . . . . Angels	21 . . . . Dodgers
5 . . . . Athletics	24 . . . . Dodgers
6 . . . . Giants	25 . . . . Reds
10 . . . . Padres	29 . . . . Rangers

INDIANS

JUNE	23 . . . . Reds
21 . . . . Brewers	26 . . . . Padres
24 . . . . Reds	27 . . . . Dodgers
28 . . . . Dodgers	31 . . . . Mariners
29 . . . . Rangers	**AUGUST**
JULY	2 . . . . Dodgers
2 . . . . Cubs	3 . . . . Cubs
3 . . . . Brewers	7 . . . . Royals
6 . . . . Royals	8 . . . . Angels
9 . . . . Padres	12 . . . . Brewers
13 . . . . Giants	13 . . . . Giants
14 . . . . Angels	15 . . . . Rangers
16 . . . . Mariners	18 . . . . Reds
19 . . . . Reds	21 . . . . Athletics
21 . . . . Athletics	25 . . . . Dodgers
	26 . . . . Brewers

REDS

JUNE	22 . . . . Dodgers
22 . . . . Dodgers	27 . . . . Brewers
23 . . . . Brewers	29 . . . . Cubs
27 . . . . Padres	31 . . . . Padres
29 . . . . Royals	**AUGUST**
JULY	3 . . . . Royals
1 . . . . Dodgers	8 . . . . Athletics
4 . . . . Athletics	11 . . . . Mariners
6 . . . . Rangers	12 . . . . Dodgers
7 . . . . Indians	16 . . . . Indians
11 . . . . Mariners	17 . . . . Giants
13 . . . . Brewers	21 . . . . Angels
17 . . . . Giants	22 . . . . Brewers
18 . . . . Cubs	23 . . . . Indians
21 . . . . Angels	27 . . . . Indians

ATHLETICS

JUNE	25 . . . . Cubs
22 . . . . Giants	29 . . . . Giants
25 . . . . Angels	31 . . . . Rangers
26 . . . . Reds	**AUGUST**
29 . . . . Cubs	3 . . . . Padres
30 . . . . Giants	4 . . . . Brewers
JULY	9 . . . . Royals
5 . . . . Dodgers	10 . . . . Indians
6 . . . . Brewers	13 . . . . Angels
10 . . . . Angels	15 . . . . Mariners
11 . . . . Royals	19 . . . . Cubs
14 . . . . Padres	20 . . . . Dodgers
16 . . . . Rangers	25 . . . . Angels
19 . . . . Mariners	26 . . . . Giants
22 . . . . Indians	28 . . . . Cubs
24 . . . . Reds	

ANGELS

JUNE	27 . . . . Giants
21 . . . . Athletics	30 . . . . Athletics
24 . . . . Cubs	31 . . . . Royals
27 . . . . Giants	**AUGUST**
JULY	3 . . . . Giants
1 . . . . Rangers	6 . . . . Dodgers
2 . . . . Mariners	9 . . . . Mariners
5 . . . . Royals	10 . . . . Reds
7 . . . . Padres	15 . . . . Padres
9 . . . . Athletics	16 . . . . Cubs
12 . . . . Reds	19 . . . . Brewers
15 . . . . Dodgers	20 . . . . Indians
17 . . . . Indians	23 . . . . Athletics
20 . . . . Brewers	24 . . . . Cubs
22 . . . . Cubs	28 . . . . Giants
26 . . . . Rangers	

GIANTS

JUNE	28 . . . . Reds
23 . . . . Cubs	30 . . . . Mariners
24 . . . . Athletics	**AUGUST**
28 . . . . Brewers	2 . . . . Brewers
29 . . . . Angels	4 . . . . Rangers
JULY	7 . . . . Dodgers
2 . . . . Dodgers	9 . . . . Padres
3 . . . . Mariners	11 . . . . Indians
8 . . . . Reds	12 . . . . Royals
9 . . . . Cubs	16 . . . . Athletics
12 . . . . Padres	18 . . . . Angels
14 . . . . Royals	21 . . . . Cubs
18 . . . . Rangers	24 . . . . Athletics
20 . . . . Athletics	27 . . . . Cubs
24 . . . . Indians	29 . . . . Angels
25 . . . . Angels	

CUBS

JUNE	27 . . . . Padres
22 . . . . Angels	28 . . . . Indians
25 . . . . Giants	**AUGUST**
27 . . . . Athletics	1 . . . . Athletics
30 . . . . Angels	2 . . . . Reds
JULY	6 . . . . Athletics
3 . . . . Reds	7 . . . . Brewers
4 . . . . Indians	12 . . . . Rangers
7 . . . . Brewers	13 . . . . Mariners
10 . . . . Giants	17 . . . . Dodgers
12 . . . . Dodgers	18 . . . . Padres
13 . . . . Rangers	22 . . . . Giants
17 . . . . Mariners	23 . . . . Royals
19 . . . . Royals	26 . . . . Angels
23 . . . . Giants	29 . . . . Athletics
24 . . . . Angels	

GULF COAST LEAGUE

ASTROS

JUNE		
22	. . . . .Marlins	28 . . . . Nationals
24	. . . . .Cardinals	30 . . . . Mets
28	. . . . Nationals	**AUGUST**
30	. . . . Mets	1 . . . . .Marlins
JULY		3 . . . . .Cardinals
2	. . . . .Marlins	7 . . . . Nationals
4	. . . . .Cardinals	9 . . . . Mets
8	. . . . Nationals	11 . . . . .Marlins
10	. . . . Mets	13 . . . . .Cardinals
12	. . . . .Marlins	17 . . . . Nationals
14	. . . . .Cardinals	19 . . . . Mets
18	. . . . Nationals	21 . . . . .Marlins
20	. . . . Mets	23 . . . . .Cardinals
22	. . . . .Marlins	27 . . . . Nationals
24	. . . . .Cardinals	29 . . . . Mets

BLUE JAYS

JUNE		
22	. . . . Phillies	26 . . . . Phillies
24	. . . . Braves	28 . . . . Braves
26	. . . . .Tigers	30 . . . . .Tigers
29	. . . . Yankees	**AUGUST**
JULY		2 . . . . Yankees
1	. . . . Pirates	5 . . . . Pirates
2	. . . . Phillies	7 . . . . Phillies
5	. . . . Braves	10 . . . . Braves
7	. . . . .Tigers	12 . . . . .Tigers
9	. . . . Yankees	14 . . . . Yankees
12	. . . . Pirates	17 . . . . Priates
14	. . . . Phillies	18 . . . . Phillies
17	. . . . Braves	20 . . . . Braves
20	. . . . .Tigers	23 . . . . .Tigers
22	. . . . Yankees	25 . . . . Yankees
23	. . . . Pirates	27 . . . . Pirates

BRAVES

JUNE		
21	. . . . .Tigers	27 . . . . .Tigers
23	. . . . .Blue Jays	29 . . . . .Blue Jays
25	. . . . Pirates	31 . . . . Pirates
28	. . . . Phillies	**AUGUST**
30	. . . . Yankees	3 . . . . Phillies
JULY		5 . . . . Yankees
3	. . . . .Tigers	6 . . . . .Tigers
6	. . . . .Blue Jays	9 . . . . .Blue Jays
8	. . . . Pirates	11 . . . . Pirates
10	. . . . Phillies	13 . . . . Phillies
13	. . . . Yankees	16 . . . . Yankees
14	. . . . .Tigers	19 . . . . .Tigers
16	. . . . .Blue Jays	21 . . . . .Blue Jays
19	. . . . Pirates	24 . . . . Pirates
21	. . . . Phillies	26 . . . . Phillies
23	. . . . Yankees	28 . . . . Yankees

CARDINALS

JUNE		
23	. . . . Mets	15 . . . . .Marlins
25	. . . . .Marlins	16 . . . . Nationals
29	. . . . .Astros	19 . . . . .Astros
JULY		23 . . . . Mets
3	. . . . Mets	25 . . . . .Marlins
5	. . . . .Marlins	26 . . . . Nationals
6	. . . . Nationals	29 . . . . .Astros
9	. . . . .Astros	**AUGUST**
13	. . . . Mets	2 . . . . Mets
		4 . . . . .Marlins

MARLINS

5 . . . . Nationals
8 . . . . .Astros
12 . . . . Mets
14 . . . . .Marlins
15 . . . . Nationals

18 . . . . .Astros
22 . . . . Mets
24 . . . . .Marlins
25 . . . . Nationals
28 . . . . .Astros

JUNE		
21	. . . . Mets	27 . . . . .Astros
24	. . . . Nationals	30 . . . . .Cardinals
30	. . . . .Cardinals	31 . . . . Mets
JULY		**AUGUST**
1	. . . . Mets	3 . . . . Nationals
4	. . . . Nationals	6 . . . . .Astros
7	. . . . .Astros	9 . . . . .Cardinals
10	. . . . .Cardinals	10 . . . . Mets
11	. . . . Mets	13 . . . . Nationals
14	. . . . Nationals	16 . . . . .Astros
17	. . . . .Astros	19 . . . . .Cardinals
20	. . . . .Cardinals	20 . . . . Mets
21	. . . . Mets	23 . . . . Nationals
24	. . . . Nationals	26 . . . . .Astros
		29 . . . . .Cardinals

METS

JUNE		
22	. . . . Nationals	26 . . . . .Marlins
25	. . . . .Astros	28 . . . . .Cardinals
26	. . . . .Marlins	**AUGUST**
28	. . . . .Cardinals	1 . . . . Nationals
JULY		4 . . . . .Astros
2	. . . . Nationals	5 . . . . .Marlins
5	. . . . .Astros	7 . . . . .Cardinals
6	. . . . .Marlins	11 . . . . Nationals
8	. . . . .Cardinals	14 . . . . .Astros
12	. . . . Nationals	15 . . . . .Marlins
15	. . . . .Astros	17 . . . . .Cardinals
16	. . . . .Marlins	21 . . . . Nationals
18	. . . . .Cardinals	24 . . . . .Astros
22	. . . . Nationals	25 . . . . .Marlins
25	. . . . .Astros	27 . . . . .Cardinals

NATIONALS

JUNE		
21	. . . . .Cardinals	23 . . . . .Astros
23	. . . . .Astros	27 . . . . Mets
27	. . . . Mets	31 . . . . .Cardinals
29	. . . . .Marlins	**AUGUST**
JULY		2 . . . . .Astros
1	. . . . .Cardinals	6 . . . . Mets
3	. . . . .Astros	8 . . . . .Marlins
7	. . . . Mets	10 . . . . .Cardinals
9	. . . . .Marlins	12 . . . . .Astros
11	. . . . .Cardinals	16 . . . . Mets
13	. . . . .Astros	18 . . . . .Marlins
17	. . . . Mets	20 . . . . .Cardinals
19	. . . . .Marlins	22 . . . . .Astros
21	. . . . .Cardinals	26 . . . . Mets
		28 . . . . .Marlins

ORIOLES

JUNE		
21	. . . . Twins	10 . . . . .Rays
23	. . . . Red Sox	12 . . . . Red Sox
26	. . . . .Rays	13 . . . . .Rays
29	. . . . Twins	15 . . . . Twins
JULY		19 . . . . Twins
1	. . . . Red Sox	21 . . . . Red Sox
2	. . . . .Rays	24 . . . . .Rays
6	. . . . Red Sox	27 . . . . Twins
7	. . . . Twins	29 . . . . .Rays
		30 . . . . .Rays

AUGUST

2	Red Sox
4	Twins
7	Rays
10	Red Sox
12	Twins
13	Rays
16	Twins
18	Red Sox
21	Rays
23	Red Sox
25	Twins
27	Rays

PHILLIES

JUNE

21	Blue Jays
23	Pirates
25	Yankees
29	Braves
30	Tigers

JULY

3	Blue Jays
6	Pirates
8	Yankees
9	Braves
13	Tigers
15	Blue Jays
16	Pirates
19	Yankees
22	Braves
23	Tigers
27	Blue Jays
29	Pirates
31	Yankees

AUGUST

2	Braves
5	Tigers
6	Blue Jays
9	Pirates
11	Yankees
14	Braves
16	Twins
19	Blue Jays
21	Pirates
24	Yankees
25	Braves
27	Tigers

PIRATES

JUNE

22	Yankees
26	Braves
29	Tigers
30	Blue Jays

JULY

5	Phillies
7	Braves
9	Tigers
13	Blue Jays
15	Yankees
17	Phillies
20	Braves
22	Tigers
24	Blue Jays
26	Yankees
28	Phillies
30	Braves

AUGUST

2	Tigers
4	Blue Jays
7	Yankees
10	Phillies
12	Braves
14	Tigers
16	Blue Jays
18	Yankees
20	Phillies
23	Braves
25	Tigers
28	Blue Jays

RED SOX

JUNE

21	Rays
24	Orioles
25	Twins
29	Rays
30	Orioles

JULY

3	Twins
5	Orioles
7	Rays
9	Twins
14	Rays
16	Orioles
17	Twins
19	Rays
22	Orioles
23	Twins
26	Rays
28	Twins
31	Twins

AUGUST

3	Orioles
4	Rays
6	Twins
9	Orioles
12	Rays
14	Twins
16	Rays
19	Orioles
20	Twins
24	Orioles
26	Rays
28	Twins

TIGERS

JUNE

22	Braves
24	Yankees
25	Blue Jays
28	Pirates

JULY

1	Phillies
2	Braves
5	Yankees
8	Blue Jays
10	Pirates
12	Phillies
15	Braves
17	Yankees
19	Blue Jays
21	Pirates
24	Phillies
25	Braves
28	Yankees
31	Blue Jays

AUGUST

3	Pirates
4	Phillies
7	Braves
10	Yankees
11	Blue Jays
13	Pirates
17	Phillies
18	Braves
20	Yankees
24	Blue Jays
26	Pirates
28	Phillies

TWINS

JUNE

22	Orioles
23	Rays
26	Red Sox
28	Orioles

JULY

1	Rays
2	Red Sox
6	Rays
8	Orioles
10	Red Sox
12	Rays
13	Red Sox
14	Orioles
20	Orioles
21	Rays
24	Red Sox
26	Orioles
29	Red Sox
30	Red Sox

AUGUST

2	Rays
5	Orioles
7	Red Sox
10	Rays
11	Red Sox
13	Orioles
17	Orioles
18	Rays
21	Red Sox
23	Rays
26	Orioles
27	Red Sox

RAYS

JUNE

22	Red Sox
24	Twins
25	Orioles
28	Red Sox
30	Twins

JULY

3	Orioles
5	Twins
8	Red Sox
9	Orioles
15	Red Sox
16	Twins
17	Orioles
20	Red Sox
22	Twins
23	Orioles
26	Red Sox
28	Orioles
31	Orioles

AUGUST

3	Twins
5	Red Sox
6	Orioles
9	Twins
11	Red Sox
14	Orioles
17	Red Sox
19	Twins
20	Orioles
24	Twins
25	Red Sox
28	Orioles

YANKEES

JUNE

21	Pirates
23	Tigers
26	Phillies
28	Blue Jays

JULY

1	Braves
3	Pirates
6	Tigers
7	Phillies
10	Blue Jays
12	Braves
14	Pirates
20	Phillies
21	Blue Jays
24	Braves
27	Pirates
9	Tigers
30	Phillies

AUGUST

3	Blue Jays
4	Braves
6	Pirates
9	Tigers
12	Phillies
13	Blue Jays
17	Braves
19	Pirates
21	Tigers
23	Phillies
26	Blue Jays
27	Braves

INDEPENDENT

AMERICAN ASSOCIATION HOME GAMES ONLY

EL PASO

MAY	
13-16	Sioux City
18-20	Fort Worth

JUNE	
1-3	Shreveport
4-6	Grand Prairie
15-17	Pensacola
18-20	Lincoln

JULY	
1-4	Shreveport

16-18	St. Paul
19-21	Grand Prairie
23-25	Pensacola

AUGUST	
2-5	Fort Worth
10-12	Grand Prairie
13-15	Pensacola
20-22	Wichita
24-26	Shreveport

FORT WORTH

MAY	
13-16	Shreveport
21-23	Lincoln
30-31	Grand Prairie

JUNE	
8-10	Grand Prairie
11-14	El Paso
18-20	Pensacola
28-30	El Paso

JULY	
4	Grand Prairie

6-8	El Paso
13-15	Pensacola
16-18	Shreveport
29-31	Shreveport

AUGUST	
1	Shreveport
6-8	Grand Prairie
10-12	Pensacola
20-22	Grand Prairie
23-25	Wichita

GRAND PRAIRIE

MAY	
14-16	Pensacola
17-19	Sioux City
25-27	Shreveport
28-29	Fort Worth

JUNE	
2-3	Fort Worth
11-13	Pensacola
14-17	Lincoln
21-23	El Paso

JULY	
1-3	Fort Worth
13-15	St. Paul
16-18	Pensacola
29-31	El Paso

AUGUST	
1	El Paso
2-4	Pensacola
13-15	Fort Worth
17-19	El Paso
27-29	Shreveport

LINCOLN

MAY	
25-27	Wichita
28-30	El Paso

JUNE	
8-10	St. Paul
11-13	Shreveport
22-24	Sioux Falls
25-27	Sioux City

JULY	
1-4	Pensacola

9-12	Sioux Falls
20-22	Wichita
23-25	Sioux Falls
28-31	Sioux City

AUGUST	
5-7	St. Paul
9-11	Wichita
16-18	Shreveport
27-29	Lincoln

PENSACOLA

MAY	
21-24	Grand Prairie
25-27	Fort Worth

JUNE	
1-3	St. Paul
4-6	Fort Worth
8-10	El Paso

21-23	Shreveport
24-26	Grand Prairie

JULY	
6-8	Shreveport
9-12	El Paso
19-21	Shreveport
29-31	Wichita

AUGUST
AUGUST	
1	Wichita
6-8	Sioux Falls

SHREVEPORT-BOSSIER

MAY	
18-18-20	Pensacola
21-23	El Paso
28-30	Pensacola

JUNE	
4-6	St. Paul
15-17	Fort Worth
18-20	Grand Prairie
24-26	El Paso
27-29	Grand Prairie

JULY	
9-12	Fort Worth
13-15	El Paso
22-25	Grand Prairie

AUGUST	
2-4	Wichita
6-8	El Paso
9	Pensacola
10-11	Sioux Falls
20-22	Pensacola

ST. PAUL

MAY	
13-15	Wichita
17-19	Lincoln
28-30	Sioux Falls

JUNE	
11-13	Sioux Falls
14-16	Sioux City
25-27	Wichita
28-30	Pensacola

JULY	
4	Wichita
6-8	Wichita
9-11	Sioux City
20-22	Fort Worth
28-31	St. Paul

AUGUST	
9-12	Sioux City
13-15	Lincoln
20-22	Lincoln
23-25	Sioux City

SIOUX CITY

MAY	
21-23	Sioux Falls
25-27	St. Paul

JUNE	
1-3	Lincoln
8-10	Shreveport
11-13	Wichita
21-24	St. Paul

JULY	
1	Sioux Falls

3-4	Sioux Falls
6-8	Lincoln
13-15	Sioux Falls
16-19	Lincoln
20	Sioux Falls
23-25	Fort Worth

AUGUST	
2-4	St. Paul
6-8	Wichita
13-15	Shreveport
20-22	Sioux Falls

SIOUX FALLS

MAY	
13-16	Lincoln
25-27	El Paso

JUNE	
1-3	Wichita
4-6	Sioux City
14-16	Wichita
18-20	St. Paul
25-27	Fort Worth
28-30	Lincoln

JULY	
2	Sioux City
6-8	Grand Prairie
16-19	Wichita
21-22	Sioux City

AUGUST	
1-3	Lincoln
17-19	St. Paul
23-25	Lincoln
26-29	St. Paul

WICHITA

MAY	
18-20	Sioux Falls
21-24	St. Paul
28-30	Sioux City

JUNE	
4-6	Lincoln
7-10	Sioux Falls
18-20	Sioux City
22-24	Fort Worth
28-30	Sioux City

JULY
1-3 . . . . St. Paul
9-12 . . . . . . Grand Prairie
13-15 . . . . Lincoln
23-25 . . . . St. Paul

AUGUST
14-16 . . . . . . Sioux Falls
17-19 . . . . . . Sioux City
27-29 . . . . El Paso

ATLANTIC LEAGUE
HOME GAMES ONLY

LABEL

APRIL
22-25 . . . . Somerset
28-29 . Southern Maryland

MAY
7-9 . . . . Long Island
11-13 . . . . .Newark
21-23 . . . . .York
28-30 . . . . Camden
31 . . . . Lancaster

JUNE
1 . . . . Lancaster
11-13 . . . . . . Somerset
14-17 . Southern Maryland
25-27 . . . . . Long Island
28-30 . . . . .Newark

JULY
8-11 . . . . .York
19-21 . . . . . Lancaster
22-25 . . . . Camden

AUGUST
3-5 . . . . .York
6-8 . . . . Camden
9-10 . . . . Lancaster
17-19 . Southern Maryland
23-26 . . . . .Newark
27-29 . . . . . Long Island

SEPTEMBER
8-9 . . . . Lancaster
10-12 . . . . Somerset

CAMDEN

APRIL
30 . . . . .Newark

MAY
1-2 . . . . .Newark
7-10 . . . . Lancaster
11-13 . . . . . . Somerset
21-23 . Southern Maryland
24-25 . . . . .York
31 . . . . Long Island

JUNE
1-3 . . . . Long Island
4-6 . . . . Bridgeport
14-17 . . . . .York
18-21 . . . . . Bridgeport
25-27 . . . . . . Lancaster

JULY
8-11 . . Southern Maryland
13-15 . . . . . . Somerset
19-21 . . Southern Maryland
30-31 . . . . . . .Newark

AUGUST
1 . . . . .Newark
3-5 . . . . Long Island
13-15 . . . . . Bridgeport
23-26 . . . . . . Somerset
27-29 . . . . . Lancaster

SEPTEMBER
7-9 . . . . Long Island
13-15 . . . . .York
16-19 . . . . .Newark

LANCASTER

APRIL
30 . . . . .York

MAY
1-2 . . . . .York
4-6 . . . . Bridgeport
14-16 . . . . Camden
17-19 . Southern Maryland
25-27 . . . . . . .Newark

JUNE
2-3 . . . . Bridgeport
4-6 . . . . Long Island
8-10 . . . . Somerset
18-20 . . . . .York
22-24 . . . . . Bridgeport
28-30 . . Southern Maryland

JULY
8-11 . . . . . . Somerset
16-18 . . . . . . Camden
26-29 . . . . . . .Newark
30-31 . . . . . Long Island

AUGUST
1 . . . . Long Island
11-12 . . . . . Bridgeport
13-15 . . . . .York
20-22 . . . . . Somerset
30-31 . . Southern Maryland

SEPTEMBER
1 . . . . Southern Maryland
2-5 . . . . Camden
13-15 . . . . .Newark
16-19 . . . . . Long Island

LONG ISLAND

APRIL
22-25 . . . . . . Lancaster
27-29 . . . . . . Somerset

MAY
11-13 . . . . .York
14-16 . . . . . Bridgeport
25-26-27 . . . . . Somerset
28-29-30 Southern Maryland

JUNE
8-10 . . . . Camden
11-13 . . . . . . Lancaster
18-20 . Southern Maryland
22-24 . . . . . . Camden

JULY
1-4 . . . . .Newark
13-15 . . . . .York
16-18 . . . . . Bridgeport
19-21 . . . . . . .Newark
26-29 . . . . . . Somerset

AUGUST
6-8 . . . . Lancaster
9-12 . . . . Camden
20-22 . . . . . . .Newark
23-26 . . . . .York

SEPTEMBER
3-6 . . . . Bridgeport
10-12 . . Southern Maryland

NEWARK

APRIL
22-25 . . . . Camden
27-29 . . . . . . Lancaster

MAY
4-6 . . . . Long Island
7-9 . . . . .York
18-20 . . . . . Bridgeport
21-23 . . . . . Long Island
28-30 . . . . . . Somerset
31 . . . . Southern Maryland

JUNE
1-3 . . . Southern Maryland
11-13 . . . . Camden
14-17 . . . . . Lancaster
25-27 . . . . .York

JULY
8-11 . . . . . Long Island
13-15 . . . . . Bridgeport
22-25 . . . . . . Somerset

AUGUST
3-5 . . . Southern Maryland
6-8 . . . . Somerset
17-19 . . . . . Lancaster
27-29 . . . . .York
31 . . . . Bridgeport

SEPTEMBER
1 . . . . Bridgeport
7-9 . . . Southern Maryland
10-12 . . . . . . Camden

SOMERSET

APRIL
30 . . . . Bridgeport

MAY
1-2 . . . . . . Bridgeport
7-10 . . Southern Maryland
18-20 . . . . . . Camden
21-23 . . . . . Lancaster
31 . . . . .York

JUNE
1 . . . . .York
4-7 . . . . .Newark
14-17 . . . . . Long Island
18-20 . . . . . . .Newark
28-30 . . . . . . Camden

JULY
1-4 . . . . Lancaster

16-18 . . Southern Maryland
19-21 . . . . .York
30-31 . . . . . . Bridgeport

AUGUST
1-2 . . . . Bridgeport
3-5 . . . . Lancaster
11-12 . . . . .York
13-15 . . . . .Newark
17-19 . . . . . Long Island
27-29 . . Southern Maryland
30-31 . . . . . . Camden

SEPTEMBER
1 . . . . Camden
6-8 . . . . .York
13-15 . . . . . Long Island
17-19 . . . . . Bridgeport

SOUTHERN MARYLAND

APRIL
30 . . . . Long Island

MAY
1-2 . . . . . . Long Island
4-6 . . . . Camden
11-13 . . . . . Lancaster
14-16 . . . . . Somerset
25-27 . . . . . Bridgeport

JUNE
4-6 . . . . .York
8-10 . . . . . . .Newark
22-24 . . . . . . .Newark
25-27 . . . . . . Somerset

JULY
1-4 . . . . Camden

13-15 . . . . . Lancaster
22-25 . . . . . Long Island
26-29 . . . . . Bridgeport
30-31 . . . . .York

AUGUST
1 . . . . .York
9-12 . . . . . . .Newark
13-15 . . . . . Long Island
20-22 . . . . . . Camden
23-26 . . . . . Lancaster

SEPTEMBER
2-5 . . . . Somerset
13-15 . . . . . Bridgeport
16-19 . . . . .York

YORK

APRIL		JULY	
22-25	. . Southern Maryland	1-4	. . . . Bridgeport
27-29	. . . . Camden	16-18	. . . . .Newark
MAY		22-25	. . . . Lancaster
4-6	. . . . Somerset	26-29	. . . . Camden
14-16	. . . . .Newark	**AUGUST**	
17-20	. . . . . . Long Island	6-8	. . Southern Maryland
28-30	. . . . Lancaster	9-10	. . . . Somerset
JUNE		17-19	. . . . Camden
2-3	. . . . Somerset	20-22	. . . . . . Bridgeport
8-10	. . . . Bridgeport	30-31	. . . . . . Long Island
11-13	. . Southern Maryland	**SEPTEMBER**	
22-24	. . . . Somerset	1	. . . . Long Island
28-30	. . . . . . Long Island	2-5	. . . . .Newark
		10-12	. . . . Lancaster

CAN-AM LEAGUE HOME GAMES ONLY

BROCKTON

MAY		19-21	. . . . Pittsfield
28-30	. . . . Worcester	30-31	. . . . Sussex
JUNE		**AUGUST**	
10	. . . . Worcester	1-2	. . . . Sussex
15-17	. . . . Pittsfield	9-11	. . . . Quebec
18-20	. . . . Worcester	12-15	. . . . . . Worcester
24-27	. . . . . . New Jersey	20-22	. . . . Sussex
29-30	. . . . Quebec	26-29	. . . . Quebec
JULY		30-31	. . . . Pittsfield
1-2	. . . . Quebec	**SEPTEMBER**	
5-7	. . . . Sussex	1	. . . . Pittsfield
11-13	. . . . Pittsfield		

NEW JERSEY

JUNE		29-31	. . . . Pittsfield
3-6	. . . . .Brockton	**AUGUST**	
8-10	. . . . Pittsfield	1	. . . . Pittsfield
18-20	. . . . Quebec	9-11	. . . . Quebec
21-23	. . . . Worcester	12-15	. . . . . . Worcester
29-30	. . . . Sussex	20-22	. . . . Sussex
JULY		26-29	. . . . Quebec
1-2	. . . . Sussex	30-31	. . . . Pittsfield
12-14	. . . . Sussex	**SEPTEMBER**	
15-17	. . . . . . .Brockton	1	. . . . Pittsfield
26-28	. . . . . . .Brockton		

PITTSFIELD

MAY		15-17	. . . . Quebec
31	. . . . New Jersey	22-25	. . . . Worcester
JUNE		26-28	. . . . Quebec
1-2	. . . . New Jersey	**AUGUST**	
3-6	. . . . Quebec	3-5	. . . . Worcester
11-13	. . . . Worcester	9-11	. . . . Sussex
18-20	. . . . Sussex	12-15	. . . . . . .Brockton
21-23	. . . . .Brockton	23-25	. . . . . . New Jersey
JULY		**SEPTEMBER**	
3-6	. . . . New Jersey	3-6	. . . . Sussex

QUEBEC

MAY		8-10	. . . . New Jersey
27-30	. . . . Pittsfield	19-21	. . . . Sussex
31	. . . . Worcester	22-25	. . . . .Brockton
JUNE		**AUGUST**	
1-2	. . . . Worcester	3-5	. . . . .Brockton
11-13	. . . . .Brockton	6-8	. . . . Sussex
15-17	. . . . Sussex	17-19	. . . . Pittsfield
24-27	. . . . Pittsfield	23-25	. . . . Worcester
JULY		**SEPTEMBER**	
3-6	. . . . Worcester	3-6	. . . . . New Jersey

SUSSEX

MAY		8-10	. . . . Pittsfield
27-30	. . . . . . New Jersey	15-17	. . . . Worcester
31	. . . . .Brockton	22-25	. . . New Jersey
JUNE		26-28	. . . . Worcester
1-2	. . . . .Brockton	**AUGUST**	
7-8	. . . . .Brockton	3-5	. . . . New Jersey
11-13	. . . . . New Jersey	12-15	. . . . Quebec
21-23	. . . . . Quebec	16-18	. . . . Worcester
JULY		23-25	. . . . .Brockton
3-4	. . . . .Brockton	26-29	. . . . Pittsfield

WORCESTER

JUNE		29-31	. . . . Quebec
3-6	. . . . Sussex	**AUGUST**	
7-9	. . . . Quebec	1	. . . . Quebec
15-17	. . . . . New Jersey	6-8	. . . . . New Jersey
24-27	. . . . . . Sussex	9-11	. . . . .Brockton
29-30	. . . . Pittsfield	20-22	. . . . Pittsfield
JULY		26-29	. . . . . . .Brockton
1-2	. . . . Pittsfield	31	. . . . Sussex
8-10	. . . . .Brockton	**SEPTEMBER**	
12-14	. . . . . . Quebec	1-2	. . . . Sussex
19-21	. . . . . New Jersey		

FRONTIER LEAGUE HOME GAMES ONLY

EVANSVILLE

MAY		9-11	. . . . .Lake Erie
21-23	. . . . .Normal	16-18	. . . . Florence
24-26	. . . . Gateway	19-21	. . . . River City
JUNE		25-27	. . . . Southern Illinois
8-10	. . . . . . Traverse City	**AUGUST**	
11-13	. . . . Oakland County	6-8	. . . . Southern Illinois
20-22	. . . . Gateway	13-15	. . . . . Kalamazoo
23-25	. . . . Florence	17-19	. . . . . Windy City
JULY		24-26	. . . . . . River City
6-8	. . . . .Washington	27-29	. . . . .Normal

FLORENCE

MAY		JULY	
26-28	. . . . Southern Illinois	6-8	. . . . .Lake Erie
28-30	. . . . Evansville	9-11	. . . . . . .Washington
JUNE		22-24	. . . . . . Evansville
2-2-3	. . . . Oakland County	28-30	. . . . . . .Normal
8-10	. . . . Oakland County	31	. . . . Gateway
11-13	. . . . . Traverse City	**AUGUST**	
17-19	. . . . . River City	1-2	. . . . Gateway
20-22	. . . . .Normal	10-12	. . . . . Kalamazoo
26-28	. . . . Southern Illinois	13-15	. . . . . Windy City
		24-26	. . . . Gateway
		27-29	. . . . . . River City

GATEWAY

MAY	
21-23	Florence
29-29	River City

JUNE	
1-3	Washington
4-6	Lake Erie
14-16	Evansville
17-19	Southern Illinois
23-25	River City

JULY	
2-4	Windy City
6-8	Kalamazoo

19-21	Normal
28-30	Evansville

AUGUST	
4-5	River City
6-8	Normal
17-19	Traverse City
20-21	Oakland County
31	Florence

SEPTEMBER	
1-2	Florence
3-5	Southern Illinois

KALAMAZOO

MAY	
25-27	Washington
28-30	Lake Erie

JUNE	
8-10	Southern Illinois
11-13	Normal
20-22	Oakland County
23-25	Washington
29-30	Gateway

JULY	
1	Gateway
2-4	River City
19-21	Oakland County
25-27	Traverse City
28-30	Windy City

AUGUST	
6-8	Windy City
17-19	Florence
20-22	Evansville
27-29	Lake Erie

LAKE ERIE

MAY	
21-23	Traverse City
25-27	Oakland County

JUNE	
1-3	River City
11-13	Gateway
14-16	Washington
20-22	Windy City
26-28	Oakland County
29-30	Florence

JULY	
1	Florence
2-4	Evansville

16-18	Windy City
19-21	Traverse City
31	Kalamazoo

AUGUST	
1-2	Kalamazoo
6-8	Oakland County
17-19	Normal
20-22	Southern Illinois
31	Washington

SEPTEMBER	
1-2	Washington
3-5	Kalamazoo

NORMAL

JUNE	
1-3	Windy City
4-6	Kalamazoo
14-16	Florence
17-19	Evansville
26-28	Gateway
29-30	Oakland County

JULY	
1	Oakland County
9-11	Traverse City
16-18	Southern Illinois

22-24	River City
25-27	Gateway
31	River City

AUGUST	
1-2	River City
3-5	Evansville
10-12	Lake Erie
20-22	Washington
24-26	Southern Illinois

SEPTEMBER	
3-5	Florence

OAKLAND COUNTY

JUNE	
4-6	Evansville
14-16	Kalamazoo

JULY	
6-8	Normal
9-11	Southern Illinois
16-18	Washington
22-24	Lake Erie

31	Washington

AUGUST	
1-2	Washington
10-12	Gateway
13-15	River City
24-26	Windy City
27-29	Traverse City
31	Kalamazoo

SEPTEMBER	
1-2	Kalamazoo

RIVER CITY

MAY	
25-27	Normal
28-30	Gateway

JUNE	
8-10	Lake Erie
11-13	Washington
20-22	Southern Illinois
26-28	Evansville

JULY	
6-8	Windy City
9-11	Kalamazoo

16-18	Gateway
25-27	Florence
28-30	Southern Illinois

AUGUST	
6-8	Florence
17-19	Traverse City
20-22	Oakland County
31	Normal

SEPTEMBER	
1-2	Normal
3-5	Evansville

SOUTHERN ILLINOIS

MAY	
20-23	River City
28-30	Normal

JUNE	
1-3	Kalamazoo
11-13	Windy City
15-16	River City
23-25	Normal
29-30	Traverse City

JULY	
1	Traverse City
2-4	Oakland County

19-21	Florence
22-24	Gateway
31	Evansville

AUGUST	
1-2	Evansville
3-5	Florence
10-12	Washington
13-15	Lake Erie
27-29	Gateway
30-31	Evansville

SEPTEMBER	
1	Evansville

TRAVERSE CITY

MAY	
28-30	Oakland County

JUNE	
1-3	Evansville
4-6	Florence
14-16	Windy City
17-19	Lake Erie
23-25	Lake Erie
26-28	Kalamazoo

JULY	
2-4	Normal
6-8	Southern Illinois

16-18	Kalamazoo
22-24	Washington
28-30	Oakland County

AUGUST	
3-5	Oakland County
10-12	Gateway
13-15	River City
24-26	Kalamazoo
31	Windy City

SEPTEMBER	
1-2	Windy City
3-5	Washington

WASHINGTON

MAY	
21-23	Oakland County
28-30	Windy City

JUNE	
4-6	River City
8-10	Gateway
17-19	Kalamazoo
20-22	Traverse City
29-30	Evansville

JULY	
1	Evansville

2-4	Florence
19-21	Windy City
25-27	Oakland County
28-30	Lake Erie

AUGUST	
3-5	Kalamazoo
6-8	Traverse City
13-15	Normal
17-19	Southern Illinois
24-26	Lake Erie

SEPTEMBER	
1-2	Kalamazoo

3-5	Windy City

WINDY CITY

MAY		
20-22	. . . . . .	Kalamazoo
25-27	. . . . . .	Traverse City

JUNE		
4-6	. . . . .	Southern Illinois
8-10	. . . .	Normal
17-19	. . .	Oakland County
23-25	. . . .	Oakland County
26-28	. . . . . .	Washington
29-30	. . . . . .	River City

JULY		
1	. . . .	River City

9-11	. . . .	Gateway
22-24	. . . . . .	Kalamazoo
25-27	. . . .	Lake Erie
31	. . . .	Traverse City

AUGUST		
1-2	. . . .	Traverse City
3-5	. . . .	Lake Erie
10-12	. . . . . .	Evansville
20-22	. . . .	Florence
27-29	. . . . . .	Washington

GOLDEN LEAGUE   HOME GAMES ONLY

CALGARY

MAY		
Maui.	. . . .	27-30

JUNE		
Orange County	. . . . . .	1-5
Victoria	. . . .	12-15
Victoria	. . . .	25-26
Edmonton	. . . .	29-30

JULY		
Edmonton	. . . .	3-4

Tijuana	. . . .	15-18
Yuma	. . . .	19-21
Edmonton	. . . . . .	23-26
Chico	. . . .	30-31

AUGUST		
Chico	. . . .	1
Tucson	. . . .	9-13
St. George	. . . . . .	14-17
Victoria	. . . . . .	26-29

CHICO

MAY		
Tijuana	. . . .	27-30

JUNE		
St. George	. . . .	1-3
Tucson	. . . .	8-10
Yuma	. . . .	11-13
Edmonton	. . . . . .	22-24
Orange County	. . . .	28-30

JULY		
St. George	. . . .	2-4

Victoria	. . . .	15-17
Orange County	. . .	23-25

AUGUST		
Yuma	. . . .	3-5
Calgary	. . . .	6-8
Maui.	. . . .	19-21
St. George	. . . . .	25-29
Calgary	. . . .	31

SEPTEMBER		
Calgary	. . . .	1-2

EDMONTON

JUNE		
Maui.	. . . .	1-5
Orange County	. . . .	8-12
Victoria	. . . .	14-15

JULY		
Calgary	. . . .	1-2
Tijuana	. . . .	6-10
Yuma	. . . .	15-18
Tijuana	. . . .	19-21

Calgary	. . . .	28-29

AUGUST		
Chico	. . . .	10-13
Tucson	. . . .	14-17
Calgary	. . . . . .	19-23
Victoria	. . . .	31

SEPTEMBER		
Victoria	. . . .	1-2

MAUI

JUNE		
Tijuana	. . . .	8-9
Tijuana	. . . .	11-13
St. George	. . . .	15-20

JULY		
Victoria	. . . .	8-11
Tucson	. . . . . .	15-18
Tucson	. . . . . .	20-21

AUGUST		
Edmonton	. . . . . .	2-4
Edmonton	. . . . . .	6-8
Yuma	. . . . . .	11-15
Yuma	. . . .	17
Orange County	. . . .	31

SEPTEMBER		
Orange County	. . . .	1
Orange County	. . .	3-6

ORANGE COUNTY

JUNE		
Calgary	. . . .	15-17
Yuma	. . . . . .	18-19
Chico	. . . .	25-26

JULY		
Maui.	. . . .	2-4
Calgary	. . . .	6-8
Tucson	. . . .	9-10
St. George	. . . . .	15-17

Chico	. . . .	18-20
Edmonton	. . . . . .	30-31

AUGUST		
Victoria	. . . . . .	2-4
Tijuana	. . . . .	14 DH
Tijuana	. . . . .	16-17
Yuma	. . . . .	19-21
Maui.	. . . . .	22-24
Tijuana	. . . . .	26-28

ST. GEORGE

MAY		
Orange County	. . . .	21-22
Orange County	. . . .	24-25
Edmonton	. . . . . .	27-29

JUNE		
Tucson	. . . .	4-5
Yuma	. . . .	7-9
Tucson	. . . . . .	22-24
Edmonton	. . . . .	25-26
Maui.	. . . . . .	28-30

JULY		
Calgary	. . . .	9-11
Victoria	. . . . .	19-21
Tucson	. . . . . .	26-28
Yuma	. . . . . .	30-31

AUGUST		
Yuma	. . . .	1
Orange County	. . . .	6-9
Victoria	. . . . .	19-21

SEPTEMBER		
Chico	. . . . . .	3-6

TIJUANA

MAY		
Chico	. . . .	21-25

JUNE		
Chico	. . . .	4-6
Tucson	. . . . . .	15-17
Calgary	. . . . .	18-19
Maui.	. . . . . .	22-24
Yuma	. . . . . .	25-27

JULY		
Maui.	. . . . .	23-25

Orange County	. . . .	27-29
Victoria	. . . . . .	30-31

AUGUST		
Victoria	. . . . . .	1
St. George	. . . . .	2-5
Orange County	. . . .	11-13
Tucson	. . . . .	22-24
Yuma	. . . . . .	31

SEPTEMBER		
Yuma	. . . . . .	1
Calgary	. . . . . .	3-6

TUCSON

MAY		
Edmonton	. . . . . .	19-22
Calgary	. . . . .	23-25

JUNE		
Victoria	. . . .	1-3
St. George	. . . .	11-13
Chico	. . . . . .	18-20
Maui.	. . . . .	25-27
Yuma	. . . . .	29-30

JULY		
Yuma	. . . . . .	1

Yuma	. . . . . .	4-5
Chico	. . . . . .	6-8
St. George	. . . .	23-25
Maui.	. . . . .	29-31

AUGUST		
Tijuana	. . . . .	19-21
Edmonton	. . . . .	26-29
St. George	. . . . .	31

SEPTEMBER		
St. George	. . . . .	1-2
Yuma	. . . . .	3-4

VICTORIA

MAY		
Maui.	. . . . . .	21-25
Orange County	. . . .	27-30

JUNE		
Calgary	. . . . . .	8-10
Edmonton	. . . .	18-20
Calgary	. . . . .	21-24
Tijuana	. . . . .	29-30

JULY		
Tijuana	. . . . . .	1-3

Yuma	. . . . . .	23-25
Calgary	. . . . .	26-28

AUGUST		
Tucson	. . . . . .	5-8
St. George	. . . .	11-13
Chico	. . . . .	14-17

SEPTEMBER		
Edmonton	. . . . .	3-6

YUMA

MAY
Calgary 19-22
Edmonton 23-25
Tucson 27-29

JUNE
Tijuana 1-3
Victoria 4-6
Chico 15-17
Orange County 21-24

JULY
Tucson 2-3
St. George 6-8
Chico 9-11
Maui. 27-28

AUGUST
Tijuana 6-9
Victoria 22-24
Maui. 25-29

NORTHERN LEAGUE — HOME GAMES ONLY

FARGO-MOORHEAD

MAY
21-23 . . . . Joliet
24-27 . . . . . Lake County

JUNE
7-10 . . . . . . Schaumburg
11-13 . . . . . Kansas City
24-27 . . . . .Gary
28-30 . . . . .Rockford

JULY
1 . . . . .Rockford

8-11 . . . . . . Schaumburg
16-18 . . . . . . Winnipeg
19-22 . . . . .Gary
23-25 . . . . Joliet

AUGUST
6-8. . . . . .Rockford
9-12 . . . . . Kansas City
19-22 . . . . . . Winnipeg
23-25 . . . . . Lake County

GARY

MAY
20-23 . . . . . . Kansas City
24-25 . . . . . . .Rockford
31 . . . . Winnipeg

JUNE
1-2. . . . . Winnipeg
4-6. . . . . . Lake County
10 . . . . .Rockford
18-20 . . . . . . .Rockford
28-30 . . . . Joliet

JULY
5-7. . . . .Fargo-Moorhead

9-11 . . . . . . Kansas City
23-25 . . . . . Lake County
26-28 . . .Fargo-Moorhead

AUGUST
2-4. . . . . Winnipeg
13-15 . . . . . Lake County
16-18 . . . . . Schaumburg
20-22 . . . . . .Rockford
27-29 . . . . Joliet
30-31 . . . . . Schaumburg

SEPTEMBER
1-2. . . . . . . Schaumburg

JOLIET

MAY
28-31 . . . . . Lake County

JUNE
1-3. . . . . .Rockford
8-10 . . . . . . Lake County
15-17 . . .Fargo-Moorhead
18-20 . . . . . . Winnipeg
24-27 . . . . . . Kansas City

JULY
1-4. . . . . Winnipeg
19-20-21-22 . . . .Rockford

29-30-31 . . . . .Gary

AUGUST
1 . . . . .Gary
6-8. . . . . . . Schaumburg
19-22 . . . . . . Kansas City
23-26 . . . . . Schaumburg
31 . . . .Fargo-Moorhead

SEPTEMBER
1-2 . . .Fargo-Moorhead
3-6. . . . . .Gary

KANSAS CITY

MAY
28-31 . . .Fargo-Moorhead
31 . . . . Lake County

JUNE
1-2. . . . . . . Lake County
4-6. . . . . Joliet
14-17 . . . . .Gary
18-20 . . . . . Schaumburg
21-23 . . . . . Lake County

JULY
2-4. . . . .Fargo-Moorhead
5-7. . . . . Winnipeg
16-18 . . . . Joliet
20-22 . . . . . Schaumburg
23-25 . . . . .Rockford

AUGUST
3-5. . . . . Joliet
13-15 . . . . . . .Rockford
16-18 . . . . . . Winnipeg

23-25 . . . . .Gary

SEPTEMBER
3-6. . . . .Fargo-Moorhead

LAKE COUNTY

JUNE
11-13 . . . . .Gary
15-17 . . . . . . Winnipeg
18-20 . . .Fargo-Moorhead
24-25 . . . . . Schaumburg
27 . . . . Schaumburg
28-30 . . . . . . Winnipeg

JULY
2 . . . . .Gary
5-7. . . . . Joliet
9-11 . . . . .Rockford
26-29 . . . . . . Kansas City

30-31 . . . . Winnipeg

AUGUST
1 . . . . Winnipeg
2-4. . . . .Fargo-Moorhead
5-8. . . . . .Gary
16-18 . . . . Joliet
19-22 . . . . . Schaumburg
31 . . . . Kansas City

SEPTEMBER
1-2. . . . . . . Kansas City
3-6. . . . . .Rockford

ROCKFORD

MAY
20-23 . . . . . Schaumburg
26-27 . . . . . Kansas City
28-30 . . . . Winnipeg

JUNE
4-6. . .Fargo-Moorhead
8-9. . . . . .Gary
11-13 . . . . Joliet
21-23 . . .Fargo-Moorhead

JULY
2 . . . . Schaumburg
3-4. . . . . . . Lake County

15-18 . . . . . Lake County
27-29 . . . . . . Winnipeg
30-31 . . . . . . Kansas City

AUGUST
1 . . . . Kansas City
2-5. . . . . . . Schaumburg
10-12 . . . . Joliet
16-18 . . .Fargo-Moorhead
26-28 . . . . . Kansas City
31 . . . . Winnipeg

SEPTEMBER
1-2 . . . . Winnipeg

SCHAUMBURG

MAY
25-27 . . . . . Kansas City
28-30 . . . . .Gary
31 . . . . .Fargo-Moorhead

JUNE
1-2. . . . .Fargo-Moorhead
11-13 . . . . Winnipeg
14-16 . . . . . . .Rockford
21-23 . . . . Joliet
26 . . . . Lake County
28-30 . . . . . . Kansas City

JULY
1 . . . . Kansas City

3-4. . . . . .Gary
5-7. . . . . .Rockford
16-18 . . . . .Gary
26-28 . . . . Joliet
30-31 . .Fargo-Moorhead

AUGUST
1 . . . . . .Fargo-Moorhead
9-12 . . . . .Gary
13-15 . . . . Joliet
27-29 . . . . . Lake County

SEPTEMBER
3-5. . . . . Winnipeg

WINNIPEG

MAY
20-23 . . . . . Lake County
24-27 . . . . Joliet

JUNE
4-6. . . . . . . Schaumburg
7-10 . . . . . . Kansas City
21-23 . . . . .Gary
24-27 . . . . .Rockford

JULY
8-11 . . . . Joliet
19-22 . . . . . Lake County
23-25 . . . . . Schaumburg

AUGUST
6-8. . . . . . . Kansas City
9-12 . . . . .Gary
13-15 . . .Fargo-Moorhead
23-25 . . . . .Rockford
26-29 . . .Fargo-Moorhead

COLLEGE

COLLEGE ORGANIZATIONS

NATIONAL COLLEGIATE ATHLETIC ASSOCIATION

Mailing Address: PO Box 6222, Indianapolis, IN 46206. **Telephone:** (317) 917-6222. **Fax:** (317) 917-6826 (championships), 917-6710 (baseball). **E-Mail Addresses:** dpoppe@ncaa.org (Dennis Poppe), rbuhr@ncaa.org (Randy Buhr), dleech@ncaa.org (Damani Leech), jhamilton@ncaa.org (J.D. Hamilton), (Chad Tolliver) (ctolliver@ncaa.org), ryurk@ncaa.org (Russ Yurk), aholman@ncaa.org (Anthony Holman). **Websites:** www.ncaa.org, www.ncaa.com.

Interim President: Dr. Jim Isch. **Vice President for Division I Baseball and Football:** Dennis Poppe. **Director, Baseball:** Damani Leech. **Associate Director, Championships:** Randy Buhr; Coordinator for Division I Baseball and Football, Chad Tolliver. **Division II Assistant Director, Championships:** Russ Yurk. **Division III Associate Director, Championships:** Anthony Holman. **Media Contact, Division I College World Series:** J.D. Hamilton. **Contact, Statistics:** Sean Straziscar, Jeff Williams.

Chairman, Division I Baseball Committee: Tim Weiser (Deputy Commissioner, Big 12 Conference). **Division I Baseball Committee:** John Anderson (head coach, Minnesota), Mark LaBarbera (athletic director, Valparaiso), Mark Marquess (head coach, Stanford), Bobby Staub (athletic director, Louisiana-Monroe).

Assistant Athletics Director: Gary Overton (East Carolina University). **Athletics Director, Director of Athletics:** John P. Hardt (Bucknell), Lynn W. Thompson (Bethune-Cookman), Chris Monasch (St. John's). **Commissioner:** Kyle Kallander (Big South Conference).

Chairman, Division II Baseball Committee: Jeff Schaly (Assistant Athletic Director, Lynn University). **Chairman, Division III Baseball Committee:** Jack McKiernan (Associate Athletic Director, Kean). **2010 National Convention:** Jan. 13-16 at Atlanta

2010 CHAMPIONSHIP TOURNAMENTS

NCAA DIVISION I
64th College World Series . . . . Omaha, June 19-29/30
Super Regionals (8) . . . . Campus sites, June 11-14
Regionals (16). . . . . Campus sites, June 4-7

NCAA DIVISION II
43rd World Series. .USA Baseball National Training Complex, May 22-29.
Regionals (8). . . . . Campus sites, May 13-17.

NCAA DIVISION III
35th World Series. . . . . Appleton, Wis., May 28-June 1
Regionals (8). . . . . Campus sites, May 19-23

NATIONAL ASSOCIATION OF INTERCOLLEGIATE ATHLETICS

Mailing Address: 1200 Grand Blvd., Kansas City, MO 64106. **Telephone:** (816) 595-8000. **Fax:** (816) 595-8200. **Website:** www.naia.org.

President/CEO: Jim Carr. **VP for Championships:** Lori Thomas. **Manager, Championship Sports:** Scott McClure. **Director, Sports Information:** Chad Waller. **President, Coaches Association:** Denney Crabaugh.

2010 CHAMPIONSHIP TOURNAMENT

Opening round: May 18-21, campus locations.
Avista-NAIA World Series: May 28-June 4, Lewiston, Idaho.

NATIONAL JUNIOR COLLEGE ATHLETIC ASSOCIATION

Mailing Address: 1755 Telstar Dr., Suite 103, Colorado Springs, CO 80920. **Telephone:** (719) 590-9788. **Fax:** (719) 590-7324. **Website:** www.njcaa.org.

Executive Director: Mary Ellen Leight. **Director, Division I Baseball Tournament:** Jamie Hamilton. **Director, Division II Baseball Tournament:** Billy Mayberry. **Director, Division III Baseball Tournament:** Tim Drain. **Director, Media Relations:** Mark Krug.

2010 CHAMPIONSHIP TOURNAMENTS

DIVISION I
World Series . . . . Grand Junction, Colo., May 29-June 5

DIVISION II
World Series . . . . Enid, Okla., May 29-June 5

DIVISION III
World Series . . . . Tyler, Texas, May 22-28

CALIFORNIA COMMUNITY COLLEGE COMMISSION ON ATHLETICS

Mailing Address: 2017 O St., Sacramento, CA 95814. **Telephone:** (916) 444-1600. **Fax:** (916) 444-2616. **E-Mail Address:** ccarter@coasports.org, jboggs@coasports.org. **Website:** www.coasports.org.

Executive Director: Carlyle Carter. **Director, Member Services:** Debra Wheeler. **Assistant Director, Sports Information/Communications:** Jason Boggs.

2010 CHAMPIONSHIP TOURNAMENT

State Championship . . . . Fresno, Calif., May 21-23

NORTHWEST ATHLETIC ASSOCIATION OF COMMUNITY COLLEGES

Mailing Address: Clark College TGB 121, 1933 Fort Vancouver Way, Vancouver, WA 98663-3598. **Telephone:** (360) 992-2833. **Fax:** (360) 696-6210. **Website:** www.nwaacc.org. **E-Mail Address:** nwaacc@clark.edu.

Executive Director: Dick McClain. **Executive Assistant:** Carol Hardin. **Director, Marketing:** Charlie Warner. **Sports Information Director:** Tracy Swisher.

2010 CHAMPIONSHIP TOURNAMENT

NWAACC Championship . . . . Longview, Wash., May 27-31

AMERICAN BASEBALL COACHES ASSOCIATION

Office Address: 108 S. University Ave., Suite 3, Mount Pleasant, MI 48858-2327. **Telephone:** (989) 775-3300. **Fax:** (989) 775-3600. **E-Mail Address:** abca@abca.org. **Website:** www.abca.org.

Executive Director: Dave Keilitz. **Assistant to Executive Director:** Betty Rulong. **Membership/Convention Coordinator:** Nick Phillips. **Assistant Coordinator:** Juahn Clark.

Chairman: Jack Kaiser. **President:** Joe Roberts (Armstrong Atlantic State, Ga.).

2011 National Convention: Jan. 6-9 at Gaylord Opryland Hotel in Nashville.

NCAA DIVISION I CONFERENCES

AMERICA EAST CONFERENCE

Mailing Address: 215 First Street, Suite 140, Cambridge, MA 02142. **Telephone:** (617) 695-6369. **Fax:** (617) 695-6385. **E-Mail Address:** hanna@americaeast.com. **Website:** www.americaeast.com.

Baseball Members (First Year): Albany (2002), Binghamton (2002), Hartford (1990), Maine (1990), Maryland-Baltimore County (2004), Stony Brook (2002).

Assistant Director, Communications: Leslie Hanna

2010 Tournament: Four teams, double-elimination. May 26-28 at highest-seeded team.

ATLANTIC COAST CONFERENCE

Office Address: 4512 Weybridge Lane, Greensboro, NC 27407. **Mailing Address:** PO Drawer ACC, Greensboro, NC 27417. **Telephone:** (336) 851-6062. **Fax:** (336) 854-8797. **E-Mail Address:** sphillips@theacc.org. **Website:** www.theacc.com.

Baseball Members (First Year): Boston College (2006), Clemson (1954), Duke (1954), Florida State (1992), Georgia Tech (1980), Maryland (1954), Miami (2005), North Carolina (1954), North Carolina State (1954), Virginia (1955), Virginia Tech (2005), Wake Forest (1954).

Assistant Director, Comunications: Steve Phillips.

2010 Tournament: Eight teams, group play. May 26-30 at Greensboro, N.C.

ATLANTIC SUN CONFERENCE

Mailing Address: 3370 Vineville Ave., Suite 108-B, Macon, GA 31204. **Telephone:** (478) 474-3394. **Fax:** (478) 474-4272. **E-Mail Addresses:** emoyer@atlanticsun.org; jsymonds@atlanticsun.org **Website:** www.atlantic-sun.org.

Baseball Members (First Year): Belmont (2002), Campbell (1995), East Tennessee State (2006), Florida Gulf Coast (2008), Jacksonville (1999), Kennesaw State (2006), Lipscomb (2004), Mercer (1979), North Florida (2006), South Carolina Upstate (2008), Stetson (1986).

Director, Communications: Eric Moyer, assisted by Jeff Symonds.

2010 Tournament: Six teams, double-elimination. May 26-29 at Nashville (Lipscomb).

ATLANTIC 10 CONFERENCE

Mailing Address: 11827 Canon Blvd., Suite 200 Newport News, VA 23606. **Telephone:** (757) 706-3040. **Fax:** (757) 706-3042. **E-Mail Address:** shaug@atlantic10.org. **Website:** www.atlantic10.org.

Baseball Members (First Year): Charlotte (2006), Dayton (1996), Duquesne (1977), Fordham (1996), George Washington (1977), LaSalle (1996), Massachusetts (1977), Rhode Island (1981), Richmond (2002), St. Bonaventure (1980), Saint Joseph's (1983), Saint Louis (2006), Temple (1983), Xavier (1996).

Assistant Commissioner: Stephen Haug

2010 Tournament: Six teams, double elimination. May 27-30 at Campbell's Field, Camden, N.J.

BIG EAST CONFERENCE

Mailing Address: 222 Richmond St., Suite 110, Providence, RI 02903. **Telephone:** (401) 453-0660. **Fax:** (401) 751-8540. **E-Mail Address:** jgust@bigeast.org. **Website:** www.bigeast.org.

Baseball Members (First Year): Cincinnati (2006), Connecticut (1985), Georgetown (1985), Louisville (2006), Notre Dame (1996), Pittsburgh (1985), Rutgers (1996), St. John's (1985), Seton Hall (1985), South Florida (2006), Villanova (1985), West Virginia (1996).

Director, Communications: Chuck Sullivan.

2010 Championship: Eight teams, double-elimination. May 26-30 at Clearwater, Fla.

BIG SOUTH CONFERENCE

Mailing Address: 7233 Pineville-Matthews Rd, Suite 100, Charlotte, NC 28226. **Telephone:** (704) 341-7990. **Fax:** (704) 341-7991. **E-Mail Address:** marks@bigsouth.org. **Website:** www.bigsouthsports.com.

Baseball Members (First Year): Charleston Southern (1983), Coastal Carolina (1983), Gardner-Webb (2009), High Point (1999), Liberty (1991), UNC Asheville (1985), Presbyterian (2009), Radford (1983), Virginia Military Institute (2004), Winthrop (1983).

Assistant Commissioner, Public Relations: Mark Simpson.

2010 Tournament: Eight teams, single-elimination in first round followed by six-team double-elimination. May 25-29 at Rock Hill, S.C.

BIG TEN CONFERENCE

Mailing Address: 1500 W. Higgins Rd., Park Ridge, IL 60068. **Telephone:** (847) 696-1010. **Fax:** (847) 696-1110. **E-Mail Addresses:** schipman@bigten.org; vtodryk@bigten.org. **Website:** www.bigten.org.

Baseball Members (First Year): Illinois (1896), Indiana (1906), Iowa (1906), Michigan (1896), Michigan State (1950), Minnesota (1906), Northwestern (1898), Ohio State (1913), Penn State (1992), Purdue (1906).

Assistant Commissioner, Communications: Scott Chipman. **Assistant Director, Communications:** Valerie Todryk Krebs.

2010 Tournament: Six teams, double-elimination. May 26-29 at Bill Davis Stadium in Columbus, Ohio.

BIG 12 CONFERENCE

Mailing Address: 400 E. John Carpenter Freeway, Irving, TX 75062. **Telephone:** (469) 524-1000. **E-Mail Address:** carmen@big12sports.com. **Website:** www.big-12sports.com.

Baseball Members (First Year): Baylor (1997), Kansas (1997), Kansas State (1997), Missouri (1997), Nebraska (1997), Oklahoma (1997), Oklahoma State (1997), Texas (1997), Texas A&M (1997), Texas Tech (1997).

Assistant Director, Communications: Carmen Branch.

2010 Tournament: Two divisions, pool play format. May 26-30 at AT&T Bricktown Ballpark, Oklahoma City.

BIG WEST CONFERENCE

Mailing Address: 2 Corporate Park, Suite 206, Irvine, CA 92606. **Telephone:** (949) 261-2525. **Fax:** (949) 261-2528. **E-Mail Address:** jstcyr@bigwest.org. **Website:** www.bigwest.org.

Baseball Members (First Year): Cal Poly (1997), UC Davis (2008), UC Irvine (2002), UC Riverside (2002), UC Santa Barbara (1970), Cal State Fullerton (1975), Cal State Northridge (2001), Long Beach State (1970), Pacific (1972).

Associate Information Director: Julie St. Cyr.

2010 Tournament: None.

COLONIAL ATHLETIC ASSOCIATION

Mailing Address: 8625 Patterson Ave., Richmond, VA 23229. **Telephone:** (804) 754-1616. **Fax:** (804) 754-1830. **E-Mail Address:** rwashburn@caasports.com. **Website:** www.caasports.com.

Baseball Members (First Year): Delaware (2002), George Mason (1986), Georgia State (2006), Hofstra

(2002), James Madison (1986), UNC Wilmington (1986), Northeastern (2006), Old Dominion (1992), Towson (2002), Virginia Commonwealth (1996), William & Mary (1986).

Sports Information Director: Rob Washburn.

2010 Tournament: Four teams, double-elimination. May 27-29 at Wilmington, N.C. (UNC Wilmington).

CONFERENCE USA

Mailing Address: 5201 N. O'Connor Blvd., Suite 300, Irving, TX 75039. **Telephone:** (214) 774-1300. **Fax:** (214) 496-0055. **E-Mail Address:** rdanderson@c-usa.org. **Website:** www.conferenceusa.com.

Baseball Members (First Year): East Carolina (2002), Houston (1997), Marshall (2006), Memphis (1996), Rice (2006), Southern Miss (1996), Tulane (1996), UAB (1996), UCF (2006),.

Assistant Commissioner, Baseball Operations: Russell Anderson.

2010 Tournament: Six-team, two-division pool play. May 26-29 at Houston (University of Houston).

GREAT WEST CONFERENCE

Mailing Address: PO Box 9344, Naperville, IL 60567. **Telephone:** (630) 428-4492. **Fax:** (630) 548-0705. **E-Mail Address:** martin@gwconference.org. **Website:** www. greatwestconference.org.

Baseball Members (First Year): Chicago State (2010), Houston Baptist (2010), New Jersey Tech (2010), New York Tech (2010), North Dakota (2010), Northern Colorado (2010), Texas-Pan American (2010), Utah Valley (2010).

Media Relations Assistant: Cliff Martin.

2010 Tournament: Unavailable.

HORIZON LEAGUE

Mailing Address: 201 S. Capitol Ave., Suite 500, Indianapolis, IN 46225. **Telephone:** (317) 237-5621. **Fax:** (317) 237-5620. **E-Mail Address:** msegal@horizonleague. org. **Website:** www.horizonleague.org.

Baseball Members (First Year): Butler (1979), Cleveland State (1994), Illinois-Chicago (1994), Wisconsin-Milwaukee (1994), Valparaiso (2008), Wright State (1994), Youngstown State (2002).

Director, Communications: Matt Segal.

2010 Tournament: Six teams, double-elimination. May 26-29 at U.S. Steel Yard in Gary, Ind. (Valparaiso).

IVY LEAGUE

Mailing Address: 228 Alexander Rd., Second Floor, Princeton, NJ 08544. **Telephone:** (609) 258-6426. **Fax:** (609) 258-1690. **E-Mail Address:** alex@ivyleaguesports. com. **Website:** www.ivyleaguesports.com.

Baseball Members (First Year): Rolfe—Brown (1948), Dartmouth (1930), Harvard (1948), Yale (1930). Gehrig—Columbia (1930), Cornell (1930), Pennsylvania (1930), Princeton (1930).

Assistant Director, Communications: Alex Searle.

2010 Tournament: Best-of-three series between division champions. May 8-9 at team with best overall record.

METRO ATLANTIC ATHLETIC CONFERENCE

Mailing Address: 712 Amboy Ave., Edison, NJ 08837. **Telephone:** (732) 738-5455. **Fax:** (732) 738-8366. **E-Mail Address:** jill.skotarczak@maac.org. **Website:** www. maacsports.com.

Baseball Members (First Year): Canisius (1990), Fairfield (1982), Iona (1982), Manhattan (1982), Marist (1998), Niagara (1990), Rider (1998), St. Peter's (1982), Siena (1990).

Assistant Commissioner, Media Relations: Jill Skotarczak.

2010 Tournament: Four teams, double-elimination. May 26-29 at Fishkill, N.Y. (Marist).

MID-AMERICAN CONFERENCE

Mailing Address: 24 Public Square, 15th Floor, Cleveland, OH 44113. **Telephone:** (216) 566-4622. **Fax:** (216) 858-9622. **E-Mail Address:** jguy@mac-sports.com. **Website:** www.mac-sports.com.

Baseball Members (First Year): Akron (1992), Ball State (1973), Bowling Green State (1952), Buffalo (2001), Central Michigan (1971), Eastern Michigan (1971), Kent State (1951), Miami (1947), Northern Illinois (1997), Ohio (1946). Toledo (1950), Western Michigan (1947).

Director, Communications: Jeremy Guy.

2010 Tournament: Eight teams (two division winners, six wild-card teams with next-best conference winning percentage), double-elimination. May 26-29 at VA Memorial Stadium (Chillicothe, Ohio).

MID-EASTERN ATHLETIC CONFERENCE

Mailing Address: 222 Central Park Ave., Suite 1150, Virginia Beach, VA 23462. **Telephone:** (757) 416-7100. **Fax:** (757) 416-7109. **E-Mail Address:** rashids@themeac. com; porterp@themeac.com. **Website:** www.meacsports.com.

Baseball Members (First Year): Bethune-Cookman (1979), Coppin State (1985), Delaware State (1970), Florida A&M (1979), Maryland Eastern Shore (1970), Norfolk State (1998), North Carolina A&T (1970).

Assistant Director, Media Relations/Baseball Contact: Sahar Abdur-Rashid.

2010 Tournament: Six teams, double-elimination. May 20-23, 2010 in Daytona Beach, Florida (Bethune-Cookman).

MISSOURI VALLEY CONFERENCE

Mailing Address: 1818 Chouteau Ave., St. Louis, MO 63103. **Telephone:** (314) 421-0339. **Fax:** (314) 421-3505. **E-Mail Address:** kbriscoe@mvc.org. **Website:** www.mvc. org.

Baseball Members (First Year): Bradley (1955), Creighton (1976), Evansville (1994), Illinois State (1980), Indiana State (1976), Missouri State (1990), Southern Illinois (1974), Wichita State (1945).

Assistant Director, Communications: Kelli Briscoe.

2010 Tournament: Eight-team tournament with two four-team brackets mirroring the format of the College World Series, with the winners of each four-team bracket meeting in a single championship game. May 19-23 at Wichita.

MOUNTAIN WEST CONFERENCE

Mailing Address: 15455 Gleneagle Dr., Suite 200, Colorado Springs, CO 80921. **Telephone:** (719) 488-4050. **Fax:** (719) 487-7241. **E-Mail Address:** kmelcher@ themwc.com. **Website:** www.themwc.com.

Baseball Members (First Year): Air Force (2000), BYU (2000), UNLV (2000), New Mexico (2000), San Diego State (2000), TCU (2006), Utah (2000).

Director, Communications: Kim Melcher.

2010 Tournament: Six teams, double-elimination. May 25-29 at San Diego (San Diego State).

NORTHEAST CONFERENCE

Mailing Address: 399 Campus Drive, Somerset, NJ 08873. **Telephone:** (732) 469-0440. **Fax:** (732) 469-0744. **E-Mail Address:** rratner@northeastconference.org. **Website:** www.northeastconference.org.

Baseball Members (First Year): Bryant (2010), Central Connecticut State (1999), Fairleigh Dickinson (1981), Long Island (1981), Monmouth (1985), Mount St. Mary's (1989), Quinnipiac (1999), Sacred Heart (2000), Wagner (1981).

Associate Commissioner: Ron Ratner.

2010 Tournament: Four teams, double-elimination. May 20-22. Site TBA.

OHIO VALLEY CONFERENCE

Mailing Address: 215 Centerview Dr., Suite 115, Brentwood, TN 37027. **Telephone:** (615) 371-1698. **Fax:** (615) 371-1788. **E-Mail Address:** kschwartz@ovc.org. **Website:** www.ovcsports.com.

Baseball Members (First Year): Austin Peay State (1962), Eastern Illinois (1996), Eastern Kentucky (1948), Jacksonville State (2003), Morehead State (1948), Murray State (1948), Southeast Missouri State (1991), Tennessee-Martin (1992), Tennessee Tech (1949).

Assistant Commissioner: Kyle Schwartz.

2010 Tournament: Six teams, double-elimination. May 26-30 at Jackson, Tenn.

PACIFIC-10 CONFERENCE

Mailing Address: 1350 Treat Blvd., Suite 500. **Telephone:** (925) 932-4411. **Fax:** (925) 932-4601. **Website:** www.pac-10.org.

Baseball Members (First Year): Arizona (1979), Arizona State (1979), California (1916), UCLA (1928), Oregon (1916-1981, 2009) Oregon State (1916), Southern California (1923), Stanford (1918), Washington (1916), Washington State (1919).

Public Relations Contacts: Victor Rodriguez, Natalia Ciccone.

2010 Tournament: None.

PATRIOT LEAGUE

Mailing Address: 3773 Corporate Pkwy., Suite 190, Center Valley, PA 18034. **Telephone:** (610) 289-1963. **Fax:** (610) 289-1952. **E-Mail Address:** mdougherty@patriot-league.com. **Website:** www.patriotleague.org

Baseball Members (First Year): Army (1993), Bucknell (1991), Holy Cross (1991), Lafayette (1991), Lehigh (1991), Navy (1993).

Assistant Director, Media Relations: Matt Dougherty.

2010 Tournament: Four teams, May 15-16 and May 22-23 at site of higher seeds.

SOUTHEASTERN CONFERENCE

Mailing Address: 2201 Richard Arrington Blvd. N., Birmingham, AL 35203. **Telephone:** (205) 458-3000. **Fax:** (205) 458-3030. **E-Mail Address:** cdunlap@sec.org. **Website:** www.secsports.com.

Baseball Members (First Year): East—Florida (1933), Georgia (1933), Kentucky (1933), South Carolina (1992), Tennessee (1933), Vanderbilt (1933). West—Alabama (1933), Arkansas (1992), Auburn (1933), Louisiana State (1933), Mississippi (1933), Mississippi State (1933).

Associate Director, Media Relations: Chuck Dunlap.

2010 Tournament: Eight teams, modified double-elimination. May 26-30 at Hoover, Ala.

SOUTHERN CONFERENCE

Mailing Address: 702 N. Pine St., Spartanburg, SC 29303. **Telephone:** (864) 591-5100. **Fax:** (864) 591-4282. **E-Mail Address:** jcaskey@socon.org. **Website:** www.soconsports.com.

Baseball Members (First Year): Appalachian State (1971), College of Charleston (1998), The Citadel (1936),

Davidson (1991), Elon (2004), Furman (1936), Georgia Southern (1991), UNC Greensboro (1997), Samford (2009), Western Carolina (1976), Wofford (1997).

Media Relations: Jonathan Caskey.

2010 Tournament: Eight teams, double-elimination. May 26-30 at Joseph P. Riley, Jr. Park, Charleston, S.C.

SOUTHLAND CONFERENCE

Mailing Address: 2600 Network Blvd., Suite 150, Frisco, Texas 75034. **Telephone:** (972) 422-9500. **Fax:** (972) 422-9225. **E-Mail Address:** tlamb@southland.org. **Website:** www.southland.org.

Baseball Members (First Year): Central Arkansas (2007), Lamar (1999), McNeese State (1973), Nicholls State (1992), Northwestern State (1988), Sam Houston State (1988), Southeastern Louisiana (1998), Stephen F. Austin (2006), Texas-Arlington (1964), Texas-San Antonio (1992), Texas A&M-Corpus Christi (2007), Texas State (1988).

Baseball Contact/Assistant Commissioner: Todd Lamb.

2010 Tournament: Two four-team brackets, double-elimination. May 26-29 at Whataburger Field, Corpus Christi, Texas.

SOUTHWESTERN ATHLETIC CONFERENCE

Mailing Address: A.G. Gaston Building, 1527 Fifth Ave. N., Birmingham, AL 35203. **Telephone:** (205) 252-7573, ext. 111. **Fax:** (205) 252-9997. **E-Mail Address:** d.lewis@swac.org. **Website:** www.swac.org.

Baseball Members (First Year): East—Alabama A&M (2000), Alabama State (1982), Alcorn State (1962), Jackson State (1958), Mississippi Valley State (1968). West—Arkansas-Pine Bluff (1999), Grambling State (1958), Prairie View A&M (1920), Southern (1934), Texas Southern (1954).

Assistant Commissioner, Media Relations: Duane Lewis.

2010 Tournament: Eight teams, double-elimination. May 26-30 Jackson, Miss. (Jackson State).

SUMMIT LEAGUE

Mailing Address: 340 W. Butterfield Rd., Suite 3-D, Elmhurst, IL 60126. **Telephone:** (630) 516-0661. **Fax:** (630) 516-0673. **E-Mail Addresses:** brauer@thesummitleague.org, mette@thesummitleague.org. **Website:** www.thesummitleague.org.

Baseball Members (First Year): Centenary (2004), IPFW (2008), North Dakota State (2008), Oakland (2000), Oral Roberts (1998), South Dakota State (2008), Southern Utah (2000), Western Illinois (1984).

Director, Communications: David Brauer. **Associate Director (baseball contact):** Greg Mette.

2010 Tournament: Four teams, double-elimination. May 27-29 at Tulsa. (Oral Roberts).

SUN BELT CONFERENCE

Mailing Address: 601 Poydras St, Suite 2355, New Orleans, LA 70130. **Telephone:** (504) 299-9066. **Fax:** (504) 299-9068. **E-Mail Address:** nunez@sunbeltsports.org. **Website:** www.sunbeltsports.org.

Baseball Members (First Year): Arkansas-Little Rock (1991), Arkansas State (1991), Florida Atlantic (2007), Florida International (1999), Louisiana-Lafayette (1991), Louisiana-Monroe (2007), Middle Tennessee (2001), New Orleans (1976/1991), South Alabama (1976), Troy (2006), Western Kentucky (1982).

Director, Media Relations: Keith Nunez.

2010 Tournament: Eight teams, double-elimination. May 26-29 at Murfreesboro, Tenn. (Middle Tennessee State).

WEST COAST CONFERENCE

Mailing Address: 1250 Bayhill Dr., Suite 101, San Bruno, CA 94066. **Telephone:** (650) 873-8622. **Fax:** (650) 873-7846. **E-Mail Addresses:** jwilson@westcoast.org; apatel@westcoast.org. **Website:** www.wccsports.com.

Baseball Members (First Year): Gonzaga (1996), Loyola Marymount (1968), Pepperdine (1968), Portland (1996), Saint Mary's (1968), San Diego (1979), San Francisco (1968), Santa Clara (1968).

Director, Communications: Jae Wilson. **Associate Director, Communications:** Anish Patel.

2010 Tournament: None.

WESTERN ATHLETIC CONFERENCE

Mailing Address: 9250 East Costilla Ave., Suite 300, Englewood, CO 80112. **Telephone:** (303) 799-9221. **Fax:** (303) 799-3888. **E-Mail Address:** jerickson@wac.org. **Website:** www.wacsports.com.

Baseball Members (First Year): Fresno State (1993), Hawaii (1980), Louisiana Tech (2002), Nevada (2001), New Mexico State (2006), Sacramento State (2006), San Jose State (1997).

Commissioner: Karl Benson. **Senior Associate Commissioner:** Jeff Hurd. **Director, Sports Information:** Jason Erickson.

2010 Tournament: Six teams, double elimination. May 27-30 at Mesa, Ariz.

NCAA DIVISION I TEAMS

*Recruiting coordinator

AIR FORCE FALCONS

Conference: Mountain West.
Mailing Address: 2170 Field House Drive, USAF Academy, CO 80840. **Website:** goairforcefalcons.com.
Head Coach: Mike Hutcheon. **Assistant Coaches:** Scott Marchand, Matt Radmacher, *Chandler Rose. **Telephone:** (719) 333-0835. **Baseball SID:** Nick Arseniak. **Telephone:** (719) 333-9251. **Fax:** (719) 333-3798.
Home Field: Falcon Field. **Seating Capacity:** 1,000. **Outfield Dimensions:** LF—349, CF—400, RF—316. **Press Box Telephone:** (719) 333-3472.

AKRON ZIPS

Conference: Mid-American (East).
Mailing Address: University of Akron, Rhodes Arena, Akron, OH 44325. **Website:** www.GoZips.com.
Head Coach: Pat Bangtson. **Assistant Coaches:** Kurt Davidson, *Brian Donohew. **Telephone:** (330) 972-7290. **Baseball SID:** Rita Chinyere. **Telephone:** (330) 972-7171. **Fax:** (330) 374-8844.
Home Field: Lee Jackson Field. **Seating Capacity:** 1,500. **Outfield Dimensions:** LF—330, CF—400, RF—330. **Press Box Telephone:** (330) 972-8896.

ALABAMA CRIMSON TIDE

Conference: Southeastern (West).
Mailing Address: PO Box 870393, Tuscaloosa, AL 35487-0393. **Website:** www.rolltide.com.
Head Coach: Mitch Gaspard. **Assistant Coaches:** Bobby Barbier, Kyle Bunn, *Dax Norris. **Telephone:** (205) 348-4029. **Baseball SID:** Barry Allen. **Telephone:** (205) 348-8836. **Fax:** (205) 348-8840.
Home Field: Sewell-Thomas Stadium. **Seating Capacity:** 6,571. **Outfield Dimensions:** LF—325, CF—400, RF—325. **Press Box Telephone:** (205) 348-4927.

ALABAMA A&M BULLDOGS

Conference: Southwestern Athletic.
Mailing Address: PO Box 1597, Normal, AL 35762. **Website:** www.aamusports.com.
Head Coach: Demetrius Mitchell. **Assistant Coaches:** Unavailable. **Telephone:** (256) 372-4004. **Baseball SID:** Thomas Galbraith. **Telephone:** (256) 372-4005. **Fax:** (256) 851-5919.

ALABAMA STATE HORNETS

Conference: Southwestern Athletic.
Mailing Address: 915 S. Jackson St, Montgomery, AL 36101. **Website:** www.bamastatesports.com.
Head Coach: Larry Watkins. **Assistant Coach:** Tony Macon. **Telephone:** (334) 229-4228. **Baseball SID:** La Tonia Thirston. **Telephone:** (334) 229-5211. **Fax:** (334) 262-2971.

ALABAMA-BIRMINGHAM BLAZERS

Conference: Conference USA.
Mailing Address: U 236, 1530 3rd Ave S., Birmingham, AL 35294. **Website:** www.uabsports.com
Head Coach: Brian Shoop. **Assistant Coaches:** Josh Hopper, Ron Polk, *Perry Roth. **Telephone:** (205) 934-5181. **Baseball SID:** Tyson Mathews. **Telephone:** (205) 996-2576. **Fax:** (205) 934-7505.
Home Field: Young Memorial Field. **Seating Capacity:** 1,000. **Outfield Dimensions:** LF—330, CF—400, RF—330. **Press Box Telephone:** (Telephone: 205) 934 0200.

ALBANY GREAT DANES

Conference: America East.
Mailing Address: 1400 Washington Ave, PE Bldg 123, Albany, NY 12222. **Website:** www.ualbanysports.com.
Head Coach: Jon Mueller. **Assistant Coaches:** Garett Baron, *Drew Pearce. **Telephone:** (518) 442-3014. **Baseball SID:** Brianna LaBrecque. **Telephone:** (518) 442-5733. **Fax:** (518) 442-3139.
Home Field: Varsity Field. **Seating Capacity:** 1,000. **Outfield Dimensions:** LF—345, CF—375, RF—325.

ALCORN STATE BRAVES

Conference: Southwestern Athletic.
Mailing Address: 1000 ASU Drive, Alcorn State, MS 39096. **Website:** www.alcornsports.com.
Head Coach: Barret Rey. **Assistant Coaches:** David Gomez, Kevin Vital. **Telephone:** (601) 877-4090. **Baseball SID:** LLJuna Weir. **Telephone:** (601) 877-6509. **Fax:** (601) 877-3821.

APPALACHIAN STATE MOUNTAINEERS

Conference: Southern.
Mailing Address: Appalachian State University, Owens Field House, Boone, NC 28607. **Website:** www.goasu.com
Head Coach: Chris Pollard. **Assistant Coaches:** *Matt Boykin, Josh Jordan, Craig Scheffler. **Telephone:** (828) 262-6097. **Baseball SID:** Mike Flynn. **Telephone:** (828) 262-2845. **Fax:** (828) 262-6106.
Home Field: Beaver Field at Jim and Bettie Smith Stadium. **Seating Capacity:** 1,000. **Outfield Dimensions:** LF—330, CF—400, RF—330. **Press Box Telephone:** (828) 262-2016.

ARIZONA WILDCATS

Conference: Pacific-10.
Mailing Address: McKale Center, 1 National Championship Drive, Tucson, AZ 85721-0096. **Website:** www.arizonaathletics.com.

Head Coach: Andy Lopez. **Assistant Coaches:** Shaun Cole, Brett Scyphers, *Mark Wasikowski. **Telephone:** (520) 621-4102. **Baseball SID:** Blair Willis. **Telephone:** (520) 621-0914. **Fax:** (520) 621-2681.

Home Field: Jerry Kindall Field at Frank Sancet Stadium. **Seating Capacity:** 6,500. **Outfield Dimensions:** LF—360, CF—400, RF—360. **Press Box Telephone:** (520) 621-4440.

ARIZONA STATE SUN DEVILS

Conference: Pacific-10.

Mailing Address: 500 East Veteran's Way Tempe, AZ 85287. **Website:** www.TheSunDevils.com.

Head Coach: Tim Esmay. **Assistant Coaches:** Mike Benjamin, *Travis Jewett, Ken Knutson. **Telephone:** (480) 965-3677. **Baseball SID:** Randy Policar. **Telephone:** (480) 965-6594. **Fax:** (480) 965-5408.

Home Field: Winkles Field-Packard Stadium at Brock Ballpark. **Seating Capacity:** 3,879. **Outfield Dimensions:** LF—338, CF—395, RF—338. **Press Box Telephone:** (480) 727-7253.

ARKANSAS RAZORBACKS

Conference: Southeastern (West).

Mailing Address: 1255 S. Razorback Rd, Fayetteville, AR 72702. **Website:** www.arkansasrazorbacks.com.

Head Coach: Dave Van Horn. **Assistant Coaches:** *Todd Butler, Dave Jorn. **Telephone:** (479) 575-3655. **Baseball SID:** Zach Lawson. **Telephone:** (479) 575-7089. **Fax:** (479) 575-7481.

Home Field: Baum Stadium. **Seating Capacity:** 10,737. **Outfield Dimensions:** LF—320, CF—400, RF—320. **Press Box Telephone:** (479) 575-4141.

ARKANSAS STATE RED WOLVES

Conference: Sun Belt.

Mailing Address: PO Box 1000, State University, AR 72467. **Website:** www.asuindians.com.

Head Coach: Tommy Raffo. **Assistant Coaches:** *Chris Cook, *Justin Meccage. **Telephone:** (870) 972-2700. **Baseball SID:** Van Provence. **Telephone:** (870) 972-2707. **Fax:** (870) 972-3367.

Home Field: Tomlinson Stadium Kell Field. **Seating Capacity:** 1,500. **Outfield Dimensions:** LF—335, CF—400, RF—335. **Press Box Telephone:** (870) 972-3383.

ARKANSAS-LITTLE ROCK TROJANS

Conference: Sun Belt.

Mailing Address: 2801 S. University Ave, Little Rock, AR 72204. **Website:** www.ualrtrojans.com.

Head Coach: Scott Norwood. **Assistant Coaches:** Jeremy Haworth, *Dirk Kinney, J.J. Yant. **Telephone:** (501) 663-8095. **Baseball SID:** Joe Angolia. **Telephone:** (501) 569-3449. **Fax:** (501) 683-7002.

Home Field: Gary Hogan Field. **Seating Capacity:** 1,000. **Outfield Dimensions:** LF—330, CF—400, RF—325. **Press Box Telephone:** (501) 351-1060.

ARKANSAS-PINE BLUFF GOLDEN LIONS

Conference: Southwestern Athletic.

Mailing Address: 1200 N. University Dr, Mail Slot 4949, Pine Bluff, AR 71601. **Website:** www.uapblionsroar.com.

Head Coach: Michael Bumpers. **Assistant Coaches:** Willie Smith, *Michael Wilson. **Telephone:** (870) 575-8089. **Baseball SID:** Andrew Roberts. **Telephone:** (870) 575-7949. **Fax:** (870) 575-7880.

Home Field: Torii Hunter Baseball Complex. **Seating Capacity:** 2,500. **Outfield Dimensions:** LF—330, CF—400, RF—330.

ARMY BLACK KNIGHTS

Conference: Patriot.

Mailing Address: 639 Howard Rd, West Point, NY 10996. **Website:** www.goarmysports.com.

Head Coach: Joe Sottolano. **Assistant Coaches:** Anthony DeCicco, Matt Reid. **Telephone:** (845) 938-3712. **Baseball SID:** Bob Beretta. **Telephone:** (845) 938-6416. **Fax:** (845) 446-2556.

AUBURN TIGERS

Conference: Southeastern (West).

Mailing Address: PO Box 351, Auburn, AL 36830. **Website:** www.auburntigers.com.

Head Coach: John Pawlowski. **Assistant Coaches:** *Scott Foxhall, Link Jarrett, Ty Megahee. **Telephone:** (334) 844-4975. **Baseball SID:** Dan Froehlich. **Telephone:** (334) 844-9803. **Fax:** (334) 844-9807.

Home Field: Plainsman Park. **Seating Capacity:** 4,096. **Outfield Dimensions:** LF—315, CF—385, RF—331. **Press Box Telephone:** (334) 844-4138.

AUSTIN PEAY STATE GOVERNORS

Conference: Ohio Valley.

Mailing Address: Baseball Office, Box 4515, Clarksville, TN 37044. **Website:** www.letsgopeay.com.

Head Coach: Gary McClure. **Assistant Coaches:** Justin Dedman, Jake Peterson, *Joel Mangrum. **Telephone:** (931) 221-6266. **Baseball SID:** Cody Bush. **Telephone:** (931) 221-7561. **Fax:** (931) 221-7830.

Home Field: Raymond C. **Hand Park. Seating Capacity:** 2,000. **Outfield Dimensions:** LF—321, CF—392, RF—327. **Press Box Telephone:** (931) 221-7406.

BALL STATE CARDINALS

Conference: Mid-American (West).

Mailing Address: HP 245, Muncie, IN 47306. **Website:** www.ballstatesports.com.

Head Coach: Greg Beals. **Assistant Coaches:** Alex Marconi, Mike Stafford. **Telephone:** (765) 285-8226. **Baseball SID:** Matt McCollester. **Telephone:** (765) 285-8242. **Fax:** (765) 285-8929.

Home Field: Ball Diamond. **Seating Capacity:** 1,500. **Outfield Dimensions:** LF—330, CF—400, RF—330. **Press Box Telephone:** (765) 285-8932.

BAYLOR BEARS

Conference: Big 12 (South).

Mailing Address: 1612 South University Parks Dr, Waco, TX 76706. **Website:** www.baylorbears.com.

Head Coach: Steve Smith. **Assistant Coaches:** Steve Johnigan, Trevor Mote, *Mitch Thompson. **Telephone:** (254) 710-3029. **Baseball SID:** David Kaye. **Telephone:** (254) 710-4389.

Home Field: Baylor Ballpark. **Seating Capacity:** 5,000. **Outfield Dimensions:** LF—330, CF—400, RF—330. **Press Box Telephone:** (254) 754-5546.

BELMONT BRUINS

Conference: Atlantic Sun.

Mailing Address: 1900 Belmont Blvd, Nashville, TN 37212. **Website:** belmontbruins.cstv.com.

Head Coach: Dave Jarvis. **Assistant Coaches:** *Matt Barnett, Scott Hall. **Telephone:** (615) 460-6166. **Baseball SID:** Brian Karst. **Telephone:** (615) 460-8237. **Fax:** (615) 460-5584.

Home Field: Shelby Park. **Seating Capacity:** 1,000. **Outfield Dimensions:** LF—327, CF—400, RF—327.

BETHUNE-COOKMAN WILDCATS

Conference: Mid-Eastern Athletic.
Mailing Address: 640 Dr. Mary McLeod Bethune Blvd, Daytona Beach, FL 32114. **Website:** www.bccathletics.com.
Head Coach: Mervyl Melendez. **Assistant Coaches:** Jason Arnold, Drew Clark, Jose Vasquez. **Telephone:** (386) 481-2224. **Baseball SID:** Mark Johnson. **Telephone:** (386) 481-2206. **Fax:** (386) 481-2238.

BINGHAMTON BEARCATS

Conference: America East.
Mailing Address: Binghamton University, Events Center Office #110, Binghamton, NY, 13902. **Website:** bubearcats.com.
Head Coach: Tim Sinicki. **Assistant Coaches:** Ed Folli, *Ryan Hurba, Andy Hutchings. **Telephone:** (607) 777-2525. **Baseball SID:** John Hartrick. **Telephone:** (607) 777-6800. **Fax:** (607) 777-4597.
Home Field: Varsity Field. **Seating Capacity:** Unavailable. **Outfield Dimensions:** LF—315, CF—390, RF—315.

BOSTON COLLEGE EAGLES

Conference: Atlantic Coast (Atlantic).
Mailing Address: 140 Commonwealth Ave, Chestnut Hill, MA 02467. **Website:** bceagles.cstv.com.
Head Coach: Mik Aoki. **Assistant Coaches:** Steve Englert, *Joe Hastings, Jesse Woods. **Telephone:** (617) 552-2674. **Baseball SID:** Matt Lynch. **Telephone:** (617) 552-2193. **Fax:** (617) 552-4903.
Home Field: Shea Field. **Seating Capacity:** 1,000. **Outfield Dimensions:** LF—330, CF—410, RF—318.

BOWLING GREEN STATE FALCONS

Conference: Mid-American (East).
Mailing Address: 201 Doyt Perry Stadium East, Bowling Green, OH 43403. **Website:** www.bgsufalcons.com.
Head Coach: Danny Schmitz. **Assistant Coaches:** *Rick Blanc, Spencer Schmitz. **Telephone:** (419) 372-7065. **Baseball SID:** Ryan Gasser. **Telephone:** (419) 372-7015. **Fax:** (419) 372-6015.
Home Field: Warren E. Steller. **Seating Capacity:** 1,100. **Outfield Dimensions:** LF—340, CF—400, RF—340. **Press Box Telephone:** (419) 372-1234.

BRADLEY BRAVES

Conference: Missouri Valley.
Mailing Address: 1501 W. Bradley Ave, Peoria, IL 61625. **Website:** www.bubraves.com.
Head Coach: Elvis Dominguez. **Assistant Coaches:** *John Corbin, Sean Lyons. **Telephone:** (309) 677-2684. **Baseball SID:** Anthony Dobson. **Telephone:** (309) 677-3788. **Fax:** (309) 677-2626.
Home Field: O'Brien Field. **Seating Capacity:** 7,500. **Outfield Dimensions:** LF—310, CF—400, RF—310. **Press Box Telephone:** (309) 680-4045.

BRIGHAM YOUNG COUGARS

Conference: Mountain West.
Mailing Address: 30 SFH, BYU, Provo, UT 84602. **Website:** www.byucougars.com.
Head Coach: Vance Law. **Assistant Coaches:** Bobby Applegate, Casey Nelson, *Ryan Roberts. **Telephone:** (801) 422-5049. **Baseball SID:** Ralph Zobell. **Telephone:** (801) 422-9769. **Fax:** (801) 422-0633.
Home Field: Larry H. Miller Field. **Seating Capacity:** 2,204. **Outfield Dimensions:** LF—345, CF—400, RF—345. **Press Box Telephone:** (801) 422-4041.

BROWN BEARS

Conference: Ivy League (Rolfe).
Mailing Address: 235 Hope St, Box 1932, Providence, RI 02912. **Website:** www.BrownBears.com.
Head Coach: Marek Drabinski. **Assistant Coaches:** Dave Cunningham, Brian Murphy. **Telephone:** (401) 863-3090. **Baseball SID:** Isaac Goodling. **Telephone:** (401) 863-6069. **Fax:** (401) 863-6069.
Home Field: Murray Stadium. **Seating Capacity:** 1,000. **Outfield Dimensions:** LF—340, CF—405, RF—330. **Press Box Telephone:** (401) 863-9427.

BRYANT BULLDOGS

Conference: Northeast.
Mailing Address: 1150 Douglas Pike, Smithfield, RI 02917. **Website:** www.bryantbulldogs.com.
Head Coach: Jamie Pinzino. **Assistant Coaches:** Kevin Cobb, Andy Koocher, *Matt Ponte. **Telephone:** (401) 323-6397. **Baseball SID:** Jason Sullivan. **Telephone:** (401) 323-6072. **Fax:** (401) 232-6361.
Home Field: Bryant Baseball Complex. **Seating Capacity:** Unavailable. **Outfield Dimensions:** LF—330, CF—400, RF—330.

BUCKNELL BISON

Conference: Patriot.
Mailing Address: Bucknell University, Moore Ave, Lewisburg, PA 17837. **Website:** www.bucknellbison.com.
Head Coach: Gene Depew. **Assistant Coaches:** Jim Gulden, *Scott Heather, A.J. Yoder. **Telephone:** (570) 577-3593. **Baseball SID:** Todd Merriett. **Telephone:** (570) 577-3488. **Fax:** (570) 577-1660.
Home Field: Depew Field. **Seating Capacity:** 500. **Outfield Dimensions:** LF—330, CF—400, RF—330. **Press Box Telephone:** (570) 428-5393.

BUFFALO BULLS

Conference: Mid-American (East).
Mailing Address: University at Buffalo, Division of Athletics, 175 Alumni Arena, Buffalo, NY 14260. **Website:** www.buffalobulls.com.
Head Coach: Ron Torgalski. **Assistant Coaches:** *Jim Koerner, Carol Krestos, Devin McIntosh. **Telephone:** (716) 645-6834. **Baseball SID:** Will Nowadly. **Telephone:** (716) 645-5523. **Fax:** (716) 645-6840.
Home Field: Amherst Audubon Field. **Seating Capacity:** 500. **Outfield Dimensions:** LF—330, CF—400, RF—330. **Press Box Telephone:** (716) 867-1908.

BUTLER BULLDOGS

Conference: Horizon.
Mailing Address: 510 W. 49th Street, Indianapolis, IN 46208. **Website:** butlersports.com.
Head Coach: Steve Farley. **Assistant Coaches:** Jeff Brown, Bobby Segal, *Matt Tyner. **Telephone:** (317) 940-9721. **Baseball SID:** Josh Rattray. **Telephone:** (317) 940-9994. **Fax:** (317) 940-9808.
Home Field: Bulldog Park. **Seating Capacity:** 500. **Outfield Dimensions:** LF—330, CF—400, RF—330. **Press Box Telephone:** (317) 945-8943.

CALIFORNIA GOLDEN BEARS

Conference: Pacific-10.
Mailing Address: 66 Haas Pavilion, Berkeley, CA 94720. **Website:** www.calbears.com.
Head Coach: David Esquer. **Assistant Coaches:** Tony Arnerich, *Dan Hubbs, Brad Sanfillippo. **Telephone:**

(510) 643-6006. **Baseball SID:** Scott Ball. **Telephone:** (510) 643-1741. **Fax:** (510) 643-3444.

Home Field: Evans Diamond. **Seating Capacity:** 2,500. **Outfield Dimensions:** LF—320, CF—400, RF—320. **Press Box Telephone:** (510) 642-3098.

UC DAVIS AGGIES

Conference: Big West.

Mailing Address: Hickey Gym 119, One Shields Ave, Davis, CA 95616. **Website:** ucdavisaggies.com.

Head Coach: Rex Peters. **Assistant Coaches:** Jason Armstrong, *Tony Schifano, Matt Vaughn. **Telephone:** (530) 752-7513. **Baseball SID:** Amanda Piechowski. **Telephone:** (530) 752-3505. **Fax:** (530) 754-5674.

Home Field: Dobbins Stadium. **Seating Capacity:** 3,500. **Outfield Dimensions:** LF—310, CF—410, RF—310. **Press Box Telephone:** (530) 752-3673.

UC IRVINE ANTEATERS

Conference: Big West.

Mailing Address: UC Irvine, Crawford Hall, 903 W. Peltason Dr, Irvine, CA 92697-4500. **Website:** www.ucirvinesports.com.

Head Coach: Mike Gillespie. **Assistant Coaches:** Bob Macaluso, *Pat Shine, Ted Silva. **Telephone:** (949) 824-4292. **Baseball SID:** Fumi Kimura. **Telephone:** (949) 824-9474. **Fax:** (949) 824-5260.

Home Field: Anteater Ballpark. **Seating Capacity:** 3,200. **Outfield Dimensions:** LF—335, CF—405, RF—335. **Press Box Telephone:** (949) 824-9905.

UCLA BRUINS

Conference: Pacific-10.

Mailing Address: J.D. Morgan Center, 325 Westwood Plaza, Los Angeles, CA 90095. **Website:** www.uclabruins.com.

Head Coach: John Savage. **Assistant Coaches:** Steve Pearse, P.C. Shaw, *Rick Vanderhook. **Telephone:** (310) 794-2470. **Baseball SID:** Alex Timiraos. **Telephone:** (310) 206-4008. **Fax:** (310) 825-8664.

Home Field: Jackie Robinson Stadium. **Seating Capacity:** 1,250. **Outfield Dimensions:** LF—330, CF—395, RF—330. **Press Box Telephone:** (310) 794-8213.

UC RIVERSIDE HIGHLANDERS

Conference: Big West.

Mailing Address: Dept. of Athletics, UC Riverside, 900 University Ave, Riverside, CA 92521. **Website:** www.gohighlanders.com.

Head Coach: Doug Smith. **Assistant Coaches:** Randy Betten, *Nathan Choate. **Telephone:** (951) 827-5441. **Baseball SID:** John Maxwell. **Telephone:** (951) 827-5438. **Fax:** (951) 827-3569.

Home Field: UCR Sports Complex. **Seating Capacity:** 2,500. **Outfield Dimensions:** LF—330, CF—400, RF—330.

UC SANTA BARBARA GAUCHOS

Conference: Big West.

Mailing Address: ICA Building, UC Santa Barbara, CA 93106-5200. **Website:** www.ucsbgauchos.com.

Head Coach: Bob Brontsema. **Assistant Coaches:** John Kirkgard, Jason Lefkowitz, *Tom Myers. **Telephone:** (805) 893-3690. **Baseball SID:** Matt Hurst. **Telephone:** (805) 893-8603. **Fax:** (805) 893-4537.

Home Field: Caesar Uyesaka Stadium. **Seating Capacity:** 1,000. **Outfield Dimensions:** LF—335, CF—400, RF—335. **Press Box Telephone:** (805) 893-4671.

CAL POLY MUSTANGS

Conference: Big West.

Mailing Address: 1 Grand Ave, San Luis Obispo, CA 93407-0388. **Website:** www.GoPoly.com.

Head Coach: Larry Lee. **Assistant Coaches:** Dustin Kelly, Jason Kelly, *Jesse Zepeda. **Telephone:** (805) 756-6367. **Baseball SID:** Eric Burdick. **Telephone:** (805) 756-6550. **Fax:** (805) 756-2650.

Home Field: Baggett Stadium. **Seating Capacity:** 1,734. **Outfield Dimensions:** LF—335, CF—405, RF—335. **Press Box Telephone:** (805) 756-7456.

CAL STATE BAKERSFIELD ROADRUNNERS

Conference: Independent.

Mailing Address: 9001 Stockdale Hwy-8GYM, Bakersfield, CA 93311-1022. **Website:** www.gorunners.com.

Head Coach: Bill Kernen. **Assistant Coaches:** *Dennis Machado, Jody Robinson. **Telephone:** (661) 654-2628. **Baseball SID:** Sarah Finney. **Telephone:** (661) 654-3071. **Fax:** (661) 654-6978.

Home Field: Hardt Field. **Seating Capacity:** Unavailable. **Outfield Dimensions:** LF—327, CF—390, RF—327.

CAL STATE FULLERTON TITANS

Conference: Big West.

Mailing Address: 800 N. State College Blvd, Fullerton, CA 92831. **Website:** fullertontitans.com.

Head Coach: Dave Serrano. **Assistant Coaches:** Greg Bergeron, *Sergio Brown, Gregg Wallis. **Telephone:** (657) 278-3780. **Baseball SID:** Michael Greenlee. **Telephone:** (657) 278-3081. **Fax:** (657) 278-3141.

Home Field: Goodwin Field. **Seating Capacity:** 3,500. **Outfield Dimensions:** LF—330, CF—400, RF—330. **Press Box Telephone:** (657) 278-5327.

CAL STATE NORTHRIDGE MATADORS

Conference: Big West.

Mailing Address: 18111 Nordhoff Street, Northridge, CA 91330. **Website:** gomatadors.cstv.com.

Head Coach: Steve Rousey. **Assistant Coaches:** *Mark Kertenian, Robert McKinley, Phil Van Horn. **Telephone:** (818) 677-3218. **Baseball SID:** Eric Bankston. **Telephone:** (818) 677-3860. **Fax:** (818) 677-2661.

Home Field: Matador Field. **Seating Capacity:** 1,000. **Outfield Dimensions:** LF—325, CF—395, RF—325. **Press Box Telephone:** (818) 677-4292.

CAMPBELL FIGHTING CAMELS

Conference: Atlantic Sun.

Mailing Address: 78 McKoy Dr, Buies Creek, NC 27506. **Website:** www.gocamels.com.

Head Coach: Greg Goff. **Assistant Coaches:** Aubrey Blackwell, John Caddell, *Justin Haire. **Telephone:** (910) 893-1354. **Baseball SID:** Stan Cole. **Telephone:** (910) 893-1331. **Fax:** (910) 893-1330.

Home Field: Taylor Field. **Seating Capacity:** 1,000. **Outfield Dimensions:** LF—337, CF—395, RF—328. **Press Box Telephone:** (910) 814-4781.

CANISIUS GOLDEN GRIFFINS

Conference: Metro Atlantic.

Mailing Address: 2001 Main St, Buffalo, NY 14208. **Website:** www.gogriffs.com.

Head Coach: Mike McRae. **Assistant Coaches:** Ryan Asis, *Matt Mazurek, Neil Turvey Jr. **Telephone:** (716) 888-3207. **Baseball SID:** Matt Lozar. **Telephone:** (716) 888-3756. **Fax:** (716) 888-8444.

Home Field: Demske Sports Complex. **Seating Capacity:** 1,000. **Outfield Dimensions:** LF—310, CF—400, RF—310. **Press Box Telephone:** (440) 477-3777.

CENTENARY GENTS

Conference: Summit.
Mailing Address: 2911 Centenary Blvd, Shreveport, LA 71134. **Website:** www.gocentenary.com.
Head Coach: Ed McCann. **Assistant Coaches:** Mike Diaz, Jason Stephens. **Telephone:** (318) 869-5298. **Baseball SID:** Allison McClain. **Telephone:** (318) 869-5092. **Fax:** (318) 869-5128.

CENTRAL ARKANSAS BEARS

Conference: Southland.
Mailing Address: 2401 College Ave, Conway, AR 72034. **Website:** www.ucasports.com.
Head Coach: Doug Clark. **Assistant Coaches:** *Ronnie Goodwin, Wes Johnson. **Telephone:** (501) 450-3407. **Baseball SID:** Steve East. **Telephone:** (501) 450-5743. **Fax:** (501) 450-5740.
Home Field: Bear Field. **Seating Capacity:** 1,500. **Outfield Dimensions:** LF—320, CF—400, RF—320. **Press Box Telephone:** (501) 450-5972.

CENTRAL CONNECTICUT STATE BLUE DEVILS

Conference: Northeast.
Mailing Address: 16151 Stanley St, New Britain, CT 06050. **Website:** ccsubluedevils.com.
Head Coach: Charlie Hickey. **Assistant Coaches:** Pat Hall, *Paul LaBella, Jim Ziogas. **Telephone:** (860) 832-3074. **Baseball SID:** Tom Pincince. **Telephone:** (860) 832-3089. **Fax:** (860) 832-3754.

CENTRAL FLORIDA KNIGHTS

Conference: Conference USA.
Mailing Address: PO Box 163555, Orlando, FL 32816. **Website:** ucfathletics.com.
Head Coach: Terry Rooney. **Assistant Coaches:** *Cliff Godwin, Jeff Palumbo. **Telephone:** (407) 823-0140. **Baseball SID:** Brian Ormiston. **Telephone:** (407) 823-2409. **Fax:** (407) 823-5293.
Home Field: Jay Bergman Field. **Seating Capacity:** 2,230. **Outfield Dimensions:** LF—320, CF—390, RF—320. **Press Box Telephone:** (407) 823-4487.

CENTRAL MICHIGAN CHIPPEWAS

Conference: Mid-American (West).
Mailing Address: Suite 120 Rose Center, Mt. Pleasant, MI 48859. **Website:** www.cmuchippewas.com.
Head Coach: Steve Jaksa. **Assistant Coach:** *Jeff Opalewski. **Telephone:** (989) 774-4392. **Baseball SID:** Mike Boseak. **Telephone:** (989) 774-3277. **Fax:** (989) 774-5391.
Home Field: Theunissen Stadium. **Seating Capacity:** 2,046. **Outfield Dimensions:** LF—330, CF—400, RF—330. **Press Box Telephone:** (989) 774-3594.

COLLEGE OF CHARLESTON COUGARS

Conference: Southern.
Mailing Address: 66 George St, Charleston, SC 29424. **Website:** www.cofcsports.com.
Head Coach: Monte Lee. **Assistant Coaches:** Chris Morris, *Dan Roszel, Brent Walsh. **Telephone:** (843) 953-5556. **Baseball SID:** Tony Ciuffo. **Telephone:** (843) 953-5465. **Fax:** (843) 953-6534.
Home Field: Patriots Point Field. **Seating Capacity:** 2,000. **Outfield Dimensions:** LF—300, CF—400, RF—320. **Press Box Telephone:** (843) 953-9141.

CHARLESTON SOUTHERN BUCCANEERS

Conference: Big South.
Mailing Address: PO Box 118087, Charleston, SC 29423-8087. **Website:** csusports.com.
Head Coach: Stuart Lake. **Assistant Coaches:** *Charles Assey, Sid Fallaw. **Telephone:** (843) 863-7591. **Baseball SID:** Cedrique Flemming. **Telephone:** (843) 863-7688. **Fax:** (843) 863-7676.
Home Field: Buccaneer Ballpark. **Seating Capacity:** 1,500. **Outfield Dimensions:** LF—330, CF—400, RF—330. **Press Box Telephone:** (843) 863-7764.

CHARLOTTE 49ERS

Conference: Atlantic 10.
Mailing Address: Wachovia Fieldhouse, 9201 University City Blvd, Charlotte, NC 28223. **Website:** www.charlotte49ers.com.
Head Coach: Loren Hibbs. **Assistant Coaches:** *Brandon Hall, Brett Hall, Kris Rochelle. **Telephone:** (704) 687-3935. **Baseball SID:** Ryan Rose. **Telephone:** (704) 687-6312. **Fax:** (704) 687-4918.
Home Field: Robert and Mariam Hayes Stadium. **Seating Capacity:** 3,000. **Outfield Dimensions:** LF—335, CF—390, RF—335. **Press Box Telephone:** (704) 687-5959.

CHICAGO STATE COUGARS

Conference: Great West.
Mailing Address: 9501 S. King Drive, JCC 1532, Chicago, IL 60628. **Website:** www.csu.edu/athletics.
Head Coach: Michael Caston. **Assistant Coaches:** Joshua Appelbaum, *Neal Frendling, Matt Haug. **Telephone:** (773) 995-3659. **Baseball SID:** Corey Miggins. **Telephone:** (773) 995-2217. **Fax:** (773) 821-4961.
Home Field: Gwendolyn Brooks Field. **Seating Capacity:** 800. **Outfield Dimensions:** LF—320, CF—400, RF—320.

CINCINNATI BEARCATS

Conference: Big East.
Mailing Address: 2751 O'Varsity Way, Suite 764, Cincinnati, OH 45221. **Website:** gobearcats.com.
Head Coach: Brian Cleary. **Assistant Coaches:** *J.D. Heilmann, Greg Mamula. **Telephone:** (513) 556-0566. **Baseball SID:** John Berry. **Telephone:** (513) 556-0618. **Fax:** (513) 556-0619.
Home Field: Marge Schott Stadium. **Seating Capacity:** 3,085. **Outfield Dimensions:** LF—325, CF—400, RF—325. **Press Box Telephone:** (513) 556-9645.

CITADEL BULLDOGS

Conference: Big South.
Mailing Address: 171 Moultrie St, Charleston, SC 29409. **Website:** www.citadelsports.com.
Head Coach: Fred Jordan. **Assistant Coaches:** *David Beckley, Zach Brown, Randy Carlson. **Telephone:** (843) 953-5901. **Baseball SID:** Ben Waring. **Telephone:** (843) 953-5120. **Fax:** (843) 953-6727.
Home Field: Joseph P. Riley Jr. Park. **Seating Capacity:** 6,000. **Outfield Dimensions:** LF—305, CF—398, RF—337. **Press Box Telephone:** (843) 965-4151.

CLEMSON TIGERS

Conference: Atlantic Coast (Atlantic).
Mailing Address: PO Box 31, Clemson, SC 29633. **Website:** clemsontigers.com.
Head Coach: Jack Leggett. **Assistant Coaches:** Michael Johnson, Dan Pepicelli, *Tom Riginos. **Telephone:** (864) 656-1947. **Baseball SID:** Brian Hennessy. **Telephone:**

(864) 656-1921. **Fax:** (864) 656-0299.
Home Field: Doug Kingsmore Stadium. **Seating Capacity:** 6,217. **Outfield Dimensions:** LF—320, CF—400, RF—330. **Press Box Telephone:** (864) 656-7731.

CLEVELAND STATE VIKINGS

Conference: Horizon.
Mailing Address: 2451 Euclid Ave, Cleveland, OH 44115. **Website:** www.csuvikings.com.
Head Coach: Kevin Kocks. **Assistant Coaches:** Shane Davis, Rob Henry, Drew Saylor. **Telephone:** (216) 687-4822. **Baseball SID:** Renee Adam. **Telephone:** (216) 687-4818. **Fax:** (216) 523-7257.
Home Field: All Pro Freight Stadium. **Seating Capacity:** 5,000. **Outfield Dimensions:** Unavailable.

COASTAL CAROLINA CHANTICLEERS

Conference: Big South.
Mailing Address: 132 Chanticleer Drive W., Conway, SC 29526. **Website:** www.GoCCUSports.com.
Head Coach: Gary Gilmore. **Assistant Coaches:** Brendan Dougherty, *Kevin Schnall, Drew Thomas. **Telephone:** (843) 349-2816. **Baseball SID:** Kent Reichert. **Telephone:** (843) 349-2840. **Fax:** (843) 349-2819.
Home Field: Charles Watson Stadium/Vrooman Field. **Seating Capacity:** 2,000. **Outfield Dimensions:** LF—320, CF—390, RF—325. **Press Box Telephone:** (843) 421-8244.

COLUMBIA LIONS

Conference: Ivy League (Gehrig).
Mailing Address: 3030 Broadway, Mail Code 1901, New York, NY 10027. **Website:** www.gocolumbialions.com.
Head Coach: Brett Boretti. **Assistant Coaches:** *Pete Maki, Jay Quinn, Jim Walsh. **Telephone:** (212) 854-8448. **Baseball SID:** Pete McHugh. **Telephone:** (212) 854-7064. **Fax:** (212) 854-8168.
Home Field: Robertson Field. **Seating Capacity:** 300. **Outfield Dimensions:** LF—330, CF—350, RF—325. **Press Box Telephone:** (917) 678-3621.

CONNECTICUT HUSKIES

Conference: Big East.
Mailing Address: 2095 Hillside Rd, Unit 1173, Storrs, CT 06269. **Website:** www.UConnHuskies.com.
Head Coach: Jim Penders. **Assistant Coaches:** *Justin Blood, Steven Malinowski, Chris Podeszwa. **Telephone:** (860) 486-4089. **Baseball SID:** Kristen Altieri. **Telephone:** (860) 486-3531. **Fax:** (860) 486-5085.
Home Field: J.O. Christian Field. **Seating Capacity:** Unavailable. **Outfield Dimensions:** LF—337, CF—400, RF—325.

COPPIN STATE

Conference: Mid-Eastern Athletic.
Mailing Address: 2500 W. North Ave, Baltimore, MD 21216. **Website:** www.coppinstatesports.com.
Head Coach: Mike Scolinos. **Assistant Coaches:** Eric Franc, *Brian Magnani. **Telephone:** (410) 951-3723. **Baseball SID:** Roger McAfee. **Telephone:** (410) 951-3729. **Fax:** (410) 951-3717.
Home Field: Joe Cannon Stadium. **Seating Capacity:** 2,000. **Outfield Dimensions:** Unavailable.

CORNELL BIG RED

Conference: Ivy League (Rolfe).
Mailing Address: Cornell Baseball, Teagle Hall, Campus Rd, Ithaca, NY 14853. **Website:** cornellbigred.com.

Head Coach: Bill Walkenbach. **Assistant Coaches:** Tom Ford, *Scott Marsh. **Telephone:** (607) 255-3812. **Baseball SID:** Kevin Zeis. **Telephone:** (607) 255-5627. **Fax:** (607) 255-9791.
Home Field: Hoy Field. **Seating Capacity:** 500. **Outfield Dimensions:** LF—315, CF—400, RF—325. **Press Box Telephone:** (603) 748-1268.

CREIGHTON BLUEJAYS

Conference: Missouri Valley.
Mailing Address: 2500 California Ave, Omaha, NE 68178. **Website:** www.gocreighton.com.
Head Coach: Ed Servais. **Assistant Coaches:** Brent Alwine, *Rob Smith, Brandon Tormoehlen. **Telephone:** (402) 280-2483. **Baseball SID:** Matt Marek. **Telephone:** (402) 280-5801. **Fax:** (402) 280-2459.
Home Field: Creighton Sports Complex. **Seating Capacity:** 1,000. **Outfield Dimensions:** LF—330, CF—400, RF—330. **Press Box Telephone:** (402) 280-1676.

DALLAS BAPTIST PATRIOTS

Conference: Independent.
Mailing Address: 3000 Mt. Creek Parkway, Dallas, TX 75211. **Website:** www.dbu.edu/athletics.
Head Coach: Dan Heefner. **Assistant Coaches:** *Nate Frieling, Brad Welker, Travis Wyckoff. **Telephone:** (214) 333-5327. **Baseball SID:** Tyler Knox. **Telephone:** (214) 333-5346. **Fax:** (214) 333-5306.
Home Field: Patriot Field. **Seating Capacity:** 1,500. **Outfield Dimensions:** LF—330, CF—400, RF—330. **Press Box Telephone:** (214) 333-5542.

DARTMOUTH BIG GREEN

Conference: Ivy League (Rolfe).
Mailing Address: 6083 Alumni Gym, Hanover, NH 03755. **Website:** dartmouthsports.com.
Head Coach: Bob Whalen. **Assistant Coaches:** Jonathan Anderson, Tom Carlson, *Nicholas Enriquez. **Telephone:** (603) 646-2477. **Baseball SID:** Rick Bender. **Telephone:** (603) 646-1030. **Fax:** (603) 646-1286.
Home Field: Rolfe Field at Biondi Park. **Seating Capacity:** 2,000. **Outfield Dimensions:** LF—325, CF—402, RF—340. **Press Box Telephone:** (603) 646-6937.

DAVIDSON WILDCATS

Conference: Southern.
Mailing Address: Box 7158, Davidson, NC 28035. **Website:** www.davidsonwildcats.com.
Head Coach: Dick Cooke. **Assistant Coaches:** Toby Bicknell, Tod Gross, *Mike Zandler. **Telephone:** (704) 894-2368. **Baseball SID:** Lauren Biggers. **Telephone:** (704) 894-2815. **Fax:** (704) 894-2636.
Home Field: Wilson Field. **Seating Capacity:** 700. **Outfield Dimensions:** LF—320, CF—385, RF—325. **Press Box Telephone:** (704) 894-2740.

DAYTON FLYERS

Conference: Atlantic 10.
Mailing Address: 300 College Park, Dayton, OH 45469. **Website:** daytonflyers.com.
Head Coach: Tony Vittorio. **Assistant Coaches:** Terry Bell, Brian Harrison, Todd Linklater. **Telephone:** (937) 229-4456. **Baseball SID:** Seth Illiames. **Telephone:** (937) 229-4419. **Fax:** (937) 229-4461.
Home Field: Time Warner Cable Stadium. **Seating Capacity:** 1,500. **Outfield Dimensions:** LF—325, CF—400, RF—325.

DELAWARE FIGHTIN' BLUE HENS

Conference: Colonial Athletic.
Mailing Address: 629 South College Ave, Newark, DE 19716. **Website:** www.bluehens.com.
Head Coach: Jim Sherman. **Assistant Coaches:** Mel Bacon, *Dan Hammer, Brian Walker. **Telephone:** (302) 831-8596. **Baseball SID:** Kenny Kline. **Telephone:** (302) 831-2186. **Fax:** (302) 831-8653.
Home Field: Bob Hannah Stadium. **Seating Capacity:** 1,300. **Outfield Dimensions:** LF—330, CF—400, RF—330. **Press Box Telephone:** (302) 831-4122.

DELAWARE STATE HORNETS

Conference: Mid-Eastern Athletic.
Mailing Address: 1200 N. Dupont Hwy, Dover, DE 19901. **Website:** www.dsuhornets.com.
Head Coach: J.P. Blandin. **Assistant Coach:** Michael August, Scott Shockley, Russ Steinhorn. **Telephone:** (302) 857-6035. **Baseball SID:** Dennis Jones. **Telephone:** (302) 857-6068. **Fax:** (302) 857-6069.

DUKE BLUE DEVILS

Conference: Atlantic Coast (Coastal).
Mailing Address: 118 Cameron Indoor Stadium, Durham, NC 27708. **Website:** www.goduke.com.
Head Coach: Sean McNally. **Assistant Coaches:** *Matthew Boggs, Rhett Parrott, Sean Snedeker. **Telephone:** (919) 668-0255. **Baseball SID:** Chris Cook. **Telephone:** (919) 684-8708. **Fax:** (919) 684-2489.
Home Field: Durham Bulls Athletic Park. **Seating Capacity:** 10,000. **Outfield Dimensions:** LF—330, CF—400, RF—330. **Press Box Telephone:** (919) 812-7141.

DUQUESNE DUKES

Conference: Atlantic 10.
Mailing Address: 600 Forbes Ave, Pittsburgh, PA 15282. **Website:** www.goduquesne.com.
Head Coach: Mike Wilson. **Assistant Coaches:** Ryan Juran, Jeff Minick, T.P. Waligora. **Telephone:** (412) 396-5245. **Baseball SID:** George Nieman. **Telephone:** (412) 396-5376. **Fax:** (412) 396-6210.
Home Field: Duquesne Field. **Seating Capacity:** 1,500. **Outfield Dimensions:** LF—330, CF—390, RF—330.

EAST CAROLINA PIRATES

Conference: Conference USA.
Mailing Address: 102 Clark-LeClair Stadium, Greenville, NC 27858. **Website:** www.ecupirates.com.
Head Coach: Billy Godwin. **Assistant Coaches:** Bill Jarman, *Nick Schnabel, Jeff Stevens. **Telephone:** (252) 737-1985. **Baseball SID:** Malcolm Gray. **Telephone:** (252) 737-4523. **Fax:** (252) 737-4528.
Home Field: Clark-LeClair Stadium. **Seating Capacity:** 5,000. **Outfield Dimensions:** LF—320, CF—400, RF—320. **Press Box Telephone:** (252) 328-0068.

EAST TENNESSEE STATE BUCCANEERS

Conference: Atlantic Sun.
Mailing Address: PO Box 70707, Johnson City, TN 37604. **Website:** www.etsubucs.com.
Head Coach: Tony Skole. **Assistant Coaches:** Reid Casey, *Clay Greene. **Telephone:** (423) 439-4496. **Baseball SID:** Jeff Schneider. **Telephone:** (423) 439-5612. **Fax:** (423) 439-6138.
Home Field: Cardinal Park. **Seating Capacity:** 2,000. **Outfield Dimensions:** LF—325, CF—430, RF—320. **Press Box Telephone:** (423) 741-5297.

EASTERN ILLINOIS PANTHERS

Conference: Ohio Valley.
Mailing Address: 600 Lincoln Avenue, Charleston, IL 61920. **Website:** www.EIUpanthers.com.
Head Coach: Jim Schmitz. **Assistant Coaches:** James Conrad, *Skylar Meade. **Telephone:** (217) 581-2522. **Baseball SID:** Ben Turner. **Telephone:** (217) 581-7020. **Fax:** (217) 581-6434.
Home Field: Coaches Stadium. **Seating Capacity:** 550. **Outfield Dimensions:** LF—340, CF—380, RF—340. **Press Box Telephone:** (217) 581-8464.

EASTERN KENTUCKY COLONELS

Conference: Ohio Valley.
Mailing Address: 521 Lancaster Ave, Richmond, KY 40475. **Website:** www.ekusports.com.
Head Coach: Jason Stein. **Assistant Coaches:** *Jerry Edwards, Shawn Thompson, Todd Weaver. **Telephone:** (859) 622-2128. **Baseball SID:** Steve Fohl. **Telephone:** (859) 622-1253. **Fax:** (859) 622-5108.
Home Field: Turkey Hughes. **Seating Capacity:** 1,000. **Outfield Dimensions:** LF—340, CF—415, RF—330. **Press Box Telephone:** (859)622-2128.

EASTERN MICHIGAN EAGLES

Conference: Mid-American (West).
Mailing Address: 200 Bowen Field House, Ypsilanti, MI 48197. **Website:** www.emueagles.com.
Head Coach: Jay Alexander. **Assistant Coaches:** Aaron Hepner, *Andrew Maki, Dan O'Brien. **Telephone:** (734) 487-0315. **Baseball SID:** Dan Wyar. **Telephone:** (734) 487-0317. **Fax:** (734) 485-3840.
Home Field: Oestrike Stadium. **Seating Capacity:** 1,200. **Outfield Dimensions:** LF—330, CF—390, RF—330. **Press Box Telephone:** (734) 481-9328.

ELON PHOENIX

Conference: Southern.
Mailing Address: 2500 Campus Box, Elon, NC 27244. **Website:** www.elonphoenix.com.
Head Coach: Mike Kennedy. **Assistant Coaches:** Nick Brannon, Robbie Huffstetler, *Greg Starbuck. **Telephone:** (336) 278-6741. **Baseball SID:** Chris Rash. **Telephone:** (336) 278-6712. **Fax:** (336) 278-6768.
Home Field: Latham Park. **Seating Capacity:** 2,000. **Outfield Dimensions:** LF—317, CF—385, RF—327. **Press Box Telephone:** (336) 278-6788.

EVANSVILLE PURPLE ACES

Conference: Missouri Valley.
Mailing Address: 1800 Lincoln Ave, Evansville, IN 47722. **Website:** www.gopurpleaces.com.
Head Coach: Wes Carroll. **Assistant Coaches:** Mike Gilner, Josh Reynolds, *Marc Wagner. **Telephone:** (812) 488-2059. **Baseball SID:** Tom Benson. **Telephone:** (812) 488-1152. **Fax:** (812) 488-2090.
Home Field: Charles H. Braun Stadium. **Seating Capacity:** 1,200. **Outfield Dimensions:** LF—330, CF—400, RF—330. **Press Box Telephone:** (812) 479-2587.

FAIRFIELD STAGS

Conference: Metro Atlantic.
Mailing Address: 1073 North Benson Rd, Fairfield, CT 06824. **Website:** www.fairfieldstags.com.
Head Coach: John Slosar. **Assistant Coaches:** Adam Taraska, Dennis Whalen. **Telephone:** (203) 254-4000, ext. 2605. **Baseball SID:** Kelly McCarthy. **Telephone:** (203) 254-4000 ext. 2877. **Fax:** (203) 254-4117.
Home Field: Alumni Baseball Diamond. **Seating**

Capacity: Unavailable. Outfield Dimensions: LF—330, CF—400, RF—330.

FAIRLEIGH DICKINSON KNIGHTS

Conference: Northeast.
Mailing Address: 1000 River Rd, Teaneck, NJ 07666. Website: fduknights.com.
Head Coach: Jerry Defabbia. Assistant Coaches: *Todd Leathers, Alan Sandberg. Telephone: (201) 692-2245. Baseball SID: Sara Naggar. Telephone: (201) 692-2208. Fax: (201) 692-9361.

FLORIDA GATORS

Conference: Southeastern.
Mailing Address: University Athletic Association, PO Box 14485; Gainesville, FL 32604. Website: www.GatorZone.com.
Head Coach: Kevin O'Sullivan. Assistant Coaches: Craig Bell, Don Norris, Brad Weitzel. Telephone: (352) 375-4683, ext. 4457. Baseball SID: John Hines. Telephone: (352) 375-4683, ext. 6130. Fax: (352) 375-4809.
Home Field: Alfred A. McKethan Stadium at Perry Field. Seating Capacity: 5,500. Outfield Dimensions: LF—329, CF—400, RF—325. Press Box Telephone: (352) 375-4683.

FLORIDA A&M RATTLERS

Conference: Mid-Eastern Athletic.
Mailing Address: 1835 Wahnish Way, Tallahassee, FL 32307. Website: famurattlersports.com.
Head Coach: Robert Lucas. Assistant Coaches: Brett Richardson, Kentaus Carter. Telephone: (850) 599-3202. Baseball SID: Ronnie Johnson. Telephone: (850) 599-3736. Fax: (850) 599-3206.

FLORIDA ATLANTIC OWLS

Conference: Sun Belt.
Mailing Address: 777 Glades Rd, Boca Raton, FL 33431. Website: www.fausports.com.
Head Coach: John McCormack. Assistant Coaches: Brad Frick, *Jason Jackson, Ben Sanderson. Telephone: (561) 297-1055. Baseball SID: Jered Smith. Telephone: (561) 756-0653. Fax: (561) 297-0142.
Home Field: FAU Stadium. Seating Capacity: 2,500. Outfield Dimensions: LF—330, CF—400, RF—330. Press Box Telephone: (561) 297-3455.

FLORIDA GULF COAST EAGLES

Conference: Atlantic Sun.
Mailing Address: 10501 FGCU Blvd, South Fort Myers, FL 33965. Website: www.fgcuathletics.com.
Head Coach: Dave Tollett. Assistant Coaches: Paul Fibbe, Forrest Martin, *Rusty McKee. Telephone: (239) 590-7051. Baseball SID: Chris Perry. Telephone: (239) 590-7012. Fax: (239) 590-7014.
Home Field: Swanson Stadium. Seating Capacity: 1,800. Outfield Dimensions: LF—330, CF—400, RF—330. Press Box Telephone: (239) 590-7012.

FLORIDA INTERNATIONAL GOLDEN PANTHERS

Conference: Sun Belt.
Mailing Address: 11200 SW 8th St, Miami, FL 33199. Website: www.fiusports.com.
Head Coach: Turtle Thomas. Assistant Coaches: *Sean Allen, Frank Damas, Jose Gutierrez. Telephone: (305) 348-3166. Baseball SID: Mat Ratner. Telephone: (305) 348-1496. Fax: (305) 348-2963.
Home Field: FIU Stadium. Seating Capacity: 2,000. Outfield Dimensions: LF—325, CF—400, RF—325. Press Box Telephone: (561) 441-8057.

FLORIDA STATE SEMINOLES

Conference: Atlantic Coast (Atlantic).
Mailing Address: 403 Stadium Drive West, Room D0107, Tallahassee, FL 32306. Website: www.seminoles.com.
Head Coach: Mike Martin. Assistant Coaches: Brian Hoop, Mike Martin Jr., *Jamey Shouppe. Telephone: (850) 644-1073. Baseball SID: Jason Leturmy. Telephone: (850) 644-5656. Fax: (850) 644-3820.
Home Field: Dick Howser Stadium. Seating Capacity: 6,700. Outfield Dimensions: LF—340, CF—400, RF—320. Press Box Telephone: (850) 644-1553.

FORDHAM RAMS

Conference: Atlantic 10.
Mailing Address: 441 E. Fordham Rd, Bronx, NY 10458. Website: www.fordhamsports.com.
Head Coach: Nick Restaino. Assistant Coaches: Trevor Brown, Andrew Lang, Mark Stevens. Telephone: (718) 817-4292. Baseball SID: Unavailable. Telephone: (718) 817-4243. Fax: (718) 817-4244.
Home Field: Houlihan Park at Jack Coffey Field. Seating Capacity: 1,000. Outfield Dimensions: LF—330, CF—400, RF—330. Press Box Telephone: (718) 817-0773.

FRESNO STATE BULLDOGS

Conference: Western Athletic.
Mailing Address: 1510 E. Shaw Ave, Suite 103, Fresno, CA 93710. Website: gobulldogs.com.
Head Coach: Mike Batesole. Assistant Coaches: *Matt Curtis, Pat Waer. Telephone: (559) 278-2178. Baseball SID: Theresa Kurtz. Telephone: (559) 244-5619. Fax: (559) 244-6032.
Home Field: Beiden Field. Seating Capacity: 3,575. Outfield Dimensions: LF—330, CF—400, RF—330. Press Box Telephone: (559) 278-7678.

FURMAN PALADINS

Conference: Southern.
Mailing Address: 3300 Poinsett Highway, Greenville, SC 29613. Website: furmanpaladins.com.
Head Coach: Ron Smith. Assistant Coaches: Britt Rheames, Jeff Whitfield. Telephone: (864) 294-2146. Baseball SID: Hunter Reid. Telephone: (864) 294-2061. Fax: (864) 294-3061.

GARDNER-WEBB RUNNING BULLDOGS

Conference: Atlantic Sun.
Mailing Address: PO Box 877, Boiling Springs, NC 28017. Website: www.gwusports.com.
Head Coach: Rusty Stroupe. Assistant Coaches: Jason Burke, *Kent Cox, Michael Lewis. Telephone: (704) 406-4421. Baseball SID: Marc Rabb. Telephone: (704) 406-4355. Fax: (704) 406-4739.

GEORGE MASON PATRIOTS

Conference: Colonial Athletic.
Mailing Address: 4400 University Dr, Fairfax, VA 22030. Website: gomason.com.
Head Coach: Bill Brown. Assistant Coaches: *Steve Hay, Robbie Jacobsen, Kyle Werman. Telephone: (703) 993-3282. Baseball SID: Richard Coco. Telephone: (703) 993-3264. Fax: (703) 993-3259.
Home Field: Hap Spuhler Field. Seating Capacity: 900. Outfield Dimensions: LF—320, CF—400, RF—320.

GEORGE WASHINGTON COLONIALS

Conference: Atlantic 10.
Mailing Address: 600 22nd Street NW, Washington, DC 20052. **Website:** gwsports.cstv.com.
Head Coach: Steve Mrowka. **Assistant Coaches:** Tim Brown, *Pat O'Brien. **Telephone:** (202) 994-7399. **Baseball SID:** Simon Ogus. **Telephone:** (202) 994-0339.

GEORGETOWN HOYAS

Conference: Big East.
Mailing Address: McDonough Arena, 37th & O Streets, Washington DC 20057. **Website:** guhoyas.com.
Head Coach: Pete Wilk. **Assistant Coaches:** J.J. Brock, *Curtis Brown, Matt Kirby. **Telephone:** (202) 687-2462. **Baseball SID:** Drew Wiseman. **Telephone:** (202) 687-6591. **Fax:** (202) 687-2491.
Home Field: Shirley Povich Field. **Seating Capacity:** 1,500. **Outfield Dimensions:** LF—330, CF—375, RF—330. **Press Box Telephone:** (267) 304-2440.

GEORGIA BULLDOGS

Conference: Southeastern (East).
Mailing Address: One Selig Circle, Athens, GA 30602. **Website:** www.georgiadogs.com.
Head Coach: David Perno. **Assistant Coaches:** *Jason Eller, Justin Holmes, Brady Wiederhold. **Telephone:** (706) 542-7971. **Baseball SID:** Christopher Lakos. **Telephone:** (706) 542-1621. **Fax:** (706) 542-7993.
Home Field: Foley Field. **Seating Capacity:** 3,291. **Outfield Dimensions:** LF—350, CF—404, RF—314. **Press Box Telephone:** (706) 542-6161.

GEORGIA SOUTHERN EAGLES

Conference: Southern.
Mailing Address: PO Box 8095, Statesboro GA 30460. **Website:** www.georgiasoutherneagles.com.
Head Coach: Rodney Hennon. **Assistant Coaches:** Dennis Dove, B.J. Green, *Mike Tidick. **Telephone:** (912) 478-7360. **Baseball SID:** Rose Carter. **Telephone:** (912) 478-0352. **Fax:** (912) 478-1063.
Home Field: JI Clements Stadium. **Seating Capacity:** 3,000. **Outfield Dimensions:** LF—325, CF—385, RF—325. **Press Box Telephone:** (912) 478-5764.

GEORGIA STATE PANTHERS

Conference: Colonial Athletic.
Mailing Address: 125 Decatur St, Suite 201, Atlanta, GA 30329. **Website:** www.georgiastatesports.com.
Head Coach: Greg Frady. **Assistant Coaches:** Nick Hogan, Blaine McFerrin, *Brad Stromdahl. **Telephone:** (404) 413-4077. **Baseball SID:** Mike Holmes. **Telephone:** (404) 413-4033. **Fax:** (404) 413-4035.
Home Field: The Field at Panthersville. **Seating Capacity:** 1,000. **Outfield Dimensions:** LF—334, CF—385, RF—338. **Press Box Telephone:** (404) 241-9850.

GEORGIA TECH YELLOW JACKETS

Conference: Atlantic Coast (Coastal).
Mailing Address: 150 Bobby Dodd Way, Atlanta, GA 30332. **Website:** www.ramblinwreck.com.
Head Coach: Danny Hall. **Assistant Coaches:** Tom Kinkelaar, *Bryan Prince, Matt White. **Telephone:** (404) 894-5471. **Baseball SID:** Mike Huff. **Telephone:** (404) 385-2959. **Fax:** (404) 894-1248.
Home Field: Russ Chandler Stadium. **Seating Capacity:** 4,157. **Outfield Dimensions:** LF—328, CF—400, RF—334. **Press Box Telephone:** (404) 894-3167.

GONZAGA BULLDOGS

Conference: West Coast.
Mailing Address: 502 E. Boone Ave, Spokane, WA 99258. **Website:** gozags.com.
Head Coach: Mark Machtolf. **Assistant Coaches:** Bobby Carlson, *Danny Evans, Steve Bennett. **Telephone:** (509) 313-4227. **Baseball SID:** Bobby Alworth. **Telephone:** (509) 313-4227. **Fax:** (509) 313-5730.
Home Field: Patterson Baseball Complex and Washington Trust Field. **Seating Capacity:** 1,500. **Outfield Dimensions:** LF—328, CF—398, RF—328. **Press Box Telephone:** (509) 279-1005.

GRAMBLING STATE TIGERS

Conference: Southwestern Athletic.
Mailing Address: PO Box 868, Grambling, LA 71245. **Website:** www.gsutigers.com.
Head Coach: James Cooper. **Assistant Coach:** Scott Joshua. **Telephone:** (318) 274-6204. **Baseball SID:** Roderick Mosley. **Telephone:** (318) 274-6562.

HARTFORD HAWKS

Conference: America East.
Mailing Address: Sports Center, 200 Bloomfield Ave, West Hartford, CT 06117. **Website:** www.hartfordhawks.com.
Head Coach: Jeff Calcaterra. **Assistant Coaches:** Inaki Ormaechea, *Jerry Shank, Brian Stasaitis. **Telephone:** (860) 768-5760. **Baseball SID:** Sam Angell. **Telephone:** (860) 768-4620. **Fax:** (860) 768-4068.
Home Field: Fiondella Field. **Seating Capacity:** 1,500. **Outfield Dimensions:** LF—325, CF—400, RF—325.

HARVARD CRIMSON

Conference: Ivy League (Rolfe).
Mailing Address: 65 North Harvard St, Boston, MA 02163. **Website:** www.gocrimson.com.
Head Coach: Joe Walsh. **Assistant Coaches:** Kristaps Aldins, Aaron Landes, *Tom Lo Ricco. **Telephone:** (617) 495-2629. **Baseball SID:** Kurt Svoboda. **Telephone:** (617) 495-2206. **Fax:** (617) 495-2130.

HAWAII RAINBOWS

Conference: Western Athletic.
Mailing Address: 1337 Lower Campus Rd, Honolulu, HI 96822. **Website:** hawaiiathletics.com.
Head Coach: Mike Trapasso. **Assistant Coaches:** Keith Komeiji, *Chad Konishi. **Telephone:** (808) 956-6247. **Baseball SID:** Pakalani Bello. **Telephone:** (808) 956-7506. **Fax:** (808) 956-4470.
Home Field: Les Murakami Stadium. **Seating Capacity:** 4,312. **Outfield Dimensions:** LF—325, CF—385, RF—325. **Press Box Telephone:** (808) 956-6253.

HIGH POINT PANTHERS

Conference: Big South.
Mailing Address: 833 Montlieu Ave, High Point, NC 27262. **Website:** highpointpanthers.com.
Head Coach: Craig Cozart. **Assistant Coaches:** Daniel Latham, *Bryan Peters, Rich Wallace. **Telephone:** (336) 841-9190. **Baseball SID:** Erika Carrubba. **Telephone:** (336) 841-4640. **Fax:** (336) 841-9182.
Home Field: Coy O. Williard Baseball Stadium. **Seating Capacity:** 550. **Outfield Dimensions:** LF—350, CF—400, RF—330. **Press Box Telephone:** (336) 841-3077.

HOFSTRA PRIDE

Conference: Colonial Athletic.
Mailing Address: 228 PFC, 230 Hofstra University, Hempstead, NY 11549. **Website:** www.gohofstra.com.
Head Coach: Patrick Anderson. **Assistant Coaches:** Kelly Haynes, James Lally, *John Russo. **Telephone:** (516) 463-5065. **Baseball SID:** Len Skoros. **Telephone:** (516) 463-4602. **Fax:** (516) 463-5033.
Home Field: University Field. **Seating Capacity:** 500. **Outfield Dimensions:** LF—331, CF—380, RF—340.

HOLY CROSS CRUSADERS

Conference: Patriot.
Mailing Address: One College Street, Worcester, MA 01610. **Website:** goholycross.com.
Head Coach: Greg DiCenzo. **Assistant Coaches:** Kevin Gately, Jeff Kane, *Gabe Ribas. **Telephone:** (508) 793-2753. **Baseball SID:** Meredith Cook. **Telephone:** (508) 793-2780.
Home Field: Fitton Field. **Seating Capacity:** 3,000. **Outfield Dimensions:** LF—332, CF—385, RF—313.

HOUSTON COUGARS

Conference: Conference USA.
Mailing Address: 3100 Cullen Blvd, Houston, TX 77204. **Website:** UHCougars.com.
Head Coach: Rayner Noble. **Assistant Coaches:** Jorge Garza, *Russell Stockton, Travis Tully. **Telephone:** (713) 743-9396. **Baseball SID:** Jamie Zarda. **Telephone:** (713) 743-9406. **Fax:** (713) 743-9411.
Home Field: Cougar Field. **Seating Capacity:** 2,000. **Outfield Dimensions:** LF—330, CF—390, RF—330. **Press Box Telephone:** (713) 743-0840.

HOUSTON BAPTIST HUSKIES

Conference: Great West.
Mailing Address: 7502 Fondren Rd, Houston, TX 77074. **Website:** www.hbuhuskies.com.
Head Coach: Jared Moon. **Assistant Coaches:** Chris Hill, Steve Hughes. **Telephone:** (281) 649-3332. **Baseball SID:** Jeff Sutton. **Telephone:** (281) 649-3098. **Fax:** (281) 649-3496.

ILLINOIS FIGHTING ILLINI

Conference: Big Ten.
Mailing Address: 1700 S. Fourth St, Champaign, IL 61820. **Website:** www.fightingillini.com.
Head Coach: Dan Hartleb. **Assistant Coaches:** *Eric Snider, Jeff Thomas, Ken Westray. **Telephone:** (217) 244-8144. **Baseball SID:** Ben Taylor. **Telephone:** (217) 244-5045. **Fax:** (217) 333-5540.
Home Field: Illinois Field. **Seating Capacity:** 1,500. **Outfield Dimensions:** LF—330, CF—400, RF—330. **Press Box Telephone:** (217) 333-1227.

ILLINOIS STATE REDBIRDS

Conference: Missouri Valley.
Mailing Address: Illinois State Athletic Media Relations, 202 Horton Field House, Normal, IL 61671. **Website:** GoRedbirds.com.
Head Coach: Mark Kingston. **Assistant Coaches:** Mike Current, *Bo Durkac, Billy Mohl. **Telephone:** (309) 438-5709. **Baseball SID:** Kevin McCarty. **Telephone:** (309) 428-3249. **Fax:** (309) 438-5634.
Home Field: Duffy Bass Field. **Seating Capacity:** 2,000. **Outfield Dimensions:** LF—330, CF—400, RF—330.

ILLINOIS-CHICAGO FLAMES

Conference: Horizon.
Mailing Address: 839 W. Roosevelt Rd, MC 195, Chicago, IL 60608. **Website:** uicflames.cstv.com.
Head Coach: Mike Dee. **Assistant Coaches:** John Flood, *Mike Nall, Sean McDermott. **Telephone:** (312) 996-8645. **Baseball SID:** John Jaramillo. **Telephone:** (312) 996-5880. **Fax:** (312) 996-8349.
Home Field: Les Miller Field. **Seating Capacity:** 1,000. **Outfield Dimensions:** LF—330, CF—400, RF—330. **Press Box Telephone:** (312) 355-1190.

INDIANA HOOSIERS

Conference: Big Ten.
Mailing Address: 1001 E. 17th St, Bloomington IN 47408. **Website:** iuhoosiers.com.
Head Coach: Tracy Smith. **Assistant Coaches:** Dustin Coffman, Ben Greenspan, *Ty Neal. **Telephone:** (812) 855-1680. **Baseball SID:** Matt Brady. **Telephone:** (812) 856-0215. **Fax:** (812) 855-9401.
Home Field: Sembower Field. **Seating Capacity:** 1,500. **Outfield Dimensions:** LF—330, CF—400, RF—330. **Press Box Telephone:** (812) 855-4787.

INDIANA STATE SYCAMORES

Conference: Missouri Valley.
Mailing Address: 401 N. 4th St, Terre Haute, IN 47809. **Website:** gosycamores.com.
Head Coach: Rick Heller. **Assistant Coaches:** *Tyler Herbst, Max Hutson, Brian Smiley. **Telephone:** (812) 237-4051. **Baseball SID:** Danny Pfrank. **Telephone:** (812) 237-4160. **Fax:** (812) 237-4157.
Home Field: Bob Warn Field. **Seating Capacity:** 2,000. **Outfield Dimensions:** LF—340, CF—410, RF—340. **Press Box Telephone:** (812) 237-4187.

IPFW MASTODONS

Conference: Summit.
Mailing Address: 2101 E. Coliseum Blvd, Fort Wayne, IN 46805. **Website:** gomastodons.com.
Head Coach: Bobby Pierce. **Assistant Coaches:** Grant Birely, *Josh Schultz. **Telephone:** (260) 481-5480. **Baseball SID:** Rudy Yovich. **Telephone:** (260) 481-6646. **Fax:** (260) 481-6002.

IONA GAELS

Conference: Metro Atlantic.
Mailing Address: 715 North Ave, New Rochelle, NY 10801. **Website:** icgaels.com.
Head Coach: Pat Carey. **Assistant Coaches:** Rob DiToma, James LaSala, Chuck Todd. **Telephone:** (914) 633-2319. **Baseball SID:** Brian Beyrer. **Telephone:** (914) 633-2334. **Fax:** (914) 633-2072.
Home Field: Salesian Field. **Seating Capacity:** 450. **Outfield Dimensions:** LF—301, CF—401, RF—320. **Press Box Telephone:** (914) 497-3136.

IOWA HAWKEYES

Conference: Big Ten.
Mailing Address: 232 Carver Hawkeye Arena, Iowa City, IA 52242. **Website:** www.hawkeyesports.com.
Head Coach: Jack Dahm. **Assistant Coaches:** *Ryan Brownlee, Zach Dillon, Chris Maliszewski. **Telephone:** (319) 335-9389. **Baseball SID:** Matt Weitzel. **Telephone:** (319) 335-9411.
Home Field: Duane Banks Field. **Seating Capacity:** 3,000. **Outfield Dimensions:** LF—330, CF—400, RF—330. **Press Box Telephone:** (319) 335-9520.

JACKSON STATE TIGERS

Conference: Southwestern Athletic.
Mailing Address: JSU Box 18060, Jackson, MS 39217-0660. **Website:** www.jsutigers.com.
Head Coach: Omar Johnson. **Assistant Coaches:** Ralph Johnson, Anton Shinhoster, Kevin Whiteside. **Telephone:** (601) 979-3930. **Baseball SID:** Jamea Adams-Ginyard. **Telephone:** (601) 979-2274. **Fax:** (601) 979-2000.
Home Field: Robert "Bob" Braddy Sr. **Field. Seating Capacity:** 800. **Outfield Dimensions:** LF—325, CF—400, RF—325.

JACKSONVILLE DOLPHINS

Conference: Atlantic Sun.
Mailing Address: 2800 University Blvd N., Jacksonville, FL 32211. **Website:** judolphins.com.
Head Coach: Terry Alexander. **Assistant Coaches:** Mike McCallister, *Tim Montez, Tommy Murphy. **Telephone:** (904) 256-7412. **Baseball SID:** Josh Ellis. **Telephone:** (904) 256-7402. **Fax:** (904) 256-7424.
Home Field: John Sessions Stadium. **Seating Capacity:** 3,000. **Outfield Dimensions:** LF—340, CF—405, RF—340. **Press Box Telephone:** (904) 256-7588.

JACKSONVILLE STATE GAMECOCKS

Conference: Ohio Valley.
Mailing Address: 700 Pelham Rd North, Jacksonville, AL 36265. **Website:** www.jsugamecocksports.com.
Head Coach: Jim Case. **Assistant Coaches:** *Steve Gillispie, Travis Janssen, Shayne Kelley. **Telephone:** (256) 782-5367. **Baseball SID:** Greg Seitz. **Telephone:** (256) 782-5279. **Fax:** (256) 782-5958.
Home Field: Rudy Abbott Field. **Seating Capacity:** 1,500. **Outfield Dimensions:** LF—330, CF—400, RF—335. **Press Box Telephone:** (256) 782-5533.

JAMES MADISON DUKES

Conference: Colonial Athletic.
Mailing Address: 395 South High St, MSC 6925, Memorial Hall, Harrisonburg, VA 22807. **Website:** jmusports.com.
Head Coach: Joe McFarland. **Assistant Coaches:** Jason Middleton, *Jay Sullenger, Ted White. **Telephone:** (540) 568-5510. **Baseball SID:** Kevin Warner. **Telephone:** (540) 568-6154. **Fax:** (540) 568-3703.
Home Field: Veterans Memorial Park. **Seating Capacity:** 1,200. **Outfield Dimensions:** LF—340, CF—400, RF—320. **Press Box Telephone:** (540) 568-6545.

KANSAS JAYHAWKS

Conference: Big 12.
Mailing Address: Allen Fieldhouse, 1651 Naismith Dr, Lawrence, KS 66045. **Website:** www.kuathletics.com.
Head Coach: Ritch Price. **Assistant Coaches:** Kevin Frady, Ryan Graves, *John Szefc. **Telephone:** (785) 864-7907. **Baseball SID:** Mike Cummings. **Telephone:** (785) 864-3575. **Fax:** (785) 864-7944.
Home Field: Hoglund Ballpark. **Seating Capacity:** 2,500. **Outfield Dimensions:** LF—330, CF—392, RF—330. **Press Box Telephone:** (785) 864-4037.

KANSAS STATE WILDCATS

Conference: Big 12.
Mailing Address: 1800 College Ave, Manhattan, KS 66502. **Website:** www.kstatesports.com.
Head Coach: Brad Hill. **Assistant Coaches:** Anthony Everman, *Sean McCann, Andy Sawyers. **Telephone:** (785) 532-3926. **Baseball SID:** Ryan Lackey. **Telephone:**
(785) 532-7708. **Fax:** (785) 532-6093.
Home Field: Tointon Family Stadium. **Seating Capacity:** 2,331. **Outfield Dimensions:** LF—340, CF—400, RF—325. **Press Box Telephone:** (785) 532-5801.

KENNESAW STATE OWLS

Conference: Atlantic Sun.
Mailing Address: 1000 Chastain Rd, Kennesaw, GA 30144. **Website:** ksuowls.com.
Head Coach: Mike Sansing. **Assistant Coaches:** Kevin Erminio, D.J. King, *Derrick Tucker. **Telephone:** (770) 423-6264. **Baseball SID:** Jason Hanes. **Telephone:** (678) 797-2562. **Fax:** (770) 423-6555.
Home Field: Stillwell Stadium. **Seating Capacity:** 1,065. **Outfield Dimensions:** LF—331, CF—400, RF—330.

KENT STATE GOLDEN FLASHES

Conference: Mid-American (East).
Mailing Address: 234 MAC Center, Kent, OH 44242. **Website:** www.kentstatesports.com.
Head Coach: Scott Stricklin. **Assistant Coaches:** Mike Birkbeck, *Scott Daeley, Doug Sanders. **Telephone:** (330) 672-8432. **Baseball SID:** Matthew Lofton. **Telephone:** (330) 672-2254. **Fax:** (330) 672-2112.
Home Field: Schoonover Stadium. **Seating Capacity:** 1,148. **Outfield Dimensions:** LF—330, CF—415, RF—320. **Press Box Telephone:** (330) 672-3696.

KENTUCKY WILDCATS

Conference: Southeastern (East).
Mailing Address: Joe Craft Center, 338 Lexington Ave, Lexington, KY 40506. **Website:** www.ukathletics.com.
Head Coach: Gary Henderson. **Assistant Coaches:** *Brad Bohannon, Brian Green, Keith Vorhoff. **Telephone:** (859) 257-8988. **Baseball SID:** Brent Ingram. **Telephone:** (859) 257-3838. **Fax:** (859) 323-4310.
Home Field: Cliff Hagan Stadium. **Seating Capacity:** 3,000. **Outfield Dimensions:** LF—340, CF—390, RF—310. **Press Box Telephone:** (859) 257-9011.

LA SALLE EXPLORERS

Conference: Atlantic 10.
Mailing Address: 1900 West Olney Ave, Box 805, Philadelphia, PA 19141. **Website:** www.goexplorers.com.
Head Coach: *Mike Lake. **Assistant Coaches:** Mike Dertouzos, Toby Fisher. **Telephone:** (215) 951-1995. **Baseball SID:** Marc Mullen. **Telephone:** (215) 951-1633. **Fax:** (215) 951-1694. **Fax:** (215) 951-1694.
Home Field: Hank DeVincent Field. **Seating Capacity:** 1,000. **Outfield Dimensions:** LF—305, CF—458, RF—321.

LAFAYETTE LEOPARDS

Conference: Patriot.
Mailing Address: Kirby Sports Center, Easton, PA 18042. **Website:** www.goleopards.com.
Head Coach: Joe Kinney. **Assistant Coaches:** *Rick Clagett, Gregg Durrah, Brandt Godshalk. **Telephone:** (610) 330-5476. **Baseball SID:** Katie Meier. **Telephone:** (610) 330-5518. **Fax:** (610) 330-5519.
Home Field: Kamine Stadium. **Seating Capacity:** 500. **Outfield Dimensions:** LF—332, CF—403, RF—335.

LAMAR CARDINALS

Conference: Southland.
Mailing Address: PO Box 10066, Beaumont, TX, 77710. **Website:** lamarcardinals.com.

Head Coach: Jim Gilligan. Assistant Coaches: Matt Gore, Scott Hatten, *Jim Ricklefson. Telephone: (409) 880-8315. Baseball SID: Rush Wood. Telephone: (409) 880-7845. Fax: (409) 880-2338.

Home Field: Vincent-Beck Stadium. Seating Capacity: 3,500. Outfield Dimensions: LF—325, CF—380, RF—325. Press Box Telephone: (409) 880-8327.

LE MOYNE DOLPHINS

Conference: Independent.
Mailing Address: 1419 Salt Springs Rd, Syracuse, NY 13214. Website: www.lemoynedolphins.com.
Head Coach: Steve Owens. Assistant Coaches: *Scott Cassidy, Scott Landers, Corey O'Neill. Telephone: (315) 445-4415. Baseball SID: Craig Lane. Telephone: (315) 445-4412. Fax: (315) 445-4678.
Home Field: Dick Rockwell Field. Seating Capacity: 2,500. Outfield Dimensions: LF—314, CF—375, RF—337.

LEHIGH MOUNTAIN HAWKS

Conference: Patriot.
Mailing Address: 641 Taylor St, Bethlehem, PA 18015. Website: www.lehighsports.com.
Head Coach: Sean Leary. Assistant Coaches: John Bisco, Kyle Collina, *Brian Hirschberg. Telephone: (610) 758-4315. Baseball SID: Garrett Falk. Telephone: (610) 758-5101. Fax: (610) 758-4407.
Home Field: Lehigh Field. Seating Capacity: 250. Outfield Dimensions: LF—320, CF—400, RF—320.

LIBERTY FLAMES

Conference: Big South.
Mailing Address: 1971 University Blvd, Lynchburg, VA 24502. Website: www.libertyflames.com.
Head Coach: Jim Toman. Assistant Coaches: *Jason Murray, Garrett Quinn, Adam Ward. Telephone: (434) 582-2103. Baseball SID: Ryan Bomberger. Telephone: (434) 582-2605. Fax: (434) 582-2076.
Home Field: Worthington Stadium. Seating Capacity: 1,000. Outfield Dimensions: LF—325, CF—390, RF—325. Press Box Telephone: (434) 582-2914.

LIPSCOMB BISONS

Conference: Atlantic Sun.
Mailing Address: 1 University Park Dr, Nashville, TN 37204. Website: lipscombsports.com.
Head Coach: Jeff Forehand. Assistant Coaches: *Chris Collins, Tyler Shrout. Telephone: (615) 966-5716. Baseball SID: Trevor Garrett. Telephone: (615) 966-5990. Fax: (615) 966-1806.
Home Field: Dugan Field. Seating Capacity: 1,500. Outfield Dimensions: LF—330, CF—405, RF—330. Press Box Telephone: (615) 479-3794.

LONG BEACH STATE DIRTBAGS

Conference: Big West.
Mailing Address: 1250 Bellflower Blvd, Long Beach, CA 90840. Website: www.longbeachstate.com.
Head Coach: Mike Weathers. Assistant Coaches: T.J. Bruce, Troy Buckley, *Andy Rojo. Telephone: (562) 985-7548. Baseball SID: Roger Kirk. Telephone: (562) 985-8569. Fax: (562) 985-8197.
Home Field: Blair Field. Seating Capacity: 3,200. Outfield Dimensions: LF—348, CF—400, RF—348.

LONG ISLAND BLACKBIRDS

Conference: Northeast.
Mailing Address: 1 University Plaza, Brooklyn, NY 11201. Website: www.liuathletics.com.

Head Coach: Don Maines. Assistant Coaches: *Craig Noto, Dan Pirillo, Chris Reyes. Telephone: (718) 488-1538. Baseball SID: Shawn Sweeney. Telephone: (718) 488-1307. Fax: (718) 488-3302.
Home Field: LIU Field. Seating Capacity: 500. Outfield Dimensions: LF—315, CF—416, RF—315.

LONGWOOD LANCERS

Conference: Independent.
Mailing Address: 201 High St, Farmville, VA 23909. Website: www.longwoodlancers.com.
Head Coach: Buddy Bolding. Assistant Coaches: Brian McCullough, *Brett Mooney, Jonathan Quigley. Telephone: (434) 395-2352. Baseball SID: Greg Prouty. Telephone: (434) 395-2097. Fax: (434) 395-2568.
Home Field: Charles Buddy Bolding Stadium. Seating Capacity: 500. Outfield Dimensions: LF—335, CF—400, RF—335. Press Box Telephone: (434) 395-2710.

LOUISIANA STATE FIGHTING TIGERS

Conference: Southeastern (West).
Mailing Address: PO Box 25095, Baton Rouge, LA 70894. Website: www.LSUsports.net.
Head Coach: Paul Mainieri. Assistant Coaches: Will Davis, *David Grewe, Javi Sanchez. Telephone: (225) 578-4148. Baseball SID: Bill Franques. Telephone: (225) 578-2527. Fax: (225) 578-1861.
Home Field: Alex Box Stadium. Seating Capacity: 9,200. Outfield Dimensions: LF—330, CF—405, RF—330. Press Box Telephone: (225) 578-4149.

LOUISIANA TECH BULLDOGS

Conference: Western Athletic.
Mailing Address: PO Box 3166, Ruston, LA 71272. Website: www.latechsports.com.
Head Coach: Wade Simoneaux. Assistant Coaches: Spud Adams, Fran Andermann, *Brian Rountree. Telephone: (318) 257-5318. Baseball SID: John Sella. Telephone: (318) 257-5071.
Home Field: J.C. Love Field at Pat Patterson Park. Seating Capacity: 3,500. Outfield Dimensions: LF—315, CF—385, RF—325. Press Box Telephone: (318) 257-3144.

LOUISIANA-LAFAYETTE RAGIN' CAJUNS

Conference: Sun Belt.
Mailing Address: 201 Reinhardt Dr, Cox Communications Athletic Complex, Lafayette, LA 70506. Website: www.ragincajuns.com.
Head Coach: Tony Robichaux. Assistant Coaches: Anthony Babineaux, Brooks Badeaux, *Mike Trahan. Telephone: (337) 482-6189. Baseball SID: Matt Hebert. Telephone: (337) 482-6330. Fax: (337) 482-6529.
Home Field: M.L. "Tigue" Moore Field. Seating Capacity: 3,755. Outfield Dimensions: LF—330, CF—400, RF—330. Press Box Telephone: (337) 851-2255.

LOUISIANA-MONROE WARHAWKS

Conference: Sun Belt.
Mailing Address: 308 Warhawk Way, Monroe, LA 71209. Website: www.ulmwarhawks.com.
Head Coach: Jeff Schexnaider. Assistant Coaches: Cory Barton, Jared Harrell, Lantz Wheeler. Telephone: (318) 342-3591. Baseball SID: Adam Prendergast. Telephone: (318) 342-5463.
Home Field: Warhawk Field. Seating Capacity: 1,800. Outfield Dimensions: LF—330, CF—400, RF—330. Press Box Telephone: (318) 342-5476.

LOUISVILLE CARDINALS

Conference: Big East.
Mailing Address: 215 Central Ave, Louisville, KY 40292. **Website:** www.UofLSports.com.
Head Coach: Dan McDonnell. **Assistant Coaches:** Xan Barksdale, *Chris Lemonis, Roger Williams. **Telephone:** (502) 852-0103. **Baseball SID:** Garett Wall. **Telephone:** (502) 852-3088. **Fax:** (502) 852-7401.
Home Field: Jim Patterson Stadium. **Seating Capacity:** 2,500. **Outfield Dimensions:** LF—330, CF—402, RF—330. **Press Box Telephone:** (502) 852-3700.

LOYOLA MARYMOUNT LIONS

Conference: West Coast.
Mailing Address: 1 LMU Drive, Los Angeles, CA 90045. **Website:** lmulions.com.
Head Coach: Jason Gill. **Assistant Coaches:** *Andrew Keehn, Scott Walter, Jeff Walker. **Telephone:** (310) 338-2949. **Baseball SID:** Tyler Geivett. **Telephone:** (310) 338-7638. **Fax:** (310) 338-2703.
Home Field: Page Stadium. **Seating Capacity:** 600. **Outfield Dimensions:** LF—326, CF—413, RF—330. **Press Box Telephone:** (310) 338-3046.

MAINE BLACK BEARS

Conference: America East.
Mailing Address: 5747 Memorial Gym, Orono, ME 04469. **Website:** www.goblackbears.com.
Head Coach: Steve Trimper. **Assistant Coaches:** *Mike Cole, Aaron Izaryk. **Telephone:** (207) 581-1090. **Baseball SID:** Laura Reed. **Telephone:** (207) 581-3646. **Fax:** (207) 581-3297.
Home Field: Mahaney Diamond. **Seating Capacity:** 4,400. **Outfield Dimensions:** LF—330, CF—400, RF—330. **Press Box Telephone:** (207) 581-1049.

MANHATTAN JASPERS

Conference: Metro Atlantic.
Mailing Address: 4513 Manhattan College Pkwy, Riverdale, NY 10471. **Website:** www.gojaspers.com.
Head Coach: Kevin Leighton. **Assistant Coaches:** Ryan Darcy, *Jason Spaulding. **Telephone:** (718) 862-7936. **Baseball SID:** Stephen Dombroski. **Telephone:** (718) 862-7228. **Fax:** (718) 862-8020.
Home Field: Van Cortlandt Park. **Seating Capacity:** 500. **Outfield Dimensions:** LF—320, CF—398, RF—320.

MARIST RED FOXES

Conference: Metro Atlantic.
Mailing Address: 3399 North Road, Poughkeepsie, NY 12601. **Website:** goredfoxes.com.
Head Coach: Chris Tracz. **Assistant Coaches:** John McGorty, Joe Michalski. **Telephone:** (845) 575-3699, ext 2570. **Baseball SID:** Mike Ferraro. **Telephone:** (845) 575-3699, ext 3321.

MARSHALL THUNDERING HERD

Conference: Conference USA.
Mailing Address: 2001 3rd Ave, Huntington, WV 25715. **Website:** herdzone.com.
Head Coach: Jeff Waggoner. **Assistant Coaches:** George Brumfield, Tim Donnelly, *Joe Renner. **Telephone:** (304) 696-5277. **Baseball SID:** Ben Warnick. **Telephone:** (304) 696-4662. **Fax:** (304) 696-2325.
Home Field: Appalachian Power Park. **Seating Capacity:** 4,500. **Outfield Dimensions:** LF—330, CF—400, RF—320.

MARYLAND TERRAPINS

Conference: Atlantic Coast (Atlantic).
Mailing Address: Comcast Center, 1 Terrapin Trail, College Park, MD 20742. **Website:** umterps.com.
Head Coach: Erik Bakich. **Assistant Coaches:** *Dan Burton, Sean Kenny, Nolan Neiman. **Telephone:** (301) 314-1845. **Baseball SID:** Justin Moore. **Telephone:** (301) 314-7068. **Fax:** (301) 314-9094.
Home Field: Shipley Field. **Seating Capacity:** 2,500. **Outfield Dimensions:** LF—320, CF—380, RF—325. **Press Box Telephone:** (301) 314-0379.

MARYLAND-BALTIMORE COUNTY RETRIEVERS

Conference: America East.
Mailing Address: 1000 Hilltop Circle, Baltimore, MD 21250. **Website:** www.umbcretrievers.com.
Head Coach: John Jancuska. **Assistant Coaches:** Greg Beckman, Kevin Daly, *Bob Mumma. **Telephone:** (410) 455-2239. **Baseball SID:** Tom Fenstermaker. **Telephone:** (410) 455-1530. **Fax:** (410) 455-3994.
Home Field: Baseballfactory Field at UMBC. **Seating Capacity:** 1,000. **Outfield Dimensions:** LF—330, CF—360, RF—340.

MARYLAND-EASTERN SHORE HAWKS

Conference: Mid-Eastern.
Mailing Address: William P. Hytche Athletic Center, One Backbone Rd, Princess Anne, MD 21853. **Website:** umeshawks.com.
Head Coach: Will Gardner. **Assistant Coaches:** Eric Armstrong, Zach Farry. **Telephone:** (410) 651-8158. **Baseball SID:** Tyler Birnbaum. **Telephone:** (410) 651-7888. **Fax:** (410) 651-7514.
Home Field: Hawk Stadium. **Seating Capacity:** 1,000. **Outfield Dimensions:** LF—340, CF—400, RF—340.

MASSACHUSETTS MINUTEMEN

Conference: Atlantic 10.
Mailing Address: 131 Commonwealth Ave, Amherst, MA 01003. **Website:** umassathletics.com.
Head Coach: Mike Stone. **Assistant Coaches:** Ernie May, *Mike Sweeney. **Telephone:** (413) 545-3120. **Baseball SID:** Jillian Jakuba. **Telephone:** (413) 577-0053. **Fax:** (413) 545-1404.
Home Field: Earl Lorden Field. **Seating Capacity:** Unavailable. **Outfield Dimensions:** LF—330, CF—400, RF—330. **Press Box Telephone:** (413) 420-3116.

MCNEESE STATE COWBOYS

Conference: Southland.
Mailing Address: 615 Bienville Street, Lake Charles, LA 70607. **Website:** mcneesesports.com.
Head Coach: Terry Burrows. **Assistant Coaches:** *Bubbs Merrill, Clay Van Hook. **Telephone:** (337) 475-5484. **Baseball SID:** Louis Bonnette. **Telephone:** (337) 475-5207. **Fax:** (337) 475-5202.
Home Field: Cowboy Diamond. **Seating Capacity:** 2,000. **Outfield Dimensions:** LF—330, CF—400, RF—330. **Press Box Telephone:** (337) 475-8007.

MEMPHIS TIGERS

Conference: Conference USA.
Mailing Address: 570 Normal, Memphis, TN 38152. **Website:** www.gotigersgo.com.
Head Coach: Daron Schoenrock. **Assistant Coaches:** Fred Corral, Derrick Dunbar *Jerry Zulli. **Telephone:** (901) 678-2452. **Baseball SID:** Jason Redd. **Telephone:** (901) 734-4640. **Fax:** (901) 678-4131.
Home Field: FedEx Park. **Seating Capacity:** 2,000.

Outfield Dimensions: LF—318, CF—380, RF—317.

MERCER BEARS

Conference: Atlantic Sun.
Mailing Address: 1400 Coleman Ave, Macon, GA 31207. **Website:** www.mercerbears.com.
Head Coach: Craig Gibson. **Assistant Coaches:** Tim Boeth, Jason Miller, *Brent Shade. **Telephone:** (478) 301-2396. **Baseball SID:** Jason Farhadi. **Telephone:** (478) 301-5218. **Fax:** (478) 301-5350.
Home Field: Claude Smith Field. **Seating Capacity:** 500. **Outfield Dimensions:** LF—330, CF—400, RF—320. **Press Box Telephone:** (478) 301-2339.

MIAMI HURRICANES

Conference: Atlantic Coast (Coastal).
Mailing Address: 5821 San Amaro Dr, Coral Gables, FL 33146. **Website:** www.hurricanesports.com.
Head Coach: Jim Morris. **Assistant Coaches:** *J.D. Arteaga, Joe Mercadante, Roger Tomas. **Telephone:** (305) 284-4171. **Baseball SID:** Rob Dunning. **Telephone:** (305) 284-3230. **Fax:** (305) 284-2807.
Home Field: Alex Rodriguez Park at Mark Light Field. **Seating Capacity:** 5,000. **Outfield Dimensions:** LF—330, CF—400, RF—330. **Press Box Telephone:** (305) 284-8192.

MIAMI (OHIO) REDHAWKS

Conference: Mid-American (East).
Mailing Address: 120 Withrow Court, Oxford, OH 45056. **Website:** www.muredhawks.com.
Head Coach: Dan Simonds. **Assistant Coaches:** *Ben Bachmann, Danny Hayden, Jeremy Ison. **Telephone:** (513) 529-6631. **Baseball SID:** Michael Weisman. **Telephone:** (513) 529-1601. **Fax:** (513) 529-6729.
Home Field: McKie Field at Hayden Park. **Seating Capacity:** 1,000. **Outfield Dimensions:** LF—332, CF—400, RF—343. **Press Box Telephone:** (513) 529-4331.

MICHIGAN WOLVERINES

Conference: Big Ten.
Mailing Address: 1000 South State St, Ann Arbor, MI 48109. **Website:** www.mgoblue.com.
Head Coach: Rich Maloney. **Assistant Coaches:** *Matt Husted, Bob Keller, Mike Penn. **Telephone:** (734) 647-4550. **Baseball SID:** Matt Fancett. **Telephone:** (734) 647-1726. **Fax:** (734) 647-1188.
Home Field: Wilpon Complex/Ray Fisher Stadium. **Seating Capacity:** 3,500. **Outfield Dimensions:** LF—312, CF—395, RF—320. **Press Box Telephone:** (734) 647-1283.

MICHIGAN STATE SPARTANS

Conference: Big Ten.
Mailing Address: 304 Jenison Field House, East Lansing, MI 48824. **Website:** msuspartans.com.
Head Coach: Jake Boss. **Assistant Coaches:** Jake Boss Sr., Billy Gernon, *Mark Van Ameyde. **Telephone:** (517) 355-4486. **Baseball SID:** Jeff Barnes. **Telephone:** (517)355-2271. **Fax:** (517) 353-9636.
Home Field: McLane Stadium. **Seating Capacity:** 2,500. **Outfield Dimensions:** LF—330, CF—410, RF—305. **Press Box Telephone:** (517) 353-3009.

MIDDLE TENNESSEE STATE BLUE RAIDERS

Conference: Sun Belt.
Mailing Address: PO Box 90, Murfreesboro, TN 37132. **Website:** www.goblueraiders.com.
Head Coach: Steve Peterson. **Assistant Coaches:** *Jim McGuire, Mike McLaury, John Peterson. **Telephone:** (615)

898-2984. **Baseball SID:** Jessica Stauffacher. **Telephone:** (615) 904-8115. **Fax:** (615) 898-5626.
Home Field: Reese Smith Field. **Seating Capacity:** 2,100. **Outfield Dimensions:** LF—330, CF—390, RF—330. **Press Box Telephone:** (615) 898-2117.

MINNESOTA GOLDEN GOPHERS

Conference: Big Ten.
Mailing Address: University of Minnesota, 516 15th Ave SE, Minneapolis, MN 55455. **Website:** www.gophersports.com.
Head Coach: John Anderson. **Assistant Coaches:** *Rob Fornasiere, Todd Oakes, Lee Swenson. **Telephone:** (612) 625-4057. **Baseball SID:** Steve Geller. **Telephone:** (612) 624-9396. **Fax:** (612) 625-0359.
Home Field: Metrodome. **Seating Capacity:** 48,000. **Outfield Dimensions:** LF—340, CF—408, RF—327. **Press Box Telephone:** (612) 210-2380.

MISSISSIPPI REBELS

Conference: Southeastern (West).
Mailing Address: Ole Miss Baseball Office, University Place, University, MS 38677. **Website:** www.OleMissSports.com.
Head Coach: Mike Bianco. **Assistant Coaches:** Rob Francis, *Carl Lafferty, Matt Mossberg. **Telephone:** (662) 915-6643. **Baseball SID:** Bill Bunting. **Telephone:** (662) 915-1083. **Fax:** (662) 915-7006.
Home Field: Oxford University Stadium/Swayze Field. **Seating Capacity:** 10,323. **Outfield Dimensions:** LF—330, CF—390, RF—330. **Press Box Telephone:** (662) 915-7858.

MISSISSIPPI STATE BULLDOGS

Conference: Southeastern (West).
Mailing Address: PO Box 5327, Mississippi State, MS 39762. **Website:** www.mstateathletics.com.
Head Coach: John Cohen. **Assistant Coaches:** Lane Burroughs, *Butch Thompson. **Telephone:** (662) 325-3597. **Baseball SID:** Joe Dier. **Telephone:** (662) 325-8040. **Fax:** (662) 325-3600.
Home Field: Dudy Noble Field/Polk-DeMent Stadium. **Seating Capacity:** 15,000. **Outfield Dimensions:** LF—330, CF—390, RF—326. **Press Box Telephone:** (662) 325-3776.

MISSISSIPPI VALLEY STATE DELTA DEVILS

Conference: Southwestern Athletic.
Mailing Address: 14000 Highway 82 West, No. 7246, Itta Bena, MS 38941. **Website:** www.mvsu.edu/athletics.
Head Coach: Doug Shanks. **Assistant Coach:** Aaron Stevens. **Telephone:** (662) 254-3834. **Baseball SID:** William Bright Jr. **Telephone:** (662) 254-3011. **Fax:** (662) 254-3639.

MISSOURI TIGERS

Conference: Big 12.
Mailing Address: 100 Mizzou Athletic Training Complex, Columbia, MO 65211. **Website:** mutigers.com.
Head Coach: Tim Jamieson. **Assistant Coaches:** Evan Pratte, *Tony Vitello, Travis Wendte. **Telephone:** (573) 882-1917. **Baseball SID:** Josh Murray. **Telephone:** (573) 882-0711.
Home Field: Taylor Stadium at Simmons Field. **Seating Capacity:** 3,000. **Outfield Dimensions:** LF—340, CF—400, RF—340. **Press Box Telephone:** (573) 884-8912.

MISSOURI STATE BEARS

Conference: Missouri Valley.
Mailing Address: 901 S. National Ave, Springfield, MO 65897. **Website:** www.missouristatebears.com.
Head Coach: Keith Guttin. **Assistant Coaches:** *Paul Evans, Brent Thomas. **Telephone:** (417) 836-4497. **Baseball SID:** Ben Adamson. **Telephone:** (417) 836-4584. **Fax:** (417) 836-4868.
Home Field: Hammons Field. **Seating Capacity:** 8,000. **Outfield Dimensions:** LF—315, CF—400, RF—330. **Press Box Telephone:** (417) 863-0395, ext. 3070.

MONMOUTH HAWKS

Conference: Northeast.
Mailing Address: 400 Cedar Ave, West Long Branch, NJ, 07764. **Website:** www.gomuhawks.com.
Head Coach: Dean Ehehalt. **Assistant Coaches:** Jeff Barbalinardo, Jimmy Belanger *Karl Nonemaker. **Telephone:** (732) 263 5186. **Baseball SID:** Chris Tobin. **Telephone:** (732) 263 5180. **Fax:** (732) 571-3535.
Home Field: MU Baseball Field. **Seating Capacity:** 500. **Outfield Dimensions:** LF—320, CF—380, RF—320.

MOREHEAD STATE EAGLES

Conference: Ohio Valley.
Mailing Address: Allen Field, Morehead, KY 40351. **Website:** www.msueagles.com.
Head Coach: Jay Sorg. **Assistant Coaches:** Dillion Lawson, *Jason Neal, C.J. Wamsley. **Telephone:** (606) 783-2881. **Baseball SID:** Drew Dickerson. **Telephone:** (606) 783-2557. **Fax:** (606) 783-5035.
Home Field: Allen Field. **Seating Capacity:** 1,500. **Outfield Dimensions:** LF—320, CF—370, RF—310.

MOUNT ST. MARY'S MOUNTAINEERS

Conference: Northeast.
Mailing Address: 16300 Old Emmitsburg Rd, Emmitsburg, MD 21727. **Website:** www.mountathletics.com.
Head Coach: Scott Thomson. **Assistant Coaches:** Eric Smith. **Telephone:** (301) 447-3806. **Baseball SID:** Mark Vandergrift. **Telephone:** (301) 447-5384. **Fax:** (301) 447-5300.

MURRAY STATE THOROUGHBREDS

Conference: Ohio Valley.
Mailing Address: 217 Stewart Stadium, Murray, KY, 42071. **Website:** goracers.com.
Head Coach: Rob McDonald. **Assistant Coaches:** Dan Skirka, *Paul Wyczawski. **Telephone:** (270) 809-4892. **Baseball SID:** John Brush. **Telephone:** (270) 809-7044. **Fax:** (270) 809-3814.
Home Field: Reagan Field. **Seating Capacity:** 800. **Outfield Dimensions:** LF—330, CF—400, RF—330. **Press Box Telephone:** (270) 809-5650.

NAVY MIDSHIPMEN

Conference: Patriot.
Mailing Address: 566 Brownson Rd, Annapolis, MD 21402. **Website:** navysports.com.
Head Coach: Paul Kostacopoulos. **Assistant Coaches:** *Scott Friedholm, Matt Reynolds. **Telephone:** (410) 293-5571. **Baseball SID:** Jonathan Maggart. **Telephone:** (410) 293-8771. **Fax:** (410) 293-8954.
Home Field: Terwilliger Brothers Field at Max Bishop Stadium. **Seating Capacity:** 1,500. **Outfield Dimensions:** LF—323, CF—397, RF—304. **Press Box Telephone:** (410) 293-5431.

NEBRASKA CORNHUSKERS

Conference: Big 12.
Mailing Address: 403 Line Drive Circle, Suite B, Lincoln, NE 68588. **Website:** huskers.com.
Head Coach: Mike Anderson. **Assistant Coaches:** *Dave Bingham, Eric Newman, Nate Thompson. **Telephone:** (402) 472-2269. **Baseball SID:** Shamus McKnight. **Telephone:** (402) 472-7772. **Fax:** (402) 472-2005.
Home Field: Hawks Field at Haymarket Park. **Seating Capacity:** 8,486. **Outfield Dimensions:** LF—335, CF—395, RF—325. **Press Box Telephone:** (402) 434-6861.

NEVADA WOLF PACK

Conference: Western Athletic.
Mailing Address: 1664 N. Virginia St, Reno, NV 89557. **Website:** www.nevadawolfpack.com.
Head Coach: Gary Powers. **Assistant Coaches:** Chris Pfatenhauer, *Stan Stolte, Kevin Tucker. **Telephone:** (775) 682-6978. **Baseball SID:** Jack Kuestermeyer. **Telephone:** (775) 682-6984. **Fax:** (775) 784-4386.
Home Field: Peccole Park. **Seating Capacity:** 3,000. **Outfield Dimensions:** LF—340, CF—401, RF—340. **Press Box Telephone:** (775) 784-1585.

NEVADA-LAS VEGAS REBELS

Conference: Mountain West.
Mailing Address: 4505 S. Maryland Parkway, Las Vegas, NV 89154. **Website:** unlvrebels.com.
Head Coach: Buddy Gouldsmith. **Assistant Coaches:** Robert Fenn, *David Martinez, Jeff Prieto. **Telephone:** (702) 895-3499. **Baseball SID:** Bryan Haines. **Telephone:** (702) 895-3764. **Fax:** (702) 895-0989.
Home Field: Earl E. Wilson Stadium. **Seating Capacity:** 3,000. **Outfield Dimensions:** LF—335, CF—400, RF—335. **Press Box Telephone:** (702) 895-1595.

NEW JERSEY TECH HIGHLANDERS

Conference: Great West.
Mailing Address: University Heights, Newark, NJ 07102-1982. **Website:** www.njithighlanders.com.
Head Coach: Brian Callahan. **Assistant Coaches:** Chris Reardon, Ed Ward. **Telephone:** (973) 596-5827. **Baseball SID:** Tim Camp. **Telephone:** (973) 596-8461. **Fax:** (973) 596-8295.

NEW MEXICO LOBOS

Conference: Mountain West.
Mailing Address: 1401 University Blvd SE, Albuquerque, NM 87131. **Website:** golobos.com.
Head Coach: Ray Birmingham. **Assistant Coaches:** *Ken Jacome, Pat Leach, Chad Tidwell. **Telephone:** (505) 925-5720. **Baseball SID:** Daniel Archuleta. **Telephone:** (505) 925-5854. **Fax:** (505) 925-5529.
Home Field: Isotopes Park. **Seating Capacity:** 11,124. **Outfield Dimensions:** LF—335, CF—400, RF—335. **Press Box Telephone:** (505) 688-2364.

NEW MEXICO STATE AGGIES

Conference: Western Athletic.
Mailing Address: Regents Row Athletics Complex, MSC 3145, 1 Regents Row, Las Cruces, NM 88001-8001. **Website:** nmstatesports.com.
Head Coach: Rocky Ward. **Assistant Coaches:** J.T. Bloodworth, *Chase Tidwell, Gary Ward. **Telephone:** (575) 646-5813. **Baseball SID:** Eddie Morelos. **Telephone:** (575) 646-1885. **Fax:** (575) 646-2425.
Home Field: Presley-Askew Field. **Seating Capacity:** 1,000. **Outfield Dimensions:** LF—340, CF—400, RF—340.

NEW ORLEANS PRIVATEERS

Conference: Sun Belt.
Mailing Address: 6601 Franklin Ave, New Orleans, LA 70148. **Website:** www.unoprivateers.com.
Head Coach: Bruce Peddie. **Assistant Coaches:** *Scott Biesecker, Jason Walck. **Telephone:** (504) 280-7253. **Baseball SID:** Rob Broussard. **Telephone:** (504) 280-7027. **Fax:** (504) 280-3977.
Home Field: Maestri Field at Privateer Park. **Seating Capacity:** 4,200. **Outfield Dimensions:** LF—330, CF—405, RF—330. **Press Box Telephone:** (504) 280-3874.

NEW YORK TECH BEARS

Conference: Great West.
Mailing Address: PO Box 8000, Old Westbury, NY 11568. **Website:** www.nyit.edu/athletics.
Head Coach: Bob Hirschfield. **Assistant Coaches:** Mike Caulfield, Ron McKay. **Telephone:** (516) 686-7513. **Baseball SID:** Ben Arcuri. **Telephone:** (516) 686-7504. **Fax:** (516) 686-1219.

NIAGARA EAGLES

Conference: Metro Atlantic.
Mailing Address: PO Box 2009, Niagara University, NY 14109. **Website:** www.purpleeagles.com.
Head Coach: Rob McCoy. **Assistant Coaches:** Dan Cevette, Devin Greeno, Jessel Mangal. **Telephone:** (716) 286-7361. **Baseball SID:** Kevin Carver. **Telephone:** (716) 286-8586. **Fax:** (716) 286-8582.

NICHOLLS STATE COLONELS

Conference: Southland.
Mailing Address: PO Box 2032, Thibodaux, LA 70310. **Website:** geauxcolonels.com.
Head Coach: Chip Durham. **Assistant Coaches:** Chris Prothro, Stephen Tharp, *Seth Thibodeaux. **Telephone:** (985) 448-4808. **Baseball SID:** Charlie Gillingham. **Telephone:** (985) 448-4282. **Fax:** (985) 448-4814.
Home Field: Ray Didier Field. **Seating Capacity:** 3,000. **Outfield Dimensions:** LF—340, CF—400, RF—330.

NORFOLK STATE SPARTANS

Conference: Mid-Eastern Athletic.
Mailing Address: 700 Park Ave, Norfolk, VA 23504. **Website:** www.nsuspartans.com.
Head Coach: Claudell Clark. **Assistant Coaches:** A.J. Corbin, Quentin Jones. **Telephone:** (757) 823-8196. **Baseball SID:** Matt Michalec. **Telephone:** (757) 823-2628. **Fax:** (757) 823-8218.
Home Field: Marty L. Miller Field. **Seating Capacity:** 1,500. **Outfield Dimensions:** LF—330, CF—404, RF—318. **Press Box Telephone:** (757) 823-8196.

NORTH CAROLINA TAR HEELS

Conference: Atlantic Coast (Coastal).
Mailing Address: PO Box 2126, Chapel Hill, NC 27515. **Website:** tarheelblue.com.
Head Coach: Mike Fox. **Assistant Coaches:** Scott Forbes, *Scott Jackson, Matt McCay. **Telephone:** (919) 962-2351. **Baseball SID:** Chris Gallo. **Telephone:** (919) 962-1160. **Fax:** (919) 962-0612.
Home Field: Bryson Field at Boshamer Stadium. **Seating Capacity:** 4,100. **Outfield Dimensions:** LF—335, CF—400, RF—340. **Press Box Telephone:** (919) 962-3509.

NORTH CAROLINA A&T AGGIES

Conference: Mid-Eastern Athletic.
Mailing Address: 1601 E. Market St, Greensboro, NC 27411-0001. **Website:** www.ncataggies.com.
Head Coach: Keith Shumate. **Assistant Coaches:** Austin Love, Tim Wilson. **Telephone:** (336) 334-7371. **Baseball SID:** Brian Holloway. **Telephone:** (336) 334-7141. **Fax:** (336) 334-7181.
Home Field: War Memorial Stadium. **Seating Capacity:** 2,500. **Outfield Dimensions:** LF—327, CF—400, RF—327.

NORTH CAROLINA CENTRAL EAGLES

Conference: Independent.
Mailing Address: 1801 Fayetteville St, Durham, NC 27707. **Website:** www.nccueaglepride.com.
Head Coach: Henry White. **Assistant Coaches:** Chris Smith, Michael Swann, Ken Valentine. **Telephone:** (919) 530-6723. **Baseball SID:** Reah Nicholson. **Telephone:** (919) 530-6892. **Fax:** (919) 530-5426.

NORTH CAROLINA STATE WOLFPACK

Conference: Atlantic Coast (Atlantic).
Mailing Address: 1081 Varsity Drive, Campus Box 8505, Raleigh, NC 27695. **Website:** gopack.com.
Head Coach: Elliott Avent. **Assistant Coaches:** Chris Hart, *Tom Holliday, Brian Ward. **Telephone:** (919) 515-3613. **Baseball SID:** Bruce Winkworth. **Telephone:** (919) 515-1182. **Fax:** (919) 515-3624.
Home Field: Doak Field at Dail Park. **Seating Capacity:** 2,500. **Outfield Dimensions:** LF—320, CF—400, RF—330. **Press Box Telephone:** (919) 819-3035.

UNC ASHEVILLE BULLDOGS

Conference: Big South.
Mailing Address: One University Heights, Justice Gymnasium, Asheville, NC 28804. **Website:** www.uncabulldogs.com.
Head Coach: Tom Smith. **Assistant Coaches:** Joe John, *Aaron Rembert, Kenny Smith. **Telephone:** (828) 251-6920. **Baseball SID:** Mike Gore. **Telephone:** (828) 251-6923. **Fax:** (828) 251-6386.
Home Field: McCormick Field. **Seating Capacity:** 4,000. **Outfield Dimensions:** LF—326, CF—370, RF—297. **Press Box Telephone:** (828) 254-5125.

UNC GREENSBORO SPARTANS

Conference: Southern.
Mailing Address: 1400 Spring Garden St, Greensboro, NC 27412. **Website:** www.uncgspartans.com.
Head Coach: Mike Gaski. **Assistant Coaches:** *Jamie Athas, Dustin Ijames. **Telephone:** (336) 334-3247. **Baseball SID:** David Percival. **Telephone:** (336) 334-5615. **Fax:** (336) 334-3182.
Home Field: UNCG Baseball Stadium. **Seating Capacity:** 3,500. **Outfield Dimensions:** LF—340, CF—405, RF—340. **Press Box Telephone:** (336) 334-3885.

UNC WILMINGTON SEAHAWKS

Conference: Colonial Athletic.
Mailing Address: 601 South College Rd, Wilmington, NC 28403. **Website:** www.uncwsports.com.
Head Coach: Mark Scalf. **Assistant Coaches:** Daniel Hargrave, *Randy Hood, Jason Howell. **Telephone:** (910) 962-3570. **Baseball SID:** Tom Riordan. **Telephone:** (910) 962-4099. **Fax:** (910) 962-3001.
Home Field: Brooks Field. **Seating Capacity:** 3,500. **Outfield Dimensions:** LF—340, CF—380, RF—340. **Press Box Telephone:** (910) 395-5141.

NORTH DAKOTA FIGHTING SIOUX

Conference: Great West.
Mailing Address: Hyslop Sports Center, Room 120, 2751 2nd Ave N., Stop 9013, Grand Forks, NC 58202. **Website:** www.fightingsioux.com.
Head Coach: Jeff Dodson. **Assistant Coaches:** Brian DeVillers, J.C. Field, Eric Hoffman. **Telephone:** (701) 777-4038. **Baseball SID:** Ryan Powell. **Telephone:** (701) 777-2986. **Fax:** (701) 777-4352.

NORTH DAKOTA STATE BISON

Conference: Summit.
Mailing Address: NDSU Dept 1200, PO Box 6050, Fargo, ND 58108-6050. **Website:** www.gobison.com.
Head Coach: Tod Brown. **Assistant Coaches:** *David Pearson, Steve Montgomery, Kole Zimmerman. **Telephone:** (701) 231-8853. **Baseball SID:** Ryan Perreault. **Telephone:** (701) 231-8331. **Fax:** (701) 231-8022.
Home Field: Newman Outdoor Field. **Seating Capacity:** 4,513. **Outfield Dimensions:** LF—318, CF—408, RF—314. **Press Box Telephone:** (701) 235-5204.

NORTH FLORIDA OSPREYS

Conference: Atlantic Sun.
Mailing Address: 1 UNF Drive, Jacksonville, FL 32224. **Website:** www.unfospreys.com.
Head Coach: Dusty Rhodes. **Assistant Coaches:** Smoke Laval, *Judd Loveland, Bob Shepherd. **Telephone:** (904) 620-1556. **Baseball SID:** Chris Whitehead. **Telephone:** (904) 620-4029. **Fax:** (904) 620-2821.
Home Field: Harmon Stadium. **Seating Capacity:** 1,000. **Outfield Dimensions:** LF—325, CF—400, RF—325. **Press Box Telephone:** (904) 620-1557.

NORTHEASTERN HUSKIES

Conference: Colonial Athletic.
Mailing Address: 219 Cabot Center, 360 Huntington Ave, Boston, MA 02115. **Website:** www.gonu.com.
Head Coach: Neil McPhee. **Assistant Coaches:** Caleb Ginsberg, Mike Glavine, Patrick Mason. **Telephone:** (617) 373-3657. **Baseball SID:** Thomas Chen. **Telephone:** (617) 373-4154. **Fax:** (617) 373-3152.
Home Field: Parsons Field. **Seating Capacity:** 3,000. **Outfield Dimensions:** LF—330, CF—400, RF—342.

NORTHERN COLORADO BEARS

Conference: Great West.
Mailing Address: 208 Butler-Hancock Athletic Center, Box 117, Greeley, CO 80639. **Website:** uncbears.com.
Head Coach: Kevin Smallcomb. **Assistant Coach:** Wes Sells, Ryan Strain. **Telephone:** (970) 351-1714. **Baseball SID:** Heather Kennedy. **Telephone:** (970) 351-1065. **Fax:** (970) 351-1995.

NORTHERN ILLINOIS HUSKIES

Conference: Mid-American (West).
Mailing Address: 209 Convocation Center, 1525 W. Lincoln Highway, DeKalb, IL 60115. **Website:** niuhuskies.com.
Head Coach: Ed Mathey. **Assistant Coaches:** *Steve Joslyn, Ray Napientek, Jason Smith. **Telephone:** (815) 753-2225. **Baseball SID:** Zach Peters. **Telephone:** (815) 753-9572. **Fax:** (815) 753-7700.
Home Field: Ralph McKinzie Field. **Seating Capacity:** 2,000. **Outfield Dimensions:** LF—312, CF—400, RF—322. **Press Box Telephone:** (815) 753-8094.

NORTHWESTERN WILDCATS

Conference: Big Ten.
Mailing Address: 1501 Central St, Evanston, IL 60208. **Website:** nusports.com.
Head Coach: Paul Stevens. **Assistant Coaches:** Joe Keenan, *Jon Mikrut, Tim Stoddard. **Telephone:** (847) 491-4652. **Baseball SID:** Nick Brilowski. **Telephone:** (847) 467-3831. **Fax:** (847) 491-8818.
Home Field: Rocky Miller Park. **Seating Capacity:** 1,000. **Outfield Dimensions:** LF—330, CF—400, RF—320. **Press Box Telephone:** (847) 491-4200.

NORTHWESTERN STATE DEMONS

Conference: Southland.
Mailing Address: Athletic Fieldhouse, Natchitoches, LA 71497. **Website:** www.nsudemons.com.
Head Coach: Jon Paul Davis. **Assistant Coaches:** Mike Jaworski, *Jeff McCannon, Philip Miller. **Telephone:** (318) 357-4139. **Baseball SID:** Matthew Bonnette. **Telephone:** (318) 357-6469. **Fax:** (318) 357-4515.
Home Field: Brown Stroud Field. **Seating Capacity:** 1,200. **Outfield Dimensions:** LF—320, CF—400, RF—330. **Press Box Telephone:** (318) 357-4606.

NOTRE DAME FIGHTING IRISH

Conference: Big East.
Mailing Address: Frank Eck Stadium, Notre Dame, IN 46556. **Website:** und.com.
Head Coach: Dave Schrage. **Assistant Coaches:** Dave Dangler, *Scott Lawler, Graham Sikes. **Telephone:** (574) 631-6366. **Baseball SID:** Michael Bertsch. **Telephone:** (574) 631-7516. **Fax:** (574) 631-7941.
Home Field: Frank Eck Stadium. **Seating Capacity:** 2,500. **Outfield Dimensions:** LF—330, CF—400, RF—330. **Press Box Telephone:** (574) 631-9018.

OAKLAND GOLDEN GRIZZLIES

Conference: Summit.
Mailing Address: 2200 N. Squirrel Athletics Center, Rochester, MI 48309. **Website:** www.ougrizzlies.com.
Head Coach: John Musachio. **Assistant Coaches:** Del Young. **Telephone:** (248) 370-4059. **Baseball SID:** Mike Bond. **Telephone:** (248) 370-3123. **Fax:** (248) 370-3138.
Home Field: OU Baseball Field. **Seating Capacity:** 500. **Outfield Dimensions:** LF—325, CF—390, RF—308.

OHIO BOBCATS

Conference: Mid-American (East).
Mailing Address: N117 Convocation Center, Athens, OH 45701. **Website:** www.ohiobobcats.com.
Head Coach: Joe Carbone. **Assistant Coaches:** Scott Malinowski, *Andrew See. **Telephone:** (740) 593-1180. **Baseball SID:** Jason Corriher. **Telephone:** (740) 593-1298. **Fax:** (740) 597-1838.
Home Field: Bob Wren Stadium. **Seating Capacity:** 4,000. **Outfield Dimensions:** LF—340, CF—405, RF—340. **Press Box Telephone:** (740) 593-0526.

OHIO STATE BUCKEYES

Conference: Big Ten.
Mailing Address: 650 Borror Drive, Suite 250, Columbus, Ohio 43210. **Website:** www.ohiostatebuckeyes.com.
Head Coach: Bob Todd. **Assistant Coaches:** *Greg Cypret, Pete Jenkins, Eric Parker. **Telephone:** (614) 292-1075. **Baseball SID:** Jerry Emig. **Telephone:** (614) 688-0343. **Fax:** (614) 292-8547.
Home Field: Bill Davis Stadium. **Seating Capacity:** 4,450. **Outfield Dimensions:** LF—330, CF—400, RF—

330. **Press Box Telephone:** (614) 292-0021.

OKLAHOMA SOONERS

Conference: Big 12.
Mailing Address: 401 W. Imhoff, Norman, OK 73019.
Website: www.soonersports.com.
Head Coach: Sunny Golloway. **Assistant Coaches:**
Mike Bell, Russell Raley, *Tim Tadlock. **Telephone:** (405)
325-8354. **Baseball SID:** Craig Moran. **Telephone:** (405)
325-6449. **Fax:** (405) 325-7623.
Home Field: L. Dale Mitchell Park. **Seating Capacity:**
2,700. **Outfield Dimensions:** LF—335, CF—411, RF—
335. **Press Box Telephone:** (405) 325-8363.

OKLAHOMA STATE COWBOYS

Conference: Big 12.
Mailing Address: 220 Athletics Center, Stillwater, OK
74078. **Website:** www.okstate.com.
Head Coach: Frank Anderson. **Assistant Coaches:**
Greg Evans, *Billy Jones, Dax Leone. **Telephone:** (405)
744-5849. **Baseball SID:** Wade McWhorter. **Telephone:**
(405) 744-7853. **Fax:** (405) 744-7754.
Home Field: Allie P. Reynolds Stadium. **Seating
Capacity:** 4,000. **Outfield Dimensions:** LF—330, CF—
398, RF—330. **Press Box Telephone:** (405) 744-5757.

OLD DOMINION MONARCHS

Conference: Colonial Athletic.
Mailing Address: Athletic Admin. Bldg., Norfolk, VA
23529-0201. **Website:** www.odusports.com.
Head Coach: Jerry Meyers. **Assistant Coaches:** *Nate
Goulet, Travis Huffman, Tag Montague. **Telephone:** (757)
683-4230. **Baseball SID:** Carol Hudson. **Telephone:** (757)
683-3372. **Fax:** (757) 683-3119.
Home Field: Bud Metheny Complex. **Seating
Capacity:** 2,500. **Outfield Dimensions:** LF—325, CF—
395, RF—325. **Press Box Telephone:** (757) 683-5036.

ORAL ROBERTS GOLDEN EGALES

Conference: Summit.
Mailing Address: 7777 S. Lewis Ave, Tulsa, OK 74147.
Website: www.orugoldeneagles.com.
Head Coach: Rob Walton. **Assistant Coaches:** Wes
Davis, Ryan Folmar, *Ryan Neill. **Telephone:** (918) 495-
7130. **Baseball SID:** Cris Belvin. **Telephone:** (918) 495-
7181. **Fax:** (918) 495-7142.
Home Field: J.L. Johnson Stadium. **Seating Capacity:**
2,500. **Outfield Dimensions:** LF—330, CF—400, RF—
330. **Press Box Telephone:** (918) 495-7165.

OREGON DUCKS

Conference: Pacific-10.
Mailing Address: 2727 Leo Harris Parkway, Eugene,
OR 97401. **Website:** www.goducks.com.
Head Coach: George Horton. **Assistant Coaches:**
*Andrew Checketts, Mike Kirby, Jay Uhlman. **Telephone:**
(541) 346-5576. **Baseball SID:** Andria Wenzel. **Telephone:**
(541) 346-0962. **Fax:** (541) 346-5449.
Home Field: PK Park. **Seating Capacity:** 3,717.
Outfield Dimensions: LF—335, CF—400, RF—325.
Press Box Telephone: (916) 838-2346.

OREGON STATE BEAVERS

Conference: Pacific-10.
Mailing Address: 103 Gill Coliseum, Corvallis, OR
97331. **Website:** www.osubeavers.com.
Head Coach: Pat Casey. **Assistant Coaches:** Pat
Bailey, *Marty Lees, Nate Yeskie. **Telephone:** (541) 737-
2825. **Baseball SID:** Hank Hager. **Telephone:** (541) 737-
7472. **Fax:** (541) 737-3072.

Home Field: Goss Stadium. **Seating Capacity:** 3,248.
Outfield Dimensions: LF—330, CF—400, RF—330.
Press Box Telephone: (541) 737-7475.

PACIFIC TIGERS

Conference: Big West.
Mailing Address: 3601 Pacific Ave, Stockton, CA
95211. **Website:** pacifictigers.com.
Head Coach: Ed Sprague. **Assistant Coaches:** *Don
Barbara, Chris McCormack, Mike McCormick. **Telephone:**
(209) 946-2709. **Baseball SID:** Monique Moyal.
Telephone: (209) 946-2289. **Fax:** (209) 946-2757.
Home Field: Klein Family Field. **Seating Capacity:**
2,000. **Outfield Dimensions:** LF—314, CF—405, RF—
325. **Press Box Telephone:** (209) 946-2722.

PENN QUAKERS

Conference: Ivy League (Gehrig).
Mailing Address: James D. Dunning Coaches Center,
235 South 33rd Street, Philadelphia, PA 19104. **Website:**
www.pennathletics.com.
Head Coach: John Cole. **Assistant Coaches:** Jon Cross,
John Yurkow. **Telephone:** (215) 898-6282. **Baseball SID:**
Ben Stockwell. **Telephone:** (215) 898-6128. **Fax:** (215)
898-1747.
Home Field: Meiklejohn Stadium. **Seating Capacity:**
900. **Outfield Dimensions:** LF—325, CF—380, RF—355.

PENN STATE NITTANY LIONS

Conference: Big Ten.
Mailing Address: 112 Bryce Jordan Center, University
Park, PA 16802. **Website:** www.GoPSUsports.com.
Head Coach: Robbie Wine. **Assistant Coaches:** Jason
Bell, *Eric Folmar, Will Hoover. **Telephone:** (814) 863-
0239. **Baseball SID:** Justin Lefleur. **Telephone:** (814)
865-1757. **Fax:** (814) 863-3165.
Home Field: Medlar Field at Lubrano Park. **Seating
Capacity:** 5,406. **Outfield Dimensions:** LF—325, CF—
399, RF—320.

PEPPERDINE WAVES

Conference: West Coast.
Mailing Address: 24255 Pacific Coast Hwy, Malibu,
CA 90263. **Website:** www.PepperdineSports.com.
Head Coach: Steve Rodriguez. **Assistant Coaches:**
Rick Hirtensteiner, *Jon Strauss, Joe Wilkins. **Telephone:**
(310) 506-4371. **Baseball SID:** Chris Macaluso.
Telephone: (310) 506-4333. **Fax:** (310) 506-4322.
Home Field: Eddy D. Field Stadium. **Seating Capacity:**
1,800. **Outfield Dimensions:** LF—330, CF—400, RF—
330. **Press Box Telephone:** (310) 456-4598.

PITTSBURGH PANTHERS

Conference: Big East.
Mailing Address: 212 Fitzgerald Field House,
Pittsburgh PA 15261. **Website:** pittsburghpanthers.com.
Head Coach: Joe Jordano. **Assistant Coaches:** Ryan
Leahy, *Danny Lopaze, Brandon Rowan. **Telephone:**
(412) 648-8208. **Baseball SID:** Mendy Nestor. **Telephone:**
(412) 648-1018. **Fax:** (412) 648-8248.
Home Field: Trees Field. **Seating Capacity:** 500.
Outfield Dimensions: LF—300, CF—405, RF—330.
Press Box Telephone: (412) 849-9470.

PORTLAND PILOTS

Conference: West Coast.
Mailing Address: 5000 North Willamette Blvd,
Portland, OR 97203. **Website:** www.portlandpilots.com.
Head Coach: Chris Sperry. **Assistant Coaches:** Tucker
Brack, *Larry Casian, Dale Stebbins. **Telephone:** (503)

943-7707. **Baseball SID:** Adam Linnman. **Telephone:** (503) 943-7731. **Fax:** (503) 943-7242.
Home Field: Joe Etzel Field. **Seating Capacity:** Unavailable. **Outfield Dimensions:** LF—350, CF—390, RF—340.

PRAIRIE VIEW A&M PANTHERS

Conference: Southwestern Athletic.
Mailing Address: PO Box 519 MS 1500, Prairie View, TX 77446. **Website:** sports.pvamu.edu.
Head Coach: Waskyla Cullivan. **Assistant Coaches:** *Byron Carter. **Telephone:** (936) 261 9121. **Baseball SID:** Reginald Rouzan. **Telephone:** (936) 261-9106. **Fax:** (936) 261-9159.

PRESBYTERIAN BLUE HOSE

Conference: Big South.
Mailing Address: 105 Ashland Ave, Clinton, SC 29325. **Website:** www.gobluehose.com
Head Coach: Elton Pollock. **Assistant Coaches:** Kevin Davis, Chris Edwards, *Mark Johnson. **Telephone:** (864) 833-8236. **Baseball SID:** Brent Hager. **Telephone:** (864) 833-8252. **Fax:** (864) 833-8323.
Home Field: Baseball Complex. **Seating Capacity:** 500. **Outfield Dimensions:** LF—325, CF—400, RF—325.

PRINCETON TIGERS

Conference: Ivy League (Gehrig).
Mailing Address: Jadwin Gymnasium, Princeton, NJ 08544. **Website:** www.GoPrincetonTigers.com.
Head Coach: Scott Bradley. **Assistant Coaches:** *Lloyd Brewer, Jeremy Meccage. **Telephone:** (609) 258-5059. **Baseball SID:** Yariv Amir. **Telephone:** (609) 258-5701. **Fax:** (609) 258-2399.
Home Field: Clarke Field. **Seating Capacity:** 500. **Outfield Dimensions:** LF—335, CF—400, RF—325. **Press Box Telephone:** (609) 462-0248.

PURDUE BOILERMAKERS

Conference: Big Ten.
Mailing Address: 1225 Northwestern Ave, West Lafayette, IN 47907. **Website:** purduesports.com.
Head Coach: Doug Schreiber. **Assistant Coaches:** Bobby Bartow, Jeff Duncan, Ryan Sawyers. **Telephone:** (765) 494-3998. **Baseball SID:** Matt Rector. **Telephone:** (765) 494-3196. **Fax:** (765) 494-5447.
Home Field: Lambert Field. **Seating Capacity:** 1,100. **Outfield Dimensions:** LF—340, CF—408, RF—340. **Press Box Telephone:** (765) 494-1522.

QUINNIPIAC BOBCATS

Conference: Northeast.
Mailing Address: 275 Mount Carmel Ave, Hamden, CT 06518. **Website:** quinnipiacbobcats.com.
Head Coach: *Dan Gooley. **Assistant Coaches:** Dan Scarpa, Joe Tonelli. **Telephone:** (203) 582-8966. **Baseball SID:** Ken Sweeten. **Telephone:** (203) 582-8625. **Fax:** (203) 582-5385.
Home Field: Quinnipiac Field. **Seating Capacity:** 1,000. **Outfield Dimensions:** Unavailable. **Press Box Telephone:** (203) 859-8529.

RADFORD HIGHLANDERS

Conference: Big South.
Mailing Address: PO Box 6913, Radford, VA 24142. **Website:** www.ruhighlanders.com.
Head Coach: Joe Raccuia. **Assistant Coaches:** *Brian Anderson, Rick Olivieri, Allen Rice. **Telephone:** (540) 831-5881. **Baseball SID:** Patrick Reed. **Telephone:** (540) 831-5211. **Fax:** (540) 831-6095.

Home Field: Radford University Baseball Field. **Seating Capacity:** 1,000. **Outfield Dimensions:** LF—330, CF—400, RF—330. **Press Box Telephone:** (540) 257-1159.

RHODE ISLAND RAMS

Conference: Atlantic 10.
Mailing Address: 3 Keaney Rd, Suite One, Kingston, RI 02881. **Website:** gorhody.com.
Head Coach: Jim Foster. **Assistant Coaches:** *Steve Breitbach, Eric Cirella, Idris Liasu. **Telephone:** (401) 874-4550. **Baseball SID:** Jodi Pontbriand. **Telephone:** (401) 874-5356. **Fax:** (401) 874-5354.
Home Field: Bill Beck Field. **Seating Capacity:** Unavailable. **Outfield Dimensions:** LF—330, CF—400, RF—330.

RICE OWLS

Conference: Conference USA.
Mailing Address: 6100 Main St, MS 547, Houston, TX 77251. **Website:** www.riceowls.com.
Head Coach: Wayne Graham. **Assistant Coaches:** Patrick Hallmark, *David Pierce, *Mike Taylor. **Telephone:** (713) 348-8864. **Baseball SID:** John Sullivan. **Telephone:** (713) 348-5636. **Fax:** (713) 348-6019.
Home Field: Reckling Park. **Seating Capacity:** 5,700. **Outfield Dimensions:** LF—330, CF—400, RF—330. **Press Box Telephone:** (713) 348-4931.

RICHMOND SPIDERS

Conference: Atlantic 10.
Mailing Address: The Robins Center, Richmond, VA 23173. **Website:** RichmondSpiders.com.
Head Coach: Mark McQueen. **Assistant Coaches:** Joey Haug, Chad Oxendine, *Ryan Wheeler. **Telephone:** (804) 289-8391. **Baseball SID:** Mike DeGeorge. **Telephone:** (804) 287-6313. **Fax:** (804) 289-8820.
Home Field: Pitt Field. **Seating Capacity:** 600. **Outfield Dimensions:** LF—320, CF—380, RF—320. **Press Box Telephone:** (804) 289-8714.

RIDER BRONCS

Conference: Metro Atlantic.
Mailing Address: 2083 Lawrenceville Road, Lawrenceville, NJ 08648. **Website:** www.gobroncs.com.
Head Coach: Barry Davis. **Assistant Coaches:** Pat Horvath, Ray Scipione, Jaime Steward. **Telephone:** (609) 896-5055. **Baseball SID:** Bud Focht. **Telephone:** (609) 896-5138. **Fax:** (609) 896-0341.

RUTGERS SCARLET KNIGHTS

Conference: Big East.
Mailing Address: Louis Brown Athletic Center, 83 Rockafeller Rd, Piscataway, NJ 08854. **Website:** www. scarletknights.com.
Head Coach: Fred Hill. **Assistant Coaches:** Jay Blackwell, Rick Freeman, *Darren Fenster. **Telephone:** (732) 445-7834. **Baseball SID:** Doug Drabik. **Telephone:** (732) 445-7884. **Fax:** (732) 445-3063.
Home Field: Bainton Field. **Seating Capacity:** 1,500. **Outfield Dimensions:** LF—330, CF—410, RF—320. **Press Box Telephone:** (732) 921-1067.

SACRAMENTO STATE HORNETS

Conference: Western Athletic.
Mailing Address: 6000 J Street, Sacramento, CA 95819-6099. **Website:** www.hornetsports.com.
Head Coach: John Smith. **Assistant Coaches:** Jim Barr, John Callahan, *Reggie Christiansen. **Telephone:** (916) 278-7225. **Baseball SID:** J.D. Fox. **Telephone:** (916)

278-6896. **Fax:** (916) 278-5429.
Home Field: Hornet Field. **Seating Capacity:** 1,267. **Outfield Dimensions:** LF—333, CF—400, RF—333. **Press Box Telephone:** (209) 210-8858.

SACRED HEART PIONEERS

Conference: Northeast.
Mailing Address: 5151 Park Ave, Fairfield, CT 06825. **Website:** www.sacredheartpioneers.com.
Head Coach: Nick Giaguinto. **Assistant Coaches:** Earl Mathewson, Wayne Mazzoni. **Telephone:** (203) 365-7632. **Baseball SID:** Gene Gumbs. **Telephone:** (203) 396-8127. **Fax:** (203) 371-7889.

ST. BONAVENTURE BONNIES

Conference: Atlantic 10.
Mailing Address: PO Box G, Reilly Center, St. Bonaventure, NY 14778. **Website:** gobonnies.com.
Head Coach: Larry Sudbrook. **Assistant Coaches:** Nick LaBella, Kieran Malone, Rick Pillitteri. **Telephone:** (716) 375-2641. **Baseball SID:** Patrick Pierson. **Telephone:** (716) 375-2575. **Fax:** (716) 375-2383.
Home Field: Fred Handler Park. **Seating Capacity:** Unavailable. **Outfield Dimensions:** LF—330, CF—402, RF—330.

ST. JOHN'S RED STORM

Conference: Big East.
Mailing Address: 8000 Utopia Parkway, Queens, NY 11439. **Website:** www.redstormsports.com.
Head Coach: Ed Blankmeyer. **Assistant Coaches:** Scott Brown, *Mike Hampton, Jeffrey Quiros. **Telephone:** (718) 990-6148. **Baseball SID:** Tim Brown. **Telephone:** (718) 990-1521. **Fax:** (718) 969-8468.
Home Field: Kaiser Stadium. **Seating Capacity:** 3,500. **Outfield Dimensions:** LF—325, CF—400, RF—325. **Press Box Telephone:** (718) 990-2725.

ST. JOSEPH'S HAWKS

Conference: Atlantic 10.
Mailing Address: 5600 City Ave, Philadelphia, PA 19131. **Website:** sjuhawks.com.
Head Coach: Fritz Hamburg. **Assistant Coaches:** *Jake Gill, Greg Manco. **Telephone:** (610) 660-1718. **Baseball SID:** Joe Greenwich. **Telephone:** (610) 660-1738. **Fax:** (610) 660-1724.
Home Field: Campbell's Field. **Seating Capacity:** 6,425. **Outfield Dimensions:** LF—325, CF—405, RF—325.

SAINT LOUIS BILLIKENS

Conference: Atlantic 10.
Mailing Address: 3303 Laclede Ave, Saint Louis, MO 63103. **Website:** www.slubillikens.com.
Head Coach: Darin Hendrickson. **Assistant Coaches:** Will Bradley, Danny Jackson, *Kevin Moulder. **Telephone:** (314) 977-3172. **Baseball SID:** Brian Kunderman. **Telephone:** (314) 977-3346. **Fax:** (314) 977-3178.
Home Field: Billiken Sports Center. **Seating Capacity:** 500. **Outfield Dimensions:** LF—330, CF—403, RF—330. **Press Box Telephone:** (314) 808-4868.

ST. MARY'S GAELS

Conference: West Coast.
Mailing Address: 1928 Saint Mary's Rd, Moraga, CA 94575. **Website:** www.smcgaels.com.
Head Coach: Jedd Soto. **Assistant Coaches:** *Lloyd Acosta, Mike McCormack, Gape Zappin. **Telephone:** (925) 631-4637. **Baseball SID:** Rich Davi. **Telephone:** (925) 631-4402. **Fax:** (925) 631-4405.

Home Field: Louis Guisto Field. **Seating Capacity:** 1,000. **Outfield Dimensions:** LF—340, CF—400, RF—340. **Press Box Telephone:** (925) 376-3906.

ST. PETER'S PEACOCKS

Conference: Metro Atlantic.
Mailing Address: 2641 Kennedy Blvd, Jersey City, NJ 07306. **Website:** www.spc.edu/pages/408.asp.
Head Coach: Derek England. **Assistant Coaches:** Ben Cueto, Tim Nagurka, *Corky Thompson. **Telephone:** (201) 761-7318. **Baseball SID:** David Freeman. **Telephone:** (201) 761-7315. **Fax:** (201) 761-7317.

SAM HOUSTON STATE BEARKATS

Conference: Southland.
Mailing Address: PO Box 2268, Huntsville, TX 77341. **Website:** gobearkats.com.
Head Coach: Mark Johnson. **Assistant Coaches:** Chris Berry, Jim Blair. **Telephone:** (936) 294-1731. **Baseball SID:** Paul Ridings. **Telephone:** (936) 294-1764. **Fax:** (936) 294-3538.

SAMFORD BULLDOGS

Conference: Ohio Valley.
Mailing Address: Samford Athletics, 800 Lakeshore Dr, Birmingham, AL 35229. **Website:** samfordsports.com.
Head Coach: Casey Dunn. **Assistant Coaches:** *Tony David, Mick Fieldbinder, Rucker Taylor. **Telephone:** (205) 726-2134. **Baseball SID:** Joey Mullins. **Telephone:** (205) 726-2799. **Fax:** (205) 726-2545.
Home Field: Joe Lee Griffin Field. **Seating Capacity:** 1,000. **Outfield Dimensions:** LF—330, CF—390, RF—335. **Press Box Telephone:** (205) 726-4167.

SAN DIEGO TOREROS

Conference: West Coast.
Mailing Address: 5998 Alcala Park, San Diego, CA 92110. **Website:** www.usdtoreros.com.
Head Coach: Rich Hill. **Assistant Coaches:** *Jay Johnson, Tyler Kincaid, Ramon Orozco. **Telephone:** (619) 260-5953. **Baseball SID:** Chris Loucks. **Telephone:** (619) 260-7930. **Fax:** (619) 260-2213.
Home Field: Cunningham Stadium. **Seating Capacity:** 1,200. **Outfield Dimensions:** LF—309, CF—395, RF—329. **Press Box Telephone:** (619) 260-8829.

SAN DIEGO STATE AZTECS

Conference: Mountain West.
Mailing Address: 5500 Campanile Dr, San Diego, CA 92182. **Website:** www.goaztecs.com.
Head Coach: Tony Gwynn. **Assistant Coaches:** Mark Martinez, Brock Ungricht, *Eric Valenzuela. **Telephone:** (619) 594-6889. **Baseball SID:** Dave Kuhn. **Telephone:** (619) 594-5242. **Fax:** (619) 582-6541.
Home Field: Tony Gwynn Stadium. **Seating Capacity:** 3,000. **Outfield Dimensions:** LF—340, CF—410, RF—340. **Press Box Telephone:** (619) 594-4103.

SAN FRANCISCO DONS

Conf Conference: West Coast.
Mailing Address: 2130 Fulton Street, San Francisco, CA 94117-1080. **Website:** www.usfdons.com.
Head Coach: Nino Giarratano. **Assistant Coaches:** *Matt Hobbs, Troy Nakamura, Jon Norfolk. **Telephone:** (415) 422-2934. **Baseball SID:** Jordan Wilcox. **Telephone:** (415) 422-6161. **Fax:** (415) 422-2929.
Home Field: Benedetti Diamond. **Seating Capacity:** 2,000. **Outfield Dimensions:** LF—301, CF—400, RF—305. **Press Box Telephone:** (415) 422-2919.

SAN JOSE STATE SPARTANS

Conference: Western Athletic.
Mailing Address: 1393 S. 7th Street, San Jose, CA 95112. **Website:** www.sjsuspartans.com.
Head Coach: Sam Piraro. **Assistant Coaches:** Tom Kunis, *Jeff Pritchard, Brian Yocke. **Telephone:** (408) 924-1255. **Baseball SID:** Doga Gur. **Telephone:** (408) 924-1211. **Fax:** (408) 924-1291.
Home Field: Municipal Stadium. **Seating Capacity:** 5,200. **Outfield Dimensions:** LF—320, CF—390, RF—320. **Press Box Telephone:** (408) 924-7276.

SANTA CLARA BRONCOS

Conference: West Coast.
Mailing Address: 500 El Camino Real, Santa Clara, CA 95053. **Website:** www.santaclarabroncos.com.
Head Coach: Mark O'Brien. **Assistant Coaches:** Chad Baum, Shawn Epidendio, *Mike Zirelli. **Telephone:** (408) 554-4680. **Baseball SID:** Nick Mirkovich. **Telephone:** (408) 554-4659. **Fax:** (408) 554-6969.
Home Field: Stephen Schott Stadium. **Seating Capacity:** 2,200. **Outfield Dimensions:** LF—340, CF—402, RF—335. **Press Box Telephone:** (408) 554-4752.

SAVANNAH STATE TIGERS

Conference: Independent.
Mailing Address: 3219 College St, Savannah, GA 31404. **Website:** www.ssuathletics.com.
Head Coach: Carlton Hardy. **Assistant Coaches:** Emmanuel Wheeler. **Telephone:** (912) 356-2801. **Baseball SID:** Opio Mashariki. **Telephone:** (912) 356-2446. **Fax:** (912) 353-5287.

SEATTLE REDHAWKS

Conference: Independent.
Mailing Address: 901 12th Ave, PO Box 222000, Seattle, WA 98122. **Website:** www.goseattleu.com.
Head Coach: Donny Harrel. **Assistant Coaches:** Casey Powell, Dave Wainhouse. **Telephone:** (206) 398-4399. **Baseball SID:** Jason Behenna. **Telephone:** (206) 296-5915. **Fax:** (206) 296-2154.

SETON HALL PIRATES

Conference: Big East.
Mailing Address: 400 South Orange Ave, South Orange, NJ 07079. **Website:** www.shupirates.com.
Head Coach: Rob Sheppard. **Assistant Coaches:** Chris Bagley, Phil Cundari. **Telephone:** (973) 761-9557. **Baseball SID:** Joe Montefusco. **Telephone:** (973) 761-9493. **Fax:** (073) 761-9061.
Home Field: Owen T. Carroll Field. **Seating Capacity:** 1,000. **Outfield Dimensions:** LF—315, CF—401, RF—330. **Press Box Telephone:** (973) 670-2752.

SIENA SAINTS

Conference: Metro Atlantic.
Mailing Address: 515 Loudon Rd, Loudonville, NY 12211. **Website:** www.sienasaints.com.
Head Coach: Tony Rossi. **Assistant Coaches:** Phil Cahill, Keith Glasser, Jimmy Jackson. **Telephone:** (518) 786-5044. **Baseball SID:** Jason Rich. **Telephone:** (518) 783-2411. **Fax:** (518) 783-2992.
Home Field: Siena Field. **Seating Capacity:** 500. **Outfield Dimensions:** LF—300, CF—400, RF—325.

SOUTH ALABAMA JAGUARS

Conference: Sun Belt.
Mailing Address: 1209 Mitchell Center, Mobile, AL 36688. **Website:** www.usajaguars.com.
Head Coach: Steve Kittrell. **Assistant Coaches:** Alan Luckie, Scot Sealy, *Seth Von Behren. **Telephone:** (251) 460-6876. **Baseball SID:** Charlie Nichols. **Telephone:** (251) 414-8017. **Fax:** (251) 460-7297.
Home Field: Stanky Field. **Seating Capacity:** 3,575. **Outfield Dimensions:** LF—330, CF—400, RF—330. **Press Box Telephone:** (251) 461-1842.

SOUTH CAROLINA GAMECOCKS

Conference: Southeastern (East).
Mailing Address: 1300 Rosewood Dr, Columbia, SC 29208. **Website:** www.gamecocksonline.com.
Head Coach: Ray Tanner. **Assistant Coaches:** Mark Calvi, Sammy Esposito, *Chad Holbrook. **Telephone:** (803) 777-0116. **Baseball SID:** Andrew Kitick. **Telephone:** (803) 777-5257. **Fax:** (803) 777-2967.
Home Field: Carolina Stadium. **Seating Capacity:** 8,242. **Outfield Dimensions:** LF—325, CF—400, RF—325. **Press Box Telephone:** (803) 777-6648.

SOUTH CAROLINA-UPSTATE SPARTANS

Conference: Atlantic Sun.
Mailing Address: 800 University Way, Spartanburg, SC 29303. **Website:** upstatespartans.cstv.com.
Head Coach: Matt Fincher. **Assistant Coaches:** Grant Rembert, *Russell Triplett. **Telephone:** (864) 503-5135. **Baseball SID:** Joe Guistina. **Telephone:** (864) 503-5152. **Fax:** (864) 503-5127.
Home Field: Harley Park. **Seating Capacity:** 500. **Outfield Dimensions:** LF—325, CF—402, RF—325. **Press Box Telephone:** (864) 503-5058.

SOUTH DAKOTA STATE JACKRABBITS

Conference: Summit.
Mailing Address: 2820 HPER Center, Brookings, SD 57007. **Website:** gojacks.com.
Head Coach: Ritchie Price. **Assistant Coaches:** *Jake Angier, Ryan Overland. **Telephone:** (605) 688-5027. **Baseball SID:** Jason Hove. **Telephone:** (605) 688-4623. **Fax:** (605) 688-5999.
Home Field: Erv Huether Field. **Seating Capacity:** 400. **Outfield Dimensions:** LF—330, CF—400, RF—330. **Press Box Telephone:** (605) 695-1827.

SOUTH FLORIDA BULLS

Conference: Big East.
Mailing Address: 4202 E. Fowler Ave, ATH 100, Tampa, FL 33620. **Website:** www.GoUSFBulls.com.
Head Coach: Lelo Prado. **Assistant Coaches:** *Lazer Collazo, Bryant Ward. **Telephone:** (813) 974-2504. **Baseball SID:** Brad Borghetti. **Telephone:** (813) 974-4029. **Fax:** (813) 974-4029.
Home Field: Red McEwen Field. **Seating Capacity:** 1,500. **Outfield Dimensions:** LF—375, CF—400, RF—375. **Press Box Telephone:** (813) 410-1194.

SOUTHEAST MISSOURI STATE REDHAWKS

Conference: Ohio Valley.
Mailing Address: 1 University Plaza, MS 0200, Cape Girardeau, MO 63701. **Website:** gosoutheast.com.
Head Coach: Mark Hogan. **Assistant Coaches:** Chris Cafalone, Dave Lawson, *Rick McCarty. **Telephone:** (573) 986-6002. **Baseball SID:** Brett Maikowski. **Telephone:** (573) 651-2294. **Fax:** (573) 651-2810.
Home Field: Capaha Field. **Seating Capacity:** 2,000.

Outfield Dimensions: LF—335, CF—400, RF—335.

SOUTHEASTERN LOUISIANA LIONS

Conference: Southland.
Mailing Address: SLU 10309, Hammond, LA 70402.
Website: www.lionsports.net.
Head Coach: Jay Artigues. **Assistant Coaches:** Justin Cryer, *Justin Hill, Matt Riser. **Telephone:** (985) 549-3566. **Baseball SID:** Matt Sullivan. **Telephone:** (985) 549-2142. **Fax:** (985) 549-3495.
Home Field: Pat Kennelly Diamond at Alumni Field. **Seating Capacity:** 3,000. **Outfield Dimensions:** LF—320, CF—365-400-365, RF—320.

SOUTHERN JAGUARS

Conference: Southwestern Athletic.
Mailing Address: Baseball Office, F.G. Clark Center, Harding Blvd, Baton Rouge, LA 70813. **Website:** gojagsports.com.
Head Coach: Roger Cador. **Assistant Coach:** *Fernando Puebla. **Telephone:** (225) 771-2513. **Baseball SID:** Kevin Manns. **Telephone:** (225) 771-2601. **Fax:** (225) 771-4400.
Home Field: Lee-Hines Field. **Seating Capacity:** 1,500. **Outfield Dimensions:** LF—360, CF—395, RF—325.

SOUTHERN CALIFORNIA TROJANS

Conference: Pacific-10.
Mailing Address: Dedeaux Field, 1021 Childs Way, Los Angeles, CA 90089-0731. **Website:** usctrojans.com.
Head Coach: Chad Kreuter. **Assistant Coaches:** Frank Cruz, Tom House, *Doyle Wilson. **Telephone:** (213) 740-5762. **Baseball SID:** Jason Pommier. **Telephone:** (213) 740-3807. **Fax:** (213) 740-7584.
Home Field: Dedeaux Field. **Seating Capacity:** 2,500. **Outfield Dimensions:** LF—335, CF—395, RF—335. **Press Box Telephone:** (213) 748 3449.

SOUTHERN ILLINOIS SALUKIS

Conference: Missouri Valley.
Mailing Address: 118 Lingle Hall, SIU Arena, Carbondale, IL 62901-6620. **Website:** siusalukis.com.
Head Coach: Dan Callahan. **Assistant Coaches:** Tim Dixon, *Ken Henderson, Brian Neal. **Telephone:** (618) 453-2802. **Baseball SID:** Jason Clay. **Telephone:** (618) 453-5470. **Fax:** (618) 453-2648.
Home Field: Abe Martin Field. **Seating Capacity:** 2,000. **Outfield Dimensions:** LF—340, CF—390, RF—340. **Press Box Telephone:** (618) 453-3794.

SOUTHERN ILLINOIS-EDWARDSVILLE COUGARS

Conference: Independent.
Mailing Address: Box 1129 SIUE, Edwardsville, IL 62026. **Website:** www.siuecougars.com.
Head Coach: Gary Collins. **Assistant Coach:** Kurt Calvert, Tony Stoecklin. **Telephone:** (618) 650-2331. **Baseball SID:** Eric Hess. **Telephone:** (618) 650-3608. **Fax:** (618) 650-2296.

SOUTHERN MISSISSIPPI GOLDEN EAGLES

Conference: Conference USA.
Mailing Address: 118 College Dr, No. 5161, Hattiesburg, MS 39401. **Website:** www.southernmiss.com.
Head Coach: Scott Berry. **Assistant Coaches:** *Chad Caillet, Michael Fererico, Richy Harrelson. **Telephone:** (601) 266-5427. **Baseball SID:** Jason Kirksey. (601) 266-5332. **Fax:** (601) 266-4507.
Home Field: Pete Taylor Park. **Seating Capacity:** 6,600. **Outfield Dimensions:** LF—340, CF—400, RF—

340. **Press Box Telephone:** (601) 266-5684.

SOUTHERN UTAH THUNDERBIRDS

Conference: Summit.
Mailing Address: 351 West University Blvd, Cedar City, UT 84720. **Website:** www.suutbirds.com.
Head Coach: David Eldredge. **Assistant Coaches:** Matt Hollod, Chase Hudson, Keli'l Zablan. **Telephone:** (435) 327-0452. **Baseball SID:** Kyle Cottam. **Telephone:** (435) 586-7752. **Fax:** (435) 586-5444.
Home Field: Thunderbird Park. **Seating Capacity:** 500. **Outfield Dimensions:** LF—345, CF—410, RF—330.

STANFORD CARDINAL

Conference: Pacific-10.
Mailing Address: 641 E. Campus Dr, Stanford, CA 94305. **Website:** gostanford.com.
Head Coach: Mark Marquess. **Assistant Coaches:** Rusty Filter, *Dean Stotz. **Telephone:** (650) 723-4528. **Baseball SID:** Niall Adler. **Telephone:** (650) 725-2959. **Fax:** (650) 725-2957.
Home Field: Klein Field at Sunken Diamond. **Seating Capacity:** 4,000. **Outfield Dimensions:** LF—335, CF—400, RF—335. **Press Box Telephone:** (650) 723-4629.

STEPHEN F. AUSTIN STATE LUMBERJACKS

Conference: Southland.
Mailing Address: PO Box 13010, SFA Station, Nacogdoches, TX 75962. **Website:** www.sfajacks.com.
Head Coach: Johnny Cardenas. **Assistant Coaches:** *Chris Connally, Chad Massengale. **Telephone:** (936) 468-5982. **Baseball SID:** Ben Rikard. **Telephone:** (936) 468-5801. **Fax:** (936) 468-4593.
Home Field: Jaycees Field. **Seating Capacity:** 1,000. **Outfield Dimensions:** LF—330, CF—400, RF—300. **Press Box Telephone:** (936) 559-8344.

STETSON HATTERS

Conference: Atlantic Sun.
Mailing Address: 421 N. Woodland Blvd, DeLand, FL 32723. **Website:** www.gohatters.com.
Head Coach: Pete Dunn. **Assistant Coaches:** Clint Chrysler, *Mark Leavitt, Chris Roberts. **Telephone:** (386) 822-8106. **Baseball SID:** Dean Watson. **Telephone:** (386) 822-8130. **Fax:** (386) 822-7486.
Home Field: Melching Field. **Seating Capacity:** 2,500. **Outfield Dimensions:** LF—335, CF—403, RF—335. **Press Box Telephone:** (386) 736-7360.

STONY BROOK SEAWOLVES

Conference: America East.
Mailing Address: Indoor Sports Complex, Stony Brook, NY 11794-3500. **Website:** goseawolves.cstv.com.
Head Coach: Matt Senk. **Assistant Coaches:** Mike Marron, *Joe Pennucci, Jordan Wyckoff. **Telephone:** (631) 632-9226. **Baseball SID:** Jeremy Cohen. **Telephone:** (631) 632-6328. **Fax:** (631) 632-8841.
Home Field: University Field. **Seating Capacity:** 1,000. **Outfield Dimensions:** LF—330, CF—400, RF—330.

TEMPLE OWLS

Conference: Atlantic 10.
Mailing Address: 1700 North Broad St, Philadelphia, PA. **Website:** www.owlsports.com.
Head Coach: Rob Valli. **Assistant Coaches:** Joe Agnello, *Chuck Ristano. **Telephone:** (214) 204-8639. **Baseball SID:** Alex Samuelian. **Telephone:** (215) 204-7446. **Fax:** (215) 204-7499.
Home Field: Skip Wilson Field. **Seating Capacity:** 1000. **Outfield Dimensions:** LF—330, CF—400, RF—

330. **Press Box Telephone:** (609) 969-0975.

TENNESSEE VOLUNTEERS

Conference: Southeastern (East).
Mailing Address: 1720 Volunteer Blvd, Knoxville, TN 37996. **Website:** www.UTsports.com.
Head Coach: Todd Raleigh. **Assistant Coaches:** Jason Beverlin, Nate Headley, *Bradley LeCroy. **Telephone:** (865) 974-1223. **Baseball SID:** Cameron Harris. **Telephone:** (865) 974-8876. **Fax:** (865) 974-8875.
Home Field: Lindsey Nelson. **Seating Capacity:** 5,000. **Outfield Dimensions:** LF—320, CF—390, RF—320. **Press Box Telephone:** (865) 974-3376.

TENNESSEE TECH GOLDEN EAGLES

Conference: Ohio Valley.
Mailing Address: Box 5057, Cookeville, TN 38505. **Website:** www.ttusports.com.
Head Coach: Matt Bragga. **Assistant Coaches:** *Larry Bragga, Chris Cole, Justin Hogan. **Telephone:** (931) 372-3925. **Baseball SID:** Nick Heidelberger. **Telephone:** (931) 372-3923. **Fax:** (931) 372-3114.
Home Field: Howell Bush Stadium. **Seating Capacity:** 1,000. **Outfield Dimensions:** LF—331, CF—405, RF—329.

TENNESSEE-MARTIN SKYHAWKS

onference: Ohio Valley.
Mailing Address: 1037 Elam Center, Martin, TN 38238. **Website:** www.utmsports.com.
Head Coach: Victor Cates. **Assistant Coaches:** Trevor Berryhill, Brad Goss, Joe Scarano. **Telephone:** (731) 881-7337. **Baseball SID:** Joe Lofaro. **Telephone:** (731) 881-7632. **Fax:** (731) 881-7624.
Home Field: Skyhawk Field. **Seating Capacity:** 300. **Outfield Dimensions:** LF—330, CF—385, RF—330.

TEXAS LONGHORNS

Conference: Big 12.
Mailing Address: 2100 San Jacinto Boulevard, 327 Bellmont Hall, Austin, TX 78712. **Website:** www.TexasSports.com.
Head Coach: Augie Garrido. **Assistant Coaches:** *Tommy Harmon, Skip Johnson, Tommy Nicholson. **Telephone:** (512) 471-1404. **Baseball SID:** Thomas Dick. **Telephone:** (512) 471-6039. **Fax:** (512) 471-6040.
Home Field: UFCU Disch Falk Field. **Seating Capacity:** 6,876. **Outfield Dimensions:** LF—340, CF—400, RF—320.

TEXAS A&M AGGIES

Conference: Big 12.
Mailing Address: PO Box 30017, College Station, TX 77842-3017. **Website:** AggieAthletics.com.
Head Coach: Rob Childress. **Assistant Coaches:** Matt Deggs, Mike Clement, *Justin Seely. **Telephone:** (979) 845-4810. **Baseball SID:** Matt Simon. **Telephone:** (979) 862-5451. **Fax:** (979) 845-6825.
Home Field: Olsen Field. **Seating Capacity:** 7,053. **Outfield Dimensions:** LF—330, CF—400, RF—330. **Press Box Telephone:** (979) 458-3604.

TEXAS A&M-CORPUS CHRISTI ISLANDERS

Conference: Southland.
Mailing Address: 6300 Ocean Drive, Unit 5719, Corpus Christi, TX 78412. **Website:** www.goislanders.com.
Head Coach: Scott Malone. **Assistant Coaches:** Blaze Lambert, *Chris Ramirez, Marty Smith. **Telephone:** (361) 825-3412. **Baseball SID:** Aaron Ames. **Telephone:** (361)

825-3410. **Fax:** (361) 825-3218.
Home Field: Whataburger Field. **Seating Capacity:** 8,000. **Outfield Dimensions:** LF—327, CF—400, RF—315. **Press Box Telephone:** (361) 561-4665.

TEXAS CHRISTIAN HORNED FROGS

Conference: Mountain West.
Mailing Address: 2900 Stadium Dr, Fort Worth, TX 76129. **Website:** www.gofrogs.com.
Head Coach: Jim Schlossnagle. **Assistant Coaches:** Randy Mazey, Ryan Shotzberger, *Todd Whitting. **Telephone:** (817) 257-5354. **Baseball SID:** Brandie Davidson. **Telephone:** (817) 257-7479. **Fax:** (817) 257-7964.
Home Field: Lupton Stadium. **Seating Capacity:** 3,500. **Outfield Dimensions:** LF—330, CF—400, RF—330. **Press Box Telephone:** (817) 257-7966.

TEXAS SOUTHERN TIGERS

Conference: Southwestern Athletic.
Mailing Address: H&PE Building, Room 111, 3100 Cleburne Ave, Houston, TX 77004. **Website:** www.tsu.edu/athletics.
Head Coach: Michael Robertson. **Assistant Coaches:** Cory Alexander, Torik Harrison, Candy Robinson. **Telephone:** (713) 313-4315. **Baseball SID:** Rodney Bush. **Telephone:** (713) 313-7603. **Fax:** (713) 313-1045.

TEXAS STATE BOBCATS

Conference: Southland.
Mailing Address: 601 University Dr, San Marcos, TX 78666. **Website:** txstatebobcats.com.
Head Coach: Ty Harrington. **Assistant Coaches:** Jeremy Fikac, *Derek Matlock, Steven Trout. **Telephone:** (512) 245-8395. **Baseball SID:** Amber Arterberry. **Telephone:** (512) 245-4692. **Fax:** (512) 245-8387.
Home Field: Bobcat Field. **Seating Capacity:** 2,000. **Outfield Dimensions:** LF—370, CF—395, RF—330.

TEXAS TECH RED RAIDERS

Conference: Big 12.
Mailing Address: Box 43021, 6th and Boston Ave, Lubbock, TX 79409. **Website:** www.texastech.com.
Head Coach: Dan Spencer. **Assistant Coaches:** Ed Gustafson, Andy Jarvis, *Trent Petrie. **Telephone:** (806) 742-3355. **Baseball SID:** Blayne Beal. **Telephone:** (806) 742-2770. **Fax:** (806) 742-1970.
Home Field: Dan Law Field. **Seating Capacity:** 5,026. **Outfield Dimensions:** LF—330, CF—405, RF—330. **Press Box Telephone:** (806) 742-3688.

TEXAS-ARLINGTON MAVERICKS

Conference: Southland.
Mailing Address: 1309 West Mitchell Street, Arlington, TX 76019. **Website:** utamavs.com.
Head Coach: Darin Thomas. **Assistant Coaches:** Mark Flatten, *Jay Sirianni, Fuller Smith. **Telephone:** (817) 272-2542. **Baseball SID:** Scott Lacefield. **Telephone:** (817) 272-2239. **Fax:** (817) 272-5037.
Home Field: Clay Gould Ballpark. **Seating Capacity:** 1,600. **Outfield Dimensions:** LF—330, CF—400, RF—330. **Press Box Telephone:** (817) 462-4225.

TEXAS-PAN AMERICAN BRONCS

Conference: Independent.
Mailing Address: 1201 W. University Drive, Edinburg, TX 78539. **Website:** utpabroncs.com.
Head Coach: Manny Mantrana. **Assistant Coaches:** Norbert Lopez, *Stephen Piercefield. **Telephone:** (956) 381-2235. **Baseball SID:** Bernie Saenz. **Telephone:** (956)

381-2240. **Fax:** (956) 381-2261.

TEXAS-SAN ANTONIO ROADRUNNERS

Conference: Southland.
Mailing Address: One UTSA Circle, San Antonio, TX 78249-0691. **Website:** www.goutsa.com.
Head Coach: Sherman Corbett. **Assistant Coaches:** Brett Lawler, Josh Lee, *Jason Marshall. **Telephone:** (210) 458-4805. **Baseball SID:** Brian Hernandez. **Telephone:** (210) 458-4907. **Fax:** (210) 458-4569.
Home Field: Roadrunner Field. **Seating Capacity:** 800. **Outfield Dimensions:** LF—335, CF—405, RF—340. **Press Box Telephone:** (210) 458-4612.

TOLEDO ROCKETS

Conference: Mid-American (West).
Mailing Address: 2801 West Bancroft St, MS-408, Toledo, OH 43606. **Website:** utrockets.com.
Head Coach: Cory Mee. **Assistant Coaches:** *Josh Bradford, Nick McIntyre, Matt Talarico. **Telephone:** (419) 530-6263. **Baseball SID:** Brian DeBenedictis. **Telephone:** (419) 530-4919. **Fax:** (419) 530-4428.
Home Field: Scott Park. **Seating Capacity:** 1,000. **Outfield Dimensions:** LF—330, CF—400, RF—330. **Press Box Telephone:** (419) 530-3089.

TOWSON TIGERS

Conference: Colonial Athletic.
Mailing Address: 8000 York Road, Towson, MD 21252-0001. **Website:** www.towsontigers.com.
Head Coach: Mike Gottlieb. **Assistant Coaches:** Lance Mauck, *Scott Roane. **Telephone:** (410) 704-3775. **Baseball SID:** Dan O'Connell. **Telephone:** (410) 704-3102. **Fax:** (410) 704-3861.
Home Field: John B. Schuerholz Park. **Seating Capacity:** 1,200. **Outfield Dimensions:** LF—312, CF—424, RF—302. **Press Box Telephone:** (410) 704-5810.

TROY TROJANS

Conference: Sun Belt.
Mailing Address: 5000 Veterans Stadium Dr, Troy, AL 36082. **Website:** www.TroyTrojans.com.
Head Coach: Bobby Pierce. **Assistant Coaches:** Jeff Crane, Eric House, *Mark Smartt. **Telephone:** (334) 670-3489. **Baseball SID:** Ricky Hazel. **Telephone:** (334) 670-3832. **Fax:** (334) 670-5665.
Home Field: Riddle-Pace Field. **Seating Capacity:** 2,000. **Outfield Dimensions:** LF—340, CF—400, RF—310. **Press Box Telephone:** (334) 670-5701.

TULANE GREEN WAVE

Conference: Conference USA.
Mailing Address: James Wilson Center, New Orleans, LA 70118-5698. **Website:** www.TulaneGreenWave.com.
Head Coach: Rick Jones. **Assistant Coaches:** Jack Cressend, Jake Gautreau, *Chad Sutter. **Telephone:** (504) 862-8239. **Baseball SID:** Unavailable. **Telephone:** (504) 862-8240. **Fax:** (504) 862-8569.
Home Field: Greer Field at Turchin Stadium. **Seating Capacity:** 5,000. **Outfield Dimensions:** LF—325, CF—400, RF—325. **Press Box Telephone:** (504) 862-8224.

UTAH UTES

Conference: Mountain West.
Mailing Address: 1825 E. South Campus Dr, Salt Lake City, UT 84112. **Website:** utahutes.com.
Head Coach: Bill Kinneberg. **Assistant Coaches:** *Mike Crawford, Bryan Kinneberg, Pete Flores. **Telephone:** (801) 581-3526. **Baseball SID:** Brooke Frederickson. **Telephone:** (801) 581-8302. **Fax:** (801) 581-4358.

Home Field: Spring Mobile Ballpark. **Seating Capacity:** 15,000. **Outfield Dimensions:** LF—320, CF—410, RF—315.

UTAH VALLEY WOLVERINES

Conference: Independent.
Mailing Address: 800 W. University Parkway, Orem, UT 84058. **Website:** www.WolverineGreen.com.
Head Coach: Eric Madsen. **Assistant Coaches:** *Dave Carter, Mike Martin, Adam Openshaw. **Telephone:** (801) 863-6509. **Baseball SID:** Clint Burgi. **Telephone:** (801) 863-8644. **Fax:** (801) 863-8813.
Home Field: Brent Brown Ballpark. **Seating Capacity:** 5,000. **Outfield Dimensions:** LF—312, CF—408, RF—315. **Press Box Telephone:** (801) 362-1548.

VALPARAISO CRUSADERS

Conference: Horizon.
Mailing Address: 1009 Union St, Valparaiso, IN 46383. **Website:** www.valpoathletics.com.
Head Coach: Tracy Woodson. **Assistant Coaches:** Josh Dietz, Brian Schmack. **Telephone:** (219) 464-5239. **Baseball SID:** Ryan Wronkowicz. **Telephone:** (219) 464-5232. **Fax:** (219) 464-5762.
Home Field: Emory G. Bauer Field. **Seating Capacity:** 500. **Outfield Dimensions:** LF—330, CF—400, RF—330. **Press Box Telephone:** (219) 464-6006.

VANDERBILT COMMODORES

Conference: Southeastern (East).
Mailing Address: 2601 Jess Neely Dr, Nashville, TN 37212. **Website:** www.vucommodores.com.
Head Coach: Tim Corbin. **Assistant Coaches:** Larry Day, *Josh Holliday, Derek Johnson. **Telephone:** (615) 322-7725. **Baseball SID:** Thomas Samuel. **Telephone:** (615) 343-0020. **Fax:** (615) 343-7064.
Home Field: Hawkins Field. **Seating Capacity:** 4,100. **Outfield Dimensions:** LF—315, CF—400, RF—335. **Press Box Telephone:** (615) 320-0436.

VILLANOVA WILDCATS

Conference: Big East.
Mailing Address: 800 Lancaster Ave, Villanova, PA 19085. **Website:** villanova.com.
Head Coach: Joe Godri. **Assistant Coaches:** *Jim Carone, Rod Johnson, Dave Miller. **Telephone:** (610) 519-4529. **Baseball SID:** David Berman. **Telephone:** (610) 519-4122. **Fax:** (610) 519-6884.
Home Field: Villanova Ballpark at Plymouth. **Seating Capacity:** 750. **Outfield Dimensions:** LF—330, CF—405, RF—330. **Press Box Telephone:** (860) 490-6398.

VIRGINIA CAVALIERS

Conference: Atlantic Coast (Coastal).
Mailing Address: PO Box 400853, Charlottesville, VA 22904-4853. **Website:** www.virginiasports.com.
Head Coach: Brian O'Connor. **Assistant Coaches:** Karl Kuhn, *Kevin McMullan, Eddie Smith. **Telephone:** (434) 982-4932. **Baseball SID:** Andy Fledderjohann. **Telephone:** (434) 982-5131. **Fax:** (434) 982-5525.
Home Field: Davenport Field. **Seating Capacity:** 3,600. **Outfield Dimensions:** LF—335, CF—408, RF—335. **Press Box Telephone:** (434) 244-4071.

VIRGINIA COMMONWEALTH RAMS

Conference: Colonial Athletic.
Mailing Address: 1300 W. Broad Street, Richmond, VA 23284. **Website:** www.vcuathletics.com.
Head Coach: Paul Keyes. **Assistant Coaches:** Tim Haynes, *Shawn Stiffler. **Telephone:** (804) 828-4820.

Baseball SID: Mitchell Moore. **Telephone:** (804) 828-8496. **Fax:** (804) 828-4938.
Home Field: The Diamond. **Seating Capacity:** 12,134. **Outfield Dimensions:** LF—330, CF—402, RF—330. **Press Box Telephone:** (302) 593-0115.

VIRGINIA MILITARY INSTITUTE KEYDETS

Conference: Big South.
Mailing Address: Virginia Military Institute, Lexington, VA 24450. **Website:** www.VMIKeydets.com.
Head Coach: Marlin Ikenberry. **Assistant Coaches:** Kwan Evans, Jonathan Hadra, *Ryan Mau. **Telephone:** (540) 464-7609. **Baseball SID:** Christian Hoffman. **Telephone:** (540) 464-7514. **Fax:** (540) 464-7583.
Home Field: Gray-Minor Stadium. **Seating Capacity:** 1,400. **Outfield Dimensions:** LF—330, CF—395, RF—335. **Press Box Telephone:** (540) 460-6920.

VIRGINIA TECH HOKIES

Conference: Atlantic Coast (Coastal).
Mailing Address: 460 Jamerson Athletic Center, Blacksburg, VA 24061. **Website:** www.hokiesports.com.
Head Coach: Pete Hughes. **Assistant Coaches:** *Mike Gambino, Mike Kunigonis, Dave Turgeon. **Telephone:** (540) 231-3671. **Baseball SID:** Matt Kovatch. **Telephone:** (540) 231-1894. **Fax:** (540) 231-6984.
Home Field: English Field. **Seating Capacity:** 4,000. **Outfield Dimensions:** LF—330, CF—400, RF—330. **Press Box Telephone:** (540) 231-8974.

WAGNER SEAHAWKS

Conference: Northeast.
Mailing Address: Spiro Sports Center, One Campus Rd, Staten Island, NY 10301. **Website:** wagnerathletics.com.
Head Coach: Joe Litterio. **Assistant Coaches:** Jason Jurgens, Billy Malloy, Ray Montanez. **Telephone:** (718) 390-3154. **Baseball SID:** Kevin Ross. **Telephone:** (718) 390-3215. **Fax:** (718) 420-4015.
Home Field: Richmond County Bank Ballpark. **Seating Capacity:** 6,900. **Outfield Dimensions:** LF—320, CF—390, RF—318. **Press Box Telephone:** (716) 969-6126.

WAKE FOREST DEMON DEACONS

Conference: Atlantic Coast (Atlantic).
Mailing Address: 211 Wingate Drive, 310 Miller Center, Winston-Salem, NC 27109. **Website:** wakeforestsports.com.
Head Coach: Tom Walter. **Assistant Coaches:** Grant Achilles, Bill Cilento, *Dennis Healy. **Telephone:** (336) 758-5570. **Baseball SID:** Chad Crunk. **Telephone:** (336) 758-5842. **Fax:** (336) 758-5140.
Home Field: Wake Forest Ballpark. **Seating Capacity:** 6,000. **Outfield Dimensions:** LF—325, CF—390, RF—325.

WASHINGTON HUSKIES

Conference: Pacific-10.
Mailing Address: Box 354070, Seattle, WA 98195. **Website:** www.gohuskies.com.
Head Coach: Lindsay Meggs. **Assistant Coaches:** Greg Moore, *Dave Nakama, Kevin Ticen. **Telephone:** (206) 543-9365. **Baseball SID:** Jeff Bechthold. **Telephone:** (206) 685-7910. **Fax:** (206) 543-5000.
Home Field: Husky Ballpark. **Seating Capacity:** 1500. **Outfield Dimensions:** LF—327, CF—395, RF—317. **Press Box Telephone:** (206) 685-1994.

WASHINGTON STATE COUGARS

Conference: Pacific-10.
Mailing Address: Bohler Athletic Complex M-40, Pullman, WA 99163. **Website:** wsucougars.cstv.com.
Head Coach: Donnie Marbut. **Assistant Coaches:** *Spencer Allen, Gabe Boruff, Gregg Swenson. **Telephone:** (509) 335-0332. **Baseball SID:** Craig Lawson. **Telephone:** (509) 335-0265. **Fax:** (509) 335-0267.
Home Field: Bailey-Brayton Field. **Seating Capacity:** 3,500. **Outfield Dimensions:** LF—330, CF—400, RF—335. **Press Box Telephone:** (509) 335-2684.

WEST VIRGINIA MOUNTAINEERS

Conference: Big East.
Mailing Address: PO Box 0877, Morgantown, WV 26507. **Website:** www.msnsportsnet.com.
Head Coach: Greg Van Zant. **Assistant Coaches:** Tad Reida, *Pat Sherald, Jake Weghorst. **Telephone:** (304) 293-9881. **Baseball SID:** Steve Stone. **Telephone:** (304) 293-2821. **Fax:** (304) 293-4105.
Home Field: Hawley Field. **Seating Capacity:** 1,500. **Outfield Dimensions:** LF—325, CF—390, RF—325. **Press Box Telephone:** (304) 293-5988.

WESTERN CAROLINA CATAMOUNTS

Conference: Southern.
Mailing Address: Ramsey Center, Cullowhee, NC 28723. **Website:** catamountsports.com.
Head Coach: Bobby Moranda. **Assistant Coaches:** *Alan Beck, David Haverstick, Bruce Johnson. **Telephone:** (828) 227-7338. **Baseball SID:** Daniel Hooker. **Telephone:** (828) 227-2339. **Fax:** (828) 227-7688.
Home Field: Childress Field/Hennon Stadium. **Seating Capacity:** 1,500. **Outfield Dimensions:** LF—325, CF—390, RF—325. **Press Box Telephone:** (828) 227-7020.

WESTERN ILLINOIS FIGHTING LEATHERNECKS

Conference: Summit.
Mailing Address: 204 Western Hall, 1 University Circle, Macomb, IL 61455. **Website:** www.wiuathletics.com.
Head Coach: Mike Villano. **Assistant Coaches:** Brock Bainter. **Telephone:** (309) 298-1521. **Baseball SID:** Ryan Bower. **Telephone:** (309) 298-1133. **Fax:** (309) 298-1960.
Home Field: Alfred D. Boyer Stadium. **Seating Capacity:** 500. **Outfield Dimensions:** LF—330, CF—400, RF—330. **Press Box Telephone:** (309) 298-1190.

WESTERN KENTUCKY HILLTOPPERS

Conference: Sun Belt.
Mailing Address: 1605 Avenue of Champions, Bowling Green, KY 42101. **Website:** www.wkusports.com.
Head Coach: Chris Finwood. **Assistant Coaches:** *Blake Allen, Casey Hamilton, Matt Myers. **Telephone:** (270) 745-2277. **Baseball SID:** Michael Schroeder. **Telephone:** (270) 745-4298. **Fax:** (270) 745-3444.
Home Field: Nick Denes Field. **Seating Capacity:** 1,500. **Outfield Dimensions:** LF—330, CF—400, RF—330. **Press Box Telephone:** (270) 745-6941.

WESTERN MICHIGAN BRONCOS

Conference: Mid-American (West).
Mailing Address: 1903 West Michigan Ave, Kalamazoo, MI 49008. **Website:** www.wmubroncos.com.
Head Coach: Randy Ford. **Assistant Coaches:** *Scott Demetral, Tom Grant. **Telephone:** (269) 386-3205. **Baseball SID:** Kristin Keirns. **Telephone:** (269) 387-4123.

Fax: (269) 387-4139.
Home Field: Robert J. Bobb Stadium at Hyames Field. **Seating Capacity:** 2500. **Outfield Dimensions:** LF—325, CF—400, RF—340. **Press Box Telephone:** (269) 387-8210.

WICHITA STATE SHOCKERS

Conference: Missouri Valley.
Mailing Address: 1845 Fairmount, Campus Box 18, Wichita, KS 67260-0018. **Website:** www.goshockers.com.
Head Coach: Gene Stephenson. **Assistant Coaches:** Brandon Hall, *Brent Kemnitz, Jim Thomas. **Telephone:** (316) 978-3636. **Baseball SID:** Tami Cutler. **Telephone:** (316) 978-5559. **Fax:** (316) 978-3336.
Home Field: Eck Stadium. **Seating Capacity:** 7,851. **Outfield Dimensions:** LF—330, CF—390, RF—330. **Press Box Telephone:** (316) 978-3390.

WILLIAM & MARY TRIBE

Conference: Colonial Athletic.
Mailing Address: PO Box 399, Williamsburg, VA 23187. **Website:** www.tribeathletics.com.
Head Coach: Frank Leoni. **Assistant Coaches:** George Fisher, Kyle Padgett, *Jad Prachniak. **Telephone:** (757) 221-3399. **Baseball SID:** Scott Burns. **Telephone:** (757) 221-3344. **Fax:** (757) 221-2989.
Home Field: Plumeri Park. **Seating Capacity:** 1,200. **Outfield Dimensions:** LF—330, CF—400, RF—330. **Press Box Telephone:** (757) 221-3562.

WINTHROP EAGLES

Conference: Big South.
Mailing Address: 1162 Eden Terrace Road, Rock Hill, SC 29733. **Website:** www.winthropeagles.com.
Head Coach: Joe Hudak. **Assistant Coaches:** Kyle DiEduardo, *Mike McGuire, Jeff Stanek. **Telephone:** (803) 323-2129. **Baseball SID:** Wesley Herring. **Telephone:** (803) 323-2129. **Fax:** (803) 323-2433.
Home Field: The Winthrop Ballpark. **Seating Capacity:** 1,800. **Outfield Dimensions:** LF—325, CF—390, RF—325. **Press Box Telephone:** (803) 323-2155.

WISCONSIN-MILWAUKEE PANTHERS

Conference: Horizon.
Mailing Address: 3409 N. Downer Ave, Milwaukee, WI 53201. **Website:** uwmpanthers.com.
Head Coach: Scott Doffek. **Assistant Coaches:** *Cory Bigler, Mike Goetz, Steve Sanfilippo. **Telephone:** (414) 229-5670. **Baseball SID:** Chris Zills. **Telephone:** (414) 229-4593. **Fax:** (414) 229-6759.
Home Field: Henry Aaron Field. **Seating Capacity:** Unavailable. **Outfield Dimensions:** LF—320, CF—390, RF—320. **Press Box Telephone:** (414) 750-2090.

WOFFORD TERRIERS

Conference: Southern.
Mailing Address: 429 N. Church Street, Spartanburg, SC 29303. **Website:** athletics.wofford.edu.
Head Coach: Todd Interdonato. **Assistant Coaches:** *Dusty Blake, Anthony Dillenger, Ryan McKenzie. **Telephone:** (864) 597-4497. **Baseball SID:** Brent Williamson. **Telephone:** (864) 597-4093. **Fax:** (864) 597-4129.
Home Field: Russell C. King Field. **Seating Capacity:** 2,500. **Outfield Dimensions:** LF—325, CF—395, RF—325. **Press Box Telephone:** (864) 597-4478.

WRIGHT STATE RAIDERS

Conference: Horizon.
Mailing Address: 3640 Colonel Glenn Hwy., Dayton, OH 45435. **Website:** wsuraiders.cstv.com.
Head Coach: Rob Cooper. **Assistant Coaches:** *Greg Lovelady, Brian Meyer, Ross Oeder. **Telephone:** (937) 775-3667. **Baseball SID:** Greg Campbell. **Telephone:** (937) 775-4687. **Fax:** (937) 775-2368.
Home Field: Nischwitz Stadium. **Seating Capacity:** 750. **Outfield Dimensions:** LF—330, CF—400, RF—370. **Press Box Telephone:** (937) 602-0326.

XAVIER MUSKETEERS

Conference: Atlantic 10.
Mailing Address: 3800 Victory Parkway, Cincinnati, OH 45207. **Website:** www.goxavier.com.
Head Coach: Scoot Googins. **Assistant Coaches:** Bryan Bonner, Nick Otte, *Zach Schmidt. **Telephone:** (513) 745-2891. **Baseball SID:** Jenna Willhoit. **Telephone:** (513) 745-3961. **Fax:** (513) 745-2825.
Home Field: Hayden Field. **Seating Capacity:** 500. **Outfield Dimensions:** LF—310, CF—380, RF—310. **Press Box Telephone:** (513) 532-2781.

YALE BULLDOGS

Conference: Ivy League (Rolfe).
Mailing Address: 20 Tower Pkwy, New Haven, CT 06520. **Website:** yalebulldogs.com.
Head Coach: John Stuper. **Assistant Coaches:** *Tucker Frawley, Ray Guarino, Kevin Huber. **Telephone:** (203) 432-1466. **Baseball SID:** Drew Kingsley. **Telephone:** (203) 432-1448. **Fax:** (203) 432-1454.
Home Field: Yale Field. **Seating Capacity:** 12,000. **Outfield Dimensions:** LF—330, CF—405, RF—315.

YOUNGSTOWN STATE PENGUINS

Conference: Horizon.
Mailing Address: One University Plaza, Youngstown, OH 44555. **Website:** www.ysusports.com.
Head Coach: Rich Pasquale. **Assistant Coaches:** Craig Antush, Dan Lipari, *Tom Lipari. **Telephone:** (330) 941-3485. **Baseball SID:** John Vogel. **Telephone:** (330) 941-1480. **Fax:** (330) 941-3191.
Home Field: Eastwood Field. **Seating Capacity:** 6,000. **Outfield Dimensions:** LF—335, CF—405, RF—335. **Press Box Telephone:** (330) 505-0000, ext. 229.

AMATEUR & YOUTH

INTERNATIONAL ORGANIZATIONS

INTERNATIONAL BASEBALL FEDERATION

Headquarters: Avenue de Mon Repos 24, Case Postale 6099, 1002 Lausanne, Switzerland. **Telephone:** (+41-21) 318-82-40. **FAX:** (41-21) 318-82-41.

Website: www.ibaf.org. **E-Mail:** ibaf@ibaf.org **Year Founded:**1938.

President: Riccardo Fraccari

1st Vice President: Kazuhiro Tawa. **2nd Vice President:** Alonso Perez Gonzalez. **3rd Vice President:** Antonio Castro. **Secretary General:** Israel Roldan. **Treasurer:** Rene Laforce. **First Member at Large:** Paul Seiler. **Second Member at Large:** Tom Peng. **Third Member at Large:** Luis Melero. **Continental VP, Africa:** Ishola Williams. **Continental VP, Americas:** Eduardo De Bello. **Continental VP, Asia:** Kang Seung Kyoo. **Continental VP, Europe:** Martin Miller. **Continental VP, Oceania:** John Ostermeyer.

Manager, Media Relations: Jake Fehling. **Media Coordinator:** Joe Favorito. **Manager, Anti-Doping:** Jean-Pierre Moser. **Assistant, Special Projects:** Masaru Yokoo. **Manager, Project Development:** Ian Young.

CONTINENTAL ASSOCIATIONS

CONFEDERATION PAN AMERICANA DE BEISBOL (COPABE)

Mailing Address: Calle 3, Francisco Filos, Vista Hermosa, Edificio 74, Planta Baja Local No. 1, Panama City, Panama. **Telephone:** (507) 229-8684. **Fax:** Unavailable. **E-Mail Address:** copabe@sinfo.net.

President: Eduardo De Bello (Panama). **Secretary General:** Hector Pereyra (Dominican Republic).

AFRICAN BASEBALL/SOFTBALL ASSOCIATION

Mailing Address: Paiko Road, Changaga, Minna, Niger State, PMB 150, Nigeria. **Telephone:** (234-66) 224-555. **Fax:** (234-66) 224-555. **E-Mail Address:** absasecretariat@yahoo.com.

President: Ishola Williams (Nigeria). **Executive Director:** Friday Ichide (Nigeria). **Secretary General:** Fridah Shiroya (Kenya).

BASEBALL FEDERATION OF ASIA

Mailing Address: No. 946-16 Dogok-Dong, Kangnam-Gu, Seoul, 135-270 Korea. **Telephone:** (82-2) 572-8413. **Fax:** (82-2) 572-8416.

President: Nae-Heun Lee (Korea). **Secretary General:** Kyung-Hoon Minn (Korea).

EUROPEAN BASEBALL CONFEDERATION

Mailing Address: Otto-FleckSchneise 12, D - 60528 Frankfurt, Germany. **Telephone:** +49-69-6700-284. **Fax:** +49-69-67724-212. **E-Mail Address:** office@baseballeurope.com. **Website:** baseballeurope.com.

President: Martin Miller (Germany). **Secretary General:** Petr Ditrich (Czech Republic).

BASEBALL CONFERERATION OF OCEANIA

Mailing Address: 48 Partridge Way, Mooroolbark, Victoria 3138, Australia. **Telephone:** (61-2) 6214-1236. **Fax:** (61-3) 6214-1926. **E-Mail Address:** bcosecgeneral@baseballoceania.com. **Website:** www.baseballoceania.com.

President: John Ostermeyer (Australia). **Secretary General:** Chet Gray (Australia).

ORGANIZATIONS

INTERNATIONAL GOODWILL SERIES, INC.

Mailing Address: 982 Slate Drive, Santa Rosa, CA 95405. **Telephone:** (707) 538-0777. **E-Mail Address:** bobw.24@goodwillseries.org. **Website:** www.goodwillseries.org.

President, Goodwill Series, Inc.: Bob Williams.

INTERNATIONAL SPORTS GROUP

Mailing Address: 11430 Kestrel Rd., Klamath Falls, OR 97601. **Telephone:** (541) 882-4293. **E-Mail Address:** isg-baseball@yahoo.com. **Website:** www.isgbaseball.com.

President: Jim Jones. **Vice President:** Tom O'Connell. **Secretary/Treasurer:** Randy Town.

NATIONAL ORGANIZATIONS

USA BASEBALL

Mailing Address, Corporate Headquarters: 403 Blackwell St., Durham, NC 27701 **Telephone:** (919) 474-8721. **Fax:** (919) 474-8822. **E-Mail Address:** info@usa-baseball.com. **Website:** www.usabaseball.com.

President: Mike Gaski. **Secretary General:** Ernie Young. **Treasurer:** Jason Dobis.

Executive Director/Chief Executive Officer: Paul Seiler. **Director, Operations/Women's National Team:** Ashley Bratcher. **General Manager, Professional/National Teams:** Eric Campbell. **Chief Financial Officer:** Ray Darwin. **Director, Media/Public Relations:** Jake Fehling. **Director, 14U National Team:** Nate Logan. **Chief Operating Officer:** David Perkins. **Director, 18U National Team:** Rick Riccobono. **Director, 16U National Team:** Jeff Singer.

National Members: Amateur Athletic Union (AAU), American Amateur Baseball Congress (AABC), American Baseball Coaches Association (ABCA), American Legion Baseball, Babe Ruth Baseball, Dixie Baseball, Little League Baseball, National Amateur Baseball Federation (NABF), National Association of Intercollegiate Athletics (NAIA), National Baseball Congress (NBC), National Collegiate Athletic Association (NCAA), National Federation of State High School Athletic Associations, National High School Baseball Coaches Association (BCA), National Junior College Athletic Association (NJCAA), Police Athletic League (PAL), PONY Baseball, T-Ball USA, United States Specialty Sports Association (USSSA), YMCAs of the USA.

2010 Events

USA Baseball Professional Teams
Unavailable

USA Baseball Collegiate National Team
July 5 -11. . .Collegiate National Team Trials & Training Cary, N.C.
July 12 – 13 . . . . .USA vs. TBD N.C.
July 14 – 18 .USA vs. Korea N.C.
June 20 - 21 .USA vs. TBD TBD
July 25 – 28 . USA vs. Chinese Taipei Taipei City, Chinese Taipei
July 30 – Aug. 7. . .V FISU World Championships Tokyo, Japan

USA Baseball 18U National Team
June 22 – 28. . . .USA Baseball Tournament of Stars Cary, N.C.
June 28 – July 3 18U National Team Trials & Training Cary, N.C.
July 6 – 10 . . . . USA vs. NYC All-Stars New York, N.Y.
July 12 – 20 . . . International Friendship Series Various, Minn.
July 23 – Aug. 1. . . . . IBAF World "AAA" Championships
Thunder Bay, Canada

USA Baseball 16U National Team
June 18 – 26 . 16U Championships – West Peoria & Surprise, Ariz.
June 18 – 26 16U Championships – East Palm Beach County, Fla.
TBD . . . . 16U National Team Trials & Training TBD
TBD . . . . .COPABE Pan Am "AA" Championships TBD, Mexico

USA Baseball 14U National Team
June 18 – 2314U Championships – West Peoria & Surprise, Ariz.

June 18 – 23. . . . 14U Championships – East Lee County, Fla.
July 14 – 20 . . 14U National Team Trials & Training Cary, N.C.
July 23 – Aug. 1. . . . . . . .COPABE Pan Am "A" Championships
Managua, Nicaragua

USA Baseball Women's National Team
TBD . . . . Women's Championship Cary, N.C.
TBD . . . . Women's National Team Trials & Training Cary, N.C.
TBD . . . . IBAF Women's Baseball World Cup TBD

USA Baseball National Teams Identification Series (NTIS)
Sept. 10 – 12 . . . . 17U, 15U, 13U NTIS Cary, N.C.

USA Baseball Athlete Development Camps
June 15 – 17. . . . . .USAB ADP Camp Jupiter, Fla.
June 15 – 17. . . . . USAB ADP Camp Fort Myers, Fla.
June 15 – 17. . . . . USAB ADP Camp Peoria, Ariz.

Other Events
March 26. . . . . . . Coaches Spring Training Clinic Cary, N.C.
March 27. . . . . .Youth Spring Training Clinic Cary, N.C.
April 10. . . . . .USAB Parent & Child Clinic Cary, N.C.
June 29 – July 4 . USA Baseball NT Invitational 14U Cary, N.C.
July 6 – 11 . . . . . USA Baseball NT Invitational 16U Cary, N.C.
Sept. 3 – 6 . . . . USA Baseball Labor Day Cup Cary, N.C.
Oct. 30 . . . . Triangle Classic (12U) Cary, N.C.

BASEBALL CANADA

Mailing Address: 2212 Gladwin Cres., Suite A7, Ottawa, On-tario K1B 5N1. **Telephone:** (613) 748-5606. **FAX:** (613) 748-5767. **E-Mail Address:** info@baseball.ca. **Website:** www.baseball.ca.

Director General: Jim Baba. **Head Coach/Director, National Teams:** Greg Hamilton. **Manager, Baseball Operations:** Andre Lachance. **Manager, Media/Public Relations:** Andre Cormier. **Ad-ministrative Coordinator:** Denise Thomas.

NATIONAL BASEBALL CONGRESS

Mailing Address: 300 S. Sycamore, Wichita, KS 67213. **Telephone:** (316) 264-4625. **Fax:** (316) 264-3037. **Website:** www.nbcbaseball.com.

Year Founded: 1931.

General Manager: Josh Robertson. **Tournament Director:** Jerry Taylor.

ATHLETES IN ACTION

Mailing Address: 651 Taylor Dr., Xenia, OH 45385. **Telephone:** (937) 352-1000. **Fax:** (937) 352-1245. **E-Mail Address:** baseball@athletesinaction.org. **Website:** www.aiabaseball.org.

Director, AIA Baseball: Jason Lester. **U.S. Teams Director:** Chris Beck. **International Teams Director:** John McLaughlin. **General Manager, Great Lakes:** John Henschen. **Athletic Trainer:** Natalie McLaughlin.

SUMMER COLLEGE LEAGUES

NATIONAL ALLIANCE OF COLLEGE SUMMER BASEBALL

Telephone: (508) 404-7403. **E-Mail Address:** pga-lop@comcast.net.

Executive Director: Jeff Carter (Southern Collegiate Baseball League). **Assistant Executive Directors:** Kim Lance (Great Lakes Summer Collegiate League), David Biery (Valley Baseball League). **Secretary:** Sara Whiting (Florida Collegiate Summer League). **Treasurer:** Jim Phillips (Valley Baseball League).

Member Leagues: Atlantic Collegiate Baseball League, Cal Ripken Collegiate Summer League, Cape Cod Baseball League, Florida Collegiate Summer League, Great Lakes Summer Collegiate League, New York Collegiate Baseball League, Southern Collegiate Baseball League, Valley Baseball League.

ALASKA BASEBALL LEAGUE

Mailing Address: PO Box 2690, Palmer, AK 99645. **Telephone:** (907) 745-6401. **Fax:** (907) 746-5068. **E-Mail Address:** gmminers@gci.net.

Year Founded: 1974 (reunited, 1998).

President: Pete Christopher (Mat-Su Miners). **League Spokesperson:** Mike Baxter. **League Stats:** Dick Lobdell.

Regular Season: 45 league games and approximately 5 non-league games. **2010 Opening Date:** June 10. **Closing Date:** August 3.

Playoff Format: League champion and second-place finisher qualify for National Baseball Congress World Series.

Roster Limit: 24 plus exemption for Alaska residents. **Player Eligibility Rule:** Players with college eligibility, except drafted seniors.

ANCHORAGE BUCS

Mailing Address: PO Box 240061, Anchorage, AK 99524-0061. **Telephone:** (907) 561-2827. **Fax:** (907) 561-2920. **E-Mail Address:** admin@anchoragebucs.com. **Website:** www.anchoragebucs.com. **General Manager:** Dennis Mattingly. **Head Coach:** T.J. Bruce (Long Beach State).

ANCHORAGE GLACIER PILOTS

Mailing Address: 207 East Northern Lights Blvd #125, Anchorage, AK 99503. **Telephone:** (907) 274-3627. **Fax:** (907) 274-3628. **E-Mail Address:** gpilots@alaska.net. **Website:** www.glacierpilots.com. **General Manager:** Jon Dyson. **Head Coach:** Yogi Cox.

ATHLETES IN ACTION

Mailing Address: 651 Taylor Dr, Xenia, OH 45385. **Telephone:** (937) 352-1237. **Fax:** (937) 352-1245. **E-Mail Address:** chris.beck@athletesinaction.org. **Website:** www.aiabaseball.org. **General Manager:** Chris Beck. **Head Coach:** Chris Beck.

FAIRBANKS ALASKA GOLDPANNERS

Mailing Address: PO Box 71154, Fairbanks, AK 99707. **Telephone:** (907) 451-0095, (619) 561-4581. **Fax:** (907) 456-6429. **E-Mail Address:** addennis@cox.net. **Website:** www.goldpanners.com. **General Manager:** Don Dennis. **Head Coach:** Jim Dietz.

MAT-SU MINERS

Mailing Address: PO Box 2690, Palmer, AK 99645-2690. **Telephone:** (907) 746-4914. **Fax:** (907) 746-5068. **E-Mail Address:** generalmanager@matsuminers.org. **Website:** www.matsuminers.org. **General Manager:** Pete Christopher. **Head Coach:** Russell Raley (University of Oklahoma).

PENINSULA OILERS

Mailing Address: 601 S. Main St, Kenai, AK 99611. **Telephone:** (907) 283-7133. **Fax:** (907) 283-3390. **E-Mail Address:** shawn@oilersbaseball.com. **Website:** www.oilersbaseball.com. **General Manager:** Shawn Maltby. **Head Coach:** Dennis Machado (Cal State Bakersfield).

ATLANTIC COLLEGIATE LEAGUE

Mailing Address: 1760 Joanne Drive, Quakertown, PA 18951. **Telephone:** (215) 536-5777. **Fax:** (215) 536-5177. **E-Mail:** tbonekemper@verizon.net. **Website:** www.acbl-online.com.

Year Founded: 1967.

Commissioner: Ralph Addonizio. **President:** Tom Bonekemper. **Secretary:** Ed Kull. **Treasurer:** Bob Hoffman.

Division Structure: Wolff—Jersey, Lehigh Valley, Quakertown, Scranton. Kaiser—Long Island, North Jersey, Staten Island, Torrington. Hamptons—North Fork, Riverhead, Sag Harbor, Southampton, Westhampton.

Regular Season: 40 games. **2009 Opening Date:** June 1. **Closing Date:** Aug. 15.

All-Star Game: July 12 at St. John's University.

Playoff Format: TBD.

Roster Limit: 25 (college-eligible players only).

JERSEY PILOTS

Mailing Address: 401 Timber Dr, Berkeley Heights, NJ 07922. **Telephone:** (908) 464-8042. **E-Mail Address:** bensmookler@aol.com. **President/General Manager:** Ben Smookler. **Field Manager:** Evan Davis.

LEHIGH VALLEY CATZ

Mailing Address: 103 Logan Dr, Easton, PA 18045. **Telephone:** (610) 533-9349. **E-Mail Address:** valley-catz@hotmail.com. **Website:** www.lvcatz.com. **General Manager:** Pat O'Connell. **Field Manager:** Dennis Morgan.

LONG ISLAND COLLEGIANS

Mailing Address: 825 East Gate Blvd, Suite 101, Garden City, NY 11530. **E-Mail Address:** philpursino@gmail.com. **Website:** www.limustangsbaseball.com. **General Manager:** Phil Pursino. **Field Manager:** Chris Rojas.

NORTH FORK OSPREYS

Operated by: Hamptons Collegiate Baseball. **Telephone:** (631) 680-7870. **Website:** www.hamptonsbaseball.org. **General Manager:** Joe Finora. **Field Manager:** Shawn Epidendio.

NORTH NEW JERSEY EAGLES

Mailing Address: 107 Pleasant Avenue, Upper Saddle River, NJ 07458. **General Manager:** Doug Cinnella. **Field Manager:** Jorge Hernandez.

QUAKERTOWN BLAZERS

Telephone: (215) 536-5777. **E-Mail Address:** batpower44@hotmail.com. **Field Manager:** Mike Schneider.

RIVERHEAD TOMCATS

Operated by: Hamptons Collegiate Baseball. **Website:** www.hamptonsbaseball.org. **Field Manager:** Randy Cadin.

SAG HARBOR WHALERS

Operated by: Hamptons Collegiate Baseball. **Website:** www.hamptonsbaseball.org. **Field Manager:** Unavailable.

SOUTHAMPTON BREAKERS

Operated by: Hamptons Collegiate Baseball. **Website:** www.hamptonsbaseball.org. **Field Manager:** Andrew Lorraine.

TORRINGTON TITANS

E-Mail Address: brian@ourbaseballhaven.com. **General Manager:** Brian Leighton. **Field Manager:** Greg Hunt.

WESTHAMPTON AVIATORS

Operated by: Hamptons Collegiate Baseball. **Telephone:** (631) 466-4393. **Website:** www.hamptonsbaseball.org. **General Manager:** Henry Bramwell. **Field Manager:** Jeff Quiros.

CALIFORNIA COLLEGIATE LEAGUE

Mailing Address: 4299 Carpinteria Ave, Suite 201, Carpinteria, CA 93013. **Telephone:** (805) 684-0657. **Fax:** (805) 684-8596. **Website:** www.calsummerball.com.

Year Founded: 1993.

President: Pat Burns.

Member Clubs: Conejo Oaks, Las Vegas Baseball Club, MLB Urban Youth Academy, San Luis Obispo Blues, San Luis Obispo Rattlers, Santa Barbara Foresters, Santa Maria Valley Packers.

Regular Season: 36 games. **2010 Opening Date:** June 5. **Closing Date:** July 30.

Playoff Format: League champion and runner-up advance to NBC World Series.

Roster Limit: 33.

CAL RIPKEN COLLEGIATE LEAGUE

Address: PO Box 22471, Baltimore, MD 21203. **Telephone:** (410) 588-9900. **E-Mail:** info@calripkenleague.org. **Website:** www.calripkenleague.org.

Year Founded: 2005.

Commissioner: Robert Douglas. **Deputy Commissioner:** Jerry Wargo. **Executive Director:** Alex Thompson.

Regular Season: 42 games. **2010 Opening Date:** June 4. **Closing Date:** July 25.

All-Star Game: July 14 at Ripken Stadium in Aberdeen, Md.

Playoff Format: Four-team, double-elimination league championship series, July 28-August 1.

Roster Limit: 30 (college-eligible players 22 and under).

ALEXANDRIA ACES

Address: 1300 I Street, NW, Suite 400E, Washington, DC 20005. **Telephone:** (202) 216-8302. **E-Mail:** pat@alexandriaaces.org. **Website:** www.alexandriaaces.org. **Chairman:** Don Dinan. **President:** Patrick J. **Malone.**

Head Coach: Eric Williams.

BALTIMORE REDBIRDS

Address: 2208 Pine Hill Farms Lane, Cockeysville, MD 21030. **Telephone:** (410) 802-2220. **Fax:** (410) 785-6138. **E-Mail:** johntcarey@hotmail.com. **Website:** www.mdredbirds.com. **President:** John Carey. **Head Coach:** Mark Palmerino

BETHESDA BIG TRAIN

Address: PO Box 30306, Bethesda, MD 20824. **Telephone:** (301) 983-1006. **Fax:** (301) 652-0691. **E-Mail:** faninfo@bigtrain.org. **Website:** www.bigtrain.org. **General Manager:** Jordan Henry. **Head Coach:** Sal Colangelo.

HERNDON BRAVES

Address: 1305 Kelly Court, Herndon, VA 20170-2605. **Telephone:** (703) 973-4444. **Fax:** (703) 783-1319. **E-Mail:** herndonbraves@cox.net. **Website:** www.herndonbraves.com. **General Manager:** Chris Smith. **Team Admin:** Lisa Lombardozzi. **Head Coach:** P.J. **Mitchell.**

ROCKVILLE EXPRESS

Address: PO Box 10188, Rockville, MD 20849. **Telephone:** (301) 928-6608. **E-Mail:** info@rockvilleexpress.org. **Website:** www.rockvilleexpress.org. **President/GM:** Jim Kazunas. **Vice President:** Brad Botwin. **Head Coach:** Angelo Nicolosi.

SILVER SPRING-TAKOMA T-BOLTS

Address: 906 Glaizewood Court, Takoma Park, MD 20912. **Telephone:** (301) 270-0794. **E-Mail:** tboltsbaseball@gmail.com. **Website:** www.tbolts.org. **General Manager:** Richard O'Connor. **Head Coach:** Inaki Ormaechea.

SOUTHERN MARYLAND NATIONALS

Address: 2243 Garrity Rd, Saint Leonard, MD 20685. **Telephone:** (301) 751-6299. **E-Mail:** winegard@erols.com. **General Manager:** Don Herbert. **Head Coach:** Chuck Winegardner.

YOUSE'S ORIOLES

Address: 3 Oyster Court, Baltimore, MD 21219. **Telephone:** (410) 477-3764. **E-Mail:** tnt017@comcast.net. **Website:** www.youseorioles.org. **Head Coach:** Tim Norris.

CAPE COD LEAGUE

Mailing Address: PO Box 266, Harwich Port, MA 02646. **Telephone:** (508) 432-6909. **E-Mail:** info@capecodbaseball.org. **Website:** www.capecodbaseball.org.

Year Founded: 1885.

Commissioner: Paul Galop. **President:** Judy Walden Scarafile. **Senior Vice President:** Jim Higgins. **Vice Presidents:** Peter Ford, Chuck Sturtevant. **Deputy Commissioner:** Richard Sullivan. **Deputy Commissioner/Director, Officiating:** Sol Yas. **Treasurer/Website Manager:** Steven Wilson. **Director, Public Relations/Broadcast Media:** John Garner. **Director, Communications:** Jim McGonigle. **Director, Publications:** Lou Barnicle.

Division Structure: East—Brewster, Chatham, Harwich, Orleans, Yarmouth-Dennis. West—Bourne, Cotuit, Falmouth, Hyannis, Wareham.

Regular Season: 44 games. **2010 Opening Date:** June 13. **Closing Date:** Aug. **15.**

All-Star Game: July 28.

Playoff Format: Top four teams in each division qualify. Three rounds of best-of-three series.
Roster Limit: 25 (college-eligible players only).

BOURNE BRAVES

Mailing Address: PO Box 895, Monument Beach, MA 02553. Telephone: (508) 345-1013. Fax: (508) 759-4062. E-Mail Address: bournebravesgm@hotmail.com. Website: www.bournebraves.org. President: Thomas Fink. General Manager: Michael Carrier. Head Coach: Harvey Shapiro.

BREWSTER WHITE CAPS

Mailing Address: PO Box 2349, Brewster, MA 02631. Telephone: (508) 896-8500, ext. 147. Fax: (508) 896-9845. E-Mail Address: contact@brewsterwhitecaps, PABlatz@comcast.net. Website: www.brewsterwhite-caps.com. President: Peter Blatz. General Manager: Ned Monthie. Head Coach: Tom Myers (UC Santa Barbara).

CHATHAM ANGLERS

Mailing Address: PO Box 428, Chatham, MA 02633. Telephone: (508) 241-8382. Fax: (508) 430-8382. E-Mail Address: ruddock4@yahoo.com. Website: www.chathamas.com. President: Doug Grattan. General Manager: Andy Ruddock. Head Coach: John Schiffner.

COTUIT KETTLEERS

Mailing Address: PO Box 411, Cotuit, MA 02635. Telephone: (508) 428-3358. Fax: (508) 420-5584. E-Mail Address: info@kettleers.org. Website: www.kettleers.org. President: Paul Logan. General Manager: Bruce Murphy. Head Coach: Mike Roberts.

FALMOUTH COMMODORES

Mailing Address: PO Box 808 Falmouth, MA 02541. Telephone: (508) 472-7922. Fax: (508) 862-6011. E-Mail Address: jreilly@falcommodores.org. Website: www.falcommodores.org. President: Christine Clark. General Manager: Bob Clark. Head Coach: Jeff Trundy.

HARWICH MARINERS

Mailing Address: PO Box 201, Harwich Port, MA 02646. Telephone: (508) 432-2000. Fax: (508) 432-5357. E-Mail Address: mehendy@comcast.net. Website: www.harwichmariners.org. President: Mary Henderson. General Manager: John Reid. Head Coach: Steve Englert (Boston College).

HYANNIS METS

Mailing Address: PO Box 852, Hyannis, MA 02601. Telephone: (508) 364-3164. Fax: (508) 534-1270. E-Mail Address: bbussiere@hyannismets.org. Website: www.hyannismets.org. General Manager: Bill Bussiere. Head Coach: Chad Gassman.

ORLEANS FIREBIRDS

Mailing Address: PO Box 504, Orleans, MA 02653. Telephone: (508) 255-0793. Fax: (508) 255-2237. Website: www.orleansfirebirds.com. President: Ken Farrar. General Manager: Sue Horton. Head Coach: Kelly Nicholson.

WAREHAM GATEMEN

Mailing Address: PO Box 287, Wareham, MA 02571. Telephone: (508) 748-0287. Fax: (508) 880-2602. E-Mail Address: sheri.gay4gatemen@comcast.net. Website: www.gatemen.org. President/General Manager: Thomas Gay. Head Coach: Cooper Farris (Mississippi Gulf Coast CC).

YARMOUTH-DENNIS RED SOX

Mailing Address: PO Box 814, South Yarmouth, MA 02664. Telephone: (508) 394-9387. Fax: (508) 398-2239. E-Mail Address: jimmartin321@yahoo.com. Website: www.ydredsox.org. President: Bob Mayo. General Manager: Jim Martin. Head Coach: Scott Pickler (Cypress, Calif., CC).

CLARK GRIFFITH COLLEGIATE LEAGUE

Mailing Address: 10915 Howland Dr, Reston, VA 20191. Telephone: (703) 860-0946. Fax: (703) 860-0143. E-Mail Address: info@clarkgriffithbaseball.com. Website: www.clarkgriffithbaseball.com.
Year Founded: 1945.
Commissioner: Tom Davis. Executive Vice President: Frank Fannan. Treasurer: Tom Dellinger. Vice President/Rules Enforcement: Byron Zeigler.
Regular Season: 44 games. 2010 Opening Date: June 4. Closing Date: July 31.
Playoff Format: Top four teams, double-elimination tournament.
Roster Limit: 25 (college-eligible players only).

DC GRAYS

Mailing Address: 1406-B Leslie Ave, Alexandria, VA 22301. Telephone: (202) 315-6945. Fax: (703) 684-9702. E-Mail Address: antonio@dcgrays.net. Website: www.dcgrays.net. General Manager: Antonio Scott. Head Coach: Antonio Scott.

FAIRFAX NATIONALS

Mailing Address: 1844 Horseback Trail, Vienna, VA 22182. Telephone: (703) 201-3346. E-Mail Address: garyboss@fairfaxnationals.com. Website: www.fairfaxnationals.com. General Manager: Gary Boss. Head Coach: John Nolan

MCLEAN DODGERS

Contact Information: Unavailable.

RESTON RENEGADES

Mailing Address: 12703 Hitchcock Ct, Reston, VA 20191. Telephone: (703) 904-5081. E-Mail Address: tickets@brucehallsports.com. Website: www.brucehallsports.com. President/General Manager: Bruce Hall.

VIENNA SENATORS

Mailing Address: 308 Hillwood Ave, Suite G2, Vienna, VA 22046. Telephone: (703) 534-5081. Fax: (703) 534-5085. E-Mail Address: cburr17@hotmail.com. Website: www.viennasenators.com. President: Bill McGillicuddy. General Manager: Bob Menefee. Head Coach: Chris Burr.

COASTAL PLAIN LEAGUE

Mailing Address: 125 Quantum Street, Holly Springs, NC 27540. Telephone: (919) 852-1960. Fax: (919) 516-0852. Website: www.coastalplain.com.
Year Founded: 1997.
Chairman/CEO: Jerry Petitt. President/Commissioner: Pete Bock. Assistant Commissioner: Justin Sellers. Director of On-Field Operations: Jeff Bock.
Division Structure: North—Edenton, Outer Banks, Peninsula, Petersburg, Wilson. South—Columbia, Fayetteville, Florence, Morehead City, Wilmington. West—Asheboro, Forest City, Gastonia, Martinsville,

Thomasville.

Regular Season: 56 games (split schedule). **2010 Opening Date:** May 26. **Closing Date:** Aug. **2.**

All-Star Game: July 20 at Forest City, N.C.

Playoff Format: Three rounds, best of three in each round. Aug. 4-14.

Roster Limit: 27 (college-eligible players only).

ASHEBORO COPPERHEADS

Mailing Address: PO Box 4006, Asheboro, NC 27204. **Telephone:** (336) 460-7018. **Fax:** (336) 629-2651. **E-Mail Address:** info@teamcopperhead.com. **Website:** www.teamcopperhead.com. **Owners:** Ronnie Pugh, Steve Pugh, Doug Pugh, Mike Pugh. **General Manager:** David Camp. **Head Coach:** Donnie Wilson (College of the Sequoias, Calif.).

COLUMBIA BLOWFISH

Mailing Address: PO Box 1328, Columbia, SC 29202. **Telephone:** (803) 254-3474. **Fax:** (803) 254-4482. **E-Mail Address:** info@blowfishbaseball.com. **Website:** www.blowfishbaseball.com. **Owner:** HWS Baseball V (Michael Savit, Bill Shanahan). **General Manager:** Skip Anderson. **Head Coach:** Lee Gronkiewicz.

EDENTON STEAMERS

Mailing Address: PO Box 86, Edenton, NC 27932. **Telephone:** (252) 482-4080. **Fax:** (252) 482-1717. **E-Mail Address:** edentonsteamers@hotmail.com. **Website:** www.edentonsteamers.com. **Owner:** Edenton-Chowan Community Foundation Inc. **President/General Manager:** Katy Ebersole. **Head Coach:** Marty Smith (Texas A&M-Corpus Christi).

FAYETTEVILLE SWAMPDOGS

Mailing Address: PO Box 64691, Fayetteville, NC 28306. **Telephone:** (910) 426-5900. **Fax:** (910) 426-3544. **E-Mail Address:** info@fayettevilleswampdogs.com. **Website:** www.goswampdogs.com. **Owners:** Lew Handelsman, Darrell Handelsman. **Head Coach/Director, Operations:** Darrell Handelsman. **General Manager:** Jeremy Aagard.

FLORENCE REDWOLVES

Mailing Address: PO Box 809, Florence, SC 29503. **Telephone:** (843) 629-0700. **Fax:** (843) 629-0703. **E-Mail Address:** jamie@florenceredwolves.com. **Website:** www.florenceredwolves.com. **President:** Kevin Barth. **General Manager:** Jamie Young. **Head Coach:** Russell Carter (Blinn JC, Texas).

FOREST CITY OWLS

Mailing Address: PO Box 1062, Forest City, NC 28043. **Telephone:** (828) 245-0000. **Fax:** (828) 245-6666. **E-Mail Address:** jwolfe@forestcitybaseball.com. **Website:** www.forestcitybaseball.com. **President:** Ken Silver. **General Manager:** James Wolfe. **Head Coach:** Matt Hayes (Limestone, S.C.).

GASTONIA GRIZZLIES

Mailing Address: PO Box 177, Gastonia, NC 28053. **Telephone:** (704) 866-8622. **Fax:** (704) 864-6122. **E-Mail Address:** jesse@gastoniagrizzlies.com. **Website:** www.gastoniagrizzlies.com. **President:** Ken Silver. **General Manager:** Jesse Cole. **Head Coach:** Jason Plourde (Belmont Abbey, N.C.).

MARTINSVILLE MUSTANGS

Mailing Address: PO Box 1112, Martinsville, VA 24114. **Telephone:** (276) 403-5250. **Fax:** (276) 403-5387. **E-Mail Address:** mustangsgm28@aol.com. **Website:** www.martinsvillemustangs.com. **General Manager:** Gary Cody. **Head Coach:** Barry Powell.

MOREHEAD CITY MARLINS

Mailing Address: 1311 N. Craven Street, New Bern, NC 28560. **Telephone:** (252) 269-9767. **Fax:** (252) 637-2721. **E-Mail Address:** mcmarlins@gmail.com. **Website:** www.mhcmarlins.com. **President:** Sabrina Bengel. **Vice President:** Buddy Bengel. **General Manager:** Unavailable. **Head Coach:** Jay Bergman.

OUTER BANKS DAREDEVILS

Mailing Address: PO Box 7596, Kill Devil Hills, NC 27948. **Telephone:** (252) 441-0600. **Fax:** (252) 441-0606. **E-Mail Address:** owen@obxdaredevils.com. **Website:** www.obxdaredevils.com. **Owner:** Marcus Felton. **General Manager:** Owen Hassell. **Head Coach:** Jeff Wicker (South Carolina—Salkehatchie).

PENINSULA PILOTS

Mailing Address: PO Box 7376, Hampton, VA 23666. **Telephone:** (757) 245-2222. **Fax:** (757) 245-8030. **E-Mail Address:** jeffscott@peninsulapilots.com. **Website:** www.peninsulapilots.com. **Owner:** Henry Morgan. **General Manager:** Jeffrey Scott. **Head Coach:** Hank Morgan.

PETERSBURG GENERALS

Mailing Address: 1981 Midway Ave, Petersburg, VA 23803. **Telephone:** (804) 722-0141. **Fax:** (804) 733-7370. **E-Mail Address:** pbgenerals@aol.com. **Website:** www.generals.petersburgsports.com. **Owner:** City of Petersburg. **General Manager:** Kevin Booker. **Head Coach:** Unavailable.

THOMASVILLE HI-TOMS

Mailing Address: 7003 Ballpark Road, Thomasville, NC 27360. **Telephone:** (336) 472-8667. **Fax:** (336) 472-7198. **E-Mail Address:** info@hitoms.com. **Website:** www.hitoms.com. **President/General Manager:** Greg Suire. **Head Coach:** Tom Dorzweiler.

WILMINGTON SHARKS

Mailing Address: PO Box 15233, Wilmington, NC 28412. **Telephone:** (910) 343-5621. **Fax:** (910) 343-8932. **E-Mail Address:** info@wilmingtonsharks.com. **Website:** www.wilmingtonsharks.com. **Owners:** Lew Handelsman, Darrell Handelsman, Conor Caloia. **General Manager/Director of Operations:** Conor Caloia. **Head Coach:** Tom Fleenor (South Carolina-Sumter).

WILSON TOBS

Mailing Address: PO Box 633, Wilson, NC 27894. **Telephone:** (252) 291-8627. **Fax:** (252) 291-1224. **E-Mail Address:** wilsontobs@earthlink.net. **Website:** www.wilsontobs.com. **President:** Greg Turnage. **General Manager:** Ben Jones. **Head Coach:** Jeff Steele (Lubbock Christian, Texas).

FLORIDA COLLEGIATE SUMMER LEAGUE

Mailing Address: 1778 N. Park Ave, Suite 201, Maitland, FL 32751. **Telephone:** (321) 206-9174. **Fax:** (407) 628-8535. **E-Mail Address:** info@floridaleague.com. **Website:** www.floridaleague.com.

Year Founded: 2004.
President: Sara Whiting. **Vice President:** Rob Sitz.
Regular Season: 44 games. **2010 Opening Date:** June 3. **Closing Date:** August 5.
All-Star Game: July 14 at Sanford.
Playoff Format: Five-team, modified series tournament.
Roster Limit: 25 (college-eligible players only).

DELAND SUNS

Operated through league office. **E-Mail Address:** delandsuns@floridaleague.com. **Head Coach:** Rick Hall.

LEESBURG LIGHTNING

Mailing Address: 318 South 2nd St, Leesburg, FL 34748. **Telephone:** (352) 728-9885. **E-Mail Address:** leesburglightning@floridaleague.com. **President:** Bruce Ericson. **Head Coach:** Frank Viola.

ORLANDO MAVERICKS

Operated through league office. **E-Mail Address:** orlandomavericks@floridaleague.com. **Head Coach:** Scott Makarewicz.

SANFORD RIVER RATS

Operated through league office. **E-Mail Address:** sanfordriverrats@floridaleague.com. **Head Coach:** Davey Johnson.

WINTER PARK DIAMOND DAWGS

Operated through league office. **E-Mail Address:** winterparkdiamonddawgs@floridaleague.com. **Head Coach:** Mark Leavitt.

GREAT LAKES LEAGUE

Mailing Address: 133 W. Winter St, Delaware, OH 43015. **Telephone:** (740) 368-3527. **Fax:** (740) 368-3999. **E-Mail Address:** kalance@greatlakesleague.org. **Website:** www.greatlakesleague.org.
Year Founded: 1986.
President/Commissioner: Kim Lance.
Regular Season: 40 games. **2010 Opening Date:** June 11.
Playoff Format: Top six teams meet in playoff.
Roster Limit: 30 (college-eligible players only).

CINCINNATI STEAM

Mailing Address: 2745 Anderson Ferry Rd, Cincinnati, OH 45238. **Telephone:** (513) 922-4272. **Website:** www.cincinnatisteam.com. **General Manager:** Max McLeary. **Head Coach:** Joe Regruth.

DELAWARE COWS

Mailing Address: 2379 Sherwood Road, Bexley, OH 43209. **Telephone:** (614) 235-1111. **Website:** www.delawarecows.com. **General Manager:** Jay Sokol. **Head Coach:** Dave Koblentz.

GRAND LAKE MARINERS

Mailing Address: 717 W. **Walnut St, Coldwater, OH 45828. Telephone:** (513) 207-5977. **Website:** www.grandlakemariners.com. **General Manager:** Wayne Miller. **Head Coach:** Joe Marker.

HAMILTON JOES

Mailing Address: 6218 Greens Way, Hamilton, OH 45011. **E-mail address:** darrelgrissom@fuse.net. **General Manager:** Darrel Grissom. **Head Coach:** Darrel Grissom.

LAKE ERIE MONARCHS

Mailing Address: 26670 Cranden Dr, Perrysburg, OH 43551. **Telephone:** (734) 626-1166. **Website:** www.lakeeriemonarchs.com. **General Manager:** Jim DeSana. **Head Coach:** Mike Montgomery.

LEXINGTON HUSTLERS

Mailing Address: 1999 Richmond Rd, Suite 300, Lexington, KY 40502. **Telephone:** (859) 335-0928. **General Manager:** Adam Revelette. **Head Coach:** Bobby Wright.

LICKING COUNTY SETTLERS

Mailing Address: 958 Camden Dr, Newark, OH 43055. **Telephone:** (740) 344-1063. **Website:** www.settlersbaseball.com. **General Manager:** Unavailable. **Head Coach:** Brian Meyer

LIMA LOCOS

Mailing Address: 3588 South Conant Rd, Spencerville, OH 45887. **Telephone:** (419) 647-5242. **Website:** www.limalocos.com. **General Manager:** Steve Meyer. **Head Coach:** Gene Stechshulte.

SOUTHERN OHIO COPPERHEADS

Mailing Address: PO Box 442, Athens, OH 45701. **Telephone:** (740) 541-9284. **Website:** www.copperheadsbaseball.com. **General Manager:** David Palmer. **Head Coach:** Mike Florak.

STARK COUNTY TERRIERS

Mailing Address: 1019 35th St Northwest, Canton, OH, 44709. **Telephone:** (330) 492-9220. **Website:** www.terriersbaseballclub.com. **General Manager:** Greg Trbovich. **Head Coach:** Eric Bunnell.

XENIA ATHLETES IN ACTION

Mailing Address: 651 Taylor Dr, Xenia, OH 45385. **Telephone:** (937) 352-1239. **E-Mail Address:** john.henschen@athletesinaction.org **Website:** www.aiabaseball.org. **General Manager:** John Henschen. **Head Coach:** Josh Hulin.

JAYHAWK LEAGUE

Mailing Address: 865 Fabrique, Wichita, KS 67218. **Telephone:** (316) 942-6333. **Fax:** (316) 942-2009. **Website:** www.jayhawkbaseballleague.org.
Year Founded: 1976.
Commissioner: Bob Considine. **President:** J.D. Schneider. **Vice President:** Frank Leo. **Public Relations/Statistician:** Gary Karr. **Secretary:** Cheryl Kastner.
Regular Season: 32 games. **2009 Opening Date:** June 4.
Playoff Format: Top two teams qualify for National Baseball Congress World Series in Wichita, KS.
Roster Limit: 30 to begin season; 28 at midseason.

DERBY TWINS

Mailing Address: 1245 N. Pine Grove, Wichita, KS 67212. **Telephone:** (316) 992-3623. **Fax:** 316-667-2286. **E-mail:** derbytwins@earthlink.net. **Website:** www.derbytwins.com. **General Manager:** Jeff Wells. **Head Coach:** Jason Santangelo.

DODGE CITY A'S

Mailing Address: 2914 Center, Dodge City, KS 67801. **Telephone:** 620-225-0238. **E-mail:** no1teammom@hotmail.com. **General Manager:** Phil Stevenson. **Head Coach:** Jeremy Irlbeck.

EL DORADO BRONCOS

Mailing Address: 865 Fabrique, Wichita, KS 67218. **Telephone:** (316) 687-2309. **Fax:** (316) 942-2009. **Website:** www.eldoradobroncos.org. **General Manager:** Doug Bell. **Head Coach:** Andy Schatzley.

HAYS LARKS

Mailing Address: 2715 Walnut., Hays, KS 67601. **Telephone:** (785) 259-1430. **Fax:** (630) 848-2236. **E-Mail Address:** cbieber@sbcglobal.net. **General Manager:** Frank Leo. **Head Coach:** Frank Leo.

LIBERAL BEEJAYS

Mailing Address: PO Box 793, Liberal, KS 67901. **Telephone:** (620) 629-1162. **Fax:** (620) 624-1906. **General Manager:** Bob Carlisle. **Head Coach:** John Martin.

HAYSVILLE HEAT

Mailing Address: 417 Apple Ct., Haysville, KS 67060. **Telephone:** (316) 239-1221. **General Manager:** Dick "Chief" Twyman.

M.I.N.K. LEAGUE

(Missouri, Iowa, Nebraska, Kansas)
Mailing Address: PO Box 1155, Chillicothe, MO 64601. **Telephone:** (660) 646-2165. **Fax:** (660) 646-6933. **Email Address:** lfechtig@midwestglove.com. **Website:** www.minkleaguebaseball.com.
Year Founded: 1995.
Commissioner: Bob Steinkamp. **President:** Liz Fechtig. **Vice President:** Jeff Post. **Secretary:** Edwina Rains.
Regular Season: 34 games. **2010 Opening Date:** June 3. **Closing Date:** July 23.
Playoff Format: Top team qualifies for National Baseball Congress World Series in Wichita.
Roster Limit: 28.

CHILLICOTHE MUDCATS

Mailing Address: 426 E. Jackson, Chillicothe, MO 64601. **Telephone:** (660) 646-2165. **Fax:** (660) 646-6933. **E-Mail Address:** lfechtig@midwestglove.com. **Website:** www.chillicothemudcats.com. **General Manager:** Liz Fechtig. **Head Coach:** Unavailable.

CLARINDA A'S

Mailing Address: 225 East Lincoln, Clarinda, IA 51632. **Telephone:** (712) 542-4272. **E-Mail Address:** m.everly@mchsi.com. **Website:** www.clarindaiowa-asbaseball.org. **General Manager:** Merle Eberly. **Head Coach:** Unavailable.

EXCELSIOR SPRINGS COUGARS

Mailing Address: 4900 NE 65th Terrace, Kansas City, MO 64119. **Telephone:** (573) 280-5870. **E-Mail Address:** admmcannon@gmail.com. **Website:** Unavailable. **General Manager:** Adam Cannon.

JOPLIN OUTLAWS

Mailing Address: 5860 North Pearl, Joplin, MO 64801. **Telephone:** (417) 825-4218. **E-Mail address:** merains@mchsi.com. **Website:** www.joplinoutlaws.com. **General Manager:** Mark Rains. **Head Coach:** Unavailable.

MAC-N-SEITZ A'S

Mailing Address: 4104 NE Georgian Dr, Lee's Summit, MO 64064. **Telephone:** (816) 305-9708. **E-Mail address:** mlusardi@midwestsportsadvisors.com. **Website:** www.leaguelineup.com/mac-n-seitzcollegiate. **General**

Manager: Mike Lusardi. **Head Coach:** Unavailable.

NEVADA GRIFFONS

Mailing Address: PO Box 601, Nevada, MO 64772. **Telephone:** (417) 667-6159. **E-Mail address:** jpost@morrisonpost.com. **Website:** www.nevadagriffons.org. **President:** Padrio Cladio. **General Manager:** Jeff Post. **Head Coach:** Unavailable.

OMAHA DIAMOND SPIRIT

Mailing Address: 4618 N. 135th Ave, Omaha, NE 68164. **Telephone:** (402) 679-0206. **E-Mail address:** arkaosky@cox.net. **Website:** www.scorebook.com/spirit2006. **General Manager:** Arden Rakosky. **Head Coach:** Unavailable.

OZARK GENERALS

Mailing Address: 1336 W. F.R. Road 182, Springfield, MO 65810. **Telephone:** (417) 818-8756. **E-Mail Address:** rda160@yahoo.com. **Website:** www.generalsbaseballclub.com. **General Manager/Head Coach:** Rusty Aton.

ST. JOSEPH MUSTANGS

Mailing Address: 6200 NW 104th St, Kansas City, MO 64154. **Telephone:** (913) 238-3705. **E-Mail address:** rmuntean717@gmail.com. **Website:** www.stjoemustangs.com. **President:** Dan Gerson. **General Manager:** Rick Muntean. **Head Coach:** Unavailable.

SEDALIA BOMBERS

Mailing Address: 2201 S. Grand, Sedalia, MO 65301. **Telephone:** (660) 287-4722. **E-Mail address:** jkindle@knobnoster.k12.mo.us. **Website:** www.sedaliabombers.com. **President/General Manager/Head Coach:** Jud Kindle. **Vice President:** Ross Dey.

MOUNTAIN COLLEGIATE LEAGUE

E-Mail Address: info@mcbl.net. **Website:** www.mcbl.net.
Year Founded: 2005.
Directors: Kurt Colicchio, Ron Kailey, Gil Carbajal, Nicko Kleppinger.
Director of Umpires: Gary Weibert
Regular Season: 42 games. **2010 Opening Date:** May 28. **Closing Date:** Aug. 1.
Playoff Format: Second- and third-place teams meet in one-game playoff; winner advances to best-of-three championship series against first-place team.
All-Star Game: July 6 in Cheyenne, WY
Roster limit: 31 total, 25 active (college-eligible players only).

CHEYENNE GRIZZLIES

Telephone: (307) 631-7337. **E-Mail Address:** rkaide@aol.com. **Website:** www.cheyennegrizzlies.com. **Owner/General Manager:** Ron Kailey. **Head Coach:** Aaron Holley (University of Redlands, Calif.).

FORT COLLINS FOXES

Telephone: (970) 225-9564. **E-Mail Address:** info@fortcollinsfoxes.com. **Website:** www.fortcollinsfoxes.com. **Owner/General Manager:** Kurt Colicchio. **Head Coach:** Michael Bender (Montreat College, N.C.).

GREELEY GRAYS

Telephone: (303) 870-2523. **E-Mail Address:** rklesh@earthlink.net. **Website:** www.greeleygrays.com. **Owner:** Gil Carbajal. **General Manager:** Chris Waters. **Head Coach:** John Barnes.

LARAMIE COLTS

Telephone: (307) 760-0544. **E-Mail Address:** laramiecolts@msn.com. **Website:** www.laramiecolts.com. **Owners/Co-General Managers:** Kent & Nicko Kleppinger. **Head Coach:** Nathan Schwartz (Texas-Permian Basin)

NEW ENGLAND COLLEGIATE LEAGUE

Mailing Address: 37 Grammar School Dr, Danbury, CT 06811. **Telephone:** (203) 241-9392. **Fax:** (203) 643-2230. **Website:** www.necbl.com.

Commissioner: Mario Tiani. **Deputy Commissioner:** Everts "Eph" Mangan. **President:** John DeRosa. **Executive Vice President:** Dick Murray. **Treasurer:** Brigid Schaffer. **Secretary:** Richard Rossiter.

Division Structure: East—Laconia, Lowell, New Bedford, Newport, North Shore, Sanford. West—Bristol, Danbury, Holyoke, Keene, North Adams, Vermont.

Regular Season: 42 games. **2010 Opening Date:** June 4. **Closing Date:** July 31.

All-Star Game: July 18 at Newport.

Playoff Format: Top four teams in each division meet in best-of-three quarterfinals; winners meet in best-of-three divisional championship. Winners meet in best-of-three final for league championship.

Roster Limit: 28 (college-eligible players only).

BRISTOL NINE

Mailing Address: 525 Burnside Ave, East Hartford, CT 06108. **Telephone:** (860) 805-1132. **E-Mail Address:** d.kennedy@bristolnine.com. **Website:** www.bristolnine.com. **President:** Kevin Kelleher. **General Manager:** Dan Kennedy. **Field Manager:** Patrick Hall.

DANBURY WESTERNERS

Mailing Address: 5 Old Hayrake Rd, Danbury, CT 06811. **Telephone:** (203) 797-0897. **Fax:** (203) 792-6177. **E-Mail Address:** westerners1@aol.com. **Website:** www.danburywesterners.com. **President:** Mike Malone. **General Manager:** Terry Whalen. **Field Manager:** Jamie Shevchik.

HOLYOKE BLUE SOX

Mailing Address: 19 Cranberry Lane, Dedham, MA 01026. **Telephone:** (413) 652-9014. **E-Mail Address:** barry@wadsworthsports.net. **Website:** www.holyokesox.com. **Chairman/CEO:** Karen Wadsworth-Rella. **General Manager:** Barry Wadsworth. **Field Manager:** Darryl Morhardt.

KEENE SWAMP BATS

Mailing Address: PO Box 160, Keene, NH 03431. **Telephone:** (603) 355-7016. **Website:** www.swampbats.com. **President:** Kevin Watterson. **General Manager:** Vicki Bacon. **Field Manager:** Marty Testo.

LACONIA MUSKRATS

Mailing Address: 134 Stevens Rd, Lebanon, NH 03766. **Telephone:** (864) 380-2873. **E-Mail Address:** noah@laconiamuskrats.com. **Website:** www.laconiamuskrats.com. **Owner/General Manager:** Noah Crane. **Field Manager:** Matt Williams.

LOWELL ALL-AMERICANS

Mailing Address: PO Box 2228, Lowell, MA 01851. **Telephone:** (978) 454-5058. **Fax:** (978) 251-1211. **E-Mail Address:** info@lowellallamericans.com. **Website:** www. lowellallamericans.com. **President/General Manager:** Harry Ayotte. **Director of Operations:** Salvatore Accardi. **Field Manager:** Jeff Kane.

NEW BEDFORD BAY SOX

Mailing Address: 4 Blinkoff Ct., Torrington, CT 06790. **Telephone/Fax:** (860) 482-0450. **E-Mail Address:** kfredriksson@optonline.net. **Website:** www.nbbaysox.com. **President:** Rita M. **Hubner. General Manager:** Kirk Fredriksson. **Field Manager:** Ray Ricker.

NEWPORT GULLS

Mailing Address: PO Box 777, Newport, RI 02840. **Telephone:** (401) 845-6832. **Website:** www.newportgulls.com. **President/General Manager:** Chuck Paiva. **Vice President/Assistant GM:** Chris Patsos. **Head Coach:** Mike Coombs.

NORTH ADAMS STEEPLECATS

Mailing Address: PO Box 540, North Adams, MA 01247. **Telephone:** (413) 652-1031. **E-Mail Address:** steeplecats_gm@roadrunner.com. **Website:** www.steeplecats.com. **President:** David Bond. **General Manager:** Sean McGrath. **Field Manager:** Unavailable.

NORTH SHORE NAVIGATORS

Mailing Address: 6 Draper Rd, Wayland, MA 01778. **Telephone:** (781) 439-8029. **E-Mail Address:** philip@nsnavs.com. **Website:** www.nsnavs.com. **President:** Philip Rosenfield. **General Manager:** Peter Delani. **Head Coach:** Jason Falcon.

SANFORD MAINERS

Mailing Address: PO Box 26, 4 Washington St, Sanford, ME 04073. **Telephone:** (207) 324-0010. **Fax:** (207) 324-2227. **E-Mail Address:** jwebb@nicholswebb.com. **Website:** www.sanfordmainers.com. **General Manager:** John Webb. **Field Manager:** Aaron Izaryk.

VERMONT MOUNTAINEERS

Mailing Address: PO Box 57, East Montpelier, VT 05651. **Telephone:** (802) 223-5224. **E-Mail Address:** gmvtm@comcast.net. **Website:** www.thevermontmountaineers.com. **General Manager:** Brian Gallagher. **Field Manager:** Troy Moock.

NEW YORK COLLEGIATE BASEBALL LEAGUE

Mailing Address: 4 Creekside Ln, Rochester, NY 14624-1059. **Telephone:** (585) 314-1122. **E-Mail Address:** slehman@nycbl.com. **Website:** www.nycbl.com.

President: Stan Lehman. **Vice President:** Mark Perlo. **Treasurer:** Dan Russo. **Secretary:** Darin Williams.

Year Founded: 1978.

Member Clubs: East—Amsterdam Mohawks, Bennington Bombers, Cooperstown Hawkeyes, Glens Falls Golden Eagles, Mohawk Valley Diamondawgs, Saratoga Phillies, Watertown Wizards. West—Alleghany County Nitros, Bolivar Oilers, Elmira Pioneers, Geneva Red Wings, Hornell Dodgers, Niagara Power, Webster Yankees.

Regular season starts: June 4. **Regular season ends:** July 28.

2010 Playoffs: July 30-Aug. **8.**

Playoff Format: Eight teams, top four in each division. Best-of-three championship series format follows best of three divisional semifinals and finals.

All-Star game: July 12 at East Field, Glens Falls, N.Y.

Roster Limit: 25 (college-eligible players only).

NORTHWOODS LEAGUE

Office Address: 2900 4th St. SW, Rochester, MN 55902. **Telephone:** (507) 536-4579. **Fax:** (507) 536-4597. **Website:** www.northwoodsleague.com. **E-Mail Address:** curt@northwoodsleague.com

Year Founded: 1994.
President: Dick Radatz Jr.
Director of Operations: Curt Carstensen.
Division Structure: North—Alexandria, Brainerd, Duluth, Mankato, Rochester, St. Cloud, Thunder Bay, Willmar. South—Battle Creek, Eau Claire, Green Bay, La Crosse, Madison, Rochester, Waterloo, Wisconsin, Wisconsin Rapids.
Regular Season: 70 games (split schedule). **2009 Opening Date:** June 2. **Closing Date:** Aug. 22.
All-Star Game: July 20 at Eau Claire.
Playoff Format: First-half and second-half division winners meet in best-of-three series. Winners meet in best-of-three series for league championship.
Roster Limit: 26 (college-eligible players only).

ALEXANDRIA BEETLES

Mailing Address: 1210 Broadway, Suite #100, Alexandria, MN 56308. **Telephone:** (320) 763-8151. **Fax:** (320) 763-8152. **E-Mail Address:** alexbeetles@gmail.com. **Website:** www.alexandriabeetles.com. **General Manager:** Shawn Reilly. **Head Coach:** Scott Chisholm (Oakland City Univ.).

BATTLE CREEK BOMBERS

Mailing Address: 189 Bridge Street, Battle Creek, MI 49017. **Telephone:** (269) 962-0735. **Fax:** (269) 962-0741. **Email Address:** info@battlecreekbombers.com **Website:** www.battlecreekbombers.com. **General Manager:** Rick Lindau. **Head Coach:** TBA.

BRAINERD LAKES AREA LUNKERS

Mailing Address: PO Box 431, Brainerd, MN 56401. **Telephone:** (218) 824-3474. **Fax:** (320) 255-5228. **E-Mail Address:** info@lunkersbaseball.com. **Website:** www.lunkersbaseball.com. **General Manager:** Dustin Anaas. **Head Coach:** Ryan Levendoski (Wisconsin-Stout).

DULUTH HUSKIES

Mailing Address: 207 W. Superior St, Suite 206, Holiday Center Mall, Duluth, MN 55802. **Telephone:** (218) 786-9909. **Fax:** (218) 786-9001. **E-Mail Address:** huskies@duluthhuskies.com. **Website:** www.duluthhuskies.com. **General Manager:** Craig Smith. **Head Coach:** Daniel Hersey (Central Florida CC).

EAU CLAIRE EXPRESS

Mailing Address: 108 E. Grand Ave, Eau Claire, WI 54701. **Telephone:** (715) 839-7788. **Fax:** (715) 839-7676. **E-Mail Address:** info@eauclaireexpress.com. **Website:** www.eauclaireexpress.com. **General Manager:** Brett Schroedel. **Head Coach:** Dale Varsho.

GREEN BAY BULLFROGS

Mailing Address: 1306 Main Street, Green Bay, WI 54302. **Telephone:** (920) 497-7225. **Fax:** (920) 437-3551. **Email Address:** info@greenbaybullfrogs.com. **Website:** www.greenbaybullfrogs.com. **VP-Operations:** Jeremy Hinde. **Head Coach:** Jordan Bischel (Northwest Missouri State).

LA CROSSE LOGGERS

Mailing Address: 1223 Caledonia St, La Crosse, WI 54603. **Telephone:** (608) 796-9553. **Fax:** (608) 796-9032. **E-Mail Address:** info@lacrosseloggers.com. **Website:** www.lacrosseloggers.com. **General Manager:** Chris Goodell. **Assistant General Manager:** Ben Kapanke. **Head Coach:** Andy McKay (Sacramento City College).

MADISON MALLARDS

Mailing Address: 2920 N. Sherman Ave, Madison, WI 53704. **Telephone:** (608) 246-4277. **Fax:** (608) 246-4163. **E-Mail Address:** conor@mallardsbaseball.com. **Website:** www.mallardsbaseball.com. **General Manager:** Conor Coloia. **Head Coach:** C.J. Thieleke (Madison Area Tech).

MANKATO MOONDOGS

Mailing Address: 310 Belle Ave, Suite L-8, Mankato, MN 56001. **Telephone:** (507) 625-7047. **Fax:** (507) 625-7059. **E-Mail Address:** office@mankatomoondogs.com. **Website:** www.mankatomoondogs.com. **General Manager:** Kyle Mrozek. **Head Coach:** Mike Orchard (Central Arizona).

ROCHESTER HONKERS

Mailing Address: PO Box 482, Rochester, MN 55903. **Telephone:** (507) 289-1170. **Fax:** (507) 289-1866. **E-Mail Address:** honkers@rochesterhonkers.com. **Website:** www.rochesterhonkers.com. **General Manager:** Dan Litzinger. **Head Coach:** TBA.

ST. CLOUD RIVER BATS

Mailing Address: PO Box 5059, St. Cloud, MN 56302. **Telephone:** (320) 240-9798. **Fax:** (320) 255-5228. **E-Mail Address:** info@riverbats.com. **Website:** www.riverbats.com. **General Manager:** Wes Sharp. **Head Coach:** Gabe Boruff (Washington State).

THUNDER BAY BORDER CATS

Mailing Address: PO Box 29105, Thunder Bay, Ontario P7B 6P9. **Telephone:** (807) 766-2287. **Fax:** (807) 345-8299. **E-Mail Address:** baseball@tbaytel.net. **Website:** www.bordercatsbaseball.com. **General Manager:** Brad Jorgenson. **Head Coach:** Mike Steed.

WATERLOO BUCKS

Mailing Address: PO Box 4124, Waterloo, IA 50704. **Telephone:** (319) 232-0500. **Fax:** (319) 232-0700. **E-Mail Address:** waterloobucks@waterloobucks.com. **Website:** www.waterloobucks.com. **General Manager:** Dan Corbin. **Head Coach:** Jason Nell (Iowa Lakes CC).

WILLMAR STINGERS

Mailing Address: PO Box 201, Willmar, MN, 56201. **Telephone:** (320) 222-2010. **E-Mail Address:** ryan@willmarstingers.com. **Website:** www.willmarstingers.com. **General Manager:** Ryan Voz. **Head Coach:** Matt Hollod (Southern Utah).

WISCONSIN WOODCHUCKS

Mailing Address: PO Box 6157, Wausau, WI 54402. **Telephone:** (715) 845-5055. **Fax:** (715) 845-5015. **E-Mail Address:** info@woodchucks.com. **Website:** www.woodchucks.com. **General Manager:** Ryan Treu. **Head Coach:** Guido Aspeitia.

WISCONSIN RAPIDS

Mailing Address: 521 Lincoln St., Wisconsin Rapids, WI 54494. **Telephone:** (715) 424-5400. **E-Mail Address:** info@rapidsbaseball.com. **Website:** www.rapidsbaseball.com. **General Manager:** Liz Kern. **Head Coach:** Unavailable.

PACIFIC INTERNATIONAL LEAGUE

Mailing Address: 4400 26th Ave W, Seattle, WA 98199. **Telephone:** (206) 623-8844. **Fax:** (206) 623-8361. **E-Mail Address:** spotter@potterprinting.com. **Website:** www.pacificinternationalleague.com.

Year Founded: 1992

President: Steve Konek. **Commissioner:** Brian Gooch. **Secretary:** Steve Potter. **Treasurer:** Mark Dow.

Member Clubs: Bellevue Honkers, Burnaby Bulldogs, Coquitlam Angels, Everett Merchants, Kamloops Sundevils, Kelowna Jays, Langley Blaze, Nanaimo Coal Miners, Seattle Studs, Trail (B.C.) **franchise.**

Regular Season: 28 league games. **2010 Opening Date:** June 1.

Playoff Format: Top two teams playoff; winner goes to NBC World Series in Wichita.

Roster Limit: 30; 25 eligible for games (players must be at least 18 years old).

PROSPECT LEAGUE

Mailing Address: 59 N. Paint St. Chillicothe, OH 45601 **Telephone:** (740) 773-1444. **E-Mail Address:** commissioner@prospectleague.com. **Website:** www.prospectleague.com.

Year Founded: 1963 (as Central Illinois Collegiate League) 2009 as The Prospect League.

President: Bryan Wickline

Regular Season: 56 games. **2010 Opening Date:** June 4. **Closing Date:** Aug. 10.

All-Star Game: July 6 in Quincy, Illinois.

Playoff Format: Post-season tournament

Roster Limit: 26

BUTLER BLUESOX

Mailing Address: 1347 Gabby Avenue, Washington, PA 15301. **Telephone:** (724) 263-9874. **Fax:** (412) 440-0342. **E-Mail Address:** butlerbluesox@ymail.com. **Website:** www.butlerbluesox.net. **General Manager:** Leo Trich

CHILLICOTHE PAINTS

Mailing Address: 59 N. Paint Street, Chillicothe, OH 45601. **Telephone:** (740) 773-8326. **Fax:** (740) 773-8338. **E-Mail Address:** bwickline@chillicothepaints.com. **Website:** www.chillicothepaints.com. **Owner:** Chris Hanners. **President:** Shirley Bandy. **Vice President/General Manager:** Bryan Wickline. **Head Coach:** Brian Mannino

DANVILLE DANS

Mailing Address: PO Box 1041, Danville, IL 61832. **Telephone:** (217) 446-5521. **Fax:** (217) 446-9995. **E-Mail Address:** JeanieCooke@danvilleareainfo.com. **Website:** www.danvilledans.blogspot.com Owners/General Managers: Rick Kurth and Jeanie Cooke. **Head Coach:** Pete Paciorek

DEKALB COUNTY LINERS

Mailing Address: 164 E. Lincoln Highway, Suite 114-A, DeKalb, IL 60115. **Telephone:** (815) 508-3610 Fax: (815) 756-5164 E-mail Address: linersbaseball@gmail.com. **Website:** www.linersbaseball.com Owner: Kim Wise

DUBOIS COUNTY BOMBERS

Mailing Address: PO Box 332, Huntingburg, IN 47542. **Telephone:** (812) 683-3700. **Fax:** (812) 683-5661. **E-Mail Address:** jace_wg@yahoo.com. **Website:** www.dcbombers.com. **General Manager:** John Bigness

DUPAGE DRAGONS

Mailing Address: PO Box 3076, Lisle, IL 60532. **Telephone:** (630) 241-2255. **Fax:** (708) 784-1468. **E-Mail Address:** geoff@dupagedragons.com Website: www.dupagedragons.com. **General Manager:** Geoff Steele. **Head Coach:** Mark Viramontes.

HANNIBAL CAVEMEN

Mailing Address: Clemens Field, 403 Warren Barrett Drive, Hannibal, MO 63401. **Telephone:** (573) 221-1010. **Fax:** (573) 221-5296. **E-Mail Address:** hannibalbaseball@sbcglobal.com. **Website:** www.hannibalcavemen.com. **Owners:** Roland Hemond, Bob Hemond, Larry Owens and Dave Trogan. **Director of Baseball Operations:** Jay Hemond.

NORTHCOAST KNIGHTS

Mailing Address: 578 East 30th Street, Willowick, OH 44095. **Telephone:** (440) 339-3291. **Website:** www.northcoastknights.com.

QUINCY GEMS

Mailing Address: 300 Civic Center Plaza, Quincy, IL 62301. **Telephone:** (217) 223-1000. **Fax:** (217) 223-1330. **E-Mail Address:** rebbing@oakleylindsaycenter.com. **Website:** www.quincygems.com. **General Manager:** Rob Ebbing. **Head Coach:** Chris Martin.

RICHMOND RIVERRATS

Mailing Address: McBride Stadium, 201 NW 13th Street, Richmond, IN 47374. **Telephone:** (765) 935-7287. **Fax:** (765) 935-7529 E-Mail Address: dbeaman@richmondriverrats.com. **Website:** www.richmondriverrats.com. **General Manager:** Deanna Beaman. **Director of Business Operations:** Duke Ward. **Director of Baseball Operations:** John Cate

NASHVILLE OUTLAWS

Mailing Address: 2201 Dunn Ave, Nashville, TN 37211. **Phone:** (615) 469-0228. **Fax:** (615) 346-9405. **E-mail Address:** info@nashvilleoutlaws.com. **Website:** www.nashvilleoutlaws.com. **General Manager:** Brandon Vonderharr.

SLIPPERY ROCK SLIDERS

Mailing Address: PO Box 496, Slippery Rock, PA 16057. **Telephone:** (724) 458-8831. **E-Mail Address:** mbencic@zoominternet.net. **Website:** www.theslipperyrocksliders.com. **Owner/General Manager:** Mike Bencic

SPRINGFIELD SLIDERS

Mailing Address: 1415 North Grand Ave. E, Suite B, Springfield, IL 62702. **Telephone:** (217) 679-3511. **Fax:** (217) 679-3512. **E-Mail Address:** info@springfieldsliders.com. **Website:** www.springfieldsliders.com. **Owner:** Jesse Bolder. **Head Coach:** Jack Clark.

TERRE HAUTE REX

Mailing Address: Indiana State University Foundation, 320 Gillum Hall, Terre Haute, IN 47809. **Telephone:** (812) 237-8342 Fax: (812) 237-7797. **E-mail Address:** khoolehan@indstatefoundation.org. **General Manager:** Roland Shelton

WEST VIRGINIA MINERS

Mailing Address: 200 Stadium Drive, Beckley, WVA 25801. **Telephone:** (304) 252-7233. **Fax:** (304) 253-1998. **E-mail Address:** mike@wvminersbaseball.com. **Website:** www.wvminersbaseball.com. **General Manager:** Mike Gilligan.

SOUTHERN COLLEGIATE BASEBALL LEAGUE

Mailing Address: 103 Pine Lake Drive, Monroe, NC 28110. **Telephone:** (704) 635-7126. **Fax:** (704) 635-7371. **E-Mail Address:** SCBLCommissioner@aol.com. **Website:** www.scbl.org. **Year Founded:** 1999.

Commissioner: Bill Capps. **President:** Jeff Carter. **Vice President:** Brian Swords. **Vice President of Marketing & Development:** Mark Dudley. **Secretary:** Larry Tremitiere. **Treasurer:** Brenda Templin. **Regular Season:** 42 games. **2010 Opening Date:** June 1. **Closing Date:** July 19. **Playoff Format:** No. 1 seed hosts four-team, double-elimination tournament; begins July 23. **Roster Limit:** 30 (College-eligible players only).

ASHEVILLE REDBIRDS

Mailing Address: PO Box 17637, Asheville, NC 28816. **Telephone:** (828) 691-3679. **General Manager:** Bill Stewart. **Head Coach:** Ryan Smith.

CAROLINA CHAOS

Mailing Address: 142 Orchard Drive, Liberty, SC 29657. **Telephone:** (864) 843-3232, (864) 901-4331. **E-Mail Address:** brian_swords@carolinachaos.com. **Website:** www.carolinachaos.com. **General Manager:** Brian Swords (Southern Wesleyan, S.C.), **Head Coach:** Nathan Swords.

CAROLINA STINGERS

Mailing Address: 1793 Hickorywood Court, Fort Mill, SC 29715. **Telephone:** (803) 389-3255.
E-Mail Address: eric@carolinastingersbaseball.com. **General Manager:** Eric Fransen. **Head Coach:** Ryan Bown (Shippensburg, Pa.).

LAKE NORMAN COPPERHEADS

Mailing Address: PO Box 9723, Northcross Center Court, Huntersville, NC 28078. **Telephone:** (704) 892-1041, (704) 564-9211. **E-Mail Address:** jcarter@standpointtech.com. **Website:** www.copperheadsports.org. **General Manager:** Jeff Carter. **Head Coach:** Derek Shoe.

MORGANTON AGGIES

Mailing Address: PO Box 3448, Morganton, NC 28680. **Telephone:** (828) 438-5351. **Fax:** (828) 438-5350. **E-Mail Address:** gwleonhardt@aol.com. **General Manager:** Gary Leonhardt. **Head Coach:** Travis Howard.

SPARTANBURG BLUE EAGLES

Mailing Address: PO Box 4786, Cowpens, SC 29305. **Telephone:** (864) 444-4348. **E-Mail Address:** markdudley51@gmail.com. **General Manager:** Mark Dudley. **Head Coach:** Ryan Thomas.

STATESVILLE OWLS

Mailing Address: 8680 Shallowford Road, Lewisville, NC 27023. **Telephone:** (336) 408-1516.
E-Mail Address: hugh.mcbride@statesvilleowls.net. **President:** Jeff May. **General Manager:** Hugh McBride. **Head Coach:** Jamie Lowe (Surry CC, N.C.).

TENNESSEE TORNADO

Mailing Address: 1995 Roan Creek Road, Mountain City, TN 37683. **Telephone:** (423) 727-9111. **E-Mail Address:** tdr@maymead.com. **Owner:** Wiley Roark. **General Manager:** Tom Reese. **Head Coach:** Phillip Al-Mateen (East Tennessee State).

TEXAS COLLEGIATE LEAGUE

Mailing Address: 405 Mitchell St, Bryan, TX 77801. **Telephone:** (979) 779-7529. **Fax:** (979) 779-2398. **E-Mail Address:** info@tclbaseball.com. **Website:** www.texascollegiateleague.com.

Year Founded: 2004.
President: Uri Geva.
Regular Season: 56 games (split schedule). **2010 Opening Date:** June 2.
Playoff Format: The first- and second-half champions will be joined in the TCL playoffs by two wild card teams. Winners of the best-of-three divisional round meet in the three-game TCL Championship Series.
Roster Limit: 30 (College-eligible players only).

BRAZOS VALLEY BOMBERS

Mailing Address: 405 Mitchell St, Bryan, TX 77801. **Telephone:** (979) 799-7529. **Fax:** (979) 779-2398. **E-Mail Address:** info@bvbombers.com. **Website:** www.bvbombers.com. **Co-Owners:** Uri Geva, Kfir Jackson. **Director, Player Recruitment:** Adam Cain. **Head Coach:** Brent Alumbaugh.

COPPELL/COLLIN COUNTY COPPERHEADS

Mailing Address: 735 Plaza Blvd, Suite 200, Coppell, TX 75019. **Telephone:** (972) 745-2929. **E-Mail Address:** info@tclcopperheads.com. **Website:** www.tclcopperheads.com. **Director, General Operations:** David Apple. **Director, Finance:** Steve Pratt. **Director, Baseball Operations:** John Marston. **Head Coach:** Barry Rose.

EAST TEXAS PUMP JACKS

Physical Address: 1100 Stone Rd, Suite 120, Kilgore, TX 75662. **Mailing Address:** PO Box 2369, Kilgore, TX 75663. **Telephone:** (903) 218-4638. **Fax:** (866) 511-5449. **E-mail Address:** info@pumpjacksbaseball.com. **Website:** www.pumpjacksbaseball.com. **General Manager:** Mike Lieberman. **Head Coach:** Ben Taylor.

MCKINNEY MARSHALS

Mailing Address: 6151 Alma Rd, McKinney, TX 75070. **Telephone:** (972) 747-8248. **E-Mail Address:** info@tclmarshals.com. **Website:** www.tclmarshals.com. **Director, General Operations:** David Apple. **Director, Finance:** Steve Pratt. **Director, Baseball Operations:** Mike Henneman.

TEXAS TOMCATS

Mailing Address: 3708 N. Navarro St, Suite A, Victoria, TX 77901. **Telephone:** (361) 485-9522. **Fax:** (361) 485-0936. **E-Mail Address:** info@baseballinvictoria.com. **President:** Tracy Young. **General Manager:** Blake Koch.

VICTORIA GENERALS

Mailing Address: 3708 N. Navarro St., Suite A, Victoria, TX 77901. **Telephone:** (361) 485-9522. **Fax:** (361) 485-0936. **E-Mail Address:** info@baseballinvictoria.com. **Website:** www.victoriagenerals.com. **President:** Tracy Young. **General Manager:** Blake Koch. **Head Coach:** Chris Clemons.

VALLEY LEAGUE

Mailing Address: 58 Bethel Green Rd, Staunton, VA 24401. **Telephone:** (540) 885-8901. **Fax:** (540) 213-8255. **E-Mail Addresses:** dmbiery@wildblue.net. **Website:** www.valleyleaguebaseball.com.

Year Founded: 1961.

President: David Biery. **Executive Vice President:** Bruce Alger. **Media Relations Director:** Scott Musa. **Secretary:** Ken Newman

Regular Season: 44 games. **2010 Opening Date:** June 3. **Closing Date:** August 2.

All-Star Game: July 11 at Harrisonburg.

Playoff Format: Eight teams; best-of-three quarterfinals and semifinals; best-of-five finals.

Roster Limit: 28 (college eligible players only).

COVINGTON LUMBERJACKS

Mailing Address: PO Box 30, Covington, VA 24426. **Telephone:** (540) 958-3848. **E-Mail Address:** covingtonlumberjacks@valleyleaguebaseball.com; dizzgar10@aol.com. **Website:** www.lumberjacksbaseball.com. **Owners:** Dizzy Garten. **Head Coach:** Unavailable.

FRONT ROYAL CARDINALS

Mailing Address: 382 Morgans Ridge Road, Front Royal, VA 22630. **Telephone:** (540) 636-1882, (540) 671-9184. **Fax:** (540) 635-8746. **E-Mail Address:** frontroyalcardinals@valleyleaguebaseball.com. **Website:** www.frontroyalcardinals.com. **President:** Donna Settle. **Head Coach:** Joe Scarano

HARRISONBURG TURKS

Mailing Address: 1489 S. Main St, Harrisonburg, VA 22801. **Telephone:** (540) 434-5919. **E-Mail Address:** turksbaseball@hotmail.com. **Website:** www.harrisonburgturks.com. **Operations Manager:** Teresa Wease. **GM/Head Coach:** Bob Wease.

HAYMARKET SENATORS

Mailing Address: 15000 Graduation Dr, Haymarket, VA 20168. **Telephone:** (703) 989-5009. **E-Mail Address:** haymarketsenators@valleyleaguebaseball.com. **Website:** www.haymarketbaseball.com. **President/General Manager:** Scott Newell. **Head Coach:** Ryan Fecteau.

LURAY WRANGLERS

Mailing Address: 1203 E. Main St, Luray, VA 22835. **Telephone:** (540) 743-3338. **E-Mail Addresses:** luraywranglers@valleyleaguebaseball.com. **Website:** www.luraywranglers.com. **President:** Bill Turner. **General Manager:** Unavailable. **Head Coach:** Mike Bocock.

NEW MARKET REBELS

Mailing Address: PO Box 1127, New Market, VA 22844. **Telephone:** (540) 740-4247, (540) 740-8569. **E-Mail Address:** nmrebels@shentel.net. **Website:** www.rebelsbaseball.biz. **President/General Manager:** Bruce Alger. **Executive Vice President:** Jim Weissenborn. **Head Coach:** Corey Paluga

ROCKBRIDGE RAPIDS

Mailing Address: P.O Box 600, Lexington, VA 24450. **Telephone:** (540) 460-7502. **E-Mail Address:** rockbridgerapids@valleyleaguebaseball.com. **Website:** www.rockbridgerapids.com. **General Manager:** Ken Newman. **Head Coach:** Greg Keaton

STAUNTON BRAVES

Mailing Address: 14 Shannon Place, Staunton, VA 24401. **Telephone:** (540) 886-0987. **Fax:** (540) 886-0905. **E-Mail Address:** stauntonbraves@valleyleaguebaseball.com. **Website:** www.stauntonbravesbaseball.com. **General Manager:** Steve Cox. **Head Coach:** Lance Mauck

WAYNESBORO GENERALS

Mailing Address: PO Box 615, Waynesboro VA 22980. **Telephone:** (540) 949-0370, (540) 942-2474. **E-Mail Address:** jim_critzer@hotmail.com. **Website:** www.waynesborogenerals.com. **Owner:** Jim Critzer. **Head Coach:** Ronny Palmer.

WINCHESTER ROYALS

Mailing Address: PO Box 2485, Winchester, VA 22604. **Telephone:** (540) 667-7677. **Fax:** (540) 662-1434. **E-Mail Addresses:** winchesterroyals@valleyleaguebaseball.com, jimphill@shentel.net. **Website:** www.winchesterroyals.com. **President:** Jim Shipp. **Vice President/General Manager:** Jim Phillips. **Head Coach:** John Lowery Sr.

WOODSTOCK RIVER BANDITS

Mailing Address: PO Box 227, Woodstock, VA 22664. **Telephone:** (804) 795-5128. **Fax:** (804) 226-8706. **E-Mail Address:** woodstockriverbandits@yahoo.com. **Website:** www.woodstockriverbandits.org. **Owner/President:** Jim Yates. **General Manager:** Robert Bowman. **Head Coach:** Donn Foltz.

WEST COAST LEAGUE

Mailing Address: PO Box 8395, Portland, Oregon 97207. **Telephone:** (503) 764-9510. **E-Mail Address:** wilson@westcoastleague.com. **Website:** www.westcoastleague.com.

Year Founded: 2005.

President: Ken Wilson. **Vice President:** Bobby Brett. **Secretary:** Dan Segel. **Treasurer:** Jim Corcoran.

Division Structure: East—Kelowna, Moses Lake, Walla Walla, Wenatchee. West—Bellingham, Bend, Corvallis, Cowlitz, Kitsap.

Regular Season: 48 games. **2010 Opening Date:** June 4. **Closing Date:** Aug. 8.

All-Star Game: None.

Playoff Format: First- and second-place teams in each division meet in best-of-three semifinal series; winners advance to best-of-three championship series.

Roster Limit: 28 (college-eligible players only).

BELLINGHAM BELLS

Mailing Address: P.O. Box 28935, Bellingham, WA 98228. **Telephone:** (360) 746-0406. **E-Mail Address:** info@bellinghambells.com. **Website:** www.bellinghambells.com. **General Manager:** Justin Stottlemyre. **Head Coach:** Kevin Matthews (Skagit Valley Washington CC).

BEND ELKS

Mailing Address: PO Box 9009, Bend, OR 97708. **Telephone:** (541) 312-9259. **E-Mail Address:** richardsj@bendcable.com. **Website:** www.bendelks.com. **Owner/General Manager:** Jim Richards. **Head Coach:** Sean Kinney (Whitman College).

CORVALLIS KNIGHTS

Mailing Address: PO Box 1356, Corvallis, OR 97339. **Telephone:** (541) 752-5656. **E-Mail Address:** dan.segel@corvallisknights.com. **Website:** www.corvallisknights.com. **President:** Dan Segel. **General Manager/Head Coach:** Brooke Knight.

COWLITZ BLACK BEARS

Mailing Address: P.O. Box 1255, Longview, WA 98632. **Telephone:** (360) 703-3195. **E-Mail Address:** gwilsonagm@gmail.com. **Website:** www.cowlitzblackbears.com. **Owner:** Tony Bonacci. **General Manager:** Grant Wilson. **Head Coach:** Bryson LeBlanc (Oregon)

KELOWNA FALCONS

Mailing Address: 201-1014 Glenmore Dr, Kelowna, B.C., V1Y 4P2. **Telephone:** (250) 763-4100. **E-Mail Address:** mark@kelownafalcons.com. **Website:** www.kelownafalcons.com. **General Manager:** Mark Nonis. **Head Coach:** Kevin Frady (Kansas).

KITSAP BLUEJACKETS

Mailing Address: PO Box 68, Silverdale, WA 98383. **Telephone:** (360) 692-5566. **E-Mail Address:** ricjansmith@comcast.net. **Website:** www.kitsapbluejackets.com. **Managing Partner/General Manager:** Rick Smith. **Head Coach:** Matt Acker (Green River, Washington CC).

MOSES LAKE PIRATES

Mailing Address: 2165 Westshore Drive, Suite Arrr!, Moses Lake, WA 98837. **Telephone:** (509) 764-8200. **E-Mail Address:** bkirwan@mlpirates.com. **Website:** www.mlpirates.com. **Owner/General Manager:** Brent Kirwan. **Head Coach:** Steve Keller (Wenatchee Valley College).

WALLA WALLA SWEETS

Mailing Address: 109 E. Main Street, Walla Walla, WA 99362. **Telephone:** (509) 522-2255. **E-Mail Address:** Zachary.Fraser@pacificbaseballventures.com. **Website:** www.wallawallabaseball.com. **Managing Partner:** John Stanton. **General Manager:** Zachary Fraser. **Head Coach:** J.C. Biagi (Walla Walla Washington CC)

WENATCHEE APPLESOX

Mailing Address: PO Box 5100, Wenatchee, WA 98807. **Telephone:** (509) 665-6900. **E-Mail Address:** sales@applesox.com. **Website:** www.applesox.com. **Owner/General Manager:** Jim Corcoran. **Head Coach:** Ed Knaggs.

WCL PORTLAND

Mailing Address: 2811 N.E. Holman, Portland, Oregon 97211. **Telephone:** (503) 502-3057. **E-Mail Address:** rvance@cu-portland.edu. **Website:** www.westcoastleague.com/portland. **Year Founded:** 2009.

Commissioner: Rob Vance.

Regular Season: 25 games. **2010 Opening Date:** June 6. **Closing Date:** August 8.

All-Star Game: August 2 - All-Stars at Cowlitz Black Bears (West Coast League).

Playoff Format: First-place team faces fourth-place team and second-place team faces third-place team in best-of-three semifinal series. Winners advance to best-of-three championship series.

Roster Limit: 28 (college-eligible players only). **Teams:** Bucks, Dukes, Lobos, Ports, Stars, Toros.

WCL TRI-STATE

Mailing Address: 232 Boyle Street, Eureka, California 95503. **Telephone:** (707) 499-9075. **E-Mail Address:** wilson@westcoastleague.com. **Website:** www.westcoastleague.com/tri-state. **Year Founded:** 2009.

Commissioner: Roger Lorenzetti.

Regular Season: 24 games. **2010 Opening Date:** June 18. **Closing Date:** August 1.

All-Star Game: None.

Play-off Format: First four teams in round-robin.

Roster Limit: 28 (college-eligible players only).

FOLSOM PIONEERS

Mailing Address: 449 South Lexington Drive, Folsom, California 95630. **Telephone:** (916) 206-8616. **E-Mail Address:** sirmikecarter@gmail.com. **Website:** www.folsompioneers.com. **Owner/General Manager:** Mike Carter.

HUMBOLDT CRABS

Mailing Address: P.O. Box 4422, Arcata, California 95518. **Telephone:** (707) 845-5255. **E-Mail Address:** mfilar@pacbell.net. **Website:** www.humboldtcrabs.com. **President:** Matt Filar.

NEVADA BIGHORNS

Mailing Address: 3476 Indian Drive, Carson City, Nevada 89705. **Telephone:** (775) 721-3024. **E-Mail Address:** dyoung1544@yahoo.com. **Website:** www.nevadabighornbaseball.com. **General Manager/Coach:** Dennis Young.

SOUTHERN ORGEON RIVER DAWGS

Mailing Address: 710 Haven Road, Jacksonville, Oregon 97530. **Telephone:** (541) 601-1722. **E-Mail Address:** ccwolfcubs@msn.com. **Website:** www.baseballcharts.com/riverdawgs. **General Manager/Coach:** Chris Wolf.

REDDING COLT 45S

Mailing Address: 22636 Bridlewood Lane, Palo Cedro, California 96073. **Telephone:** (530) 308-1888. **E-Mail Address:** cadsfam@frontiernet.net. **Website:** www.ballcharts.com/reddingcolt45. **General Manager:** Greg Cadaret.

HIGH SCHOOL BASEBALL

NATIONAL FEDERATION OF STATE HIGH SCHOOL ASSOCIATIONS

Mailing Address: P.O. Box 690, Indianapolis, IN 46206. **Telephone:** (317) 972-6900. **Fax:** (317) 822-5700. **E-Mail Address:** baseball@nfhs.org. **Website:** www.nfhs.org.

Executive Director: Robert Kanaby. **Chief Operating Officer:** Bob Gardner. **Assistant Director/Baseball Rules Editor:** Elliot Hopkins. **Director, Publications/Communications:** Bruce Howard.

NATIONAL HIGH SCHOOL BASEBALL COACHES ASSOCIATION

Mailing Address: P.O. Box 12843, Tempe, AZ 85284. **Telephone:** (602) 615-0571. **Fax:** (480) 838-7133. **E-Mail Address:** rdavini@cox.net. **Website:** www.baseball-coaches.org. **Executive Director:** Ron Davini. **President:** Mark Gjormand (Madison HS, Herndon, Va.). **First Vice President:** Steve Mandl (Washington HS, New York). **Second Vice President:** Phil Clark (Bartlett, Tenn., **HS).**

2010 National Convention: Dec. 2-5, 2009 at Nashville, Tenn.

NATIONAL TOURNAMENTS

IN-SEASON

HORIZON NATIONAL INVITATIONAL

Mailing Address: Horizon High School, 5653 Sandra Terrace, Scottsdale, AZ 85254. **Telephone:** (602) 867-9003. **E-mail:** huskycoach1@yahoo.com Website: www.horizonbaseball.com

Tournament Director: Eric Kibler.

2010 Tournament: Dates unavailable.

INTERNATIONAL PAPER CLASSIC

Mailing Address: 4775 Johnson Rd., Georgetown, SC 29440. **Telephone:** (843) 527-9606, (843) 546-3807. **Fax:** (843) 546-8521. **Website:** www.ipclassic.com.

Tournament Director: Alicia Johnson.

2010 Tournament: March 4-7 (eight teams).

LIONS INVITATIONAL

Mailing Address: 3502 Lark St., San Diego CA 92103. **Telephone:** (619) 602-8650. **Fax:** (619) 239-3539. **E-Mail Address:** peter.gallagher@sdcourt.ca.gov. **Website:** www.lionsbaseball.org

Tournament Director: Peter Gallagher.

2010 Tournament: March 29-April 1

NATIONAL CLASSIC BASEBALL TOURNAMENT

Mailing Address: P.O. Box 338, Placentia, CA 92870. **Telephone:** (714) 993-2838. **Fax:** (714) 993-5350. **E-Mail Address:** placentiamustang@aol.com. **Website:** national-classic.com

Tournament Director: Todd Rogers.

2010 Tournament: April 3-8 (16 teams).

USA CLASSIC NATIONAL HIGH SCHOOL INVITATIONAL

Mailing Address: 5900 Walnut Grove Rd., Memphis, TN 38120. **Telephone:** (901) 872-8326. **Fax:** (901) 681-9443. **Email:** jdaigle@bigriver.net Web-site: www.usabaseball-stadium.org.

Tournament Organizers: John Daigle, Buster Kelso.

2010 Tournament: March 31-April 3 at USA Baseball Stadium, Millington, TN (16 teams).

POSTSEASON

SUNBELT BASEBALL CLASSIC SERIES

Mailing Address: 505 North Blvd., Edmond, OK 73034. **Telephone:** (405) 348-3839. **Fax:** (405) 340-7538

Chairman: John Schwartz.

2010 Senior Series: Norman, OK, June 21-26

2010 Junior Series: McAlester and Wilburton, OK, June 10-16

2010 Sophomore Series: Oklahoma City, OK, June 3-6

ALL-STAR GAMES/AWARDS

AFLAC HIGH SCHOOL ALL-AMERICA CLASSIC

Mailing Address: 1932 Wynnton Road, Columbus, Georgia 31999. **Telephone:** (706) 763-2827. **Fax:** (706) 320-2288. **Event Organizer:** Blue Ridge Sports & Entertainment. **Vice President, Events:** Lou Lacy. **2010 Game:** Unavailable.

UNDER ARMOUR ALL-AMERICA GAME, POWERED BY BASEBALL FACTORY

Mailing Address: 9176 Red Branch Rd., Suite M, Columbia, MD 21045. **Telephone:** 410-715-5080. **E-Mail Address:** jason@baseballfactory.com. **Website:** baseball-factory.com. **Event Organizers:** Baseball Factory, Team One Baseball. **2010 Game:** August 14.

GATORADE CIRCLE OF CHAMPIONS

(National HS Player of the Year Award)

Mailing Address: The Gatorade Company, 321 N. Clark St., Suite 24-3, Chicago, IL, 60610. **Telephone:** 312-821-1000. **Website:** www.gatorade.com

SHOWCASE EVENTS

ALL-AMERICAN BASEBALL TALENT SHOWCASES

Mailing Address: 333 Preston Ave., Unit 1, Voorhees, NJ 08043. **Telephone:** (856) 354-0201. **Fax:** (856) 354-0818. **E-Mail Address:** hitdoctor@thehitdoctor.com. **Website:** thehitdoctor.com. **National Director:** Joe Barth.

AREA CODE GAMES

Mailing Address: 23954 Madison Street, Torrance, CA 90505. **Telephone:** (310) 791-1142 x 4424. **E-Mail Address:** andrew@studentsports.com. **Website:** www.areacodebaseball.com

Event Organizer: Andrew Drennen.

2010 Area Code Games: Aug. 5-10 at Long Beach, CA (Blair Field).

ARIZONA FALL CLASSIC

Mailing Address: 6102 W. Maui Lane, Glendale, AZ 85306 **Telephone:** (602) 978-2929. **Fax:** (602) 439-4494. **E-Mail Address:** azbaseballted@msn.com. **Website:** www.azfallclassic.com.

Directors: Ted Heid, Tracy Heid.

2010 Events

Four Corner Classic (Open HS, 16 & under) . Peoria, AZ, June 4-6
Summer National Classic (2009 and Under) . Peoria, AZ, TBA
Arizona Fall Invitational . . . . Oct. 8-10
AZ Senior Fall Classic (HS seniors) . . . Peoria, AZ, Oct. 14-17
AZ Junior Fall Classic (HS juniors) . . . . Peoria, AZ, Oct. 22-24
AZ Sophomore Fall Classic . . . .
(HS sophomore and Under) . . . . Peoria, AZ, Oct. 29-31

BASEBALL FACTORY

Office Address: 9176 Red Branch Rd., Suite M, Columbia, MD 21045. **Telephone:** (800) 641-4487, (410) 715-5080. **FAX:** (410) 715-1975. **E-Mail Address:** info@baseballfactory.com. **Website:** www.baseballfactory.com.

Chief Executive Officer: Steve Sclafani. **President:** Rob Naddelman. **Executive VP, Baseball Operations:** Steve Bernhardt. **VP, Finance:** Matt Frese. **VP, Operations/Marketing:** Jason Budden. **Senior Director, Baseball Operations:** Andy Ferguson Sr. **Director, Instruction:** Matt Schilling. **VP, On-Field Events:** Jim Gemler. **Personal Recruiting Director:** Dan Mooney. **Creative Director:** Matt Kirby. **VP, Player Development:** Dan Forester.

Player Development Coordinators: Will Bach, Will Bowers, Chris Brown, Zack Bryant, Adam Darvick, Steve Nagler, John Perko, Dave Packer, Patrick Wuebben. **Director, SCR Program/UA National Tryouts:** Dave Wipkowski. **Director, Player Identification:** Josh Sunday. **Lessons Coordinator:** Joe Lake. **Client Service Coordinator:** Cecile Banas. **Senior Director, Team One Baseball:** Justin Roswell. **Team One Recruiting Specialist:** Vince Sacco. **Baseball Consultants:** Dana Cavalea (Strength and Conditioning), Doug Glanville (Consultant), Rick Sofield (Special Advisor to Baseball Operations), Mike Toomey (Scouting Consultant). **College Recruiting:** Bernadette Bechta (Academic Advisor), Dan Mooney (Senior Director of the Exclusive Program), Woody Wingfield (Director of Exclusive Program Operations). **SCR/Under Armour National Tryout Representatives:** Bryan Hoffman, Samantha

Latzes, Rob Onolfi.

Under Armour Pre-Season All-America Tournament: January 15-17 in Tucson, AZ (Kino Sports Complex)

Under Armour All-America Game: August 2010

2010 Under Armour National Tryouts/Signature College Recruiting Program Video Sessions: Various locations across the country. Year round. Open to high school players age 13 – 18. Check www.baseballfactory.com for full schedule.

BLUE-GREY CLASSIC

Mailing address: 68 Norfolk Road, Mills MA 02054. **Telephone:** (508) 376-1250. **Email address:** impact-prospects@comcast.net. **Website:** www.impact-prospects.com.

2010 events: Various dates, locations June-Sept. 2010.

COLLEGE SELECT BASEBALL

Mailing Address: P.O. Box 783, Manchester, CT 06040. **Telephone:** (800) 782-3672. **E-Mail Address:** TRhit@msn.com. **Website:** www.collegeselect.org.

Consulting Director: Tom Rizzi.

IMPACT BASEBALL

Mailing Address: P.O. Box 47, Sedalia, NC 27342. **E-Mail Address:** andypartin@aol.com. **Website:** impact-baseball.com.

Operator: Andy Partin.

2010 Showcases: January 30, Surry Community College; Feb. 13-14, Forsyth Country Day; June 14-15, Wingate University; July 19-20, TBA; August 28, University of North Carolina.

EAST COAST PROFESSIONAL SHOWCASE

Mailing Address: 2125 North Lake Avenue, Lakeland, FL 33805. **Telephone:** (863) 686-8075. **Website:** www.eastcoastproshowcase.com.

Tournament Directors: John Castleberry. **Tournament Coordinator:** Shannon Follett.

2010 Showcase: Aug. 1-4, Lakeland, FL.

PACIFIC NORTHWEST CHAMPIONSHIPS

Mailing Address: 42783 Deerhorn Road, Springfield, Or. 97478. **Telephone:** (541) 896-0841. **Email Address:** mckay@baseballnorthwest.com. **Website:** www.base-ballnorthwest.com. **Tournament Organizer:** Jeff McKay.

State Prospect Games: Southeast Idaho, June 7-10 at Hillcrest H.S. in Idaho Falls, Idaho; Southwest Idaho, June 7-10 at TBA; Montana/Wyoming, June 14-17 at Luzenac Field in Three Forks, Mont.; Southern Oregon, June 14-17 at TBA; Washington Metro, June 21-24 at TBA; Washington Northeast/Northern Idao, June 21-24 at Avista Stadium in Spokane, Wash.; Washington Metro South, June 28-July 1 at Tacoma (Wash.) CC; Oregon Mid-Valley, June 28-July 1 at Lane (Ore.) CC in Eugene, Ore.; Washington Metro North, July 5-8 at TBA; East Washington, July 12-15 at Columbia Basin (Wash.) CC in Pasco, Wash.; Washington Peninsula, July 12-15 at TBA; Washington Southwest Central, July 19-22 at Wheeler Field in Centralia, Wash.; Washington Northwest, July 19-22 at TBA; Washington Metro East, July 26-29 at TBA;

Oregon Metro, July 26-29 at Wilsonville (Ore.) H.S.

PERFECT GAME USA

Mailing Address: 1203 Rockford Road SW, Cedar Rapids, IA 52404. **Telephone:** (319) 298-2923 Fax: (319) 298-2924. **E-Mail Address:** jerry@perfectgame.org. **Website:** www.perfectgameusa.com.

President, Director: Jerry Ford. **Vice Presidents:** Andy Ford, Jason Gerst, Tyson Kimm, Allan Simpson. **International Director:** Kentaro Yasutake. **National Showcase Director:** Jim Arp. **National Tournament Director:** Taylor McCollough. **Scouting Director:** David Rawnsley. **National BCS Director:** Ben Ford. **Iowa League Director:** Steve James. **Northeast Director/Showcase Director:** Dan Kennedy. **West Coast Director:** Mike Spiers. **Scouting Coordinators:** Jeff Simpson, Greg Sabers, Kyle Noesen, Jason Piddington, Anup Sinha. **National Coordinator:** Frank Fulton.

2010 Showcase/Tournament Events: Sites across the United States, Jan. 9 – Nov. 7.

PROFESSIONAL BASEBALL INSTRUCTION—BATTERY INVITATIONAL

(for top HS pitchers and catchers)

Mailing Address: 107 Pleasant Avenue, Upper Saddle River NJ 07458. **Telephone:** (800) 282-4638. **Fax:** (201) 760-8720. **E-mail Address:** info@baseballclinics.com Website: www.baseballclinics.com/batteryinvitational.html

President: Doug Cinnella.
Senior Staff Administrator: Greg Cinnella.
General Manager/PR/Marketing: Jim Monaghan.
2010 Showcase Events: Nov. 4 & 5.

SELECTFEST BASEBALL

Mailing Address: 60 Franklin Pl., Morris Plains, NJ 07950. **Telephone:** (862) 222-6404. **E-Mail Address:** selectfest@optonline.net. **Website:** www.selectfestbaseball.org Camp Directors: Bruce Shatel.
2010 Showcase: June 25-27.

TEAM ONE BASEBALL

(A division of Baseball Factory)

Office Address: 1000 Bristol Street North, Box 17285, Newport Beach, CA 92660. **Telephone:** (800) 621-5452, (805) 451-8203. **FAX:** (949) 209-1829. **E-Mail Address:** jroswell@teamonebaseball.com. **Website:** www.teamonebaseball.com.

Senior Director: Justin Roswell. **Executive VP, Baseball Operations:** Steve Bernhardt. **Director, On-Field Sessions:** Jim Gemler.

2010 Showcases: Team One South, June 27-28 at Emory University in Atlanta; Team One Midwest, June 27-28 at Triton College in River Grove, Ill.; Team One West, July 17-18 at Vanguard University in Costa Mesa, Calif.; Team One Northeast, Aug. 9-10 at Waterfront Park in Trenton, N.J.

2010 Under Armour Tournaments: Memorial Day Classic, May 28-31 at Roger Dean Sports Complex in Jupiter, Fla.; Under Armour Southeast, June 4-8 at Roger Dean Sports Complex in Jupiter, Fla.; Under Armour Invitational, June 11-15 at Roger Dean Sports Complex in Jupiter, Fla.; Firecracker Classic, July 1-5 at Roger Dean Sports Complex in Jupiter, Fla.; Under Armour Southwest, July 29-Aug. 2 at Peoria Sports Complex in Peoria, Ariz.; Fall Classic, Sept. 24-26 at Roger Dean Sports Complex in Jupiter, Fla.; Thanksgiving Classic, Nov. 27-29 at Vanguard University in Costa Mesa, Calif.; Winter Classic, Dec. 27-30 at Kino Sports Complex in Tucson, Ariz.

TOP 96 COLLEGE COACHES CLINICS

Mailing Address: 6 Foley Dr. Southboro, MA 01772. **Telephone:** 508-481-5939

E-Mail Address: doug.henson@top96.com. **Website:** www.top96.com

Directors: Doug Henson, Dave Callum.
2010 Clinics: Various clinics throughout the United States; see website for schedule.

YOUTH BASEBALL

ALL AMERICAN AMATEUR BASEBALL ASSOCIATION

Mailing Address: 331 Parkway Dr., Zanesville, OH 43701. **Telephone:** (740) 453-8531. **Fax:** (740) 453-8531. **E-Mail Address:** clw@aol.com. **Website:** www.aaaba.us.
Year Founded: 1944.
President: Doug Pollock. **Executive Director/ Secretary:** Bob Wolfe.
2010 Events: Dates unavailable.

AMATEUR ATHLETIC UNION OF THE UNITED STATES, INC.

Mailing Address: P.O. Box 22409, Lake Buena Vista, FL 32830. **Telephone:** (407) 934-7200. **Fax:** (407) 934-7242. **E-Mail Address:** dan@aausports.org, kristy@aausports. org. **Website:** www.aaubaseball.org.
Year Founded: 1982. **Sports Manager, Baseball:** Dan Stanley

AMERICAN AMATEUR BASEBALL CONGRESS

National Headquarters: 100 West Broadway, Farmington, NM 87401. **Telephone:** (505) 327-3120. **Fax:** (505) 327-3132. **E-Mail Address:** aabc@aabc.us. **Website:** www.aabc.us.
Year Founded: 1935.
President: Richard Neely.

AMERICAN AMATEUR YOUTH BASEBALL ALLIANCE

Mailing Address: 1703 Koala Drive, Wentzville, MO 63385. **Telephone:** (636) 332-7799. **E-Mail Address:** clwjr28@aol.com. **Website:** www.aayba.com.
President, Baseball Operations: Carroll Wood.

AMERICAN LEGION BASEBALL

National Headquarters: American Legion Baseball, 700 N. Pennsylvania St., Indianapolis, IN 46204. **Telephone:** (317) 630-1213. **Fax:** (317) 630-1369. **E-Mail Address:** baseball@legion.org Website: www.baseball. legion.org.
Year Founded: 1925.
Program Coordinator: Jim Quinlan.
2010 World Series (19 and under): Aug. 13-17 at Avista Stadium, Spokane, Wash. (8 teams).
2010 Regional Tournaments (Aug. 5-9, 8 teams): Northeast—Middletown, Conn.; Mid-Atlantic—West Lawn, Pa.; Southeast—Columbia, Tenn.; Mid-South—Grand Prairie, Texas; Great Lakes—Mattoon, Ill.; Central Plains—Blue Springs, Mo.; Northwest—Spokane, Wash.; Western—Las Vegas.

BABE RUTH BASEBALL

International Headquarters: 1770 Brunswick Pike, P.O. Box 5000, Trenton, NJ 08638. **Telephone:** (609) 695-1434. **Fax:** (609) 695-2505. **E-Mail Address:** info@baberuthleague.org. **Website:** www.baberuthleague. org.
Year Founded: 1951.
President, Chief Executive Officer: Steven Tellefsen.

CONTINENTAL AMATEUR BASEBALL ASSOCIATION

Mailing Address: 1173 French Court, Maineville, Ohio 45039. **Telephone:** (513) 677-1580. **Fax:** 513-677-2586 **E-Mail Address:** lred-wine@cababaseball.com. **Website:** www.cababaseball.com.
Year Founded: 1984.
Executive Director: Larry Redwine. **Commissioner:** John Mocny. **Executive Vice President:** Fran Pell.

DIXIE YOUTH BASEBALL

Mailing Address: P.O. Box 877, Marshall, TX 75671. **Telephone:** (903) 927-2255. **Fax:** (903) 927-1846. **E-Mail Address:** dyb@dixie.org. **Website:** www.dixie.org.
Year Founded: 1955.
Commissioner: Wes Skelton.

DIXIE BOYS BASEBALL

Commissioner/Chief Executive Officer: Sandy Jones, P.O. Box 8263, Dothan, AL 36304. **Telephone:** (334) 793-3331.

DIZZY DEAN BASEBALL

Mailing Address: P.O. Box 856, Hernando, MS 38632. **Telephone:** (662) 429-4365, (423) 596-1353 E-Mail Address: dizzydeanbaseball@yahoo.com. **Website:** www.dizzydeanbbinc.org.
Year Founded: 1962.
Commissioner: Danny Phillips. **Presdient:** Jimmy Wahl. **VP:** Bobby Dunn. **Secretary:** Billy Powell. **Treasurer:** Houston Suggs.

HAP DUMONT YOUTH BASEBALL

(A Division of the National Baseball Congress)
Mailing Address: P.O. Box 83, Lexington, OK 73051. **Telephone:** (405) 899-7689. **E-Mail Address:** steve-smith@hapdumontbaseball.com. **Website:** www.hapdu-montbaseball.com; www.oabf.net
Year Founded: 1974.

LITTLE LEAGUE BASEBALL

International Headquarters: P.O. Box 3485, Williamsport, PA 17701. **Telephone:** (570) 326-1921. **Fax:** (570) 326-1074. **E-Mail Address:** headquar-ters@LL.orgWebsite: www.littleleague.org.
Year Founded: 1939.
Chairman: Dennis Lewin.
President/Chief Executive Officer: Stephen D. Keener. **Chief Financial Officer:** David Houseknecht. **Vice President, Operations:** Patrick Wilson. **Treasurer:** Melissa Singer. **Senior Communications Executive:** Lance Van Auken.

NATIONAL AMATEUR BASEBALL FEDERATION

Mailing Address: P.O. Box 705, Bowie, MD 20718. **Telephone:** (410) 721-4727. **Fax:** (410) 721-4940. **E-Mail Address:** nabf1914@aol.com. **Website:** www.nabf.com.
Year Founded: 1914.
Executive Director: Charles Blackburn.

NATIONAL ASSOCIATION OF POLICE ATHLETIC LEAGUES

Mailing Address: 658 W. Indiantown Road #201, Jupiter, FL 33458. **Telephone:** (561) 745-5535. **Fax:** (561) 745-3147. **E-Mail Address:** cop-nkid@nationalpal.org. **Website:** www.nationalpal.org.
Year Founded: 1914.
Executive Director: Mike Dillhyon. **National Program Manager:** Eric Widness.

PONY BASEBALL

International Headquarters: P.O. Box 225, Washington, PA 15301. **Telephone:** (724) 225-1060. **Fax:** (724) 225-9852. **E-Mail Address:** info@pony.org. **Website:** www.pony.org.
Year Founded: 1951.
President: Abraham Key.

REVIVING BASEBALL IN INNER CITIES

Mailing Address: 245 Park Ave., New York, NY 10167. **Telephone:** (212) 931-7800. **Fax:** (212) 949-5695.
Year Founded: 1989. **Founder:** John Young. **Vice President, Community Affairs:** Thomas C. Brasuell.
Email: rbi@mlb.com. **Website:** www.mlb.com/rbi

SUPER SERIES BASEBALL OF AMERICA

National Headquarters: 3449 East Kael Street., Mesa, AZ 85213-1773. **Telephone:** (480) 664-2998. **Fax:** (480) 664-2997. **E-Mail Address:** info@superseriesbaseball. com. **Website:** www.superseriesbaseball.com.
President: Mark Mathew

TRIPLE CROWN SPORTS

Mailing Address: 3930 Automation Way, Fort Collins, CO 80525. **Telephone:** (970) 223-6644. **Fax:** (970) 223-3636. **Websites:** www.triplecrownsports.com. **E-mail:** thad@triplecrownsports.com, sean@triplecrownsports. com. **Director, Baseball Operations:** Thad Anderson.

U.S. AMATEUR BASEBALL ASSOCIATION

Mailing Address: 7101 Lake Ballinger Way, Edmonds, WA 98026. **Telephone/Fax:** (425) 776-7130. **E-Mail Address:** usaba@usaba.com. **Website:** www.usaba.com.
Year Founded: 1969.
Executive Director: Al Rutledge. **Secretary:** Roberta Engelhart.

U.S. AMATEUR BASEBALL FEDERATION

Mailing Address: 389 Bryan Point Dr. Chula Vista, CA 91914. **Telephone:** (619) 934-2551. **Fax:** (619) 271-6659. **E-Mail Address:** usabf@cox.net. **Website:** www. usabf.com.
Year Founded: 1997.
Senior Chief Executive Officer/President: Tim Halbig.

UNITED STATES SPECIALTY SPORTS ASSOCIATION

Executive Vice President, Baseball: Don DeDonatis III, 33600 Mound Rd., Sterling Heights, MI 48310. **Telephone:** (810) 397-6410. **E-Mail Address:** michussa@aol.com.
Executive Vice President, Baseball Operations: Rick Fortuna, 6324 N. Chatham Ave., #136, Kansas City, MO 64151. **Telephone:** (816) 587-4545. **E-Mail Address:** rick@kcsports.org. **Website:** www.usssabaseball.org.
Year Founded: 1965/Baseball 1996.

WORLD WOOD BAT ASSOCIATION

(A Division of Perfect Game USA)
Mailing Address: 1203 Rockford Road SW, Cedar Rapids, IA 52404. **Telephone:** (319) 298-2923 **Fax:** (319) 298-2924. **E-Mail Address:** tay-lor@perfectgame.org **Website:** www.worldwoodbat.com.
Year Founded: 1997.
President: Andy Ford. **National Director:** Taylor McCollough. **Scouting Director:** David Rawnsley.

BASEBALL USA

Mailing Address: 2626 W. Sam Houston Pkwy. N., Houston, TX 77043. **Telephone:** (713) 690-5055. **Fax:** (713) 690-9448. **E-Mail Address:** info@baseballusa.com. **Website:** www.baseballusa.com.
President: Phil Cross. **Tournament Director:** Steve Olson

CALIFORNIA COMPETITIVE YOUTH BASEBALL

Mailing Address: P.O. Box 338, Placentia, CA 92870. **Telephone:** (714) 993-2838. **Fax:** (714) 961-6078. **E-Mail Address:** ccybnet@aol.com. **Website:** www.ccyb.net.
Tournament Director: Todd Rogers.

COCOA EXPO SPORTS CENTER

Mailing Address: 500 Friday Road, Cocoa, FL 32926. **Telephone:** (321) 639-3976. **Fax:** (321) 639-0598. **E-Mail Address:** athleticdirector@cocoaexpo.com. **Website:** www.cocoaexpo.com.
Athletic Director: Matt Yurish.
Activities: Spring training program, instructional camps, team training camps, youth tournaments.

COOPERSTOWN BASEBALL WORLD

Mailing Address: P.O. Box 530, Brick, NJ 08723. **Telephone:** (888) CBW-8750. **Fax:** (888) CBW-8720. **E-Mail:** cbw@cooperstownbaseballworld.com. **Website:** www.cooperstownbaseballworld.com
Complex Address: Cooperstown Baseball World, SUNY-Oneonta, Ravine Parkway, Oneonta, NY 13820.
President/Chairman: Eddie Einhorn. **Vice President:** Debra Sirianni.
2010 Tournaments (15 Teams Per Week): Open to 12U, 13U, 14U, 15U, 16U from July 4 through August 14.

COOPERSTOWN DREAMS PARK

Mailing Address: 330 S. Main St., Salisbury, NC 28144. **Telephone:** (704) 630-0050. **Fax:** (704) 630-0737. **E-Mail Address:** info@cooperstowndreamspark.com. **Website:** www.cooperstowndreamspark.com.

Complex Address: 4550 State Highway 28, Cooperstown, NY 13807.

Chief Executive Officer: Lou Presutti. **Program Director:** Geoff Davis.

2010 Tournaments: Weekly June 5–Aug. 28

COOPERSTOWN ALL STAR VILLAGE

Mailing Address: 4158 State Highway 23, Oneonta, N.Y. **13820. Telephone:** (800) 327-6790. **Fax:** (607) 432-1076.

DISNEY'S WIDE WORLD OF SPORTS

Mailing Address: P.O. BOX 470847, Celebration, Fl 34747. **Telephone:** (407) 938-3802. **FAX:** (407) 938-3442. **E-mail address:** wdw.sports.baseball@disney.com. **Website:** www.disneybaseball.com.

Manager, Sports Events: Scott St George. **Sports Manager:** Emily Moak. **Tournament Directory:** Al Schlazer. **Sales Manager, Baseball:** Ryan Morris. **Sports Sales Coordinator, Baseball:** Kirk Stanley.

KC SPORTS TOURNAMENTS

Mailing Address: KC Sports, 6324 N. Chatham Ave., No. 136, Kansas City, MO 64151.

Telephone: (816) 587-4545. **Fax:** (816) 587-4549. **E-Mail Addresses:** jay@kcsports.org, wally@kcsports.org. **Website:** www.kcsports.org.

Activities: USSSA Youth tournaments (ages 6-18).

Tournament Organizers: Wally Fortuna, Jay Baxter.

U.S. AMATEUR BASEBALL FEDERATION

Mailing Address: 389 Bryan Point Dr. Chula Vista, CA 91914. **Telephone:** (619) 934-2551. **Fax:** (619) 271-6659. **E-Mail Address:** usabf@cox.net. **Website:** www.usabf.com.

Year Founded: 1997. **Senior Chief Executive Officer/President:** Tim Halbig.

INSTRUCTIONAL SCHOOLS/

PRIVATE CAMPS

ACADEMY OF PRO PLAYERS

Mailing Address: 140 5th Avenue, Hawthorne, NJ 07506. **Telephone:** (973) 772-3355. **Fax:** (973) 772-4839. **Website:** www.academypro.com. **Camp Director:** Dan Gilligan.

ALL-STAR BASEBALL ACADEMY

Mailing Addresses: 650 Parkway Blvd., Broomall, PA 19008; 52 Penn Oaks Dr., West Chester, PA 19382. **Telephone:** (610) 355-2411, (610) 399-8050. **Fax:** (610) 355-2414. **E-Mail Address:** basba@allstarbaseballacademy.com. **Website:** www.allstarbaseballacademy.com. **Directors:** Mike Manning, Jim Freeman.

AMERICAN BASEBALL FOUNDATION

Mailing Address: 2660 10th Ave. South, Suite 620, Birmingham, AL 35205. **Telephone:** (205) 558-4235. **Fax:** (205) 918-0800. **E-Mail Address:** abf@asmi.org. **Website:** www.americanbaseball.org. **Executive Director:** David Osinski. **Chairman of the Board:** James R. **Andrews, M.D.**

THE BASEBALL ACADEMY

Mailing Address: IMG Academies, 5500 34th St. W., Bradenton, FL 34210. **Telephone:** (941) 755-1000. **Fax:** (941) 739-7484. **Website:** www.imgacademies.com.

AMERICA'S BASEBALL CAMPS

Mailing Address: Ben Boulware, 3020 ISSQ. Pine Lake Road #12, Sammamish, WA 98075. **Telephone:** (800) 222-8152. **Fax:** (888)-751-8989. **E-Mail Address:** info@baseballcamps.com. **Website:** www.baseballcamps.com.

BUCKY DENT'S BASEBALL SCHOOL

Mailing Address: 490 Dotterel Road, Delray Beach, FL 33444. **Telephone:** (561) 265-0280. **Fax:** (561) 278-6679. **E-Mail Address:** staff@dentbaseball.com. **Website:** www.buckydentbaseballschool.com. **VP/GM:** Larry Hoskin.

CHAMPIONS BASEBALL ACADEMY

Mailing Address: Champions Baseball Academy, 510 E. Business Way, Cincinnati, OH 45241. **Telephone:** (513) 247-9511. **Fax:** (513) 247-0040. **E-Mail Address:** toddmontgomery@championsbaseball.net. **Website:** www.championsbaseball.net.

DOYLE BASEBALL ACADEMY

Mailing Address: P.O. Box 9156, Winter Haven, FL 33883. **Telephone:** (863) 439-1000. **Fax:** (863) 294-8607. **E-Mail Address:** info@doylebaseball.com.

Website: www.doylebaseball.com. **President:** Denny Doyle. **Director:** Blake Doyle.

FROZEN ROPES TRAINING CENTERS

Mailing Address: 12 Elkay Dr., Chester, NY 10918. **Telephone:** (877) 846-5699. **Fax:** (845) 469-6742. **E-Mail Address:** info@frozenropes.com. **Website:** www.frozenropes.com. **Corporate Director:** Tony Abbatine. **Camp Director:** Dan Hummel.

MARK CRESSE BASEBALL SCHOOL

Mailing Address: 58 Fulmar Lane, Aliso Viego, CA 92656. **Telephone:** (714) 892-6145. **Fax:** (714) 892-1881. **E-Mail Address:** info@markcresse.com. **Website:** www.markcresse.com. **Owner/Founder:** Mark Cresse. **Executive Director:** Jeff Courvoisier.

US SPORTS CAMPS

Mailing Address: Mike de Surville, 750 Lindaro Street, Suite 220, San Rafael, CA 94901. **Telephone:** (415) 479-6060. **Fax:** (415) 479-6061. **E-Mail Address:** baseball@ussportscamps.com. **Website:** www.ussportscamps.com.

MOUNTAIN WEST BASEBALL ACADEMY

Mailing Address: 389 West 10000 South, South Jordan, UT 84095. **Telephone:** (801) 561-1700. **Fax:** (801) 561-1762. **E-Mail Address:** kent@utahbaseballacademy.com. **Website:** www.mountainwestbaseballacademy.com. **Director:** Bob Keyes

NORTH CAROLINA BASEBALL ACADEMY

Mailing Address: 1137 Pleasant Ridge Road, Greensboro, NC 27409. **Telephone:** (336) 931-1118. **E-Mail Address:** info@ncbaseball.com. **Website:** www.ncbaseball.com.

Owner/Director: Scott Bankhead.

PENNSYLVANIA DIAMOND BUCKS
Mailing Address: 2320 Whitetail Court, Hellertown, PA 18055. **Telephone:** (610) 838-1219, (610) 442-6998. **E-Mail Address:** jciganick@moravian.edu. **Camp Director:** Jan Ciganick. **Head of Instruction:** Chuck Ciganick.

PROFESSIONAL BASEBALL INSTRUCTION
Mailing Address: 107 Pleasant Ave., Upper Saddle River, NJ 07458. **Telephone:** (800) 282-4638 (NY/NJ), (877) 448-2220 (rest of U.S.). **Fax:** (201) 760-8820. **E-Mail Address:** info@baseballclinics.com. **Website:** www.baseballclinics.com. **President:** Doug Cinnella.

RIPKEN BASEBALL CAMPS
Mailing Address: 1427 Clarkview Rd., Suite 100, Baltimore, MD 21209. **Telephone:** (800) 486-0850. **Fax:** (410) 823-0850. **E-Mail Address:** information@ripken-baseball.com. **Website:** www.ripkenbaseball.com.

SHO-ME BASEBALL CAMP
Mailing Address: P.O. Box 2270, Branson West, MO 65737. **Telephone:** (800) 993-2267, (417) 338-5838. **Fax:** (417) 338-2610. **E-Mail Address:** info@shomebaseball.com. **Website:** www.shomebaseball.com. **Camp Director:** Christopher Schroeder. **Head of Instruction:** Dick Birmingham.

COLLEGE CAMPS
Almost all of the elite college baseball programs have summer/holiday instructional camps. Please consult the college section for listings.

SENIOR BASEBALL

MEN'S SENIOR BASEBALL LEAGUE
(25 and Over, 35 and Over, 45 and Over, 55 and Over)
Mailing Address: One Huntington Quadrangle, Suite 3N07, Melville, NY 11747. **Telephone:** (631) 753-6725. **Fax:** (631) 753-4031.
President: Steve Sigler. **Vice President:** Gary D'Ambrisi. **E-Mail Address:** info@msblnational.com. **Website:** www.msblnational.com.

MEN'S ADULT BASEBALL LEAGUE
(18 and Over)
Mailing Address: One Huntington Quadrangle, Suite 3N07, Melville, NY 11747. **Telephone:** (631) 753-6725. **Fax:** (631) 753-4031.
E-Mail Address: info@msblnational.com. **Website:** www.msblnational.com.
President: Steve Sigler. **Vice President:** Gary D'Ambrisi.

NATIONAL ADULT BASEBALL ASSOCIATION
Mailing Address: 3609 S. Wadsworth Blvd., Suite 135, Lakewood, CO 80235. **Telephone:** (800) 621-6479. **Fax:** (303) 639-6605. **E-Mail:** nabanational@aol.com. **Website:** www.dugout.org.
President: Shane Fugita.

NATIONAL AMATEUR BASEBALL FEDERATION
Mailing Address: P.O. Box 705, Bowie, MD 20718. **Telephone:** (301) 464-5460. **Fax:** (301) 352-0214. **E-Mail Address:** nabf1914@aol.com. **Website:** www.nabf.com.
Year Founded: 1914.
Executive Director: Charles Blackburn.

ROY HOBBS BASEBALL
Open (28-over), Veterans (38-over), Masters (48-over), Legends (55-over); Family Affairs Division, Classics (60-over), Seniors (65-over), Women's open
Mailing Address: 2048 Akron Peninsula Rd., Akron, OH 44313. **Telephone:** (330) 923-3400. **Fax:** (330) 923-1967. **E-Mail Address:** rhbb@royhobbs.com. **Website:** www.royhobbs.com.
President: Tom Giffen. **Vice President:** Ellen Giffen.

DIRECTORIES

- **AGENT**
- **SERVICE**

AGENT DIRECTORY

ACES, INC.
Seth Levinson, Esq.
Sam Levinson
Keith Miller
Peter Pedalino, Esq.
Mike Zimmerman
188 Montague Street
6th Floor
Brooklyn, NY 11201
Phone: 718-237-2900
Fax: 718-522-3906
aces@acesinc1.com

DOUBLE DIAMOND SPORTS MANAGEMENT
Joshua Kusinick
1 E. Broward Blvd
Suite 1400
Ft. Lauderdale, FL 33301
Phone: 954-472-1047
Fax: 954-523-7009
Joshuakusnick@aol.com

FRANK A. BLANDINO, LLC
Frank A. Blandino
204 Towne Centre Drive
Hillsborough, NJ 08844
Phone: 908-217-3226
Fax: 908-281-0596
Frank@blandinolaw.com

JENNINGS, TAYLOR, WHEELER & HALEY P.C.
David L. Taylor, Esq.
Charles T. Jennings, Esq.
11711 North Pennsylvania St.
Suite 250 Carmel, IN 46032
Phone: 317-575-7979
Fax: 317-575-7977
Dtaylor@jtwhlaw.com

METIS SPORTS MANAGEMENT, LLC
Storm T. Kirschenbaum, Esq.
132 North Old Woodward Ave
Birmingham, MI 48009
Phone: 248-594-1070
Fax: 248-281-5150
www.metissports.com
storm@metissports.com

OAK SPORTS MANAGEMENT
Michael Bonanno
Don Webster
111 Forsythe St.
Suite 406
Oakville, Ontario, CA L6K 3J9
Phone: 905-407-3277
www.oaksportsmanagement.com
michael.bonanno@
oaksportsmanagement.com
donald.webster@
oaksportsmanagement.com

PETER E. GREENBERG & ASSOCIATES
Peter E. Greenberg, Esq.
Edward L. Greenberg
Chris Leible
200 Madison Ave.
Suite 2225
New York, NY 10016
Phone: 212-334-6880
Fax: 212-334-6895
www.petergreenbergsports.com

PRO AGENTS INC.
David P. Pepe
Bill Martin, Jr.
90 Woodbridge Center Drive
Woodbridge, NJ 07095
Phone: 800-795-3454
Fax: 732-726-6688
Pepeda@wilentz.com

PRO STAR MANAGEMENT, INC.
Joe Bick
Brett Bick
1600 Scripps Center
312 Walnut Street
Cincinnati, OH 45202
Phone: 513-762-7576
Fax: 513-721-4628
www.prostarmanagement.com
prostar@fuse.net

REYNOLDS SPORTS MANAGEMENT
Larry Reynolds
Patrick Murphy
Matthew Kinzer
2155 Chicago Avenue
Suite 305
Riverside, CA 92507
Phone: 951-784-6333
Fax: 951-784-1451
www.reynoldssports.com

SOSNICK COBBE SPORTS
Matt Sosnick
Paul Cobbe
Matt Hofer
Adam Karon
Jonathan Pridie
712 Bancroft Road
#510
Walnut Creek, CA 94598
Phone: 925-890-5283
Fax: 925-476-0130
www.sosnickcobbesports.com
mattsoz@aol.com
paulcobbe@msn.com

THE SPARTA GROUP
Michael Nicotera
Gene Casaleggio
Sohail Shahpar, Esq.
140 Littleton Road
Suite 100
Parsippany, NJ 07054
Phone: 973-335-0550
Fax: 973-335-2148
www.thespartagroup.com
frontdesk@thespartagroup.com

VERRILL DANA SPORTS LAW GROUP
David S. Abramson, Esq.
One Portland Square
Portland, ME 04101
Phone: 207-774-4000
Fax: 207-774-7499
www.verrilldana.com
dabramson@verrilldana.com

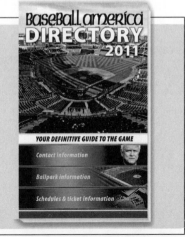

SERVICE DIRECTORY

ACCOUNTING

RESNICK AMSTERDAM LESHNER P.C.
633 Skippack Pike, Suite 300
Blue Bell, PA 19422
Phone: 215-628-8080
Fax: 215-643-2391
www.baseballaccountants.com
sxr@ral-cpa.com

APPAREL

ALL-PRO SPORTS
5341 Derry Ave., Suite P
Agoura Hills, CA 91301
Phone: 818-707-3180
Phone: 818-707-3191
www.allprosports.net/store
win@allprosports.net

MINOR LEAGUES, MAJOR DREAMS
P.O. Box 6098 Anaheim, CA 92816
Phone: 800-345-2421
Fax: 714-939-0655
www.minorleagues.com
mlmd@minorleagues.com

UNDER ARMOUR
1020 Hull St. Baltimore, MD 21230
Phone: 888-4-ARMOUR
www.baseball.underarmour.com

A/V CONTENT DELIVERY AND DISPLAY SYSTEMS

CLICK EFFECTS/SOUND & VIDEO CREATIONS, INC.
2820 Azalea Place Nashville, TN 37204
Phone: 615-460-7330
Fax: 615-460-7331
www.clickeffects.com
fkowalski@clickeffects.com

BAGS

DIAMOND BASEBALL COMPANY
11130 Warland Drive Cypress, CA 90630
Phone: 800-366-2999
Fax: 888-870-7555
www.diamond-sports.com
info@diamond-sports.com

GERRY COSBY AND COMPANY
11 Pennsylvania Plaza
New York, NY 10001
Phone: 877-563-6464
Fax: 212-967-0876
www.cosbysports.com
gcsmsg@cosbysports.com

LOUISVILLE SLUGGER
800 W Main St. Louisville, KY 40202
Phone: 800-282-2287
Fax: 502-585-1179
www.slugger.com
customer.service@slugger.com

SCHUTT SPORTS INC.
1200 E. Union Ave. Litchfield, IL 62056
Phone: 217-324-2712
Fax: 217-324-2732
www.schuttsports.com
sales@schutt-sports.com

WILSON SPORTING GOODS
8750 West Bryn Mawr Ave. 13th Floor
Chicago, IL 60631
Phone: 800-333-8326
Fax: 773-714-4595
www.wilson.com

BASEBALL CARDS

BLEACHER LEAGUE BASEBALL
526 Spruce Ave Upper Darby, PA 19082
Phone: 610-931-2110
www.bleacherleaguebaseball.com
john@bleacherleaguebaseball.com

BASEBALL BACKSTOP

L.A. STEELCRAFT PRODUCTS
1975 Lincoln Ave. Pasadena, CA 91103
Phone: 626-798-7401/800-371-2438
Fax: 626-798-1482
www.lasteelcraft.com
info@lasteelcraft.com

BASEBALLS

DIAMOND BASEBALL COMPANY
11130 Warland Drive Cypress, CA 90630
Phone: 800-366-2999
Fax: 888-870-7555
www.diamond-sports.com
info@diamond-sports.com

SWINGBUSTER, LLC
P.O. Box 534 Selma, AL 36702-0534
Phone: 877-422-8292
Fax: 334-872-2990
www.swingbuster.com
cindyloumosley@hotmail.com

WILSON SPORTING GOODS
8750 West Bryn Mawr Ave. 13th Floor
Chicago, IL 60631
Phone: 800-333-8326
Fax: 773-714-4595
www.wilson.com

BASES

SCHUTT SPORTS INC.
1200 E. Union Ave. Litchfield, IL 62056
Phone: 217-324-2712
Fax: 217-324-2732
www.schuttsports.com
sales@schutt-sports.com

BATS

BRETT BROS. SPORTS
East 9516 Montgomery St Bldg #14
Spokane Valley, WA 99206
Phone: 509-891-6435
Fax: 509-891-4156
www.brettbros.com
brettbats@aol.com

BWP BATS
80 Womeldorf Lane
Brookville, PA 15825
Phone: 814-849-0089
Fax: 814-849-8584
www.bwpbats.com
sales@bwpbats.com

DEMARINI
6435 NW Croeni Rd Hillsboro, OR 97124
Phone: 800-937-BATS
Fax: 503-531-5506
www.demarini.com

DIAMOND BASEBALL COMPANY
11130 Warland Drive Cypress, CA 90630
Phone: 800-366-2999
Fax: 888-870-7555
www.diamond-sports.com
info@diamond-sports.com

DINGER BATS
109 Kimbro St. Ridgway, IL 62979
Phone: 618-272-7250
Fax: 618-272-5905
www.dingerbats.com
info@dingerbats.com

EASTON
7855 Haskell Ave. Suite 200
Van Nuys, CA 91406
Phone: 800-632-7866
www.eastonbaseball.com

LOUISVILLE SLUGGER
800 W Main St. Louisville, KY 40202
Phone: 800-282-2287
Fax: 502-585-1179
www.slugger.com
customer.service@slugger.com

MATTINGLY SPORTS
2 Enterprise Drive Suite 407
Shelton, CT 06484
Phone: 866-627-2287
Fax: 203-944-0284
www.mattinglysports.com
marketing@mattinglybaseball.com

NIKE
One Bowerman Drive
Beaverton, OR 97005
Phone: 800-806-6453
www.nike.com

OLD HICKORY BAT COMPANY, INC.
P.O. Box 588 White House, TN 37188
Phone: 866-PRO-BATS
Fax: 615-285-051
www.oldhickorybats.com
mail@oldhickorybats.com

PHOENIX BATS
7801 Corporate Blvd, Suite E
Plain City, OH 43064
Phone: 877-598-2287
Fax: 614-873-7796
www.phoenixbats.com
lefty@phoenixbats.com

RAWLINGS
510 Maryville University Drive
Suite 110 St. Louis, MO 63141
Phone: 866-678-GEAR
www.rawlings.com

REEBOK
1895 JW Foster Blvd. Canton, MA 02021
Phone: 800-934-3566
www.reebok.com

ROCKBATS, LLC
P.O. Box 6713 Monona, WI 53716
Phone: 608-628-WOOD
Fax: 262-922-HITS
www.rockbats.com
roland@rockbats.com

SAM BAT (THE ORIGINAL MAPLE BAT)
54 Beech Street Ottawa, ON K2G 6W9
Phone: 888-SAM BATS
Phone: 613-725-3299
www.sambat.com
bats@sambat.com

SSK
514 Sebastopol Ave.
Santa Rosa, CA 95401
Phone: 707-318-3610
Fax: 707-566-6997
www.ssksports.com
robwilliams10@yahoo.com

BATTER'S HELMETS

RAWLINGS
510 Maryville University Drive
Suite 110 St. Louis, MO 63141
Phone: 866-678-GEAR
www.rawlings.com

SCHUTT SPORTS INC.
1200 E. Union Ave. Litchfield, IL 62056
Phone: 217-324-2712
Fax: 217-324-2732
www.schuttsports.com
sales@schutt-sports.com

BATTING CAGES

C&H BASEBALL, INC
2215 60th Drive East
Bradenton, FL 34203
Phone: 941-727-1533
Fax: 941-727-0588
www.chbaseball.com
info@chbaseball.com

DIAMOND BASEBALL COMPANY
11130 Warland Drive Cypress, CA 90630
Phone: 800-366-2999
Fax: 888-870-7555
www.diamond-sports.com
info@diamond-sports.com

JUGS SPORTS
11885 S.W. Herman Rd.
Tualatin, OR 97062
Phone: 800-547-6843
Fax: 503-691-1100
www.jugssports.com
stevec@jugssports.com

MASTER PITCHING MACHINE, INC.
4200 NE Birmingham Rd.
Kansas City, MO 64117
Phone: 800-878-8228
Fax: 816-452-0228
www.masterpitch.com
info@masterpitch.com

NATIONAL BATTING CAGES, INC.
P.O. Box 250
Forest Grove, OR 97116-0250
Phone: 800-547-8800
Fax: 503-357-3727
www.nationalbattingcages.com
sales@nationalbattingcages.com

NATIONAL SPORTS PRODUCTS
3441 S. 11th Ave. Eldridge, IA 52748
Phone: 800-478-6497
Fax: 800-443-8907
www.nationalsportsproducts.com
sales@nationalsportsproducts.com

WEST COAST NETTING
5075 Flightline Drive
Kingman, AZ 86401
Phone: 928-692-1144/800-854-5741
Fax: 928-692-1501
www.westcoastnetting.com
dkirkland@westcoastnetting.com

CAMPS/SCHOOLS

PROFESSIONAL BASEBALL INSTRUCTION
107 Pleasant Ave.
Upper Saddle River, NJ 07458
Phone: 800-282-4638
Fax: 201-760-8820
www.baseballclinics.com
info@baseballclinics.com

SCORE INTERNATIONAL
P.O. Box 9994 Chattanooga, TN 37412
Phone: 423-894-7111
Fax: 423-894-7303
www.scoreinternational.org
info@scoreinternational.org

CAPS/HEADWEAR

EBBETS FIELD FLANNELS, INC.
PO Box 4858 Seattle, WA 98104
Phone: 206-382-7249
Fax: 206-382-4411
www.ebbets.com
jcohen@ebbets.com

MINOR LEAGUES, MAJOR DREAMS
P.O. Box 6098 Anaheim, CA 92816
Phone: 800-345-2421
Fax: 714-939-0655
www.minorleagues.com
mlmd@minorleagues.com

OUTDOOR CAP
1200 Melissa Lane
Bentonville, AR 72712
Phone: 800-826-6047
www.outdoorcap.com
sales@outdoorcap.com

CASH REGISTERS/ P.O.S. EQUIPMENT

CASIO AMERICA, INC
570 Mt. Pleasant Ave Dover, NJ 07801
Phone: 973-361-5400
Fax: 973-537-8956
www.casio.com
lsampey@casio.com

CLEATS

ALL-PRO SPORTS
5341 Derry Ave. Suite P
Agoura Hills, CA 91301
Phone: 818-707-3180
Phone: 818-707-3191
www.allprosports.net/store
win@allprosports.net

NIKE
One Bowerman Drive
Beaverton, OR 97005
Phone: 800-806-6453
www.nike.com

REEBOK
1895 JW Foster Blvd. Canton, MA 02021
Phone: 800-934-3566
www.reebok.com

UNDER ARMOUR
1020 Hull St. Baltimore, MD 21230
Phone: 888-4-ARMOUR
www.baseball.underarmour.com

CONCESSION OPERATIONS

CASIO AMERICA INC.
670 Mt. Pleasant Ave. Dover, NJ 07801
Phone: 973-361-5400
Fax: 973-637-8979
www.casio4business.com
1sampey@casio.com

CONSULTING SERVICES

CONCESSION SOLUTIONS INC.
16022 26th Ave NE Shoreline, WA 98155
Phone: 206-440-9203
Fax: 206-440-9213
www.concessionsolutions.com
Theresa@concessionsolutions.com

EMBROIDERED EMBLEMS/ PATCHES

THE EMBLEM SOURCE
4575 West Grove Drive #500
Addison, TX 75001
Phone: 972-248-1909
Fax: 972-248-1615
www.theemblemsource.com
info@theemblemsource.com

ENGRAVED PRESENTATION BASEBALL AWARD BATS

ENGRAVEDTOLAST.COM
230 Pinetown Rd Audubon, PA 19403
Phone: 610-650-0375
www.EngravedtoLast.com
sales@EngravedtoLast.com

ENTERTAINMENT

BIRDZERK!
P.O. Box 36061 Louisville, KY 40233
Phone: 800-219-0899/502-458-4020
Fax: 502-458-0867
www.birdzerk.com
dom@birdzerk.com

BREAKIN' BBOY MCCOY
P.O. Box 36061 Louisville, KY 40233
Phone: 800-219-0899/502-458-4020
Fax: 502-458-0867
www.bboymccoy.com
dom@theskillvillegroup.com

INFLATAMANIACS
8004 Sycamore Creek
Louisville, KY 40222
Phone: 502-417-8659
Fax: 502-326-9410
www.INFLATAMANIACS.com
steven@inflatamaniacs.com

MYRON NOODLEMAN
P.O. Box 36061
Louisville, KY 40233
Phone: 800-219-0899/502-458-4020
Fax: 502-458-0867
www.myronnoodleman.com
dom@theskillvillegroup.com

SCOLLON PRODUCTIONS, INC.
P.O. Box 486 White Rock, SC 29177
Phone: 803-345-3922 x48
Fax: 803-345-9313
www.scollon.com
rick@scollon.com

TOTAL SPORTS ENTERTAINMENT + TSE GAMETIME
P.O. Box 2166 La Crosse, WI 54602
Phone: 800-962-2471
Fax: 608-782-4655
www.totalsportsentertainment.com
nancy@totalsportsentertainment.com

ZOOPERSTARS!
P.O. Box 36061 Louisville, KY 40233
Phone: 800-219-0899/502-458-4020
Fax: 502-458-0867
www.zooperstars.com
dom@zooperstars.com

FIELD CONSTRUCTION/ RENOVATION

ALPINE SERVICES, INC.
5313 Brookeville Rd.
Gaithersburg, MD 20882
Phone: 800-292-8420
Fax: 301-963-7901
www.alpineservices.com
asi@alpineservices.com

FIELD COVERS/TARPS

AER-FLO, INC.
4455 18th Street East
Bradenton, FL 34203
Phone: 800-823-7356
Fax: 941-747-2489
www.aerflo.com
jeffm@aerflo.com

BEAM CLAY
Kelsey Park Great Meadows, NJ 07838
Phone: 800-247-BEAM
Fax: 908-637-8421
www.beamclay.com
sales@partac.com
See our ad on the inside back cover!

C&H BASEBALL, INC
2215 60th Drive East
Bradenton, FL 34203
Phone: 941-727-1533
Fax: 941-727-0588
www.chbaseball.com
info@chbaseball.com

COVERMASTER INC.
100 Westmore Dr 11-D
Rexdale, ON M9V5C3
Phone: 800-387-5808
Fax: 416-742-6837
www.covermaster.com
info@covermaster.com

NATIONAL SPORTS PRODUCTS
3441 S. 11th Ave. Eldridge, IA 52748
Phone: 800-478-6497
Fax: 800-443-8907
www.nationalsportsproducts.com
sales@nationalsportsproducts.com

PROMATS ATHLETICS LLC
P.O. Box 2489 Salisbury, NC 28145
Phone: 800-678-6287
Fax: 704-603-4138
www.promatsathletics.com
mcross@promatsathletics.com

REEF INDUSTRIES, INC.
9209 Almeda Genoa Houston, TX 77075
Phone: 713-507-4251
Fax: 713-507-4295
www.reefindustries.com
ri@reefindustries.com

FIELD EQUIPMENT

DIAMOND BASEBALL COMPANY
11130 Warland Drive Cypress, CA 90630
Phone: 800-366-2999
Fax: 888-870-7555
www.diamond-sports.com
info@diamond-sports.com

FIELD WALL PADDING

BEAM CLAY
Kelsey Park Great Meadows, NJ 07838
Phone: 800-247-BEAM
Fax: 908-637-8421
www.beamclay.com
sales@partac.com
See our ad on the inside back cover!

C&H BASEBALL, INC
2215 60th Drive East
Bradenton, FL 34203
Phone: 941-727-1533
Fax: 941-727-0588
www.chbaseball.com
info@chbaseball.com \

COVERMASTER INC.
100 Westmore Dr 11-D
Rexdale, ON M9V5C3
Phone: 800-387-5808
Fax: 416-742-6837
www.covermaster.com
info@covermaster.com

NATIONAL SPORTS PRODUCTS
3441 S. 11th Ave. Eldridge, IA 52748
Phone: 800-478-6497
Fax: 800-443-8907
www.nationalsportsproducts.com
sales@nationalsportsproducts.com

PROMATS ATHLETICS LLC
P.O. Box 2489 Salisbury, NC 28145
Phone: 800-678-6287
Fax: 704-603-4138
www.promatsathletics.com
mcross@promatsathletics.com

WEST COAST NETTING
5075 Flightline Drive
Kingman, AZ 86401
Phone: 928-692-1144/800-854-5741
Fax: 928-692-1501
www.westcoastnetting.com
dkirkland@westcoastnetting.com

FIREWORKS

PYROTECNICO
P.O. Box 149 New Castle, PA 16103
Phone: 800-854-4705
Fax: 724-652-1288
www.pyrotecnico.com
info@pyrotecnico.com

GAME MANAGEMENT SOFTWARE/GAME OPS CONSULTING

TOTAL SPORTS ENTERTAINMENT + TSE GAMETIME
P.O. Box 2166 La Crosse, WI 54602
Phone: 800-962-2471
Fax: 608-782-4655
www.totalsportsentertainment.com
nancy@totalsportsentertainment.com

GIVEAWAY ITEMS

BLEACHER LEAGUE BASEBALL
526 Spruce Ave Upper Darby, PA 19082
Phone: 610-931-2110
www.bleacherleaguebaseball.com
johnr@bleacherleaguebaseball.com

COYOTE PROMOTIONS
PO Box 2212 Great Neck, NY 11021
Phone: 800-726-9683
Fax: 516-482-7425
www.coyotepromotions.com
info@coyotepromotions.com

RICO INDUSTRIES, INC./ TAG EXPRESS
7000 N. Austin Niles, IL 60714
Phone: 800-423-5856
Fax: 312-427-0190
www.ricoinc.com
jimz@ricoinc.com

GLOVES

LOUISVILLE SLUGGER
800 W Main St. Louisville, KY 40202
Phone: 800-282-2287
Fax: 502-585-1179
www.slugger.com
customer.service@slugger.com

NIKE
One Bowerman Drive
Beaverton, OR 97005
Phone: 800-806-6453
www.nike.com

OLD HICKORY BAT COMPANY, INC.
P.O. Box 588 White House, TN 37188
Phone: 866-PRO-BATS
Fax: 615-285-0572
www.oldhickorybats.com
mail@oldhickorybats.com

RAWLINGS
510 Maryville University Drive
Suite 110 St. Louis, MO 63141
Phone: 866-678-GEAR
www.rawlingsgear.com

REEBOK
1895 JW Foster Blvd. Canton, MA 02021
Phone: 800-934-3566
www.reebok.com

WILSON SPORTING GOODS
8750 West Bryn Mawr Ave. 13th Floor
Chicago, IL 60631
Phone: 800-333-8326
Fax: 773-714-4595
www.wilson.com

INSURANCE

CHUBB CUSTOM MARKET, INC.
2001 Bryan Street Suite 3400
Dallas, TX 75201
Phone: 214-721-6205
Fax: 214-754-8105
www.Chubb.com
kbeaver@chubb.com

K&K INSURANCE
1712 Magnavox Way
Fort Wayne, IN 46804
Phone: 260-459-5604
Fax: 260-459-5140
www.kandkinsurance.com
lou_valentic@kandkinsurance.com
See our ad on the inside front cover!

LANYARDS AND ID ACCESSORIES

B.I.G. BADGE USA
40 Citation Lane Lititz, PA 17543
Phone: 717-569-5797
Fax: 717-569-2390
www.bigbadgeusa.com
peg.liounis@identicard.com

MARKETING SERVICES

BLEACHER LEAGUE BASEBALL
526 Spruce Ave Upper Darby, PA 19082
Phone: 610-931-2110
www.bleacherleaguebaseball.com
johnr@bleacherleaguebaseball.com

EYELEVEL MARKETING
5478 Wilshire Blvd #210
Los Angeles, CA 90036
Phone: 323-525-0072
Fax: 323-525-0092
www.eyelevelmarketing.com
sol@eyelevelmarketing.com

PRO SPORTS MVP
16055 Tejon St. Ste 202
Colorado Springs, CO 80905
Phone: 719-227-3920
Fax: 719-227-3922
www.prosportsmvp.com
dchavez@prosportsmvp.com

MASCOTS

OLYMPUS FLAG & BANNER
9000 W. Heather Ave.
Milwaukee, WI 53224
Phone: 414-355-2010
Fax: 414-355-1931
www.olympus-flag.com
sales@olympus-flag.com

SCOLLON PRODUCTIONS, INC.
P.O. Box 486 White Rock, SC 29177
Phone: 803-345-3922 x48
Fax: 803-345-9313
www.scollon.com
rick@scollon.com

STREET CHARACTERS
#2, 2828 18 Street NE
Calgary, AB T2E 7B1
Phone: 888-MASCOTS
Fax: 403-250-3846
www.mascots.com
info@mascots.com

MUSIC/SOUND EFFECTS

CLICK EFFECTS/ SOUND & VIDEO CREATIONS, INC.
2820 Azalea Place Nashville, TN 37204
Phone: 615-460-7330
Fax: 615-460-7331
www.clickeffects.com
fkowalski@clickeffects.com

SOUND DIRECTOR
2918 SW Royal Way Gresham, OR 97080
Phone: 503-665-6869
Fax: 503-914-1812
www.sounddirector.com
jj@sounddirector.com

NETTING/POSTS

C&H BASEBALL, INC
2215 60th Drive East
Bradenton, FL 34203
Phone: 941-727-1533
Fax: 941-727-0588
www.chbaseball.com
info@chbaseball.com

JUGS SPORTS
11885 S.W. Herman Rd.
Tualatin, OR 97062
Phone: 800-547-6843
Fax: 503-691-1100
www.jugssports.com
stevec@jugssports.com

L.A. STEELCRAFT PRODUCTS
1975 Lincoln Ave. Pasadena, CA 91103
Phone: 626-798-7401/800-371-2438
Fax: 626-798-1482
www.lasteelcraft.com
info@lasteelcraft.com

MILLER NET COMPANY, INC.
PO Box 18787 Memphis, TN 38181
Phone: 800-423-6603
Fax: 901-743-6580
www.millernets.com
miller@millernets.com

NATIONAL SPORTS PRODUCTS
3441 S. 11th Ave. Eldridge, IA 52748
Phone: 800-478-6497
Fax: 800-443-8907
www.nationalsportsproducts.com
sales@nationalsportsproducts.com

PROMATS ATHLETICS LLC
P.O. Box 2489 Salisbury, NC 28145
Phone: 800-678-6287
Fax: 704-603-4138
www.promatsathletics.com
mcross@promatsathletics.com

WEST COAST NETTING
5075 Flightline Drive
Kingman, AZ 86401
Phone: 928-692-1144/800-854-5741
Fax: 928-692-1501
www.westcoastnetting.com
dkirkland@westcoastnetting.com

NOVELTY ITEMS

BLEACHER LEAGUE BASEBALL
526 Spruce Ave Upper Darby, PA 19082
Phone: 610-931-2110
www.bleacherleaguebaseball.com
johnr@bleacherleaguebaseball.com

COYOTE PROMOTIONS
PO Box 2212 Great Neck, NY 11021
Phone: 800-726-9683
Fax: 516-482-7425
www.coyotepromotions.com
info@coyotepromotions.com

PENNANTS, FOAM FINGERS & NOVELTY GIFTS

RICO INDUSTRIES, INC./ TAG EXPRESS
7000 N. Austin Niles, IL 60714
Phone: 800-423-5856
Fax: 312-427-0190
www.ricoinc.com
jimz@ricoinc.com

PITCHING AIDS

THROWTHECURVE.COM
107 Pleasant Ave.
Upper Saddle River, NJ 07458
Phone: 800-282-4638
Fax: 201-760-8820
www.throwthecurve.com

PITCHING MACHINES

ATEC
655 Spice Island Drive Sparks, NV 89431
Phone: 800-998-ATEC
Fax: 800-959-ATEC
www.atecsports.com
askATEC@wilson.com

BETTER BASEBALL
1050 Mt. Paran Rd Atlanta, GA 30327
Phone: 404-467-4313
Fax: 404-467-4573
www.betterbaseball.com
aga@betterbaseball.com

JUGS SPORTS
11885 S.W. Herman Rd.
Tualatin, OR 97062
Phone: 800-547-6843
Fax: 503-691-1100
www.jugssports.com
stevec@jugssports.com

MASTER PITCHING MACHINE, INC.
4200 NE Birmingham Rd.
Kansas City, MO 64117
Phone: 800-878-8228
Fax: 816-452-0228
www.masterpitch.com
info@masterpitch.com

PRO BATTER SPORTS
15 Old Gate Lane Milford, CT 06460
Phone: 800-513-1807/203-874-2500
Fax: 203-878-9019
www.probatter.com
abattersby@probatter.com

PITCHING TOES

ALL-PRO SPORTS
5341 Derry Ave. Suite P
Agoura Hills, CA 91301
Phone: 818-707-3180
Phone: 818-707-3191
www.allprosports.net/store
win@allprosports.net

PLAYING FIELD PRODUCTS

BEAM CLAY
Kelsey Park Great Meadows, NJ 07838
Phone: 800-247-BEAM
Fax: 908-637-8421
www.beamclay.com
sales@partac.com

See our ad on the inside back cover!

DIAMOND PRO (TXI)
1341 West Mockingbird Lane
Dallas, TX 75247
Phone: 800-228-2987
Fax: 800-640-6735
www.diamondpro.com
diamondpro@txi.com

PRO'S CHOICE
410 N. Michigan Suite 400
Chicago, IL 60611
Phone: 800-648-1166
Phone: 312-331-9525
www.proschoice1.com
proschoice@oildri.com

POINT OF SALE ITEMS

BLEACHER LEAGUE BASEBALL
526 Spruce Ave Upper Darby, PA 19082
Phone: 610-931-2110
www.bleacherleaguebaseball.com
johnr@bleacherleaguebaseball.com

CASIO AMERICA INC.
670 Mt. Pleasant Ave. Dover, NJ 07801
Phone: 973-361-5400
Fax: 973-637-8979
www.casio4business.com
1sampey@casio.com

INTERNATIONAL MICRO SYSTEMS, INC.
200 Racoosin Dr Suite 106
Aston, PA 19014
Phone: 484-482-1600
484-482-1601
www.ims-pos.com
sales-marketing@ims-pos.com

PRINTING

OLYMPUS FLAG & BANNER
9000 W. Heather Ave.
Milwaukee, WI 53224
Phone: 414-355-2010
Fax: 414-355-1931
www.olympus-flag.com
sales@olympus-flag.com

PROMOTIONS

EYELEVEL MARKETING
5478 Wilshire Blvd #210
Los Angeles, CA 90036
Phone: 323-525-0072
Fax: 323-525-0092
www.eyelevelmarketing.com
sol@eyelevelmarketing.com

PRO SPORTS MVP
16055 Tejon St. Ste 202
Colorado Springs, CO 80905
Phone: 719-227-3920
Fax: 719-227-3922
www.prosportsmvp.com
dchavez@prosportsmvp.com

PROMOTIONAL ADVENTURES
16416 Labrador St.
North Hills, CA 91343
Phone: 818-332-1381
Fax: 818-332-1395
www.promotionaladventures.com
dustin@promotionaladventures.com

TOTAL SPORTS ENTERTAINMENT + TSE GAMETIME
P.O. Box 2166 La Crosse, WI 54602
Phone: 800-962-2471
Fax: 608-782-4655
www.totalsportsentertainment.com
nancy@totalsportsentertainment.com

PROMOTIONAL ITEMS

B.I.G. BADGE USA
40 Citation Lane Lititz, PA 17543
Phone: 717-569-5797
Fax: 717-569-2390
www.bigbadgeusa.com
peg.liounis@identicard.com

BLEACHER LEAGUE BASEBALL
526 Spruce Ave Upper Darby, PA 19082
Phone: 610-931-2110
www.bleacherleaguebaseball.com
johnr@bleacherleaguebaseball.com

BRETT BROS. SPORTS
East 9516 Montgomery St Bldg #14
Spokane Valley, WA 99206
Phone: 509-891-6435
Fax: 509-891-4156
www.brettbros.com
brettbats@aol.com

RICO INDUSTRIES, INC./ TAG EXPRESS
7000 N. Austin Niles, IL 60714
Phone: 800-423-5856
Fax: 312-427-0190
www.ricoinc.com
jimz@ricoinc.com

PROTECTIVE EQUIPMENT

DIAMOND BASEBALL COMPANY
11130 Warland Drive Cypress, CA 90630
Phone: 800-366-2999
Fax: 888-870-7555
www.diamond-sports.com
info@diamond-sports.com

NUTTY BUDDY INC.
6040 E. Montecito Scottsdale, AZ 85251
Phone: 877-688-8928
www.NuttyBuddy.com
Lina@NuttyBuddy.com

SCHUTT SPORTS INC.
1200 E. Union Ave. Litchfield, IL 62056
Phone: 217-324-2712
Fax: 217-324-2732
www.schuttsports.com
sales@schutt-sports.com

WEST COAST NETTING
5075 Flightline Drive
Kingman, AZ 86401
Phone: 928-692-1144/800-854-5741
Fax: 928-692-1501
www.westcoastnetting.com
dkirkland@westcoastnetting.com

WILSON SPORTING GOODS
8750 West Bryn Mawr Ave. 13th Floor
Chicago, IL 60631
Phone: 800-333-8326
Fax: 773-714-4595
www.wilson.com

RADAR EQUIPMENT

JUGS SPORTS
11885 S.W. Herman Rd.
Tualatin, OR 97062
Phone: 800-547-6843
Fax: 503-691-1100
www.jugssports.com
stevec@jugssports.com

SPORTS SENSORS, INC.
11351 Embassy Dr.
Cincinnati, OH 45240
Phone: 888-542-9246
Fax: 513-825-8532
www.sportssensors.com
adilz@cinci.rr.com

SCOREBOARD

CLICK EFFECTS/ SOUND & VIDEO CREATIONS, INC.
2820 Azalea Place Nashville, TN 37204
Phone: 615-460-7330
Fax: 615-460-7331
www.clickeffects.com
fkowalski@clickeffects.com

SEATING

AMERICAN SEATING
401 American Seating
Grand Rapids, MI 49504
Phone: 616-732-6600
Fax: 616-732-6847
www.americanseating.com
info@amseco.com

STURDISTEEL CO.
P.O. Box 2655 Waco, TX 76702
Phone: 800-433-3116
Fax: 254-666-4472
www.sturdisteel.com
rgroppe@sturdisteel.com

SHOWCASES/ PLAYER DEVELOPMENT

PROFESSIONAL BASEBALL INSTRUCTION - BATTERY INVITATIONAL
(pitchers/catchers - early November)
107 Pleasant Avenue
Upper Saddle River, NJ 07458
Phone: 800-282-4638
Fax: 201-760-8820
greg@baseballclinics.com

SPORTING GOODS

ALL-PRO SPORTS
5341 Derry Ave. Suite P
Agoura Hills, CA 91301
Phone: 818-707-3180
Phone: 818-707-3191
www.allprosports.net/store
win@allprosports.net

JUGHEAD SPORTS
107 Pleasant Avenue
Upper Saddle River, NJ 07458
Phone: 800-282-4638
Fax: 201-760-8820
www.jugheadsports.com

STADIUM ARCHITECTS

360 ARCHITECTURE
300 West 22nd St.
Kansas City, MO 64108
Phone: 816-472-3360
www.360architecture.com
clamberth@360architecture.com

DLR GROUP
Offices Nationwide
Phone: 1-877-DLR-GROUP
www.dlrgroup.com
dberst@dlrgroup.com

POPULOUS
300 Wyandotte, Suite 300
Kansas City, MO 64105
Phone: 816-221-1500
Fax: 816-221-1578
www.populous.com

See our ad on page 13!

STEEL STADIUMS
P.O. Box 2048 Graham, TX 76450
Phone: 940-549-5700
Fax: 940-549-5723
www.steelstadiums.com
info@steelstadiums.com

SYNTHETIC TURF

A-TURF
PO Box 157 Williamsville, NY 14231
Phone: 888-777-6910
Fax: 716-204-0189
www.aturf.com
info@aturf.com

TICKETS

NATIONAL TICKET COMPANY
P.O. Box 547 Shamokin, PA 17872
Phone: 800-829-0829
Fax: 800-829-0888
www.nationalticket.com

TRAINING EQUIPMENT

ATEC
655 Spice Island Drive
Sparks, NV 89431
Phone: 800-998-ATEC
Fax: 800-959-ATEC
www.atecsports.com
askATEC@wilson.com

C&H BASEBALL, INC
2215 60th Drive East
Bradenton, FL 34203
Phone: 941-727-1533
Fax: 941-727-0588
www.chbaseball.com
info@chbaseball.com

LOUISVILLE SLUGGER
800 W Main St. Louisville, KY 40202
Phone: 800-282-2287
Fax: 502-585-1179
www.slugger.com
customer.service@slugger.com

SPORTS SENSORS, INC.
11351 Embassy Dr.
Cincinnati, OH 45240
Phone: 888-542-9246
Fax: 513-825-8532
www.sportssensors.com
adilz@cinci.rr.com

SWINGBUSTER, LLC
P.O. Box 534 Selma, AL 36702-0534
Phone: 877-422-8292
Fax: 334-872-2990
www.swingbuster.com
cindyloumosley@hotmail.com

WEST COAST NETTING
5075 Flightline Drive
Kingman, AZ 86401
Phone: 928-692-1144/800-854-5741
Fax: 928-692-1501
www.westcoastnetting.com
dkirkland@westcoastnetting.com

TRAVEL

BROACH BASEBALL TOURS
5821 Fairview Rd Suite 118
Charlotte, NC 28209
Phone: 800-849-6345
www.baseballtoursusa.com
info@broachsportstours.com

SCORE INTERNATIONAL
P.O. Box 9994 Chattanooga, TN 37412
Phone: 423-894-7111
Fax: 423-894-7303
www.scoreinternational.org
info@scoreinternational.org

SPORTS TRAVEL AND TOURS
60 Main St. P.O. Box 50
Hafield, MA 01038
Phone: 800-662-4424
Fax: 413-247-5700
www.sportstravelandtours.com
info@sportstravelandtours.com

TROPHIES/AWARDS

BALLQUBE, LC
12146 CR 4233 W Cushing, TX 75760
Phone: 800-543-1470
Fax: 903-863-5571
www.ballqube.com
www.sportsqube.com
sales@ballqube.com

TURNSTILE ADVERTISING

ENTRY MEDIA
127 West Fairbanks Ave. #417
Winter Park, FL 32789
Phone: 407-678-4446
Fax: 407-679-1658
www.entrymedia.com
martin@entrymedia.com

UNIFORMS

EBBETS FIELD FLANNELS, INC.
PO Box 4858 Seattle, WA 98104
Phone: 206-382-7249
Fax: 206-382-4411
www.ebbets.com
jcohen@ebbets.com

EYELEVEL MARKETING
5478 Wilshire Blvd #210
Los Angeles, CA 90036
Phone: 323-525-0072
Fax: 323-525-0092
www.eyelevelmarketing.com
sol@eyelevelmarketing.com

WILSON SPORTING GOODS
8750 West Bryn Mawr Ave. 13th Floor
Chicago, IL 60631
Phone: 800-333-8326
Fax: 773-714-4595
www.wilson.com

WINDSCREENS

AER-FLO, INC.
4455 18th Street East
Bradenton, FL 34203
Phone: 800-823-7356
Fax: 941-747-2489
www.aerflo.com
jeffm@aerflo.com

C&H BASEBALL, INC
2215 60th Drive East
Bradenton, FL 34203
Phone: 941-727-1533
Fax: 941-727-0588
www.chbaseball.com
info@chbaseball.com

COVERMASTER INC.
100 Westmore Dr 11-D
Rexdale, ON M9V5C3
Phone: 800-387-5808
Fax: 416-742-6837
www.covermaster.com
info@covermaster.com

NATIONAL SPORTS PRODUCTS
3441 S. 11th Ave. Eldridge, IA 52748
Phone: 800-478-6497
Fax: 800-443-8907
www.nationalsportsproducts.com
sales@nationalsportsproducts.com

PROMATS ATHLETICS LLC
P.O. Box 2489 Salisbury, NC 28145
Phone: 800-678-6287
Fax: 704-603-4138
www.promatsathletics.com
mcross@promatsathletics.com

WEST COAST NETTING
5075 Flightline Drive
Kingman, AZ 86401
Phone: 928-692-1144/800-854-5741
Fax: 928-692-1501
www.westcoastnetting.com
dkirkland@westcoastnetting.com

WRISTBANDS

NATIONAL TICKET COMPANY
P.O. Box 547 Shamokin, PA 17872
Phone: 800-829-0829
Fax: 800-829-0888
www.nationalticket.com

**Add your company to the Baseball America
2011 Agent Directory or Service Directory!**

Call 919-682-9635 x298 or email advertising@baseballamerica.com

---

MAJOR LEAGUE TEAMS

MINOR LEAGUE TEAMS

INDEPENDENT TEAMS

OTHER ORGANIZATIONS